laudenum –
opium soaked in
alcohol

refer bop. p. 102

The Broadview Anthology of Poetry

D0029004

North of Summer by Al Purdy

/

Essay 2 –
Keats Ode to Melancholy
Brown' Porphyria's Lover
My Last Duchess

notes the term
"hidden meaning"

The Broadview Anthology of Poetry

edited by

Herbert Rosengarten & Amanda Goldrick-Jones

broadview press

Canadian Cataloguing in Publication Data
The broadview anthology of poetry

Includes index.
ISBN 1-55111-006-7
1. Poetry — Collections. 2. College readers.
I Rosengarten, Herbert. II. Goldrick-Jones, Amanda

PN6101.B76 1993   808.81   C93-094404-6

Broadview Press
Post Office Box 1243
Peterborough, Ontario, Canada, K9J 7H5

in the United States of America
3576 California Road,
Orchard Park, NY 14127

in the United Kingdon
c/o Drake Marketing,
Saint Fagan's Road,
Fairwater, Cardiff, CF53AE

PRINTED IN CANADA

Broadview Press gratefully acknowledges the support of the Canada Council, the
Ontario Arts Council, the Ontario Publishing Centre,
and the Ministry of National Heritage.

Copyrights

Preface

The purpose of *The Broadview Anthology of Poetry* is to present a wide range of poetry written in English. Despite appearances, we have not compiled a historical survey, but rather a collection of poems that represent a variety of times, places, and English-speaking cultures. Our selection process was guided by a wish to combine works long accepted as part of the English-language "canon" with material not always well represented in anthologies—such as, for example, the poetry of women since the seventeenth century. We chose a chronological arrangement to suggest two general ideas: first, that much Western poetry is grounded in a shared tradition of forms, subjects, and cultural values; and secondly, that intriguing similarities—as well as sharp differences—exist in the treatments of these forms, subjects, and values over a long span of time.

Another notion implicit in the framing of this anthology is that English-language poetry has dramatically expanded within the last century. Writers in Australia and New Zealand, Canada, India, Africa, and the Caribbean all hold in common an English-language tradition that helped to shape their history and their institutions, and that laid the groundwork for new writings. The first significant anthology of Canadian poetry, *Songs of the Great Dominion* (1889), was intended to celebrate the poetic accomplishments of Canada, "the eldest daughter of the Empire" as the editor proudly referred to his country. Today, Canada and other nations that were once extensions of England, the "mother-country," are independent culturally as well as politically. Formerly colonial literatures have forged their own identities, and a host of new voices, new words, new rhythms have broadened the field of English-language poetry.

Though we have included a number of Commonwealth and post-colonial writers, constraints of space have made it impossible to offer more than a sampling of their work. Also, in trying to include as wide a selection as possible of representative work by British, Canadian, and American poets, we have had to leave out well-known long poems, or (in a few instances) have given readers only a taste of the whole by offering brief excerpts. In almost all cases, however, we have chosen to represent each poet by several poems, inviting readers to take a broader view of a given writer's work and ways of thinking.

We owe thanks to many readers and lovers of poetry who gave us the benefit of their advice in the preparation of this anthology, including Michael Keefer, Kieran Kealy, Don LePan, George Kirkpatrick, Jane Flick, Jack Foster, Margaret Blom, Andrew Busza, Bryce Gorven, Andrea Gorven, Lisa Schnell, Jeffery Donaldson, Tom Marshall, W. J. Keith, Bill New, U. Paramesewan, Wayne Tefs, and Cliff Werier. Their suggestions were invaluable, and saved us from some of the eccentricities and idiosyncrasies that often beset anthologists preoccupied with their own version of the world. Any remaining peculiarities in selection or emphasis are entirely our own.

H.J.R.
A.G.-J.

Contents

dr. prescribed opiates (handwritten margin note)

Geoffrey Chaucer

(c. 1343–1400)

from: *The Canterbury Tales*[1]

Ther was also a Nonne, a Prioresse,[2]
That of hir smiling was ful simple and coy.[3]
Hir gretteste ooth was but by sainte Loy;[4]
And she was cleped[5] madame Eglantine.
Ful wel she soong the service divine,
Entuned in hir nose ful semely;
And Frenssh she spak ful faire and fetisly,[6]
After the scole of Stratford atte Bowe[7]—
For Frenssh of Paris was to hire unknowe.
At mete[8] wel ytaught was she withalle:[9]
She leet no morsel from hir lippes falle,
Ne wette hir fingres in hir sauce deepe;
Wel coude she carye a morsel, and wel keepe[10]
That no drope ne fille upon hir brest.
In curteisye was set ful muchel hir lest.[11]
Hir over-lippe wiped she so clene
That in hir coppe ther was no ferthing[12] seene
Of grece, whan she dronken hadde hir draughte;
Ful semely after hir mete she raughte.[13]
And sikerly[14] she was of greet disport,[15]
And ful plesant, and amiable of port,[16]
And pained hire to countrefete cheere[17]
Of court, and to been estatlich[18] of manere,
And to been holden digne[19] of reverence.
But, for to speken of hir conscience,
She was so charitable and so pitous

---

1   The excerpt given here is taken from the General Prologue, in which the narrator introduces a group of pilgrims bound for Canterbury.
2   The Nun is a Mother Superior in a convent.
3   modest
4   St. Eloi, or Eligius, had been a goldsmith before becoming treasurer to the French court in the 7th century.
5   named
6   neatly, carefully
7   Stratford at the Bow, on the outskirts of London, possibly the site of the Prioress's convent
8   at the table
9   besides
10   take care
11   concern
12   small piece
13   reached
14   certainly
15   good cheer
16   mien
17   manners
18   dignified
19   deserving

She wolde weepe if that she saw a mous
Caught in a trappe, if it were deed or bledde.
Of smale houndes hadde she that she fedde
With rosted flessh, or milk and wastelbreed;[1]
But sore wepte she if oon of hem were deed,
Or if men smoot it with a yerde smerte;[2]
And al was conscience and tendre herte.
Ful semely hir wimpel pinched[3] was,
Hir nose tretys,[4] hir yen[5] greye as glas,
Hir mouth ful smal, and therto softe and reed—
But sikerly she hadde a fair forheed:
It was almost a spanne brood, I trowe,[6]
For hardily,[7] she was nat undergrowe.
Ful fetis[8] was hir cloke, as I was war;[9]
Of smal coral aboute hir arm she bar
A paire of bedes,[10] gauded al with greene,[11]
And thereon heeng a brooch of gold ful sheene,[12]
On which ther was first writen a crowned *A*,
And after, *Amor vincit omnia.*[13]

1	white bread
2	a stick sharply
3	her headdress pleated
4	well shaped
5	her eyes
6	a span [approx. nine inches] broad
7	certainly
8	neat
9	aware
10	a rosary
11	set with green "gauds," large ornamental beads set between the smaller beads marking the "aves" in a rosary
12	bright
13	(Latin) Love conquers all

English Ballads

Lord Rendal

1

'O where have you been, Lord Rendal my son,
O where have you been, my jolly young man?'
'In yonder wild woods, mother; make my bed soon,
For I'm wearied with hunting and fain would lie down.'

2

'And whom met you there, Lord Rendal my son,
And whom met you there, my jolly young man?'
'I met with my true love, mother; make my bed soon,
For I'm wearied with hunting and fain would lie down.'

3

'What got you for dinner, Lord Rendal my son,
What got you for dinner, my jolly young man?'
'A dish of small fishes, mother; make my bed soon,
For I'm wearied with hunting and fain would lie down.'

4

'What like were the fishes, Lord Rendal my son,
What like were the fishes, my jolly young man?'
'Black backs and speckled bellies: make my bed soon,
For I'm wearied with hunting and fain would lie down.'

5

'Who got the leavings, Lord Rendal my son,
Who got the leavings, my jolly young man?'
'My hawks and my hounds, mother; make my bed soon,
For I'm wearied with hunting and fain would lie down.'

6

'And what became of them, Lord Rendal my son,
And what became of them, my jolly young man?'
'They swelled and died, mother; make my bed soon,
For I'm wearied with hunting and fain would lie down.'

7

'I fear you are poisoned, Lord Rendal my son,
I fear you are poisoned, my jolly young man.'
'O yes I am dying, mother; make my bed soon,
For I'm wearied with hunting and fain would lie down.'

8

'What will you leave to your mother, Lord Rendal my son,
What will you leave to your mother, my jolly young man?'
'Four and twenty milch-kine,[1] mother; make my bed soon,
For I'm wearied with hunting and fain would lie down.'

9

'What will you leave to your father, Lord Rendal my son,
What will you leave to your father, my jolly young man?'
'My horse and the saddle, mother; make my bed soon,
For I'm wearied with hunting and fain would lie down.'

10

'What will you leave to your sister, Lord Rendal my son,
What will you leave to your sister, my jolly young man?'
'Both my gold box and rings, mother; make my bed soon,
For I'm wearied with hunting and fain would lie down.'

11

'What will you leave to your true love, Lord Rendal my son,
What will you leave to your true love, my jolly young man?'
'The tow and the halter,[2] mother; make my bed soon,
For I'm wearied with hunting and fain would lie down.'

Sir Patrick Spens

1

The King sits in Dumfermlin town
Drinking the blood-red wine:
'O, where will I get a skilly[3] skipper
Will sail this good ship of mine?'

---

1   milking cows
2   a rope with a noose
3   skillful

2

Then up and spake an eldern knight
　　Sat at the King's right knee:
'Sir Patrick Spens is the best sailor
　　That ever sailed the sea.'

3

The King has written a broad lettér
　　And sealed it with his hand,
And sent it to Sir Patrick Spens
　　Was walking on the strand.

4

'O who is the man has done this deed,
　　This ill deed done to me?
To send me out this time of the year
　　To sail upon the sea?

5

'To Norraway, to Norraway,
　　To Norraway o'er the faem.
The King's daughter of Norraway,
　　'Tis I must bring her hame.'

6

They have mounted sail on a Monday morn
　　With all the haste they may,
And they have landed in Norraway
　　Upon the Wednesday.

7

They had not been a week, a week
　　In Norraway but three,
Till lords of Norraway gan to say
　　'Ye spend all our white monie.

8

'Ye spend all our good kingis gold
　　But and[1] our queenis fee.'[2]

1　also
2　queen's dowry

'Ye lie, ye lie, ye liars loud:
    Full loud I hear you lie.

9

'For I have brought as much white monie
    As will gain¹ my men and me.
I have brought a half-fou² of good red gold
    Out o'er the sea with me.

10

'Be it wind or weet, be it snow or sleet
    Our ships must sail the morn.'
'O ever alack my master dear,
    I fear a deadly storm.

11

'I saw the new moon late yestreen³
    With the old moon in her arm.
And if we go to sea, mastér,
    I fear we'll come to harm.'

12

They had not sailed a league, a league,
    A league but barely three,
Came wind and weet and snow and sleet
    And gurly⁴ grew the sea.

13

'O where will I get a pretty boy
    Will take my steer in hand,
Till I get up to the tall topmast
    To see if I can spy land?'

14

He had not gone a step, a step,
    A step but barely ane,
When a bolt flew out of the good ship's side,
    And the salt sea it came in.

---

1   serve
2   half bushel
3   yesterday evening
4   rough

15

Come back, come back, my pretty boy,
    Lest you should come to harm.
For the salt sea's in at our coat neck,
    And out at the left arm.

16

They fetcht a web of the silken cloth,
    Another of the twine.
They wapped[1] them round the good ship's side,
    And still the sea came in.

17

Loth, loth, were our Scottish lords
    To wet their cork-heeled shoon,[2]
But yet ere all the play was played
    Their hats were wet aboon.[3]

18

O lang, lang may their ladies sit
    With their fans into their hand,
Or ever they see Sir Patrick Spens
    Come sailing to the land.

19

O lang, lang may the ladies stand
    With their gold combs in their hair
All waiting for their own dear lords
    That they shall not see mair.

20

There was Saturday and Sabbath-day,
    And Monnynday at morn,
Then featherbeds and silken sheets
    Come floating to Kinghorn.

---

1   swathed
2   shoes
3   above

21

Half over, half over to Aberdour
It is fifty fathoms deep,
And there lies good Sir Patrick Spens
With the Scots lords at his feet.

Barbara Allan

1

It was about the Martinmas[1] time,
When thick the leaves were falling,
That Sir John Graeme of the West Countrie,
Sent word for Barbara Allan.

2

His men have gone through Scarlet Town,
To the place where she was dwelling,
With: 'Haste and come to my master dear,
Gin[2] ye be Barbara Allan!

3

'There's sorrow printed on his face,
And death is o'er him stealing.
And he is sick, and very sick,
For love of Barbara Allan.'

4

'If sorrow's printed on his face
And death is o'er him stealing,
Then little better shall he be
For a sight of Barbara Allan.'

5

So hooly,[3] hooly raise she up,
And came where he was lying.
She drew the curtain by, and said:
'Young man, I think you're dying.'

---

1   11 November (the feast of St. Martin, a French bishop of the 4th Century)
2   If
3   slowly

6

'O, it's I am sick, and very sick,
    And it's all for Barbara Allan.'
'O, the better for her ye ne'er shall be,
    Though your heart's blood were spilling.

7

'Do not you mind,[1] young man,' said she,
    'How, with the townsfolk melling,[2]
Ye made the healths go round and round
    And slighted Barbara Allan?

8

'Gin now on your sickbed you lie,
    And death with you be dealing;
Why should I pity on you take?
    Farewell!' said Barbara Allan.

9

He turned his face unto the wall,
    Since she of hope had reft him,
Then hooly, hooly, raise she up
    And to his sorrow left him.

10

She had not gone of miles but two
    When she heard the dead bell ringing,
And every jow[3] the dead bell gave
    Cried: 'Woe to Barbara Allan!'

11

'O, mother, mother, make my bed,
    O, make it soft and narrow,
Since my love died for me today,
    I'll die for him tomorrow.'

---

1   remember
2   mingling
3   stroke

Sir Thomas Wyatt

(1503–1542)

The longe love, that in my thought doeth harbar[1]

The longe love, that in my thought doeth harbar
   And in myn hert doeth kepe his residence
   Into my face preseth with bold pretence,
   And therin campeth, spreding his baner.
She that me lerneth[2] to love and suffre
   And will that my trust, and lustes negligence
   Be rayned by reason, shame, and reverence
   With his hardines taketh displeasure.
Wherewithall, vnto the hertes forrest he fleith,
   Leving his entreprise with payne and cry
   And there him hideth and not appereth.
What may I do when my maister fereth,
   But, in the felde, with him to lyve and dye?
   For goode is the liff, ending faithfully.

Who so list[3] *to hounte I know where is an hynde*

Who so list to hounte I know where is an hynde;
   But as for me, helas, I may no more:
   The vayne travaill hath weried me so sore,
   I ame of theim that farthest cometh behinde;
Yet may I by no meanes my weried mynde
   Drawe from the Diere: but as she fleeth afore
   Faynting I folowe; I leve of therefore,
   Sithens[4] in a nett I seke to hold the wynde.
Who list her hount I put him owte of dowbte,
   As well as I may spend his tyme in vain:
   And graven with Diamondes in letters plain
There is written her faier neck rounde abowte:
   'Noli me tangere[5] for Cesars I ame,
   And wylde for to hold though I seme tame'.

---

1   This is Wyatt's translation of a sonnet by Petrarch; compare the translation by Surrey,
     "Love, that doth reign and live within my thought" (p.14)
2   teaches me
3   wishes, cares
4   Since
5   (Latin) 'Do not touch me,' said to have been inscribed on the collars of Caesar's hinds

Ffarewell, love, and all thy lawes for ever;

Ffarewell, love, and all thy lawes for ever;
    Thy bayted hookes shall tangill me no more;
    Senec[1] and Plato call me from thy lore,
    To perfaict welth my wit for to endever.
In blynde errour when I did perseuer,
    Thy sherpe repulce that pricketh ay so sore
    Hath taught me to sett in tryfels no store
    And scape fourth syns libertie is lever.[2]
Therefore, farewell; goo trouble yonger hertes
    And in me clayme no more authoritie;
    With idill yeuth goo use thy propertie
And theron spend thy many britill dertes:
    For hetherto though I have lost all my tyme,
    Me lusteth[3] no lenger rotten boughes to clyme.

They fle from me that sometyme did me seke

They fle from me that sometyme did me seke
With naked fote stalking in my chambre.
I have sene theim gentill tame and meke
That nowe are wyld and do not remembre
That sometyme they put theimself in daunger
To take bred at my hand; and nowe they raunge
Besely seking with a continuell chaunge.

Thancked be fortune, it hath ben othrewise
Twenty tymes better; but ons in speciall
In thyn arraye after a pleasaunt gyse
When her lose gowne from her shoulders did fall,
And she me caught in her armes long and small;[4]
Therewithall swetely did my kysse,
And softely said 'dere hert, how like you this?'

It was no dreme: I lay brode waking.
But all is torned thorough[5] my gentilnes
Into a straunge fasshion of forsaking;
And I have leve to goo of her goodeness,
And she also to use newfangilnes.[6]
But syns that I so kyndely[7] ame serued,
I would fain knowe what she hath deserued.

---

1   Seneca, Roman playwright and philosopher
2   dearer
3   I care
4   slender
5   through
6   fondness for novelty; fickleness
7   naturally

Blame not my lute, for he must sownd

Blame not my lute, for he must sownd
Of thes or that as liketh me;
For lake of wytt the lutte is bownd
To gyve suche tunes as plesithe me;
Tho my songes be somewhat strange
And spekes such words as toche they change,
     Blame not my lutte.

My lutte, alas, doth not ofend
Tho that perfors he must agre
To sownd such teunes as I entend
To sing to them that hereth me;
Then tho my songes be sumewhat plain,
And tocheth some that use to fayn,[1]
     Blame not my lutte.

My lute and strynges may not deny
But as I strike they must obay;
Brake not them than soo wrongfully,
But wryeke[2] thy selffe some wyser way;
And tho the songes whiche I endight
To qwytt[3] thy chainge with Rightfull spight,
     Blame not my lute.

Spyght askyth spight and changing change,
And falsyd faith must nedes be knowne,
The faute so grett, the case so strange,
Of Right it must abrod be blown:
Then sins that by thyn own desartte
My soinges do tell how trew thou artt,
     Blame not my lute.

Blame but thy selffe that hast mysdown[4]
And well desaruid to haue blame;
Change thou thy way so evyll bygown
And then my lute shall sownd that same;
But if tyll then my fyngeres play
By thy desartt their wontyd way,
     Blame not my lutte.

---

1   that are deceitful
2   revenge
3   requite
4   done wrong

Farewell, unknowne, for tho thow brake
My strynges in spight with grett desdayn
Yet haue I fownd owt for thy sake
Stringes for to strynge my lute agayne;
And yf perchance this folysh Ryme
Do make thee blush at any tyme
      Blame nott my lutte.

Henry Howard, Earl of Surrey

(ca. 1517–1547)

The Soote Season

The soote[1] season, that bud and bloom forth brings,
With green hath clad the hill and eke[2] the vale;
The nightingale with feathers new she sings;
The turtle[3] to her make[4] hath told her tale.
Summer is come, for every spray now springs;
The hart hath hung his old head on the pale;
The buck in brake his winter coat he flings,
The fishes float with new repairéd scale;
The adder all her slough away she slings,
The swift swallow pursueth the flies small;
The busy bee her honey now she mings.[5]
Winter is worn, that was the flowers' bale.[6]
And thus I see among these pleasant things,
Each care decays, and yet my sorrow springs.

Love, That Doth Reign and Live Within My Thought[7]

Love, that doth reign and live within my thought,
And built his seat within my captive breast,
Clad in the arms wherein with me he fought,
Oft in my face he doth his banner rest.
But she that taught me love and suffer pain,
My doubtful hope and eke[8] my hot desire
With shamefast look to shadow and refrain,
Her smiling grace converteth straight to ire.
And coward Love, then, to the heart apace
Taketh his flight, where he doth lurk and plain,[9]
His purpose lost, and dare not show his face.
For my lord's guilt thus faultless bide I pain,
Yet from my lord shall not my foot remove:
Sweet is the death that taketh end by love.

---

1   sweet
2   also
3   turtledove
4   mate
5   mingles
6   harm
7   A translation of a sonnet by Petrarch; compare Wyatt's version, "The longe love that in
     my thought doeth harbar" (p.10).
8   also
9   complain

Sir Walter Ralegh

(c. 1552–1618)

The Nimphs reply to the Sheepheard[1]

If all the world and love were young,
And truth in every Sheepheards tongue,
These pretty pleasures might me move,
To live with thee, and be thy love.

Time drives the flocks from field to fold,
When Rivers rage, and Rocks grow cold,
And Philomell[2] becommeth dombe,
The rest complaines of cares to come.

The flowers doe fade, and wanton fieldes,
To wayward winter reckoning yeeldes,
A honny tongue, a hart of gall,
Is fancies spring, but sorrowes fall.

Thy gownes, thy shooes, thy beds of Roses,
Thy cap, thy kirtle,[3] and thy poesies,
Soone breake, soone wither, soone forgotten:
In follie ripe, in reason rotten.

Thy belt of straw and Ivie buddes,
Thy Corall claspes and Amber studdes,
All these in mee no meanes can move,
To come to thee, and be thy love.

But could youth last, and love still breede,
Had ioyes no date, nor age no neede,
Then these delights my minde might move,
To live with thee, and be thy love.

---

1   written in reply to Christopher Marlowe's "The Passionate Shepherd to His Love" (p.30)
2   The nightingale. In Greek myth, Philomela was raped by King Tereus, who cut out her tongue; she was subsequently transformed into a nightingale.
3   skirt

Three thinges there bee that prosper up apace

Three thinges there bee that prosper up apace
And flourish, whilest they growe a sunder farr,
But on a day, they meet all in one place,
And when they meet, they one an other marr;
And they bee theise, the wood, the weede, the wagg.
The wood is that, which makes the Gallow tree,
The weed is that, which stringes the Hangmans bagg,
The wagg my pritty knave betokeneth thee.[1]
Marke well deare boy whilest theise assemble not,
Green springs the tree, hempe growes, the wagg is wilde,
But when they meet, it makes the timber rott,
It fretts the halter, and it choakes the childe.
   Then bless thee, and beware, and lett us praye,
   Wee part not with thee at this meeting day.

---

1   The poem was intended for Ralegh's eldest son, Walter.

Edmund Spenser

(1552–1599)

from: *Amoretti*

Sonnet XXXVII

What guyle is this, that those her golden tresses,
   She doth attyre under a net of gold:
   and with sly skill so cunningly them dresses,
   that which is gold or heare, may scarse be told?
Is it that mens frayle eyes, which gaze too bold,
   she may entangle in that golden snare:
   and being caught may craftily enfold,
   theyr weaker harts, which are not wel aware?
Take heed therefore, myne eyes, how ye doe stare
   henceforth too rashly on that guilefull net,
   in which if ever ye entrapped are,
   out of her bands ye by no meanes shall get.
Fondnesse[1] it were for any being free,
   to covet fetters, though they golden bee.

Sonnet LXXV.

One day I wrote her name upon the strand,
   but came the waves and washed it away:
   agayne I wrote it with a second hand,
   but came the tyde, and made my paynes his pray.
"Vayne man," sayd she, "that doest in vaine assay,
   a mortall thing so to immortalize,
   for I my selue shall lyke to this decay,
   and eek[2] my name bee wyped out lykewize."
"Not so," (quod I) "let baser things devize
   to dy in dust, but you shall live by fame:
   my verse your vertues rare shall eternize,
   and in the hevens wryte your glorious name.
Where whenas death shall all the world subdew,
   our loue shall live, and later life renew."

---

1   foolishness
2   also

Sonnet LXXIX

Men call you fayre, and you doe credit it,
    For that your selfe ye dayly such doe see:
    but the trew fayre, that is the gentle wit,
    and vertuous mind, is much more praysd of me.
For all the rest, how ever fayre it be,
    shall turne to nought and loose that glorious hew:[1]
    but onely that is permanent and free
    from frayle corruption, that doth flesh ensew.[2]
That is true beautie: that doth argue you
    to be divine and borne of heavenly seed:
    deriv'd from that fayre Spirit, from whom al true
    and perfect beauty did at first proceed.
He onely fayre, and what he fayre hath made,
    all other fayre lyke flowres untymely fade.

Sonnet LXXXI

Fayre is my loue, when her fayre golden heares,
    with the loose wynd ye waving chance to marke:
    fayre when the rose in her red cheekes appeares,
    or in her eyes the fyre of love does sparke.
Fayre when her brest lyke a rich laden barke,[3]
    with pretious merchandize she forth doth lay:
    fayre when that cloud of pryde, which oft doth dark
    her goodly light with smiles she drives away.
But fayrest she, when so she doth display,
    the gate with pearles and rubyes richly dight:[4]
    throgh which her words so wise do make their way
    to beare the message of her gentle spright.
The rest be works of natures wonderment,
    but this the worke of harts astonishment.

* * *

---

1   form, appearance
2   outlast
3   ship
4   adorned

Prothalamion[1]

1

Calme was the day, and through the trembling ayre,
Sweete breathing Zephyrus[2] did softly play,
A gentle spirit, that lightly did delay[3]
Hot Titan's[4] beames, which then did glyster[5] fayre:
When I whom sullein care,
Through discontent of my long fruitlesse stay
In Princes Court, and expectation vayne
Of idle hopes, which still doe fly away,
Like empty shaddowes, did aflict my brayne,
Walkt forth to ease my payne
Along the shoare of silver streaming Themmes,
Whose rutty Bancke, the which his River hemmes,
Was paynted all with variable flowers,
And all the meades adornd with daintie gemmes,
Fit to decke maydens bowres,
And crowne their Paramours,[6]
Against[7] the Brydale day, which is not long:[8]
   Sweete Themmes runne softly, till I end my song.

2

There, in a Meadow, by the Rivers side,
A Flocke of Nymphes I chauncéd to espy,
All lovely Daughters of the Flood thereby,
With goodly greenish locks all loose untyde,
As each had bene a Bryde,[9]
And each one had a little wicker basket,
Made of fine twigs entrayléd curiously,
In which they gathered flowers to fill their flasket:
And with fine Fingers, cropt full feateously[10]
The tender stalkes on hye.
Of every sort, which in that Meadow grew,
They gathered some; the Violet pallid blew,
The little Dazie, that at evening closes,

---

1   Coined by Spenser, the word "prothalamion" means a celebratory song before a marriage.
     The occasion of the poem was the double wedding of Lady Elizabeth and Lady Katherine
     Somerset, daughters of Edward Somerset, the Earl of Worcester, in 1596.
2   in Greek mythology, the west wind
3   soften
4   the sun god's
5   glisten
6   lovers
7   in expectation of
8   which is not far off
9   At the time brides would let their hair fall free during the marriage ceremony.
10   delicately

The virgin Lillie, and the Primrose trew,
With store of vermeil[1] Roses,
To decke their Bridegromes posies,
Against the Brydale day, which was not long:
   Sweete Themmes runne softly, till I end my song.

3

With that, I saw two Swannes of goodly hewe,
Come softly swimming downe along the Lee;[2]
Two fairer Birds I yet did never see:
The snow which doth the top of Pindus[3] strew,
Did never whiter shew,
Nor Jove himselfe when he a Swan would be
For love of Leda,[4] whiter did appeare:
Yet Leda was they say as white as he,
Yet not so white as these, nor nothing neare;
So purely white they were,
That even the gentle streame, the which them bare,
Seemed foule to them, and bad his billowes spare
To wet their silken feathers, least they might
Soyle their fayre plumes with water not so fayre
And marre their beauties bright,
That shone as heavens light,
Against their Brydale day, which was not long:
   Sweete Themmes runne softly, till I end my song.

4

Eftsoones the Nymphes, which now had Flowers their fill,
Ran all in haste, to see that silver brood,
As they came floating on the Christal Flood.
Whom when they sawe, they stood amazéd still,
Their wondring eyes to fill,
Them seemed they never saw a sight so fayre,
Of Fowles so lovely, that they sure did deeme
Them heavenly borne, or to be that same payre
Which through the Skie draw Venus silver Teeme,[5]
For sure they did not seeme
To be begot of any earthly Seede,
But rather Angels or of Angels breede:
Yet were they bred of Somers-heat[6] they say,

---

1   vermillion
2   possibly the River Lea, a tributary of the Thames
3   a mountain range in central and northern Greece
4   In Greek mythology, Zeus (here called Jove) assumed the form of a swan to visit Leda. One of the children born from their union was Helen of Troy.
5   According to Ovid, Venus is pulled through the air by a team of swans.
6   a play on 'Somerset,' the family name

In sweetest Season, when each Flower and weede
The earth did fresh aray,
So fresh they seemed as day,
Even as their Brydale day, which was not long:
   Sweete Themmes runne softly, till I end my song.

5

Then forth they all out of their baskets drew,
Great store of Flowers, the honour of the field,
That to the sense did fragrant odours yeild,
All which upon those goodly Birds they threw,
And all the Waves did strew,
That like old Peneus[1] Waters they did seeme,
When downe along by pleasant Tempes shore
Scattred with Flowres, through Thessaly they streeme,
That they appeare through Lillies plenteous store,
Like a Brydes Chamber flore:
Two of those Nymphes, meane while, two Garlands bound,
Of freshest Flowres which in that Mead they found,
The which presenting all in trim Array,
Their[2] snowie Foreheads therewithall they crownd,
Whil'st one did sing this Lay,
Prepared against that Day,
Against their Brydale day, which was not long:
   Sweete Themmes runne softly, till I end my song.

6

"Ye gentle Birdes, the worlds faire ornament,
And heavens glorie, whom this happie hower
Doth leade unto your lovers blisfull bower,
Joy may you have and gentle hearts content
Of your loves couplement:
And let faire Venus, that is Queene of love,
With her heart-quelling Sonne upon you smile,
Whose smile they say, hath vertue to remove
All Loves dislike, and friendships faultie guile
For ever to assoile.[3]
Let endlesse Peace your steadfast hearts accord,
And blesséd Plentie wait upon your bord,[4]
And let your bed with pleasures chast abound,
That fruitfull issue may to you afford,

---

1   the river that runs through the vale of Tempe in Thessaly
2   i.e. the swans'
3   i.e. has the power to remove any lack of affection in love, and assail [or overwhelm] the
     guile that can undermine friendship
4   board, table

Which may your foes confound,
And make your joyes redound,
Upon your Brydale day, which is not long:
   Sweete Themmes run softlie, till I end my Song."

7

So ended she, and all the rest around
To her redoubled that her undersong,[1]
Which said, their bridale daye should not be long.
And gentle Eccho from the neighbour ground,
Their accents did resound.
So forth those joyous Birdes did passe along,
Adowne the Lee, that to them murmurde low,
As he would speake, but that he lackt a tong,
Yet did by signes his glad affection show,
Making his streame run slow.
And all the foule which in his flood did dwell
Gan flock about these twaine, that did excell
The rest, so far, as Cynthia[2] doth shend[3]
The lesser starres. So they enrangéd well,
Did on those two attend,
And their best service lend,
Against their wedding day, which was not long:
   Sweete Themmes run softly, till I end my song.

8

At length they all to mery London came,
To mery London, my most kyndly Nurse,
That to me gave this Lifes first native sourse:
Though from another place I take my name,
An house of auncient fame.[4]
There when they came, whereas those bricky towres,[5]
The which on Themmes brode aged backe doe ryde,
Where now the studious Lawyers have their bowers
There whylome[6] wont the Templer Knights to byde,
Till they decayd through pride:
Next whereunto there standes a stately place,
Where oft I gaynéd giftes and goodly grace
Of that great Lord,[7] which therein wont to dwell,

---

1   refrain, chorus
2   the goddess of the moon
3   surpass
4   The poet Spenser was related to the Spencer family of Althorp, Northamptonshire.
5   the "Temple," housing law students in London; originally the home of the Knights Templar
6   formerly
7   Spenser's former patron the Earl of Leicester, who had died in 1588

Whose want too well now feeles my freendles case:
But Ah here fits not well
Olde woes but joyes to tell
Against the bridale daye, which is not long:
   Sweete Themmes runne softly, till I end my song.

9

Yet therein now doth lodge a noble Peer,[1]
Great Englands glory and the Worlds wide wonder,
Whose dreadfull name, late through all Spaine did thunder,[2]
And Hercules two pillors[3] standing neere,
Did make to quake and feare:
Faire branch of Honor, flower of Chevalrie,
That fillest England with thy triumphs fame,
Joy have thou of thy noble victorie,
And endlesse happinesse of thine owne name
That promiseth the same:
That through thy prowesse and victorious armes,
Thy country may be freed from forraine harmes:
And great Elisaes[4] glorious name may ring
Through al the world, filled with thy wide Alarmes,
Which some brave muse may sing
To ages following,
Upon the Brydale day, which is not long:
   Sweete Themmes runne softly, till I end my song.

10

From those high Towers, this noble Lord issuing,
Like Radiant Hesper[5] when his golden hayre
In th'Ocean billowes he hath Bathéd fayre,
Descended to the Rivers open viewing,
With a great traine ensuing.
Above the rest were goodly to bee seene
Two gentle Knights[6] of lovely face and feature
Beseeming well the bower of anie Queene,
With gifts of wit and ornaments of nature,
Fit for so goodly stature:
That like the twins of Jove they seemed in sight,

---

1   Robert Devereux, 2nd Earl of Essex, who, with Sir Walter Raleigh, had plundered a
     Spanish fleet at Cadiz in June 1596
2   In 1596 the Earl of Essex led a successful raid on the Spanish port of Cadiz.
3   the straits of Gibraltar
4   Elizabeth I's
5   Hesperus, the morning star
6   i.e., the prospective bridegrooms, here compared to Castor and Pollux ("the twins of
     Jove")

Which decke the Bauldricke of the Heavens[1] bright.
They two forth pacing to the Rivers side,
Received those two faire Brides, their Loves delight,
Which at th'appointed tyde,
Each one did make his Bryde,
Against their Brydale day, which is not long:
 Sweete Themmes runne softly, till I end my song.

---

1   the zodiac

Lady Mary Wroth

(1587–c.1652)

from: *Pamphilia to Amphilanthus*[1]

When Nights Black Mantle Could Most Darknes Prove

When nights black mantle could most darknes prove,
    And sleepe deaths Image did my senceses hiere
    From knowledg of my self, then thoughts did move
    Swifter then those most swiftnes need require:

In sleepe, a Chariot drawne by wing'd desire
    I sawe: wher sate bright Venus Queene of love,
    And att her feete her sonne, still adding fire
    To burning hearts which she did hold above,

Butt one hart flaming more then all the rest
    The goddess held, and putt itt to my brest,
    Deare sonne now shutt sayd she: thus must wee winn;

Hee her obay'd, and martir'd my poore hart,
    I, waking hop'd as dreames itt would depart
    Yett since: O mee: a lover I have binn.

Faulce hope which feeds butt to destroy, and spill

Faulce hope which feeds butt to destroy, and spill
    What itt first breeds; unaturall to the birth
    Of thine owne wombe; conceaving butt to kill,
    And plenty gives to make the greater dearth,

Soe Tirants doe who faulsly ruling earth
    Outwardly grace them, and with profitts fill
    Advance those who appointed are to death
    To make theyr greater falle to please theyr will.

Thus shadow they theyr wicked vile intent
    Coulering evill with a show of good
    While in faire showes theyr malice soe is spent;
    Hope kills the hart, and tirants shed the blood.

---

1   The names are those of the protagonists in Wroth's prose romance the *Countess of Montgomery's Urania* (1621); the two sonnets and the song given here come from a sequence appended to the romance. "Pamphilia"means all-loving; "Amphilanthus" mean lover of two.

For hope deluding brings us to the pride
Of our desires the farder downe to slide.

Love a child is ever criing

Love a child is ever criing,
    Please him, and hee straite is flying,
    Give him hee the more is craving
    Never satisfi'd with having;

His desires have noe measure,
    Endles folly is his treasure,
    What hee promiseth hee breaketh
    Trust nott one word that he speaketh;

Hee vowes nothing butt faulce matter,
    And to cousen[1] you hee'l flatter,
    Lett him gaine the hand hee'll leave you,
    And still glory to deseave you;

Hee will triumph in your wayling,
    And yett cause bee of your fayling,
    Thes his vertus ar, and slighter
    Ar his guiftes, his favours lighter,

Feathers ar as firme in staying
    Woulves noe fiercer in theyr praying.
    As a child then leave him crying
    Nor seeke him soe giv'n to flying.

---

1   deceive

(handwritten: Sonnet sequence)

Sir Philip Sydney

(handwritten: Stella - Star / Astrophil - lover of star)

(1554–1586)

from: *Astrophil and Stella*

(handwritten: carries on a kind of sequence)

(handwritten: looking at his inspiration)

1

(handwritten: 12 syllables each line - 6 feet / hexameter)

(handwritten: very similar form to an Eliz. sonnet)

Loving in truth, and faine in verse my love to show,   a
That the deare She might take some pleasure of my paine: b
Pleasure might cause her reade, reading might make her know,   a
Knowledge might pitie winne, and pitie grace obtaine,   b
   I sought fit words to paint the blackest face of woe,   a
Studying inventions fine, her wits to entertaine: b
Oft turning others' leaves, to see if thence would flow   a
Some fresh and fruitfull showers upon my sunne-burn'd braine.   b
   But words came halting forth, wanting Invention's stay,[1]   c
Invention, Nature's child, fled step-dame Studie's blowes,   d
And others' feete still seem'd but strangers in my way.   c
Thus great with child to speake, and helplesse in my throwes, *(handwritten: throes)*
   Biting my trewand[2] pen, beating my selfe for spite,   e
'Foole,' said my Muse to me, 'looke in thy heart and write.'   e

(handwritten: introductory poem)

(handwritten: basically he's saying he's tongue tied / she has a child in him labor-throes of child / that he wants to give birth to)

31

With how sad steps, ô Moone, thou climb'st the skies,   a
   How silently, and with how wanne a face,   b
   What, may it be that even in heav'nly place   b
That busie archer his sharpe arrowes tries?   a
Sure, if that long with *Love* acquainted eyes   a
   Can judge of *Love*, thou feel'st a Lover's case;   b
   I reade it in thy lookes, thy languisht grace,   b
To me that feele the like, thy state descries.   a
   Then ev'n of fellowship, ô Moone, tell me   c
Is constant *Love* deem'd there but want of wit?   d
Are Beauties there as proud as here they be?   c
Do they above love to be lov'd, and yet   d
   Those Lovers scorne whom that *Love* doth possesse?   e
   Do they call *Vertue* there ungratefulnesse?   e

(handwritten: Italian sonnet)

(handwritten: more idealistic than Shakespeare / Sidney is from the upper classes, / Skspre was more exposed to the / harsher realities of life)

---

1   support
2   truant

[27]

rhetorical ques.

47

What, have I thus betrayed my libertie? *a were branded to*
  Can those blacke beames such burning markes engrave *symbol*
  In my free side? or am I borne a slave, *their position*
Whose necke becomes[1] such yoke of tyranny? *a*
Or want I sense to feele my miserie? *a*
  Or sprite, disdaine of such disdaine to have? *b*
  Who for long faith, tho dayly helpe I crave, *please have*
May get no almes but scorne of beggerie.[2] *a pity of me*
  Vertue awake, Beautie but beautie is, *c*
I may, I must, I can, I will, I do *d*
Leave following that, which it is gaine to misse. *c*
Let her go. Soft, but here she comes. Go to, *d*
  Unkind, I love you not: O me, that eye *e*
  Doth make my heart give to my tongue the lie. *e*

you're lying

71

boob

Who will in fairest booke of Nature know, *a*
  How Vertue may best lodg'd in beautie be, *b*
  Let him but learne of *Love* to reade in thee, *b*
Stella, those faire lines, which true goodnesse show. *c*
There shall he find all vices' overthrow, *a*
  Not by rude force, but sweetest soveraigntie *b soveraignty*
  Of reason, from whose light those night-birds flie; *b*
That inward sunne in thine eyes shineth so. *a*
  And not content to be Perfection's heire *heir c*
Thy selfe, doest strive all minds that way to move, *d*
Who marke in thee what is in thee most faire. *c*
So while thy beautie drawes the heart to love, *d*
  As fast thy Vertue bends that love to good: *e*
  'But ah,' Desire still cries, 'give me some food.' *e*

* * *

---

1   is suited to
2   scorn for my begging

English sonnet ✓

Leave me ô Love, which reachest but to dust

Leave me ô Love, which reachest but to dust, *a*
And thou my mind aspire to higher things: *b*
Grow rich in that which never taketh rust: *a*
What ever fades, but fading pleasure brings. *b*

Draw in thy beames, and humble all thy might, *c*
To that sweet yoke, where lasting freedomes be: *d*
Which breakes the clowdes and opens forth the light, *c*
That doth both shine and give us sight to see. *d*

O take fast hold, let that light be thy guide, *e*
In this small course which birth drawes out to death,
And thinke how evill becommeth him to slide, *e*
Who seeketh heav'n, and comes of heav'nly breath. *f*
    Then farewell world, thy uttermost I see, *g*
    Eternall Love maintaine thy life in me. *g*

Italian must be Abba even though the rest will vary

said to have great sprezzatura

Petrarchan – highly artificial (in their idealism, use of fig. speech)

Christopher Marlowe

(1564–1593)

The Passionate Sheepheard to his Love

Come live with mee, and be my love,
And we will all the pleasures prove,[1]
That Vallies, groves, hills and fieldes,
Woods, or steepie mountaine yeeldes.

And wee will sit upon the Rocks,
Seeing the Sheepheards feede theyr flocks,
By shallow Rivers, to whose falls,
Melodious byrds sing Madrigalls.

And I will make thee beds of Roses,
And a thousand fragrant poesies,
A cap of flowers, and a kirtle,[2]
Imbroydred all with leaves of Mirtle.

A gowne made of the finest wooll,
Which from our pretty Lambes we pull,
Fayre linèd slippers for the cold:
With buckles of the purest gold.

A belt of straw, and Ivie buds,
With Corall clasps and Amber studs,
And if these pleasures may thee move,
Come live with mee, and be my love.

The Sheepheards Swaines shall daunce and sing,
For thy delight each May-morning.
If these delights thy minde may move;
Then live with mee, and be my love.

---

1   test, experience
2   skirt

William Shakespeare

(1564–1616)

Sonnet 18

[handwritten margin note: personifying the sun]

Shall I compare thee to a Summers day?
Thou art more lovely and more temperate:
Rough windes do shake the darling buds of Maie,
And Sommers lease hath all too short a date:
Sometime too hot the eye of heaven shines,
And often is his gold complexion dimm'd,
And every faire from faire some-time declines,
By chance, or natures changing course untrim'd:[1]
But thy eternall Sommer shall not fade,
Nor loose possession of that faire thou ow'st,
Nor shall death brag thou wandr'st in his shade,
When in eternall lines to time thou grow'st,
  So long as men can breath or eyes can see,
  So long lives this, and this gives life to thee.

[handwritten margin note: Parallelism (Beginning of a line → anaphola)]

Sonnet 29

[handwritten margin notes: personifying heaven; using metonymy; addressing heaven; really addressing God —]

When in disgrace with Fortune and mens eyes,
I all alone beweepe my out-cast state,
And trouble deafe heaven with my bootlesse[2] cries,
And looke upon my selfe and curse my fate.
Wishing me like to one more rich in hope,
Featur'd like him, like him with friends possest,
Desiring this mans art, and that mans skope,
With what I most injoy contented least,
Yet in these thoughts my selfe almost despising,
Haplye I thinke on thee, and then my state,
(Like to the Larke at breake of daye arising)
From sullen earth sings himns at Heavens gate,
  For thy sweet love remembred such welth brings,
  That then I skorne to change my state with Kings.

Sonnet 30

When to the Sessions of sweet silent thought,
I sommon up remembrance of things past,
I sigh the lacke of many a thing I sought,
And with old woes new waile my deare times waste:
Then can I drowne an eye (un-us'd to flow)
For precious friends hid in deaths dateles night,

---

1   divested of beauty
2   futile

And weepe a fresh loves long since canceld woe,
And mone th'expence of many a vannisht sight.
Then can I greeve at greevances fore-gon,
And heavily from woe to woe tell ore
The sad account of fore-bemoned mone,
Which I new pay, as if not payd before.
  But if the while I thinke on thee (deare friend)
  All losses are restord, and sorrowes end.

Sonnet 55

Not marble, nor the guilded monument,
Of Princes shall out-live this powrefull rime,
But you shall shine more bright in these contents
Then unswept stone, besmeer'd with sluttish time.
When wastefull warre shall Statues over-turne,
And broiles roote out the worke of masonry,
Nor Mars his sword, nor warres quick fire shall burne:
The living record of your memory.
Gainst death, and all oblivious enmity
Shall you pace forth, your praise shall stil finde roome,
Even in the eyes of all posterity
That weare this world out to the ending doome.[1]
  So til the judgement that your selfe arise,
  You live in this, and dwell in lovers eies.

Sonnet 73

That time of yeeare thou maist in me behold,
When yellow leaves, or none, or few doe hange
Upon those boughes which shake against the could,
Bare ruin'd quiers, where late the sweet birds sang.
In me thou seest the twi-light of such day,
As after Sun-set fadeth in the West,
Which by and by blacke night doth take away,
Deaths second selfe that seals up all in rest.
In me thou seest the glowing of such fire,
That on the ashes of his youth doth lye,
As the death bed, whereon it must expire,
Consum'd with that which it was nurrisht by.
  This thou percev'st, which makes thy love more strong
  To love that well, which thou must leave ere long.

1   the Day of Judgement

Sonnet 106

When in the Chronicle of wasted time,
I see discriptions of the fairest wights,[1]
And beautie making beautifull old rime,
In praise of Ladies dead, and lovely Knights,
Then in the blazon[2] of sweet beauties best,
Of hand, of foote, of lip, of eye, of brow,
I see their antique Pen would have exprest,
Even such a beauty as you maister now.
So all their praises are but prophesies
Of this our time, all you prefiguring,
And for they look'd but with devining eyes,
They had not still enough your worth to sing:
  For we which now behold these present dayes,
  Have eyes to wonder, but lack toungs to praise.

[margin: Kind of parallelism]

[margin: I've read all these things, all those things are but prophesies of you]

Sonnet 116

Let me not to the marriage of true mindes
Admit impediments, love is not love
Which alters when it alteration findes,
Or bends with the remover to remove.
O no, it is an ever fixed marke
That lookes on tempests and is never shaken;
It is the star to every wandring barke,
Whose worths unknowne, although his higth[3] be taken.
Lov's not Times foole, though rosie lips and cheeks
Within his bending sickles compasse come,
Love alters not with his breefe houres and weekes,
But beares it out even to the edge of doome:[4]
  If this be error and upon me proved,
  I never writ, nor no man ever loved.

[margin: ideal conception of love]

Sonnet 129

Th'expence of Spirit[5] in a waste of shame
Is lust in action, and till action, lust
Is perjurd, murdrous, bloudy, full of blame,
Savage, extreame, rude, cruell, not to trust,
Injoyd no sooner but dispised straight,

[margin: compares love to bait]

[margin: negative imagery]

[margin: Thus the]

[margin: reg. rhythm shifts the meter]

[margin: examine your own experience]

1 people
2 display, as of armorial bearings
3 altitude
4 judgement
5 life, vitality

Note of the power of the Rythm in this Sonnet

Parallelism *only metaphor in this poem*

Past reason hunted, and no sooner had *(swallowed bait)*
Past reason hated as a swollowed bayt,
On purpose layd to make the taker mad.
mad→ Made in pursut and in possession so,
Had, having, and in quest, to have extreame,
lust is 1 of 7 A blisse in proofe[1] and provd a very wo, *(c)*
deadly sins Before a joy proposd behind a dreame,
All this the world well knowes yet none knowes well,
To shun the heaven that leads men to this hell.

Sonnet 130

making fun of the Petrarchan tradition

Corall → My Mistres eyes are nothing like the Sunne,
Currall is farre more red, then her lips red,
If snow be white, why then her brests are dun:
making fun If haires be wiers, black wiers grow on her head:
of idealized I have seene Roses damaskt,[2] red and white,
love, the But no such Roses see I in her cheekes,
practise of And in some perfumes is there more delight, *connotation*
putting a Then in the breath that from my Mistres reekes. *too strong unpleasant*
woman on a I love to heare her speake, yet well I know,
pedestal That Musicke hath a farre more pleasing sound:
I graunt I never saw a goddesse goe,
parallelism My Mistres when shee walkes treads on the ground.
And yet by heaven I thinke my love as rare,
As any she beli'd with false compare.

Sonnet 146

Pyrrhic foot followed by spondee

Elizab. Printer's Poore soule the center of my sinfull earth,
but real missing My sinfull earth these rebbell powres that thee array,
words are Why dost thou pine within and suffer dearth
unknow— Painting thy outward walls so costlie gay?
alternates→ Why so large cost having so short a lease,
'Lord of' Dost thou upon thy fading mansion spend?
'Slave of' Shall wormes inheritors of this excesse
'Starved by' Eate up thy charge? is this thy bodies end?
Then soule live thou upon thy servants losse,
And let that pine to aggravat[3] thy store;
Buy tearmes divine in selling houres of drosse: *Scarcity*
Within be fed, without be rich no more,
So shalt thou feed on death, that feeds on men,
And death once dead, ther's no more dying then.

---

1 in the experience
2 ornamented with rich patterns
3 enlarge, increase

Fear no more the heat o' th' sun[1]

Fear no more the heat o' th' sun,
  Nor the furious winter's rages,
Thou thy worldly task hast done,
  Home art gone and ta'en thy wages.
Golden lads and girls all must,
As chimney-sweepers, come to dust.

Fear no more the frown o' th' great,
  Thou art past the tyrant's stroke,
Care no more to clothe and eat,
  To thee the reed is as the oak:
The sceptre, learning, physic,[2] must
All follow this and come to dust.

Fear no more the lightning-flash.
  Nor th' all-dreaded thunder-stone.[3]
Fear not slander, censure rash.
  Thou hast finish'd joy and moan.
All lovers young, all lovers must
Consign to thee and come to dust.

No exorciser harm thee!
  Nor no witchcraft charm thee!
Ghost unlaid forbear thee!
  Nothing ill come near thee!
Quiet consummation have,
And renownéd be thy grave!

Poor soul/ the cén/tér o/ my sinful earthy/

*✱-o/ is difficult to accent
- last word of line almost always accent
(except in feminine rhyme)*

---

1 from *Cymbeline* IV.ii.258-82
2 medicine
3 The noise of thunder was thought to be caused by falling meteorites.

O mistress mine, where are you roaming?[1]

O mistress mine, where are you roaming?
O stay and hear, your true love's coming,
  That can sing both high and low.
Trip no further, pretty sweeting;
Journeys end in lovers meeting,
  Every wise man's son doth know.
What is love? 'Tis not hereafter;
Present mirth hath present laughter;
  What's to come is still unsure.
In delay there lies no plenty,
Then come kiss me, sweet and twenty;
  Youth's a stuff will not endure.

---

1   from *Twelfth Night* II.iii.40-52

Thomas Campion

(1567–1620)

My Sweetest Lesbia

My sweetest Lesbia, let us live and love,
And, though the sager sort our deedes reprove,
Let us not way them: heav'ns great lampes doe dive
Into their west, and strait againe revive,
But, soone as once set is our little light,
Then must we sleepe one ever-during night.

If all would lead their lives in love like mee,
Then bloudie swords and armour should not be,
No drum nor trumpet peaceful sleeps should move,
Unles alar'me came from the campe of love:
But fooles do live, and wast their little light,
And seeke with paine their ever-during night.

When timely death my life and fortune ends,
Let not my hearse be vext with mourning friends,
But let all lovers, rich in triumph, come,
And with sweet pastimes grace my happie tombe;
And, Lesbia, close up thou my little light,
And crowne with love my ever-during night.

When Thou Must Home

When thou must home to shades of underground,
And there ariv'd, a newe admired guest,
The beauteous spirits do ingirt thee round,
White Iope,[1] blith Hellen, and the rest,
To heare the stories of thy finisht love,
From that smoothe toong whose musicke hell can move:

Then wilt thou speake of banqueting delights,
Of masks and revels which sweete youth did make,
Of Turnies and great challenges of knights,
And all these triumphes for thy beauties sake:
When thou hast told these honours done to thee,
Then tell, O tell, how thou didst murther me.

---

1   In Greek mythology, Iope (also known as Casseiopia) was renowned for her beauty.

There is a Garden in her face

There is a Garden in her face,
Where Roses and white Lillies grow;
A heav'nly paradice is that place,
Wherein all pleasant fruits doe flow.
There Cherries grow, which none may buy
Till Cherry ripe[1] themselves doe cry.

Those Cherries fayrely doe enclose
Of Orient Pearle a double row,
Which when her lovely laughter showes,
They looke like Rose-buds fill'd with snow.
Yet them nor Peere nor Prince can buy,
Till Cherry ripe themselves doe cry.

Her Eyes like Angels watch them still;
Her Browes like bended bowes doe stand,
Threatning with piercing frownes to kill
All that attempt with eye or hand
Those sacred Cherries to come nigh,
Till Cherry ripe themselves doe cry.

---

1   the cry of a London street seller

John Donne

(1572–1631)

The Good-Morrow

I wonder by my troth, what thou, and I
Did, till we lov'd? were we not wean'd till then?
But suck'd on countrey pleasures, childishly?
Or snorted we in the seaven sleepers den?[1]
T'was so; But this, all pleasures fancies bee.
If ever any beauty I did see,
Which I desir'd, and got, t'was but a dreame of thee.

And now good morrow to our waking soules,
Which watch not one another out of feare;
For love, all love of other sights controules,
And makes one little roome, an every where.
Let sea-discoverers to new worlds have gone,
Let Maps to other, worlds on worlds have showne,
Let us possesse one world, each hath one, and is one.

My face in thine eye, thine in mine appeares,
And true plaine hearts doe in the faces rest,
Where can we finde two better hemispheares
Without sharpe North, without declining West?
What ever dyes, was not mixt equally;[2]
If our two loves be one, or, thou and I
Love so alike, that none doe slacken, none can die.

The Sunne Rising

Busie old foole, unruly Sunne,
　　Why dost thou thus,
Through windowes, and through curtaines call on us?
Must to thy motions lovers seasons run?
　　Sawcy pedantique wretch, goe chide
　　Late schoole boyes and sowre prentices,
　Goe tell Court-huntsmen, that the King will ride,
　Call countrey ants to harvest offices;
Love, all alike, no season knowes, nor clyme,
Nor houres, dayes, moneths, which are the rags of time.

　　Thy beames, so reverend, and strong
　　Why shouldst thou thinke?

1　Seven Christian youths hid in a cave near Ephesus to avoid persecution by the Roman
　emperor Decius, and slept for almost 200 years.
2　According to medieval science, unless the elements in nature were in perfect equilibrium,
　they were subject to flux and mortality.

I could eclipse and cloud them with a winke,
But that I would not lose her sight so long:
    If her eyes have not blinded thine,
    Looke, and to morrow late, tell mee,
    Whether both the'India's of spice and Myne[1]
    Be where thou leftst them, or lie here with mee.
Aske for those Kings whom thou saw'st yesterday,
And thou shalt heare, All here in one bed lay.

    She'is all States, and all Princes, I,
        Nothing else is.
Princes doe but play us; compar'd to this,
All honor's mimique; All wealth alchimie.
        Thou sunne art halfe as happy'as wee,
        In that the world's contracted thus;
    Thine age askes ease, and since thy duties bee
    To warme the world, that's done in warming us.
Shine here to us, and thou art every where;
This bed thy center is, these walls, thy spheare.

Our love is colossal that others will consider us Saints

The Canonization

For Godsake hold your tongue, and let me love,
    Or chide my palsie, or my gout,
My five gray haires, or ruin'd fortune flout,
    With wealth your state, your minde with Arts improve,
        Take you a course, get you a place,
        Observe his honour, or his grace,
    Or the Kings reall, or his stamped face[2]
        Contemplate, what you will, approve,
        So you will let me love.

Alas, alas, who's injur'd by my love?
    What merchants ships have my sighs drown'd?
Who saies my teares have overflow'd his ground?
    When did my colds a forward spring remove?
        When did the heats which my veines fill
        Adde one more to the plaguie Bill?[3]
Soldiers finde warres, and Lawyers finde out still
    Litigious men, which quarrels move,
    Though she and I do love.

Call us what you will, wee are made such by love;
    Call her one, mee another flye,

---

1   East India, the source of spices; and the West Indies, the source of gold
2   i.e., on a coin
3   the lists of plague victims

We'are Tapers too, and at our owne cost die,
  And wee in us finde the'Eagle and the Dove.[1]
    The Phoenix[2] ridle hath more wit
    By us, we two being one, are it.
So to one neutrall thing both sexes fit,
  Wee dye and rise the same, and prove
  Mysterious by this love.

Wee can dye by it, if not live by love,
  And if unfit for tombes and hearse
Our legend bee, it will be fit for verse;
    And if no peece of Chronicle wee prove,
    We'll build in sonnets pretty roomes;
    As well a well wrought urne becomes
The greatest ashes, as halfe-acre tombes,
  And by these hymnes, all shall approve
  Us *Canoniz'd* for Love:

[handwritten: generally his poems have positive connotations, lot of love.]

And thus invoke us; You whom reverend love
  Made one anothers hermitage;
You, to whom love was peace, that now is rage;
  Who did the whole worlds soule contract, and drove
    Into the glasses of your eyes
    (So made such mirrors, and such spies,
  That they did all to you epitomize,)
  Countries, Townes, Courts: Beg from above
  A patterne of your love!

[handwritten: At this time, being bitten by a flea was no more dishonourable then being bitten by a mosquito]

The Flea

[handwritten: dramatic monologue found a flea, he thinks that its bitten him, then he]

Marke but this flea, and marke in this,
How little that which thou deny'st me is;
It suck'd me first, and now sucks thee,
And in this flea, our two bloods mingled bee;
Thou know'st that this cannot be said
A sinne, nor shame, nor losse of maidenhead,
  Yet this enjoyes before it wooe,
  And pamper'd swells with one blood made of two
  And this, alas, is more than wee would doe.

[handwritten: the flea doesn't even have to ask, it just takes what it wants]

[handwritten: his blood, her blood + its blood]

Oh stay, three lives in one flea spare,
Where wee almost, yea more than maryed are.
This flea is you and I, and this
Our mariage bed, and mariage temple is;

---

1   traditional symbols of strength and purity
2   a mythical bird that lived a thousand years, then arose to new life from the ashes of its
    own funeral pyre

Though parents grudge, and you, w'are met,
And cloysterd in these living walls of Jet.
Though use make you apt to kill mee,
Let not to that, selfe murder added bee,
And sacrilege, three sinnes in killing three.

Cruell and sodaine, hast thou since
Purpled thy naile, in blood of innocence?
Wherein could this flea guilty bee,
Except in that drop which it suckt from thee?
Yet thou triumph'st, and saist that thou
Find'st not thy selfe, nor mee the weaker now;
'Tis true, then learne how false, feares bee;
Just so much honor, when thou yeeld'st to mee,
Will wast, as this flea's death tooke life from thee.

(handwritten annotations: like a religious order; a black material; if you kill this flea, you also kill me + you committing suicide — what a sin!; sudden; what did it do wrong; She's trying to refute his argument; That's right you're not any weaker now how; wrong could it be to go to bed w/me? such a small thing,)

A Valediction: Forbidding Mourning

As virtuous men passe mildly away,
    And whisper to their soules, to goe,
Whilst some of their sad friends doe say,
    The breath goes now, and some say, no:

So let us melt, and make no noise,
    No teare-floods, nor sigh-tempests move,
T'were prophanation of our joyes
    To tell the layetie our love.

Moving of th'earth brings harmes and feares,
    Men reckon what it did and meant,
But trepidation of the spheares,[1]
    Though greater farre, is innocent.

Dull sublunary lovers love
    (Whose soule is sense) cannot admit
Absence, because it doth remove
    Those things which elemented it.

But we by a love, so much refin'd,
    That our selves know not what it is,
Inter-assured of the mind,
    Care lesse, eyes, lips, and hands to misse.

---

1   According to Ptolemaic theory, around the earth revolved a concentric series of spheres,
    into which were set the heavenly bodies. Enveloping all the rest was an outer sphere
    known as the "Primum Mobile" ("First Mover"), thought to give motion to the other
    spheres, and to introduce variations into the times of the equinoxes.

Our two soules therefore, which are one,
　　Though I must goe, endure not yet
A breach, but an expansion,
　　Like gold to ayery thinnesse beate.

If they be two, they are two so
　　As stiffe twin compasses are two,
Thy soule the fixt foot, makes no show
　　To move, but doth, if the'other doe.

And though it in the center sit,
　　Yet when the other far doth rome,
It leanes, and hearkens after it,
　　And growes erect, as that comes home.

Such wilt thou be to mee, who must
　　Like th'other foot, obliquely runne;
Thy firmnes drawes my circle just,
　　And makes me end, where I begunne.

The Extasie

Where, like a pillow on a bed,
　　A Pregnant banke swel'd up, to rest
The violets reclining head,
　　Sat we two, one anothers best.
Our hands were firmely cimented
　　With a fast balme, which thence did spring,
Our eye-beames twisted, and did thred
　　Our eyes, upon one double string;
So to'entergraft our hands, as yet
　　Was all the meanes to make us one,
And pictures in our eyes to get
　　Was all our propagation.
As 'twixt two equall Armies, Fate
　　Suspends uncertaine victorie,
Our soules, (which to advance their state,
　　Were gone out,) hung 'twixt her, and mee.
And whil'st our soules negotiate there,
　　Wee like sepulchrall statues lay;
All day, the same our postures were,
　　And wee said nothing, all the day.
If any, so by love refin'd,
　　That he soules language understood,
And by good love were growen all minde,
　　Within convenient distance stood,
He (though he knew not which soul spake,
　　Because both meant, both spake the same)
Might thence a new concoction take,

And part farre purer than he came.
This Extasie doth unperplex
    (We said) and tell us what we love,
Wee see by this, it was not sexe,
    Wee see, we saw not what did move:
But as all severall soules containe
    Mixture of things, they know not what,
Love, these mixt soules, doth mixe againe,
    And makes both one, each this and that.
A single violet transplant,
    The strength, the colour, and the size,
(All which before was poore, and scant,)
    Redoubles still, and multiplies.
When love, with one another so
    Interinanimates two soules,
That abler soule, which thence doth flow,
    Defects of lonelinesse controules.
Wee then, who are this new soule, know,
    Of what we are compos'd, and made,
For, th'Atomies of which we grow,
    Are soules, whom no change can invade.
But O alas, so long, so farre
    Our bodies why doe wee forbeare?
They are ours, though they are not wee, Wee are
    The intelligences,[1] they the spheares.
We owe them thankes because they thus,
    Did us, to us, at first convay,
Yeelded their forces, sense, to us,
    Nor are drosse to us, but allay.
On man heavens influence workes not so,
    But that it first imprints the ayre,[2]
Soe soule into the soule may flow,
    Though it to body first repaire.
As our blood labours to beget
    Spirits, as like soules as it can,
Because such fingers need to knit
    That subtile knot, which makes us man:
So must pure lovers soules descend
    T'affections, and to faculties,
Which sense may reach and apprehend,
    Else a great Prince in prison lies.
To'our bodies turne wee then, that so
    Weake men on love reveal'd may looke;
Loves mysteries in soules doe grow,
    But yet the body is his booke.

---

1   the angelic spirits that according to Ptolemaic theory guided the motion of the spheres
2   The influence of the stars was thought to be transmitted to people through the medium
    of the air.

And if some lover, such as wee,
　Have heard this dialogue of one,
Let him still marke us, he shall see
　Small change, when we'are to bodies gone

Holy Sonnets [*seems to have written these after his ordainment.*]

VII

[*4 corners of the world – says we imagined it*]

At the round earths imagin'd corners, blow
Your trumpets, Angells, and arise, arise
From death, you numberlesse infinities
Of soules, and to your scattred bodies goe,　[*imagine people rising from the dead.*]
All whom the flood did, and fire shall o'erthrow,
All whom warre, dearth, age, agues, tyrannies,
Despaire, law, chance, hath slaine, and you whose eyes,
Shall behold God, and never tast deaths woe.
But let them sleepe, Lord, and mee mourne a space,
For, if above all these, my sinnes abound,
'Tis late to aske abundance of thy grace,　[*at the Last Judgement*]
When wee are there; here on this lowly ground,
Teach mee how to repent; for that's as good
As if thou'hadst seal'd my pardon, with thy blood.

X

Death be not proud, though some have called thee
Mighty and dreadfull, for, thou art not soe,
For, those, whom thou think'st, thou dost overthrow,
Die not, poore death, nor yet canst thou kill mee.
From rest and sleepe, which but thy pictures bee,
Much pleasure, then from thee, much more must flow,
And soonest our best men with thee doe goe,
Rest of their bones, and soules deliverie
Thou art slave to Fate, Chance, kings, and desperate men,
And dost with poyson, warre, and sicknesse dwell,
And poppie, or charmes can make us sleepe as well,
And better than thy stroake; why swell'st thou then?
[*Italian sonnet*] One short sleepe past, wee wake eternally,
And death shall be no more; death, thou shalt die.

[*Slight rhyme*] [*sonnet*]

XIV　[*(most famous one) of the Holy Sonnets*]

[*Trinity*]

[*referring to the 3 person god.*] Batter my heart, three person'd God; for, you
As yet but knocke, breathe, shine, and seeke to mend;
That I may rise, and stand, o'erthrow mee,'and bend
Your force, to breake, blowe, burn and make me new.　[*do drastic things to my heart, I am a sinner I need the force like a tin Ken don't just shine me up a little*]
I, like an usurpt towne, to'another due,
Labour to'admit you, but Oh, to no end,
Reason your viceroy in mee, mee should defend,　[*use force on me to make me new*]

asking for direct intervention on his life

But is captiv'd, and proves weake or untrue.

I am a town captived, being besieged

Yet dearely'I love you,'and would be loved faine,

But am betroth'd unto your enemie:

Using sexual imagery;

Divorce mee,'untie, or breake that knot againe,

very serious
Divorce me
from evil

a spiritual marriage

Take mee to you, imprison mee, for I

Except you'enthrall mee, never shall be free,

Nor ever chast, except you ravish mee.

fine / both entranced + enslaved

never will I be pure unless you overwhelm/overpower me

Goodfriday, 1613. Riding Westward

Let mans Soule be a Spheare, and then, in this,
The intelligence that moves, devotion is,
And as the other Spheares, by being growne
Subject to forraigne motions, lose their owne,
And being by others hurried every day,
Scarce in a yeare their naturall forme obey:
Pleasure or businesse, so, our Soules admit
For their first mover,[1] and are whirld by it.
Hence is't, that I am carryed towards the West
This day, when my Soules forme bends toward the East.
There I should see a Sunne, by rising set,
And by that setting endlesse day beget;
But that Christ on this Crosse, did rise and fall,
Sinne had eternally benighted all.
Yet dare I'almost be glad, I do not see
That spectacle of too much weight for mee.
Who sees Gods face, that is selfe life, must dye;
What a death were it then to see God dye?
It made his owne Lieutenant Nature shrinke,
It made his footstoole crack, and the Sunne winke.
Could I behold those hands which span the Poles,
And tune all spheares at once, peirc'd with those holes?
Could I behold that endlesse height which is
Zenith to us, and our Antipodes,
Humbled below us? or that blood which is
The seat of all our Soules, if not of his,
Made durt of dust, or that flesh which was worne
By God, for his apparell, rag'd, and torne?
If on these things I durst not looke, durst I
Upon his miserable mother cast mine eye,
Who was Gods partner here, and furnish'd thus
Halfe of that Sacrifice, which ransom'd us?
Though these things, as I ride, be from mine eye,
They'are present yet unto my memory,
For that looks towards them; and thou look'st towards mee,

---

1 The outermost sphere in the Ptolemaic system, the "primum mobile," was credited with imparting motion to all the other spheres carrying the heavenly bodies.

O Saviour, as thou hang'st upon the tree;
I turne my backe to thee, but to receive
Corrections, till thy mercies bid thee leave.
O thinke mee worth thine anger, punish mee,
Burne off my rusts, and my deformity,
Restore thine Image, so much, by thy grace,
That thou may'st know mee, and I'll turne my face.

As yet/but knock, breath, shine / I seek/to mend

Ben Jonson

(1573–1637)

On my first Sonne[1]

Farewell, thou child of my right hand, and joy;
My sinne was too much hope of thee, lov'd boy,
Seven yeeres tho'wert lent to me, and I thee pay,
Exacted by thy fate, on the just day.
O, could I loose all father, now. For why
Will man lament the state he should envie?
To have so soone scap'd worlds, and fleshes rage,
And, if no other miserie, yet age?
Rest in soft peace, and, ask'd, say here doth lye
Ben. Jonson his best piece of poetrie.
For whose sake, hence-forth, all his vowes be such,
As what he loves may never like too much.

Inviting a friend to supper

To night, grave sir, both my poore house, and I
Doe equally desire your companie:
Not that we thinke us worthy such a ghest,
But that your worth will dignifie our feast,
With those that come; whose grace may make that seeme
Something, which, else, could hope for no esteeme.
It is the faire acceptance, Sir, creates
The entertaynment perfect: not the cates.[2]
Yet shall you have, to rectifie your palate,
An olive, capers, or some better sallade
Ushring the mutton; with a short-leg'd hen,
If we can get her, full of egs, and then,
Limons, and wine for sauce: to these, a coney[3]
Is not to be despair'd of, for our money;
And, though fowle, now, be scarce, yet there are clarkes,
The skie not falling, thinke we may have larkes.
Ile tell you more, and lye, so you will come:
Of partrich, pheasant, wood-cock, of which some
May yet be there; and godwit, if we can:
Knat, raile, and ruffe[4] too. How so ere, my man
Shall reade a piece of Virgil, Tacitus,
Livie, or of some better booke to us,
Of which wee'll speake our minds, amidst our meate;

---

1 Jonson's son Benjamin (Hebrew, "child of the right hand") was born in 1596 and died in 1603.
2 dishes
3 rabbit
4 small game birds

And Ile professe no verses to repeate:
To this, if ought appeare, which I not know of,
That will the pastrie, not my paper, show of.
Digestive cheese, and fruit there sure will bee;
But that, which most doth take my Muse, and mee,
Is a pure cup of rich Canary-wine,
Which is the Mermaids,[1] now, but shall be mine:
Of which had Horace, or Anacreon[2] tasted,
Their lives, as doe their lines, till now had lasted.
Tabacco, Nectar, or the Thespian spring,[3]
Are all but Luthers beere, to this I sing.
Of this we will sup free, but moderately,
And we will have no Pooly', or Parrot[4] by;
Nor shall our cups make any guiltie men:
But, at our parting, we will be, as when
We innocently met. No simple word,
That shall be utter'd at our mirthfull boord,
Shall make us sad next morning: or affright
The libertie, that wee'll enjoy to night.

Song. *To Celia*

Come my Celia, let us prove,
While we may, the sports of love;
Time will not be ours, for ever:
He, at length, our good will sever.
Spend not then his guifts in vaine.
Sunnes, that set, may rise againe:
But if once we loose this light,
'Tis, with us, perpetuall night.
Why should we deferre our joyes?
Fame, and rumor are but toyes.
Cannot we delude the eyes
Of a few poore houshold spyes?
Or his easier eares beguile,
So removed by our wile?
'Tis no sinne, loves fruit to steale,
But the sweet theft to reveale:
To be taken, to be seene,
These have crimes accounted beene.

---

1   the London tavern favoured by writers in Jonson's time
2   The Roman writer Horace (65-8 B.C.), and the Greek poet Anacreon (5th century B.C.)
     both wrote songs praising love and wine.
3   a spring on Mount Helicon in Greece, sacred to the Muses
4   Possibly a reference to known government agents. Robert Pooly or Poley was present at
     the death of Christopher Marlowe. "Parrot" may be a contemporary writer, Henry Parrot
     or Perrot.

A Hymne to God the Father

Heare mee, O God!
  A broken heart
  Is my best part:
Use still thy rod,
  That I may prove
  Therein, thy Love.

If thou hadst not
  Beene sterne to mee,
  But left me free,
I had forgot
  My selfe and thee.

For, sin's so sweet,
  As minds ill bent
  Rarely repent,
Untill they meet
  Their punishment.

Who more can crave
  Then thou hast done:
  That gav'st a Sonne,
To free a slave?
  First made of nought;
  With all since bought.

Sinne, Death, and Hell,
  His glorious Name
  Quite overcame,
Yet I rebell,
  And slight the same.

But, I'le come in,
  Before my losse,
  Me farther tosse,
As sure to win
  Under his Crosse.

To the Memory of my Beloved, the Author, Mr. William Shakespeare: and what he hath left us

To draw no envy (Shakespeare) on thy name,
Am I thus ample to thy Booke,[1] and Fame:
While I confesse thy writings to be such,
As neither Man, nor Muse, can praise too much.
'Tis true, and all mens suffrage. But these wayes
Were not the paths I meant unto thy praise:
For seeliest Ignorance on these may light,
Which, when it sounds at best, but eccho's right,
Or blinde Affection, which doth ne're advance
The truth, but gropes, and urgeth all by chance;
Or crafty Malice, might pretend this praise,
And thinke to ruine, where it seem'd to raise.
These are, as some infamous Baud, or Whore,
Should praise a Matron. What could hurt her more?
But thou art proofe against them, and indeed
Above th'ill fortune of them, or the need.
I therefore will begin. Soule of the Age!
The applause! delight! the wonder of our Stage!
My Shakespeare, rise; I will not lodge thee by
Chaucer, or Spenser, or bid Beaumont[2] lye
A little further, to make thee a roome:
Thou art a Moniment, without a tombe,
And art alive still, while thy Booke doth live,
And we have wits to read, and praise to give.
That I not mixe thee so, my braine excuses;
I meane with great, but disproportion'd Muses:
For, if I thought my judgement were of yeeres,
I should commit thee surely with thy peeres,
And tell, how farre thou didst our Lily[3] out-shine,
Or sporting Kid, or Marlowes mighty line.
And though thou hadst small Latine, and lesse Greeke,
From thence to honour thee, I would not seeke
For names; but call forth thund'ring Aeschilus,
Euripides, and Sophocles to us,
Paccuvius, Accius, him of Cordova dead,[4]
To life againe, to heare thy Buskin[5] tread,
And shake a Stage: Or, when thy Sockes were on,

---

1   the first collection of Shakespeare's plays (the "First Folio"), published in 1623, in which Jonson's poem appears
2   The playwright Francis Beaumont, together with Chaucer and Spenser, was buried in Westminster Abbey.
3   John Lyly (c. 1554–1606) and Thomas Kid (c.1557–1595), English dramatists
4   Pacuvius and Accius were Latin tragedians of the 2nd century B.C.; "him of Cordova" refers to the Roman playwright Seneca the Younger (4 B.C.-A.D. 65) who was born in Spain.
5   Thick-soled boot, conventionally worn by actors in tragedies; 'socks,' or light shoes, were associated with comedy

Leave thee alone, for the comparison
Of all, that insolent Greece, or haughtie Rome
Sent forth, or since did from their ashes come.
Triumph, my Britaine, thou hast one to showe,
To whom all Scenes[1] of Europe homage owe.
He was not of an age, but for all time!
And all the Muses still were in their prime,
When like Apollo he came forth to warme
Our eares, or like a Mercury[2] to charme!
Nature her selfe was proud of his designes,
And joy'd to weare the dressing of his lines!
Which were so richly spun, and woven so fit,
As, since, she will vouchsafe no other Wit.
The merry Greeke, tart Aristophanes,[3]
Neat Terence, witty Plautus,[4] now not please;
But antiquated, and deserted lye
As they were not of Natures family.
Yet must I not give Nature all: Thy Art,
My gentle Shakespeare, must enjoy a part.
For though the Poets matter, Nature be,
His Art doth give the fashion. And, that he,
Who casts to write a living Line, must sweat,
(Such as thine are) and strike the second heat
Upon the Muses anvile: turne the same,
(And himselfe with it) that he thinkes to frame;
Or for the lawrell, he may gaine a scorne,
For a good Poet's made, as well as borne.
And such wert thou. Looke how the fathers face
Lives in his issue, even so, the race
Of Shakespeares minde, and manners brightly shines
In his well torned, and true-filed lines:
In each of which, he seemes to shake a Lance,
As brandish't at the eyes of Ignorance.
Sweet Swan of Avon! what a sight it were
To see thee in our waters yet appeare,
And make those flights upon the bankes of Thames,
That so did take Eliza, and our James![5]
But stay, I see thee in the Hemisphere
Advanc'd, and made a Constellation there!
Shine forth, thou Starre of Poets, and with rage,
Or influence, chide, or cheere the drooping Stage;
Which, since thy flight from hence, hath mourn'd like night,
And despaires day, but for thy Volumes light.

---

1   stages
2   In Greek mythology, Apollo was the god of poetry, Hermes (Roman, Mercury) the god
    who invented the lyre.
3   Greek dramatist of the 4th century B.C.
4   Roman playwrights of the 2nd century B.C.
5   Queen Elizabeth and King James I

Robert Herrick

(1591–1674)

Corinna's going a Maying

Get up, get up for shame, the Blooming Morne
Upon her wings presents the god unshorne.[1]
    See how *Aurora*[2] throwes her faire
    Fresh-quilted colours through the aire:
    Get up, sweet-Slug-a-bed, and see
    The Dew-bespangling Herbe and Tree.
Each Flower has wept, and bow'd toward the East,
Above an houre since; yet you not drest,
    Nay! not so much as out of bed?
    When all the Birds have Mattens seyd,
    And sung their thankfull Hymnes: 'tis sin,
    Nay, profanation to keep in,
When as a thousand Virgins on this day,
Spring, sooner then the Lark, to fetch in May.

Rise; and put on your Foliage, and be seene
To come forth, like the Spring-time, fresh and greene;
    And sweet as *Flora*[3]. Take no care
    For Jewels for your Gowne, or Haire:
    Feare not; the leaves will strew
    Gemms in abundance upon you:
Besides, the childhood of the Day has kept,
Against you come, some *Orient Pearls* unwept:
    Come, and receive them while the light
    Hangs on the Dew-locks of the night:
    And *Titan* on the Eastern hill
    Retires himselfe, or else stands still
Till you come forth. Wash, dresse, be briefe in praying:
Few Beads[4] are best, when once we goe a Maying.

Come, my *Corinna*, come; and comming, marke
How each field turns a street; each street a Parke
    Made green, and trimm'd with trees: see how
    Devotion gives each House a Bough,
    Or Branch: Each Porch, each doore, ere this,
    An Arke a Tabernacle is
Made up of white-thorn neatly enterwove;
As if here were those cooler shades of love.
    Can such delights be in the street,
    And open fields, and we not see't?

---

1   Apollo, god of the sun
2   goddess of the dawn
3   goddess of flowers
4   prayers

Come, we'll abroad; and let's obay
The Proclamation made for May:
And sin no more, as we have done, by staying;
But my *Corinna*, come, let's goe a Maying.

There's not a budding Boy, or Girle, this day,
But is got up, and gone to bring in May.
    A deale of Youth, ere this, is come
    Back, and with *White-thorn* laden home.
    Some have dispatcht their Cakes and Creame,
    Before that we have left to dreame:
And some have wept, and woo'd, and plighted Troth,
And chose their Priest, ere we can cast off sloth:
    Many a green-gown has been given;
    Many a kisse, both odde and even:
    Many a glance too has been sent
    From out the eye, Loves Firmament:
Many a jest told of the Keyes betraying
This night, and Locks pickt, yet w'are not a Maying.

Come, let us goe, while we are in our prime;
And take the harmlesse follie of the time.
    We shall grow old apace, and die
    Before we know our liberty.
    Our life is short; and our dayes run
    As fast away as do's the Sunne:
And as a vapour, or a drop of raine
Once lost, can ne'r be found againe:
    So when or you or I are made
    A fable, song, or fleeting shade;
    All love, all liking, all delight
    Lies drown'd with us in endlesse night.
Then while time serves, and we are but decaying;
Come, my *Corinna*, come, let's goe a Maying.

Delight in Disorder

A sweet disorder in the dresse
Kindles in cloathes a wantonnesse:
A Lawne about the shoulders thrown
Into a fine distraction:
An erring Lace, which here and there
Enthralls the Crimson Stomacher:
A Cuffe neglectfull, and thereby
Ribbands to flow confusedly:
A winning wave (deserving Note)
In the tempestuous petticote:

A carelesse shoe-string, in whose tye
I see a wilde civility:
Doe more bewitch me, then when Art
Is too precise in every part.

Upon Julia's Clothes

When as in silks my *Julia* goes,
Then, then (me thinks) how sweetly flowes
That liquefaction of her clothes.

Next, when I cast mine eyes and see
That brave Vibration each way free;
O how that glittering taketh me!

To the Virgins, to make much of Time.

Gather ye Rose-buds while ye may,
    Old Time is still a flying:
And this same flower that smiles to day,
    To morrow will be dying.

The glorious Lamp of Heaven, the Sun,
    The higher he's a getting;
The sooner will his Race be run,
    And neerer he's to Setting.

That Age is best, which is the first,
    When Youth and Blood are warmer;
But being spent, the worse, and worst
    Times, still succeed the former.

Then be not coy, but use your time;
    And while ye may, goe marry:
For having lost but once your prime,
    You may for ever tarry.

To Blossoms

Faire pledges of a fruitfull Tree,
    Why do yee fall so fast?
    Your date is not so past;
But you may stay yet here a while,
    To blush and gently smile;
      And go at last.

What, were yee borne to be
    An houre or half's delight;
    And so to bid goodnight?
'Twas pitie Nature brought yee forth
    Meerly to shew your worth,
      And lose you quite.

But you are lovely Leaves, where we
    May read how soon things have
    Their end, though ne'r so brave:
And after they have shown their pride,
    Like you a while: They glide
      Into the Grave.

George Herbert

(1593–1633)

Easter Wings

Lord, who createdst man in wealth and store,
Though foolishly he lost the same,
Decaying more and more,
Till he became
Most poore:
With thee
O let me rise
As larks, harmoniously,
And sing this day thy victories:
Then shall the fall further the flight in me.

My tender age in sorrow did beginne:
And still with sicknesses and shame
Thou didst so punish sinne,
That I became
Most thinne.
With thee
Let me combine,
And feel this day thy victorie:
For, if I imp¹ my wing on thine,
Affliction shall advance the flight in me.

Prayer (I)

Prayer the Churches banquet, Angels age,
   Gods breath in man returning to his birth,
   The soul in paraphrase, heart in pilgrimage,
The Christian plummet sounding heav'n and earth;

Engine against th' Almightie, sinners towre,
   Reversed thunder, Christ-side-piercing spear,
   The six-daies world-transposing in an houre,
A kinde of tune, which all things heare and fear;

Softnesse, and peace, and joy, and love, and blisse,
   Exalted Manna, gladnesse of the best,
   Heaven in ordinarie, man well drest,
The milkie way, the bird of Paradise,

---

1   "Imp" means to mend a falcon's broken pinion feather by binding it to a new one.

Church-bels beyond the starres heard, the souls bloud,
The land of spices; something understood.

Jordan¹ (I)

Who sayes that fictions onely and false hair
Become a verse? Is there in truth no beautie?
Is all good structure in a winding stair?
May no lines passe, except they do their dutie
    Not to a true, but painted chair?²

Is it no verse, except enchanted groves
And sudden arbours shadow course-spunne lines?
Must purling streams refresh a lovers loves?
Must all be vail'd, while he that reades, divines,
    Catching the sense at two removes?

Shepherds are honest people; let them sing:
Riddle who list, for me, and pull for Prime:³
I envie no mans nightingale or spring;
Nor let them punish me with losse of rime,
    Who plainly say, *My God, My King.*

The Flower

    How fresh, O Lord, how sweet and clean
Are thy returns! ev'n as the flowers in spring;
    To which, besides their own demean,
The late-past frosts tributes of pleasure bring.
       Grief melts away
      Like snow in May,
As if there were no such cold thing.

    Who would have thought my shrivel'd heart
Could have recover'd greennesse? It was gone
    Quite under ground; as flowers depart
To see their mother-root, when they have blown;
      Where they together
      All the hard weather,
Dead to the world, keep house unknown.

    These are thy wonders, Lord of power,
Killing and quickning, bringing down to hell

---

1   the Holy River, across which lay the Promised Land sought by the Israelites
2   a false throne
3   drawing for a winning hand in a card game called primero

And up to heaven in an houre;
Making a chiming of a passing-bell.
      We say amisse,
      This or that is:
Thy word is all, if we could spell.

O that I once past changing were,
Fast in thy Paradise, where no flower can wither!
Many a spring I shoot up fair,
Offring[1] at heav'n, growing and groning thither:
      Nor doth my flower
      Want a spring-showre,
My sinnes and I joining together:

But while I grow in a straight line,
Still upwards bent, as if heav'n were mine own,
Thy anger comes, and I decline:
What frost to that? what pole is not the zone,
      Where all things burn,
      When thou dost turn,
And the least frown of thine is shown?

And now in age I bud again,
After so many deaths I live and write;
I once more smell the dew and rain,
And relish versing: O my onely light,
      It cannot be
      That I am he
On whom thy tempests fell all night.

These are thy wonders, Lord of love,
To make us see we are but flowers that glide:
Which when we once can finde and prove,[2]
Thou hast a garden for us, where to bide.
      Who would be more,
      Swelling through store,
Forfeit their Paradise by their pride.

---

1   aiming
2   experience

The Collar

I struck the board,[1] and cry'd, No more.
        I will abroad.
What? shall I ever sigh and pine?
My lines and life are free; free as the rode,
    Loose as the winde, as large as store.
        Shall I be still in suit?[2]
    Have I no harvest but a thorn
    To let me bloud, and not restore
What I have lost with cordiall fruit?
        Sure there was wine
Before my sighs did drie it: there was corn
    Before my tears did drown it.
    Is the yeare onely lost to me?
        Have I no bayes to crown it?
No flowers, no garlands gay? all blasted?
        All wasted?
Not so, my heart: but there is fruit,
    And thou hast hands.
    Recover all thy sigh-blown age
On double pleasures: leave thy cold dispute
Of what is fit, and not. Forsake thy cage,
        Thy rope of sands,
Which pettie thoughts have made, and made to thee
    Good cable, to enforce and draw,
        And be thy law,
While thou didst wink[3] and wouldst not see.
        Away; take heed:
        I will abroad.
Call in thy deaths head[4] there: tie up thy fears.
        He that forbears
    To suit and serve his need,
    Deserves his load.
But as I rav'd and grew more fierce and wilde
        At every word,
Me thoughts I heard one calling, *Child*:
    And I reply'd, *My Lord.*

---

1   table
2   petitioning for favour
3   close the eyes
4   a skull, an emblem of mortality seen by the penitent as a reminder of imminent death

The Pulley

When God at first made man,
Having a glasse of blessings standing by;
Let us (said he) poure on him all we can:
Let the worlds riches, which dispersed lie,
    Contract into a span.

So strength first made a way;
Then beautie flow'd, then wisdome, honour, pleasure:
When almost all was out, God made a stay,
Perceiving that alone of all his treasure
    Rest in the bottome lay.

For if I should (said he)
Bestow this jewell also on my creature,
He would adore my gifts in stead of me,
And rest in Nature, not the God of Nature:
    So both should losers be.

Yet let him keep the rest,
But keep them with repining restlessnesse:
Let him be rich and wearie, that at least,
If goodnesse leade him not, yet wearinesse
    May tosse him to my breast.

John Milton

(1608–1674)

Lycidas

[In this Monody[1] the Author bewails a learned Friend,
unfortunatly drown'd in his Passage from *Chester* on the *Irish
Seas*, 1637. And by occasion foretels the ruin of our corrupted
Clergy then in their height.]

Yet once more, O ye Laurels, and once more
Ye Myrtles brown, with Ivy[2] never sere,
I come to pluck your Berries harsh and crude,
And with forc'd fingers rude,
Shatter your leaves before the mellowing year.　　　　5
Bitter constraint, and sad occasion dear,[3]
Compels me to disturb your season due:
For *Lycidas* is dead, dead ere his prime,
Young *Lycidas*, and hath not left his peer:
Who would not sing for *Lycidas*? he knew　　　　10
Himself to sing, and build the lofty rhyme.
He must not float upon his wat'ry bier
Unwept, and welter to the parching wind,
Without the meed of some melodious tear.
　Begin then, Sisters of the sacred well,[4]　　　　15
That from beneath the seat of *Jove* doth spring,
Begin, and somewhat loudly sweep the string.
Hence with denial vain, and coy excuse,
So may some gentle Muse
With lucky words favor my destin'd Urn,　　　　20
And as he passes turn,
And bid fair peace be to my sable shroud.
For we were nurst upon the self-same hill,
Fed the same flock, by fountain, shade, and rill.
　Together both, ere the high Lawns appear'd　　　　25
Under the opening eyelids of the morn,
We drove afield, and both together heard
What time the Gray-fly winds her sultry horn,
Batt'ning[5] our flocks with the fresh dews of night,
Oft till the Star that rose, at Ev'ning, bright　　　　30
Toward Heav'n's descent had slop'd his westering wheel.
Meanwhile the Rural ditties were not mute,
Temper'd to th'Oaten Flute;
Rough *Satyrs* danc'd, and *Fauns* with clov'n heel

1　a dirge sung or recited by one mourner
2　Laurels, myrtles, and ivy are traditional symbols of poetic fame and inspiration.
3　Edward King, a Cambridge acquaintance of Milton's, was drowned on his way to Ireland
　　in August 1637.
4　i.e., the Muses, usually associated with the Pierian spring in Thessaly
5　feeding

From the glad sound would not be absent long,   35
And old *Damoetas*[1] lov'd to hear our song.
    But O the heavy change, now thou art gone,
Now thou art gone, and never must return!
Thee Shepherd, thee the Woods, and desert Caves,
With wild Thyme and the gadding Vine o'ergrown,   40
And all their echoes mourn.
The Willows and the Hazel Copses green
Shall now no more be seen,
Fanning their joyous Leaves to thy soft lays.
As killing as the Canker to the Rose,   45
Or Taint-worm to the weanling Herds that graze,
Or Frost to Flowers, that their gay wardrobe wear,
When first the White-thorn blows;
Such, *Lycidas*, thy loss to Shepherd's ear.
    Where were ye Nymphs when the remorseless deep   50
Clos'd o'er the head of your lov'd *Lycidas*?
For neither were ye playing on the steep,
Where your old *Bards*, the famous *Druids*, lie,
Nor on the shaggy top of *Mona*[2] high,
Nor yet where *Deva*[3] spreads her wizard stream: 55
Ay me, I fondly dream!
Had ye been there—for what could that have done?
What could the Muse herself that *Orpheus*[4] bore,
The Muse herself, for her enchanting son
Whom Universal nature did lament,   60
When by the rout that made the hideous roar,
His gory visage down the stream was sent,
Down the swift *Hebrus* to the *Lesbian* shore?
    Alas! What boots it with uncessant care
To tend the homely slighted Shepherd's trade,   65
And strictly meditate the thankless Muse?
Were it not better done as others use,
To sport with *Amaryllis*[5] in the shade,
Or with the tangles of *Neaera's* hair?
Fame is the spur that the clear spirit doth raise   70
(That last infirmity of Noble mind)
To scorn delights, and live laborious days;
But the fair Guerdon when we hope to find,
And think to burst out into sudden blaze,
Comes the blind *Fury*[6] with th'abhorred shears,   75

1   a conventional name for a shepherd in pastoral poetry
2   Roman name for the isle of Anglesey, off the Welsh coast
3   the river Dee in Cheshire, associated in legend with supernatural forces and prophecy
4   Orpheus, the son of the Muse Calliope, was torn apart by a "rout" (mob) of Thracian
     women; still singing, his head floated down the river Hebrus and out to the island of
     Lesbos. See Ovid's *Metamorphoses* xi.
5   conventional name in pastoral literature for a pretty shepherdess, as is Neaera
6   Atropos, one of the three Fates

And slits the thin-spun life. "But not the praise,"
Phoebus[1] repli'd, and touch'd my trembling ears;
"*Fame* is no plant that grows on mortal soil,
Nor in the glistering foil
Set off to th'world, nor in broad rumor lies,   80
But lives and spreads aloft by those pure eyes
And perfect witness of all-judging *Jove*;
As he pronounces lastly on each deed,
Of so much fame in Heav'n expect thy meed."

O Fountain *Arethuse*,[2] and thou honor'd flood,   85
Smooth-sliding *Mincius*;[3] crown'd with vocal reeds,
That strain I heard was of a higher mood:
But now my Oat proceeds,
And listens to the Herald of the Sea[4]
That came in *Neptune's* plea.   90
He ask'd the Waves, and ask'd the Felon winds,
What hard mishap hath doom'd this gentle swain?
And question'd every gust of rugged wings
That blows from off each beaked Promontory.
They knew not of his story,   95
And sage *Hippotades*[5] their answer brings,
That not a blast was from his dungeon stray'd,
The Air was calm, and on the level brine,
Sleek *Panope*[6] with all her sisters play'd.
It was that fatal and perfidious Bark   100
Built in th'eclipse, and rigg'd with curses dark,
That sunk so low that sacred head of thine.

Next *Camus*,[7] reverend Sire, went footing slow,
His Mantle hairy, and his Bonnet sedge,
Inwrought with figures dim, and on the edge   105
Like to that sanguine flower inscrib'd with woe.[8]
"Ah! Who hath reft" (quoth he) "my dearest pledge?"
Last came, and last did go,
The Pilot of the *Galilean* lake.[9]
Two massy Keys he bore of metals twain   110
(The Golden opes, the Iron shuts amain).
He shook his Mitred[10] locks, and stern bespake:
"How well could I have spar'd for thee, young swain,
Enough of such as for their bellies' sake,

---

1   Apollo, god of poetic inspiration
2   Arethusa was a fountain in Sicily, homeland of the Greek poet Theocritus.
3   Mincius was a river in Lombardy near the birthplace of the Roman poet Virgil.
4   Triton, son of Poseidon
5   Aeolus, son of Hippotes, and god of the winds
6   a Nereid, or sea-nymph
7   god of the river Cam, which passes through Cambridge
8   The hyacinth, named after the youth Hyacinthus, slain by Apollo, was said to be marked "ai, ai" (woe, woe).
9   St. Peter, who had been a fisherman on the Sea of Galilee
10 wearing a bishop's mitre

Creep and intrude and climb into the fold?   115
Of other care they little reck'ning make,
Than how to scramble at the shearers' feast,
And shove away the worthy bidden guest;
Blind mouths! that scarce themselves know how to hold
A Sheep-hook, or have learn'd aught else the least   120
That to the faithful Herdman's art belongs!
What recks it them? What need they? They are sped;
And when they list, their lean and flashy songs
Grate on their scrannel[1] Pipes of wretched straw.
The hungry Sheep look up, and are not fed,   125
But swoln with wind, and the rank mist they draw,
Rot inwardly, and foul contagion spread:
Besides what the grim Wolf with privy paw
Daily devours apace, and nothing said;
But that two-handed engine[2] at the door   130
Stands ready to smite once, and smite no more."
    Return *Alpheus*,[3] the dread voice is past
That shrunk thy streams; Return *Sicilian* Muse,
And call the Vales, and bid them hither cast
Their Bells and Flowrets of a thousand hues.   135
Ye valleys low where the mild whispers use
Of shades and wanton winds and gushing brooks,
On whose fresh lap the swart Star[4] sparely looks,
Throw hither all your quaint enamell'd eyes,
That on the green turf suck the honied showers,   140
And purple all the ground with vernal flowers.
Bring the rathe[5] Primrose that forsaken dies,
The tufted Crow-toe, and pale Jessamine,
The white Pink, and the Pansy freakt with jet,
The glowing Violet,   145
The Musk-rose, and the well-attir'd Woodbine,
With Cowslips wan that hang the pensive head,
And every flower that sad embroidery wears:
Bid *Amaranthus*[6] all his beauty shed,
And Daffadillies fill their cups with tears,   150
To strew the Laureate Hearse where *Lycid* lies.
For so to interpose a little ease,
Let our frail thoughts dally with false surmise.
Ay me! Whilst thee the shores and sounding Seas
Wash far away, where'er thy bones are hurl'd,   155
Whether beyond the stormy *Hebrides*,[7]

---

1   thin, harsh
2   an unclear reference to some agent of reform, possibly the two Houses of Parliament
3   a river in Arcady
4   Sirius, the Dog Star, whose baleful influence makes vegetation wither
5   early
6   an imaginary flower, reputed never to fade
7   islands off the west coast of Scotland

Where thou perhaps under the whelming tide
Visit'st the bottom of the monstrous world;
Or whether thou to our moist vows denied,
Sleep'st by the fable of *Bellerus*[1] old,   160
Where the great vision of the guarded Mount[2]
Looks toward *Namancos* and *Bayona's* hold;
Look homeward Angel now, and melt with ruth:
And, O ye *Dolphins*, waft the hapless youth.
    Weep no more, woeful Shepherds weep no more,   165
For *Lycidas* your sorrow is not dead,
Sunk though he be beneath the wat'ry floor,
So sinks the day-star in the Ocean bed,
And yet anon repairs his drooping head,
And tricks his beams, and with new-spangled Ore,   170
Flames in the forehead of the morning sky:
So *Lycidas*, sunk low, but mounted high,
Through the dear might of him that walk'd the waves,
Where other groves, and other streams along,
With *Nectar* pure his oozy Locks he laves,   175
And hears the unexpressive[3] nuptial Song,
In the blest Kingdoms meek of joy and love.
There entertain him all the Saints above,
In solemn troops, and sweet Societies
That sing, and singing in their glory move,   180
And wipe the tears for ever from his eyes.
Now *Lycidas*, the Shepherds weep no more;
Henceforth thou art the Genius[4] of the shore,
In thy large recompense, and shalt be good
To all that wander in that perilous flood.   185
    Thus sang the uncouth Swain to th'Oaks and rills,
While the still morn went out with Sandals gray;
He touch't the tender stops of various Quills,
With eager thought warbling his *Doric*[5] lay:
And now the Sun had stretch't out all the hills,   190
And now was dropt into the Western bay;
At last he rose, and twitch't his Mantle blue:
Tomorrow to fresh Woods, and Pastures new.

---

1   a mythical giant, said to lie buried off the coast of Land's End, the southwestern tip of England
2   St. Michael's Mount in Cornwall, guarded by the archangel St. Michael, here imagined looking south to Namancos and Bayona in northern Spain
3   inexpressible
4   guardian spirit
5   the dialect of the Greek pastoral poets

On Shakespeare

What needs my *Shakespeare* for his honour'd Bones
The labour of an age in piled Stones,
Or that his hallow'd relics should be hid
Under a Star-ypointing *Pyramid?*
Dear son of memory,[1] great heir of Fame,
What need'st thou such weak witness of thy name?
Thou in our wonder and astonishment
Hast built thyself a livelong Monument.
For whilst to th'shame of slow-endeavouring art,
Thy easy numbers flow, and that each heart
Hath from the leaves of thy unvalu'd[2] Book
Those Delphic[3] lines with deep impression took,
Then thou our fancy of itself bereaving,
Dost make us Marble with too much conceiving;
And so Sepulcher'd in such pomp dost lie,
That Kings for such a Tomb would wish to die.

How Soon Hath Time

How soon hath Time, the subtle thief of youth,
    Stol'n on his wing my three and twentieth year!
    My hasting days fly on with full career,
    But my late spring no bud or blossom show'th.
Perhaps my semblance might deceive the truth,
    That I to manhood am arriv'd so near,
    And inward ripeness doth much less appear,
    That some more timely-happy spirits endu'th.
Yet be it less or more, or soon or slow,
    It shall be still in strictest measure ev'n
    To that same lot, however mean or high,
Toward which Time leads me, and the will of Heav'n;
    All is, if I have grace to use it so,
    As ever in my great task-Master's eye.

---

1   Mnemosyne, mother of the Muses
2   invaluable
3   Apollo, god of poetry, had his temple at Delphi.

On the Late Massacre in Piemont[1]

Avenge, O Lord, thy slaughter'd Saints, whose bones
   Lie scatter'd on the Alpine mountains cold,
   Ev'n them who kept thy truth so pure of old
   When all our Fathers worship't Stocks and Stones[2]
Forget not: in thy book record their groans
   Who were thy Sheep and in their ancient Fold
   Slain by the bloody *Piemontese* that roll'd
   Mother with Infant down the Rocks. Their moans
The Vales redoubl'd to the Hills, and they
   To Heav'n. Their martyr'd blood and ashes sow
   O'er all th'*Italian* fields where still doth sway
The triple Tyrant:[3] that from these may grow
   A hundredfold, who having learnt thy way
   Early may fly the *Babylonian*[4] woe.

When I Consider How My Light Is Spent[5]

When I consider how my light is spent,
   Ere half my days, in this dark world and wide,
   And that one Talent[6] which is death to hide,
   Lodg'd with me useless, though my Soul more bent
To serve therewith my Maker, and present
   My true account, lest he returning chide,
   Doth God exact day-labour, light denied,
   I fondly ask; But patience to prevent
That murmur, soon replies, God doth not need
   Either man's work or his own gifts; who best
   Bear his mild yoke, they serve him best, his State
Is Kingly. Thousands at his bidding speed
   And post o'er Land and Ocean without rest:
   They also serve who only stand and wait.

---

1   Forces of the Duke of Savoy killed 1700 members of the Protestant Waldensian sect in
     Piedmont, a district of north-western Italy, in April 1655.
2   The Waldenses had been critical of what they saw as idolatry and materialism in the
     Roman Catholic church.
3   the Pope, who wears a three-crowned tiara
4   The Catholic Church was identified by Protestants with the decadent city of Babylon,
     whose destruction is described in Revelations 17 and 18.
5   Milton became blind in 1651, about a year before he wrote this poem.
6   a reference to the Biblical parable of the talents; see Matthew 25.14-30

Methought I Saw My Late Espoused Saint[1]

Methought I saw my late espouséd Saint
  Brought to me like *Alcestis*[2] from the grave,
  Whom *Jove's* great Son to her glad Husband gave,
  Rescu'd from death by force though pale and faint.
Mine as whom washt from spot of child-bed taint,
  Purification in the old Law[3] did save,
  And such, as yet once more I trust to have
Full sight of her in Heaven without restraint,
  Came vested all in white, pure as her mind:
  Her face was veil'd, yet to my fancied sight,
  Love, sweetness, goodness, in her person shin'd
So clear, as in no face with more delight.
  But O, as to embrace me she inclin'd,
  I wak'd, she fled, and day brought back my night.

from: *Paradise Lost: Book I*

All these[4] and more came flocking; but with looks
Downcast and damp, yet such wherein appear'd
Obscure some glimpse of joy, to have found their chief 525
Not in despair, to have found themselves not lost
In loss itself; which on his count'nance cast
Like doubtful hue: but he his wonted pride
Soon recollecting, with high words, that bore
Semblance of worth, not substance, gently rais'd
Their fainting courage, and dispell'd their fears.   530
Then straight commands that at the warlike sound
Of Trumpets loud and Clarions be uprear'd
His mighty Standard; that proud honor claim'd
Azazel[5] as his right, a Cherub tall:
Who forthwith from the glittering Staff unfurl'd   535
Th' Imperial Ensign, which full high advanc't
Shone like a Meteor streaming to the Wind
With Gems and Golden lustre rich imblaz'd,
Seraphic arms and Trophies: all the while
Sonorous metal blowing Martial sounds: 540
At which the universal Host upsent
A shout that tore Hell's Concave, and beyond

---

1   Milton's second wife, Katherine Woodcock, to whom he had been married less than two
     years when she died in 1658
2   In Greek mythology, Hercules ("Jove's great son") brings Alcestis back from death to her
     husband Admetus.
3   the law described in Leviticus 12, requiring the ritual purification of women after
     childbirth
4   the leaders among the fallen angels, responding to a summons by Satan
5   the name given in Jewish tradition to a prince of the devils

Frighted the Reign of *Chaos*[1] and old Night.
All in a moment through the gloom were seen
Ten thousand Banners rise into the Air   545
With Orient Colors waving: with them rose
A Forest huge of Spears: and thronging Helms
Appear'd, and serried Shields in thick array
Of depth immeasurable: Anon they move
In perfect *Phalanx* to the *Dorian* mood[2]   550
Of Flutes and soft Recorders; such as rais'd
To highth of noblest temper Heroes old
Arming to Battle, and instead of rage
Deliberate valor breath'd, firm and unmov'd
With dread of death to flight or foul retreat,   555
Nor wanting power to mitigate and swage
With solemn touches, troubl'd thoughts, and chase
Anguish and doubt and fear and sorrow and pain
From mortal or immortal minds. Thus they
Breathing united force with fixed thought   560
Mov'd on in silence to soft Pipes that charm'd
Their painful steps o'er the burnt soil; and now
Advanc't in view they stand, a horrid[3] Front
Of dreadful length and dazzling Arms, in guise
Of Warriors old with order'd Spear and Shield,   565
Awaiting what command their mighty Chief
Had to impose: He through the armed Files
Darts his experienc't eye, and soon traverse
The whole Battalion views, their order due,
Their visages and stature as of Gods;   570
Their number last he sums. And now his heart
Distends with pride, and hard'ning in his strength
Glories: For never since created man,
Met such imbodied force, as nam'd with these
Could merit more than that small infantry[4]   575
Warr'd on by Cranes: though all the Giant brood
Of *Phlegra*[5] with th' Heroic Race were join'd
That fought at *Thebes*[6] and *Ilium*,[7] on each side
Mixt with auxiliar Gods; and what resounds
In Fable or *Romance* of *Uther's* Son[8]   580

---

1   In Milton's cosmology, Chaos is the region of unformed matter below Heaven, out of
     which are formed both Hell and the created Universe.
2   a simple, solemn music, like that played by the Spartans preparing for battle
3   bristling (Latin "horridus")
4   According to Pliny, a race of pigmies in eastern Asia rode goats in their battles with
     cranes.
5   where the giants rose against the gods, but were defeated
6   Seven Greek warriors sought to dislodge Eteocles, son of Oedipus, from Thebes, but
     failed.
7   Troy
8   King Arthur

Begirt with *British* and *Armoric*[1] Knights;
And all who since, Baptiz'd or Infidel
Jousted in *Aspramont* or *Montalban*,[2]
Damasco, or *Marocco*, or *Trebisond*,
Or whom *Biserta* sent from *Afric* shore   585
When *Charlemain* with all his Peerage fell
By *Fontarabbia*. Thus far these beyond
Compare of mortal prowess, yet observ'd
Their dread commander: he above the rest
In shape and gesture proudly eminent   590
Stood like a Tow'r; his form had yet not lost
All her Original brightness, nor appear'd
Less than Arch-Angel ruin'd, and th' excess
Of Glory obscur'd: As when the Sun new ris'n
Looks through the Horizontal misty Air   595
Shorn of his Beams, or from behind the Moon
In dim Eclipse disastrous twilight sheds
On half the Nations, and with fear of change
Perplexes Monarchs. Dark'n'd so, yet shone
Above them all th' Arch-Angel: but his face   600
Deep scars of Thunder had intrencht, and care
Sat on his faded cheek, but under Brows
Of dauntless courage, and considerate[3] Pride
Waiting revenge: cruel his eye, but cast
Signs of remorse and passion to behold   605
The fellows of his crime, the followers rather
(Far other once beheld in bliss) condemn'd
For ever now to have thir lot in pain,
Millions of Spirits for his fault amerc't[4]
Of Heav'n, and from Eternal Splendors flung   610
For his revolt, yet faithful how they stood,
Their Glory wither'd. As when Heaven's Fire
Hath scath'd the Forest Oaks, or Mountain Pines,
With singed top thir stately growth though bare
Stands on the blasted Heath. He now prepar'd   615
To speak; whereat thir doubl'd Ranks they bend
From wing to wing, and half enclose him round
With all his Peers: attention held them mute.
Thrice he assay'd, and thrice in spite of scorn,
Tears such as Angels weep, burst forth: at last   620
Words interwove with sighs found out their way.
    "O Myriads of immortal Spirits, O Powers
Matchless, but with th' Almighty, and that strife

---

1 from Armorica, the ancient name of Brittany
2 These and the other place-names are a mingling of the real and the fictional, intended
   to recall great stories of war and chivalry, climaxed by the story of the death of Roland
   at Roncesvalles, Fontarabbia in Northern Spain.
3 deliberate, conscious
4 deprived

Was not inglorious, though th' event[1] was dire,
As this place testifies, and this dire change   625
Hateful to utter: but what power of mind
Foreseeing or presaging, from the Depth
Of knowledge past or present, could have fear'd
How such united force of Gods, how such
As stood like these, could ever know repulse?   630
For who can yet believe, though after loss,
That all these puissant Legions, whose exile
Hath emptied Heav'n, shall fail to re-ascend
Self-rais'd, and repossess their native seat?
For mee be witness all the Host of Heav'n,   635
If counsels different, or danger shunn'd
By me, have lost our hopes. But he who reigns
Monarch in Heav'n, till then as one secure
Sat on his Throne, upheld by old repute,
Consent or custom, and his Regal State   640
Put forth at full, but still his strength conceal'd,
Which tempted our attempt, and wrought our fall.
Henceforth his might we know, and know our own
So as not either to provoke, or dread
New War, provok't; our better part remains   645
To work in close design, by fraud or guile
What force effected not: that he no less
At length from us may find, who overcomes
By force, hath overcome but half his foe.
Space may produce new Worlds; whereof so rife   650
There went a fame[2] in Heav'n that he ere long
Intended to create, and therein plant
A generation, whom his choice regard
Should favor equal to the Sons of Heaven:
Thither, if but to pry, shall be perhaps   655
Our first eruption, thither or elsewhere:
For this Infernal Pit shall never hold
Celestial Spirits in Bondage, nor th' Abyss
Long under darkness cover. But these thoughts
Full Counsel must mature: Peace is despair'd,   660
For who can think Submission? War then, War
Open or understood, must be resolv'd.
    He spake: and to confirm his words, out-flew
Millions of flaming swords, drawn from the thighs
Of mighty Cherubim; the sudden blaze   665
Far round illumin'd hell: highly they rag'd
Against the Highest, and fierce with grasped Arms
Clash'd on their sounding shields the din of war,
Hurling defiance toward the Vault of Heav'n.

---

1   the outcome
2   rumour

Anne Bradstreet

(1613?–1672)

The Prologue

1

To sing of wars, of captains, and of kings,
Of cities founded, commonwealths begun,
For my mean pen are too superior things:
Or how they all, or each their dates have run
Let poets and historians set these forth,
My obscure lines shall not so dim their worth.

2

But when my wond'ring eyes and envious heart
Great Bartas'[1] sugared lines do but read o'er,
Fool I do grudge the Muses did not part
'Twixt him and me that overfluent store;
A Bartas can do what a Bartas will
But simple I according to my skill.

3

From schoolboy's tongue no rhet'ric we expect,
Nor yet a sweet consort from broken strings,
Nor perfect beauty where's a main defect:
My foolish, broken, blemished Muse so sings,
And this to mend, alas, no art is able,
'Cause nature made it so irreparable.

4

Nor can I, like that fluent sweet tongued Greek,[2]
Who lisped at first, in future times speak plain.
By art he gladly found what he did seek,
A full requital of his striving pain.
Art can do much, but this maxim's most sure:
A weak or wounded brain admits no cure.

5

I am obnoxious to each carping tongue
Who says my hand a needle better fits,

---

1   Guillaume Du Bartas (1544-1590), author of *La Semaine* (1578), an epic poem about the Creation
2   According to tradition, the Greek orator Demosthenes (c.383-322 B.C.) had to conquer a lisp before achieving his renowned fluency of speech.

A poet's pen all scorn I should thus wrong,
For such despite they cast on female wits:
If what I do prove well, it won't advance,
They'll say it's stol'n, or else it was by chance.

6

But sure the antique Greeks were far more mild
Else of our sex, why feigned they those nine
And poesy made Calliope's[1] own child;
So 'mongst the rest they placed the arts divine:
But this weak knot they will full soon untie,
The Greeks did nought, but play the fools and lie.

7

Let Greeks be Greeks, and women what they are
Men have precedency and still excel,
It is but vain unjustly to wage war;
Men can do best, and women know it well.
Preeminence in all and each is yours;
Yet grant some small acknowledgement of ours.

8

And oh ye high flown quills that soar the skies,
And ever with your prey still catch your praise,
If e'er you deign these lowly lines your eyes,
Give thyme or parsley wreath, I ask no bays;[2]
This mean and unrefined ore of mine
Will make your glist'ring gold but more to shine.

The Author to Her Book[3]

Thou ill-formed offspring of my feeble brain,
Who after birth didst by my side remain,
Till snatched from thence by friends, less wise than true
Who thee abroad, exposed to public view,
Made thee in rags, halting to th' press to trudge,
Where errors were not lessened (all may judge).
At thy return my blushing was not small,
My rambling brat (in print) should mother call,
I cast thee by as one unfit for light,

---

1   the Muse of epic poetry
2   the laurel garlands that traditionally crowned a poet
3   These lines are thought to be a preface intended for a new edition of Bradstreet's book
    The Tenth Muse, first published in 1650 without her permission.

Thy visage was so irksome in my sight;
Yet being mine own, at length affection would
Thy blemishes amend, if so I could:
I washed thy face, but more defects I saw,
And rubbing off a spot still made a flaw.
I stretched thy joints to make thee even feet,
Yet still thou run'st more hobbling than is meet;
In better dress to trim thee was my mind,
But nought save homespun cloth i' th' house I find.
In this array 'mongst vulgars may'st thou roam.
In critic's hands beware thou dost not come,
And take thy way where yet thou art not known;
If for thy father asked, say thou hadst none;
And for thy mother, she alas is poor,
Which caused her thus to send thee out of door.

Before the Birth of One of Her Children

All things within this fading world hath end,
Adversity doth still our joys attend;
No ties so strong, no friends so dear and sweet,
But with death's parting blow is sure to meet.
The sentence past is most irrevocable,
A common thing, yet oh, inevitable.
How soon, my Dear, death may my steps attend,
How soon't may be thy lot to lose thy friend,
We both are ignorant, yet love bids me
These farewell lines to recommend to thee,
That when that knot's untied that made us one,
I may seem thine, who in effect am none.
And if I see not half my days that's due,
What nature would, God grant to yours and you;
The many faults that well you know I have
Let be interred in my oblivious grave;
If any worth or virtue were in me,
Let that live freshly in thy memory
And when thou feel'st no grief, as I no harms,
Yet love thy dead, who long lay in thine arms.
And when thy loss shall be repaid with gains
Look to my little babes, my dear remains.
And if thou love thyself, or loved'st me,
These O protect from step-dame's injury.
And if chance to thine eyes shall bring this verse,
With some sad sighs honour my absent hearse;
And kiss this paper for thy love's dear sake,
Who with salt tears this last farewell did take.

To My Dear and Loving Husband

If ever two were one, then surely we.
If ever man were loved by wife, then thee;
If ever wife was happy in a man,
Compare with me, ye women, if you can.
I prize thy love more than whole mines of gold
Or all the riches that the East doth hold.
My love is such that rivers cannot quench,
Nor ought but love from thee, give recompense.
Thy love is such I can no way repay,
The heavens reward thee manifold, I pray.
Then while we live, in love let's so persevere
That when we live no more, we may live ever.

A Letter to Her Husband, Absent Upon Public Employment[1]

My head, my heart, mine eyes, my life, nay, more,
My joy, my magazine[2] of earthly store,
If two be one, as surely thou and I,
How stayest thou there, whilst I at Ipswich[3] lie?
So many steps, head from the heart to sever,
If but a neck, soon should we be together.
I, like the Earth this season, mourn in black,
My Sun is gone so far in's zodiac,
Whom whilst I 'joyed, nor storms, nor frost I felt,
His warmth such frigid colds did cause to melt.
My chilled limbs now numbed lie forlorn;
Return, return, sweet Sol, from Capricorn;[4]
In this dead time, alas, what can I more
Than view those fruits which through thy heat I bore?
Which sweet contentment yield me for a space,
True living pictures of their father's face.
O strange effect! now thou art southward gone,
I weary grow the tedious day so long;
But when thou northward to me shalt return,
I wish my Sun may never set, but burn
Within the Cancer[5] of my glowing breast,
The welcome house of him my dearest guest.
Where ever, ever stay, and go not thence,

---

1 Bradstreet's husband Simon was a member of the General Court in Boston, which was working on a scheme to unite the New England colonies.
2 storehouse
3 A town about 40 miles north of Boston, Ipswich was then a remote plantation.
4 The sun is in the sign of Capricorn in December and January.
5 The sun is in Cancer at the summer solstice.

Till nature's sad decree shall call thee hence;
Flesh of thy flesh, bone of thy bone,
I here, thou there, yet both but one.

Upon the Burning of Our House July 10th, 1666.

In silent night when rest I took
For sorrow near I did not look
I wakened was with thund'ring noise
And piteous shrieks of dreadful voice.
That fearful sound of "Fire!" and "Fire!"
Let no man know is my desire.
I, starting up, the light did spy,
And to my God my heart did cry
To strengthen me in my distress
And not to leave me succorless.
Then, coming out, beheld a space
The flame consume my dwelling place.
And when I could no longer look,
I blest His name that gave and took,
That laid my goods now in the dust.
Yea, so it was, and so 'twas just.
It was His own, it was not mine,
Far be it that I should repine;
He might of all justly bereft
But yet sufficient for us left.
When by the ruins oft I past
My sorrowing eyes aside did cast,
And here and there the places spy
Where oft I sat and long did lie:
Here stood that trunk, and there that chest,
There lay that store I counted best.
My pleasant things in ashes lie,
And them behold no more shall I.
Under thy roof no guest shall sit,
Nor at thy table eat a bit.
No pleasant tale shall e'er be told,
Nor things recounted done of old.
No candle e'er shall shine in thee,
Nor bridegroom's voice e'er heard shall be.
In silence ever shall thou lie,
Adieu, Adieu, all's vanity.[1]
Then straight I 'gin my heart to chide,
And did thy wealth on earth abide?
Didst fix thy hope on mold'ring dust?

---

1   "Vanity of vanities, saith the Preacher, vanity of vanities; all is vanity" (Ecclesiastes 1.2).

The arm of flesh didst make thy trust?
Raise up thy thoughts above the sky
That dunghill mists away may fly.
Thou hast an house on high erect,
Framed by that mighty Architect,
With glory richly furnished,
Stands permanent though this be fled.
It's purchased and paid for too
By Him who hath enough to do.
A price so vast as is unknown
Yet by His gift is made thine own;
There's wealth enough, I need no more,
Farewell, my pelf, farewell my store.
The world no longer let me love,
My hope and treasure lies above.

Andrew Marvell

(1621–1678)

The Coronet

When for the Thorns with which I long, too long,
　With many a piercing wound,
　My Saviours head have crown'd,
I seek with Garlands to redress that Wrong;
　Through every Garden, every Mead,
I gather flow'rs (my fruits are only flow'rs)
　Dismantling all the fragrant Towers
That once adorn'd my Shepherdesses head.
And now when I have summ'd up all my store,
　Thinking (so I my self deceive)
　So rich a Chaplet thence to weave
As never yet the king of Glory wore:
　Alas I find the Serpent old
　That, twining in his speckled breast,
　About the flow'rs disguis'd does fold,
　With wreaths of Fame and Interest[1].
Ah, foolish Man, that would'st debase with them,
And mortal Glory, Heavens Diadem!
But thou who only could'st the Serpent tame,
Either his slipp'ry knots at once untie,
And disentangle all his winding Snare:
Or shatter too with him my curious frame:
And let these wither, so that he may die,
Though set with Skill and chosen out with Care.
That they, while Thou on both their Spoils dost tread,
May crown thy Feet, that could not crown thy Head.

A Dialogue between the Soul and Body

Soul

　　O Who shall, from this Dungeon, raise
A Soul enslav'd so many wayes?
With bolts of Bones, that fetter'd stands
In Feet; and manacled in Hands.
Here blinded with an Eye; and there
Deaf with the drumming of an Ear.
A Soul hung up, as 'twere, in Chains
Of Nerves, and Arteries, and Veins.
Tortur'd, besides each other part,
In a vain Head, and double Heart.

1　self-interest, self-advancement

Body

O who shall me deliver whole,
From bonds of this Tyrannic Soul?
Which, stretcht upright, impales me so,
That mine own Precipice I go;
And warms and moves this needless[1] Frame:
(A Fever could but do the same.)
And, wanting where its spight to try,
Has made me live to let me dye.
A Body that could never rest,
Since this ill Spirit it possest.

Soul

What Magick could me thus confine
Within anothers Grief to pine?
Where whatsoever it complain,
I feel, that cannot feel, the pain.
And all my Care its self employes,
That to preserve, which me destroys:
Constrain'd not only to indure
Diseases, but, whats worse, the Cure:
And ready oft the Port to gain,
Am Shipwrackt into Health again.

Body

But Physick[2] yet could never reach
The Maladies Thou me dost teach;
Whom first the Cramp of Hope does Tear:
And then the Palsie Shakes of Fear.
The Pestilence of Love does heat:
Or Hatred's hidden Ulcer eat.
Joy's chearful Madness does perplex:
Or Sorrow's other Madness vex.
Which Knowledge forces me to know;
And Memory will not foregoe.
What but a Soul could have the wit
To build me up for Sin so fit?
So Architects do square and hew
Green Trees that in the Forest grew.

---

1   having no want
2   medicine

ANDREW MARVELL

To his Coy Mistress

Had we but World enough, and Time,
This coyness Lady were no crime.
We would sit down, and think which way
To walk, and pass our long Loves Day.
Thou by the *Indian Ganges* side
Should'st Rubies find: I by the Tide
Of *Humber*[1] would complain. I would
Love you ten years before the Flood:
And you should, if you please, refuse
Till the Conversion of the *Jews*.[2]
My vegetable Love should grow
Vaster than Empires, and more slow.
An hundred years should go to praise
Thine Eyes, and on thy Forehead Gaze.
Two hundred to adore each Breast:
But thirty thousand to the rest.
An Age at least to every part,
And the last Age should show your Heart.
For Lady you deserve this State;
Nor would I love at lower rate.
   But at my back I alwaies hear,
Times winged Charriot hurrying near:
And yonder all before us lye
Deserts of vast Eternity.
Thy Beauty shall no more be found;
Nor, in thy marble Vault, shall sound
My ecchoing Song: then Worms shall try
That long preserv'd Virginity:
And your quaint Honour turn to dust;
And into ashes all my Lust.
The Grave's a fine and private place,
But none I think do there embrace.
   Now therefore, while the youthful hew
Sits on thy skin like morning glew,
And while thy willing Soul transpires
At every pore with instant Fires,
Now let us sport us while we may;
And now, like am'rous birds of prey,
Rather at once our Time devour,
Than languish in his slow-chapt[3] pow'r.
Let us roll all our Strength, and all
Our sweetness, up into one Ball:
And tear our Pleasures with rough strife,

---

1   the river that flows through Hull, Marvell's home town in northeastern England
2   an event popularly believed to occur just before the Last Judgement
3   slow-jawed

[81]

*carpe diem -
to
Seize the day*

Thorough the Iron gates of Life.
Thus, though we cannot make our Sun
Stand still, yet we will make him run.

*We'll give the
Sun a run
for his money*

The Definition of Love

i

My Love is of a birth as rare
As 'tis for object strange and high:
It was begotten by despair
Upon Impossibility.

ii

Magnanimous Despair alone
Could show me so divine a thing,
Where feeble Hope could ne'r have flown
But vainly flapt its Tinsel Wing.

iii

And yet I quickly might arrive
Where my extended Soul is fixt,
But Fate does Iron wedges drive,
And alwaies crouds it self betwixt.

iv

For Fate with jealous Eye does see
Two perfect Loves; nor lets them close;[1]
Their union would her ruine be,
And her Tyrannick pow'r depose.

v

And therefore her Decrees of Steel
Us as the distant Poles have plac'd,
(Though Loves whole World on us doth wheel)
Not by themselves to be embrac'd.

vi

Unless the giddy Heaven fall,
And Earth some new Convulsion tear;

---

1   come together

And, us to joyn, the World should all
Be cramp'd into a *Planisphere*.[1]

vii

As Lines so Loves *oblique* may well
Themselves in every Angle greet:
But ours so truly *Paralel,*
Though infinite can never meet.

viii

Therefore the Love which us doth bind,
But Fate so enviously debarrs,
Is the Conjunction of the Mind,
And Opposition of the Stars.

The Garden

i

How vainly men themselves amaze
To win the Palm, the Oke, or Bayes;[2]
And their uncessant Labours see
Crown'd from some single Herb or Tree,
Whose short and narrow verged Shade
Does prudently their Toyles upbraid;
While all Flow'rs and all Trees do close
To weave the Garlands of repose.

ii

Fair quiet, have I found thee here,
And Innocence thy Sister dear!
Mistaken long, I sought you then
In busie Companies of Men.
Your sacred Plants, if here below,
Only among the Plants will grow.
Society is all but rude,
To this delicious Solitude.

---

1   a map formed by the plane projection of a sphere
2   honours conferred for military, civic, or poetic achievement respectively

iii

No white nor red[1] was ever seen
So am'rous as this lovely green.
Fond Lovers, cruel as their Flame,
Cut in these Trees their Mistress name.
Little, Alas, they know, or heed,
How far these Beauties Hers exceed!
Fair Trees! where s'ere your barkes I wound
No Name shall but your own be found.

iv

When we have run our Passions heat,
Love hither makes his best retreat.
The *Gods*, that mortal Beauty chase,[2]
Still in a Tree did end their race.
Apollo hunted *Daphne* so,
Only that She might Laurel grow.
And *Pan* did after *Syrinx* speed,
Not as a Nymph, but for a Reed.

iv

What wond'rous Life in this I lead!
Ripe Apples drop about my head;
The Luscious Clusters of the Vine
Upon my Mouth do crush their Wine;
The Nectaren, and curious[3] Peach,
Into my hands themselves do reach;
Stumbling on Melons, as I pass,
Insnar'd with Flow'rs, I fall on Grass.

vi

Mean while the Mind, from pleasures less,
Withdraws into its happiness:
The Mind, that Ocean where each kind
Does streight its own resemblance find;
Yet it creates, transcending these,
Far other Worlds, and other Seas;
Annihilating all that's made
To a green Thought in a green Shade.

---

1   i.e., of a woman's complexion
2   The stories of Apollo's pursuit of Daphne, and of Pan's pursuit of Syrinx, are told in
     the first book of Ovid's *Metamorphoses*.
3   rare, exquisite

vii

Here at the Fountains sliding foot,
Or at some Fruit-tree's mossy root,
Casting the Bodies Vest aside,
My Soul into the boughs does glide:
There like a Bird it sits, and sings,
Then whets,[1] and combs its silver Wings;
And, till prepar'd for longer flight,
Waves in its Plumes the various Light.

viii

Such was that happy Garden-state,
While Man there walk'd without a Mate:
After a Place so pure, and sweet,
What other Help could yet be meet!
But 'twas beyond a Mortal's share
To wander solitary there:
Two Paradises 'twere in one
To live in Paradise alone.

ix

How well the skilful Gardner drew
Of flow'rs and herbes this Dial new;
Where from above the milder Sun
Does through a fragrant Zodiack run;
And, as it works, th' industrious Bee
Computes its time as well as we.
How could such sweet and wholsome Hours
Be reckon'd but with herbs and flow'rs!

---

1   preens

Margaret Cavendish, Duchess of Newcastle

(1624?–1674)

The Poetresses Petition

Like to a Feavers pulse my heart doth beat,
For fear my Book some great repulse should meet.
If it be naught, let her in silence lye,
Disturbe her not, let her in quiet dye;
Let not the Bells of your dispraise ring loud,
But wrap her up in silence as a Shrowd;
Cause black oblivion on her Hearse to hang,
Instead of Tapers, let darke night there stand;
Instead of Flowers to the grave her strow
Before her Hearse, sleepy, dull Poppy throw;
Instead of Scutcheons,[1] let my Teares be hung,
Which greife and sorrow from my eyes out wrung:
Let those that beare her Corps, no Jesters be,
But sad, and sober, grave Mortality:
No Satyr Poets to her Funerall come;
No Altars rays'd to write Inscriptions on:
Let dust of all forgetfulnesse be cast
Upon her Corps, there let them lye and waste:
Nor let her rise againe; unlesse some know,
At Judgements some good Merits shee can shew;
Then shee shall live in Heavens of high praise:
And for her glory, Garlands of fresh Bayes.[2]

Natures Cook

Death is the cook of Nature; and we find
Meat dressed several ways to please her mind.
Some meats she roasts with fevers, burning hot,
And some she boils with dropsies in a pot.
Some for jelly consuming by degrees,
And some with ulcers, gravy out to squeeze.
Some flesh as sage she stuffs with gouts, and pains,
Others for tender meat hangs up in chains.
Some in the sea she pickles up to keep,
Others, as brawn is soused,[3] those in wine steep.
Some with the pox,[4] chops flesh, and bones so small,
Of which she makes a French fricasse withal.
Some on gridirons of calentures[5] is broiled,

---

1   in heraldry, the shield-shaped tablets displaying a family's armorial bearings
2   the laurel garlands bestowed on poets
3   as pork flesh is pickled
4   syphilis
5   delirious fevers

And some is trodden on, and so quite spoiled.
But those are baked, when smothered they do die,
By hectic fevers some meat she doth fry.
In sweat sometimes she stews with savoury smell,
A hodge-podge of diseases tasteth well.
Brains dressed with apoplexy to Nature's wish,
Or swims with sauce of megrims[1] in a dish.
And tongues she dries with smoke from stomachs ill,
Which as the second course she sends up still.
Then Death cuts throats, for blood-puddings to make,
And puts them in the guts, which colics rack.
Some hunted are by Death, for deer that's red.
Or stall-fed oxen, knocked on the head.
Some for bacon by Death are singed, or scaled,
Then powdered up with phlegm, and rheum that's salt.

A Woman drest by Age

A milk-white hair-lace wound up all her hairs,
And a deaf coif did cover both her ears,
A sober countenance about her face she ties,
And a dim sight doth cover half her eyes,
About her neck a kercher of coarse skin,
Which Time had crumpled, and worn creases in,
Her gown was turned to melancholy black,
Which loose did hang upon her sides and back,
Her stockings cramps had knit, red worsted gout,
And pains as garters tied her legs about.
A pair of palsy gloves her hands drew on,
With weakness stitched, and numbness trimmed upon.
Her shoes were corns, and hard skin sewed together,
Hard skin were soles, and corns the upper leather.
A mantle of diseases laps her round,
And thus she's dressed, till Death lays her in ground.

---

1 migraine headaches

Katherine Philips

(1631–1664)

A marryd state affords but little Ease

A marry^d state affords but little Ease
The best of husbands are so hard to please
This in wifes Carefull faces you may spell
Tho they desemble their misfortunes well
A virgin state is crown'd with much content
Its allways happy as its inocent
No Blustering husbands to create yr fears
No pangs of child birth to extort yr tears
No childrens crys for to offend your ears
Few wordly crosses to distract yr prayers
Thus are you freed from all the cares that do
Attend on matrymony & a husband too
Therefore Mad^m be advised by me
Turn turn apostate to loves Levity
Supress wild nature if she dare rebell
Theres no such thing as leading Apes in hell[1]

L'Amitie: To Mrs M. Awbrey[2]

Soule of my soule! my Joy, my crown, my friend!
A name which all the rest doth comprehend;
How happy are we now, whose souls are grown,
By an incomparable mixture, One:
Whose well acquainted minds are now as neare
As Love, or vows, or secrets can endeare.
I have no thought but what's to thee reveal'd,
Nor thou desire that is from me conceal'd.
Thy heart locks up my secrets richly set,
And my brest is thy private cabinet.
Thou shedst no teare but what my moisture lent,
And if I sigh, it is thy breath is spent.
United thus, what horrour can appeare
Worthy our sorrow, anger, or our feare?
Let the dull world alone to talk and fight,
And with their vast ambitions nature fright;
Let them despise so inocent a flame,
While Envy, pride, and faction play their game:
But we by Love sublim'd so high shall rise,

---

1   a proverbial punishment for spinsters; see *Much Ado About Nothing*, II.i.44
2   Mary Aubrey (1631-1700) was a schoolfriend of Philips's.

To pitty Kings, and Conquerours despise,
Since we that sacred union[1] have engrost,
Which they and all the sullen world have lost.

Friendship's Mysterys: to my dearest Lucasia[2]

1

Come, my Lucasia, since we see
    That miracles men's faith do move
By wonder and by Prodigy
    To the dull, angry world let's prove
    There's a religion in our Love.

2

For though we were design'd t'agree,
    That fate no liberty destroys,
But our election[3] is as free
    As Angells, who with greedy choice
    Are yet determin'd to their Joys.

3

Our hearts are doubled by their loss,
    Here mixture is addition grown;
We both diffuse, and both engrosse:
    And we, whose minds are so much one,
    Never, yet ever, are alone.

4

We court our own captivity,
    Then Thrones more great and innocent:
'Twere banishment to be set free,
    Since we weare fetters whose intent
    Not bondage is, but Ornament.

---

1   i.e., the union of souls. In this and other poems, Philips explores the nature of ideal
    Platonic friendship between women.
2   "Lucasia" was the name Philips gave to Anne Owen, a friend to whom she addressed
    some of her poems on female friendship. It is the name of a character in William
    Cartwright's play *The Lady Errant* (1636).
3   In Calvinist doctrine, "election" refers to the predestination of souls to salvation.

5

Divided Joys are tedious found,
 And griefs united easyer grow:
We are our selves but by rebound,
 And all our titles shuffled so,
 Both Princes, and both subjects too.

6

Our hearts are mutuall victims lay'd,
 While they (such power in friendship ly's)
Are Altars, Priests, and off'rings made,
 And each heart which thus kindly dy's,
 Grows deathless by the sacrifise.

John Dryden

(1631–1700)

To the Memory of Mr. Oldham[1]

Farewel, too little and too lately known,
Whom I began to think and call my own;
For sure our Souls were near ally'd; and thine
Cast in the same Poetick mould with mine.
One common Note on either Lyre did strike,
And Knaves and Fools we both abhorr'd alike:
To the same Goal did both our Studies drive,
The last set out the soonest did arrive.
Thus *Nisus*[2] fell upon the slippery place,
While his young Friend perform'd and won the Race.
O early ripe! to thy abundant store
What could advancing Age have added more?
It might (what Nature never gives the young)
Have taught the numbers of thy native Tongue.
But Satyr needs not those, and Wit will shine
Through the harsh cadence of a rugged line.
A noble Error, and but seldom made,
When Poets are by too much force betray'd.
Thy generous fruits, though gather'd ere their prime
Still shew'd a quickness; and maturing time
But mellows what we write to the dull sweets of Rime.
Once more, hail and farewel; farewel thou young,
But ah too short, *Marcellus*[3] of our Tongue;
Thy Brows with Ivy, and with Laurels bound;
But Fate and gloomy Night encompass thee around.

---

1   John Oldham (1653-83), author of *Satires upon the Jesuits* (1681)
2   Nisus, leading in a footrace, slipped in a patch of blood, but in his fall brought down
    his nearest rival and thus allowed his dear friend Euryalus to take the prize (Virgil, *Aeneid*
    Book 5).
3   Chosen to succeed Caesar Augustus, Marcus Claudius Marcellus died at twenty.

To the Pious Memory of the Accomplisht Young Lady

Mrs. Anne Killigrew,

Excellent in the two Sister-Arts of Poësie, and Painting.

An ODE[1]

I

Thou Youngest Virgin-Daughter of the Skies,
Made in the last Promotion of the Blest;
Whose Palmes, new pluckt from Paradise,
In spreading Branches more sublimely rise,
Rich with Immortal Green above the rest: 5
Whether, adopted to some Neighbouring Star,
Thou rol'st above us, in thy wand'ring Race,
   Or, in Procession fixt and regular,
   Mov'd with the Heavens Majestick Pace;
   Or, call'd to more Superiour Bliss,   10
Thou tread'st, with Seraphims, the vast Abyss:
What ever happy Region is thy place,
Cease thy Celestial Song a little space;
(Thou wilt have Time enough for Hymns Divine,
   Since Heav'ns Eternal Year is thine.)   15
Hear then a Mortal Muse thy Praise rehearse,
     In no ignoble Verse;
But such as thy own voice did practise here,
When thy first Fruits of Poesie were giv'n;
To make thy self a welcome Inmate there: 20
   While yet a young Probationer,
     And Candidate of Heav'n.

II

If by Traduction[2] came thy Mind,
   Our Wonder is the less to find
A Soul so charming from a Stock so good;   25
Thy Father was transfus'd into thy Blood:
So wert thou born into the tuneful strain,
(An early, rich, and inexhausted Vain.)
   But if thy Praeexisting Soul
   Was form'd, at first, with Myriads more,   30
It did through all the Mighty Poets roul,
   Who *Greek* or *Latine* Laurels wore,

---

1   Anne Killigrew was a poet and painter who died of smallpox in 1685.
2   the doctrine that the soul, as well as the body, is transmitted by the parents to the child

And was that *Sappho*[1] last, which once it was before.
  If so, then cease thy flight, *O Heav'n-born Mind!*
  Thou hast no Dross to purge from thy Rich Ore: 35
  Nor can thy Soul a fairer Mansion find,
  Than was the Beauteous Frame she left behind:
Return, to fill or mend the Quire, of thy Celestial kind.

III

  May we presume to say, that at thy Birth,
New joy was sprung in Heav'n, as well as here on Earth. 40
  For sure the Milder Planets did combine
  On thy Auspicious Horoscope to shine,
  And ev'n the most Malicious were in Trine.[2]
    Thy Brother-Angels at thy Birth
    Strung each his Lyre, and tun'd it high,   45
    That all the People of the Skie
  Might know a Poetess was born on Earth.
      And then if ever, Mortal Ears
      Had heard the Musick of the Spheres!
      And if no clust'ring Swarm of Bees[3]   50
On thy sweet Mouth distill'd their golden Dew,
    'Twas that, such vulgar Miracles,
    Heav'n had not Leasure to renew:
  For all the Blest Fraternity of Love
Solemniz'd there thy Birth, and kept thy Holyday above. 55

IV

  O Gracious God! How far have we
Prophan'd thy Heav'nly Gift of Poesy?
Made prostitute and profligate the Muse,
Debas'd to each obscene and impious use,
  Whose Harmony was first ordain'd Above   60
For Tongues of Angels, and for Hymns of Love?
O wretched We! why were we hurry'd down
    This lubrique and adult'rate age,
    (Nay added fat Pollutions of our own)
    T' increase the steaming Ordures of the Stage?   65
What can we say t' excuse our *Second Fall?*
Let this thy *Vestal,* Heav'n, attone for all!

  Her *Arethusian* Stream[4] remains unsoil'd,

---

1   a Greek lyric poet of the 7th century B.C., born on the island of Lesbos
2   in astrological terms, in favourable positions relative to one another, and thus positive
    in their influence
3   A swarm of bees is said to have alighted on the lips of the infant Plato, foretelling his
    eloquence.
4   Arethusa was a Greek nymph who was pursued by the river-god Alpheus, and changed

Unmixt with Forreign Filth, and undefil'd,
Her Wit was more than Man, her Innocence a Child!   70

V

Art she had none, yet wanted none:
For Nature did that Want supply,
So rich in Treasures of her Own,
She might our boasted Stores defy:
Such Noble Vigour did her Verse adorn,   75
That it seem'd borrow'd, where 'twas only born.
Her Morals too were in her Bosome bred
   By great Examples daily fed,
What in the best of Books, her Fathers Life, she read.
And to be read her self she need not fear,   80
Each Test, and ev'ry Light, her Muse will bear,
Though *Epictetus*[1] with his Lamp were there.
Ev'n Love (for Love sometimes her Muse exprest)
Was but a *Lambent-flame* which play'd about her Brest:
Light as the Vapours of a Morning Dream,   85
So cold herself, whilst she such Warmth exprest,
'Twas *Cupid* bathing in *Diana's* Stream.

VI

Born to the Spacious Empire of the *Nine*,[2]
One would have thought, she should have been content
To manage well that Mighty Government: 90
But what can young ambitious Souls confine?
   To the next Realm she stretcht her Sway,
   For *Painture* neer adjoyning lay,
A plenteous Province, and alluring Prey.
A *Chamber of Dependences* was fram'd,   95
(As Conquerors[3] will never want Pretence,
   When arm'd, to justifie the Offence)
And the whole Fief, in right of Poetry she claim'd.
The Country open lay without Defence:
For Poets frequent In-rodes there had made,   100
   And perfectly could represent
The Shape, the Face, with ev'ry Lineament;
And all the large Demains which the *Dumb-sister*[4] sway'd,

---

by Artemis into a fountain in Sicily; but Alpheus mingled his stream with the fountain,
thus uniting them.
1   a Stoic philosopher (c.A.D.60-140)
2   the nine Muses of the arts
3   An allusion to recent annexations by Louis XIV of France, who legitimised his takeover
   of Alsace and Luxembourg in 1679 through pseudo-parliamentary bodies called
   "chambres de réunion."
4   i.e., the Muse of painting

All bow'd beneath her Government,
   Receiv'd in Triumph wheresoe're she went.   105
Her Pencil drew, what e're her Soul design'd,
And oft the happy Draught surpass'd the Image in her Mind.
   The *Sylvan* Scenes of Herds and Flocks,
   And fruitful Plains and barren Rocks,
   Of shallow Brooks that flow'd so clear,   110
   The Bottom did the Top appear;
   Of deeper too and ampler Flouds,
   Which as in Mirrors, shew'd the Woods;
   Of lofty Trees with Sacred Shades,
   And Perspectives of pleasant Glades,   115
   Where Nymphs of brightest Form appear,
   And shaggy Satyrs standing neer,
   Which them at once admire and fear.
   The Ruines too of some Majestick Piece,
   Boasting the Pow'r of ancient *Rome* or *Greece*,   120
   Whose Statues, Freezes, Columns broken lie,
   And though deface't, the Wonder of the Eie,
   What Nature, Art, bold Fiction e're durst frame,
   Her forming Hand gave Feature to the Name.
   So strange a Concourse ne're was seen before,   125
But when the peopl'd Ark the whole Creation bore.

VII

The Scene then chang'd, with bold Erected Look
Our Martial King[1] the sight with Reverence strook:
For not content t' express his Outward Part,
Her hand call'd out the Image of his Heart,   130
His Warlike Mind, his Soul devoid of Fear,
His High-designing Thoughts, were figur'd there,
As when, by Magick, Ghosts are made appear.
   Our Phenix Queen[2] was portrai'd too so bright,
Beauty alone could Beauty take so right: 135
Her Dress, her Shape, her matchless Grace,
Were all observ'd, as well as heav'nly Face.
With such a Peerless Majesty she stands,
As in that Day she took the Crown from Sacred hands:
Before a Train of Heroins was seen,   140
In *Beauty* foremost, as in Rank, the Queen!
  Thus nothing to her *Genius* was deny'd,
But like a Ball of Fire the further thrown,
   Still with a greater Blaze she shone,
And her bright Soul broke out on ev'ry side.   145

---

1   James II
2   Mary of Modena. The phoenix is a mythical bird that appears only once a thousand
    years.

What next she had design'd, Heaven only knows,
To such Immod'rate Growth her Conquest rose,
That Fate alone its Progress could oppose.

VIII

Now all those Charmes, that blooming Grace,
The well-proportion'd Shape, and beauteous Face,   150
Shall never more be seen by Mortal Eyes;
In Earth the much lamented Virgin lies!
  Not Wit, nor Piety could Fate prevent;
  Nor was the cruel *Destiny* content
    To finish all the Murder at a Blow,   155
To sweep at once her Life, and Beauty too;
But, like a hardn'd Fellon, took a pride
    To work more Mischievously slow,
    And plunder'd first, and then destroy'd.
O double Sacriledge on things Divine,   160
To rob the Relique, and deface the Shrine!
    But thus *Orinda*[1] dy'd:
  Heav'n, by the same Disease, did both translate,
As equal were their Souls, so equal was their Fate.

IX

Mean time her Warlike Brother[2] on the Seas   165
  His waving Streamers to the Winds displays,
And vows for his Return, with vain Devotion, pays.
    Ah, Generous Youth, that Wish forbear,
    The Winds too soon will waft thee here!
    Slack all thy Sailes, and fear to come,   170
Alas, thou know'st not, Thou art wreck'd at home!
No more shalt thou behold thy Sisters Face,
Thou hast already had her last Embrace.
But look aloft, and if thou ken'st[3] from far,
Among the *Pleiad's*[4] a New-kindl'd Star,   175
If any sparkles, than the rest, more bright,
'Tis she that shines in that propitious Light.

X

When in mid-Aire, the Golden Trump shall sound,
  To raise the Nations under ground;

---

1   pseudonym of the poet Katherine Philips (1631-64), who died of smallpox
2   Henry Killigrew was a naval officer.
3   if thou see'st
4   The Pleiades were the seven daughters of Atlas who were pursued by Orion, until he
     and they were turned into constellations.

When in the Valley of *Jehosaphat*,[1]   180
The Judging God shall close the Book of Fate;
   And there the last Assizes keep,
      For those who Wake, and those who Sleep;
         When ratling Bones together fly,
From the four Corners of the Skie,   185
When Sinews o're the Skeletons are spread,
Those cloath'd with Flesh, and Life inspires the Dead:
The Sacred Poets first shall hear the Sound,
   And formost from the Tomb shall bound:
For they are cover'd with the lightest Ground   190
And streight, with in-born Vigour, on the Wing,
Like mounting Larkes, to the New Morning sing.
There *Thou*, Sweet Saint, before the Quire shalt go,
As Harbinger of Heav'n, the Way to show,
The Way which thou so well hast learn'd below.   195

from: *Absalom and Achitophel*[2]

Th' inhabitants of old *Jerusalem*[3]   85
Were *Jebusites*[4]: the Town so call'd from them;
And their's the Native right—
But when the chosen people[5] grew more strong,
The rightfull cause at length became the wrong:
And every loss the men of *Jebus* bore,   90
They still were thought God's enemies the more.
Thus, worn and weaken'd, well or ill content,
Submit they must to *David's* Government:
Impoverisht, and depriv'd of all Command,
Their Taxes doubled as they lost their Land,   95
And, what was harder yet to flesh and blood,
Their Gods disgrac'd, and burnt like common wood.
This set the Heathen Priesthood in a flame;
For Priests of all Religions are the same:
Of whatsoe'r descent their Godhead be,   100
Stock, Stone, or other homely pedigree,
In his defence his Servants are as bold
As if he had been born of beaten gold.

---

1   Ezekiel 37; Joel 3.12
2   In a thinly veiled parallel between the Biblical story of King David and the situation of
    England under Charles II, Dryden describes the struggle between the King, who sought
    to preserve the succession for his Catholic son James, and those who feared a Catholic
    monarchy and wanted to make the Protestant Duke of Monmouth (Charles's illegitimate
    son) the next-in-line to the throne. Charles II is represented as David; Monmouth is
    Absalom; and the Earl of Shaftesbury appears as Achitophel, who in the Biblical story
    conspired with Absalom against David (see 2 Samuel 13-18).
3   London
4   Catholics
5   the Protestants

The *Jewish Rabbins*[1] thô their Enemies,
In this conclude them honest men and wise: 105
For 'twas their duty, all the Learned think,
T'espouse his Cause by whom they eat and drink.
From hence began that Plot,[2] the Nation's Curse,
Bad in it self, but represented worse.
Rais'd in extremes, and in extremes decry'd; 110
With Oaths affirm'd, with dying Vows deny'd.
Not weigh'd, or winnow'd by the Multitude;
But swallow'd in the Mass, unchew'd and Crude.
Some Truth there was, but dash'd and brew'd with Lyes;
To please the Fools, and puzzle all the Wise. 115
Succeeding times did equal folly call,
Believing nothing, or believing all.
Th' *Egyptian*[3] Rites the *Jebusites* imbrac'd;
Where Gods were recommended by their Tast.[4]
Such savory Deities must needs be good, 120
As serv'd at once for Worship and for Food.
By force they could not Introduce these Gods;
For Ten to One, in former days was odds.
So Fraud was us'd, (the Sacrificers trade,)
Fools are more hard to Conquer than Perswade. 125
Their busie Teachers mingled with the *Jews*;
And rak'd, for Converts, even the Court and Stews:[5]
Which *Hebrew* Priests the more unkindly took,
Because the Fleece accompanies the Flock.
Some thought they God's Anointed meant to Slay 130
By Guns, invented since full many a day:
Our Authour swears it not; but who can know
How far the Devil and *Jebusites* may go?
This Plot, which fail'd for want of common Sense,
Had yet a deep and dangerous Consequence: 135
For, as when raging Fevers boyl the Blood,
The standing Lake soon floats into a Flood;
And every hostile Humour,[6] which before
Slept quiet in its Channels, bubbles o'r:
So, several Factions from this first Ferment, 140
Work up to Foam, and threat the Government.
Some by their Friends, more by themselves thought wise,
Oppos'd the Power, to which they could not rise.

1 i.e., the Protestant clergy
2 The "Popish Plot" of 1678 was the fabrication of Titus Oates, who swore that he had
   evidence of a Jesuit plot to overthrow the monarchy. His accusations led to the deaths
   of many innocent people.
3 Here Egypt stands for France.
4 the Catholic doctrine of transubstantiation
5 brothels
6 In ancient physiology, the body's health was determined by the balance and proportion
   of the bodily "humours" or fluids (blood, phlegm, yellow bile, and black bile).

Some had in Courts been Great, and thrown from thence,
Like Feinds, were harden'd in Impenitence.   145
Some by their Monarch's fatal mercy grown,
From Pardon'd Rebels, Kinsmen to the Throne;
Were rais'd in Power and publick Office high:
Strong Bands, if Bands ungratefull men could tye.
  Of these the false *Achitophel* was first: 150
A Name to all succeeding Ages Curst.
For close Designs, and crooked Counsels fit;
Sagacious, Bold, and Turbulent of wit:
Restless, unfixt in Principles and Place;
In Power unpleas'd, impatient of Disgrace.   155
A fiery Soul, which working out its way,
Fretted the Pigmy Body to decay:
And o'r inform'd the Tenement of Clay.
A daring Pilot in extremity;
Pleas'd with the Danger, when the Waves went high   160
He sought the Storms; but for a Calm unfit,
Would Steer too nigh the Sands, to boast his Wit.
Great Wits are sure to Madness near ally'd;
And thin Partitions do their Bounds divide:
Else, why should he, with Wealth and Honour blest,   165
Refuse his Age the needful hours of Rest?
Punish a Body which he coud not please;
Bankrupt of Life, yet Prodigal of Ease?
And all to leave, what with his Toyl he won,
To that unfeather'd, two Leg'd thing, a Son: 170
Got, while his Soul did hudled Notions try;
And born a shapeless Lump, like Anarchy.
In Friendship False, Implacable in Hate:
Resolv'd to Ruine or to Rule the State.
To Compass this the Triple Bond[1] he broke;   175
The Pillars of the publick Safety shook:
And fitted *Israel*[2] for a Foreign Yoke.
Then, seiz'd with Fear, yet still affecting Fame,
Usurp'd a Patriott's All-attoning Name.
So easie still it proves in Factious Times,   180
With publick Zeal to cancel private Crimes:
How safe is Treason, and how sacred ill,
Where none can sin against the Peoples Will:
Where Crouds can wink; and no offence be known,
Since in anothers guilt they find their own.   185
Yet, Fame deserv'd, no Enemy can grudge;
The Statesman we abhor, but praise the Judge.

---

1   On Shaftesbury's advice, England broke its alliance with Holland and Sweden, joining
    instead with France to wage war on Holland in 1672.
2   i.e., England

In *Israels* Courts ne'r sat an *Abbethdin*[1]
With more discerning Eyes, or Hands more clean:
Unbrib'd, unsought, the Wretched to redress;   190
Swift of Dispatch, and easie of Access.
Oh, had he been content to serve the Crown,
With vertues only proper to the Gown;
Or, had the rankness of the Soyl been freed
From Cockle, that opprest the Noble seed: 195
David, for him his tunefull Harp had strung,
And Heaven had wanted one Immortal song.
But wilde Ambition loves to slide, not stand;
And Fortunes Ice prefers to Vertues Land:
Achitophel, grown weary to possess   200
A lawfull Fame, and lazy Happiness;
Disdain'd the Golden fruit to gather free,
And lent the Croud his Arm to shake the Tree.
Now, manifest of Crimes, contriv'd long since,
He stood at bold Defiance with his Prince: 205
Held up the Buckler of the Peoples Cause,
Against the Crown; and sculk'd behind the Laws.
The wish'd occasion of the Plot he takes,
Some Circumstances finds, but more he makes.
By buzzing Emissaries, fills the ears   210
Of listning Crowds, with Jealosies and Fears
Of Arbitrary Counsels brought to light,
And proves the King himself a *Jebusite*:
Weak Arguments! which yet he knew full well,
Were strong with People easie to Rebell.   215
For, govern'd by the *Moon*, the giddy *Jews*
Tread the same track when she the Prime renews:
And once in twenty Years, their Scribes Record,
By natural Instinct they change their Lord.

---

1   A chief magistrate in the Jewish court; here, the reference is to Shaftesbury's brief term
    of appointment as Charles's Lord Chancellor.

Aphra Behn

(1640–1689)

Love in fantastick Triumph sat[1]

Love in fantastick Triumph sat,
    Whilst bleeding Hearts around him flow'd,
For whom fresh Pains he did create,
    And strange Tyrannick Pow'r he shew'd;
From thy bright Eyes he took his Fires,
    Which round about in sport he hurl'd;
But 'twas from mine he took Desires,
    Enough t'undo the amorous World.

From me he took his Sighs and Tears,
    From thee his Pride and Cruelty;
From me his Languishments and Fears,
    And ev'ry killing Dart from thee:
Thus thou, and I, the God have arm'd,
    And set him up a Deity;
But my poor Heart alone is harm'd,
    Whilst thine the Victor is, and free.

To Alexis in Answer to his Poem against Fruition. Ode.[2]

Ah hapless sex! who bear no charms,
But what like lightning flash and are no more,
    False fires sent down for baneful harms,
Fires which the fleeting Lover feebly warms
    And given like past Beboches[3] o're,
    Like Songs that please (thô bad,) when new,
    But learn'd by heart neglected grew.

In vain did Heav'n adorn the shape and face
With Beautyes which by Angels forms it drew:
In vain the mind with brighter Glories Grace,
While all our joys are stinted to the space
    Of one betraying enterview,
With one surrender to the eager will
We're short-liv'd nothing, or a real ill.

---

1   a song from Behn's play *Abdelazar*
2   This is a response to a poem preceding Behn's in the collection *Lycidus; or the Lover in Fashion* (1688).
3   perhaps a misprint for "Deboches," debauches

Since Man with that inconstancy was born,
To love the absent, and the present scorn,
  Why do we deck, why do we dress
  For such a short-liv'd happiness?
  Why do we put Attraction on,

Since either way tis we must be undon?
  They fly if Honour take our part,
  Our Virtue drives 'em o're the field.
  We lose 'em by too much desert,
  And Oh! they fly us if we yeild.
Ye Gods! is there no charm in all the fair
To fix this wild, this faithless, wanderer?

  Man! our great business and our aim,
  For whom we spread our fruitless snares,
No sooner kindles the designing flame,
  But to the next bright object bears
The Trophies of his conquest and our shame:
  Inconstancy's the good supream
The rest is airy Notion, empty Dream!

  Then, heedless Nymph, be rul'd by me
  If e're your Swain the bliss desire;
  Think like *Alexis* he may be
  Whose wisht Possession damps his fire;
  The roving youth in every shade
Has left some sighing and abandon'd Maid,
For tis a fatal lesson he has learn'd,
After fruition ne're to be concern'd.

The Disappointment

I

One day the Amorous *Lysander,*
By an impatient Passion sway'd,
Surpriz'd fair *Cloris*, that lov'd Maid,
Who could defend her self no longer.
All things did with his Love conspire;
The gilded Planet of the Day,
In his gay Chariot drawn by Fire,
Was now descending to the Sea,
And left no Light to guide the World,
But what from *Cloris* Brighter Eyes was hurld.

II

In a lone Thicket made for Love,
Silent as yielding Maids Consent,

She with a Charming Languishment,
Permits his Force, yet gently strove;
Her Hands his Bosom softly meet,
But not to put him back design'd,
Rather to draw 'em on inclin'd:
Whilst he lay trembling at her Feet,
Resistance 'tis in vain to show;
She wants the pow'r to say—*Ah! What d'ye do?*

III

Her Bright Eyes sweet, and yet severe,
Where Love and Shame confus'dly strive,
Fresh Vigor to *Lysander* give;
And breathing faintly in his Ear,
She cry'd—*Cease, Cease—your vain Desire,*
Or I'll call out—What would you do?
My Dearer Honour ev'n to You
I cannot, must not give—Retire,
Or take this Life, whose chiefest part
I gave you with the Conquest of my Heart.

IV

But he as much unus'd to Fear,
As he was capable of Love,
The blessed minutes to improve,
Kisses her Mouth, her Neck, her Hair;
Each Touch her new Desire Alarms,
His burning trembling Hand he prest
Upon her swelling Snowy Brest,
While she lay panting in his Arms.
All her Unguarded Beauties lie
The Spoils and Trophies of the Enemy.

V

And now without Respect or Fear,
He seeks the Object of his Vows,
(His Love no Modesty allows)
By swift degrees advancing—where
His daring Hand that Altar seiz'd,
Where Gods of Love do sacrifice:
That Awful Throne, that Paradice
Where Rage is calm'd, and Anger pleas'd;
That Fountain where Delight still flows,
And gives the Universal World Repose.

VI

Her Balmy Lips incountring his,
Their Bodies, as their Souls, are joyn'd;
Where both in Transports Unconfin'd
Extend themselves upon the Moss.
Cloris half dead and breathless lay;
Her soft Eyes cast a Humid Light,
Such as divides the Day and Night;
Or falling Stars, whose Fires decay:
And now no signs of Life she shows,
But what in short-breath'd Sighs returns and goes.

VII

He saw how at her Length she lay;
He saw her rising Bosom bare;
Her loose thin *Robes*, through which appear
A Shape design'd for Love and Play;
Abandon'd by her Pride and Shame.
She does her softest Joys dispence,
Off'ring her Virgin-Innocence
A Victim to Loves Sacred Flame;
While the o'er-Ravish'd Shepherd lies
Unable to perform the Sacrifice.

VIII

Ready to taste a thousand Joys,
The too transported hapless Swain
Found the vast Pleasure turn'd to Pain;
Pleasure which too much Love destroys:
The willing Garments by he laid,
And Heaven all open'd to his view,
Mad to possess, himself he threw
On the Defenceless Lovely Maid.
But Oh what envying God conspires
To snatch his Power, yet leave him the Desire!

IX

Nature's Support, (without whose Aid
She can no Humane Being give)
It self now wants the Art to live;
Faintness its slack'ned Nerves invade:
In vain th' inraged Youth essay'd
To call its fleeting Vigor back,
No motion 'twill from Motion take;
Excess of Love his Love betray'd:
In vain he Toils, in vain Commands;
The Insensible fell weeping in his Hand.

X

In this so Amorous Cruel Strife,
Where Love and Fate were too severe,
The poor *Lysander* in despair
Renounc'd his Reason with his Life:
Now all the brisk and active Fire
That should the Nobler Part inflame,
Serv'd to increase his Rage and Shame,
And left no Spark for New Desire:
Not all her Naked Charms cou'd move
Or calm that Rage that had debauch'd his Love.

XI

Cloris returning from the Trance
Which Love and soft Desire had bred,
Her timerous Hand she gently laid
(Or guided by Design or Chance)
Upon that Fabulous *Priapus*,[1]
That Potent God, as Poets feign;
But never did young *Shepherdess*,
Gath'ring of Fern upon the Plain,
More nimbly draw her Fingers back,
Finding beneath the verdant Leaves a Snake:

XII

Than *Cloris* her fair Hand withdrew,
Finding that God of her Desires
Disarm'd of all his Awful Fires,
And Cold as Flow'rs bath'd in the Morning Dew.
Who can the *Nymph's* Confusion guess?
The Blood forsook the hinder Place,
And strew'd with Blushes all her Face,
Which both Disdain and Shame exprest:
And from *Lysander's* Arms she fled,
Leaving him fainting on the Gloomy Bed.

XIII

Like Lightning through the Grove she hies,
Or *Daphne* from the *Delphick God*,[2]
No Print upon the grassey Road
She leaves, t' instruct Pursuing Eyes.

---

1   Priapus was a god of fertility, often represented with an enlarged phallus.
2   In Greek mythology, Daphne was a nymph pursued by Apollo, and transformed into a
    bay tree. Apollo's temple was at Delphi.

The Wind that wanton'd in her Hair,
And with her Ruffled Garments plaid,
Discover'd in the Flying Maid
All that the Gods e'er made, if Fair.
So *Venus*, when her *Love* was slain,[1]
With Fear and Haste flew o'er the Fatal Plain.

XIV

The *Nymph's* Resentments none but I
Can well Imagine or Condole:
But none can guess *Lysander's* Soul,
But those who sway'd his Destiny.
His silent Griefs swell up to Storms,
And not one God his Fury spares;
He curs'd his Birth, his Fate, his Stars;
But more the *Shepherdess's* Charms,
Whose soft bewitching Influence
Had Damn'd him to the *Hell* of Impotence.

---

1   Venus's lover Adonis was slain by a boar.

Lady Mary Chudleigh

(1656–1710)

To the Ladies

Wife and servant are the same,
But only differ in the name:
For when that fatal knot is tied,
Which nothing, nothing can divide,
When she the word *Obey* has said,
And man by law supreme has made,
Then all that's kind is laid aside,
And nothing left but state and pride.
Fierce as an eastern prince he grows,
And all his innate rigour shows:
Then but to look, to laugh, or speak,
Will the nuptial contract break.
Like mutes, she signs alone must make,
And never any freedom take,
But still be governed by a nod,
And fear her husband as her god:
Him still must serve, him still obey,
And nothing act, and nothing say,
But what her haughty lord thinks fit,
Who, with the power, has all the wit.
Then shun, oh! shun that wretched state,
And all the fawning flatterers hate.
Value yourselves, and men despise:
You must be proud, if you'll be wise.

The Resolve

For what the world admires I'll wish no more,
    Nor court that airy nothing of a name:
Such flitting shadows let the proud adore,
    Let them be suppliants for an empty fame.

If Reason rules within, and keeps the throne,
    While the inferior faculties obey,
And all her laws without reluctance own,
    Accounting none more fit, more just than they;

If Virtue my free soul unsullied keeps,
    Exempting it from passion and from stain,
If no black guilty thoughts disturb my sleeps,
    And no past crimes my vexed remembrance pain;

If, though I pleasure find in living here,
    I yet can look on death without surprise;
If I've a soul above the reach of fear,
    And which will nothing mean or sordid prize;

A soul, which cannot be depressed by grief,
   Nor too much raised by the sublimest joy,
Which can, when troubled, give itself relief,
   And to advantage all its thoughts employ:

Then am I happy in my humble state,
   Although not crowned with glory nor with bays:[1]
A mind, that triumphs over vice and fate,
   Esteems it mean to court the world for praise.

---

1   the laurel garlands awarded to poets

Anne Finch, Countess Of Winchilsea

(1661–1720)

The Introduction

Did I, my lines intend for publick view,
How many censures, wou'd their faults persue,
Some wou'd, because such words they do affect,
Cry they're insipid, empty, uncorrect.
And many have attain'd, dull and untaught,
The name of Witt, only by finding fault.
True judges might condemn their want of witt,
And all might say, they're by a Woman writt.
Alas! a woman that attempts the pen,
Such an intruder on the rights of men,
Such a presumptuous Creature, is esteem'd,
The fault, can by no vertue be redeem'd.
They tell us, we mistake our sex and way;
Good breeding, fassion, dancing, dressing, play
Are the accomplishments we shou'd desire;
To write, or read, or think, or to enquire
Wou'd cloud our beauty, and exaust our time,
And interrupt the Conquests of our prime;
Whilst the dull mannage, of a servile house
Is held by some, our outmost art, and use.
 Sure 'twas not ever thus, nor are we told
Fables, of Women that excell'd of old;
To whom, by the diffusive hand of Heaven
Some share of witt, and poetry was given.
On that glad day, on which the Ark[1] return'd,
The holy pledge, for which the Land had mourn'd,
The joyfull Tribes, attend itt on the way,
The Levites do the sacred Charge convey,
Whilst various Instruments, before itt play;
Here, holy Virgins in the Concert joyn,
The louder notes, to soften, and refine,
And with alternate verse, compleat the Hymn Devine.
Loe! the yong Poet,[2] after Gods own heart,
By Him inspired, and taught the Muses Art,
Return'd from Conquest, a bright Chorus meets,
That sing his slayn ten thousand in the streets.
In such loud numbers they his acts declare,
Proclaim the wonders, of his early war,
That Saul upon the vast applause does frown,
And feels itts mighty thunder shake the Crown.

---

1 the Ark of the Covenant, brought by King David to Jerusalem amidst much rejoicing (1 Chronicles 15)
2 David, who was praised in song and dance by women when he and Saul returned from their victory over the Philistines (1 Samuel 18)

What, can the threat'n'd Judgment now prolong?
Half of the Kingdom is already gone;
The fairest half, whose influence guides the rest,
Have David's Empire, o're their hearts confess't.
  A Woman here,[1] leads fainting Israel on,
She fights, she wins, she tryumphs with a song,
Devout, Majestick, for the subject fitt,
And far above her arms, exalts her witt,
Then, to the peacefull, shady Palm withdraws,
And rules the rescu'd Nation, with her Laws.
How are we fal'n, fal'n by mistaken rules?
And Education's, more then Nature's fools,
Debarr'd from all improve-ments of the mind,
And to be dull, expected and dessigned;
And if some one wou'd Soar above the rest,
With warmer fancy, and ambition press't,
So strong, th' opposing faction still appears,
The hopes to thrive, can ne're outweigh the fears,
Be caution'd then my Muse, and still retir'd;
Nor be dispis'd, aiming to be admir'd;
Conscious of wants, still with contracted wing,
To some few freinds, and to thy sorrows sing;
For groves of Lawrell,[2] thou wert never meant;
Be dark enough thy shades, and be thou there content.

A Nocturnal Reverie

In such a *Night*, when every louder Wind
Is to its distant Cavern safe confin'd;
And only gentle *Zephyr* fans his Wings,
And lonely *Philomel*,[3] still waking, sings;
Or from some Tree, fam'd for the *Owl's* delight,
She, hollowing[4] clear, directs the Wand'rer right:
In such a *Night*, when passing Clouds give place,
Or thinly vail the Heav'ns mysterious Face;
When in some River, overhung with Green,
The waving Moon and trembling Leaves are seen;
When freshen'd Grass now bears it self upright,
And makes cool Banks to pleasing Rest invite,
Whence springs the *Woodbind*, and the *Bramble-Rose*,
And where the sleepy *Cowslip* shelter'd grows;
Whilst now a paler Hue the *Foxglove* takes,

---

1   Deborah the prophetess sang praises to God for the victory of the Israelites over the Canaanites (Judges 4 and 5).
2   i.e., for public acclaim, signified by the awarding of laurel garlands
3   the nightingale
4   calling out, shouting

Yet checquers still with Red the dusky brakes
When scatter'd *Glow-worms*, but in Twilight fine,
Shew trivial Beauties watch their Hour to shine;
Whilst *Salisb'ry*[1] stands the Test of every Light,
In perfect Charms, and perfect Virtue bright:
When Odours, which declin'd repelling Day,
Thro' temp'rate Air uninterrupted stray;
When darken'd Groves their softest Shadows wear,
And falling Waters we distinctly hear;
When thro' the Gloom more venerable shows
Some ancient Fabrick, awful in Repose,
While Sunburnt Hills their swarthy Looks conceal,
And swelling Haycocks thicken up the Vale:
When the loos'd *Horse* now, as his Pasture leads,
Comes slowly grazing thro' th' adjoining Meads,
Whose stealing Pace, and lengthen'd Shade we fear,
Till torn up Forage in his Teeth we hear:
When nibbling *Sheep* at large pursue their Food,
And unmolested Kine rechew the Cud;
When *Curlews* cry beneath the Village-walls,
And to her straggling Brood the *Partridge* calls;
Their shortliv'd Jubilee the Creatures keep,
Which but endures, whilst Tyrant-*Man* do's sleep;
When a sedate Content the Spirit feels,
And no fierce Light disturb, whilst it reveals;
But silent Musings urge the Mind to seek
Something, too high for Syllables to speak;
Till the free Soul to a compos'dness charm'd,
Finding the Elements of Rage disarm'd,
O'er all below a solemn Quiet grown,
Joys in th' inferiour World, and thinks it like her Own:
In such a *Night* let Me abroad remain,
Till Morning breaks, and All's confus'd again;
Our Cares, our Toils, our Clamours are renew'd,
Or Pleasures, seldom reach'd, again pursu'd.

---

1   possibly the poet's friend Lady Salisbury

The Unequal Fetters

Cou'd we stop the time that's flying
   Or recall itt when 'tis past
Put far off the day of Dying
   Or make Youth for ever last
To Love wou'd then be worth our cost.

But since we must loose those Graces
   Which at first your hearts have wonne
And you seek for in new Faces
   When our Spring of Life is done
It wou'd but urdge our ruine on.

Free as Nature's first intention
   Was to make us, I'll be found
Nor by subtle Man's invention
   Yeild to be in Fetters bound
By one that walks a freer round.

Mariage does but slightly tye Men
   Whil'st close Pris'ners we remain
They the larger Slaves of Hymen[1]
   Still are begging Love again
At the full length of all their chain.

---

1   the god of marriage

Jonathan Swift

(1667–1745)

A Description of the Morning

Now hardly here and there a Hackney-Coach
Appearing, show'd the Ruddy Morns Approach.
Now *Betty* from her Masters Bed had flown,
And softly stole to discompose her own.
The Slipshod Prentice from his Masters Door,
Had par'd the Dirt, and Sprinkled round the Floor.
Now *Moll* had whirl'd her Mop with dext'rous Airs,
Prepar'd to Scrub the Entry and the Stairs.
The Youth with Broomy Stumps began to trace
The Kennel-Edge,[1] where Wheels had worn the Place.
The Smallcoal-Man was heard with Cadence deep,
'Till drown'd in Shriller Notes of *Chimney-Sweep*.
Duns at his Lordships Gate began to meet,
And Brickdust *Moll* had Scream'd through half a Street.
The Turnkey now his Flock returning sees,
Duly let out a Nights to Steal for Fees.
The watchful Bailiffs take their silent Stands,
And School-Boys lag with Satchels in their Hands.

A Description of a City Shower

Careful Observers may fortel the Hour
(By sure Prognosticks) when to dread a Show'r:
While Rain depends, the pensive Cat gives o'er
Her Frolicks, and pursues her Tail no more.
Returning Home at Night, you'll find the Sink[2]
Strike your offended Sense with double Stink.
If you be wise, then go not far to Dine,
You spend in Coach-hire more than save in Wine.
A coming Show'r your shooting Corns presage,
Old Aches throb, your hollow Tooth will rage.
Sauntring in Coffee-house is *Dulman* seen;
He damns the Climate, and complains of Spleen[3].

Mean while the South rising with dabbled Wings,
A Sable Cloud a-thwart the Welkin flings,
That swill'd more Liquor than it could contain,
And like a Drunkard gives it up again.
Brisk *Susan* whips her Linen from the Rope,
While the first drizzling Show'r is born aslope,

---

1   edge of the gutter
2   sewer
3   the fashionable illness of melancholy

Such is that Sprinkling which some careless Quean
Flirts on you from her Mop, but not so clean.
You fly, invoke the Gods; then turning, stop
To rail; she singing, still whirls on her Mop.
Not yet, the Dust had shun'd th' unequal Strife,
But aided by the Wind, fought still for Life;
And wafted with its Foe by violent Gust,
'Twas doubtful which was Rain, and which was Dust.
Ah! where must needy Poet seek for Aid,
When Dust and Rain at once his Coat invade;
Sole Coat, where Dust cemented by the Rain,
Erects the Nap, and leaves a cloudy Stain.

Now in contiguous Drops the Flood comes down
Threat'ning with Deluge this *Devoted* Town.
To Shops in Crouds the dagled[1] Females fly,
Pretend to cheapen Goods,[2] but nothing buy.
The Templer[3] spruce, while ev'ry Spout's a-broach,
Stays till 'tis fair, yet seems to call a Coach.
The tuck'd-up Sempstress walks with hasty Strides,
While Streams run down her oil'd Umbrella's Sides.
Here various Kinds by various Fortunes led,
Commence Acquaintance underneath a Shed.
Triumphant Tories, and desponding Whigs,
Forget their Fewds, and join to save their Wigs.
Box'd in a Chair the Beau impatient sits,
While Spouts run clatt'ring o'er the Roof by Fits;
And ever and anon with frightful Din
The Leather[4] sounds, he trembles from within.
So when *Troy* Chair-men bore the Wooden Steed,
Pregnant with *Greeks,* impatient to be freed,
(Those Bully *Greeks,* who, as the Moderns do,
Instead of paying Chair-men, run them thro'.)
Laoco'n[5] struck the Outside with his Spear,
And each imprison'd Hero quak'd for Fear.

Now from all Parts the swelling Kennels[6] flow,
And bear their Trophies with them as they go:
Filth of all Hues and Odours seem to tell
What Streets they sail'd from, by the Sight and Smell.
They, as each Torrent drives, with rapid Force

---

1   bemired, muddied
2   to bargain for goods
3   a law student, from one of the Inns of Temple in London
4   The roof of a sedan chair was made of leather.
5   the Trojan priest who tried to dissuade the Trojans from allowing the wooden horse into Troy
6   gutters

From *Smithfield*, or St. *Pulchre's* shape their Course,[1]
And in huge Confluent join at *Snow-Hill* Ridge,
Fall from the *Conduit* prone to *Holborn-Bridge*.
Sweepings from Butchers Stalls, Dung, Guts, and Blood,
Drown'd Puppies, stinking Sprats, all drench'd in Mud,
Dead Cats and Turnip-Tops come tumbling down the Flood.

---

1   The torrents started from Smithfield Market and St. Sepulchre's Church at Newgate, then flowed down Snow Hill into Fleet Ditch (the modern Fleet Street) which was crossed by Holborn Bridge.

Alexander Pope

(1688-1744)

from: *An Essay on Criticism*

I

'Tis hard to say, if greater Want of Skill
Appear in *Writing* or in *Judging* ill;
But, of the two, less dang'rous is th' Offence,
To tire our *Patience*, than mis-lead our *Sense*:
Some few in *that*, but Numbers err in *this*,   5
Ten Censure wrong for one who Writes amiss;
A *Fool* might once *himself* alone expose,
Now *One* in *Verse* makes many more in *Prose*.
    'Tis with our *Judgments* as our *Watches*, none
Go just *alike*, yet each believes his own.   10
In *Poets* as true *Genius* is but rare,
True *Taste* as seldom is the Critick's Share;
Both must alike from Heav'n derive their Light,
These *born* to Judge, as well as those to Write.
Let such teach others who themselves excell,   15
And *censure freely* who have *written well*.
Authors are partial to their *Wit*, 'tis true,
But are not *Criticks* to their *Judgment* too?
    Yet if we look more closely, we shall find
Most have the *Seeds* of Judgment in their Mind;   20
Nature affords at least a *glimm'ring Light*;
The *Lines*, tho' touch'd but faintly, are drawn right.
But as the slightest Sketch, if justly trac'd,
Is by ill *Colouring* but the more disgrac'd,
So by *false Learning* is *good Sense* defac'd;   25
Some are bewilder'd in the Maze of Schools,
And some made *Coxcombs* Nature meant but *Fools*.
In search of *Wit* these lose their *common Sense*,
And then turn Criticks in their own Defence.
Each burns alike, who can, or cannot write,   30
Or with a *Rival's* or an *Eunuch's* spite.
All *Fools* have still an Itching to deride,
And fain *wou'd* be upon the *Laughing Side*:
If *Maevius*[1] Scribble in *Apollo's* spight,
There are, who *judge* still *worse* than he can *write*.   35
    Some have at first for *Wits*, then *Poets* past,
Turn'd *Criticks* next, and prov'd plain *Fools* at last;
Some neither can for *Wits* nor *Criticks* pass,
As heavy Mules are neither *Horse* nor *Ass*.
Those half-learn'd Witlings, num'rous in our Isle,   40

---

1   a type name for a bad or foolish poet

As half-form'd Insects on the Banks of *Nile*;[1]
Unfinish'd Things, one knows not what to call,
Their Generation's so *equivocal*:
To tell[2] 'em, wou'd a *hundred Tongues* require,
Or *one vain Wit's*, that might a hundred tire.   45
   But *you* who seek to *give* and *merit* Fame,
And justly bear a Critick's noble Name,
Be sure *your self* and your own *Reach* to know,
How far your *Genius, Taste,* and *Learning* go;
Launch not beyond your Depth, but be discreet,   50
And mark *that Point* where Sense and Dulness *meet.*
   Nature to all things fix'd the Limits fit,
And wisely curb'd proud Man's pretending Wit:
As on the *Land* while *here* the *Ocean* gains,
In *other Parts* it leaves wide sandy Plains;   55
Thus in the *Soul* while *Memory* prevails,
The solid Pow'r of *Understanding* fails;
Where Beams of warm *Imagination* play,
The *Memory's* soft Figures melt away.
One *Science* only will one *Genius* fit;   60
So *vast* is Art, so *narrow* Human Wit:
Not only bounded to *peculiar Arts*,
But oft in *those*, confin'd to *single Parts*.
Like Kings we lose the Conquests gain'd before,
By vain Ambition still to make them more: 65
Each might his *sev'ral Province* well command,
Wou'd all but *stoop* to what they *understand.*
   First follow NATURE, and your Judgment frame
By her just Standard, which is still the same:
Unerring Nature, still divinely bright,   70
One *clear, unchang'd,* and *Universal* Light,
Life, Force, and Beauty, must to all impart,
At once the *Source,* and *End,* and *Test* of Art.
Art from that Fund each *just Supply* provides,
Works *without Show,* and *without Pomp* presides: 75
In some fair Body thus th' informing Soul
With Spirits feeds, with Vigour fills the whole,
Each Motion guides, and ev'ry Nerve sustains;
It self unseen, but in th' *Effects,* remains.
Some, to whom Heav'n in Wit has been profuse,   80
Want as much more, to turn it to its use;
For *Wit* and *Judgment* often are at strife,
Tho' meant each other's Aid, like *Man* and *Wife.*
'Tis more to *guide* than *spur* the Muse's Steed;
Restrain his Fury, than provoke his Speed;   85

---

1   The ancients believed that the fertile mud of the Nile created forms of life.
2   count

The winged Courser,[1] like a gen'rous Horse,
Shows most true Mettle when you *check* his Course.
   Those RULES of old *discover'd*, not *devis'd*,
Are *Nature* still, but *Nature Methodiz'd*;
Nature, like *Liberty*, is but restrain'd   90
By the same Laws which first *herself* ordain'd.

                    *   *   *

                       II

   Thus Criticks, of less *Judgment* than *Caprice*,   285
Curious, not *Knowing*, not *exact*, but *nice*,[2]
Form *short Ideas*; and offend in *Arts*
(As most in *Manners*) by a *Love to Parts*.
   Some to *Conceit*[3] alone their Taste confine,
And glitt'ring Thoughts struck out at ev'ry Line;   290
Pleas'd with a Work where nothing's just or fit;
One *glaring Chaos* and *wild Heap of Wit*:
Poets like Painters, thus, unskill'd to trace
The *naked Nature* and the *living Grace*,
With *Gold* and *Jewels* cover ev'ry Part,   295
And hide with *Ornaments* their *Want of Art*.
True Wit is *Nature* to Advantage drest,
What oft was *Thought*, but ne'er so well *Exprest*,
Something, whose Truth convinc'd at Sight we find,
That gives us back the Image of our Mind: 300
As Shades more sweetly recommend the Light,
So modest Plainness sets off sprightly Wit;
For *Works* may have more *Wit* than does 'em good,
As *Bodies* perish through Excess of *Blood*.
   Others for *Language* all their Care express,   305
And value *Books*, as Women *Men*, for *Dress*:
Their Praise is still—*The Stile is excellent:*
The *Sense*, they humbly take upon Content.
Words are like *Leaves*; and where they most abound,
Much *Fruit* of *Sense* beneath is rarely found.   310
False Eloquence, like *the Prismatic Glass*,
Its gawdy Colours spreads on *ev'ry place;*
The Face of Nature we no more Survey,
All glares *alike*, without *Distinction* gay:
But true *Expression*, like th' unchanging *Sun*,   315
Clears, and *improves* whate'er it shines upon,
It *gilds* all Objects, but it *alters* none.
Expression is the *Dress* of *Thought*, and still

---

1   Pegasus, the winged horse in Greek legend, favoured by the Muses
2   critical, punctilious in taste or judgement
3   witty or extravagant figures of speech

Appears more *decent* as more *suitable*;
A vile Conceit in pompous Words exprest,   320
Is like a Clown[1] in regal Purple drest;
For diff'rent *Styles* with diff'rent *Subjects* sort,
As several Garbs with Country, Town, and Court.
Some by *Old Words* to Fame have made Pretence;
Ancients in *Phrase,* meer Moderns in their *Sense!*   325
Such *labour'd Nothings,* in so *strange* a Style,
Amaze th'unlearn'd and make the Learned *Smile.*
Unlucky, as *Fungoso*[2] in the Play,
These Sparks with aukward Vanity display
What the Fine Gentleman wore *Yesterday!*   330
And but so mimick ancient Wits at best,
As Apes our Grandsires in their *Doublets drest.*
In *Words,* as *Fashions,* the same Rule will hold;
Alike Fantastick, if *too New,* or *Old;*
Be not the first by whom the *New* are try'd,   335
Nor yet the *last* to lay the *Old* aside.
   But most by *Numbers*[3] judge a Poet's Song,
And *smooth* or *rough,* with them, is *right* or *wrong*;
In the bright *Muse* tho' thousand *Charms* conspire,
Her *Voice* is all these tuneful Fools admire,   340
Who haunt *Parnassus* but to please their Ear,
Not mend their Minds; as some to *Church* repair,
Not for the *Doctrine,* but the *Musick* there.
These *Equal Syllables* alone require,
Tho' oft the Ear the *open Vowels* tire,   345
While *Expletives* their feeble Aid *do* join,
And ten low Words oft creep in one dull Line,
While they ring round the same *unvary'd Chimes,*
With sure *Returns* of still *expected Rhymes.*
Where-e'er you find the *cooling Western Breeze,*   350
In the next Line, it *whispers thro' the Trees*;
If *Chrystal Streams with pleasing Murmurs creep,*
The Reader's threaten'd (not in vain) with *Sleep.*
Then, at the *last,* and *only* Couplet fraught
With some *unmeaning* Thing they call a *Thought,*   355
A *needless Alexandrine* ends the Song,
That like a wounded Snake, drags its slow length along.
Leave such to tune their own dull Rhimes, and know
What's *roundly smooth,* or *languishingly slow;*
And praise the *Easie Vigor* of a Line,   360
Where *Denham's* Strength, and *Waller's*[4] Sweetness join.

---

1   a rustic or ill-bred man
2   a character in Ben Jonson's *Every Man out of His Humour,* (1600) who seeks to be a
    courtier, but is always behind the fashion
3   versification
4   Denham and Waller were English poets of the 17th century.

True Ease in Writing comes from Art, not Chance,
As those move easiest who have learn'd to dance.
'Tis not enough no Harshness gives Offence,
The *Sound* must seem an *Eccho* to the *Sense*.   365
Soft is the Strain when *Zephyr* gently blows,
And the *smooth Stream* in *smoother Numbers* flows;
But when loud Surges lash the sounding Shore,
The *hoarse, rough Verse* shou'd like the *Torrent* roar.
When *Ajax*[1] strives, some Rock's vast Weight to throw,   370
The Line too *labours,* and the Words move *slow;*
Not so, when swift *Camilla*[2] scours the Plain,
Flies o'er th'unbending Corn, and skims along the Main.
Hear how *Timotheus*[3] vary'd Lays surprize,
And bid Alternate Passions fall and rise!   375
While, at each Change, the Son of *Lybian Jove*[4]
Now *burns* with Glory, and then *melts* with Love;
Now his *fierce Eyes* with *sparkling Fury* glow;
Now *Sighs* steal out, and *Tears begin to flow:*
Persians and *Greeks* like *Turns of Nature* found,   380
And the *World's Victor* stood subdu'd by *Sound!*
The Pow'rs of Musick all our Hearts allow;
And what *Timotheus* was, is *Dryden* now.

* * *

---

1   one of the Greek warriors that lay siege to Troy
2   a swift-footed warrior-maiden in Virgil's *Aeneid*
3   a celebrated musician and poet of the 4th century B.C.
4   Alexander the Great, who claimed descent from the Egyptian god Ammon, identified
    with Greek Zeus and Roman Jupiter or Jove.

from: *The Rape of the Lock*[1]

Canto I

What dire Offence from am'rous Causes springs,
What mighty Contests rise from trivial Things,
I sing—This Verse to *Caryll,*[2] Muse! is due;
This, ev'n *Belinda*[3] may vouchsafe to view:
Slight is the Subject, but not so the Praise,　　　　　　5
If She inspire, and He approve my Lays.
　Say what strange Motive, Goddess! cou'd compel
A well-bred *Lord* t'assault a gentle *Belle?*
Oh say what stranger Cause, yet unexplor'd,
Cou'd make a gentle *Belle* reject a *Lord?*　　　　　　10
In Tasks so bold, can Little Men engage,
And in soft Bosoms dwells such mighty Rage?
　Sol thro' white Curtains shot a tim'rous Ray,
And op'd those Eyes that must eclipse the Day;
Now Lapdogs give themselves the rowzing Shake,　　　15
And sleepless Lovers, just at Twelve, awake:
Thrice rung the Bell, the Slipper knock'd the Ground,
And the press'd Watch return'd a silver Sound.
Belinda still her downy Pillow prest,
Her Guardian *Sylph*[4] prolong'd the balmy Rest.　　　20
'Twas he had summon'd to her silent Bed
The Morning-Dream that hover'd o'er her Head.
A Youth more glitt'ring than a *Birth-night Beau,*[5]
(That ev'n in Slumber caus'd her Cheek to glow)
Seem'd to her Ear his winning Lips to lay,　　　　　　25
And thus in Whispers said, or seem'd to say.
　Fairest of Mortals, thou distinguish'd Care
Of thousand bright Inhabitants of Air!
If e'er one Vision touch'd thy infant Thought,
Of all the Nurse and all the Priest have taught,　　　30
Of airy Elves by Moonlight Shadows seen,
The silver Token,[6] and the circled Green,[7]
Or Virgins visited by Angel-Pow'rs,
With Golden Crowns and Wreaths of heav'nly Flow'rs,

1　The poem was written in 1711 to mend a breach between two families caused by the
　　theft of a lock of hair. Pope sought to make light of the matter by treating it in mock-
　　heroic style, using the language and devices of epic poetry to stress the triviality of the
　　event.
2　Pope's friend John Caryll, at whose suggestion the poem was written
3　Arabella Fermor, whose lock of hair had been stolen by Lord Petre (the "well-bred lord")
4　Pope has adapted a scheme from Rosicrucian lore, whereby the four elements are
　　inhabited by spirits called sylphs, gnomes, nymphs, and salamanders, who embody
　　different aspects of human temperament.
5　a courtier dressed in finery to celebrate the monarch's birthday
6　a silver coin left by fairies in return for a drink of cream
7　rings of grass thought to be made by fairies

Hear and believe! thy own Importance know,   35
Nor bound thy narrow Views to Things below.
Some secret Truths from Learned Pride conceal'd,
To Maids alone and Children are reveal'd:
What tho' no Credit doubting Wits may give?
The Fair and Innocent shall still believe.   40
Know then, unnumber'd Spirits round thee fly,
The light *Militia* of the lower Sky;
These, tho' unseen, are ever on the Wing,
Hang o'er the *Box*,[1] and hover round the *Ring*.[2]
Think what an Equipage thou hast in Air,   45
And view with scorn *Two Pages* and a *Chair*.[3]
As now your own, our Beings were of old,
And once inclos'd in Woman's beauteous Mold;
Thence, by a soft Transition, we repair
From earthly Vehicles to these of Air.   50
Think not, when Woman's transient Breath is fled,
That all her Vanities at once are dead:
Succeeding Vanities she still regards,
And tho' she plays no more, o'erlooks the Cards.
Her joy in gilded Chariots, when alive,   55
And Love of *Ombre*,[4] after Death survive.
For when the Fair in all their Pride expire,
To their first Elements[5] their Souls retire:
The Sprights of fiery Termagants in Flame
Mount up, and take a *Salamander's*[6] Name.   60
Soft yielding Minds to Water glide away,
And sip with *Nymphs,* their Elemental Tea.
The graver Prude sinks downward to a *Gnome,*
In search of Mischief still on Earth to roam.
The light Coquettes in *Sylphs* aloft repair,   65
And sport and flutter in the Fields of Air.
   Know farther yet; Whoever fair and chaste
Rejects Mankind, is by some *Sylph* embrac'd:
For Spirits, freed from mortal Laws, with ease
Assume what Sexes and what Shapes they please.   70
What guards the Purity of melting Maids,
In Courtly Balls, and Midnight Masquerades,
Safe from the treach'rous Friend, the daring Spark,
The Glance by Day, the Whisper in the Dark;

---

1   i.e., in the theatre
2   the fashionable promenade in Hyde Park
3   a sedan chair
4   a card game
5   According to ancient lore, each person is made up of a combination of the elements of
     air, fire, earth, and water, which create the "humours" that govern our minds and bodies.
     One or other of these humours will predominate, making us melancholic, sanguine,
     phlegmatic, or choleric.
6   The salamander was a mythical lizard fabled to live in fire.

When kind Occasion prompts their warm Desires,   75
When Musick softens, and when Dancing fires?
'Tis but their *Sylph,* the wise Celestials know,
Tho' *Honour* is the Word with Men below.
    Some Nymphs there are, too conscious of their Face,
For Life predestin'd to the *Gnomes'* Embrace.   80
These swell their Prospects and exalt their Pride,
When Offers are disdain'd, and Love deny'd.
Then gay Ideas[1] crowd the vacant Brain;
While Peers and Dukes, and all their sweeping Train,
And Garters, Stars, and Coronets appear,   90
And in soft Sounds, *Your Grace* salutes their Ear.
'Tis these that early taint the Female Soul,
Instruct the Eyes of young *Coquettes* to roll,
Teach Infant-Cheeks a bidden Blush to know,
And little Hearts to flutter at a *Beau.*   95
    Oft when the World imagine Women stray,
The *Sylphs* thro' mystick Mazes guide their Way,
Thro' all the giddy Circle they pursue,
And old Impertinence expel by new.
What tender Maid but must a Victim fall   95
To one Man's Treat, but for another's Ball?
When *Florio* speaks, what Virgin could withstand,
If gentle *Damon* did not squeeze her Hand?
With varying Vanities, from ev'ry Part,
They shift the moving Toyshop of their Heart;   100
Where Wigs with Wigs, with Sword-knots Sword-knots strive,
Beaus banish Beaus, and Coaches Coaches drive.
This erring Mortals Levity may call,
Oh blind to Truth! the *Sylphs* contrive it all.
    Of these am I, who thy Protection claim,   105
A watchful Sprite, and *Ariel* is my Name.
Late, as I rang'd the Crystal Wilds of Air,
In the clear Mirror of thy ruling *Star*
I saw, alas! some dread Event impend,
Ere to the Main this Morning Sun descend.   110
But Heav'n reveals not what, or how, or where:
Warn'd by thy *Sylph,* oh Pious Maid beware!
This to disclose is all thy Guardian can.
Beware of all, but most beware of Man!
    He said; when *Shock,* who thought she slept too long,   115
Leapt up, and wak'd his Mistress with his Tongue.
'Twas then *Belinda!* if Report say true,
Thy Eyes first open'd on a *Billet-doux;*
Wounds, Charms, and *Ardors,* were no sooner read,
But all the Vision vanish'd from thy Head.   120

---

1   images

And now, unveil'd, the *Toilet* stands display'd,
Each Silver Vase in mystic Order laid.
First, rob'd in White, the Nymph intent adores
With Head uncover'd, the *Cosmetic* Pow'rs.
A heav'nly Image in the Glass appears,   125
To that she bends, to that her Eyes she rears;
Th'inferior Priestess, at her Altar's side,
Trembling, begins the sacred Rites of Pride.
Unnumber'd Treasures ope at once, and here
The various Off'rings of the World appear;   130
From each she nicely culls with curious Toil,
And decks the Goddess with the glitt'ring Spoil.
This Casket *India's* glowing Gems unlocks,
And all *Arabia* breathes from yonder Box.
The Tortoise here and Elephant unite,   135
Transform'd to *Combs,* the speckled and the white.
Here Files of Pins extend their shining Rows,
Puffs, Powders, Patches, Bibles, Billet-doux.
Now awful Beauty puts on all its Arms;
The Fair each moment rises in her Charms,   140
Repairs her Smiles, awakens ev'ry Grace,
And calls forth all the Wonders of her Face;
Sees by Degrees a purer Blush arise,
And keener Lightnings quicken in her Eyes.
The busy *Sylphs* surround their darling Care;   145
These set the Head, and those divide the Hair,
Some fold the Sleeve, while others plait the Gown;
And *Betty's*[1] prais'd for Labours not her own.

---

1   Betty is Belinda's maid.

Lady Mary Wortley Montagu

(1689–1762)

The Resolve

Whilst thirst of praise, and vain desire of fame,
In every age, is every woman's aim;
With courtship pleased, of silly toasters proud;
Fond of a train, and happy in a crowd;
On each poor fool bestowing some kind glance;
Each conquest owing to some loose advance;
Whilst vain coquets affect to be pursued,
And think they're virtuous, if not grossly lewd;
Let this great maxim be my virtue's guide:
In part she is to blame, who has been tried,
He comes too near, that comes to be denied.

from: *Six Town Eclogues*

Saturday: The Small-Pox[1]

Flavia

The wretched Flavia, on her couch reclined,
Thus breathed the anguish of a wounded mind.
A glass reversed in her right hand she bore,
For now she shunned the face she sought before.
   'How am I changed! alas! how am I grown
A frightful spectre, to myself unknown!
Where's my complexion? where the radiant bloom,
That promised happiness for years to come?
Then, with what pleasure I this face surveyed!
To look once more, my visits oft delayed!
Charmed with the view, a fresher red would rise
And a new life shot sparkling from my eyes!
Ah! faithless glass, my wonted bloom restore!
Alas! I rave, that bloom is now no more!
   'The greatest good the gods on men bestow,
Ev'n youth itself, to me is useless now.
There was a time (oh! that I could forget!)
When opera-tickets poured before my feet;
And at the Ring,[2] where brightest beauties shine,
The earliest cherries of the spring were mine.
Witness, O Lillie, and thou, Motteux,[3] tell,

---

1 Montagu herself suffered a serious attack of small-pox in 1715. Subsequently she became
   a pioneer in encouraging the use of inoculation against the disease.
2 the Ring in Hyde Park, a fashionable promenade
3 Both shopkeepers: Charles Lillie was a perfumer, and Peter Motteux sold Oriental goods.

How much japan these eyes have made you sell.
With what contempt ye saw me oft despise
The humble offer of the raffled prize;
For at each raffle still the prize I bore,
With scorn rejected, or with triumph wore.
Now beauty's fled, and presents are no more.
  'For me the patriot has the House forsook,
And left debates to catch a passing look;
For me the soldier has soft verses writ;
For me the beau has aimed to be a wit.
For me the wit to nonsense was betrayed;
The gamester has for me his dun delayed,
And overseen the card I would have paid.
The bold and haughty by success made vain,
Awed by my eyes, has trembled to complain:
The bashful squire, touched with a wish unknown,
Has dared to speak with spirit not his own:
Fired by one wish, all did alike adore;
Now beauty's fled, and lovers are no more.
  'As round the room I turn my weeping eyes,
New unaffected scenes of sorrow rise.
Far from my sight that killing picture bear,
The face disfigure, or the canvas tear!
That picture, which with pride I used to show,
The lost resemblance but upbraids me now.
And thou, my toilette, where I oft have sat,
While hours unheeded passed in deep debate,
How curls should fall, or where a patch to place;
If blue or scarlet best became my face;
Now on some happier nymph your aid bestow;
On fairer heads, ye useless jewels, glow!
No borrowed lustre can my charms restore,
Beauty is fled, and dress is now no more.
  'Ye meaner beauties, I permit you shine;
Go, triumph in the hearts that once were mine;
But, midst your triumphs with confusion know,
'Tis to my ruin all your charms ye owe.
Would pitying heaven restore my wonted mien,
Ye still might move unthought of and unseen:
But oh, how vain, how wretched is the boast
Of beauty faded, and of empire lost!
What now is left but weeping to deplore
My beauty fled, and empire now no more?
  'Ye cruel chymists, what withheld your aid?
Could no pomatums¹ save a trembling maid?
How false and trifling is that art you boast;

---

1   ointments

No art can give me back my beauty lost!
In tears, surrounded by my friends I lay,
Masked o'er, and trembling at the light of day;
Mirmillo came my fortune to deplore
(A golden-headed cane well carved he bore):
"Cordials", he cried, "my spirits must restore!"
Beauty is fled, and spirit is no more!
Galen[1] the grave, officious Squirt was there,
With fruitless grief and unavailing care:
Machaon[2] too, the great Machaon known
By his red cloak and his superior frown;
"And why," he cried, "this grief and this despair?
You shall again be well, again be fair;
Believe my oath" (with that an oath he swore);
False was his oath! my beauty is no more.

'Cease, hapless maid, no more thy tale pursue,
Forsake mankind, and bid the world adieu.
Monarchs and beauties rule with equal sway,
All strive to serve, and glory to obey:
Alike unpitied when deposed they grow,
Men mock the idol of their former vow.

'Adieu, ye parks—in some obscure recess,
Where gentle streams will weep at my distress,
Where no false friend will in my grief take part,
And mourn my ruin with a joyful heart;
There let me live in some deserted place,
There hide in shades this lost inglorious face.
Plays, operas, circles, I no more must view!
My toilette, patches, all the world, adieu!'

---

1   Montagu uses the name of the Greek physician of the second century B.C. as a type-name
     for a doctor.
2   the name of one of the Greek surgeons in the Trojan war, used also by Samuel Garth
     in his burlesque poem *The Dispensary* (1699)

from: *Verses Addressed to the Imitator of the First Satire of the Second Book of Horace*[1]

[A Reply to Alexander Pope]

When God created thee, one would believe
He said the same as to the snake of Eve:
'To human race antipathy declare,
'Twixt them and thee be everlasting war.'[2]
But oh! the sequel of the sentence dread,
And whilst you bruise their heel, beware your head.
  Nor think thy weakness shall be thy defence,
The female scold's protection in offence.
Sure 'tis as fair to beat who cannot fight,
As 'tis to libel those who cannot write.
And if thou draw'st thy pen to aid the law,
Others a cudgel, or a rod, may draw.
  If none with vengeance yet thy crimes pursue,
Or give thy manifold affronts their due;
If limbs unbroken, skin without a stain,
Unwhipped, unblanketed, unkicked, unslain,
That wretched little carcase you retain,
The reason is, not that the world wants eyes,
But thou'rt so mean, they see, and they despise:
When fretful porcupine,[3] with rancorous will,
From mounted back shoots forth a harmless quill,
Cool the spectators stand; and all the while
Upon the angry little monster smile.
Thus 'tis with thee:—whilst impotently safe,
You strike unwounding, we unhurt can laugh.
'Who but must laugh, this bully when he sees,
A puny insect shivering at a breeze?'[4]
One over-matched by every blast of wind,
Insulting and provoking all mankind.
  Is this the thing to keep mankind in awe,
'To make those tremble who escape the law?'[5]
Is this the ridicule to live so long,
'The deathless satire and immortal song?'
No: like thy self-blown praise, thy scandal flies;

---

1   In her youth, Lady Mary had met and corresponded with Alexander Pope, but their relations deteriorated after she derided his declaration of love. They attacked one another in a series of poems and pamphlets. This poem, published in March 1733, is a response to an insult by Pope in his *First Satire of the Second Book of Horace*, issued in February 1733.

2   See Genesis 3.14-15.

3   See *Hamlet* I.v.20.

4   from Pope's "Epistle to Burlington," 107-8

5   This and the next two lines are adapted from Pope's *The First Satire of the Second Book*, 118, 69, 79-80.

And, as we're told of wasps, it stings and dies.
  If none do yet return th' intended blow,
You all your safety to your dullness owe:
But whilst that armour thy poor corpse defends,
'Twill make thy readers few, as are thy friends:
Those, who thy nature loathed, yet loved thy art,
Who liked thy head, and yet abhorred thy heart:
Chose thee to read, but never to converse,
And scorned in prose him whom they prized in verse:
Even they shall now their partial error see,
Shall shun thy writings like thy company;
And to thy books shall ope their eyes no more
Than to thy person they would do their door.
  Nor thou the justice of the world disown,
That leaves thee thus an outcast and alone;
For though in law to murder be to kill,
In equity the murder's in the will:
Then whilst with coward-hand you stab a name,
And try at least t'assassinate our fame,
Like the first bold assassin's be thy lot,
Ne'er be thy guilt forgiven, or forgot;
But, as thou hat'st, be hated by mankind,
And with the emblem of thy crooked mind
Marked on thy back, like Cain,[1] by God's own hand,
Wander, like him, accursèd through the land.

---

1   See Genesis 4.15.

Thomas Gray

(1716–1771)

Ode on the Death of a Favourite Cat, Drowned in a Tub of Gold Fishes

'Twas on a lofty vase's side,
Where China's gayest art had dy'd
  The azure flowers, that blow;
Demurest of the tabby kind,
The pensive Selima[1] reclin'd,
  Gazed on the lake below.

Her conscious tail her joy declar'd;
The fair round face, the snowy beard,
  The velvet of her paws,
Her coat, that with the tortoise vies,
Her ears of jet, and emerald eyes,
  She saw; and purr'd applause.

Still had she gaz'd; but 'midst the tide
Two angel forms were seen to glide,
  The Genii of the stream:
Their scaly armour's Tyrian hue[2]
Thro' richest purple to the view
  Betray'd a golden gleam.

The hapless Nymph with wonder saw:
A whisker first and then a claw,
  With many an ardent wish,
She stretch'd in vain to reach the prize.
What female heart can gold despise?
  What Cat's averse to fish?

Presumptuous Maid! with looks intent
Again she stretch'd, again she bent,
  Nor knew the gulf between.
(Malignant Fate sat by, and smil'd)
The slipp'ry verge her feet beguil'd,
  She tumbled headlong in.

---

1   the name of Horace Walpole's cat, drowned in a china cistern
2   purple

Eight times emerging from the flood
She mew'd to ev'ry watry God,
   Some speedy aid to send.
No Dolphin came, no Nereid[1] stirr'd:
Nor cruel *Tom*, nor *Susan* heard.
   A Fav'rite has no friend!

From hence, ye Beauties, undeceiv'd,
Know, one false step is ne'er retriev'd,
   And be with caution bold.
Not all that tempts your wand'ring eyes
And heedless hearts, is lawful prize;
   Nor all, that glisters, gold.

Elegy Written in a Country Church-Yard

The Curfew tolls the knell of parting day,
The lowing herd wind slowly o'er the lea,
The ploughman homeward plods his weary way,
And leaves the world to darkness and to me.

Now fades the glimmering landscape on the sight,   5
And all the air a solemn stillness holds,
Save where the beetle wheels his droning flight,
And drowsy tinklings lull the distant folds;

Save that from yonder ivy-mantled tow'r
The moping owl does to the moon complain   10
Of such, as wand'ring near her secret bow'r,
Molest her ancient solitary reign.

Beneath those rugged elms, that yew-tree's shade,
Where heaves the turf in many a mould'ring heap,
Each in his narrow cell for ever laid,   15
The rude[2] Forefathers of the hamlet sleep.

The breezy call of incense-breathing Morn,
The swallow twitt'ring from the straw-built shed,
The cock's shrill clarion, or the ecchoing horn,
No more shall rouse them from their lowly bed.   20

For them no more the blazing hearth shall burn,
Or busy houswife ply her evening care:
No children run to lisp their sire's return,
Or climb his knees the envied kiss to share.

---

1   a sea-nymph, one of the daughters of Nereus
2   uneducated, ignorant

Oft did the harvest to their sickle yield,   25
Their furrow oft the stubborn glebe[1] has broke;
How jocund did they drive their team afield!
How bow'd the woods beneath their sturdy stroke!

Let not Ambition mock their useful toil,   30
Their homely joys, and destiny obscure;
Nor Grandeur hear with a disdainful smile,
The short and simple annals of the poor.

The boast of heraldry, the pomp of pow'r,
And all that beauty, all that wealth e'er gave,
Awaits alike th' inevitable hour.   35
The paths of glory lead but to the grave.

Nor you, ye Proud, impute to These the fault,
If Mem'ry o'er their Tomb no Trophies raise,
Where thro' the long-drawn isle and fretted vault
The pealing anthem swells the note of praise.   40

Can storied urn or animated[2] bust
Back to its mansion call the fleeting breath?
Can Honour's voice provoke[3] the silent dust,
Or Flatt'ry sooth the dull cold ear of Death?

Perhaps in this neglected spot is laid   45
Some heart once pregnant with celestial fire,
Hands, that the rod of empire might have sway'd,
Or wak'd to extasy the living lyre.

But Knowledge to their eyes her ample page
Rich with the spoils of time did ne'er unroll;   50
Chill Penury repress'd their noble rage,
And froze the genial current of the soul.

Full many a gem of purest ray serene,
The dark unfathom'd caves of ocean bear:
Full many a flower is born to blush unseen,   55
And waste its sweetness on the desert air.

Some village-Hampden,[4] that with dauntless breast
The little Tyrant of his fields withstood;

---

1   earth, field
2   lifelike
3   call forth
4   John Hampden (1594-1643), Member of Parliament, led the resistance against the imposition of unfair taxes by Charles I. He died in a skirmish in the Civil War.

Some mute inglorious Milton here may rest,
Some Cromwell guiltless of his country's blood.   60

Th' applause of list'ning senates to command,
The threats of pain and ruin to despise,
To scatter plenty o'er a smiling land,
And read their hist'ry in a nation's eyes,

Their lot forbad: nor circumscrib'd alone   65
Their growing virtues, but their crimes confin'd;
Forbad to wade through slaughter to a throne,
And shut the gates of mercy on mankind,

The struggling pangs of conscious truth to hide,
To quench the blushes of ingenuous shame,   70
Or heap the shrine of Luxury and Pride
With incense kindled at the Muse's flame.

Far from the madding crowd's ignoble strife,
Their sober wishes never learn'd to stray;
Along the cool sequester'd vale of life   75
They kept the noiseless tenor of their way.

Yet ev'n these bones from insult to protect
Some frail memorial still erected nigh,
With uncouth rhimes and shapeless sculpture deck'd,
Implores the passing tribute of a sigh.   80

Their name, their years, spelt by th' unletter'd muse,
The place of fame and elegy supply:
And many a holy text around she strews,
That teach the rustic moralist to die.

For who to dumb Forgetfulness a prey,   85
This pleasing anxious being e'er resign'd,
Left the warm precincts of the chearful day,
Nor cast one longing ling'ring look behind?

On some fond breast the parting soul relies,
Some pious drops the closing eye requires;   90
Ev'n from the tomb the voice of Nature cries,
Ev'n in our Ashes live their wonted Fires.

For thee, who mindful of th' unhonour'd Dead
Dost in these lines their artless tale relate;
If chance, by lonely contemplation led,   95
Some kindred Spirit shall inquire thy fate,

Haply some hoary-headed Swain may say,
'Oft have we seen him at the peep of dawn
'Brushing with hasty steps the dews away
'To meet the sun upon the upland lawn.   100

'There at the foot of yonder nodding beech
'That wreathes its old fantastic roots so high,
'His listless length at noontide wou'd he stretch,
'And pore upon the brook that babbles by.

'Hard by yon wood, now smiling as in scorn,   105
'Mutt'ring his wayward fancies he wou'd rove,
'Now drooping, woeful wan, like one forlorn,
'Or craz'd with care, or cross'd in hopeless love.

'One morn I miss'd him on the custom'd hill,
'Along the heath and near his fav'rite tree;   110
'Another came; nor yet beside the rill,
'Nor up the lawn, nor at the wood was he;

'The next with dirges due in sad array
'Slow thro' the church-way path we saw him born.
'Approach and read (for thou can'st read) the lay,   115
'Grav'd on the stone beneath yon aged thorn.'

The EPITAPH.

Here rests his head upon the lap of Earth
A Youth to Fortune and to Fame unknown,
Fair Science frown'd not on his humble birth,
And Melancholy mark'd him for her own.

Large was his bounty, and his soul sincere,
Heav'n did a recompence as largely send:
He gave to Mis'ry all he had, a tear,
He gain'd from Heav'n ('twas all he wish'd) a friend.

No farther seek his merits to disclose,
Or draw his frailties from their dread abode,
(There they alike in trembling hope repose)
The bosom of his Father and his God.

Sonnet on the Death of Richard West[1]

In vain to me the smileing Mornings shine,
And redning Phoebus lifts his golden Fire:
The Birds in vain their amorous Descant joyn;
Or chearful Fields resume their green Attire:
These Ears, alas! for other Notes repine,
A different Object do these Eyes require.
My lonely Anguish melts no Heart, but mine;
And in my Breast the imperfect Joys expire.
Yet Morning smiles the busy Race to chear,
And new-born Pleasure brings to happier Men:
The Fields to all their wonted Tribute bear:
To warm their little Loves the Birds complain:
I fruitless mourn to him, that cannot hear,
And weep the more, because I weep in vain.

---

1   Richard West, a schoolfriend of the poet's, died on 1 June 1742, aged 25.

Christopher Smart

(1722–1771)

from: *Jubilate Agno*[1] *(fragment B)*

[My Cat Jeoffry[2]]

For I will consider my Cat Jeoffry.
For he is the servant of the Living God duly and daily serving him.
For at the first glance of the glory of God in the East he worships
      in his way.
For is this done by wreathing his body seven times round with
elegant quickness.
For then he leaps up to catch the musk, which is the blessing of God
upon his prayer.
For he rolls upon prank to work it in.
For having done duty and received blessing he begins to consider
      himself.
For this he performs in ten degrees.
For first he looks upon his fore paws to see if they are clean.
For secondly he kicks up behind to clear away there.
For thirdly he works it upon stretch with the fore-paws extended.
For fourthly he sharpens his paws by wood.
For fifthly he washes himself.
For Sixthly he rolls upon wash.
For Seventhly he fleas himself, that he may not be interrupted upon
      the beat.
For Eighthly he rubs himself against a post.
For Ninthly he looks up for his instructions.
For Tenthly he goes in quest of food.
For having consider'd God and himself he will consider his neighbor.
For if he meets another cat he will kiss her in kindness.
For when he takes his prey he plays with it to give it a chance.
For one mouse in seven escapes by his dallying.
For when his day's work is done his business more properly begins.
For he keeps the Lord's watch in the night against the adversary.
For he counteracts the powers of darkness by his electrical skin &
      glaring eyes.
For he counteracts the Devil, who is death, by brisking about the
life.
For in his morning orisons he loves the sun and the sun loves him.
For he is of the tribe of Tiger.
For the Cherub Cat is a term of the Angel Tiger.[3]
For he has the subtlety and hissing of a serpent, which in goodness

---

1   Rejoice in the Lamb.
2   Smart's cat kept him company during the years of his confinement in a madhouse (1759-
     63), during which period he wrote *Jubilate Agno.*
3   a kind of equation, in which a cat is to a tiger as a cherub is to an angel; i.e., Jeoffry is
     a small tiger.

he suppresses.
For he will not do destruction if he is well-fed, neither will he spit
    without provocation.
For he purrs in thankfulness, when God tells him he's a good Cat.
For he is an instrument for the children to learn benevolence upon.
For every house is incomplete without him & a blessing is lacking in
    the spirit.
For the Lord commanded Moses concerning the cats at the
departure of the Children of Israel from Egypt.
For every family had one cat at least in the bag.[1]
For the English Cats are the best in Europe.
For he is the cleanest in the use of his fore-paws of any quadrupede.
For the dexterity of his defence is an instance of the love of God to
    him exceedingly.
For he is the quickest to his mark of any creature.
For he is tenacious of his point.
For he is a mixture of gravity and waggery.
For he knows that God is his Saviour.
For there is nothing sweeter than his peace when at rest.
For there is nothing brisker than his life when in motion.
For he is of the Lord's poor and so indeed is he called by
    benevolence perpetually—Poor Jeoffry! poor Jeoffry! the rat
    has bit thy throat.
For I bless the name of the Lord Jesus that Jeoffry is better.
For the divine spirit comes about his body to sustain it in complete
    cat.
For his tongue is exceeding pure so that it has in purity what it
    wants In music.
For he is docile and can learn certain things.
For he can set up with gravity which is patience upon approbation.
For he can fetch and carry, which is patience in employment.
For he can jump over a stick which is patience upon proof positive.
For he can spraggle upon waggle at the word of command.
For he can jump from an eminence into his master's bosom.
For he can catch the cork and toss it again.
For he is hated by the hypocrite and miser.
For the former is afraid of detection.
For the latter refuses the charge.
For he camels his back to bear the first notion of business.
For he is good to think on, if a man would express himself neatly.
For he made a great figure in Egypt for his signal services.
For he killed the Icneumon-rat[2] very pernicious by land.
For his ears are so acute that they sting again.
For from this proceeds the passing quickness of his attention.
For by stroking of him I have found out electricity.
For I perceived God's light about him both wax and fire.

---

1   a fanciful notion, since cats are not mentioned in the Bible
2   The ichneumon, a carnivore related to the mongoose, was worshipped by the Egyptians.

For the Electrical fire is the spiritual substance, which God sends
from heaven to sustain the bodies both of man and beast.
For God has blessed him in the variety of his movements.
For, though he cannot fly, he is an excellent clamberer.
For his motions upon the face of the earth are more than any other
    quadrupede.
For he can tread to all the measures upon the music.
For he can swim for life.
For he can creep.

Mary Leapor

(1722–1746)

Strephon to Celia.[1] A Modern Love-Letter

MADAM
             I hope you'll think it's true
I deeply am in love with you,
When I assure you t' other day,
As I was musing on my way,
At thought of you I tumbled down
Directly in a deadly swoon:
And though 'tis true I'm something better,
Yet I can hardly spell my letter:
And as the latter you may view,
I hope you'll think the former true.
You need not wonder at my flame,
For you are not a mortal dame:
I saw you dropping from the skies;
And let dull idiots swear your eyes
With love their glowing breast inspire,
I tell you they are flames of fire,
That scorch my forehead to a cinder,
And burn my very heart to tinder.
Your breast so mighty cold, I trow,
Is made of nothing else but snow:
Your hands (no wonder they have charms)
Are made of ivory like your arms.
Your cheeks, that look as if they bled,
Are nothing else but roses red.
Your lips are coral very bright,
Your teeth—though numbers out of spite
May say they're bones—yet 'twill appear
They're rows of pearl exceeding dear.

Now, madam, as the chat goes round,
I hear you have ten thousand pound:
But that as I a trifle hold,
Give me your person, dem[2] your gold;
Yet for your own sake 'tis secured,
I hope—your houses too insured;
I'd have you take a special care,
And of false mortgages beware;
You've wealth enough 'tis true, but yet
You want a friend to manage it.
Now such a friend you soon might have,

---

1   stock names for lovers. "Strephon" is the name Sidney gives to a lovesick shepherd in his prose romance *Arcadia* (1593).
2   i.e., damn

By fixing on your humble slave;
Not that I mind a stately house,
Or value money of a louse;
But your five hundred pounds a year,
I would secure it for my dear:
Then smile upon your slave, that lies
Half murdered by your radiant eyes;
Or else this very moment dies—
Strephon

An Essay on Woman

Woman, a pleasing but a short-lived flower,
Too soft for business and too weak for power:
A wife in bondage, or neglected maid;
Despised, if ugly; if she's fair, betrayed.
'Tis wealth alone inspires every grace,
And calls the raptures to her plenteous face.
What numbers for those charming features pine,
If blooming acres round her temples twine!
Her lip the strawberry, and her eyes more bright
Than sparkling Venus in a frosty night;
Pale lilies fade and, when the fair appears,
Snow turns a negro and dissolves in tears,
And, where the charmer treads her magic toe,
On English ground Arabian odours grow;
Till mighty Hymen[1] lifts his sceptred rod,
And sinks her glories with a fatal nod,
Dissolves her triumphs, sweeps her charms away,
And turns the goddess to her native clay.

But, Artemisia,[2] let your servant sing
What small advantage wealth and beauties bring.
Who would be wise, that knew Pamphilia's fate?
Or who be fair, and joined to Sylvia's mate?
Sylvia, whose cheeks are fresh as early day,
As evening mild, and sweet as spicy May:
And yet that face her partial husband tires,
And those bright eyes, that all the world admires.
Pamphilia's wit who does not strive to shun,
Like death's infection or a dog-day's sun?
The damsels view her with malignant eyes,
The men are vexed to find a nymph so wise:
And wisdom only serves to make her know

---

1   god of marriage
2   Leapor's name for Bridget Fremantle, the daughter of a local clergyman, who took a
close interest in her work. Artemisia was the name of a warrior queen of Halicarnassus.

The keen sensation of superior woe.
The secret whisper and the listening ear,
The scornful eyebrow and the hated sneer,
The giddy censures of her babbling kind,
With thousand ills that grate a gentle mind,
By her are tasted in the first degree,
Though overlooked by Simplicus and me.
Does thirst of gold a virgin's heart inspire,
Instilled by nature or a careful sire?
Then let her quit extravagance and play,
The brisk companion and expensive tea,
To feast with Cordia in her filthy sty
On stewed potatoes or on mouldy pie;
Whose eager eyes stare ghastly at the poor,
And fright the beggars from her hated door;
In greasy clouts[1] she wraps her smoky chin,
And holds that pride's a never-pardoned sin.

If this be wealth, no matter where it falls;
But save, ye Muses, save your Mira's walls:
Still give me pleasing indolence and ease,
A fire to warm me and a friend to please.

Since, whether sunk in avarice or pride,
A wanton virgin or a starving bride,
Or wondering crowds attend her charming tongue,
Or, deemed an idiot, ever speaks the wrong;
Though nature armed us for the growing ill
With fraudful cunning and a headstrong will;
Yet, with ten thousand follies to her charge,
Unhappy woman's but a slave at large.

The Epistle of Deborah Dough

Dearly beloved Cousin, these
Are sent to thank you for your cheese;
The price of oats is greatly fell:
I hope your children all are well
(Likewise the calf you take delight in),
As I am at this present writing.
But I've no news to send you now;
Only I've lost my brindled cow,
And that has greatly sunk my dairy.
But I forgot our neighbour Mary;
Our neighbour Mary—who, they say,

---

1   rags

Sits scribble-scribble all the day,
And making—what—I can't remember;
But sure 'tis something like December;
A frosty morning[1]—let me see—
O! now I have it to a T:
She throws away her precious time
In scrawling nothing else but rhyme;
Of which, they say, she's mighty proud,
And lifts her nose above the crowd;
Though my young daughter Cicely
Is taller by a foot than she,
And better learned (as people say);
Can knit a stocking in a day;
Can make a pudding, plump and rare;
And boil her bacon to an hair;
Will coddle apples nice and green,
And fry her pancakes—like a queen.

But there's a man, that keeps a dairy,
Will clip the wings of neighbour Mary:
Things wonderful they talk of him,
But I've a notion 'tis a whim.
Howe'er, 'tis certain he can make
Your rhymes as thick as plums in cake;
Nay more, they say that from the pot
He'll take his porridge, scalding hot,
And drink 'em down;—and yet they tell ye
Those porridge shall not burn his belly;
A cheesecake o'er his head he'll throw,
And when 'tis on the stones below,
It shan't be found so much as quaking,
Provided 'tis of his wife's making.
From this some people would infer
That this good man's a conjuror:
But I believe it is a lie;
I never thought him so, not I,
Though Win'fred Hobble who, you know,
Is plagued with corns on every toe,
Sticks on his verse with fastening spittle,
And says it helps her feet a little.
Old Frances too his paper tears,
And tucks it close behind his ears;
And (as she told me t'other day)
It charmed her toothache quite away.

---

1   Leapor is preparing us for a pun on "rime" amd "rhyme" four lines below.

Now as thou'rt better learned than me,
Dear Cos', I leave it all to thee
To judge about this puzzling man,
And ponder wisely—for you can.

Now Cousin, I must let you know
That, while my name is Deborah Dough,
I shall be always glad to see ye,
And what I have, I'll freely gi' ye.

'Tis one o'clock, as I'm a sinner;
The boys are all come home to dinner,
And I must bid you now farewell.
I pray remember me to Nell;
And for your friend I'd have you know
Your loving Cousin,
                              Deborah Dough

William Cowper

(1731–1800)

On The Death of Mrs. Throckmorton's Bulfinch

Ye nymphs! if e'er your eyes were red
With tears o'er hapless fav'rites shed,
   O share Maria's grief!
Her fav'rite, even in his cage,
(What will not hunger's cruel rage?)
   Assassin'd by a thief.

Where Rhenus[1] strays his vines among,
The egg was laid from which he sprung,
   And though by nature mute,
Or only with a whistle blest,
Well-taught he all the sounds express'd
   Of flagelet or flute.

The honours of his ebon poll
Were brighter than the sleekest mole,
   His bosom of the hue
With which Aurora decks the skies,
When piping winds shall soon arise,
   To sweep away the dew.

Above, below, in all the house,
Dire foe alike of bird and mouse,
   No cat had leave to dwell;
And Bully's cage supported stood
On props of smoothest-shaven wood,
   Large-built and lattic'd well.

Well-lattic'd—but the grate, alas!
Not rough with wire of steel or brass,
   For Bully's plumage sake,
But smooth with wands from Ouse's[2] side,
With which, when neatly peel'd and dried,
   The swains their baskets make.

Night veil'd the pole: all seem'd secure:
When led by instinct sharp and sure,
   Subsistence to provide,
A beast forth sallied on the scout,
Long-back'd, long-tail'd, with whisker'd snout,
   And badger-colour'd hide.

---

1   the Latin name for the Rhine river
2   the river Ouse, in Buckinghamshire

He, ent'ring at the study-door,
Its ample area 'gan explore;
 And something in the wind
Conjectur'd, sniffing round and round,
Better than all the books he found,
 Food chiefly for the mind.

Just then, by adverse fate impress'd,
A dream disturb'd poor Bully's rest;
 In sleep he seem'd to view
A rat fast-clinging to the cage,
And, screaming at the sad presage,
 Awoke and found it true.

For, aided both by ear and scent,
Right to his mark the monster went—
 Ah, muse! forbear to speak
Minute the horrours that ensu'd;
His teeth were strong, the cage was wood—
 He left poor Bully's beak.

O had he made that too his prey;
That beak, whence issu'd many a lay
 Of such mellifluous tone,
Might have repaid him well, I wote,
For silencing so sweet a throat,
 Fast stuck within his own.

Maria weeps—The Muses mourn—
So, when by Bacchanalians torn,
 On Thracian Hebrus' side
The tree-enchanter Orpheus[1] fell,
His head alone remain'd to tell
 The cruel death he died.

The Poplar-Field

The poplars are fell'd, farewell to the shade
And the whispering sound of the cool colonnade,
The winds play no longer, and sing in the leaves,
Nor Ouse on his bosom their image receives.

---

1 Orpheus was so skilled a player on the lyre that all of Nature was spellbound by his
music. For the manner of his death, see the note on the reference to Orpheus in Milton's
"Lycidas" (p. 63 above).

Twelve years have elaps'd since I last took a view
Of my favourite field and the bank where they grew,
And now in the grass behold they are laid,
And the tree is my seat that once lent me a shade.

The blackbird has fled to another retreat
Where the hazels afford him a screen from the heat,
And the scene where his melody charm'd me before,
Resounds with his sweet-flowing ditty no more.

My fugitive years are all hasting away,
And I must ere long lie as lowly as they,
With a turf on my breast, and a stone at my head,
Ere another such grove shall arise in its stead.

'Tis a sight to engage me, if any thing can,
To muse on the perishing pleasures of man;
Though his life be a dream, his enjoyments, I see,
Have a being less durable even than he.

from: *The Task: Book II*

[On Slavery]

Oh for a lodge in some vast wilderness,
Some boundless contiguity of shade,
Where rumour of oppression and deceit,
Of unsuccessful or successful war
Might never reach me more. My ear is pain'd,   5
My soul is sick with ev'ry day's report
Of wrong and outrage with which earth is fill'd.
There is no flesh in man's obdurate heart,
It does not feel for man. The nat'ral bond
Of brotherhood is sever'd as the flax   10
That falls asunder at the touch of fire.
He finds his fellow guilty of a skin
Not colour'd like his own, and having pow'r
T' inforce the wrong, for such a worthy cause
Dooms and devotes[1] him as his lawful prey.   15
Lands intersected by a narrow frith
Abhor each other. Mountains interposed
Make enemies of nations who had else
Like kindred drops been mingled into one.
Thus man devotes his brother, and destroys;   20

---

1   curses or dooms (an obsolete usage)

And worse than all, and most to be deplored
As human nature's broadest, foulest blot,
Chains him, and tasks him, and exacts his sweat
With stripes, that mercy with a bleeding heart
Weeps when she sees inflicted on a beast.   25
Then what is man? And what man seeing this,
And having human feelings, does not blush
And hang his head, to think himself a man?
I would not have a slave to till my ground,
To carry me, to fan me while I sleep,   30
And tremble when I wake, for all the wealth
That sinews bought and sold have ever earn'd.
No: dear as freedom is, and in my heart's
Just estimation priz'd above all price,
I had much rather be myself the slave   35
And wear the bonds, than fasten them on him.
We have no slaves at home.—Then why abroad?
And they themselves once ferried o'er the wave
That parts us, are emancipate and loos'd.
Slaves cannot breathe in England;[1] if their lungs   40
Receive our air, that moment they are free,
They touch our country and their shackles fall.
That's noble, and bespeaks a nation proud
And jealous of the blessing. Spread it then,
And let it circulate through ev'ry vein   45
Of all your empire. That where Britain's power
Is felt, mankind may feel her mercy too.
   Sure there is need of social intercourse,
Benevolence and peace and mutual aid
Between the nations, in a world that seems   50
To toll the death-bell of its own decease,
And by the voice of all its elements
To preach the gen'ral doom. When were the winds
Let slip with such a warrant to destroy,
When did the waves so haughtily o'erleap   55
Their ancient barriers, deluging the dry?
Fires from beneath, and meteors from above
Portentous, unexampled, unexplained,
Have kindled beacons in the skies and th' old
And crazy earth has had her shaking fits   60
More frequent, and forgone her usual rest.
Is it a time to wrangle, when the props
And pillars of our planet seem to fail,
And Nature with a dim and sickly eye
To wait the close of all? But grant her end   65
More distant, and that prophecy demands

---

1   From 1772 West Indian planters were forbidden to keep slaves in England, since slavery
was forbidden by English law.

A longer respite, unaccomplished yet;
Still they are frowning signals, and bespeak
Displeasure in his breast who smites the earth
Or heals it, makes it languish or rejoice.   70
And 'tis but seemly, that where all deserve
And stand exposed by common peccancy
To what no few have felt, there should be peace,
And brethren in calamity should love.

* * *

The Cast-Away

Obscurest night involv'd the sky,
  Th' Atlantic billows roar'd,
When such a destin'd wretch as I
  Wash'd headlong from on board,
Of friends, of hope, of all bereft,
His floating home for ever left.

No braver chief could Albion boast
  Than he with whom he went,
Nor ever ship left Albion's coast
  With warmer wishes sent.
He lov'd them both, but both in vain,
Nor him beheld, nor her again.

Not long beneath the whelming brine
  Expert to swim, he lay;
Nor soon he felt his strength decline
  Or courage die away;
But wag'd with death a lasting strife
Supported by despair of life.

He shouted: nor his friends had fail'd
  To check the vessel's course,
But so the furious blast prevail'd
  That, pitiless perforce,
They left their outcast mate behind,
And scudded still before the wind.

Some succour yet they could afford;
  And, such as storms allow,
The cask, the coop, the floated cord
  Delay'd not to bestow.
But he, they knew, nor ship nor shore,
Whate'er they gave, should visit more.

Nor, cruel as it seem'd, could he
  Their haste, himself, condemn,
Aware that flight in such a sea
  Alone could rescue *them*;
Yet bitter felt it still to die
Deserted, and his friends so nigh.

He long survives who lives an hour
  In ocean, self-upheld:
And so long he with unspent pow'r
  His destiny repell'd:
And ever as the minutes flew,
Entreated help, or cried—'Adieu!'

At length, his transient respite past,
  His comrades, who before
Had heard his voice in ev'ry blast,
  Could catch the sound no more:
For then, by toil subdued, he drank
The stifling wave, and then he sank.

No poet wept him, but the page
  Of narrative sincere
That tells his name, his worth, his age,
  Is wet with Anson's[1] tear;
And tears by bards or heroes shed
Alike immortalize the dead.

I, therefore, purpose not or dream,
  Descanting on his fate,
To give the melancholy theme
  A more enduring date;
But mis'ry still delights to trace
Its semblance in another's case.

No voice divine the storm allay'd,
  No light propitious shone;
When, snatch'd from all effectual aid,
  We perish'd, each alone;
But I, beneath a rougher sea,
And whelm'd in deeper gulfs than he.

---

1 Cowper's poem is based on an incident in George Anson's account of his voyage around
   the world in 1740-44.

Anna Laetitia Barbauld

(1743–1825)

The Mouse's Petition to Dr. Priestley[1]

*Found in the trap where he had been contained all night by
Dr. Priestley, for the sake of making experiments with different
kinds of air.*

O hear a pensive prisoner's prayer,
    For liberty that sighs;
And never let thine heart be shut
    Against the wretch's cries!

For here forlorn and sad I sit,
    Within the wiry grate;
And tremble at th' approaching morn,
    Which brings impending fate.

If e'er thy breast with freedom glowed,
    And spurned a tyrant's chain,
Let not thy strong oppressive force
    A free-born mouse detain!

O do not stain with guiltless blood
    Thy hospitable hearth!
Nor triumph that thy wiles betrayed
    A prize so little worth.

The scattered gleanings of a feast
    My frugal meals supply;
But if thine unrelenting heart
    That slender boon deny,—

The cheerful light, the vital air,
    Are blessings widely given;
Let Nature's commoners enjoy
    The common gifts of Heaven.

The well-taught philosophic mind
    To all compassion gives;
Casts round the world an equal eye,
    And feels for all that lives.

If mind,—as ancient sages taught,—
    A never dying flame,

---

1   Joseph Priestley (1733-1804), the philosopher and chemist who discovered oxygen, was a
tutor at the academy where Barbauld's father taught.

Still shifts through matter's varying forms,
  In every form the same;

Beware, lest in the worm you crush,
  A brother's soul you find;
And tremble lest thy luckless hand
  Dislodge a kindred mind.

Or, if this transient gleam of day
  Be *all* of life we share,
Let pity plead within thy breast
  That little *all* to spare.

So may thy hospitable board
  With health and peace be crowned;
And every charm of heartfelt ease
  Beneath thy roof be found.

So when destruction lurks unseen,
  Which men, like mice, may share,
May some kind angel clear thy path,
  And break the hidden snare.

The Rights of Woman[1]

Yes, injured Woman! rise, assert thy right!
Woman! too long degraded, scorned, opprest;
O born to rule in partial Law's despite,
Resume thy native empire o'er the breast!

Go forth arrayed in panoply divine;
That angel pureness which admits no stain;
Go, bid proud Man his boasted rule resign,
And kiss the golden sceptre of thy reign.

Go, gird thyself with grace; collect thy store
Of bright artillery glancing from afar;
Soft melting tones thy thundering cannon's roar,
Blushes and fears thy magazine of war.

Thy rights are empire: urge no meaner claim,—
Felt, not defined, and if debated, lost;
Like sacred mysteries, which withheld from fame,
Shunning discussion, are revered the most.

---

1   An allusion to Mary Wollstonecraft's *Vindication of the Rights of Woman* (1792), published
    three or four years before Barbauld wrote this poem.

Try all that wit and art suggest to bend
Of thy imperial foe the stubborn knee;
Make treacherous Man thy subject, not thy friend;
Thou mayst command, but never canst be free.

Awe the licentious, and restrain the rude;
Soften the sullen, clear the cloudy brow:
Be, more than princes' gifts, thy favours sued;—
She hazards all, who will the least allow.

But hope not, courted idol of mankind,
On this proud eminence secure to stay;
Subduing and subdued, thou soon shalt find
Thy coldness soften, and thy pride give way.

Then, then, abandon each ambitious thought;
Conquest or rule thy heart shall feebly move,
In Nature's school, by her soft maxims taught,
That separate rights are lost in mutual love.

Washing–Day

> . . . and their voice,
> *Turning again towards childish treble, pipes*
> *And whistles in its sound.——*

The Muses are turned gossips; they have lost
The buskined step,[1] and clear high-sounding phrase,
Language of gods. Come then, domestic Muse,
In slipshod measure loosely prattling on
Of farm or orchard, pleasant curds and cream,   5
Or drowning flies, or shoe lost in the mire
By little whimpering boy, with rueful face;
Come, Muse, and sing the dreaded Washing-Day.
Ye who beneath the yoke of wedlock bend,
With bowed soul, full well ye ken the day   10
Which week, smooth sliding after week, brings on
Too soon;— for to that day nor peace belongs
Nor comfort;— ere the first gray streak of dawn,
The red-armed washers come and chase repose.
Nor pleasant smile, nor quaint device of mirth,   15
E'er visited that day: the very cat,
From the wet kitchen scared and reeking hearth,
Visits the parlour,— an unwonted guest.
The silent breakfast-meal is soon dispatched;

---

1   a reference to the boots worn by actors in tragic drama

Uninterrupted, save by anxious looks   20
Cast at the lowering sky, if sky should lower.
From that last evil, O preserve us, heavens!
For should the skies pour down, adieu to all
Remains of quiet: then expect to hear
Of sad disasters,— dirt and gravel stains   25
Hard to efface, and loaded lines at once
Snapped short,—and linen-horse by dog thrown down,
And all the petty miseries of life.
Saints have been calm while stretched upon the rack,
And Guatimozin[1] smiled on burning coals;   30
But never yet did housewife notable
Greet with a smile a rainy washing-day.
—But grant the welkin[2] fair, require not thou
Who call'st thyself perchance the master there,
Or study swept, or nicely dusted coat,   35
Or usual 'tendance;—ask not, indiscreet,
Thy stockings mended, though the yawning rents
Gape wide as Erebus;[3] nor hope to find
Some snug recess impervious: shouldst thou try
The 'customed garden walks, thine eye shall rue   40
The budding fragrance of thy tender shrubs,
Myrtle or rose, all crushed beneath the weight
Of coarse checked apron,—with impatient hand
Twitched off when showers impend: or crossing lines
Shall mar thy musings, as the wet cold sheet   45
Flaps in thy face abrupt. Woe to the friend
Whose evil stars have urged him forth to claim
On such a day the hospitable rites!
Looks, blank at best, and stinted courtesy,
Shall he receive. Vainly he feeds his hopes   50
With dinner of roast chicken, savoury pie,
Or tart or pudding:—pudding he nor tart
That day shall eat; nor, though the husband try,
Mending what can't be helped, to kindle mirth
From cheer deficient, shall his consort's brow   55
Clear up propitious:—the unlucky guest
In silence dines, and early slinks away.
I well remember, when a child, the awe
This day struck into me; for then the maids,
I scarce knew why, looked cross, and drove me from them: 60
Nor soft caress could I obtain, nor hope
Usual indulgencies; jelly or creams,
Relic of costly suppers, and set by
For me their petted one; or buttered toast,

---

1   a king of Mexico tortured by Cortes
2   sky
3   in Greek mythology, a place of darkness on the way to Hades

When butter was forbid; or thrilling tale   65
Of ghost or witch, or murder—so I went
And sheltered me beside the parlour fire:
There my dear grandmother, eldest of forms,
Tended the little ones, and watched from harm,
Anxiously fond, though oft her spectacles   70
With elfin cunning hid, and oft the pins
Drawn from her ravelled stocking, might have soured
One less indulgent.—
At intervals my mother's voice was heard,
Urging dispatch: briskly the work went on,   75
All hands employed to wash, to rinse, to wring,
To fold, and starch, and clap, and iron, and plait.
Then would I sit me down, and ponder much
Why washings were. Sometimes through hollow bowl
Of pipe amused we blew, and sent aloft   80
The floating bubbles; little dreaming then
To see, Mongolfier,[1] thy silken ball
Ride buoyant through the clouds—so near approach
The sports of children and the toils of men.
Earth, air, and sky, and ocean, hath its bubbles,   85
And verse is one of them—this most of all.

---

1   The brothers Jacques and Joseph Montgolfier made the first ascent in a hot-air balloon
    in 1783.

William Blake

(1757–1827)

How sweet I roam'd from field to field

How sweet I roam'd from field to field,
  And tasted all the summer's pride,
'Till I the prince of love beheld,
  Who in the sunny beams did glide!

He shew'd me lilies for my hair,
  And blushing roses for my brow;
He led me through his gardens fair,
  Where all his golden pleasures grow.

With sweet May dews my wings were wet,
  And Phoebus fir'd my vocal rage;
He caught me in his silken net,
  And shut me in his golden cage.

He loves to sit and hear me sing,
  Then, laughing, sports and plays with me;
Then stretches out my golden wing,
  And mocks my loss of liberty.

from: *Songs of Innocence*

The Lamb

  Little lamb, who made thee?
    Dost thou know who made thee,
  Gave thee life and bid thee feed
  By the stream and o'er the mead—
  Gave thee clothing of delight,
  Softest clothing, woolly bright,
  Gave thee such a tender voice,
  Making all the vales rejoice?
    Little lamb, who made thee,
    Dost thou know who made thee?

    Little lamb, I'll tell thee,
    Little lamb, I'll tell thee!
  He is called by thy name,
  For he calls himself a Lamb;
  He is meek and he is mild,
  He became a little child:
  I a child, and thou a lamb,
  We are called by his name.
    Little lamb, God bless thee,
    Little lamb, God bless thee!

The Chimney Sweeper

When my mother died I was very young,
And my father sold me while yet my tongue
Could scarcely cry 'weep! 'weep! 'weep! 'weep!
So your chimneys I sweep, & in soot I sleep.

There's little Tom Dacre, who cried when his head,
That curl'd like a lamb's back, was shav'd; so I said,
'Hush Tom! never mind it, for when your head's bare,
You know that the soot cannot spoil your white hair.'

And so he was quiet, & that very night,
As Tom was a-sleeping he had such a sight!
That thousands of sweepers, Dick, Joe, Ned, & Jack,
Were all of them lock'd up in coffins of black;

And by came an Angel who had a bright key,
And he open'd the coffins & set them all free;
Then down a green plain leaping, laughing they run,
And wash in a river and shine in the Sun.

Then naked & white, all their bags left behind,
They rise upon clouds and sport in the wind.
And the Angel told Tom, if he'd be a good boy,
He'd have God for his father & never want joy.

And so Tom awoke; and we rose in the dark,
And got with our bags & our brushes to work.
Tho' the morning was cold, Tom was happy & warm;
So if all do their duty, they need not fear harm.

Holy Thursday[1]

'Twas on a Holy Thursday, their innocent faces clean,
The children walking two & two, in red & blue & green;
Grey-headed beadles walk'd before with wands as white as snow,
Till into the high dome of Paul's they like Thames' waters flow.

O what a multitude they seem'd, these flowers of London town!
Seated in companies they sit with radiance all their own.
The hum of multitudes was there, but multitudes of lambs,
Thousands of little boys & girls raising their innocent hands.

---

1   In the Anglican Church, Ascension Day, the fortieth day after Easter. It was the custom
on this day to take the children of the poor in procession to a service at St. Paul's
Cathedral.

Now like a mighty wind they raise to heaven the voice of song,
Or like harmonious thunderings the seats of Heaven among.
Beneath them sit the aged men, wise guardians of the poor:
Then cherish pity, lest you drive an angel from your door.

* * *

from: *Songs of Experience*

London

I wander thro' each charter'd street
Near where the charter'd Thames does flow,
And mark in every face I meet
Marks of weakness, marks of woe.

In every cry of every Man,
In every Infant's cry of fear,
In every voice, in every ban,
The mind-forg'd manacles I hear.

How the Chimney-sweeper's cry
Every black'ning Church appalls,
And the hapless Soldier's sigh
Runs in blood down Palace walls.

But most thro' midnight streets I hear
How the youthful Harlot's curse
Blasts the new-born Infant's tear,
And blights with plagues the marriage hearse.

The Tyger

Tyger! Tyger! burning bright
In the forests of the night,
What immortal hand or eye
Could frame thy fearful symmetry?

In what distant deeps or skies
Burnt the fire of thine eyes?
On what wings dare he aspire?
What the hand dare seize the fire?

And what shoulder, & what art,
Could twist the sinews of thy heart?
And when thy heart began to beat,
What dread hand? & what dread feet?

What the hammer? What the chain?
In what furnace was thy brain?
What the anvil? what dread grasp
Dare its deadly terrors clasp?

When the stars threw down their spears
And water'd heaven with their tears,
Did he smile his work to see?
Did he who made the Lamb make thee?

Tyger! Tyger! burning bright
In the forests of the night,
What immortal hand or eye
Dare frame thy fearful symmetry?

The Sick Rose

O Rose, thou art sick:
The invisible worm
That flies in the night,
In the howling storm,

Has found out thy bed
Of crimson joy;
And his dark secret love
Does thy life destroy.

The Chimney-Sweeper

A little black thing among the snow
Crying 'weep! 'weep! in notes of woe!
'Where are thy father & mother, say?'
'They are both gone up to the church to pray.

'Because I was happy upon the heath
And smil'd among the winter's snow,
They clothed me in the clothes of death
And taught me to sing the notes of woe.

'And because I am happy & dance & sing,
They think they have done me no injury,
And are gone to praise God & his Priest & King,
Who make up a heaven of our misery.'

Holy Thursday

Is this a holy thing to see
In a rich and fruitful land—
Babes reduc'd to misery,
Fed with cold and usurous hand?

Is that trembling cry a song?
Can it be a song of joy?
And so many children poor?
It is a land of poverty!

And their sun does never shine,
And their fields are bleak & bare,
And their ways are fill'd with thorns;
It is eternal winter there.

For where-e'er the sun does shine,
And where-e'er the rain does fall,
Babe can never hunger there,
Nor poverty the mind appall.

* * *

from: *Milton*

And did those feet in ancient time[1]
Walk upon England's mountains green?
And was the holy Lamb of God
On England's pleasant pastures seen?

And did the Countenance Divine
Shine forth upon our clouded hills?
And was Jerusalem builded here
Among these dark Satanic mills?

Bring me my bow of burning gold;
Bring me my arrows of desire;
Bring me my spear—O clouds, unfold!
Bring me my Chariot of fire!

I will not cease from Mental Fight,
Nor shall my Sword sleep in my hand,
Till we have built Jerusalem,
In England's green & pleasant Land.

---

1   According to ancient legend, Christ came to England with Joseph of Arimathea.

Robert Burns

(1759–1796)

To a Louse

On seeing one on a lady's bonnet at church

Ha! whare ye gaun, ye crowlin ferlie?[1]
Your impudence protects you sairly;[2]
I canna say but ye strunt[3] rarely
    Owre gauze and lace,
Tho faith! I fear ye dine but sparely
    On sic a place.

Ye ugly, creepin, blastit wonner,[4]
Detested, shunn'd by saunt an sinner,
How daur ye set your fit[5] upon her—
    Sae fine a lady!
Gae somewhere else and seek your dinner
    On some poor body.

Swith![6] in some beggar's hauffet[7] squattle;[8]
There ye may creep, and sprawl,[9] and sprattle,[10]
Wi' ither kindred, jumping cattle;
    In shoals and nations;
Whare horn nor bane[11] ne'er daur unsettle
    Your thick plantations.

Now haud you there! ye're out o sight,
Below the fatt'rils,[12] snug an tight,
Na, faith ye yet![13] ye'll no be right,
    Till ye've got on it—
The vera tapmost, tow'rin height
    O Miss's bonnet.

My sooth! right bauld ye set your nose out,
As plump an grey as onie grozet:[14]

---

1   crawling marvel
2   severely
3   move with assurance
4   accursed wonder
5   foot
6   Quickly!
7   lock of hair
8   squat
9   crawl
10   struggle
11   a comb made of horn or bone
12   ribbons
13   confound you!
14   gooseberry

O for some rank, mercurial rozet,[1]
    Or fell, red smeddum,[2]
I'd gie you sic a hearty dose o't,
    Wad dress your droddum![3]

I wad na been surpris'd to spy
You on an auld wife's flainen toy;[4]
Or aiblins[5] some bit duddie boy,[6]
    On's wyliecoat;[7]
But Miss's fine Lunardi![8] fye!
    How daur ye do't?

O Jeany, dinna toss your head,
An set your beauties a' abread![9]
Ye little ken what cursed speed
    The blastie's[10] makin!
Thae winks an finger-ends, I dread,
    Are notice takin!

O wad some Power the giftie gie us
To see oursels as ithers see us!
It wad frae monie a blunder free us,
    An foolish notion:
What airs in dress an gait wad lea'e us,
    An ev'n devotion!

Holy Willie's Prayer[11]

And send the godly in a pet to pray—POPE

O Thou that in the Heavens does dwell,
Wha, as it pleases best Thysel,
Sends ane to Heaven, an ten to Hell,
    A' for Thy glory,
And no for onie guid or ill
    They've done before Thee!

---

1   resin
2   pungent red powder (an insecticide)
3   thrash you!
4   flannel cap
5   perhaps
6   little ragged boy
7   flannel undershirt
8   a balloon-shaped bonnet, named after a famous Italian balloonist of the time
9   widely
10   malevolent creature
11   The poem satirizes a self-righteous Calvinistic elder of Mauchline, who had brought moral charges against Burns's friend Gavin Hamilton.

I bless and praise Thy matchless might,
When thousands Thou hast left in night,
That I am here before Thy sight,
 For gifts an grace
A burning and a shining light
 To a' this place.

What was I, or my generation,
That I should get sic exaltation?[1]
I, wha deserv'd most just damnation
 For broken laws,
Sax thousand years ere my creation,
 Thro Adam's cause!

When from my mither's womb I fell,
Thou might hae plung'd me deep in Hell,
To gnash my gooms, and weep and wail,
 In burning lakes,
Whare damned devils roar and yell,
 Chain'd to their stakes.

Yet I am here a chosen sample,
To show Thy grace is great and ample:
I'm here a pillar o' Thy temple,
 Strong as a rock,
A guide, a buckler,[2] and example,
 To a' Thy flock!

But yet, O Lord! confess I must,
At times I'm fash'd[3] wi' fleshy lust:
An sometimes, too, in warldly trust,
 Vile self gets in;
But Thou remembers we are dust,
 Defil'd wi' sin.

O Lord! yestreen,[4] Thou kens,[5] wi' Meg—
Thy pardon I sincerely beg—
O, may't ne'er be a livin plague
 To my dishonour!
An I'll ne'er lift a lawless leg
 Again upon her.

---

1 Holy Willy exults in the belief that he has been chosen for salvation as one of the elect.
2 a shield
3 troubled
4 yesterday evening
5 thou knowest

Besides, I farther maun avow,
Wi' Leezie's lass, three times I trow[1]—
But, Lord, that Friday I was fou,[2]
    When I cam near her,
Or else, Thou kens, Thy servant true
    Wad never steer[3] her.

Maybe Thou lets this fleshy thorn
Buffet Thy servant e'en and morn,
Lest he owre proud and high should turn,
    That he's sae gifted:
If sae, Thy han' maun[4] e'en be borne,
    Until Thou lift it.

Lord, bless Thy chosen in this place,
For here Thou has a chosen race!
But God confound their stubborn face,
    An blast their name,
Wha bring Thy elders to disgrace
    An open shame.

Lord, mind Gau'n Hamilton's deserts:
He drinks, an swears, an plays at cartes,
Yet has sae monie[5] takin arts,
    Wi' great and sma',
Frae God's ain Priest the people's hearts
    He steals awa.

And when we chasten'd him therefore,
Thou kens how he bred sic a splore,[6]
And set the warld in a roar
    O laughin at us;
Curse Thou his basket and his store,
    Kail[7] an potatoes!

Lord, hear my earnest cry and pray'r,
Against that Presbyt'ry o Ayr![8]
Thy strong right hand, Lord, mak it bare
    Upo' their heads!

---

1   trust
2   drunk
3   bother, agitate
4   must
5   so many
6   such an uproar
7   vegetable broth
8   the ecclesiastical court that found Gavin Hamilton innocent of the charge brought against him

Lord, visit them, an dinna spare,
  For their misdeeds!

O Lord, my God! that glib-tongu'd Aiken,[1]
My vera heart and flesh are quakin,
To think how we stood sweatin, shakin,
  An pish'd wi' dread,
While he, wi' hingin lip, an snakin,
  Held up his head.

Lord, in Thy day o' vengeance try him!
Lord, visit them wha did employ him!
And pass not in Thy mercy by them,
  Nor hear their pray'r,
But for Thy people's sake destroy them,
  An dinna spare.

But, Lord, remember me and mine
Wi' mercies temporal and divine,
That I for grace an gear[2] may shine,
  Excell'd by nane,
And a' the glory shall be Thine—
  Amen, Amen!

The Banks O Doon

Ye banks and braes o' bonie Doon,
  How can ye bloom sae fresh and fair;
How can ye chant, ye little birds,
  And I sae weary, fu' o' care!
Thou'll break my heart, thou warbling bird,
  That wantons thro' the flowering thorn:
Thou minds me o' departed joys,
  Departed, never to return.

Oft hae I rov'd by bonie Doon,
  To see the rose and woodbine twine;
And ilka bird sang o' its Luve,
  And fondly sae did I o' mine.
Wi' lightsome heart I pu'd a rose,
  Fu' sweet upon its thorny tree!
And my fause Luver staw[3] my rose,
  But, ah! he left the thorn wi' me.

---

1   Hamilton's defence counsel, Robert Aiken
2   goods, possessions
3   stole

A Red, Red Rose

O my Luve's like a red, red rose,
  That's newly sprung in June;
O my Luve's like the melodie
  That's sweetly played in tune.—

As fair art thou, my bonnie lass,
  So deep in luve am I;
And I will love thee still, my dear,
  Till a' the seas gang dry.—

Till a' the seas gang dry, my dear,
  And the rocks melt wi' the sun:
O I will love thee still, my dear,
  While the sands o' life shall run.—

And fare thee weel, my only Luve,
  And fare thee weel awhile!
And I will come again, my Luve,
  Though it were ten thousand mile!—

William Wordsworth

(1770–1850)

Lines Composed a few miles above Tintern Abbey, on Revisiting the banks of the Wye during a tour. July 13, 1798

Five years have past;[1] five summers, with the length
Of five long winters! and again I hear
These waters, rolling from their mountain-springs
With a soft inland murmur.—Once again
Do I behold these steep and lofty cliffs,
That on a wild secluded scene impress
Thoughts of more deep seclusion; and connect
The landscape with the quiet of the sky.
The day is come when I again repose
Here, under this dark sycamore, and view
These plots of cottage-ground, these orchard-tufts,
Which at this season, with their unripe fruits,
Are clad in one green hue, and lose themselves
'Mid groves and copses. Once again I see
These hedge-rows, hardly hedge-rows, little lines
Of sportive wood run wild: these pastoral farms,
Green to the very door; and wreaths of smoke
Sent up, in silence, from among the trees!
With some uncertain notice, as might seem
Of vagrant dwellers in the houseless woods,
Or of some Hermit's cave, where by his fire
The Hermit sits alone.

          These beauteous forms,
Through a long absence, have not been to me
As is a landscape to a blind man's eye:
But oft, in lonely rooms, and 'mid the din
Of towns and cities, I have owed to them
In hours of weariness, sensations sweet,
Felt in the blood, and felt along the heart;
And passing even into my purer mind,
With tranquil restoration:—feelings too
Of unremembered pleasure: such, perhaps,
As have no slight or trivial influence
On that best portion of a good man's life,
His little, nameless, unremembered, acts
Of kindness and of love. Nor less, I trust,
To them I may have owed another gift,

---

1   Wordsworth had first visited the Wye Valley in Monmouthshire, Wales, in August 1793.

Of aspect more sublime; that blessed mood
In which the burthen of the mystery,
In which the heavy and the weary weight
Of all this unintelligible world,
Is lightened:—that serene and blessed mood,
In which the affections gently lead us on,—
Until, the breath of this corporeal frame
And even the motion of our human blood
Almost suspended, we are laid asleep
In body, and become a living soul:
While with an eye made quiet by the power
Of harmony, and the deep power of joy,
We see into the life of things.
                                    If this
Be but a vain belief, yet, oh! how oft—
In darkness and amid the many shapes
Of joyless daylight; when the fretful stir
Unprofitable, and the fever of the world,
Have hung upon the beatings of my heart—
How oft, in spirit, have I turned to thee,
O sylvan Wye! thou wanderer thro' the woods,
How often has my spirit turned to thee!

    And now, with gleams of half-extinguished thought,
With many recognitions dim and faint,
And somewhat of a sad perplexity,
The picture of the mind revives again:
While here I stand, not only with the sense
Of present pleasure, but with pleasing thoughts
That in this moment there is life and food
For future years. And so I dare to hope,
Though changed, no doubt, from what I was when first
I came among these hills; when like a roe
I bounded o'er the mountains, by the sides
Of the deep rivers, and the lonely streams,
Wherever nature led: more like a man
Flying from something that he dreads than one
Who sought the thing he loved. For nature then
(The coarser pleasures of my boyish days,
And their glad animal movements all gone by)
To me was all in all.—I cannot paint
What then I was. The sounding cataract
Haunted me like a passion: the tall rock,
The mountain, and the deep and gloomy wood,
Their colours and their forms, were then to me
An appetite; a feeling and a love,
That had no need of a remoter charm,
By thought supplied, nor any interest
Unborrowed from the eye.—That time is past,
And all its aching joys are now no more,
And all its dizzy raptures. Not for this

Faint I, nor mourn nor murmur; other gifts
Have followed; for such loss, I would believe,
Abundant recompense. For I have learned
To look on nature, not as in the hour
Of thoughtless youth; but hearing oftentimes
The still, sad music of humanity,
Nor harsh nor grating, though of ample power
To chasten and subdue. And I have felt
A presence that disturbs me with the joy
Of elevated thoughts; a sense sublime
Of something far more deeply interfused,
Whose dwelling is the light of setting suns,
And the round ocean and the living air,
And the blue sky, and in the mind of man:
A motion and a spirit, that impels
All thinking things, all objects of all thought,
And rolls through all things. Therefore am I still
A lover of the meadows and the woods,
And mountains; and of all that we behold
From this green earth; of all the mighty world
Of eye, and ear,—both what they half create,
And what perceive; well pleased to recognise
In nature and the language of the sense
The anchor of my purest thoughts, the nurse
The guide, the guardian of my heart, and soul
Of all my moral being.
                Nor perchance,
If I were not thus taught, should I the more
Suffer my genial spirits[1] to decay:
For thou art with me here upon the banks
Of this fair river; thou my dearest Friend,[2]
My dear, dear Friend; and in thy voice I catch
The language of my former heart, and read
My former pleasures in the shooting lights
Of thy wild eyes. Oh! yet a little while
May I behold in thee what I was once,
My dear, dear Sister! and this prayer I make,
Knowing that Nature never did betray
The heart that loved her; 'tis her privilege,
Through all the years of this our life, to lead
From joy to joy: for she can so inform
The mind that is within us, so impress
With quietness and beauty, and so feed
With lofty thoughts, that neither evil tongues,
Rash judgments, nor the sneers of selfish men,
Nor greetings where no kindness is, nor all

---

1   creative powers
2   his sister and constant companion, Dorothy

The dreary intercourse of daily life,
Shall e'er prevail against us, or disturb
Our cheerful faith, that all which we behold
Is full of blessings. Therefore let the moon
Shine on thee in thy solitary walk;
And let the misty mountain-winds be free
To blow against thee: and, in after years,
When these wild ecstasies shall be matured
Into a sober pleasure; when thy mind
Shall be a mansion for all lovely forms,
Thy memory be as a dwelling-place
For all sweet sounds and harmonies; oh! then,
If solitude, or fear, or pain, or grief,
Should be thy portion, with what healing thoughts
Of tender joy wilt thou remember me,
And these my exhortations! Nor, perchance—
If I should be where I no more can hear
Thy voice, nor catch from thy wild eyes these gleams
Of past existence—wilt thou then forget
That on the banks of this delightful stream
We stood together; and that I, so long
A worshipper of Nature, hither came
Unwearied in that service: rather say
With warmer love—oh! with far deeper zeal
Of holier love. Nor wilt thou then forget,
That after many wanderings, many years
Of absence, these steep woods and lofty cliffs,
And this green pastoral landscape, were to me
More dear, both for themselves and for thy sake!

Strange fits of passion have I known

Strange fits of passion have I known:
And I will dare to tell,
But in the Lover's ear alone,
What once to me befell

When she I loved looked every day
Fresh as a rose in June,
I to her cottage bent my way,
Beneath an evening-moon.

Upon the moon I fixed my eye,
All over the wide lea;
With quickening pace my horse drew nigh
Those paths so dear to me.

And now we reached the orchard-plot;
And, as we climbed the hill,

The sinking moon to Lucy's cot
Came near, and nearer still.

In one of those sweet dreams I slept,
Kind Nature's gentlest boon!
And all the while my eyes I kept
On the descending moon.

My horse moved on; hoof after hoof
He raised, and never stopped:
When down behind the cottage roof,
At once, the bright moon dropped.

What fond and wayward thoughts will slide
Into a Lover's head!
"O mercy!" to myself I cried,
"If Lucy should be dead!"

She dwelt among the untrodden ways

She dwelt among the untrodden ways
        Beside the springs of Dove,[1]
A Maid whom there were none to praise
        And very few to love:

A violet by a mossy stone
        Half hidden from the eye!
—Fair as a star, when only one
        Is shining in the sky.

She lived unknown, and few could know
        When Lucy ceased to be;
But she is in her grave, and, oh,
        The difference to me!

I travelled among unknown men

I travelled among unknown men,
        In lands beyond the sea;
Nor, England! did I know till then
        What love I bore to thee.

'Tis past, that melancholy dream!
        Nor will I quit thy shore

---

1   a name given to several rivers in England, one of which is in the Lake District

A second time; for still I seem
　To love thee more and more.

Among thy mountains did I feel
　The joy of my desire;
And she I cherished turned her wheel
　Beside an English fire.

Thy mornings showed, thy nights concealed,
　The bowers where Lucy played;
And thine too is the last green field
　That Lucy's eyes surveyed.

Three years she grew in sun and shower

Three years she grew in sun and shower,
Then Nature said, "A lovelier flower
On earth was never sown;
This Child I to myself will take;
She shall be mine, and I will make
A Lady of my own.

"Myself will to my darling be
Both law and impulse: and with me
The Girl, in rock and plain,
In earth and heaven, in glade and bower,
Shall feel an overseeing power
To kindle or restrain.

"She shall be sportive as the fawn
That wild with glee across the lawn
Or up the mountain springs;
And hers shall be the breathing balm,
And hers the silence and the calm
Of mute insensate things.

"The floating-clouds their state shall lend
To her; for her the willow bend;
Nor shall she fail to see
Even in the motions of the Storm
Grace that shall mould the Maiden's form
By silent sympathy.

"The stars of midnight shall be dear
To her; and she shall lean her ear
In many a secret place
Where rivulets dance their wayward round,
And beauty born of murmuring sound
Shall pass into her face.

"And vital feelings of delight
Shall rear her form to stately height,
Her virgin bosom swell;
Such thoughts to Lucy I will give
While she and I together live
Here in this happy dell."

Thus Nature spake—The work was done—
How soon my Lucy's race was run!
She died, and left to me
This heath, this calm, and quiet scene;
The memory of what has been,
And never more will be.

A slumber did my spirit seal

A slumber did my spirit seal;
  I had no human fears:
She seemed a thing that could not feel
  The touch of earthly years.

No motion has she now, no force;
  She neither hears nor sees;
Rolled round in earth's diurnal[1] course,
  With rocks, and stones, and trees.

a nature poet -
this poem is in praise of the city (London)

Composed Upon Westminster Bridge, September 3, 1802

Italian Sonnet

Earth has not anything to show more fair: *a*
Dull would he be of soul who could pass by *b*
A sight so touching in its majesty: *b*
This City now doth, like a garment, wear *a*
The beauty of the morning; silent, bare, *a*
Ships, towers, domes, theatres, and temples lie *b*
Open unto the fields, and to the sky; *b*
All bright and glittering in the smokeless air. *a*
everything is soaked w/ the sunlight
Never did sun more beautifully steep *c*
In his first splendour, valley, rock, or hill; *d*
Ne'er saw I, never felt, a calm so deep! *c*
The river glideth at his own sweet will: *d*
Dear God! the very houses seem asleep; *c*
And all that mighty heart is lying still! *d*

---

1   daily

His illegitimate child

It is a beauteous evening, calm and free

It is a beauteous evening, calm and free, *Nature reflection*
The holy time is quiet as a Nun
Breathless with adoration; the broad sun
Is sinking down in its tranquillity;
The gentleness of heaven broods o'er the Sea:
Listen! the mighty Being is awake,
And doth with his eternal motion make
A sound like thunder—everlastingly. *← archaic diction*
Dear Child! dear Girl![1] that walkest with me here, *Who walk →*
If thou appear untouched by solemn thought, *← She doesn't*
Thy nature is not therefore less divine: *see to think about serious things*
Thou liest in Abraham's bosom all the year;
And worshipp'st at the Temple's inner shrine,
God being with thee when we know it not.

Abraham of the Bible to be very close to God.

London, 1802

(only)

Milton! thou shouldst be living at this hour: *last sonnet writer*
England hath need of thee: she is a fen
Of stagnant waters: altar, sword, and pen, *1660-1790*
Fireside, the heroic wealth of hall and bower,
Have forfeited their ancient English dower
Of inward happiness. We are selfish men;
Oh! raise us up, return to us again;
And give us manners, virtue, freedom, power.
Thy soul was like a Star, and dwelt apart;
Thou hadst a voice whose sound was like the sea:
Pure as the naked heavens, majestic, free,
So didst thou travel on life's common way,
In cheerful godliness; and yet thy heart
The lowliest duties on herself did lay. *Now the sonnet is becoming more popular.*

Milton

Nuns fret not at their convent's narrow room

similar to the Italian sonnet

Nuns fret not at their convent's narrow room; *a*
And hermits are contented with their cells; *b*
And students with their pensive citadels; *b*
Maids at the wheel, the weaver at his loom, *a*
Sit blithe and happy; bees that soar for bloom, *a*
High as the highest Peak of Furness-fells, *b*
Will murmur by the hour in foxglove bells; *b*
In truth the prison, unto which we doom *a*

being contd
st something simple (Nuns, hermits) reinforced
style & idea complex poetical division

fortress of learning
student can go to the library like the library to think & study

---

1   Caroline Vallon, Wordsworth's child by his former lover Annette Vallon. The occasion
was a visit he paid to France in 1802.

Experiment w/ a sonnet.

Ourselves, no prison is: and hence for me,
In sundry moods, 'twas pastime to be bound
Within the Sonnet's scanty plot of ground;
Pleased if some Souls (for such there needs must be)
Who have felt the weight of too much liberty,
Should find brief solace there, as I have found.

Ode: Intimations of Immortality

From Recollections of Early Childhood

The child is father of the Man;
And I could wish my days to be
Bound each to each with natural piety.[1]

I

There was a time when meadow, grove, and stream,
The earth, and every common sight,
    To me did seem
    Apparelled in celestial light,
The glory and the freshness of a dream.
It is not now as it hath been of yore;—
    Turn wheresoe'er I may,
    By night or day,
The things which I have seen I now can see no more.

II

    The Rainbow comes and goes,
    And lovely is the Rose,
    The Moon doth with delight
Look round her when the heavens are bare;
    Waters on a starry night
    Are beautiful and fair;
  The sunshine is a glorious birth;
  But yet I know, where'er I go,
That there hath past away a glory from the earth.

III

Now, while the birds thus sing a joyous song,
  And while the young lambs bound
    As to the tabor's sound,
To me alone there came a thought of grief:

---

1   These lines are from Wordsworth's poem "My heart leaps up."

A timely utterance gave that thought relief,
    And I again am strong:
The cataracts blow their trumpets from the steep;
No more shall grief of mine the season wrong;
I hear the Echoes through the mountains throng,
The Winds come to me from the fields of sleep,
    And all the earth is gay;
        Land and sea
    Give themselves up to jollity,
      And with the heart of May
Doth every Beast keep holiday;—
      Thou Child of Joy
Shout round me, let me hear thy shouts, thou happy Shep-
herd-boy!

IV

Ye blessèd Creatures, I have heard the call
   Ye to each other make; I see
The heavens laugh with you in your jubilee;
    My heart is at your festival,
    My head hath its coronal,
The fulness of your bliss, I feel—I feel it all.
    Oh evil day! if I were sullen
    While Earth herself is adorning,
      This sweet May-morning,
    And the Children are culling
      On every side,
    In a thousand valleys far and wide,
    Fresh flowers; while the sun shines warm,
And the Babe leaps up on his Mother's arm:—
    I hear, I hear, with joy I hear!
    —But there's a Tree, of many, one,
A single Field which I have looked upon,
Both of them speak of something that is gone:
    The Pansy at my feet
    Doth the same tale repeat:
Whither is fled the visionary gleam?
Where is it now, the glory and the dream?

V

Our birth is but a sleep and a forgetting:[1]
The Soul that rises with us, our life's Star,

---

1   Wordsworth here develops a neoplatonic notion that the immortal soul is separated from
eternal truths by its birth into matter, and gradually loses contact with "the vision
splendid."

Hath had elsewhere its setting,
   And cometh from afar:
Not in entire forgetfulness,
And not in utter nakedness,
But trailing clouds of glory do we come
   From God, who is our home:
Heaven lies about us in our infancy!
Shades of the prison-house begin to close
   Upon the growing Boy,
      But He
Beholds the light, and whence it flows,
   He sees it in his joy;
The Youth, who daily farther from the east
   Must travel, still is Nature's Priest,
   And by the vision splendid
   Is on his way attended;
At length the Man perceives it die away,
And fade into the light of common day.

VI

Earth fills her lap with pleasures of her own;
Yearnings she hath in her own natural kind,
And, even with something of a Mother's mind,
   And no unworthy aim,
   The homely Nurse doth all she can
To make her Foster-child, her Inmate Man,
   Forget the glories he hath known,
And that imperial palace whence he came.

VII

Behold the Child among his new-born blisses,
A six years' Darling of a pigmy size!
See, where 'mid work of his own hand he lies,
Frettied by sallies of his mother's kisses,
With light upon him from his father's eyes!
See, at his feet, some little plan or chart,
Some fragment from his dream of human life,
Shaped by himself with newly-learned art;
   A wedding or a festival,
   A mourning or a funeral;
    And this hath now his heart,
   And unto this he frames his song:
    Then will he fit his tongue
To dialogues of business, love, or strife;
   But it will not be long
   Ere this be thrown aside,
   And with new joy and pride
The little Actor cons another part;

Filling from time to time his "humorous stage"[1]
With all the Persons, down to palsied Age,
That Life brings with her in her equipage;
    As if his whole vocation
    Were endless imitation.

VIII

Thou, whose exterior semblance doth belie
    Thy soul's immensity;
Thou best Philosopher, who yet dost keep
Thy heritage, thou Eye among the blind,
That, deaf and silent, read'st the eternal deep,
Haunted for ever by the eternal mind,—
    Mighty Prophet! Seer blest!
    On whom those truths do rest,
Which we are toiling all our lives to find,
In darkness lost, the darkness of the grave;
Thou, over whom thy Immortality
Broods like the Day, a Master o'er a Slave,
A Presence which is not to be put by;
Thou little Child, yet glorious in the might
Of heaven-born freedom on thy being's height,
Why with such earnest pains dost thou provoke
The years to bring the inevitable yoke,
Thus blindly with thy blessedness at strife?
Full soon thy Soul shall have her earthly freight,
And custom lie upon thee with a weight,
Heavy as frost, and deep almost as life!

IX

    O joy! that in our embers
    Is something that doth live,
    That nature yet remembers
    What was so fugitive!
The thought of our past years in me doth breed
Perpetual benediction: not indeed
For that which is most worthy to be blest;
Delight and liberty, the simple creed
Of Childhood, whether busy or at rest,
With new-fledged hope still fluttering in his breast:—
    Not for these I raise
    The song of thanks and praise;
    But for those obstinate questionings
    Of sense and outward things,

---

1   from Samuel Daniel's dedicatory sonnet to *Musophilus* (1599)

Fallings from us, vanishings;
Blank misgivings of a Creature
Moving about in worlds not realised,
High instincts before which our mortal Nature
Did tremble like a guilty Thing surprised:
But for those first affections,
Those shadowy recollections,
Which, be they what they may,
Are yet the fountain light of all our day,
Are yet a master light of all our seeing;
Uphold us, cherish, and have power to make
Our noisy years seem moments in the being
Of the eternal Silence: truths that wake,
To perish never;
Which neither listlessness, nor mad endeavour,
Nor Man nor Boy,
Nor all that is at enmity with joy,
Can utterly abolish or destroy!
Hence in a season of calm weather
Though inland far we be,
Our Souls have sight of that immortal sea
Which brought us hither,
Can in a moment travel thither,
And see the Children sport upon the shore,
And hear the mighty waters rolling evermore.

X

Then sing, ye Birds, sing, sing a joyous song!
And let the young Lambs bound
As to the tabor's sound!
We in thought will join your throng,
Ye that pipe and ye that play,
Ye that through your hearts to-day
Feel the gladness of the May!
What though the radiance which was once so bright
Be now for ever taken from my sight,
Though nothing can bring back the hour
Of splendour in the grass, of glory in the flower;
We will grieve not, rather find
Strength in what remains behind;
In the primal sympathy
Which having been must ever be;
In the soothing thoughts that spring
Out of human suffering;
In the faith that looks through death,
In years that bring the philosophic mind.

XI

And O, ye Fountains, Meadows, Hills, and Groves,
Forebode not any severing of our loves!
Yet in my heart of hearts I feel your might;
I only have relinquished one delight
To live beneath your more habitual sway.
I love the Brooks which down their channels fret,
Even more than when I tripped lightly as they;
The innocent brightness of a new-born Day
      Is lovely yet;
The Clouds that gather round the setting sun
Do take a sober colouring from an eye
That hath kept watch o'er man's mortality;
Another race hath been, and other palms are won.
Thanks to the human heart by which we live,
Thanks to its tenderness, its joys, and fears,
To me the meanest flower that blows can give
Thoughts that do often lie too deep for tears.

Samuel Taylor Coleridge

(1772–1834)

Kubla Khan[1]

Or, a Vision in a Dream. A Fragment.[2]

In Xanadu did Kubla Khan
A stately pleasure-dome decree:
Where Alph,[3] the sacred river, ran
Through caverns measureless to man
    Down to a sunless sea.
So twice five miles of fertile ground
With walls and towers were girdled round:
And there were gardens bright with sinuous rills,
Where blossomed many an incense-bearing tree;
And here were forests ancient as the hills,
Enfolding sunny spots of greenery.

But oh! that deep romantic chasm which slanted
Down the green hill athwart a cedarn cover!
A savage place! as holy and enchanted
As e'er beneath a waning moon was haunted
By woman wailing for her demon-lover!
And from this chasm, with ceaseless turmoil seething,
As if this earth in fast thick pants were breathing,
A mighty fountain momently[4] was forced:
Amid whose swift half-intermitted burst
Huge fragments vaulted like rebounding hail,
Or chaffy grain beneath the thresher's flail:
And 'mid these dancing rocks at once and ever
It flung up momently the sacred river.
Five miles meandering with a mazy motion
Through wood and dale the sacred river ran,
Then reached the caverns measureless to man,
And sank in tumult to a lifeless ocean:
And 'mid this tumult Kubla heard from far
Ancestral voices prophesying war!
    The shadow of the dome of pleasure
    Floated midway on the waves;
    Where was heard the mingled measure
    From the fountain and the caves.

---

1   The historical Kublai Khan (c.1215-1294), a descendant of Gengis Khan, founded the
    Mongol dynasty in China.

2   According to Coleridge, this poem resulted from a drug-induced dream, which Coleridge
    was prevented from recapturing in its entirety because of an unwanted caller ("a person
    on business from Porlock"). Many of the details were evidently suggested by Coleridge's
    reading of Purchas his Pilgrimage, by Samuel Purchas (1613).

3   suggested by the Greek river Alpheus

4   at every moment

It was a miracle of rare device,   35
A sunny pleasure-dome with caves of ice!

    A damsel with a dulcimer
    In a vision once I saw:
    It was an Abyssinian maid,
    And on her dulcimer she played,
    Singing of Mount Abora.[1]
    Could I revive within me
    Her symphony and song,
    To such a deep delight 'twould win me,
That with music loud and long,
I would build that dome in air,
That sunny dome! those caves of ice!
And all who heard should see them there,
And all should cry, Beware! Beware!
His flashing eyes, his floating hair!
Weave a circle round him thrice,
And close your eyes with holy dread,
For he on honey-dew hath fed,
And drunk the milk of Paradise.

Frost At Midnight

The Frost performs its secret ministry,
Unhelped by any wind. The owlet's cry
Came loud—and hark, again! loud as before.
The inmates of my cottage, all at rest,
Have left me to that solitude, which suits
Abstruser musings: save that at my side
My cradled infant[2] slumbers peacefully.
'Tis calm indeed! so calm, that it disturbs
And vexes meditation with its strange
And extreme silentness. Sea, hill, and wood,
This populous village! Sea, and hill, and wood,
With all the numberless goings-on of life,
Inaudible as dreams! the thin blue flame
Lies on my low-burnt fire, and quivers not;
Only that film, which fluttered on the grate,[3]
Still flutters there, the sole unquiet thing.
Methinks, its motion in this hush of nature
Gives it dim sympathies with me who live,

---

1   possibly suggested by Mount Amara in Abyssinia, mentioned by Milton in *Paradise Lost*
    IV.28
2   Coleridge's son Hartley
3   Ash or soot fluttering on the grate: "In all parts of the kingdom these films are called
    strangers and supposed to portend the arrival of some absent friend" (Coleridge's note).

Making it a companionable form,
Whose puny flaps and freaks the idling Spirit
By its own moods interprets, every where
Echo or mirror seeking of itself,
And makes a toy of Thought.

                            But O! how oft,
How oft, at school,[1] with most believing mind,
Presageful, have I gazed upon the bars,
To watch that fluttering *stranger*! and as oft
With unclosed lids, already had I dreamt
Of my sweet birth-place,[2] and the old church-tower,
Whose bells, the poor man's only music, rang
From morn to evening, all the hot Fair-day,
So sweetly, that they stirred and haunted me
With a wild pleasure, falling on mine ear
Most like articulate sounds of things to come!
So gazed I, till the soothing things, I dreamt,
Lulled me to sleep, and sleep prolonged my dreams!
And so I brooded all the following morn,
Awed by the stern preceptor's face, mine eye
Fixed with mock study on my swimming book:
Save if the door half opened, and I snatched
A hasty glance, and still my heart leaped up,
For still I hoped to see the *stranger's* face,
Townsman, or aunt, or sister more beloved,
My play-mate when we both were clothed alike!

    Dear Babe, that sleepest cradled by my side,
Whose gentle breathings, heard in this deep calm,
Fill up the interspersed vacancies
And momentary pauses of the thought!
My babe so beautiful! it thrills my heart
With tender gladness, thus to look at thee,
And think that thou shalt learn far other lore,
And in far other scenes! For I was reared
In the great city, pent 'mid cloisters dim,
And saw nought lovely but the sky and stars.
But *thou*, my babe! shalt wander like a breeze
By lakes and sandy shores, beneath the crags
Of ancient mountain, and beneath the clouds,
Which image in their bulk both lakes and shores
And mountain crags: so shalt thou see and hear
The lovely shapes and sounds intelligible
Of that eternal language, which thy God
Utters, who from eternity doth teach

---

1   From the age of nine, Coleridge attended Christ's Hospital, London.
2   Ottery St. Mary, Devonshire

Himself in all, and all things in himself.
Great universal Teacher! he shall mould
Thy spirit, and by giving make it ask.

    Therefore all seasons shall be sweet to thee,
Whether the summer clothe the general earth
With greenness, or the redbreast sit and sing
Betwixt the tufts of snow on the bare branch
Of mossy apple-tree, while the nigh thatch
Smokes in the sun-thaw; whether the eave-drops fall
Heard only in the trances of the blast,
Or if the secret ministry of frost
Shall hang them up in silent icicles,
Quietly shining to the quiet Moon.

Dejection: An Ode

Late, late yestreen[1] I saw the new Moon,
With the old Moon in her arms;
And I fear, I fear, my Master dear!
We shall have a deadly storm.
       Ballad of Sir Patrick Spence

I

Well! If the Bard was weather-wise, who made
  The grand old ballad of Sir Patrick Spence,
  This night, so tranquil now, will not go hence
Unroused by winds, that ply a busier trade
Than those which mould yon cloud in lazy flakes,
Or the dull sobbing draft, that moans and rakes
Upon the strings of this Aeolian lute,[2]
    Which better far were mute.
  For lo! the New-moon winter-bright!
  And overspread with phantom light,
  (With swimming phantom light o'erspread
  But rimmed and circled by a silver thread)
I see the old Moon in her lap, foretelling
  The coming-on of rain and squally blast.
And oh! that even now the gust were swelling,
  And the slant night-shower driving loud and fast!
Those sounds which oft have raised me, whilst they awed,
    And sent my soul abroad,
Might now perhaps their wonted impulse give,
Might startle this dull pain, and make it move and live!

---

1   yesterday evening
2   a stringed instrument that sounds notes when played upon by the wind

II

A grief without a pang, void, dark, and drear,
A stifled, drowsy, unimpassioned grief,
Which finds no natural outlet, no relief,
   In word, or sigh, or tear—
O Lady![1] in this wan and heartless mood,
To other thoughts by yonder throstle[2] wooed,
  All this long eve, so balmy and serene,
Have I been gazing on the western sky,
  And its peculiar tint of yellow green:
And still I gaze—and with how blank an eye!
And those thin clouds above, in flakes and bars,
That give away their motion to the stars;
Those stars, that glide behind them or between,
Now sparkling, now bedimmed, but always seen:
Yon crescent Moon, as fixed as if it grew
In its own cloudless, starless lake of blue;
I see them all so excellently fair,
I see, not feel, how beautiful they are!

III

   My genial spirits[3] fail;
   And what can these avail
To lift the smothering weight from off my breast?
   It were a vain endeavour,
   Though I should gaze forever
On that green light that lingers in the west:
I may not hope from outward forms to win
The passion and the life, whose fountains are within.

IV

O Lady! we receive but what we give,
And in our life alone does Nature live:
Ours is her wedding garment, ours her shroud!
  And would we aught behold, of higher worth,
Than that inanimate cold world allowed
To the poor loveless ever-anxious crowd,
  Ah! from the soul itself must issue forth
A light, a glory, a fair luminous cloud
   Enveloping the Earth—
And from the soul itself must there be sent

---

1   Coleridge originally addressed his poem to Sara Hutchinson, the sister of Mary
     Hutchinson, Wordsworth's fiancée.
2   song-thrush
3   native powers

A sweet and potent voice, of its own birth,
Of all sweet sounds the life and element!

V

O pure of heart! thou needest not ask of me
What this strong music in the soul may be!
What, and wherein it doth exist,
This light, this glory, this fair luminous mist,
This beautiful and beauty-making power.
Joy, virtuous Lady! Joy that ne'er was given,
Save to the pure, and in their purest hour,
Life, and Life's effluence, cloud at once and shower,
Joy, Lady! is the spirit and the power,
Which, wedding Nature to us, gives in dower
A new Earth and new Heaven,
Undreamt of by the sensual and the proud—
Joy is the sweet voice, Joy the luminous cloud—
We in ourselves rejoice!
And thence flows all that charms or ear or sight,
All melodies the echoes of that voice,
All colours a suffusion from that light.

VI

There was a time when, though my path was rough,
This joy within me dallied with distress,
And all misfortunes were but as the stuff
Whence Fancy made me dreams of happiness:
For hope grew round me, like the twining vine,
And fruits, and foliage, not my own, seemed mine.
But now afflictions bow me down to earth:
Nor care I that they rob me of my mirth;
But oh! each visitation
Suspends what nature gave me at my birth,
My shaping spirit of Imagination.
For not to think of what I needs must feel,
But to be still and patient, all I can;
And haply by abstruse research to steal
From my own nature all the natural man—
This was my sole resource, my only plan:
Till that which suits a part infects the whole,
And now is almost grown the habit of my soul.

VII

Hence, viper thoughts, that coil around my mind,
Reality's dark dream!
I turn from you, and listen to the wind,
Which long has raved unnoticed. What a scream
Of agony by torture lengthened out

That lute sent forth! Thou Wind, that rav'st without,
  Bare crag, or mountain tairn,[1] or blasted tree,
Or pine-grove whither woodman never clomb,
Or lonely house, long held the witches' home,
  Methinks were fitter instruments for thee,
Mad Lutanist! who in this month of showers,
Of dark-brown gardens, and of peeping flowers,
Makest Devils' yule, with worse than wintry song,
The blossoms, buds, and timorous leaves among.
  Thou Actor, perfect in all tragic sounds!
Thou mighty Poet, e'en to frenzy bold!
    What tellest thou now about?
  'Tis of the rushing of an host in rout,
With groans, of trampled men, with smarting wounds—
At once they groan with pain, and shudder with the cold!
But hush! there is a pause of deepest silence!
  And all that noise, as of a rushing crowd,
With groans, and tremulous shudderings—all is over—
  It tells another tale, with sounds less deep and loud!
    A tale of less affright,
    And tempered with delight,
As Otway's[2] self had framed the tender lay,—
    'Tis of a little child
    Upon a lonesome wild,
Not far from home, but she hath lost her way:
And now moans low in bitter grief and fear,
And now screams loud, and hopes to make her mother hear.

VIII

'Tis midnight, but small thoughts have I of sleep:
Full seldom may my friend such vigils keep!
Visit her, gentle Sleep! with wings of healing,
  And may this storm be but a mountain-birth,
May all the stars hang bright above her dwelling,
  Silent as though they watched the sleeping Earth!
    With light heart may she rise,
    Gay fancy, cheerful eyes,
  Joy lift her spirit, joy attune her voice;
To her may all things live, from pole to pole,
Their life the eddying of her living soul!
  O simple spirit, guided from above,
Dear Lady! friend devoutest of my choice,
Thus mayest thou ever, evermore rejoice.

---

1   small mountain lake
2   Thomas Otway (1652-85), dramatist

George Gordon, Lord Byron

(1788–1824)

She Walks In Beauty

I

She walks in beauty, like the night
Of cloudless climes and starry skies;
And all that's best of dark and bright
Meet in her aspect and her eyes:
Thus mellow'd to that tender light
Which heaven to gaudy day denies.

II

One shade the more, one ray the less,
Had half impair'd the nameless grace
Which waves in every raven tress,
Or softly lightens o'er her face;
Where thoughts serenely sweet express
How pure, how dear their dwelling-place.

III

And on that cheek, and o'er that brow,
So soft, so calm, yet eloquent,
The smiles that win, the tints that glow,
But tell of days in goodness spent,
A mind at peace with all below,
A heart whose love is innocent!

So We'll Go No More A-Roving

1

So we'll go no more a-roving
    So late into the night,
Though the heart be still as loving,
    And the moon be still as bright.

2

For the sword outwears its sheath,
    And the soul wears out the breast,
And the heart must pause to breathe,
    And Love itself have rest.

3

Though the night was made for loving,
And the day returns too soon,
Yet we'll go no more a-roving
By the light of the moon.

Stanzas written on the road between Florence and Pisa

Oh, talk not to me of a name great in story;
The days of our youth are the days of our glory;
And the myrtle and ivy of sweet two-and-twenty
Are worth all your laurels, though ever so plenty.

What are garlands and crowns to the brow that is wrinkled?
'Tis but as a dead flower with May-dew besprinkled.
Then away with all such from the head that is hoary!
What care I for the wreaths that can *only* give glory!

Oh Fame!—if I e'er took delight in thy praises,
'Twas less for the sake of thy high-sounding phrases,
Than to see the bright eyes of the dear one discover,
She thought that I was not unworthy to love her.

There chiefly I sought thee, *there* only I found thee;
Her glance was the best of the rays that surround thee;
When it sparkled o'er aught that was bright in my story,
I knew it was love, and I felt it was glory.

from: *Childe Harold's Pilgrimage*

(canto III, stanzas 68–75)

LXVIII

Lake Leman[1] woos me with its crystal face,
The mirror where the stars and mountains view
The stillness of their aspect in each trace
Its clear depth yields of their far height and hue:
There is too much of man here, to look through
With a fit mind the might which I behold;
But soon in me shall Loneliness renew
Thoughts hid, but not less cherish'd than of old,
Ere mingling with the herd had penn'd me in their fold.

---

1   Lake Geneva in Switzerland

LXIX

To fly from, need not be to hate, mankind:
All are not fit with them to stir and toil,
Nor is it discontent to keep the mind
Deep in its fountain, lest it overboil
In the hot throng, where we become the spoil
Of our infection, till too late and long
We may deplore and struggle with the coil,[1]
In wretched interchange of wrong for wrong
Midst a contentious world, striving where none are strong.

LXX

There, in a moment, we may plunge our years
In fatal penitence, and in the blight
Of our own soul turn all our blood to tears,
And colour things to come with hues of Night;
The race of life becomes a hopeless flight
To those that walk in darkness: on the sea,
The boldest steer but where their ports invite,
But there are wanderers o'er Eternity
Whose bark drives on and on, and anchor'd ne'er shall be.

LXXI

Is it not better, then, to be alone,
And love Earth only for its earthly sake?
By the blue rushing of the arrowy Rhône,[2]
Or the pure bosom of its nursing lake,
Which feeds it as a mother who doth make
A fair but froward infant her own care,
Kissing its cries away as these awake;—
Is it not better thus our lives to wear,
Than join the crushing crowd, doom'd to inflict or bear?

LXXII

I live not in myself, but I become
Portion of that around me; and to me
High mountains are a feeling, but the hum
Of human cities torture: I can see
Nothing to loathe in nature, save to be
A link reluctant in a fleshly chain,
Class'd among creatures, when the soul can flee,

---

1   turmoil
2   the river that flows out of Lake Geneva on its way into France

And with the sky, the peak, the heaving plain
Of ocean, or the stars, mingle, and not in vain.

LXXIII

And thus I am absorb'd, and this is life:
I look upon the peopled desert past,
As on a place of agony and strife,
Where, for some sin, to sorrow I was cast,
To act and suffer, but remount at last
With a fresh pinion; which I feel to spring,
Though young, yet waxing vigorous, as the blast
Which it would cope with, on delighted wing,
Spurning the clay-cold bonds which round our being cling.

LXXIV

And when, at length, the mind shall be all free
From what it hates in this degraded form,
Reft of its carnal life, save what shall be
Existent happier in the fly and worm,—
When elements to elements conform,
And dust is as it should be, shall I not
Feel all I see, less dazzling, but more warm?
The bodiless thought? the Spirit of each spot?
Of which, even now, I share at times the immortal lot?

LXXV

Are not the mountains, waves, and skies, a part
Of me and of my soul, as I of them?
Is not the love of these deep in my heart
With a pure passion? should I not contemn
All objects, if compared with these? and stem
A tide of suffering, rather than forego
Such feelings for the hard and worldly phlegm
Of those whose eyes are only turn'd below,
Gazing upon the ground, with thoughts which dare not glow?

* * *

The Prisoner of Chillon[1]

I

My hair is grey, but not with years,
    Nor grew it white,
    In a single night,
As men's have grown from sudden fears:
My limbs are bow'd, though not with toil,
But rusted with a vile repose,
For they have been a dungeon's spoil,
And mine has been the fate of those
To whom the goodly earth and air
Are bann'd, and barr'd—forbidden fare;
But this was for my father's faith
I suffer'd chains and courted death;
That father perish'd at the stake
For tenets he would not forsake;
And for the same his lineal race
In darkness found a dwelling-place;
We were seven[2]—who now are one,
Six in youth and one in age,
Finish'd as they had begun,
Proud of Persecution's rage;
One in fire, and two in field,
Their belief with blood have seal'd:
Dying as their father died,
For the God their foes denied;—
Three were in a dungeon cast,
Of whom this wreck is left the last.

II

There are seven pillars of Gothic mould,
In Chillon's dungeons deep and old,
There are seven columns massy and grey,
Dim with a dull imprison'd ray,
A sunbeam which hath lost its way,
And through the crevice and the cleft
Of the thick wall is fallen and left:
Creeping o'er the floor so damp,
Like a marsh's meteor lamp:[3]
And in each pillar there is a ring,

---

1   The poem was written in 1816 after Byron had visited the Castle of Chillon by Lake Geneva. It is based on the story of François Bonivard (1496-1570), a priest imprisoned for six years in Chillon because of his opposition to the tyranny of Duke Charles III of Savoy.
2   The historical Bonivard had only two brothers, who did not accompany him to prison.
3   a will o' the wisp; the light caused by marsh gas

And in each ring there is a chain;
That iron is a cankering thing,
For in these limbs its teeth remain,
With marks that will not wear away,
Till I have done with this new day,
Which now is painful to these eyes,
Which have not seen the sun so rise
For years—I cannot count them o'er,
I lost their long and heavy score
When my last brother droop'd and died,
And I lay living by his side.

III

They chained us each to a column stone,
And we were three—yet, each alone;
We could not move a single pace,
We could not see each other's face,
But with that pale and livid light
That made us strangers in our sight:
And thus together—yet apart,
Fetter'd in hand, but join'd in heart,
'Twas still some solace, in the dearth
Of the pure elements of earth,
To hearken to each other's speech,
And each turn comforter to each
With some new hope or legend old,
Or song heroically bold;
But even these at length grew cold.
Our voices took a dreary tone,
An echo of the dungeon stone,
A grating sound—not full and free
As they of yore were wont to be, —
It might be fancy—but to me
They never sounded like our own.

IV

I was the eldest of the three,
And to uphold and cheer the rest
I ought to do—and did my best—
And each did well in his degree.
The youngest, whom my father loved,
Because our mother's brow was given
To him—with eyes as blue as heaven,
For him my soul was sorely moved:
And truly might it be distress'd
To see such bird in such a nest;
For he was beautiful as day—
(When day was beautiful to me
As to young eagles being free)—

A polar day, which will not see
A sunset till its summer's gone,
Its sleepless summer of long light,
The snow-clad offspring of the sun:
And thus he was as pure and bright,
And in his natural spirit gay,
With tears for nought but others' ills,
And then they flow'd like mountain rills,
Unless he could assuage the woe
Which he abhorr'd to view below.

V

The other was as pure of mind,
But form'd to combat with his kind;
Strong in his frame, and of a mood
Which 'gainst the world in war had stood,
And perished in the foremost rank
With joy:—but not in chains to pine:
His spirit wither'd with their clank.
I saw it silently decline—
And so perchance in sooth did mine:
But yet I forced it on to cheer
Those relics of a home so dear.
He was a hunter of the hills,
Had follow'd there the deer and wolf;
To him this dungeon was a gulf,
And fetter'd feet the worst of ills.

VI

Lake Leman[1] lies by Chillon's walls:
A thousand feet in depth below
Its massy waters meet and flow;
Thus much the fathom-line was sent
From Chillon's snow-white battlement,
Which round about the wave inthrals:
A double dungeon wall and wave
Have made—and like a living grave.
Below the surface of the lake
The dark vault lies wherein we lay,
We heard it ripple night and day;
Sounding o'er our heads it knocked;
And I have felt the winter's spray
Wash through the bars when winds were high
And wanton in the happy sky;

---

1   Lake Geneva

And then the very rock hath rock'd
And I have felt it shake, unshock'd,
Because I could have smiled to see
The death that would have set me free.

VII

I said my nearer brother pined,
I said his mighty heart declined,
He loathed and put away his food;
It was not that 'twas coarse and rude,
For we were used to hunters' fare,
And for the like had little care:
The milk drawn from the mountain goat
Was changed for water from the moat,
Our bread was such as captives' tears
Have moisten'd many a thousand years,
Since man first pent his fellow men
Like brutes within an iron den;
But what were these to us or him?
These wasted not his heart or limb:
My brother's soul was of that mould
Which in a palace had grown cold,
Had his free breathing been denied
The range of the steep mountain's side;
But why delay the truth?—he died.
I saw, and could not hold his head,
Nor reach his dying hand—nor—dead,—
Though hard I strove, but strove in vain,
To rend and gnash my bonds in twain.
He died—and they unlock'd his chain,
And scoop'd for him a shallow grave
Even from the cold earth of our cave.
I begg'd them, as a boon, to lay
His corse in dust whereon the day
Might shine—it was a foolish thought,
But then within my brain it wrought,
That even in death his freeborn breast
In such a dungeon could not rest.
I might have spared my idle prayer—
They coldly laugh'd—and laid him there:
The flat and turfless earth above
The being we so much did love;
His empty chain above it leant,
Such murder's fitting monument!

VIII

But he, the favourite and the flower,
Most cherish'd since his natal hour,
His mother's image in fair face,

The infant love of all his race,
His martyr'd father's dearest thought,
My latest[1] care, for whom I sought
To hoard my life, that his might be
Less wretched now, and one day free;
He, too, who yet had held untired
A spirit natural or inspired—
He, too, was struck, and day by day
Was wither'd on the stalk away.
Oh, God! it is a fearful thing
To see the human soul take wing
In any shape, in any mood:—
I've seen it rushing forth in blood,
I've seen it on the breaking ocean
Strive with a swoln convulsive motion,
I've seen the sick and ghastly bed
Of Sin delirious with its dread;
But these were horrors—this was woe
Unmix'd with such—but sure and slow:
He faded, and so calm and meek,
So softly worn, so sweetly weak,
So tearless, yet so tender—kind,
And grieved for those he left behind;
With all the while a cheek whose bloom
Was as a mockery of the tomb,
Whose tints as gently sunk away
As a departing rainbow's ray—
An eye of most transparent light,
That almost made the dungeon bright,
And not a word of murmur—not
A groan o'er his untimely lot,—
A little talk of better days,
A little hope my own to raise,
For I was sunk in silence—lost
In this last loss, of all the most;
And then the sighs he would suppress
Of fainting nature's feebleness,
More slowly drawn, grew less and less:
I listen'd, but I could not hear—
I call'd, for I was wild with fear;
I knew 'twas hopeless, but my dread
Would not be thus admonished;
I call'd, and thought I heard a sound—
I burst my chain with one strong bound,
And rush'd to him:—I found him not,
I only stirr'd in this black spot,

---

1   last

I only lived—*I* only drew
The accursed breath of dungeon-dew;
The last—the sole—the dearest link
Between me and the eternal brink,
Which bound me to my failing race,
Was broken in this fatal place.
One on the earth, and one beneath—
My brothers—both had ceased to breathe:
I took that hand which lay so still,
Alas! my own was full as chill;
I had not strength to stir, or strive,
But felt that I was still alive—
A frantic feeling, when we know
That what we love shall ne'er be so.
   I know not why
   I could not die,
I had no earthly hope—but faith,
And that forbade a selfish death.

IX

What next befell me then and there
I know not well—I never knew—
First came the loss of light, and air,
And then of darkness too:
I had no thought, no feeling—none—
Among the stones I stood a stone,
And was, scarce conscious what I wist,
As shrubless crags within the mist;
For all was blank, and bleak, and grey,
It was not night—it was not day,
It was not even the dungeon light,
So hateful to my heavy sight.
But vacancy absorbing space,
And fixedness—without a place;
There were no stars—no earth—no time—
No check—no change—no good—no crime—
But silence, and a stirless breath
Which neither was of life nor death;
A sea of stagnant idleness,
Blind, boundless, mute, and motionless!

X

A light broke in upon my brain,—
It was the carol of a bird;
It ceased, and then it came again,
The sweetest song ear ever heard,
And mine was thankful till my eyes
Ran over with the glad surprise,
And they that moment could not see

I was the mate of misery;
But then by dull degrees came back
My senses to their wonted track,
I saw the dungeon walls and floor
Close slowly round me as before,
I saw the glimmer of the sun
Creeping as it before had done,
But through the crevice where it came
The bird was perch'd, as fond and tame,
And tamer than upon the tree;
A lovely bird, with azure wings,
And song that said a thousand things,
And seem'd to say them all for me!
I never saw its like before,
I ne'er shall see its likeness more:
It seem'd like me to want a mate,
But was not half so desolate.
And it was come to love me when
None lived to love me so again,
And cheering from my dungeon's brink,
Had brought me back to feel and think.
I know not if it late were free,
Or broke its cage to perch on mine,
But knowing well captivity,
Sweet bird! I could not wish for thine!
Or if it were, in winged guise,
A visitant from Paradise;
For—Heaven forgive that thought! the while
Which made me both to weep and smile;
I sometimes deem'd that it might be
My brother's soul come down to me;
But then at last away it flew,
And then 'twas mortal—well I knew,
For he would never thus have flown,
And left me twice so doubly lone,—
Lone—as the corse within its shroud,
Lone—as a solitary cloud.
A single cloud on a sunny day,
While all the rest of heaven is clear,
A frown upon the atmosphere,
That hath no business to appear
When skies are blue, and earth is gay.

XI

A kind of change came in my fate,
My keepers grew compassionate;
I know not what had made them so,
They were inured to sights of woe,
But so it was:—my broken chain
With links unfasten'd did remain,

And it was liberty to stride
Along my cell from side to side,
And up and down, and then athwart,
And tread it over every part;
And round the pillars one by one,
Returning where my walk begun,
Avoiding only, as I trod,
My brothers' graves without a sod;
For if I thought with heedless tread
My step profaned their lowly bed,
My breath came gaspingly and thick,
And my crush'd heart fell blind and sick.

XII

I made a footing in the wall,
It was not therefrom to escape,
For I had buried one and all
Who loved me in a human shape;
And the whole earth would henceforth be
A wider prison unto me;
No child—no sire—no kin had I,
No partner in my misery;
I thought of this, and I was glad,
For thought of them had made me mad;
But I was curious to ascend
To my barr'd windows, and to bend
Once more, upon the mountains high,
The quiet of a loving eye.

XIII

I saw them—and they were the same,
They were not changed like me in frame;
I saw their thousand years of snow
On high—their wide long lake below,
And the blue Rhône[1] in fullest flow;
I heard the torrents leap and gush,
O'er channell'd rock and broken bush;
I saw the white-wall'd distant town,
And whiter sails go skimming down;
And then there was a little isle,
Which in my very face did smile,
The only one in view;
A small green isle, it seem'd no more,
Scarce broader than my dungeon floor,

---

1   the Rhone river, which flows out of Lake Geneva

But in it there were three tall trees,
And o'er it blew the mountain breeze
And by it there were waters flowing,
And on it there were young flowers growing,
Of gentle breath and hue.
The fish swam by the castle wall,
And they seem'd joyous each and all;
The eagle rode the rising blast,
Methought he never flew so fast
As then to me he seem'd to fly,
And then new tears came in my eye,
And I felt troubled—and would fain
I had not left my recent chain;
And when I did descend again,
The darkness of my dim abode
Fell on me as a heavy load;
It was as is a new-dug grave,
Closing o'er one we sought to save,—
And yet my glance, too much oppress'd,
Had almost need of such a rest.

XIV

It might be months, or years, or days,
I kept no count—I took no note,
I had no hope my eyes to raise,
And clear them of their dreary mote;
At last men came to set me free,
I ask'd not why, and reck'd not where.
It was at length the same to me,
Fetter'd or fetterless to be,
I learn'd to love despair.
And thus when they appear'd at last,
And all my bonds aside were cast,
These heavy walls to me had grown
A hermitage—and all my own!
And half I felt as they were come
To tear me from a second home:
With spiders I had friendship made,
And watch'd them in their sullen trade,
Had seen the mice by moonlight play,
And why should I feel less than they?
We were all inmates of one place,
And I, the monarch of each race,
Had power to kill—yet, strange to tell!
In quiet we had learn'd to dwell—
My very chains and I grew friends,
So much a long communion tends
To make us what we are:—even I
Regain'd my freedom with a sigh.

* * *

On This Day I Complete My Thirty-sixth Year

Missolonghi, 22nd January, 1824

1

'Tis time this heart should be unmoved,
Since others it hath ceased to move:
Yet, though I cannot be beloved,
Still let me love!

2

My days are in the yellow leaf;[1]
The flowers and fruits of Love are gone;
The worm, the canker, and the grief
Are mine alone!

3

The fire that on my bosom preys
Is lone as some Volcanic isle;
No torch is kindled at its blaze—
A funeral pile!

4

The hope, the fear, the jealous care,
The exalted portion of the pain
And power of love, I cannot share,
But wear the chain.

5

But 'tis not *thus*—and 'tis not *here*—
Such thoughts should shake my soul, nor *now*,
Where Glory decks the hero's bier,
Or binds his brow.

---

1   an allusion to *Macbeth*, V.iii.25

6

The Sword, the Banner, and the Field,
  Glory and Greece, around me see!
The Spartan, borne upon his shield,
    Was not more free.

7

Awake! (not Greece—she *is* awake!)
  Awake, my spirit! Think through *whom*
Thy life-blood tracks its parent lake,
    And then strike home!

8

Tread those reviving passions down,
  Unworthy manhood!—unto thee
Indifferent should the smile or frown
    Of Beauty be.

9

If thou regret'st thy youth, *why live?*
  The land of honourable death
Is here:—up to the Field, and give
    Away thy breath!

10

Seek out—less often sought than found—
  A soldier's grave, for thee the best;
Then look around, and choose thy ground,
    And take thy Rest.

from: *Don Juan*[1]

CC

My poem's epic, and is meant to be
   Divided in twelve books; each book containing,
With Love, and War, a heavy gale at sea,
   A list of ships, and captains, and kings reigning,
New characters; the episodes are three:
   A panoramic view of Hell's in training,
After the style of Virgil and of Homer,
So that my name of Epic's no misnomer.

CCI

All these things will be specified in time,
   With strict regard to Aristotle's rules,[2]
The *Vade Mecum*[3] of the true sublime,
   Which makes so many poets, and some fools:
Prose poets like blank-verse, I'm fond of rhyme,
   Good workmen never quarrel with their tools;
I've got new mythological machinery,
And very handsome supernatural scenery.

CCII

There's only one slight difference between
   Me and my epic brethren gone before,
And here the advantage is my own, I ween
   (Not that I have not several merits more,
But this will more peculiarly be seen)
   They so embellish, that 'tis quite a bore
Their labyrinth of fables to thread through,
Whereas this story's actually true.

CCIII

If any person doubt it, I appeal
   To History, Tradition, and to Facts,
To newspapers, whose truth all know and feel,
   To plays in five, and operas in three acts
All these confirm my statement a good deal,

---

1   Byron's epic poem is divided into 16 cantos, published between 1819 and 1824. Byron died before he could complete the poem.
2   the rules of dramatic and epic poetry as described in Aristotle's *Poetics*
3   Latin, "go with me": a generic title for guides and handbooks

But that which more completely faith exacts
Is, that myself, and several now in Seville,
Saw Juan's last elopement with the Devil.[1]

CCIV

If ever I should condescend to prose,
    I'll write poetical commandments, which
Shall supersede beyond all doubt all those
    That went before; in these I shall enrich
My text with many things that no one knows,
    And carry precept to the highest pitch:
I'll call the work "Longinus[2] o'er a Bottle,
Or, Every Poet his own Aristotle."

CCV

Thou shalt believe in Milton, Dryden, Pope;
    Thou shalt not set up Wordsworth, Coleridge, Southey;
Because the first is crazed beyond all hope,
    The second drunk, the third so quaint and mouthy:
With Crabbe it may be difficult to cope,
    And Campbell's Hippocrene[3] is somewhat drouthy:
Thou shall not steal from Samuel Rogers, nor
Commit—flirtation with the muse of Moore.[4]

CCVI

Thou shall not covet Mr. Sotheby's Muse,[5]
    His Pegasus,[6] nor anything that's his;
Thou shalt not bear false witness like "the Blues"[7]
    (There's one, at least, is very fond of this);
Thou shalt not write, in short, but what I choose:
    This is true criticism, and you may kiss—
Exactly as you please, or not,—the rod;
But if you don't, I'll lay it on, by G—d!

---

1   In most versions of the story of Don Juan, the heartless seducer is eventually delivered
    over to devils.
2   Greek rhetorician of the first or second century A.D., supposed author of a treatise on
    the sublime
3   a fountain on Mount Helicon, sacred to the Muses
4   George Crabbe (1754-1832), Thomas Campbell (1777-1814), Samuel Rogers (1763-1855),
    and Thomas Moore (1779-1852) were minor poets of the time.
5   William Sotheby (1757-1833), a minor poet and translator
6   the winged horse symbolizing poetic inspiration
7   intellectual women ("bluestockings"); the "one" in the next line is a reference to his wife,
    Annabella Milbanke, from whom he separated in 1816.

CCVII

If any person should presume to assert
   This story is not moral, first, I pray,
That they will not cry out before they're hurt,
   Then that they'll read it o'er again, and say
(But, doubtless nobody will be so pert)
   That this is not a moral tale, though gay
Besides, in Canto Twelfth, I mean to show;
The very place where wicked people go.

CCVIII

If, after all, there should be some so blind
   To their own good this warning to despise,
Led by some tortuosity of mind,
   Not to believe my verse and their own eyes,
And cry that they "the moral cannot find,';
   I tell him, if a clergyman, he lies"
Should captains the remark, or critics, make,
They also lie too—under a mistake.

CCIX

The public approbation I expect,
   And beg they'll take my word about the moral,
Which I with their amusement will connect
   (So children cutting teeth receive a coral);
Meantime they'll doubtless please to recollect
   My epical pretensions to the laurel[1]:
For fear some prudish readers should grow skittish,
I've bribed my Grandmother's Review—the British.[2]

CCX

I sent it in a letter to the Editor,
   Who thanked me duly by return of post—
I'm for a handsome article his creditor;
   Yet, if my gentle Muse he please to roast
And break a promise after having made it her,
   Denying the receipt of what it cost,
And smear his page with gall instead of honey,
All I can say is—that he had the money.

---

1   the garland bestowed upon poets
2   Byron had been attacked by *The British Review* for his supposed immorality. After the
    publication of this canto, the *Review* solemnly denied Byron's claim to have bribed the
    editor.

CCXI

I think that with this holy new alliance
  I may ensure the public, and defy
All other magazines of art or science,
  Daily, or monthly, or three monthly; I
Have not essayed to multiply their clients,
  Because they tell me 'twere in vain to try,
And that the Edinburgh Review and Quarterly
Treat a dissenting author very martyrly.

CCXII

"Non ego hoc ferrem calidus juventa
  Consule Planco,"[1] Horace said, and so
Say I; by which quotation there is meant a
  Hint that some six or seven good years ago
(Long ere I dreamt of dating from the Brenta[2])
  I was most ready to return a blow,
And would not brook at all this sort of thing
In my hot youth—when George the Third was King.

CCXIII

But now at thirty years my hair is grey—
  (I wonder what it will be like at forty?
I thought of a peruke the other day—)
  My heart is not much greener; and, in short, I
Have squandered my whole summer while 'twas May,
  And feel no more the spirit to retort; I
Have spent my life, both interest and principal,
And deem not, what I deemed—my soul invincible

CCXIV

No more—no more—Oh! never more on me
  The freshness of the heart can fall like dew,
Which out of all the lovely things we see
  Extracts emotions beautiful and new,
Hived in our bosoms like the bag o' the bee.
  Think'st thou the honey with those objects grew?
Alas! 'twas not in them, but in thy power
To double even the sweetness of a flower

---

1   "I would not have borne this in my hot youth, when Plancus was consul" (Horace, *Odes*
    III, 14)
2   Byron was writing in Venice, through which flows the river Brenta.

CCXV

No more—no more—Oh! never more, my heart,
  Canst thou be my sole world, my universe!
Once all in all, but now a thing apart,
  Thou canst not be my blessing or my curse:
The illusion's gone for ever, and thou art
  Insensible, I trust, but none the worse,
And in thy stead I've got a deal of judgment,
Though Heaven knows how it ever found a lodgment.

CCXVI

My days of love are over, me no more
  The charms of maid, wife, and still less of widow,
Can make the fool of which they made before,—
  In short, I must not lead the life I did do;
The credulous hope of mutual minds is o'er,
  The copious use of claret is forbid too,
So for a good old gentlemanly vice
I think I must take up with avarice.

CCXVII

Ambition was my idol, which was broken
  Before the shrines of Sorrow, and of Pleasure;
And the two last have left me many a token
  O'er which reflection may be made at leisure:
Now, like Friar Bacon's Brazen Head, I've spoken,
  "Time is, Time was, Time's past[1]"—a chymic[2] treasure
Is glittering Youth, which I have spent betimes—
My heart in passion, and my head on rhymes.

CCXVIII

What is the end of Fame? 'tis but to fill
  A certain portion of uncertain paper:
Some liken it to climbing up a hill,
  Whose summit, like all hills, is lost in vapour;
For this men write, speak, preach, and heroes kill,
  And bards burn what they call their "midnight taper,"
To have, when the original is dust,
A name, a wretched picture and worse bust.

---

1 the words spoken by the Brazen Head in Robert Greene's play *Friar Bacon and Friar Bungay* (1594)
2 alchemic, associated with magical power

CCXIX

What are the hopes of man? Old Egypt's King
   Cheops erected the first Pyramid
And largest, thinking it was just the thing
   To keep his memory whole, and mummy hid;
But somebody or other rummaging,
   Burglariously broke his coffin's lid:
Let not a monument give you or me hopes,
Since not a pinch of dust remains of Cheops.

CCXX

But I, being fond of true philosophy,
   Say very often to myself, "Alas!
All things that have been born were born to die,
   And flesh (which Death mows down to hay) is grass;
You've passed your youth not so unpleasantly,
   And if you had it o'er again—'twould pass—
So thank your stars that matters are no worse,
And read your Bible, sir, and mind your purse."

CCXXI

But for the present, gentle reader! and
   Still gentler purchaser! the Bard—that's I—
Must, with permission, shake you by the hand,
   And so—"your humble servant, and Good-bye!"
We meet again, if we should understand
   Each other, and if not, I shall not try
Your patience further than by this short sample—
'Twere well if others followed my example.

CCXXII

"Go, little Book, from this my solitude!
   I cast thee on the waters—go thy ways!
And if, as I believe, thy vein be good,
   The World will find thee after many days."
When Southey's read, and Wordsworth understood
   I can't help putting in my claim to praise—
The four first rhymes are Southey's[1] every line:
For God's sake, reader! take them not for mine.

* * *

---

[1]   The lines are taken from the conclusion to Robert Southey's *Epilogue to the Lay of the Laureate.* Southey (1774-1843) had been appointed Poet Laureate in 1813.

Percy Bysshe Shelley

(1792–1822)

Mont Blanc[1]

Lines written in the vale of Chamouni

I

The everlasting universe of things
Flows through the mind, and rolls its rapid waves,
Now dark—now glittering—now reflecting gloom—
Now lending splendour, where from secret springs
The source of human thought its tribute brings
Of waters,—with a sound but half its own,
Such as a feeble brook will oft assume
In the wild woods, among the mountains lone,
Where waterfalls around it leap for ever,
Where woods and winds contend, and a vast river
Over its rocks ceaselessly bursts and raves.

II

Thus thou, Ravine of Arve[2]—dark, deep Ravine—
Thou many-coloured, many-voicèd vale,
Over whose pines, and crags, and caverns sail
Fast cloud-shadows and sunbeams: awful scene,
Where Power in likeness of the Arve comes down
From the ice-gulfs that gird his secret throne,
Bursting through these dark mountains like the flame
Of lightning through the tempest;—thou dost lie,
Thy giant brood of pines around thee clinging,
Children of elder time, in whose devotion
The chainless winds still come and ever came
To drink their odours, and their mighty swinging
To hear—an old and solemn harmony;
Thine earthly rainbows stretched across the sweep
Of the aethereal waterfall, whose veil
Robes some unsculptured image;[3] the strange sleep
Which when the voices of the desert fail
Wraps all in its own deep eternity;—
Thy caverns echoing to the Arve's commotion,
A loud, lone sound no other sound can tame;
Thou art pervaded with that ceaseless motion,
Thou art the path of that unresting sound—
Dizzy Ravine! and when I gaze on thee

---

1 the highest mountain in the French Alps
2 the river Arve, which flows through the Valley of Chamonix in southeastern France
3 an image not made by human agency

I seem as in a trance sublime and strange
To muse on my own separate fantasy,
My own, my human mind, which passively
Now renders and receives fast influencings,
Holding an unremitting interchange
With the clear universe of things around;
One legion of wild thoughts, whose wandering wings
Now float above thy darkness, and now rest
Where that or thou art no unbidden guest,
In the still cave of the witch Poesy,
Seeking among the shadows that pass by
Ghosts of all things that are, some shade of thee,
Some phantom, some faint image; till the breast
From which they fled recalls them, thou art there!

III

Some say that gleams of a remoter world
Visit the soul in sleep,—that death is slumber,
And that its shapes the busy thoughts outnumber
Of those who wake and live.—I look on high;
Has some unknown omnipotence unfurled
The veil of life and death? or do I lie
In dream, and does the mightier world of sleep
Spread far around and inaccessibly
Its circles? For the very spirit fails,
Driven like a homeless cloud from steep to steep
That vanishes among the viewless gales!
Far, far above, piercing the infinite sky,
Mont Blanc appears,—still, snowy, and serene—
Its subject mountains their unearthly forms
Pile around it, ice and rock; broad vales between
Of frozen floods, unfathomable deeps,
Blue as the overhanging heaven, that spread
And wind among the accumulated steeps;
A desert peopled by the storms alone,
Save when the eagle brings some hunter's bone,
And the wolf tracks her there—how hideously
Its shapes are heaped around! rude, bare, and high,
Ghastly, and scarred, and riven.—Is this the scene
Where the old Earthquake-daemon[1] taught her young
Ruin? Were these their toys? or did a sea
Of fire envelop once this silent snow?
None can reply—all seems eternal now.
The wilderness has a mysterious tongue
Which teaches awful doubt, or faith so mild,

---

1   "Daemons" are natural forces, imaged as supernatural beings.

So solemn, so serene, that man may be,
But for such faith,[1] with nature reconciled;
Thou hast a voice, great Mountain, to repeal
Large codes of fraud and woe; not understood
By all, but which the wise, and great, and good
Interpret, or make felt, or deeply feel.

IV

The fields, the lakes, the forests, and the streams,
Ocean, and all the living things that dwell
Within the daedal[2] earth; lightning, and rain,
Earthquake, and fiery flood, and hurricane,
The torpor of the year when feeble dreams
Visit the hidden buds, or dreamless sleep
Holds every future leaf and flower;—the bound
With which from that detested trance they leap;
The works and ways of man, their death and birth,
And that of him and all that his may be;
All things that move and breathe with toil and sound
Are born and die; revolve, subside, and swell.
Power dwells apart in its tranquillity,
Remote, serene, and inaccessible:
And *this*, the naked countenance of earth,
On which I gaze, even these primaeval mountains
Teach the adverting mind. The glaciers creep
Like snakes that watch their prey, from their far fountains,
Slow rolling on; there, many a precipice,
Frost and the Sun in scorn of mortal power
Have piled: dome, pyramid, and pinnacle,
A city of death, distinct with many a tower
And wall impregnable of beaming ice.
Yet not a city, but a flood of ruin
Is there, that from the boundaries of the sky
Rolls its perpetual stream; vast pines are strewing
Its destined path, or in the mangled soil
Branchless and shattered stand; the rocks, drawn down
From yon remotest waste, have overthrown
The limits of the dead and living world,
Never to be reclaimed. The dwelling-place
Of insects, beasts, and birds, becomes its spoil
Their food and their retreat for ever gone,
So much of life and joy is lost. The race
Of man flies far in dread; his work and dwelling
Vanish, like smoke before the tempest's stream,

---

1   i.e., only through such faith
2   Elaborately, intricately formed: Daedalus was the craftsman who fashioned the intricate Labyrinth in Crete.

And their place is not known. Below, vast caves
Shine in the rushing torrents' restless gleam,
Which from those secret chasms in tumult welling
Meet in the vale, and one majestic River,[1]
The breath and blood of distant lands, for ever
Rolls its loud waters to the ocean-waves,
Breathes its swift vapours to the circling air.

V

Mont Blanc yet gleams on high:—the power is there,
The still and solemn power of many sights,
And many sounds, and much of life and death.
In the calm darkness of the moonless nights,
In the lone glare of day, the snows descend
Upon that Mountain; none beholds them there,
Nor when the flakes burn in the sinking sun,
Or the star-beams dart through them:—Winds contend
Silently there, and heap the snow with breath
Rapid and strong, but silently! Its home
The voiceless lightning in these solitudes
Keeps innocently, and like vapour broods
Over the snow. The secret Strength of things
Which governs thought, and to the infinite dome
Of Heaven is as a law, inhabits thee!
And what were thou, and earth, and stars, and sea,
If to the human mind's imaginings
Silence and solitude were vacancy?

Ozymandias[2]

I met a traveller from an antique land
Who said: Two vast and trunkless legs of stone
Stand in the desert . . . Near them, on the sand,
Half sunk, a shattered visage lies, whose frown,
And wrinkled lip, and sneer of cold command,
Tell that its sculptor well those passions read
Which yet survive, stamped on these lifeless things,
The hand that mocked them, and the heart that fed:
And on the pedestal these words appear:
'My name is Ozymandias, king of kings:
Look on my works, ye Mighty, and despair!'
Nothing beside remains. Round the decay
Of that colossal wreck, boundless and bare
The lone and level sands stretch far away.

---

1 the Rhone, which flows out of Lake Geneva down to the Mediterranean
2 the Greek name for Rameses II, pharoah of Egypt in the thirteenth century B.C.

[211]

Sonnet: England in 1819

An old, mad, blind, despised, and dying king,[1]—
Princes, the dregs of their dull race, who flow
Through public scorn,—mud from a muddy spring,—
Rulers who neither see, nor feel, nor know,
But leech-like to their fainting country cling,
Till they drop, blind in blood, without a blow,—
A people starved and stabbed in the untilled field,[2]—
An army, which liberticide and prey
Makes as a two-edged sword to all who wield,—
Golden and sanguine laws which tempt and slay;
Religion Christless, Godless—a book sealed;
A Senate,—Time's worst statute[3] unrepealed,—
Are graves, from which a glorious Phantom may
Burst, to illumine our tempestuous day.

Ode to the West Wind

I

O wild West Wind, thou breath of Autumn's being,
Thou, from whose unseen presence the leaves dead
Are driven, like ghosts from an enchanter fleeing,

Yellow, and black, and pale, and hectic red,[4]
Pestilence-stricken multitudes: O thou,
Who chariotest to their dark wintry bed

The wingèd seeds, where they lie cold and low,
Each like a corpse within its grave, until
Thine azure sister of the Spring shall blow

Her clarion[5] o'er the dreaming earth, and fill
(Driving sweet buds like flocks to feed in air)
With living hues and odours plain and hill;

Wild Spirit, which art moving everywhere;
Destroyer and preserver; hear, oh, hear!

---

1   George III, king from 1760 to his death in 1820, periodically suffered from insanity, and
    in 1811 he was replaced by his son the Prince of Wales, who ruled as Prince Regent.
2   a reference to the "Peterloo massacre" of August 1819, when soldiers attacked a meeting
    of parliamentary reformers in St. Peter's Field in Manchester and killed six people
3   probably an allusion to the legal disabilities imposed on Catholics and Dissenters in
    England for several centuries
4   the flushed colour often associated with the fever of consumptive diseases
5   shrill-sounding trumpet

full of self-pity
yet enormous
energy of
rejuvination,
or does the wind
at does the wind

PERCY BYSSHE SHELLEY

II

Thou on whose stream, mid the steep sky's commotion, a
Loose clouds like earth's decaying leaves are shed, b
Shook from the tangled boughs of Heaven and Ocean, a

Angels of rain and lightning: there are spread b
On the blue surface of thine aëry surge, c
Like the bright hair uplifted from the head b

Of some fierce Maenad,[1] even from the dim verge c
Of the horizon to the zenith's height, d
The locks of the approaching storm. Thou dirge c

Of the dying year, to which this closing night d
Will be the dome of a vast sepulchre, e
Vaulted with all thy congregated might d

Of vapours, from whose solid atmosphere e
Black rain, and fire, and hail will burst: oh, hear! e

III

Thou who didst waken from his summer dreams a
The blue Mediterranean, where he lay, b
Lulled by the coil of his crystàlline streams, a

Beside a pumice isle in Baiae's bay,[2] b
And saw in sleep old palaces and towers c
Quivering within the wave's intenser day, b

All overgrown with azure moss and flowers c
So sweet, the sense faints picturing them! Thou d
For whose path the Atlantic's level powers c

Cleave themselves into chasms, while far below d
The sea-blooms and the oozy woods which wear e
The sapless foliage of the ocean, know d

Thy voice, and suddenly grow gray with fear,[3] e
And tremble and despoil themselves: oh, hear! e

ends 3/5 sechims

---

1   a female votary of Dionysus, the Greek god of wine
2   an island of porous lava in the Bay of Baiae, a favourite resort of the ancient Romans,
     near Naples
3   "The vegetation at the bottom of the sea, of rivers, and of lakes, sympathizes with that
     of the land in the change of seasons, and is consequently influenced by the winds which
     announce it" (Shelley's note).

following falling of leaves is a continuation of nature's cycle.

IV

If I were a dead leaf thou mightest bear; *a*
If I were a swift cloud to fly with thee; *b*
A wave to pant beneath thy power, and share *a*

The impulse of thy strength, only less free *b*
Than thou, O uncontrollable! If even *c*
I were as in my boyhood, and could be *b*

The comrade of thy wanderings over Heaven, *c*
As then, when to outstrip thy skiey speed *d*
Scarce seemed a vision; I would ne'er have striven *c*

As thus with thee in prayer in my sore need. *d*
Oh, lift me as a wave, a leaf, a cloud! *e*
I fall upon the thorns of life! I bleed! *d*

A heavy weight of hours has chained and bowed *e*
One too like thee: tameless, and swift, and proud. *e*

V

Make me thy lyre, even as the forest is: *a*
What if my leaves are falling like its own! *b*
The tumult of thy mighty harmonies *a*

Will take from both a deep, autumnal tone, *b*
Sweet though in sadness. Be thou, Spirit fierce, *c*
My spirit! Be thou me, impetuous one! *b*

Drive my dead thoughts over the universe *c*
Like withered leaves to quicken a new birth! *d*
And, by the incantation of this verse, *c*

Scatter, as from an unextinguished hearth *d*
Ashes and sparks, my words among mankind! *e*
Be through my lips to unawakened earth *d*

The trumpet of a prophecy! O, Wind, *e*
If Winter comes, can Spring be far behind? *e* *hope for the future*

Shelley is the unacknowledged legislator of thy world. Chid radical views of politics would like his words be spark to the mankind.

Lots of exclamation points.

The Cloud

I bring fresh showers for the thirsting flowers,
    From the seas and the streams;
I bear light shade for the leaves when laid
    In their noonday dreams.
From my wings are shaken the dews that waken
    The sweet buds every one,

When rocked to rest on their mother's breast,
  As she dances about the sun.
I wield the flail of the lashing hail,
  And whiten the green plains under,
And then again I dissolve it in rain,
  And laugh as I pass in thunder.

I sift the snow on the mountains below,
  And their great pines groan aghast;
And all the night 'tis my pillow white,
  While I sleep in the arms of the blast.
Sublime on the towers of my skiey bowers,
  Lightning my pilot sits;
In a cavern under is fettered the thunder,
  It struggles and howls at fits;[1]
Over earth and ocean, with gentle motion,
  This pilot is guiding me,
Lured by the love of the genii[2] that move
  In the depths of the purple sea;
Over the rills, and the crags, and the hills,
  Over the lakes and the plains,
Wherever he dream, under mountain or stream,
  The Spirit he loves remains;
And I[3] all the while bask in Heaven's blue smile,
  Whilst he is dissolving in rains.

The sanguine Sunrise, with his meteor eyes,
  And his burning plumes outspread,[4]
Leaps on the back of my sailing rack,[5]
  When the morning star shines dead;
As on the jag of a mountain crag,
  Which an earthquake rocks and swings,
An eagle alit one moment may sit
  In the light of its golden wings.
And when Sunset may breathe, from the lit sea beneath,
  Its ardours of rest and of love,
And the crimson pall of eve may fall
  From the depth of Heaven above,
With wings folded I rest, on mine aëry nest,
  As still as a brooding dove.

That orbèd maiden with white fire laden,
  Whom mortals call the Moon,

---

1   spasmodically, fitfully
2   Lightning, the cloud's "pilot", is positive atmospheric electricity which is drawn down by the negatively charged earth.
3   i.e., the upper part of the cloud
4   the sun's corona
5   a mass of high clouds driven by the wind

Glides glimmering o'er my fleece-like floor,
  By the midnight breezes strewn;
And wherever the beat of her unseen feet,
  Which only the angels hear,
May have broken the woof of my tent's thin roof,
  The stars peep behind her and peer;
And I laugh to see them whirl and flee,
  Like a swarm of golden bees,
When I widen the rent in my wind-built tent,
  Till the calm rivers, lakes, and seas,
Like strips of the sky fallen through me on high,
  Are each paved with the moon and these.

I bind the Sun's throne with a burning zone,[1]
  And the Moon's with a girdle of pearl;
The volcanoes are dim, and the stars reel and swim,
  When the whirlwinds my banner unfurl.
From cape to cape, with a bridge-like shape,
  Over a torrent sea,
Sunbeam-proof, I hang like a roof,—
  The mountains its columns be.
The triumphal arch through which I march
  With hurricane, fire, and snow,
When the Powers of the air are chained to my chair,
  Is the million-coloured bow;
The sphere-fire above its soft colours wove,
  While the moist Earth was laughing below.

I am the daughter of Earth and Water,
  And the nursling of the Sky;
I pass through the pores of the ocean and shores;
  I change, but I cannot die.
For after the rain when with never a stain
  The pavilion of Heaven is bare,
And the winds and sunbeams with their convex gleams
  Build up the blue dome of air,[2]
I silently laugh at my own cenotaph,
  And out of the caverns of rain,
Like a child from the womb, like a ghost from the tomb,
  I arise and unbuild it again.

---

1 belt
2 the blue of the sky, created by the filtering of sunbeams through the earth's atmosphere

To a Skylark

Hail to thee, blithe Spirit!
  Bird thou never wert,
That from Heaven, or near it,
  Pourest thy full heart
In profuse strains of unpremeditated art.

  Higher still and higher
    From the earth thou springest
Like a cloud of fire;
    The blue deep thou wingest,
And singing still dost soar, and soaring ever singest.

  In the golden lightning
    Of the sunken sun,
O'er which clouds are bright'ning,
    Thou dost float and run;
Like an unbodied joy whose race is just begun.

  The pale purple even
    Melts around thy flight;
Like a star of Heaven,
    In the broad daylight
Thou art unseen, but yet I hear thy shrill delight,

  Keen as are the arrows
    Of that silver sphere,[1]
Whose intense lamp narrows
    In the white dawn clear
Until we hardly see—we feel that it is there.

  All the earth and air
    With thy voice is loud,
As, when night is bare,
    From one lonely cloud
The moon rains out her beams, and Heaven is overflowed.

  What thou art we know not;
    What is most like thee?
From rainbow clouds there flow not
    Drops so bright to see
As from thy presence showers a rain of melody.

---

1   Venus as the morning star

Like a Poet hidden
   In the light of thought,
Singing hymns unbidden,
   Till the world is wrought
To sympathy with hopes and fears it heeded not:

   Like a high-born maiden
    In a palace-tower,
Soothing her love-laden
    Soul in secret hour
With music sweet as love, which overflows her bower:

   Like a glow-worm golden
    In a dell of dew,
Scattering unbeholden
    Its aëreal hue
Among the flowers and grass, which screen it from the view!

   Like a rose embowered
    In its own green leaves,
By warm winds deflowered,
    Till the scent it gives
Makes faint with too much sweet those heavy-wingèd thieves:

   Sound of vernal showers
    On the twinkling grass,
Rain-awakened flowers,
    All that ever was
Joyous, and clear, and fresh, thy music doth surpass:

   Teach us, Sprite or Bird,
    What sweet thoughts are thine:
I have never heard
    Praise of love or wine
That panted forth a flood of rapture so divine.

   Chorus Hymeneal,[1]
    Or triumphal chant,
Matched with thine would be all
    But an empty vaunt,
A thing wherein we feel there is some hidden want.

---

1   pertaining to marriage; Hymen was the Greek god of marriage.

What objects are the fountains
   Of thy happy strain?
What fields, or waves, or mountains?
   What shapes of sky or plain?
What love of thine own kind? what ignorance of pain?

With thy clear keen joyance
   Languor cannot be:
Shadow of annoyance
   Never came near thee:
Thou lovest—but ne'er knew love's sad satiety.

Waking or asleep,
   Thou of death must deem
Things more true and deep
   Than we mortals dream,
Or how could thy notes flow in such a crystal stream?

We look before and after,
   And pine for what is not:
Our sincerest laughter
   With some pain is fraught;
Our sweetest songs are those that tell of saddest thought.

Yet if we could scorn
   Hate, and pride, and fear;
If we were things born
   Not to shed a tear,
I know not how thy joy we ever should come near.

Better than all measures
   Of delightful sound,
Better than all treasures
   That in books are found,
Thy skill to poet were, thou scorner of the ground!

Teach me half the gladness
   That thy brain must know,
Such harmonious madness
   From my lips would flow
The world should listen then—as I am listening now.

Italian Sonnet ✓

John Keats – loves Classical Mythology

(1795–1821)

On First Looking into Chapman's Homer[1]

very excited to have found a good translation of his beloved Classics. Turns his excitement & excitement to the direction of the excitement caused by travel.

Much have I travell'd in the realms of gold,   a
And many goodly states and kingdoms seen;   b
Round many western islands have I been   b
Which bards in fealty to Apollo hold.   *god of literature*   a
Oft of one wide expanse had I been told   a
    That deep-brow'd Homer ruled as his demesne;[2]   *Chapman*
    Yet did I never breathe its pure serene[3]   b   *made it*
Till I heard Chapman speak out loud and bold: c   *possible for*
Then felt I like some watcher of the skies   *all that Keats to experience*
    When a new planet swims into his ken;   *that travel to the*
Or like stout Cortez[4] when with eagle eyes   c   *Classics*
    He star'd at the Pacific—and all his men   d
Look'd at each other with a wild surmise—   c
    Silent, upon a peak in Darien.   d

ENG Sonnet ✓

When I have fears that I may cease to be

When I have fears that I may cease to be   a
    Before my pen has glean'd my teeming brain,   b
Before high piled books, in charactry,[5]
    Hold like rich garners the full ripen'd grain;   b
When I behold, upon the night's starr'd face,   c
    Huge cloudy symbols of a high romance,   d
And think that I may never live to trace   c
    Their shadows, with the magic hand of chance;   d
And when I feel, fair creature of an hour,   e
    That I shall never look upon thee more,   f
Never have relish in the fairy power   e
    Of unreflecting love;—then on the shore   f
Of the wide world I stand alone, and think   g
    Till love and fame to nothingness do sink.   g

---

1   George Chapman (c. 1559-1634) published his translation of the *Iliad* and the *Odyssey* in 1611-1616.
2   realm, possession
3   calm, clear expanse of air
4   Keats makes a minor error, in that it was Balboa, not Cortez, who crossed the Isthmus of Panama ("Darien") in 1513, and found himself at the Pacific Ocean.
5   the letters, or characters, forming the alphabet

If by dull rhymes our English must be chain'd

If by dull rhymes our English must be chain'd,
  And, like Andromeda,[1] the sonnet sweet
    Fetter'd, in spite of pained loveliness;
Let us find out, if we must be constrain'd,
  Sandals more interwoven and complete
To fit the naked foot of Poesy;
    Let us inspect the lyre, and weigh the stress
Of every chord, and see what may be gain'd
  By ear industrious, and attention meet;
    Misers of sound and syllable, no less
Than Midas[2] of his coinage, let us be
  Jealous of dead leaves in the bay wreath crown;[3]
So, if we may not let the muse be free,
  She will be bound with garlands of her own.

La Belle Dame sans Merci:

A Ballad

1

O what can ail thee, knight at arms,
  Alone and palely loitering?
The sedge has wither'd from the lake,
  And no birds sing.

2

O what can ail thee, knight at arms,
  So haggard and so woe-begone?
The squirrel's granary is full,
  And the harvest's done.

3

I see a lily on thy brow
  With anguish moist and fever dew,
And on thy cheeks a fading rose
  Fast withereth too.

---

1   the daughter of Cassiopeia who was chained to a rock as a sacrifice to a sea-monster,
     but rescued by Perseus
2   the legendary king of Phrygia, whose touch turned everything to gold
3   the traditional symbol of poetic achievement

4

I met a lady in the meads,
   Full beautiful, a fairy's child;
Her hair was long, her foot was light,
   And her eyes were wild.

5

I made a garland for her head,
   And bracelets too, and fragrant zone;[1]
She look'd at me as she did love,
   And made sweet moan.

6

I set her on my pacing steed,
   And nothing else saw all day long,
For sidelong would she bend, and sing
   A fairy's song.

7

She found me roots of relish sweet,
   And honey wild, and manna dew,
And sure in language strange she said—
   I love thee true.

8

She took me to her elfin grot,
   And there she wept, and sigh'd full sore,
And there I shut her wild wild eyes
   With kisses four.

9

And there she lulled me asleep,
   And there I dream'd—Ah! woe betide!
The latest[2] dream I ever dream'd
   On the cold hill's side.

10

I saw pale kings, and princes too,
   Pale warriors, death pale were they all;

---

1   belt, girdle
2   last

JOHN KEATS

They cried—"La belle dame sans merci
Hath thee in thrall!"

11

I saw their starv'd lips in the gloam[1]
With horrid warning gaped wide,
And I awoke and found me here
On the cold hill's side.

12

And this is why I sojourn here,
Alone and palely loitering,
Though the sedge is wither'd from the lake,
And no birds sing.

Ode to a Nightingale

1

My heart aches, and a drowsy numbness pains
My sense, as though of hemlock[2] I had drunk,
Or emptied some dull opiate to the drains
One minute past, and Lethe-wards[3] had sunk:
'Tis not through envy of thy happy lot,
But being too happy in thine happiness,—
That thou, light-winged Dryad[4] of the trees,
In some melodious plot
Of beechen green, and shadows numberless,
Singest of summer in full-throated ease.

2

O, for a draught of vintage! that hath been
Cool'd a long age in the deep-delved earth,
Tasting of Flora[5] and the country green,
Dance, and Provençal[6] song, and sunburnt mirth!
O for a beaker full of the warm South,
Full of the true, the blushful Hippocrene,[7]
With beaded bubbles winking at the brim,

1   gloaming, twilight
2   a poison made from the hemlock herb
3   Lethe was the river in Hades whose waters brought forgetfulness.
4   wood-nymph
5   Roman goddess of flowers
6   from Provence, the region in France associated with troubadors
7   water from the spring on Mount Helicon, sacred to the Muses

He would like to take a journey into some realm of the imagination

And purple-stained mouth;
That I might drink, and leave the world unseen,
And with thee fade away into the forest dim:

3

Fade far away, dissolve, and quite forget
    What thou among the leaves hast never known,
The weariness, the fever, and the fret
    Here, where men sit and hear each other groan;
Where palsy shakes a few, sad, last gray hairs,
Where youth grows pale, and spectre-thin, and dies;
Where but to think is to be full of sorrow
    And leaden-eyed despairs,
Where Beauty cannot keep her lustrous eyes,
    Or new Love pine at them beyond to-morrow.

Means shaky written not long after his brother dies of TB.

4

Away! away! for I will fly to thee,
    Not charioted by Bacchus[1] and his pards,[2]
But on the viewless wings of Poesy,
    Though the dull brain perplexes and retards:
Already with thee! tender is the night,
    And haply[3] the Queen-Moon is on her throne,
        Cluster'd around by all her starry Fays;[4]
            But here there is no light,
Save what from heaven is with the breezes blown
    Through verdurous glooms and winding mossy ways.

5

I cannot see what flowers are at my feet,
    Nor what soft incense hangs upon the boughs,
But, in embalmed[5] darkness, guess each sweet
    Wherewith the seasonable month endows
The grass, the thicket, and the fruit-tree wild;
    White hawthorn, and the pastoral eglantine;
Fast fading violets cover'd up in leaves;
        And mid-May's eldest child,
The coming musk-rose, full of dewy wine,
    The murmurous haunt of flies on summer eves.

He is in some kind of grove where he can listen but not see. He can only smell the flowers

---

1   the Roman god of wine
2   leopards
3   perhaps
4   fairies
5   fragrant, perfumed

[handwritten: fascinated w/ philosophy]

6

[handwritten: person in the dark or dark person]

Darkling I listen; and, for many a time
I have been half in love with easeful Death,
Call'd him soft names in many a mused rhyme,
    To take into the air my quiet breath;
Now more than ever seems it rich to die,
    To cease upon the midnight with no pain,
        While thou art pouring forth thy soul abroad
            In such an ecstasy!
Still wouldst thou sing, and I have ears in vain—
    To thy high requiem become a sod.

[handwritten: seeming longing for death - He'd almost like to give up. He is thinking that now would be a good time to die.]

[handwritten: done in the honor of the dead]

7

Thou wast not born for death, immortal Bird!
    No hungry generations tread thee down;
The voice I hear this passing night was heard
    In ancient days by emperor and clown:
Perhaps the self-same song that found a path
    Through the sad heart of Ruth,[1] when, sick for home,
        She stood in tears amid the alien corn;
            The same that oft-times hath
Charm'd magic casements, opening on the foam
    Of perilous seas, in faery lands forlorn.

[handwritten: As long as humans have heard this bird, they have sung the same song - they will always be, thus, immortal bird.]

8

Forlorn! the very word is like a bell
    To toll me back from thee to my sole self!
Adieu! the fancy cannot cheat so well
    As she is fam'd to do, deceiving elf.
Adieu! adieu! thy plaintive anthem fades
    Past the near meadows, over the still stream,
        Up the hill-side; and now 'tis buried deep
            In the next valley-glades:
Was it a vision, or a waking dream?
    Fled is that music:—Do I wake or sleep?

[handwritten: fancy = imagination]

[handwritten: Questioning that hypnotic(?) state - b/n sleep + wake]

[handwritten: 3rd line from bottom in each stanza is in trimeter (6 syllables) unusual]

_____

1   an allusion to the biblical story in the Book of Ruth

JOHN KEATS

Ode on a Grecian Urn

1

Thou still unravish'd bride of quietness,
   Thou foster-child of silence and slow time,
Sylvan historian, who canst thus express
   A flowery tale more sweetly than our rhyme:
What leaf-fring'd legend haunts about thy shape
   Of deities or mortals, or of both,
     In Tempe or the dales of Arcady?[1]
   What men or gods are these? What maidens loth?
What mad pursuit? What struggle to escape?
     What pipes and timbrels? What wild ecstasy?[2]

2

Heard melodies are sweet, but those unheard
   Are sweeter; therefore, ye soft pipes, play on;
Not to the sensual ear, but, more endear'd,
   Pipe to the spirit ditties of no tone:
Fair youth, beneath the trees, thou canst not leave
   Thy song, nor ever can those trees be bare;
     Bold lover, never, never canst thou kiss,
Though winning near the goal—yet, do not grieve;
   She cannot fade, though thou hast not thy bliss,
For ever wilt thou love, and she be fair!

3

Ah, happy, happy boughs! that cannot shed
   Your leaves, nor ever bid the spring adieu;
And, happy melodist, unwearied,
   For ever piping songs for ever new;
More happy love! more happy, happy love!
   For ever warm and still to be enjoy'd,
     For ever panting, and for ever young;
All breathing human passion far above,
   That leaves a heart high-sorrowful and cloy'd,
     A burning forehead, and a parching tongue.

4

Who are these coming to the sacrifice?
   To what green altar, O mysterious priest,

---

1   regions of ancient Greece symbolic of ideal pastoral beauty
2   The vase appears to depict a Dionysian ritual, in which participants would sometimes attain a state of frenzy.

contemplating the eternal work of god.

JOHN KEATS

the heifer will always be on the way to be sacrificed but it is art + never will be

Lead'st thou that heifer lowing at the skies,
  And all her silken flanks with garlands drest?
What little town by river or sea shore,
  Or mountain-built with peaceful citadel,
    Is emptied of this folk, this pious morn?
And, little town, thy streets for evermore
  Will silent be, and not a soul to tell
    Why thou art desolate, can e'er return.

The urn survived not the person. His poems surviving but Keats is dead.

5

fascinated w/ philosophy of art =>
what is the status of art.

O Attic[1] shape! Fair attitude! with brede
  Of marble men and maidens overwrought,[2]
With forest branches and the trodden weed;
  Thou, silent form, dost tease us out of thought
    As doth eternity: Cold Pastoral!
  When old age shall this generation waste,
    Thou shalt remain, in midst of other woe
    Than ours, a friend to man, to whom thou say'st,
  "Beauty is truth, truth beauty,"—that is all
    Ye know on earth, and all ye need to know.

another paradox

Preserves + does not preserve

very controversial, worries people

several interpretations are made

beauty is a truth

Ode on Melancholy

1

No, no, go not to Lethe,[3] neither twist
  Wolf's-bane,[4] tight-rooted, for its poisonous wine;
Nor suffer thy pale forehead to be kiss'd
  By nightshade, ruby grape of Proserpine;[5]
Make not your rosary of yew-berries,[6]
  Nor let the beetle,[7] nor the death-moth[8] be
    Your mournful Psyche, nor the downy owl
A partner in your sorrow's mysteries;[9]
  For shade to shade will come too drowsily,
    And drown the wakeful anguish of the soul.

---

1   from Attica, the region around Athens
2   decorated with an interwoven pattern
3   the river of Hades whose waters induce forgetfulness
4   a poisonous plant, like nightshade in line 4
5   queen of the underworld
6   The yew-tree is traditionally associated with death.
7   the black beetle, or scarab, revered by the ancient Egyptians and placed in their tombs
8   the death's-head moth, whose markings resemble a skull. Keats may also be alluding to ancient representations of the soul (psyche) as a butterfly or moth, depicted as fluttering out of the mouth of the deceased.
9   religious rites

2

But when the melancholy fit shall fall
   Sudden from heaven like a weeping cloud,
That fosters the droop-headed flowers all,
   And hides the green hill in an April shroud;
Then glut thy sorrow on a morning rose,
   Or on the rainbow of the salt sand-wave,
     Or on the wealth of globed peonies;
Or if thy mistress some rich anger shows,
   Emprison her soft hand, and let her rave,
     And feed deep, deep upon her peerless eyes.

3

She dwells with Beauty—Beauty that must die;
   And Joy, whose hand is ever at his lips
Bidding adieu; and aching Pleasure nigh,
   Turning to poison while the bee-mouth sips:
Ay, in the very temple of Delight
   Veil'd Melancholy has her sovran shrine,
Though seen of none save him whose strenuous tongue
   Can burst Joy's grape against his palate fine;
His soul shall taste the sadness of her might,
   And be among her cloudy trophies hung.

an ode to Autumn
no as complex as the Grecian urn, yet incredibly crafted

To Autumn

1

Season of mists and mellow fruitfulness, *a*
   Close bosom-friend of the maturing sun; *b*
Conspiring with him how to load and bless *a*
   With fruit the vines that round the thatch-eves run; *b*
To bend with apples the moss'd cottage-trees, *c*
   And fill all fruit with ripeness to the core; *d*
     To swell the gourd, and plump the hazel shells *e*
   With a sweet kernel; to set budding more, *d*
And still more, later flowers for the bees, *c*
Until they think warm days will never cease, *c*
     For summer has o'er-brimm'd their clammy cells. *e*

start the near the cottage

2

Who hath not seen thee oft amid thy store?
   Sometimes whoever seeks abroad may find
Thee sitting careless on a granary floor,
   Thy hair soft-lifted by the winnowing wind;
Or on a half-reap'd furrow sound asleep,
   Drows'd with the fume of poppies, while thy hook

moved to the fields

personifying autumn and staying in 2nd stanza, Autumn is described as a person lang. is considerably simplified fields of imagery in comparison to previous odes

Spares the next swath and all its twined flowers:
And sometimes like a gleaner thou dost keep
Steady thy laden head across a brook;
Or by a cyder-press, with patient look,
Thou watchest the last oozings hours by hours.

3

Where are the songs of spring? Ay, where are they?
Think not of them, thou hast thy music too,—
While barred clouds bloom the soft-dying day,
And touch the stubble-plains with rosy hue;
Then in a wailful choir the small gnats mourn
Among the river sallows,[1] borne aloft
Or sinking as the light wind lives or dies;
And full-grown lambs loud bleat from hilly bourn;[2]
Hedge-crickets sing; and now with treble soft
The red-breast whistles from a garden-croft;
And gathering swallows twitter in the skies.

moving out to the sky

clarification / personification of autumn // more impersonal & indirect personification it's fading as the day

Swallows are going to migrate

(3?) 5 movements
pre-harvest period
harvest "
post harvest "
each unit has a diff. time of day

his approach to death

1. morning — so often misty.
2. day — activities (work) that go on in the day
3. night. approaching coming to an end

starts w/ kinesthetic imagery, then visual imagery (this is how we see autumn) than sound ". (ends w/ all the sounds) Voral
Kinesthetic feeling, physical awareness touch, physical sensations

Prof. really likes this poem

1   willow-trees
2   hilly region; or possibly, a hillside stream

Ralph Waldo Emerson

(1803–1882)

The Snow-Storm

Announced by all the trumpets of the sky,
Arrives the snow, and, driving o'er the fields,
Seems nowhere to alight: the whited air
Hides hills and woods, the river, and the heaven,
And veils the farm-house at the garden's end.
The sled and traveller stopped, the courier's feet
Delayed, all friends shut out, the housemates sit
Around the radiant fireplace, enclosed
In a tumultuous privacy of storm.

    Come see the north wind's masonry.
Out of an unseen quarry evermore
Furnished with tile, the fierce artificer
Curves his white bastions with projected roof
Round every windward stake, or tree, or door.
Speeding, the myriad-handed, his wild work
So fanciful, so savage, nought cares he
For number or proportion. Mockingly,
On coop or kennel he hangs Parian[1] wreaths;
A swan-like form invests the hidden thorn;
Fills up the farmer's lane from wall to wall,
Maugre[2] the farmer's sighs; and at the gate
A tapering turret overtops the work.
And when his hours are numbered, and the world
Is all his own, retiring, as he were not,
Leaves, when the sun appears, astonished Art
To mimic in slow structures, stone by stone,
Built in an age, the mad wind's night-work,
The frolic architecture of the snow.

---

1   The island of Paros in Greece was noted for its fine white marble.
2   despite

Blight

Give me truths;
For I am weary of the surfaces,
And die of inanition. If I knew
Only the herbs and simples[1] of the wood,
Rue, cinquefoil, gill, vervain and agrimony,
Blue-vetch and trillium, hawkweed, sassafras,
Milkweeds and murky brakes, quaint pipes and sundew,
And rare and virtuous roots, which in these woods
Draw untold juices from the common earth,
Untold, unknown, and I could surely spell
Their fragrance, and their chemistry apply
By sweet affinities to human flesh,
Driving the foe and stablishing the friend,—
O, that were much, and I could be a part
Of the round day, related to the sun
And planted world, and full executor
Of their imperfect functions.
But these young scholars, who invade our hills,
Bold as the engineer who fells the wood,
And travelling often in the cut he makes,
Love not the flower they pluck, and know it not,
And all their botany is Latin names.
The old men studied magic in the flowers,
And human fortunes in astronomy,
And an omnipotence in chemistry,
Preferring things to names, for these were men,
Were unitarians of the united world,
And, wheresoever their clear eye-beams fell,
They caught the footsteps of the SAME. Our eyes
Are armed, but we are strangers to the stars,
And strangers to the mystic beast and bird,
And strangers to the plant and to the mine.
The injured elements say, 'Not in us';
And night and day, ocean and continent,
Fire, plant and mineral say, 'Not in us';
And haughtily return us stare for stare.
For we invade them impiously for gain;
We devastate them unreligiously,
And coldly ask their pottage, not their love.
Therefore they shove us from them, yield to us
Only what to our griping toil is due;
But the sweet affluence of love and song,
The rich results of the divine consents
Of man and earth, of world beloved and lover,

---

1   the herbs with medicinal properties

The nectar and ambrosia, are withheld;
And in the midst of spoils and slaves, we thieves
And pirates of the universe, shut out
Daily to a more thin and outward rind,
Turn pale and starve. Therefore, to our sick eyes,
The stunted trees look sick, the summer short,
Clouds shade the sun, which will not tan our hay,
And nothing thrives to reach its natural term;
And life, shorn of its venerable length,
Even at its greatest space is a defeat,
And dies in anger that it was a dupe;
And, in its highest noon and wantonness,
Is early frugal, like a beggar's child;
Even in the hot pursuit of the best aims
And prizes of ambition, checks its hand,
Like Alpine cataracts frozen as they leaped,
Chilled with a miserly comparison
Of the toy's purchase with the length of life.

Terminus[1]

It is time to be old,
To take in sail:—
The god of bounds,
Who sets to seas a shore,
Came to me in his fatal rounds,
And said: 'No more!
No farther shoot
Thy broad ambitious branches, and thy root.
Fancy departs: no more invent;
Contract thy firmament
To compass of a tent.
There's not enough for this and that,
Make thy option which of two;
Economize the failing river,
Not the less revere the Giver,
Leave the many and hold the few.
Timely wise accept the terms,
Soften the fall with wary foot;
A little while
Still plan and smile,
And,—fault of novel germs,—
Mature the unfallen fruit.
Curse, if thou wilt, thy sires,
Bad husbands of their fires,

---

1   the name of the Roman god of boundaries

Who, when they gave thee breath,
Failed to bequeath
The needful sinew stark[1] as once,
The Baresark[2] marrow to thy bones,
But left a legacy of ebbing veins,
Inconstant heat and nerveless reins,—
Amid the Muses, left thee deaf and dumb,
Amid the gladiators, halt and numb.'

As the bird trims her to the gale,
I trim myself to the storm of time,
I man the rudder, reef the sail,
Obey the voice at eve obeyed at prime:
'Lowly faithful, banish fear,
Right onward drive unharmed;
The port, well worth the cruise, is near,
And every wave is charmed.'

---

1   strong
2   "Baresark" (bare shirt) or "berserker" was the name given to fierce Norse warriors who fought in their shirts, without armour.

Elizabeth Barrett Browning

(1806–1861)

[handwritten annotation: as they're a bit / racy, she wanted / people to / think they're / just translation]

from: *Sonnets from the Portuguese*

[handwritten annotation: Browning's pet / name for her— / Portuguese / (she had / dark skin)]

Sonnet XXII

When our two souls stand up erect and strong,
Face to face, silent, drawing nigh and nigher,
Until the lengthening wings break into fire
At either curvèd point,—what bitter wrong
Can the earth do to us, that we should not long
Be here contented? Think. In mounting higher,
The angels would press on us and aspire
To drop some golden orb of perfect song
Into our deep, dear silence. Let us stay
Rather on earth, Belovèd,—where the unfit
Contrarious moods of men recoil away
And isolate pure spirits, and permit
A place to stand and love in for a day,
With darkness and the death-hour rounding it.

[handwritten annotation: how of the most famous / sonnets of all time—]

Sonnet XLIII

How do I love thee? Let me count the ways.
I love thee to the depth and breadth and height
My soul can reach, when feeling out of sight
For the ends of Being and ideal Grace.
I love thee to the level of everyday's
Most quiet need, by sun and candlelight.
I love thee freely, as men strive for Right;
I love thee purely, as they turn from Praise.
I love thee with the passion put to use
In my old griefs, and with my childhood's faith.
I love thee with a love I seemed to lose
With my lost saints,—I love thee with the breath,
Smiles, tears, of all my life!—and, if God choose,
I shall but love thee better after death.

* * *

A Musical Instrument

I

What was he doing, the great god Pan,
  Down in the reeds by the river?
Spreading ruin and scattering ban,
Splashing and paddling with hoofs of a goat,
And breaking the golden lilies afloat
  With the dragon-fly on the river.

II

He tore out a reed, the great god Pan,
  From the deep cool bed of the river:
The limpid water turbidly ran,
And the broken lilies a-dying lay,
And the dragon-fly had fled away,
  Ere he brought it out of the river.

III

High on the shore sate the great god Pan,
  While turbidly flowed the river;
And hacked and hewed as a great god can,
With his hard bleak steel at the patient reed,
Till there was not a sign of a leaf indeed
  To prove it fresh from the river.

IV

He cut it short, did the great god Pan,
  (How tall it stood in the river!)
Then drew the pith, like the heart of a man,
Steadily from the outside ring,
And notched the poor dry empty thing
  In holes, as he sate by the river.

V

'This is the way,' laughed the great god Pan,
  (Laughed while he sate by the river,)
'The only way, since gods began
To make sweet music, they could succeed.'
Then, dropping his mouth to a hole in the reed,
  He blew in power by the river.

VI

Sweet, sweet, sweet, O Pan!
  Piercing sweet by the river!
Blinding sweet, O great god Pan!
The sun on the hill forgot to die,
And the lilies revived, and the dragon-fly
  Came back to dream on the river.

VII

Yet half a beast is the great god Pan,
  To laugh as he sits by the river,
Making a poet out of a man:
The true gods sigh for the cost and pain,—
For the reed which grows nevermore again
  As a reed with the reeds in the river.

from: *Aurora Leigh: Book I*

(lines 384–465)

                    So it was.
I broke the copious curls upon my head
In braids, because she liked[1] smooth-ordered hair.
I left off saying my sweet Tuscan words[2]
Which still at any stirring of the heart
Came up to float across the English phrase
As lilies (*Bene* or *Che che*[3]), because
She liked my father's child to speak his tongue.
I learnt the collects[4] and the catechism,
The creeds,[5] from Athanasius back to Nice,
The Articles,[6] the Tracts *against* the times[7]
(By no means Buonaventure's 'Prick of Love'),[8]
And various popular synopses of
Inhuman doctrines never taught by John,[9]
Because she liked instructed piety.

---

1 The "she" here is Aurora's maiden aunt, to whom the orphaned girl has been sent after
   the death of her father.
2 Aurora had been brought up in Italy.
3 It is well; no, no
4 short prayers, varying with the season or occasion
5 The Athanasian and the Nicene creeds are articles of Christian faith.
6 the thirty-nine "Articles," or doctrinal principles of the Anglican Church
7 John Henry Newman and other high Anglicans published between 1833 and 1841 a series
   of *Tracts for the Times*, critical of the Church of England.
8 an allusion to the doctrine of St. Buonaventure that love is a greater force than reason
   in the search for understanding
9 St. John

I learnt my complement of classic French
(Kept pure of Balzac[1] and neologism)
And German also, since she liked a range
Of liberal education—tongues,[2] not books.
I learnt a little algebra, a little
Of the mathematics—brushed with extreme flounce
The circle of the sciences, because
She misliked women who are frivolous.
I learnt the royal genealogies
Of Oviedo,[3] the internal laws
Of the Burmese empire—by how many feet
Mount Chimborazo[4] outsoars Tenerife,[5]
What navigable river joins itself
To Lara,[6] and what census of the year five
Was taken at Klagenfurt[7]—because she liked
A general insight into useful facts.
I learnt much music—such as would have been
As quite impossible in Johnson's day[8]
As still it might be wished—fine sleights of hand
And unimagined fingering, shuffling off
The hearer's soul through hurricanes of notes
To a noisy Tophet;[9] and I drew . . . costumes
From French engravings, nereids[10] neatly draped
(With smirks of simmering godship)—I washed in
Landscapes from nature (rather say, washed out).
I danced the polka and Cellarius,[11]
Spun glass, stuffed birds, and modelled flowers in wax,
Because she liked accomplishments in girls.
I read a score of books on womanhood
To prove, if women do not think at all,
They may teach thinking (to a maiden-aunt
Or else the author)—books that boldly assert
Their right of comprehending husband's talk
When not too deep, and even of answering
With pretty 'may it please you,' or 'so it is'—
Their rapid insight and fine aptitude,
Particular worth and general missionariness,
As long as they keep quiet by the fire

---

1   Honoré de Balzac (1799-1850), French novelist
2   languages
3   a 16th century Spanish historian
4   a mountain in the Andes
5   a mountain in the Canary Islands
6   a town in Spain
7   a town in Austria
8   When told that the piece of music being played by a young woman was very difficult, Samuel Johnson replied, "I would it had been impossible."
9   a place near Jerusalem associated with human sacrifice; a type of hell
10 sea-nymphs
11 a French "quadrille mazurka," a drawing room dance popular in the 1840s

And never say 'no' when the world says 'ay,'
For that is fatal—their angelic reach
Of virtue, chiefly used to sit and darn,
And fatten household sinners—their, in brief,
Potential faculty in everything
Of abdicating power in it: she owned
She liked a woman to be womanly,
And English women, she thanked God and sighed
(Some people always sigh in thanking God),
Were models to the universe. And last
I learnt cross-stitch, because she did not like
To see me wear the night with empty hands
A-doing nothing. So, my shepherdess
Was something after all (the pastoral saints
Be praised for't), leaning lovelorn with pink eyes
To match her shoes, when I mistook the silks;
Her head uncrushed by that round weight of hat
So strangely similar to the tortoise-shell
Which slew the tragic poet.[1]
           By the way,
The works of women are symbolical.
We sew, sew, prick our fingers, dull our sight,
Producing what? A pair of slippers, sir,
To put on when you're weary—or a stool
To stumble over and vex you . . . 'curse that stool!'
Or else at best, a cushion, where you lean
And sleep, and dream of something we are not
But would be for your sake. Alas, alas!
This hurts most, this—that, after all, we are paid
The worth of our work, perhaps.

from: *Aurora Leigh: Book V*

(lines 139–213)

The critics say that epics have died out
With Agamemnon and the goat-nursed gods;
I'll not believe it. I could never deem
As Payne Knight[2] did (the mythic mountaineer
Who travelled higher than he was born to live,
And showed sometimes the goitre in his throat
Discoursing of an image seen through fog),
That Homer's heroes measured twelve feet high.
They were but men—his Helen's hair turned gray

---

1   According to tradition, an eagle dropped a tortoise on the bald head of the Greek
     playwright Aeschylus, and killed him.
2   Richard Payne Knight, a classical scholar (1750-1824)

Like any plain Miss Smith's who wears a front;[1]
And Hector's infant whimpered at a plume[2]
As yours last Friday at a turkey-cock.
All actual heroes are essential men,
And all men possible heroes: every age,
Heroic in proportions, double-faced,
Looks backward and before, expects a morn
And claims an epos.[3]
                    Ay, but every age
Appears to souls who live in't (ask Carlyle)[4]
Most unheroic. Ours, for instance, ours:
The thinkers scout it, and the poets abound
Who scorn to touch it with a finger-tip:
A pewter age—mixed metal, silver-washed;
An age of scum, spooned off the richer past,
An age of patches for old gaberdines,
An age of mere transition, meaning nought
Except that what succeeds must shame it quite
If God please. That's wrong thinking, to my mind,
And wrong thoughts make poor poems.
                                Every age,
Through being beheld too close, is ill-discerned
By those who have not lived past it. We'll suppose
Mount Athos carved, as Alexander schemed,[5]
To some colossal statue of a man.
The peasants, gathering brushwood in his ear,
Had guessed as little as the browsing goats
Of form or feature of humanity
Up there—in fact, had travelled five miles off
Or ere the giant image broke on them,
Full human profile, nose and chin distinct,
Mouth, muttering rhythms of silence up the sky
And fed at evening with the blood of suns;
Grand torso—hand, that flung perpetually
The largesse of a silver river down
To all the country pastures. 'Tis even thus
With times we live in—evermore too great
To be apprehended near.
                        But poets should
Exert a double vision; should have eyes
To see near things as comprehensively
As if afar they took their point of sight,

---

1   a false front of hair, worn over the temple
2   In the *Iliad*, Hector's child is frightened by his father's helmet and crest.
3   an epic poem
4   a reference to Thomas Carlyle's *Heroes and Hero-Worship* (1841)
5   Alexander the Great was said to have contemplated carving Mount Athos into the statue
    of a conqueror, from whose outstretched hand water would pour to irrigate the land
    beneath.

And distant things as intimately deep
As if they touched them. Let us strive for this.
I do distrust the poet who discerns
No character or glory in his times,
And trundles back his soul five hundred years,
Past moat and drawbridge, into a castle-court,
To sing—oh, not of lizard or of toad
Alive i' the ditch there—'twere excusable,
But of some black chief, half knight, half sheep-lifter,
Some beauteous dame, half chattel and half queen,
As dead as must be, for the greater part,
The poems made on their chivalric bones;
And that's no wonder: death inherits death.

Nay, if there's room for poets in this world
A little overgrown (I think there is),
Their sole work is to represent the age,
Their age, not Charlemagne's[1]—this live, throbbing age,
That brawls, cheats, maddens, calculates, aspires,
And spends more passion, more heroic heat,
Betwixt the mirrors of its drawing-rooms,
Than Roland[2] with his knights at Roncesvalles.
To flinch from modern varnish, coat or flounce,
Cry out for togas and the picturesque,
Is fatal—foolish too. King Arthur's self
Was commonplace to Lady Guinevere;
And Camelot to minstrels seemed as flat
As Fleet Street to our poets.

* * *

---

1   Charlemagne (742-814), King of the Franks and Emperor of the West
2   The medieval "Chanson de Roland" recounts how Roland, a great peer in the service of
    Charlemagne, perished in an heroic action at Roncesvalles.

Henry Wadsworth Longfellow

(1807–1882)

The Tide Rises, the Tide Falls

The tide rises, the tide falls,
The twilight darkens, the curlew calls;
Along the sea-sands damp and brown
The traveller hastens toward the town,
    And the tide rises, the tide falls.

Darkness settles on roofs and walls,
But the sea, the sea in the darkness calls;
The little waves, with their soft, white hands,
Efface the footprints in the sands,
    And the tide rises, the tide falls.

The morning breaks; the steeds in their stalls
Stamp and neigh, as the hostler calls;
The day returns, but nevermore
Returns the traveller to the shore,
    And the tide rises, the tide falls.

Snow-Flakes.

Out of the bosom of the Air,
    Out of the cloud-folds of her garments shaken,
Over the woodlands brown and bare,
    Over the harvest-fields forsaken,
        Silent, and soft, and slow
        Descends the snow,

Even as our cloudy fancies take
    Suddenly shape in some divine expression,
Even as the troubled heart doth make
    In the white countenance confession,
        The troubled sky reveals
        The grief it feels.

This is the poem of the air,
    Slowly in silent syllables recorded;
This is the secret of despair,
    Long in its cloudy bosom hoarded,
        Now whispered and revealed
        To wood and field.

In the Churchyard at Cambridge.

In the village churchyard she lies,
Dust is in her beautiful eyes,
    No more she breathes, nor feels, nor stirs;
At her feet and at her head
Lies a slave to attend the dead,
    But their dust is white as hers.

Was she, a lady of high degree,
So much in love with the vanity
    And foolish pomp of this world of ours?
Or was it Christian charity,
And lowliness and humility,
    The richest and rarest of all dowers?

Who shall tell us? No one speaks,
No colour shoots into those cheeks,
    Either of anger or of pride,
At the rude question we have asked,
Nor will the mystery be unmasked
    By those who are sleeping at her side.

Hereafter?—And do you think to look
On the terrible pages of that Book
    To find her failings, faults, and errors?
Ah, you will then have other cares,
In your own shortcomings and despairs,
    In your own secret sins and terrors!

My Lost Youth

Often I think of the beautiful town[1]
    That is seated by the sea;
Often in thought go up and down
The pleasant streets of that dear old town,
    And my youth comes back to me.
        And a verse of a Lapland song
        Is haunting my memory still:
        "A boy's will is the wind's will,
And the thoughts of youth are long, long thoughts."[2]

I can see the shadowy lines of its trees,
    And catch, in sudden gleams,
The sheen of the far-surrounding seas,

---

1   Portland, Maine, Longfellow's home town
2   The refrain was suggested by some lines in a seventeenth-century history of Lapland.

And islands that were the Hesperides[1]
  Of all my boyish dreams.
    And the burden of that old song,
    It murmurs and whispers still:
    "A boy's will is the wind's will,
And the thoughts of youth are long, long thoughts."

I remember the black wharves and the slips
  And the sea-tides tossing free;
And Spanish sailors with bearded lips,
And the beauty and mystery of the ships,
  And the magic of the sea.
    And the voice of that wayward song
    Is singing and saying still:
    "A boy's will is the wind's will,
And the thoughts of youth are long, long thoughts."

I remember the bulwarks by the shore
  And the fort upon the hill;[2]
The sunrise gun, with its hollow roar,
The drum-beat repeated o'er and o'er,
  And the bugle wild and shrill.
    And the music of that old song
    Throbs in my memory still:
    "A boy's will is the wind's will,
And the thoughts of youth are long, long thoughts."

I remember the sea-fight far away,[3]
  How it thundered o'er the tide!
And the dead captains, as they lay
In their graves, o'erlooking the tranquil bay
  Where they in battle died.
    And the sound of that mournful song
    Goes through me with a thrill:
    "A boy's will is the wind's will,
And the thoughts of youth are long, long thoughts."

I can see the breezy dome of groves,
  The shadows of Deering's Woods;
And the friendships old and the early loves
Come back with a Sabbath sound, as of doves

---

1   The Hesperides were the three sisters who guarded the golden apples received by Hera
    (wife of Zeus) as a marriage gift. Like many other writers, Longfellow uses the name to
    describe the place where the apples grew.
2   Fort St. Lawrence
3   "This was the engagement between the *Enterprise* and *Boxer* off the harbor of Portland,
    in which both captains were slain. They were buried side by side in the cemetery on
    Mountjoy" (Longfellow's note). The incident took place in 1813, during the war between
    the Americans and the British.

In quiet neighbourhoods.
  And the verse of that sweet old song,
    It flutters and murmurs still:
    "A boy's will is the wind's will,
And the thoughts of youth are long, long thoughts."

I remember the gleams and glooms that dart
  Across the schoolboy's brain;
The song and the silence in the heart,
That in part are prophecies, and in part
  Are longings wild and vain.
    And the voice of that fitful song
    Sings on, and is never still:
    "A boy's will is the wind's will,
And the thoughts of youth are long, long thoughts."

There are things of which I may not speak;
  There are dreams that cannot die;
There are thoughts that make the strong heart weak
And bring a pallor into the cheek,
  And a mist before the eye.
    And the words of that fatal song
    Come over me like a chill:
    "A boy's will is the wind's will,
And the thoughts of youth are long, long thoughts."

Strange to me now are the forms I meet
  When I visit the dear old town;
But the native air is pure and sweet,
And the trees that o'ershadow each well-known street
  As they balance up and down,
    Are singing the beautiful song,
    Are sighing and whispering still:
    "A boy's will is the wind's will,
And the thoughts of youth are long, long thoughts."

And Deering's Woods are fresh and fair,
  And with joy that is almost pain
My heart goes back to wander there,
And among the dreams of the days that were,
  I find my lost youth again.
    And the strange and beautiful song,
    The groves are repeating it still:
    "A boy's will is the wind's will,
And the thoughts of youth are long, long thoughts."

Divina Commedia[1]

I

Oft have I seen at some cathedral door
    A labourer, pausing in the dust and heat,
    Lay down his burden, and with reverent feet
    Enter, and cross himself, and on the floor
Kneel to repeat his paternoster[2] o'er;
    Far off the noises of the world retreat;
    The loud vociferations of the street
    Become an undistinguishable roar.
So, as I enter here from day to day,
    And leave my burden at this minster gate,
    Kneeling in prayer, and not ashamed to pray,
The tumult of the time disconsolate
    To inarticulate murmurs dies away,
    While the eternal ages watch and wait.

II

How strange the sculptures that adorn these towers.
    This crowd of statues, in whose folded sleeves
    Birds build their nests; while canopied with leaves
    Parvis[3] and portal bloom like trellised bowers,
And the vast minster seems a cross of flowers!
    But fiends and dragons on the gargoyled eaves
    Watch the dead Christ between the living thieves
    And, underneath, the traitor Judas lowers!
Ah! from what agonies of heart and brain,
    What exultations trampling on despair,
    What tenderness, what tears, what hate of wrong,
What passionate outcry of a soul in pain,
    Uprose this poem of the earth and air,
    The mediaeval miracle of song!

III

I enter, and I see thee in the gloom
    Of the long aisles, O poet saturnine![4]
    And strive to make my steps keep pace with thine.
    The air is filled with some unknown perfume:
The congregation of the dead make room

---

1   These sonnets were written as introductions to Longfellow's translation of Dante's *Divine Comedy* (1865-67).
2   "our father": the first words of the Lord's prayer
3   a court or portico before a church
4   Dante himself

For thee to pass; the votive tapers shine;
Like rooks that haunt Ravenna's[1] groves of pine
The hovering echoes fly from tomb to tomb.
From the confessionals I hear arise
Rehearsals of forgotten tragedies,
And lamentations from the crypts below;
And then a voice celestial, that begins
With the pathetic words, "Although your sins
As scarlet be," and ends with "as the snow."[2]

IV

With snow-white veil and garments as of flame,
She stands before thee,[3] who so long ago
Filled thy young heart with passion and the woe
From which thy song and all its splendours came;
And while with stern rebuke she speaks thy name,
The ice about thy heart melts as the snow
On mountain heights, and in swift overflow
Comes gushing from thy lips in sobs of shame.
Thou makest full confession; and a gleam,
As of the dawn on some dark forest cast,
Seems on thy lifted forehead to increase;
Lethe and Eunoë[4]—the remembered dream
And the forgotten sorrow—bring at last
That perfect pardon which is perfect peace.

V

I lift mine eyes, and all the windows blaze
With forms of saints and holy men who died,
Here martyred and hereafter glorified;
And the great Rose[5] upon its leaves displays
Christ's Triumph, and the angelic roundelays
With splendour upon splendour multiplied;
And Beatrice again at Dante's side
No more rebukes, but smiles her words of praise.
And then the organ sounds, and unseen choirs
Sing the old Latin hymns of peace and love
And benedictions of the Holy Ghost;
And the melodious bells among the spires

---

1   a city admired by Dante, and in which he died in 1301
2   Isaiah 1.18
3   Beatrice, who both in life and in death was Dante's inspiration
4   In Greek mythology, Lethe is the river of forgetfulness; Eunoe, the river of good memories. In the Purgatorio, Dante drinks of both.
5   In the *Paradiso*, Dante sees Christ, the Virgin and the saints as a many-petaled rose.

O'er all the house-tops and through heaven above
Proclaim the elevation of the Host![1]

VI

O star of morning and of liberty!
    O bringer of the light, whose splendour shines
    Above the darkness of the Apennines,
    Forerunner of the day that is to be!
The voices of the city and the sea,
    The voices of the mountains and the pines,
    Repeat thy song, till the familiar lines
    Are footpaths for the thought of Italy!
Thy flame is blown abroad from all the heights,
    Through all the nations, and a sound is heard,
    As of a mighty wind, and men devout,
Strangers of Rome, and the new proselytes,
    In their own language hear thy wondrous word,
    And many are amazed and many doubt.

---

1   the consecrated bread of the communion sacrament

Edgar Allan Poe

(1809–1849)

The City in the Sea

Lo! Death has reared himself a throne
In a strange city lying alone
Far down within the dim West,
Where the good and the bad and the worst and the best
Have gone to their eternal rest.
There shrines and palaces and towers
(Time-eaten towers that tremble not!)
Resemble nothing that is ours.
Around, by lifting winds forgot,
Resignedly beneath the sky
The melancholy waters lie.

No rays from the holy heaven come down
On the long night-time of that town;
But light from out the lurid sea
Streams up the turrets silently—
Gleams up the pinnacles far and free—
Up domes—up spires—up kingly halls—
Up fanes[1]—up Babylon-like walls[2]—
Up shadowy long-forgotten bowers
Of sculptured ivy and stone flowers—
Up many and many a marvellous shrine
Whose wreathéd friezes intertwine
The viol, the violet, and the vine.

Resignedly beneath the sky
The melancholy waters lie.
So blend the turrets and shadows there
That all seem pendulous in air,
While from a proud tower in the town
Death looks gigantically down.

There open fanes and gaping graves
Yawn level with the luminous waves;
But not the riches there that lie
In each idol's diamond eye—
Not the gaily-jewelled dead
Tempt the waters from their bed;
For no ripples curl, alas!
Along that wilderness of glass—
No swellings tell that winds may be

---

1   temples
2   Babylon was the capital of ancient Babylonia, here seen as a symbol of sin and decadence,
    doomed to suffer divine retribution.

Upon some far-off happier sea—
No heavings hint that winds have been
On seas less hideously serene.

But lo, a stir is in the air!
The wave—there is a movement there!
As if the towers had thrust aside,
In slightly sinking, the dull tide—
As if their tops had feebly given
A void within the filmy Heaven.
The waves have now a redder glow—
The hours are breathing faint and low—
And when, amid no earthly moans,
Down, down that town shall settle hence.
Hell, rising from a thousand thrones,[1]
Shall do it reverence.

Dream-Land

By a route obscure and lonely,
Haunted by ill angels only,
Where an Eidolon,[2] named NIGHT,
On a black throne reigns upright,
I have reached these lands but newly
From an ultimate dim Thule[3]—
From a wild weird clime that lieth, sublime,
        Out of SPACE—out of TIME.

Bottomless vales and boundless floods
And chasms, and caves, and Titan woods,
With forms that no man can discover
For the tears that drip all over;
Mountains toppling evermore
Into seas without a shore;
Seas that restlessly aspire,
Surging, unto skies of fire;
Lakes that endlessly outspread
Their lone waters—lone and dead,—
Their still waters—still and chilly
With the snows of the lolling lily.

By the lakes that thus outspread
Their lone waters, lone and dead,—
Their sad waters, sad and chilly

---

1   an allusion to the Book of Isaiah 14.9
2   image; phantom
3   in ancient geography, the northernmost habitable regions of the earth

With the snows of the lolling lily,—
By the mountains—near the river
Murmuring lowly, murmuring ever,—
By the grey woods,—by the swamp
Where the toad and the newt encamp,—
By the dismal tarns and pools
     Where dwell the Ghouls,—

By each spot the most unholy—
In each nook most melancholy,—
There the traveller meets, aghast,
Sheeted Memories of the Past—
Shrouded forms that start and sigh
As they pass the wanderer by—
White-robed forms of friends long given,
In agony, to the Earth—and Heaven.

For the heart whose woes are legion
'Tis a peaceful, soothing region—
For the spirit that walks in shadow
'Tis—oh 'tis an Eldorado!¹
But the traveller, travelling through it,
May not—dare not openly view it;
Never its mysteries are exposed
To the weak human eye unclosed;
So wills its King, who hath forbid
The uplifting of the fringéd lid;
And thus the sad Soul that here passes
Beholds it but through darkened glasses.

By a route obscure and lonely,
Haunted by ill angels only,
Where an Eidolon, named NIGHT,
On a black throne reigns upright,
I have wandered home but newly
From this ultimate dim Thule.

---

1   literally, "the golden": a lost city of legendary wealth in South America

The Sleeper

At midnight, in the month of June,
I stand beneath the mystic moon.
An opiate vapour, dewy, dim,
Exhales from out her golden rim,
And, softly dripping, drop by drop,
Upon the quiet mountain top,
Steals drowsily and musically
Into the universal valley.
The rosemary[1] nods upon the grave;
The lily lolls upon the wave;
Wrapping the fog about its breast,
The ruin moulders into rest;
Looking like Lethë,[2] see! the lake
A conscious slumber seems to take,
And would not, for the world, awake.
All Beauty sleeps!—and lo! where lies
Irenë, with her Destinies!

Oh, lady bright! can it be right—
This window open to the night?
The wanton airs, from the tree-top,
Laughingly through the lattice drop—
The bodiless airs, a wizard rout,
Flit through thy chamber in and out,
And wave the curtain canopy
So fitfully—so fearfully—
Above the closed and fringéd lid
'Neath which thy slumb'ring soul lies hid,
That, o'er the floor and down the wall,
Like ghosts the shadows rise and fall!
Oh, lady dear, hast thou no fear?
Why and what are thou dreaming here?
Sure thou art come o'er far-off seas,
A wonder to these garden trees!
Strange is thy pallor! strange thy dress!
Strange, above all, thy length of tress,
And this all solemn silentness!

The lady sleeps! Oh, may her sleep,
Which is enduring, so be deep!
Heaven have her in its sacred keep!
This chamber changed for one more holy,
This bed for one more melancholy,
I pray to God that she may lie

---

1   a flower associated with remembrance
2   the river of forgetfulness in Hades

Forever with unopened eye,
While the pale sheeted ghosts go by!

My love, she sleeps! Oh, may her sleep,
As it is lasting, so be deep!
Soft may the worms about her creep!
Far in the forest, dim and old,
For her may some tall vault unfold—
Some vault that oft hath flung its black
And wingéd pannels fluttering back,
Triumphant, o'er the crested palls,
Of her grand family funerals—
Some sepulchre, remote, alone,
Against whose portal she hath thrown,
In childhood, many an idle stone—
Some tomb from out whose sounding door,
She ne'er shall force an echo more,
Thrilling to think, poor child of sin!
It was the dead who groaned within.

The Haunted Palace

In the greenest of our valleys
    By good angels tenanted,
Once a fair and stately palace—
    Radiant palace—reared its head.
In the monarch Thought's dominion—
    It stood there!
Never seraph spread a pinion
    Over fabric half so fair!

Banners yellow, glorious, golden,
    On its roof did float and flow—
(This—all this—was in the olden
    Time long ago)
And every gentle air that dallied,
    In that sweet day,
Along the ramparts plumed and pallid,
    A wingèd odor went away.

Wanderers in that happy valley,
    Through two luminous windows, saw
Spirits moving musically,
    To a lute's well-tunèd law,
Round about a throne where, sitting,
    Porphyrogene,
In state his glory well befitting
    The ruler of the realm was seen.

---

1   literally, "born in the purple": one born into a ruling family

And all with pearl and ruby glowing
  Was the fair palace door,
Through which came flowing, flowing, flowing,
  And sparkling evermore,
A troop of Echoes whose sweet duty
  Was but to sing,
In voices of surpassing beauty,
  The wit and wisdom of their king.

But evil things, in robes of sorrow,
  Assailed the monarch's high estate.
(Ah, let us mourn!—for never morrow
  Shall dawn upon him, desolate!)
And round about his home the glory
  That blushed and bloomed,
Is but a dim-remembered story
  Of the old-time entombed.

And travellers, now, within that valley,
  Through the encrimsoned windows see
Vast forms that move fantastically
  To a discordant melody,
While, like a ghastly rapid river,
  Through the pale door
A hideous throng rush out forever
  And laugh—but smile no more.

To Helen

Helen, thy beauty is to me
  Like those Nicéan[1] barks[2] of yore,
That gently, o'er a perfumed sea,
  The weary, way-worn wanderer bore
  To his own native shore.

On desperate seas long wont to roam,
  Thy hyacinth hair,[3] thy classic face,
Thy Naiad[4] airs have brought me home
  To the glory that was Greece
  And the grandeur that was Rome.

---

1   Poe may have been alluding to Nicaea (modern Nice), a Greek colony which became an
     important trading centre under the Romans.
2   vessels
3   hair clustered in curls, like the flower named after the handsome youth Hyacinthus
4   water-nymph

Lo! in yon brilliant window-niche
How statue-like I see thee stand!
The agate lamp within thy hand,[1]
Ah! Psyche,[2] from the regions which
Are Holy Land!

---

1   In Greek legend, the youth Leander would swim the Hellespont each night to be with
    Hero, a priestess of Aphrodite, who would guide him by holding up a lighted torch.
2   the beautiful woman who was Cupid's lover; also the Greek word for soul

Alfred, Lord Tennyson

(1809–1892)

The Lady of Shalott

Part I

On either side the river lie
Long fields of barley and of rye,
That clothe the wold[1] and meet the sky;
And through the field the road runs by
  To many-towered Camelot;
And up and down the people go,
Gazing where the lilies blow
Round an island there below,
  The island of Shalott.

Willows whiten, aspens quiver,
Little breezes dusk and shiver
Through the wave that runs for ever
By the island in the river
  Flowing down to Camelot.
Four gray walls, and four gray towers,
Overlook a space of flowers,
And the silent isle imbowers
  The Lady of Shalott.

By the margin, willow-veiled,
Slide the heavy barges trailed
By slow horses; and unhailed
The shallop[2] flitteth silken-sailed
  Skimming down to Camelot:
But who hath seen her wave her hand?
Or at the casement seen her stand?
Or is she known in all the land,
  The Lady of Shalott?

Only reapers, reaping early
In among the bearded barley,
Hear a song that echoes cheerly
From the river winding clearly,
  Down to towered Camelot:
And by the moon the reaper weary,
Piling sheaves in uplands airy,
Listening, whispers 'Tis the fairy
  Lady of Shalott.'

---

1 a tract of undulating land
2 a light open boat

Part II

There she weaves by night and day
A magic web with colours gay.
She has heard a whisper say,
A curse is on her if she stay
    To look down to Camelot.
She knows not what the curse may be,
And so she weaveth steadily,
And little other care hath she,
    The Lady of Shalott.

And moving through a mirror clear
That hangs before her all the year,
Shadows of the world appear.
There she sees the highway near
    Winding down to Camelot:
There the river eddy whirls,
And there the surly village-churls,
And the red cloaks of market girls,
    Pass onward from Shalott.

Sometimes a troop of damsels glad,
An abbot on an ambling pad,[1]
Sometimes a curly shepherd-lad,
Or long-haired page in crimson clad,
    Goes by to towered Camelot;
And sometimes through the mirror blue
The knights come riding two and two:
She hath no loyal knight and true,
    The Lady of Shalott.

But in her web she still delights
To weave the mirror's magic sights,
For often through the silent nights
A funeral, with plumes and lights
    And music, went to Camelot:
Or when the moon was overhead,
Came two young lovers lately wed;
'I am half sick of shadows,' said
    The Lady of Shalott.

---

1   an easy-paced horse

Part III

A bow-shot from her bower-eaves,
He rode between the barley-sheaves,
The sun came dazzling through the leaves,
And flamed upon the brazen greaves[1]
    Of bold Sir Lancelot.
A red-cross knight[2] for ever kneeled
To a lady in his shield,
That sparkled on the yellow field,
    Beside remote Shalott.

The gemmy bridle glittered free,
Like to some branch of stars we see
Hung in the golden Galaxy.
The bridle bells rang merrily
    As he rode down to Camelot:
And from his blazoned baldric[3] slung
A mighty silver bugle hung,
And as he rode his armour rung,
    Beside remote Shalott.

All in the blue unclouded weather
Thick-jewelled shone the saddle-leather,
The helmet and the helmet-feather
Burned like one burning flame together,
    As he rode down to Camelot.
As often through the purple night,
Below the starry clusters bright,
Some bearded meteor, trailing light,
    Moves over still Shalott.

His broad clear brow in sunlight glowed;
On burnished hooves his war-horse trode;
From underneath his helmet flowed
His coal-black curls as on he rode,
    As he rode down to Camelot.
From the bank and from the river
He flashed into the crystal mirror,
'Tirra lirra,' by the river
    Sang Sir Lancelot.

She left the web, she left the loom,
She made three paces through the room,
She saw the water-lily bloom,

---

1   armour protecting the leg from knee to ankle
2   "Redcrosse" is the Christian knight in Spenser's epic poem *The Fairie Queene*.
3   a sash displaying his armorial bearings

She saw the helmet and the plume,
    She looked down to Camelot.
Out flew the web and floated wide;
The mirror cracked from side to side;
'The curse is come upon me,' cried
    The Lady of Shalott.

Part IV

In the stormy east-wind straining,
The pale yellow woods were waning,
The broad stream in his banks complaining,
Heavily the low sky raining
    Over towered Camelot;
Down she came and found a boat
Beneath a willow left afloat,
And round about the prow she wrote
    The Lady of Shalott.

And down the river's dim expanse
Like some bold seër in a trance,
Seeing all his own mischance—
With a glassy countenance
    Did she look to Camelot.
And at the closing of the day
She loosed the chain, and down she lay;
The broad stream bore her far away,
    The Lady of Shalott.

Lying, robed in snowy white
That loosely flew to left and right—
The leaves upon her falling light—
Through the noises of the night
    She floated down to Camelot:
And as the boat-head wound along
The willowy hills and fields among,
They heard her singing her last song,
    The Lady of Shalott.

Heard a carol, mournful, holy,
Chanted loudly, chanted lowly,
Till her blood was frozen slowly,
And her eyes were darkened wholly,
    Turned to towered Camelot.
For ere she reached upon the tide
The first house by the water-side,
Singing in her song she died,
    The Lady of Shalott.

Under tower and balcony,
By garden-wall and gallery,

A gleaming shape she floated by,
Dead-pale between the houses high,
   Silent into Camelot.
Out upon the wharfs they came,
Knight and burgher, lord and dame,
And round the prow they read her name,
   The Lady of Shalott.

Who is this? and what is here?
And in the lighted palace near
Died the sound of royal cheer;
And they crossed themselves for fear,
   All the knights at Camelot:
But Lancelot mused a little space;
He said, 'She has a lovely face;
God in his mercy lend her grace,
   The Lady of Shalott.'

The Lotos-Eaters[1]

'Courage!' he said,[2] and pointed toward the land,
'This mounting wave will roll us shoreward soon.'
In the afternoon they came unto a land
In which it seemèd always afternoon.
All round the coast the languid air did swoon,
Breathing like one that hath a weary dream.
Full-faced above the valley stood the moon;
And like a downward smoke, the slender stream
Along the cliff to fall and pause and fall did seem.

A land of streams! some, like a downward smoke,
Slow-dropping veils of thinnest lawn, did go;
And some through wavering lights and shadows
    broke,
Rolling a slumbrous sheet of foam below.
They saw the gleaming river seaward flow
From the inner land: far off, three mountain-tops,
Three silent pinnacles of agèd snow,
Stood sunset-flushed: and, dewed with showery
    drops,
Up-clomb the shadowy pine above the woven copse.

The charmèd sunset lingered low adown
In the red West: through mountain clefts the dale
Was seen far inland, and the yellow down

---

1   based on an episode in the *Odyssey*, Book 9
2   The speaker is Ulysses addressing his weary companions.

Bordered with palm, and many a winding vale
And meadow, set with slender galingale;[1]
A land where all things always seemed the same!
And round about the keel with faces pale,
Dark faces pale against that rosy flame,
The mild-eyed melancholy Lotos-eaters came.

Branches they bore of that enchanted stem,
Laden with flower and fruit, whereof they gave
To each, but whoso did receive of them,
And taste, to him the gushing of the wave
Far far away did seem to mourn and rave
On alien shores; and if his fellow spake,
His voice was thin, as voices from the grave;
And deep-asleep he seemed, yet all awake,
And music in his ears his beating heart did make.

They sat them down upon the yellow sand,
Between the sun and moon upon the shore;
And sweet it was to dream of Fatherland,
Of child, and wife, and slave; but evermore
Most weary seemed the sea, weary the oar,
Weary the wandering fields of barren foam.
Then some one said, 'We will return no more;'
And all at once they sang, 'Our island home[2]
Is far beyond the wave; we will no longer roam.'

Choric Song

I

There is sweet music here that softer falls
Than petals from blown roses on the grass,
Or night-dews on still waters between walls
Of shadowy granite, in a gleaming pass;
Music that gentlier on the spirit lies,
Than tired eyelids upon tired eyes;
Music that brings sweet sleep down from the blissful
        skies.
Here are cool mosses deep,
And through the moss the ivies creep,
And in the stream the long-leaved flowers weep,
And from the craggy ledge the poppy hangs in
        sleep.

---

1   a tall sedge plant
2   Ithaca

II

Why are we weighed upon with heaviness,
And utterly consumed with sharp distress,
While all things else have rest from weariness?
All things have rest: why should we toil alone,
We only toil, who are the first of things,
And make perpetual moan,
Still from one sorrow to another thrown:
Nor ever fold our wings,
And cease from wanderings,
Nor steep our brows in slumber's holy balm;
Nor harken what the inner spirit sings,
'There is no joy but calm!'
Why should we only toil, the roof and crown of
        things?

III

Lo! in the middle of the wood,
The folded leaf is wooed from out the bud
With winds upon the branch, and there
Grows green and broad, and takes no care,
Sun-steeped at noon, and in the moon
Nightly dew-fed; and turning yellow
Falls, and floats adown the air.
Lo! sweetened with the summer light,
The full-juiced apple, waxing over-mellow,
Drops in a silent autumn night.
All its allotted length of days,
The flower ripens in its place,
Ripens and fades, and falls, and hath no toil,
Fast-rooted in the fruitful soil.

IV

Hateful is the dark-blue sky,
Vaulted o'er the dark-blue sea.
Death is the end of life; ah, why
Should life all labour be?
Let us alone. Time driveth onward fast,
And in a little while our lips are dumb.
Let us alone. What is it that will last?
All things are taken from us, and become
Portions and parcels of the dreadful Past.
Let us alone. What pleasure can we have
To war with evil? Is there any peace
In ever climbing up the climbing wave?
All things have rest, and ripen toward the grave
In silence; ripen, fall and cease:
Give us long rest or death, dark death, or dreamful

ease.
How sweet it were, hearing the downward stream,
With half-shut eyes ever to seem
Falling asleep in a half-dream!
To dream and dream, like yonder amber light,
Which will not leave the myrrh-bush on the height;
To hear each other's whispered speech;
Eating the Lotos day by day,
To watch the crisping ripples on the beach,
And tender curving lines of creamy spray;
To lend our hearts and spirits wholly
To the influence of mild-minded melancholy;
To muse and brood and live again in memory,
With those old faces of our infancy
Heaped over with a mound of grass,
Two handfuls of white dust, shut in an urn of brass!

VI

Dear is the memory of our wedded lives,
And dear the last embraces of our wives
And their warm tears: but all hath suffered change:
For surely now our household hearths are cold:
Our sons inherit us: our looks are strange:
And we should come like ghosts to trouble joy.
Or else the island princes over-bold
Have eat our substance, and the minstrel sings
Before them of the ten years' war in Troy,
And our great deeds, as half-forgotten things.
Is there confusion in the little isle?
Let what is broken so remain.
The Gods are hard to reconcile:
'Tis hard to settle order once again.
There is confusion worse than death,
Trouble on trouble, pain on pain,
Long labour unto agèd breath,
Sore task to hearts worn out by many wars
And eyes grown dim with gazing on the pilot-stars.

VII

But, propt on beds of amaranth[1] and moly,[2]
How sweet (while warm airs lull us, blowing lowly)
With half-dropt eyelid still,
Beneath a heaven dark and holy,
To watch the long bright river drawing slowly

---

1   a legendary flower that never fades
2   an enchanted herb, given by Hermes to Ulysses as a charm against the sorceries of Circe

His waters from the purple hill—
To hear the dewy echoes calling
From cave to cave through the thick-twinèd vine—
To watch the emerald-coloured water falling
Through many a woven acanthus[1]-wreath divine!
Only to hear and see the far-off sparkling brine,
Only to hear were sweet, stretched out beneath the
    pine.

VIII

The Lotos blooms below the barren peak:
The Lotos blows by every winding creek:
All day the wind breathes low with mellower tone:
Through every hollow cave and alley lone
Round and round the spicy downs the yellow
    Lotos-dust is blown.
We have had enough of action, and of motion we,
Rolled to starboard, rolled to larboard, when the
    surge was seething free,
Where the wallowing monster spouted his foam-
    fountains in the sea.
Let us swear an oath, and keep it with an equal
    mind,
In the hollow Lotos-land to live and lie reclined
On the hills like Gods together, careless of
    mankind.
For they lie beside their nectar, and the bolts are
    hurled
Far below them in the valleys, and the clouds are
    lightly curled
Round their golden houses, girdled with the gleaming
    world:
Where they smile in secret, looking over wasted
    lands,
Blight and famine, plague and earthquake, roaring
    deeps and fiery sands,
Clanging fights, and flaming towns, and
    sinking ships, and praying hands.
But they smile, they find a music centred in a
    doleful song
Steaming up, a lamentation and an ancient tale of
    wrong,
Like a tale of little meaning though the words are
    strong;
Chanted from an ill-used race of men that cleave the

---

1   a plant with spiny leaves.

soil,
Sow the seed, and reap the harvest with enduring
    toil,
Storing yearly little dues of wheat, and wine and oil;
Till they perish and they suffer—some, 'tis
    whispered—down in hell
Suffer endless anguish, others in Elysian valleys[1]
    dwell,
Resting weary limbs at last on beds of asphodel.[2]
Surely, surely, slumber is more sweet than toil,
    the shore
Than labour in the deep mid-ocean, wind and wave
    and oar;
Oh rest ye, brother mariners, we will not wander
    more.

[handwritten: gone for 10yrs in Trojan war / 10yrs to get home]

[handwritten: dramatic monologue]

[handwritten: Odysseus = Ulysses[3] from Odyssey / The Roman version / cursed by Poseidon / & Homer]

It little profits that an idle king,
By this still hearth, among these barren crags,
Matched with an agèd wife,[4] I mete and dole
Unequal laws unto a savage race,
That hoard, and sleep, and feed, and know not me.

I cannot rest from travel: I will drink
Life to the lees: all times I have enjoyed
Greatly, have suffered greatly, both with those
That loved me, and alone; on shore, and when
Through scudding drifts the rainy Hyades[5]
Vext the dim sea: I am become a name;
For always roaming with a hungry heart
Much have I seen and known; cities of men
And manners, climates, councils, governments,
Myself not least, but honoured of them all;
And drunk delight of battle with my peers,
Far on the ringing plains of windy Troy.
I am a part of all that I have met;
Yet all experience is an arch wherethrough
Gleams that untravelled world, whose margin fades
For ever and for ever when I move.
How dull it is to pause, to make an end,
To rust unburnished, not to shine in use!

[handwritten: reputation of a name in oft times is a great thing.]

---

1   After death, those favoured by the gods are sent to Elysium, the Islands of the Blessed.
2   a flower of the lily family, said to provide sustenance to the dead
3   Tennyson combines the Homeric story of Ulysses' return to Ithaca after the Trojan War
    with Dante's account (*Inferno* xxvi) of his further voyage into the unknown.
4   Penelope
5   a group of stars associated with the coming of rain

enormous admirer of Keats

As though to breathe were life. Life piled on life
Were all too little, and of one to me
Little remains: but every hour is saved
From that eternal silence, something more,
A bringer of new things; and vile it were
For some three suns to store and hoard myself,
And this gray spirit yearning in desire
To follow knowledge like a sinking star,
Beyond the utmost bound of human thought.

This is my son, mine own Telemachus, *all through the*
To whom I leave the sceptre and the isle— *Odyssy trying to*
Well-loved of me, discerning to fulfil *find his father*
This labour, by slow prudence to make mild
A rugged people, and through soft degrees
Subdue them to the useful and the good.
Most blameless is he, centred in the sphere
Of common duties, decent not to fail
In offices of tenderness, and pay
Meet adoration to my household gods,
When I am gone. He works his work, I mine.

There lies the port; the vessel puffs her sail:
There gloom the dark broad seas. My mariners,
Souls that have toiled, and wrought, and thought with me—
That ever with a frolic welcome took
The thunder and the sunshine, and opposed
Free hearts, free foreheads—you and I are old;
Old age hath yet his honour and his toil;
Death closes all: but something ere the end,
Some work of noble note, may yet be done,
Not unbecoming men that strove with Gods. *Goes from rhetoric*
The lights begin to twinkle from the rocks: *to physical*
The long day wanes: the slow moon climbs: the deep *description*
Moans round with many voices. Come, my friends,
'Tis not too late to seek a newer world.
Push off, and sitting well in order smite
The sounding furrows; for my purpose holds
To sail beyond the sunset, and the baths
Of all the western stars,[1] until I die.
It may be that the gulfs will wash us down:
It may be we shall touch the Happy Isles,[2]
And see the great Achilles,[3] whom we knew.
Though much is taken, much abides; and though

---

1 According to the ancient Greeks, the flat earth was surrounded by a body of water into
   which the stars descended at night.
2 Elysium, the Islands of the Blessed
3 a famed Greek warrior, killed at Troy

We are not now that strength which in old days
Moved earth and heaven; that which we are, we are;
One equal temper of heroic hearts,
Made weak by time and fate, but strong in will
To strive, to seek, to find, and not to yield.

Break, Break, Break

Break, break, break,
  On thy cold gray stones, O Sea!
And I would that my tongue could utter
  The thoughts that arise in me.

O well for the fisherman's boy,
  That he shouts with his sister at play!
O well for the sailor lad,
  That he sings in his boat on the bay!

And the stately ships go on
  To their haven under the hill;
But O for the touch of a vanished hand,
  And the sound of a voice that is still!

Break, break, break
  At the foot of thy crags, O Sea!
But the tender grace of a day that is dead
  Will never come back to me.

from: *In Memoriam   A. H. H.*[1]

Obiit MDCCCXXXIII[2]

I

I held it truth, with him who sings[3]
  To one clear harp in divers tones,
  That men may rise on stepping-stones
Of their dead selves to higher things.

But who shall so forecast the years
  And find in loss a gain to match?
  Or reach a hand through time to catch
The far-off interest of tears?

Let Love clasp Grief lest both be drowned,
  Let darkness keep her raven gloss:
  Ah, sweeter to be drunk with loss,
To dance with death, to beat the ground,

Than that the victor Hours should scorn
  The long result of love, and boast,
  'Behold the man that loved and lost,
But all he was is overworn.'

VII

Dark house,[4] by which once more I stand
  Here in the long unlovely street,
  Doors, where my heart was used to beat
So quickly, waiting for a hand,

A hand that can be clasped no more—
  Behold me, for I cannot sleep,
  And like a guilty thing I creep
At earliest morning to the door.

He is not here; but far away
  The noise of life begins again,
  And ghastly through the drizzling rain
On the bald street breaks the blank day.

---

1   Begun in 1833 and completed in 1849, *In Memoriam* is Tennyson's tribute to his close
    friend Arthur Henry Hallam, who died at twenty-two. It is also a record of the poet's
    spiritual progress from despair to hope.
2   Died 1833
3   the German poet Goethe
4   Hallam's house on Wimpole Street in London

XI

Calm is the morn without a sound,
  Calm as to suit a calmer grief,
  And only through the faded leaf
The chestnut pattering to the ground:

Calm and deep peace on this high wold,
  And on these dews that drench the furze,
  And all the silvery gossamers
That twinkle into green and gold:

Calm and still light on yon great plain
  That sweeps with all its autumn bowers,
  And crowded farms and lessening towers,
To mingle with the bounding main:

Calm and deep peace in this wide air,
  These leaves that redden to the fall;
  And in my heart, if calm at all,
If any calm, a calm despair:

Calm on the seas, and silver sleep,
  And waves that sway themselves in rest,
  And dead calm in that noble breast
Which heaves but with the heaving deep.

XXVII

I envy not in any moods
  The captive void of noble rage,
  The linnet born within the cage,
That never knew the summer woods:

I envy not the beast that takes
  His license in the field of time,
  Unfettered by the sense of crime,
To whom a conscience never wakes;

Nor, what may count itself as blest,
  The heart that never plighted troth
  But stagnates in the weeds of sloth;
Nor any want-begotten rest.

I hold it true, whate'er befall;
  I feel it, when I sorrow most;
  'Tis better to have loved and lost
Than never to have loved at all.

L

Be near me when my light is low,
　　When the blood creeps, and the nerves prick
　　And tingle; and the heart is sick,
And all the wheels of Being slow.
Be near me when the sensuous frame
　　Is racked with pangs that conquer trust;
　　And Time, a maniac scattering dust,
And Life, a Fury slinging flame.

Be near me when my faith is dry,
　　And men the flies of latter spring,
　　That lay their eggs, and sting and sing
And weave their petty cells and die.

Be near me when I fade away,
　　To point the term of human strife,
　　And on the low dark verge of life
The twilight of eternal day.

LIV

O, yet we trust that somehow good
　　Will be the final goal of ill,
　　To pangs of nature, sins of will,
Defects of doubt, and taints of blood;

That nothing walks with aimless feet;
　　That not one life shall be destroy'd,
　　Or cast as rubbish to the void,
When God hath made the pile complete;

That not a worm is cloven in vain;
　　That not a moth with vain desire
　　Is shrivell'd in a fruitless fire,
Or but subserves another's gain.

Behold, we know not anything; .
　　I can but trust that good shall fall
　　At last—far off—at last, to all,
And every winter change to spring.

So runs my dream; but what am I?
　　An infant crying in the night;
　　An infant crying for the light,
And with no language but a cry.

LV

The wish, that of the living whole
   No life may fail beyond the grave,
   Derives it not from what we have
The likest God within the soul?

Are God and Nature then at strife,
   That Nature lends such evil dreams?
   So careful of the type[1] she seems,
So careless of the single life;

That I, considering everywhere
   Her secret meaning in her deeds,
   And finding that of fifty seeds
She often brings but one to bear,

I falter where I firmly trod,
   And falling with my weight of cares
   Upon the great world's altar-stairs
That slope through darkness up to God,

I stretch lame hands of faith, and grope,
   And gather dust and chaff, and call
   To what I feel is Lord of all,
And faintly trust the larger hope.

LVI

'So careful of the type?' but no.
   From scarpèd cliff[2] and quarried stone
   She[3] cries, 'A thousand types are gone:
I care for nothing, all shall go.

'Thou makest thine appeal to me:
   I bring to life, I bring to death:
   The spirit does but mean the breath:
I know no more.' And he, shall he,

Man, her last work, who seemed so fair,
   Such splendid purpose in his eyes,
   Who rolled the psalm to wintry skies,
Who built him fanes[4] of fruitless prayer,

---

1   species
2   a cliff worn or cut away to expose the strata
3   nature
4   temples

Who trusted God was love indeed
   And love Creation's final law—
   Though Nature, red in tooth and claw
With ravine, shrieked against his creed—

Who loved, who suffered countless ills,
   Who battled for the True, the Just,
   Be blown about the desert dust,
Or sealed[1] within the iron hills?

No more? A monster then, a dream,
   A discord. Dragons of the prime,
   That tare[2] each other in their slime,
Were mellow music matched with him.

O life as futile, then, as frail!
   O for thy voice[3] to soothe and bless!
   What hope of answer, or redress?
Behind the veil, behind the veil.

CVI

Ring out, wild bells, to the wild sky,
   The flying cloud, the frosty light:
   The year is dying in the night;
Ring out, wild bells, and let him die.

Ring out the old, ring in the new,
   Ring, happy bells, across the snow:
   The year is going, let him go;
Ring out the false, ring in the true.

Ring out the grief that saps the mind,
   For those that here we see no more;
   Ring out the feud of rich and poor,
Ring in redress to all mankind.

Ring out a slowly dying cause,
   And ancient forms of party strife;
   Ring in the nobler modes of life,
With sweeter manners, purer laws.

Ring out the want, the care, the sin,
   The faithless coldness of the times;

---

1   as fossils
2   archaic form of "tore"
3   i.e., Hallam's

Ring out, ring out my mournful rhymes,
But ring the fuller minstrel in.

Ring out false pride in place and blood,
    The civic slander and the spite;
    Ring in the love of truth and right,
Ring in the common love of good.

Ring out old shapes of foul disease;
    Ring out the narrowing lust of gold;
    Ring out the thousand wars of old,
Ring in the thousand years of peace.

Ring in the valiant man and free,
    The larger heart, the kindlier hand;
    Ring out the darkness of the land,
Ring in the Christ that is to be.

CXVIII

Contemplate all this work of Time,
    The giant labouring in his youth;
    Nor dream of human love and truth,
As dying Nature's earth and lime;

But trust that those we call the dead
    Are breathers of an ampler day
    For ever nobler ends. They say,
The solid earth whereon we tread

In tracts of fluent heat began,
    And grew to seeming-random forms,
    The seeming prey of cyclic storms,
Till at the last arose the man;

Who throve and branched from clime to clime,
    The herald of a higher race,
    And of himself in higher place,
If so he type this work of time

Within himself, from more to more;
    Or, crowned with attributes of woe
    Like glories, move his course, and show
That life is not as idle ore,

But iron dug from central gloom,
    And heated hot with burning fears,
    And dipt in baths of hissing tears,
And battered with the shocks of doom

To shape and use. Arise and fly
  The reeling Faun, the sensual feast;
  Move upward, working out the beast,
And let the ape and tiger die.

* * *

Crossing the Bar[1]

Sunset and evening star,
  And one clear call for me!
And may there be no moaning of the bar,
  When I put out to sea,

But such a tide as moving seems asleep,
  Too full for sound and foam,
When that which drew from out the boundless deep
  Turns again home.

Twilight and evening bell,
  And after that the dark!
And may there be no sadness of farewell,
  When I embark;

For though from out our bourne[2] of Time and Place
  The flood may bear me far,
I hope to see my Pilot face to face
  When I have crost the bar.

---

1   A bar is a sand bank at the entrance to a harbour
2   boundary

handwritten note: admirer of shelly

handwritten note: Browning wants to understand the nature of [human] evil

Robert Browning

(1812–1889)

handwritten note: -comes from a series "madhouse cells"

handwritten note: meter - most lines have 8 syllables, some 7 or 9

handwritten note: Iambic meter

Porphyria's Lover

The rain set early in to-night, *a*
  The sullen wind was soon awake, *b*
It tore the elm-tops down for spite, *a*
  And did its worst to vex the lake: *b*
  I listened with heart fit to break. *b*
When glided in Porphyria; straight *a*
  She shut the cold out and the storm,
And kneeled and made the cheerless grate
  Blaze up, and all the cottage warm;
  Which done, she rose, and from her form
Withdrew the dripping cloak and shawl,
  And laid her soiled gloves by, untied
Her hat and let the damp hair fall,
  And, last, she sat down my my side
  And called me. When no voice replied,
She put my arm about her waist,
  And made her smooth white shoulder bare,
And all her yellow hair displaced,
  And, stooping, made my cheek lie there
  And spread, o'er all, her yellow hair,
Murmuring how she loved me—she
  Too weak, for all her heart's endeavor,
To set its struggling passion free
  From pride, and vainer ties dissever,
  And give herself to me forever.
But passion sometimes would prevail,
  Nor could to-night's gay feast restrain
A sudden thought of one so pale
  For love of her, and all in vain:
  So, she was come through wind and rain.
Be sure I looked up at her eyes
  Happy and proud; at last I knew
Porphyria worshipped me; surprise
  Made my heart swell, and still it grew
  While I debated what to do.
That moment she was mine, mine, fair,
  Perfectly pure and good: I found
A thing to do, and all her hair
  In one long yellow string I wound
  Three times her little throat around
And strangled her. No pain felt she;
  I am quite sure she felt no pain.
As a shut bud that hold a bee,
  I warily oped her lids: again
  Laughed the blue eyes without a stain.
And I untightened next the tress
  About her neck, her cheek once more

handwritten note: Oh, she really loves me, I'm going to pursue this moment

[handwritten: The psychotic speaking — no one blushes while dead if they're kissed.]

Blushed bright beneath my burning kiss:
   I propped her head up as before
   Only, this time my shoulder bore,
Her head, which droops upon it still:
   The smiling rosy little head,
So glad it has its utmost will,
   That all it scorned at once is fled,
   And I, its love, am gained instead!
Porphyria's love: she guessed not how
   Her darling one wish would be heard.
And thus we sit together now,
   And all night long we have not stirred,
   And yet God has not said a word!

[handwritten: God has not intervened, must have been OK]

Soliloquy of the Spanish Cloister

[handwritten: Life in a monastery]

I

[handwritten: 1st to be Not written in iambic meter]

Gr-r-r—there go, my heart's abhorrence!
   Water your damned flower-pots, do!
If hate killed men, Brother Lawrence,
   God's blood, would not mine kill you!
What? your myrtle-bush wants trimming?
   Oh, that rose has prior claims—
Needs its leaden vase filled brimming?
   Hell dry you up with its flames!

[handwritten: he (the speaker) hates Brother Lawrence, he's too nice, drives him crazy, grass always has such advice, etc.]

II

At the meal we sit together:
   Salve Tibi![1] I must hear
Wise talk of the kind of weather,
   Sort of season, time of year:
Not a plenteous cork-crop: scarcely
   Dare we hope oak-galls,[2] *I doubt:*
What's the Latin name for "parsley"?
What's the Greek name for Swine's Snout?[3]

[handwritten: 2 monks, I hate the other for being too goody-goody the other doesn't even realize what's going on.]

III

Whew! We'll have our platter burnished,
   Laid with care on our own shelf!
With a fire-new spoon we're furnished,
   And a goblet for ourself,

---

1   Hail to thee!
2   abnormal growths on the bark of oak-trees, used in tanning and in making ink
3   dandelion (in Latin, rostrum porcinum)

Rinsed like something sacrificial
Ere 'tis fit to touch our chaps[1]—
Marked with L. for our initial!
(He-he! There his lily snaps!)

Snaps (Kills)
the Brother's
favorite flower

IV

Saint, forsooth! While brown Dolores
Squats outside the Convent bank
With Sanchicha, telling stories,
Steeping tresses in the tank,
Blue-black, lustrous, thick like horsehairs,
—Can't I see his dead eye glow,
Bright as 't were a Barbary corsair's?[2]
(That is, if he'd let it show!)

He sees
his women,
he feels
the lust
but he
Phrases
that he's
sure that
Br. Lawrence felt the lust.

V

When he finishes refection,[3]
Knife and fork he never lays
Cross-wise, to my recollection,
As do I, in Jesu's praise.
I the Trinity illustrate,
Drinking watered orange-pulp—
In three sips the Arian frustrate;[4]
While he drains his at one gulp.

Terribly
trivial.
'Office Politics'

VI

Oh, those melons? If he's able
We're to have a feast! so nice!
One goes to the Abbot's table,
All of us get each a slice.
How go on your flowers? None double?
Not one fruit-sort can you spy?
Strange!—And I, too, at such trouble,
Keep them close-nipped on the sly!

terrible
rage

VII

There's a great text in Galatians,[5]
Once you trip on it, entails
Twenty-nine distinct damnations,

---

1   jaws
2   a pirate from the Barbary coast of North Africa
3   dinner
4   The followers of Arius (256-336) denied the doctrine of the Holy Trinity.
5   In Galatians 5.19-21 St. Paul catalogues various "works of the flesh" that would lead to damnation.

One sure, if another fails:
If I trip him just a-dying,
  Sure of heaven as sure can be,
Spin him round and send him flying
  Off to hell, a Manichee?[1]

VIII

porno

Or, my scrofulous French novel
  On grey paper with blunt type!
Simply glance at it, you grovel
  Hand and foot in Belial's gripe:[2]
If I double down its pages
  At the woeful sixteenth print,
When he gathers his greengages,
  Ope a sieve and slip it in't?

I'll show this book to the Br. + he'll be damned

IX

Or, there's Satan!—one might venture
  Pledge one's soul to him, yet leave
Such a flaw in the indenture
  As he'd miss till, past retrieve,
Blasted lay that rose-acacia
  We're so proud of! Hy, Zy, Hine[3] . . .
'St, there's Vespers![4] *Plena gratia*
  Ave, Virgo![5] Gr-r-r—you swine!

Gr-r-r- There | go, my | hearts ab|horrence!
Water | your damned | flower-pots | do !
If hate | killed men, | Brother | Lawrence

trochaic tetrameter

• most poets give
flower as 1 syllable
• this is also a
catalectic
trochaic foot

---

1   one who believes in the heretical doctrine of a dualistic universe
2   in the grip of the devil
3   Perhaps the beginning of a curse against Brother Lawrence, or an obscure incantation
     to the Devil; editors have not been able to agree on the meaning of these words.
4   A bell has sounded for evening prayers.
5   "Full of grace, Hail Virgin!" The normal order of this prayer ("Hail Virgin, full of grace")
     is twisted by the warped speaker.

ROBERT BROWNING

My Last Duchess[1]

FERRARA

That's my last Duchess painted on the wall,
Looking as if she were alive. I call
That piece a wonder, now: Fra Pandolf's[2] hands
Worked busily a day, and there she stands.
Will't please you sit and look at her? I said
"Fra Pandolf" by design, for never read
Strangers like you that pictured countenance,
The depth and passion of its earnest glance,
But to myself they turned (since none puts by
The curtain I have drawn for you, but I)
And seemed as they would ask me, if they durst,
How such a glance came there; so, not the first
Are you to turn and ask thus. Sir, 't was not
Her husband's presence only, called that spot
Of joy into the Duchess' cheek: perhaps
Fra Pandolf chanced to say "Her mantle laps
Over my lady's wrist too much," or "Paint
Must never hope to reproduce the faint
Half-flush that dies along her throat": such stuff
Was courtesy, she thought, and cause enough
For calling up that spot of joy. She had
A heart—how shall I say?—too soon made glad,
Too easily impressed; she liked whate'er
She looked on, and her looks went everywhere.
Sir, 't was all one! My favour at her breast,
The dropping of the daylight in the West,
The bough of cherries some officious fool
Broke in the orchard for her, the white mule
She rode with round the terrace—all and each
Would draw from her alike the approving speech,
Or blush, at least. She thanked men,—good! but thanked
Somehow—I know not how—as if she ranked
My gift of a nine-hundred-years-old name
With anybody's gift. Who'd stoop to blame
This sort of trifling? Even had you skill
In speech—(which I have not)—to make your will
Quite clear to such an one, and say, "Just this
Or that in you disgusts me; here you miss,

---

1   Based on events in the life of Alfonso II, first Duke of Ferrara in Italy, whose first wife
    died in 1561 under suspicious circumstances after three years of marriage. Upon her
    death the Duke entered into negotiations with an agent of Count Ferdinand I of Tyrol,
    whose daughter he married in 1565.
2   an imaginary painter, just as "Claus of Innsbruck" is an imaginary sculptor

extraordinary connoisseur but cold-blooded murderer
He doesn't say directly that he killed her, gave the orders.

Or there exceed the mark"—and if she let
Herself be lessoned so, nor plainly set
Her wits to yours, forsooth, and made excuse,
—E'en then would be some stooping; and I choose
Never to stoop. Oh sir, she smiled, no doubt,
Whene'er I passed her; but who passed without
Much the same smile? This grew; I gave commands;
Then all smiles stopped together. There she stands
As if alive. Will 't please you rise? We'll meet
The company below, then. I repeat,
The Count your master's known munificence
Is ample warrant that no just pretence
Of mine for dowry will be disallowed;
Though his fair daughter's self, as I avowed
At starting, is my object. Nay, we'll go
Together down, sir. Notice Neptune, though,
Taming a sea-horse, thought a rarity,
Which Claus of Innsbruck cast in bronze for me!

I will not come down to that level, that ordinary kind of people

he's so proud of the painting bk its so lifelike + yet he had her killed.

He's most proud of the blushing in the painting which is also the reason for why he killed her.

Your master is so generous that I'm sure there will be no problem w/ the dowry.

trying to flatter her to the ambassador as if he's not marrying her merely for monetary reason.

The Bishop Orders His Tomb at Saint Praxed's Church[1]

ROME, 15—

note the reference to Poseidon training the horse. Like training his wife.

Poseidon is a powerful figure, one the Duke would want to be identified with.

Vanity, saith the preacher, vanity![2]
Draw round my bed: is Anselm keeping back?
Nephews—sons mine . . . ah God, I know not!
    Well—
She, men would have to be your mother once,
Old Gandolf envied me, so fair she was!
What's done is done, and she is dead beside,
Dead long ago, and I am Bishop since,
And as she died so must we die ourselves,
And thence ye may perceive the world's a dream.
Life, how and what is it? As here I lie
In this state-chamber, dying by degrees,
Hours and long hours in the dead night, I ask
"Do I live, am I dead?" Peace, peace seems all.
Saint Praxed's ever was the church for peace;
And so, about this tomb of mine. I fought
With tooth and nail to save my niche, ye know:
—Old Gandolf cozened[3] me, despite my care;
Shrewd was that snatch from out the corner South
He graced his carrion with, God curse the same!

---

1   The Bishop and his rival Gandolf are imaginary; the church is real, and named after a
      Roman virgin of the second century who gave her wealth to the poor.
2   an echo of Ecclesiastes 1.2
3   deceived

[279]

Yet still my niche is not so cramped but thence
One sees the pulpit o' the epistle-side,[1]
And somewhat of the choir, those silent seats,
And up into the aery dome where live
The angels, and a sunbeam's sure to lurk:
And I shall fill my slab of basalt[2] there,
And 'neath my tabernacle[3] take my rest,
With those nine columns round me, two and two,
The odd one at my feet where Anselm stands:
Peach-blossom marble all, the rare, the ripe
As fresh-poured red wine of a mighty pulse.[4]
—Old Gandolf with his paltry onion-stone,[5]
Put me where I may look at him! True peach,
Rosy and flawless: how I earned the prize!
Draw close: that conflagration of my church
—What then? So much was saved if aught were missed!
My sons, ye would not be my death? Go dig
The white-grape vineyard where the oil-press stood,
Drop water gently till the surface sink,
And if ye find . . . Ah God, I know not, I! . . .
Bedded in store of rotten fig-leaves soft,
And corded up in a tight olive-frail,[6]
Some lump, ah God, of *lapis lazuli*,[7]
Big as a Jew's head cut off at the nape,
Blue as a vein o'er the Madonna's breast . . .
Sons, all have I bequeathed you, villas, all,
That brave Frascati[8] villa with its bath,
So, let the blue lump poise between my knees,
Like God the Father's globe on both his hands
Ye worship in the Jesu Church[9] so gay,
For Gandolf shall not choose but see and burst!
Swift as a weaver's shuttle fleet our years:[10]
Man goeth to the grave, and where is he?[11]
Did I say basalt for my slab, sons? Black[12]—
'T was ever antique-black I meant! How else
Shall ye contrast my frieze to come beneath?
The bas-relief in bronze ye promised me,

---

1   During Mass, the Epistle is read from the right side of the altar, as one faces it.
2   a dark volcanic rock
3   tent-like canopy
4   a pulpy mash of fermented grapes
5   an inferior marble
6   a basket for olives
7   rich blue stone
8   a town near Rome, favoured as a resort
9   a Jesuit church in Rome, in which the figure of an angel sits on the altar, holding a large ball of lapis lazuli
10   adapted from Job 7.6
11   adapted from Job 7.9
12   black marble

Those Pans and Nymphs ye wot of, and perchance
Some tripod, thyrsus, with a vase or so,[1]
The Saviour at his sermon on the mount,
Saint Praxed in a glory, and one Pan
Ready to twitch the Nymph's last garment off,
And Moses with the tables[2] . . . but I know
Ye mark me not! What do they whisper thee,
Child of my bowels, Anselm? Ah, ye hope
To revel down my villas while I gasp
Bricked o'er with beggar's mouldy travertine[3]
Which Gandolf from his tomb-top chuckles at!
Nay, boys, ye love me—all of jasper,[4] then!
'T is jasper ye stand pledged to, lest I grieve
My bath must needs be left behind, alas!
One block, pure green as a pistachio-nut,
There's plenty jasper somewhere in the world—
And have I not Saint Praxed's ear to pray
Horses for ye, and brown Greek manuscripts,
And mistresses with great smooth marbly limbs?
—That's if ye carve my epitaph aright,
Choice Latin, picked phrase, Tully's[5] every word,
No gaudy ware like Gandolf's second line—
Tully, my masters? Ulpian[6] serves his need!
And then how I shall lie through centuries,
And hear the blessed mutter of the mass,
And see God made and eaten all day long,
And feel the steady candle-flame, and taste
Good strong thick stupefying incense-smoke!
For as I lie here, hours of the dead night,
Dying in state and by such slow degrees,
I fold my arms as if they clasped a crook,[7]
And stretch my feet forth straight as stone can point,
And let the bedclothes, for a mortcloth,[8] drop
Into great laps and folds of sculptor's-work:
And as yon tapers dwindle, and strange thoughts
Grow, with a certain humming in my ears,
About the life before I lived this life,
And this life too, popes, cardinals and priests,
Saint Praxed at his sermon on the mount,
Your tall pale mother with her talking eyes,

---

1   Implements of pagan worship; the tripod was a stool used by priestesses of Delphi, and
      the thyrsus was a staff carried in Bacchanalian processions.
2   the tablets containing the ten commandments
3   limestone
4   coloured quartz
5   Marcus Tullius Cicero (106-43 B.C.), a Roman writer renowned for the elegance of his
      style
6   Domitius Ulpianus (A.D. 170-228), an inferior Roman writer
7   a bishop's staff
8   the pall that covers a coffin or a body

And new-found agate urns as fresh as day,
And marble's language, Latin pure, discreet,
—Aha, ELUCESCEBAT[1] quoth our friend?
No Tully, said I, Ulpian at the best!
Evil and brief hath been my pilgrimage.[2]
All *lapis*, all, sons! Else I give the Pope
My villas! Will ye ever eat my heart?
Ever your eyes were as a lizard's quick,
They glitter like your mother's for my soul,
Or ye would heighten my impoverished frieze,
Piece out its starved design, and fill my vase
With grapes, and add a vizor[3] and a Term,[4]
And to the tripod ye would tie a lynx
That in his struggle throws the thyrsus down,
To comfort me on my entablature[5]
Whereon I am to lie till I must ask
"Do I live, am I dead?" There, leave me, there!
For ye have stabbed me with ingratitude
To death—ye wish it—God, ye wish it! Stone—
Gritstone,[6] a-crumble! Clammy squares which sweat
As if the corpse they keep were oozing through—
And no more *lapis* to delight the world!
Well, go! I bless ye. Fewer tapers there,
But in a row: and, going, turn your backs
—Ay, like departing altar-ministrants,
And leave me in my church, the church for peace,
That I may watch at leisure if he leers—
Old Gandolf, at me, from his onion-stone,
As still he envied me, so fair she was!

---

1 "He was illustrious." This epitaph on Gandolf's tomb is in the less pure style of a writer
   like Ulpian; Ciceronian Latin would read "Elucebat."
2 an allusion to Genesis 47.9
3 part of a helmet
4 a tapering pillar, ending in a sculptured head or bust
5 the platform supporting a statue
6 coarse sandstone

Fra Lippo Lippi[1]

I am poor brother Lippo, by your leave!
You need not clap your torches to my face.
Zooks,[2] what's to blame? you think you see a monk!
What, 'tis past midnight, and you go the rounds,
And here you catch me at an alley's end
Where sportive ladies leave their doors ajar?
The Carmine's my cloister:[3] hunt it up,
Do,—harry out, if you must show your zeal,
Whatever rat, there, haps on his wrong hole,
And nip each softling of a wee white mouse,
Weke, weke, that's crept to keep him company!
Aha, you know your betters? Then, you'll take
Your hand away that's fiddling on my throat,
And please to know me likewise. Who am I?
Why, one, sir, who is lodging with a friend
Three streets off—he's a certain . . . how d'ye call?
Master—a . . . Cosimo of the Medici,[4]
In the house that caps the corner. Boh! you were best!
Remember and tell me, the day you're hanged,
How you affected such a gullet's-gripe![5]
But you, sir, it concerns you that your knaves
Pick up a manner nor discredit you:
Zooks, are we pilchards, that they sweep the streets
And count fair prize what comes into their net?
He's Judas to a tittle,[6] that man is!
Just such a face! Why, sir, you make amends.
Lord, I'm not angry! Bid your hangdogs go
Drink out this quarter-florin to the health
Of the munificent House that harbours me
(And many more beside, lads! more beside!)
And all's come square again. I'd like his face—
His, elbowing on his comrade in the door
With the pike and lantern,—for the slave that holds
John Baptist's head a-dangle by the hair
With one hand ('Look you, now,' as who should say)
And his weapon in the other, yet unwiped!
It's not your chance to have a bit of chalk,
A wood-coal or the like? or you should see!
Yes, I'm the painter, since you style me so.
What, brother Lippo's doings, up and down,

---

1   Lippo Lippi, Florentine painter and friar (1406-1469)
2   gadzooks, a mild oath
3   Santa Maria del Carmine, the Florentine church and cloister of the Carmelite order of
     friars
4   a Florentine banker, a member of the most powerful family in Florence
5   i.e., how you dared to grasp the throat of one such as I
6   That man (one of the watchmen) looks exactly like Judas.

You know them and they take you?[1] like enough!
I saw the proper twinkle in your eye—
'Tell you, I liked your looks at very first.
Let's sit and set things straight now, hip to haunch.
Here's spring come, and the nights one makes up bands
To roam the town and sing out carnival,[2]
And I've been three weeks shut within my mew,
A-painting for the great man, saints and saints
And saints again. I could not paint all night—
Ouf! I leaned out of window for fresh air.
There came a hurry of feet and little feet,
A sweep of lute-strings, laughs, and whifts of song,—
Flower o' the broom,
Take away love, and our earth is a tomb!
Flower o' the quince,
I let Lisa go, and what good in life since?
Flower o' the thyme—and so on. Round they went.
Scarce had they turned the corner when a titter
Like the skipping of rabbits by moonlight,—three slim shapes,
And a face that looked up . . . zooks, sir, flesh and blood,
That's all I'm made of! Into shreds it went,
Curtain and counterpane and coverlet,
All the bed furniture—a dozen knots,
There was a ladder! Down I let myself,
Hands and feet, scrambling somehow, and so dropped,
And after them. I came up with the fun
Hard by St. Laurence,[3] hail fellow, well met,—
Flower o' the rose,
If I've been merry, what matter who knows?
And so as I was stealing back again
To get to bed and have a bit of sleep
Ere I rise up to-morrow and go work
On Jerome[4] knocking at his poor old breast
With his great round stone to subdue the flesh,
You snap me of the sudden. Ah, I see!
Though your eye twinkles still, you shake your head—
Mine's shaved,—a monk, you say—the sting's in that!
If Master Cosimo announced himself,
Mum's the word naturally; but a monk!
Come, what am I a .beast for? tell us, now!
I was a baby when my mother died
And father died and left me in the street.
I starved there, God knows how, a year or two
On fig-skins, melon-parings, rinds and shucks,

---

1   they captivate you?
2   the festivities preceding the beginning of Lent
3   the church of San Lorenzo in Florence
4   an ascetic saint of the fourth century A.D.

Refuse and rubbish. One fine frosty day,
My stomach being empty as your hat,
The wind doubled me up and down I went.
Old Aunt Lapaccia[1] trussed me with one hand,
(Its fellow was a stinger as I knew)
And so along the wall, over the bridge,
By the straight cut to the convent. Six words there,
While I stood munching my first bread that month:
'So, boy, you're minded,' quoth the good fat father
Wiping his own mouth, 'twas refection-time,[2]—
To quit this very miserable world?
'Will you renounce' . . . 'the mouthful of bread?' thought I;
By no means! Brief, they made a monk of me;
I did renounce the world, its pride and greed,
Palace, farm, villa, shop and banking-house,
Trash, such as these poor devils of Medici
Have given their hearts to—all at eight years old.
Well, sir, I found in time, you may be sure,
'Twas not for nothing—the good bellyful,
The warm serge and the rope that goes all round,
And day-long blessed idleness beside!
'Let's see what the urchin's fit for'—that came next.
Not overmuch their way, I must confess.
Such a to-do! they tried me with their books:
Lord, they'd have taught me Latin in pure waste!
Flower o' the clove,
All the Latin I construe is, 'amo I love!
But, mind you, when a boy starves in the streets
Eight years together, as my fortune was,
Watching folk's faces to know who will fling
The bit of half-stripped grape-bunch he desires,
And who will curse or kick him for his pains,—
Which gentleman processional and fine,
Holding a candle to the Sacrament,
Will wink and let him lift a plate and catch
The droppings of the wax to sell again,
Or holla for the Eight[3] and have him whipped,—
How say I?—nay, which dog bites, which lets drop
His bone from the heap of offal in the street,—
Why, soul and sense of him grow sharp alike,
He learns the look of things, and none the less
For admonition from the hunger-pinch.
I had a store of such remarks, be sure,
Which, after I found leisure, turned to use.

---

1 The aunt who took care of Lippi for six years after he was orphaned; see Vasari's *Lives of the Painters* (1550).
2 meal time
3 the Florentine magistrates

I drew men's faces on my copy-books,
Scrawled them within the antiphonary's marge,[1]
Joined legs and arms to the long music-notes,
Found eyes and nose and chin for A's and B's,
And made a string of pictures of the world
Betwixt the ins and outs of verb and noun,
On the wall, the bench, the door. The monks looked black.
'Nay,' quoth the Prior, 'turn him out, d'ye say?
In no wise. Lose a crow and catch a lark.
What if at last we get our man of parts,
We Carmelites, like those Camaldolese
And Preaching Friars,[2] to do our church up fine
And put the front on it that ought to be!'
And hereupon he bade me daub away.
Thank you! my head being crammed, the walls a blank,
Never was such prompt disemburdening.
First, every sort of monk, the black and white,
I drew them, fat and lean: then, folk at church,
From good old gossips waiting to confess
Their cribs[3] of barrel-droppings, candle-ends,—
To the breathless fellow at the altar-foot,
Fresh from his murder, safe and sitting there
With the little children round him in a row
Of admiration, half for his beard and half
For that white anger of his victim's son
Shaking a fist at him with one fierce arm,
Signing himself with the other because of Christ
(Whose sad face on the cross sees only this
After the passion of a thousand years)
Till some poor girl, her apron o'er her head,
(Which the intense eyes looked through) came at eve
On tiptoe, said a word, dropped in a loaf,
Her pair of earrings and a bunch of flowers
(The brute took growling), prayed, and so was gone.
I painted all, then cried, ' 'Tis ask and have;
Choose, for more's ready!'—laid the ladder flat,
And showed my covered bit of cloister-wall.
The monks closed in a circle and praised loud
Till checked, taught what to see and not to see,
Being simple bodies,—'That's the very man!
Look at the boy who stoops to pat the dog!
That woman's like the Prior's niece who comes
To care about his asthma: it's the life!'
But there my triumph's straw-fire flared and funked;[4]

---

1   the margin of his choral hymn-book
2   Benedictine and Dominican religious orders
3   petty thefts
4   went up in smoke

Their betters took their turn to see and say:
The Prior and the learned pull a face
And stopped all that in no time. 'How? what's here?
Quite from the mark of painting, bless us all!
Faces, arms, legs and bodies like the true
As much as pea and pea! it's devil's-game!
Your business is not to catch men with show,
With homage to the perishable clay,
But lift them over it, ignore it all,
Make them forget there's such a thing as flesh.
Your business is to paint the souls of men—
Man's soul, and it's a fire, smoke . . . no, it's not . . .
It's vapour done up like a new-born babe—
(In that shape when you die it leaves your mouth)
It's . . . well, what matters talking, it's the soul!
Give us no more of body than shows soul!
Here's Giotto,[1] with his Saint a-praising God,
That sets up praising,—why not stop with him?
Why put all thoughts of praise out of our head
With wonder at lines, colours, and what not?
Paint the soul, never mind the legs and arms!
Rub all out, try at it a second time.
Oh, that white smallish female with the breasts,
She's just my niece . . . Herodias,[2] I would say,—
Who went and danced and got men's heads cut off!
Have it all out!' Now, is this sense, I ask?
A fine way to paint soul, by painting body
So ill, the eye can't stop there, must go further
And can't fare worse! Thus, yellow does for white
When what you put for yellow's simply black,
And any sort of meaning looks intense
When all beside itself means and looks nought.
Why can't a painter lift each foot in turn,
Left foot and right foot, go a double step,
Make his flesh liker and his soul more like,
Both in their order? Take the prettiest face,
The Prior's niece . . . patron-saint—is it so pretty
You can't discover if it means hope, fear,
Sorrow or joy? won't beauty go with these?
Suppose I've made her eyes all right and blue,
Can't I take breath and try to add life's flash,
And then add soul and heighten them threefold?
Or say there's beauty with no soul at all—
(I never saw it—put the case the same—)
If you get simple beauty and nought else,

---

1   Florentine painter (c.1267-1337)
2   the mother of Salome; it was Salome, not Herodias, who danced for King Herod and
    obtained the head of John the Baptist as reward.

You get about the best thing God invents:
That's somewhat: and you'll find the soul you have missed,
Within yourself, when you return him thanks.
'Rub all out!' Well, well, there's my life, in short,
And so the thing has gone on ever since.
I'm grown a man no doubt, I've broken bounds:
You should not take a fellow eight years old
And make him swear to never kiss the girls.
I'm my own master, paint now as I please—
Having a friend, you see, in the Corner-house![1]
Lord, it's fast holding by the rings in front—
Those great rings serve more purposes than just
To plant a flag in, or tie up a horse!
And yet the old schooling sticks, the old grave eyes
Are peeping o'er my shoulder as I work,
The heads shake still—'It's art's decline, my son!
You're not of the true painters, great and old;
Brother Angelico's the man, you'll find;
Brother Lorenzo[2] stands his single peer:
Fag on at flesh, you'll never make the third!'
Flower o' the pine,
You keep your mistr . . . manners, and I'll stick to mine!
I'm not the third, then: bless us, they must know!
Don't you think they're the likeliest to know,
They with their Latin? So, I swallow my rage,
Clench my teeth, suck my lips in tight, and paint
To please them—sometimes do and sometimes don't;
For, doing most, there's pretty sure to come
A turn, some warm eve finds me at my saints—
A laugh, a cry, the business of the world—
(Flower o' the peach,
Death for us all, and his own life for each!)
And my whole soul revolves, the cup runs over,
The world and life's too big to pass for a dream,
And I do these wild things in sheer despite,
And play the fooleries you catch me at,
In pure rage! The old mill-horse, out at grass
After hard years, throws up his stiff heels so,
Although the miller does not preach to him
The only good of grass is to make chaff.
What would men have? Do they like grass or no—
May they or mayn't they? all I want's the thing
Settled for ever one way. As it is,
You tell too many lies and hurt yourself:
You don't like what you only like too much,
You do like what, if given you at your word,

---

1   the Medici palace
2   the painters Fra Angelico (1387-1455) and his teacher Lorenzo Monaco (1370-1425)

You find abundantly detestable.
For me, I think I speak as I was taught;
I always see the garden and God there
A-making man's wife: and, my lesson learned,
The value and significance of flesh,
I can't unlearn ten minutes afterwards.
You understand me: I'm a beast, I know.
But see, now—why, I see as certainly
As that the morning-star's about to shine,
What will hap some day. We've a youngster here
Comes to our convent, studies what I do,
Slouches and stares and lets no atom drop:
His name is Guidi[1]—he'll not mind the monks—
They call him Hulking Tom, he lets them talk—
He picks my practice up—he'll paint apace,
I hope so—though I never live so long,
I know what's sure to follow. You be judge!
You speak no Latin more than I, belike,
However, you're my man, you've seen the world
—The beauty and the wonder and the power,
The shapes of things, their colours, lights and shades,
Changes, surprises,—and God made it all!
—For what? Do you feel thankful, ay or no,
For this fair town's face, yonder river's line,
The mountain round it and the sky above,
Much more the figures of man, woman, child,
These are the frame to? What's it all about?
To be passed over, despised? or dwelt upon,
Wondered at? oh, this last of course!—you say.
But why not do as well as say,—paint these
Just as they are, careless what comes of it?
God's works—paint anyone, and count it crime
To let a truth slip. Don't object, 'His works
Are here already; nature is complete:
Suppose you reproduce her—(which you can't)
There's no advantage! you must beat her, them'
For, don't you mark? we're made so that we love
First when we see them painted, things we have passed
Perhaps a hundred times nor cared to see;
And so they are better, painted—better to us,
Which is the same thing. Art was given for that;
God uses us to help each other so,
Lending our minds out. Have you noticed, now,
Your cullion's[2] hanging face? A bit of chalk,
And trust me but you should, though! How much more,

---

1   Tommaso Guidi (1401-1428), nicknamed Masaccio (hulking, slovenly); probably Lippi's
     teacher rather than his pupil
2   rascal's

If I drew higher things with the same truth!
That were to take the Prior's pulpit-place,
Interpret God to all of you! Oh, oh,
It makes me mad to see what men shall do
And we in our graves! This world's no blot for us,
Nor blank; it means intensely, and means good:
To find its meaning is my meat and drink.
'Ay, but you don't so instigate to prayer!'
Strikes in the Prior: 'when your meaning's plain
It does not say to folk—remember matins,
Or, mind you fast next Friday!' Why, for this
What need of art at all? A skull and bones,
Two bits of stick nailed crosswise, or, what's best,
A bell to chime the hour with, does as well.
I painted a Saint Laurence¹ six months since
At Prato,² splashed the fresco³ in fine style:
'How looks my painting, now the scaffold's down?'
I ask a brother: 'Hugely,' he returns—
'Already not one phiz⁴ of your three slaves
Who turn the Deacon off his toasted side,
But's scratched and prodded to our heart's content,
The pious people have so eased their own
With coming to say prayers there in a rage:
We get on fast to see the bricks beneath.
Expect another job this time next year,
For piety and religion grow i' the crowd—
Your painting serves its purpose!' Hang the fools!
—That is—you'll not mistake an idle word
Spoke in a huff by a poor monk, God wot,
Tasting the air this spicy night which turns
The unaccustomed head like Chianti wine!
Oh, the church knows! don't misreport me, now!
It's natural a poor monk out of bounds
Should have his apt word to excuse himself:
And hearken how I plot to make amends.
I have bethought me: I shall paint a piece
. . . There's for you! Give me six months, then go, see
Something in Sant' Ambrogio's!⁵ Bless the nuns!
They want a cast⁶ o' my office. I shall paint
God in the midst, Madonna and her babe,
Ringed by a bowery flowery angel-brood,
Lilies and vestments and white faces, sweet

---

1 St. Laurence was burned alive in 258 A.D.
2 a town near Florence
3 a painting on a newly-plastered wall
4 face
5 a convent church in Florence for which Lippi painted "Coronation of the Virgin," described in the lines that follow
6 sample of my work

As puff on puff of grated orris-root[1]
When ladies crowd to Church at midsummer.
And then in the front, of course a saint or two—
Saint John,[2] because he saves the Florentines,
Saint Ambrose, who puts down in black and white
The convent's friends and gives them a long day,
And Job, I must have him there past mistake,
The man of Uz[3] (and Us without the z,
Painters who need his patience). Well, all these
Secured at their devotion, up shall come
Out of a corner when you least expect,
As one by a dark stair into a great light,
Music and talking, who but Lippo! I!—
Mazed, motionless and moonstruck—I'm the man!
Back I shrink—what is this I see and hear?
I, caught up with my monk's things by mistake,
My old serge gown and rope that goes all round,
I, in this presence, this pure company!
Where's a hole, where's a corner for escape?
Then steps a sweet angelic slip of a thing
Forward, puts out a soft palm—'Not so fast!'
—Addresses the celestial presence, 'nay—
He made you and devised you, after all,
Though he's none of you! Could Saint John there draw—
His camel-hair[4] make up a painting-brush?
We come to brother Lippo for all that,
Iste perfecit opus!'[5] So, all smile—
I shuffle sideways with my blushing face
Under the cover of a hundred wings
Thrown like a spread of kirtles[6] when you're gay
And play hot cockles, all the doors being shut,
Till, wholly unexpected, in there pops
The hothead husband! Thus I scuttle off
To some safe bench behind, not letting go
The palm of her, the little lily thing
That spoke the good word for me in the nick,
Like the Prior's niece . . . Saint Lucy, I would say.
And so all's saved for me, and for the church
A pretty picture gained. Go, six months hence!
Your hand, sir, and good-bye: no lights, no lights!
The street's hushed, and I know my own way back,
Don't fear me! There's the grey beginning. Zooks!

---

1   the perfumed powder made from the roots of irises
2   the patron saint of Florence
3   see Job 1.1
4   "And John was clothed with camel's hair" (Mark 1.6).
5   "This man brought the work to completion!"
6   skirts

Emily Brontë

(1818–1848)

The Old Stoic

Riches I hold in light esteem;
  And Love I laugh to scorn;
And lust of fame was but a dream
  That vanished with the morn:

And if I pray, the only prayer
  That moves my lips for me
Is, 'Leave the heart that now I bear,
  And give me liberty!'

Yes, as my swift days near their goal,
  'Tis all that I implore;
In life and death, a chainless soul,
  With courage to endure.

Shall Earth no more inspire thee

Shall Earth no more inspire thee,
Thou lonely dreamer now?
Since passion may not fire thee
Shall Nature cease to bow?

Thy mind is ever moving
In regions dark to thee;
Recall its useless roving—
Come back and dwell with me.

I know my mountain breezes
Enchant and soothe thee still—
I know my sunshine pleases
Despite thy wayward will.

When day with evening blending
Sinks from the summer sky,
I've seen thy spirit bending
In fond idolatry.

I've watched thee every hour;
I know my mighty sway,
I know my magic power
To drive thy griefs away.

Few hearts to mortals given
On earth so wildly pine;
Yet none would ask a Heaven
More like this Earth than thine.

Then let my winds caress thee;
Thy comrade let me be—
Since nought beside can bless thee,
Return and dwell with me.

Remembrance

Cold in the earth—and the deep snow piled above thee,
  Far, far removed, cold in the dreary grave!
Have I forgot, my only Love, to love thee,
  Severed at last by Time's all-severing wave?

Now, when alone, do my thoughts no longer hover
  Over the mountains, on that northern shore,
Resting their wings where heath and fern-leaves cover
  Thy noble heart for ever, ever more?

Cold in the earth—and fifteen wild Decembers,
  From those brown hills, have melted into spring:
Faithful, indeed, is the spirit that remembers
  After such years of change and suffering!

Sweet Love of youth, forgive, if I forget thee,
  While the world's tide is bearing me along;
Other desires and other hopes beset me,
  Hopes which obscure, but cannot do thee wrong!

No later light has lightened up my heaven,
  No second morn has ever shone for me;
All my life's bliss from thy dear life was given,
  All my life's bliss is in the grave with thee.

But when the days of golden dreams had perished,
  And even Despair was powerless to destroy;
Then did I learn how existence could be cherished,
  Strengthened, and fed without the aid of joy.

Then did I check the tears of useless passion,
  Weaned my young soul from yearning after thine;
Sternly denied its burning wish to hasten
  Down to that tomb already more than mine.

And, even yet, I dare not let it languish,
  Dare not indulge in memory's rapturous pain;
Once drinking deep of that divinest anguish,
  How could I seek the empty world again?

No Coward Soul

No coward soul is mine
No trembler in the world's storm-troubled sphere
I see Heaven's glories shine
And Faith shines equal arming me from Fear

O God within my breast
Almighty ever-present Deity
Life, that in me hast rest
As I Undying Life, have power in Thee

Vain are the thousand creeds
That move men's hearts, unutterably vain,
Worthless as withered weeds
Or idlest froth amid the boundless main

To waken doubt in one
Holding so fast by thy infinity
So surely anchored on
The steadfast rock of Immortality.

With wide-embracing love
Thy spirit animates eternal years
Pervades and broods above,
Changes, sustains, dissolves, creates and rears

Though Earth and moon were gone
And suns and universes ceased to be
And thou wert left alone
Every Existence would exist in thee.

There is not room for Death
Nor atom that his might could render void
Since thou art Being and Breath
And what thou art may never be destroyed.

Often rebuked, yet always back returning

Often rebuked, yet always back returning
  To those first feelings that were born with me,
And leaving busy chase of wealth and learning
  For idle dreams of things which cannot be:

To-day, I will seek not the shadowy region;
  Its unsustaining vastness waxes drear;
And visions rising, legion after legion,
  Bring the unreal world too strangely near.

I'll walk, but not in old heroic traces,
  And not in paths of high morality,
And not among the half-distinguished faces,
  The clouded forms of long-past history.

I'll walk where my own nature would be leading:
  It vexes me to choose another guide:
Where the gray flocks in ferny glens are feeding;
  Where the wild wind blows on the mountain side.

What have those lonely mountains worth revealing?
  More glory and more grief than I can tell:
The earth that wakes *one* human heart to feeling
  Can centre both the worlds of Heaven and Hell.

Arthur Hugh Clough

(1819–1861)

The Latest Decalogue[1]

Thou shalt have one God only; who
Would be at the expense of two?
No graven images may be
Worshipped, except the currency:
Swear not at all; for for thy curse
Thine enemy is none the worse:
At church on Sunday to attend
Will serve to keep the world thy friend:
Honour thy parents; that is, all
From whom advancement may befall:
Thou shalt not kill; but needst not strive
Officiously to keep alive:
Do not adultery commit;
Advantage rarely comes of it:
Thou shalt not steal; an empty feat,
When it's so lucrative to cheat:
Bear not false witness; let the lie
Have time on its own wings to fly:
Thou shalt not covet; but tradition
Approves all forms of competition.

The sum of all is, thou shalt love,
If any body, God above:
At any rate shall never labour
More than thyself to love thy neighbour.

Say not the struggle nought availeth

Say not the struggle nought availeth,
    The labour and the wounds are vain,
The enemy faints not, nor faileth,
    And as things have been, things remain.

If hopes were dupes, fears may be liars;
    It may be, in yon smoke concealed,
Your comrades chase e'en now the fliers,
    And, but for you, possess the field.

For while the tired waves, vainly breaking,
    Seem here no painful inch to gain,
Far back through creeks and inlets making

---

1   The first decalogue was the Ten Commandments.

Came, silent, flooding in, the main,

And not by eastern windows only,
    When daylight comes, comes in the light,
In front the sun climbs slow, how slowly,
    But westward, look, the land is bright.

from: *Dipsychus*

'There is no God,' the wicked saith,
    'And truly it's a blessing,
For what he might have done with us
    It's better only guessing.'

'There is no God,' a youngster thinks,
    'Or really, if there may be,
He surely didn't mean a man
    Always to be a baby.'

'There is no God, or if there is,'
    The tradesman thinks,''twere funny
If he should take it ill in me
    To make a little money.'

'Whether there be,' the rich man says,
    'It matters very little,
For I and mine, thank somebody,
    Are not in want of victual.'

Some others, also, to themselves
    Who scarce so much as doubt it,
Think there is none, when they are well,
    And do not think about it.

But country folks who live beneath
    The shadow of the steeple;
The parson and the parson's wife,
    And mostly married people;

Youths green and happy in first love,
    So thankful for illusion;
And men caught out in what the world
    Calls guilt, in first confusion;

And almost every one when age,
    Disease, or sorrows strike him,
Inclines to think there is a God,
    Or something very like Him.

Walt Whitman

(1819–1892)

from: *Song of Myself*

(Sections 20 - 21)

20

Who goes there? hankering, gross, mystical, nude,
How is it I extract strength from the beef I eat?

What is a man anyhow? what am I? what are you?

All I mark as my own you shall offset it with your own,
Else it were time lost listening to me.

I do not snivel that snivel the world over,
That months are vacuums and the ground but wallow and filth.

Whimpering and truckling fold with powders[1] for invalids, con-
      formity goes to the fourth-remov'd,
I wear my hat as I please indoors or out.

Why should I pray? why should I venerate and be ceremonious?

Having pried through the strata, analyzed to a hair, counsel'd with
      doctors and calculated close,
I find no sweeter fat than sticks to my own bones.

In all people I see myself, none more and not one a barley-corn
      less,
And the good or bad I say of myself I say of them.

I know I am solid and sound,
To me the converging objects of the universe perpetually flow,
All are written to me, and I must get what the writing means.

I know I am deathless,
I know this orbit of mine cannot be swept by a carpenter's
      compass,
I know I shall not pass like a child's carlacue[2] cut with a burnt
      stick at night.

---

1   Doses of medicinal powder were wrapped in small papers.
2   curlicue; a fancy twist, as a flourish with a pen

I know I am august,
I do not trouble my spirit to vindicate itself or be understood,
I see that the elementary laws never apologize,
(I reckon I behave no prouder than the level I plant my house by,
    after all.)

I exist as I am, that is enough,
If no other in the world be aware I sit content,
And if each and all be aware I sit content.

One world is aware and by far the largest to me, and that is
    myself,
And whether I come to my own to-day or in ten thousand or ten
    million years,
I can cheerfully take it now, or with equal cheerfulness I can wait.

My foothold is tenon'd and mortis'd in granite,
I laugh at what you call dissolution,
And I know the amplitude of time.

21

I am the poet of the Body and I am the poet of the Soul,
The pleasures of heaven are with me and the pains of hell are
    with me,
The first I graft and increase upon myself, the latter I translate
    into a new tongue.

I am the poet of the woman the same as the man,
And I say it is as great to be a woman as to be a man,
And I say there is nothing greater than the mother of men.

I chant the chant of dilation or pride,
We have had ducking and deprecating about enough,
I show that size is only development.

Have you outstript the rest? are you the President?
It is a trifle, they will more than arrive there every one, and still
    pass on.

I am he that walks with the tender and growing night,
I call to the earth and sea half-held by the night.

Press close bare-bosom'd night—press close magnetic nourishing
    night!
Night of south winds—night of the large few stars!
Sill nodding night—mad naked summer night.

Smile O voluptuous cool-breath'd earth!
Earth of the slumbering and liquid trees!

Earth of departed sunset—earth of the mountains misty-topt!
Earth of the vitreous pour of the full moon just tinged with blue!
Earth of shine and dark mottling the tide of the river!
Earth of the limpid gray of clouds brighter and clearer for my sake!
Far-swooping elbow'd earth—rich apple-blossom'd earth!
Smile, for your lover comes.

Prodigal, you have given me love—therefore I to you give love!
O unspeakable passionate love.

* * *

When I Heard the Learn'd Astronomer

When I heard the learn'd astronomer,
When the proofs, the figures, were ranged in columns before me,
When I was shown the charts and diagrams, to add, divide, and
    measure them,
When I sitting heard the astronomer where he lectured with much
    applause in the lecture-room,
How soon unaccountable I became tired and sick,
Till rising and gliding out I wander'd off by myself,
In the mystical moist night-air, and from time to time,
Look'd up in perfect silence at the stars.

Vigil Strange I Kept on the Field One Night

Vigil strange I kept on the field one night;
When you my son and my comrade dropt at my side that day,
One look I but gave which your dear eyes return'd with a look I
    shall never forget,
One touch of your hand to mine O boy, reach'd up as you lay on
    the ground,
Then onward I sped in the battle, the even-contested battle,
Till late in the night reliev'd to the place at last again I made my
    way,
Found you in death so cold dear comrade, found your body son
    of responding kisses, (never again on earth responding,)
Bared your face in the starlight, curious the scene, cool blew the
    moderate night-wind,
Long there and then in vigil I stood, dimly around me the battle-
    field spreading,
Vigil wondrous and vigil sweet there in the fragrant silent night,
But not a tear fell, not even a long-drawn sigh, long, long I gazed,
Then on the earth partially reclining sat by your side leaning my
    chin in my hands,
Passing sweet hours, immortal and mystic hours with you dearest
    comrade—not a tear, not a word,
Vigil of silence, love and death, vigil for you my son and my

soldier,
As onward silently stars aloft, eastward new ones upward stole,
Vigil final for you brave boy, (I could not save you, swift was your
  death,
I faithfully loved you and cared for you living, I think we shall
  surely meet again,)
Till at latest lingering of the night, indeed just as the dawn
  appear'd,
My comrade I wrapt in his blanket, envelop'd well his form,
Folded the blanket well, tucking it carefully over head and care-
  fully under feet,
And there and then and bathed by the rising sun, my son in his
  grave, in his rude-dug grave I deposited,
Ending my vigil strange with that, vigil of night and battle-field
  dim,
Vigil for boy of responding kisses, (never again on earth
  responding,)
Vigil for comrade swiftly slain, vigil I never forget, how as day
  brighten'd,
I rose from the chill ground and folded my soldier well in his
  blanket,
And buried him where he fell.

Cavalry Crossing a Ford

A line in long array where they wind betwixt green islands,
They take a serpentine course, their arms flash in the sun—hark to the
  musical clank,
Behold the silvery river, in it the splashing horses loitering stop to
  drink,
Behold the brown-faced men, each group, each person a picture, the
  negligent rest on the saddles,
Some emerge on the opposite bank, others are just entering the ford—
  while,
Scarlet and blue and snowy white,
The guidon[1] flags flutter gayly in the wind.

A Noiseless Patient Spider

A noiseless patient spider,
I mark'd where on a little promontory it stood isolated,
Mark'd how to explore the vacant vast surrounding,
It launch'd forth filament, filament, filament, out of itself,
Ever unreeling them, ever tirelessly speeding them.

---

1   a forked flag carried by mounted troops

And you O my soul where you stand,
Surrounded, detached, in measureless oceans of space,
Ceaselessly musing, venturing, throwing, seeking the spheres to
    connect them,
Till the bridge you will need be form'd, till the ductile anchor
    hold,
Till the gossamer thread you fling catch somewhere, O my soul.

To a Locomotive in Winter

Thee for my recitative,
Thee in the driving storm even as now, the snow, the winter-day
    declining,
Thee in thy panoply, thy measur'd dual throbbing and thy beat
    convulsive,
Thy black cylindric body, golden brass and silvery steel,
Thy ponderous side-bars, parallel and connecting rods, gyrating,
    shuttling at thy sides,
Thy metrical, now swelling pant and roar, now tapering in the
    distance,
Thy great protruding head-light fix'd in front,
Thy long, pale, floating vapor-pennants, tinged with delicate
    purple,
The dense and murky clouds out-belching from thy smoke-stack,
Thy knitted frame, thy springs and valves, the tremulous twinkle
    of thy wheels,
Thy train of cars behind, obedient, merrily following,
Through gale or calm, now swift, now slack, yet steadily
    careering;
Type of the modern—emblem of motion and power—pulse of
    the continent,
For once come serve the Muse and merge in verse, even as here
    I see thee,
With storm and buffeting gusts of wind and falling snow,
By day thy warning ringing bell to sound its notes,
By night thy silent signal lamps to swing.

Fierce-throated beauty!
Roll through my chant with all thy lawless music, thy swinging
    lamps at night,
Thy madly-whistled laughter, echoing, rumbling like an earth-
    quake, rousing all,
Law of thyself complete, thine own track firmly holding,
(No sweetness debonair of tearful harp or glib piano thine,)
Thy trills of shrieks by rocks and hills return'd,
Launch'd o'er the prairies wide, across the lakes,
To the free skies unpent and glad and strong.

Herman Melville

(1819–1891)

The House-top

A Night Piece

July 1863

No sleep. The sultriness pervades the air
And binds the brain—a dense oppression, such
As tawny tigers feel in matted shades,
Vexing their blood and making apt for ravage.
Beneath the stars the roofy desert spreads
Vacant as Libya. All is hushed near by.
Yet fitfully from far breaks a mixed surf
Of muffled sound, the Atheist roar of riot.
Yonder, where parching Sirius[1] set in drought,
Balefully glares red Arson—there—and there.
The Town is taken by its rats—ship-rats
And rats of the wharves. All civil charms
And priestly spells which late held hearts in awe—
Fear-bound, subjected to a better sway
Than sway of self; these like a dream dissolve,
And man rebounds whole aeons back in nature.
Hail to the low dull rumble, dull and dead,
And ponderous drag that shakes the wall.
Wise Draco[2] comes, deep in the midnight roll
Of black artillery; he comes, though late;
In code corroborating Calvin's[3] creed
And cynic tyrannies of honest kings;
He comes, nor parleys; and the Town, redeemed,
Gives thanks devout; nor, being thankful, heeds
The grimy slur on the Republic's faith implied,
Which holds that Man is naturally good,
And—more—is Nature's Roman, never to be scourged.

---

1   the Dog-Star, associated with the heat of summer
2   Athenian legislator whose code of laws (promulgated in 621 B.C.) was noted for its severity
3   John Calvin (1509-64), the stern Protestant reformer who preached the doctrine of human corruption and original sin

The Maldive Shark[1]

About the Shark, phlegmatical one,
Pale sot of the Maldive sea,
The sleek little pilot-fish, azure and slim,
How alert in attendance be.
From his saw-pit of mouth, from his charnel of maw
They have nothing of harm to dread,
But liquidly glide on his ghastly flank
Or before his Gorgonian[2] head;
Or lurk in the port of serrated teeth
In white triple tiers of glittering gates,
And there find a haven when peril's abroad,
An asylum in jaws of the Fates!
They are friends; and friendly they guide him to prey,
Yet never partake of the treat—
Eyes and brains to the dotard lethargic and dull,
Pale ravener of horrible meat.

Art

In placid hours well-pleased we dream
Of many a brave unbodied scheme.
But form to lend, pulsed life create,
What unlike things must meet and mate:
A flame to melt—a wind to freeze;
Sad patience—joyous energies;
Humility—yet pride and scorn;
Instinct and study; love and hate;
Audacity—reverence. These must mate,
And fuse with Jacob's mystic heart,
To wrestle with the angel[3]—Art.

---

1   The Maldive Islands are in the Indian Ocean.
2   The Gorgon was a monster so hideous that it turned to stone anyone who met its gaze.
3   See Genesis 32.24–32.

Matthew Arnold

(1822–1888)

Shakespeare

Others abide our question. Thou art free.
We ask and ask—Thou smilest and art still,
Out-topping knowledge. For the loftiest hill,
Who to the stars uncrowns his majesty,

Planting his steadfast footsteps in the sea,
Making the heaven of heavens his dwelling-place,
Spares but the cloudy border of his base
To the foil'd searching of mortality;

And thou, who didst the stars and sunbeams know,
Self-school'd, self-scann'd, self-honor'd, self-secure,
Didst tread on earth unguess'd at.—Better so!

All pains the immortal spirit must endure,
All weakness which impairs, all griefs which bow,
Find their sole speech in that victorious brow.

Isolation. To Marguerite

We were apart; yet, day by day,
I bade my heart more constant be.
I bade it keep the world away,
And grow a home for only thee;
Nor fear'd but thy love likewise grew,
Like mine, each day, more tried, more true.

The fault was grave! I might have known,
What far too soon, alas! I learn'd—
The heart can bind itself alone,
And faith may oft be unreturn'd.
Self-sway'd our feelings ebb and swell—
Thou lov'st no more;—Farewell! Farewell!

Farewell!—and thou, thou lonely heart,
Which never yet without remorse
Even for a moment didst depart
From thy remote and spheréd course
To haunt the place where passions reign—
Back to thy solitude again!

Back! with the conscious thrill of shame
Which Luna[1] felt, that summer-night,
Flash through her pure immortal frame,
When she forsook the starry height
To hang over Endymion's sleep
Upon the pine-grown Latmian steep.

Yet she, chaste queen, had never proved[2]
How vain a thing is mortal love,
Wandering in Heaven, far removed.
But thou hast long had place to prove
This truth—to prove, and make thine own:
'Thou hast been, shalt be, art, alone.'

Or, if not quite alone, yet they
Which touch thee are unmating things—
Ocean and clouds and night and day;
Lorn autumns and triumphant springs;
And life, and others' joy and pain,
And love, if love, of happier men.

Of happier men—for they, at least,
Have *dream'd* two human hearts might blend
In one, and were through faith released
From isolation without end
Prolong'd; nor knew, although not less
Alone than thou, their loneliness.

To Marguerite—Continued

Yes! in the sea of life enisled,
With echoing straits between us thrown
Dotting the shoreless watery wild,
We mortal millions live *alone*.
The islands feel the enclasping flow,
And then their endless bounds they know.

But when the moon their hollows lights,
And they are swept by balms of spring,
And in their glens, on starry nights,
The nightingales divinely sing;
And lovely notes, from shore to shore,
Across the sounds and channels pour—

---

1   Diana, the goddess of chastity and the moon, fell in love with the shepherd Endymion
     when she saw him sleeping on Mount Latmos.
2   experienced

Oh! then a longing like despair
Is to their farthest caverns sent;
For surely once, they feel, we were
Parts of a single continent!
Now round us spreads the watery plain—
Oh might our marges meet again!

Who ordered, that their longing's fire
Should be, as soon as kindled, cooled?
Who renders vain their deep desire?—
A God, a God their severance ruled!
And bade betwixt their shores to be
The unplumb'd, salt, estranging sea.

Dover Beach

The sea is calm tonight.
The tide is full, the moon lies fair
Upon the straits;—on the French coast the light
Gleams and is gone; the cliffs of England stand,
Glimmering and vast, out in the tranquil bay.
Come to the window, sweet is the night-air!

Only, from the long line of spray
Where the sea meets the moon-blanched land,
Listen! you hear the grating roar
Of pebbles which the waves draw back, and fling,
At their return, up the high strand,
Begin, and cease, and then again begin,
With tremulous cadence slow, and bring
The eternal note of sadness in.

Sophocles long ago
Heard it on the Aegaean, and it brought
Into his mind the turbid ebb and flow
Of human misery; we
Find also in the sound a thought,
Hearing it by this distant northern sea.

The Sea of Faith
Was once, too, at the full, and round earth's shore
Lay like the folds of a bright girdle furled.
But now I only hear
Its melancholy, long, withdrawing roar,
Retreating, to the breath
Of the night-wind, down the vast edges drear
And naked shingles of the world.

Ah, love, let us be true
To one another! for the world, which seems

To lie before us like a land of dreams,
So various, so beautiful, so new,
Hath really neither joy, nor love, nor light,
Nor certitude, nor peace, nor help for pain;
And we are here as on a darkling plain
Swept with confused alarms of struggle and flight,
Where ignorant armies clash by night.[1]

The Buried Life

Light flows our war of mocking words, and yet,
Behold, with tears mine eyes are wet!
I feel a nameless sadness o'er me roll.
Yes, yes, we know that we can jest,
We know, we know that we can smile!
But there's a something in this breast,
To which thy light words bring no rest,
And thy gay smiles no anodyne.
Give me thy hand, and hush awhile,
And turn those limpid eyes on mine,
And let me read there, love! thy inmost soul.

Alas! is even love too weak
To unlock the heart, and let it speak?
Are even lovers powerless to reveal
To one another what indeed they feel?
I knew the mass of men conceal'd
Their thoughts, for fear that if reveal'd
They would by other men be met
With blank indifference, or with blame reproved;
I knew they lived and moved
Tricked in disguises, alien to the rest
Of men, and alien to themselves—and yet
The same heart beats in every human breast!

But we, my love!—doth a like spell benumb
Our hearts, our voices?—must we too be dumb?

Ah! well for us, if even we,
Even for a moment, can get free
Our heart, and have our lips unchain'd;
For that which seals them hath been deep-ordain'd!

Fate, which foresaw
How frivolous a baby man would be—

---

1   an allusion to Thucydides' description of the Battle of Epipolae (413 B.C.) in *The History
of the Peloponnesian War*

By what distractions he would be possess'd,
How he would pour himself in every strife,
And well-nigh change his own identity—
That it might keep from his capricious play
His genuine self, and force him to obey
Even in his own despite his being's law,
Bade through the deep recesses of our breast
The unregarded river of our life
Pursue with indiscernible flow its way;
And that we should not see
The buried stream, and seem to be
Eddying at large in blind uncertainty,
Though driving on with it eternally.

But often, in the world's most crowded streets,
But often, in the din of strife,
There rises an unspeakable desire
After the knowledge of our buried life;
A thirst to spend our fire and restless force
In tracking out our true, original course;
A longing to inquire
Into the mystery of this heart which beats
So wild, so deep in us—to know
Whence our lives come and where they go.
And many a man in his own breast then delves,
But deep enough, alas! none ever mines.
And we have been on many thousand lines,
And we have shown, on each, spirit and power;
But hardly have we, for one little hour,
Been on our own line, have we been ourselves—
Hardly had skill to utter one of all
The nameless feelings that course through our breast,
But they course on for ever unexpress'd.

And long we try in vain to speak and act
Our hidden self, and what we say and do
Is eloquent, is well—but 'tis not true!
And then we will no more be rack'd
With inward striving, and demand
Of all the thousand nothings of the hour
Their stupefying power;
Ah yes, and they benumb us at our call!
Yet still, from time to time, vague and forlorn,
From the soul's subterranean depth upborne
As from an infinitely distant land,
Come airs, and floating echoes, and convey
A melancholy into all our day.

Only—but this is rare—
When a beloved hand is laid in ours,
When, jaded with the rush and glare

Of the interminable hours,
Our eyes can in another's eyes read clear,
When our world-deafen'd ear
Is by the tones of a loved voice caress'd—
A bolt is shot back somewhere in our breast,
And a lost pulse of feeling stirs again.
The eye sinks inward, and the heart lies plain,
And what we mean, we say, and what we would, we know.
A man becomes aware of his life's flow,
And hears its winding murmur; and he sees
The meadows where it glides, the sun, the breeze.

And there arrives a lull in the hot race
Wherein he doth for ever chase
That flying and elusive shadow, rest.
An air of coolness plays upon his face,
And an unwonted calm pervades his breast.
And then he thinks he knows
The hills where his life rose,
And the sea where it goes.

Dante Gabriel Rossetti

(1828–1882)

The Blessed Damozel

The blessed damozel[1] leaned out
   From the gold bar of Heaven;
Her eyes were deeper than the depth
   Of waters stilled at even;
She had three lilies in her hand,
   And the stars in her hair were seven.

Her robe, ungirt from clasp to hem,
   No wrought flowers did adorn,
But a white rose of Mary's gift,
   For service meetly worn;
Her hair that lay along her back
   Was yellow like ripe corn.

Herseemed she scarce had been a day
   One of God's choristers;
The wonder was not yet quite gone
   From that still look of hers;
Albeit, to them she left, her day
   Had counted as ten years.

(To one, it is ten years of years.
   . . . Yet now, and in this place,
Surely she leaned o'er me—her hair
   Fell all about my face. . . .
Nothing: the autumn fall of leaves.
   The whole year sets apace.)

It was the rampart of God's house
   That she was standing on;
By God built over the sheer depth
   The which is Space begun;
So high, that looking downward thence
   She scarce could see the sun.

It lies in Heaven, across the flood
   Of ether, as a bridge.
Beneath, the tides of day and night
   With flame and darkness ridge
The void, as low as where this earth
   Spins like a fretful midge.

---

1   archaic form of "damsel"

Around her, lovers, newly met
  In joy no sorrow claims,
Spoke evermore among themselves
  Their rapturous new names;
And the souls mounting up to God
  Went by her like thin flames.

And still she bowed herself and stooped
  Out of the circling charm;
Until her bosom must have made
  The bar she leaned on warm,
And the lilies lay as if asleep
  Along her bended arm.

From the fixed place of Heaven she saw
  Time like a pulse shake fierce
Through all the worlds. Her gaze still strove
  Within the gulf to pierce
Its path; and now she spoke as when
  The stars sang in their spheres.[1]

The sun was gone now; the curled moon
  Was like a little feather
Fluttering far down the gulf; and now
  She spoke through the still weather.
Her voice was like the voice the stars
  Had when they sang together.

(Ah sweet! Even now, in that bird's song,
  Strove not her accents there,
Fain to be hearkened? When those bells
  Possessed the mid-day air,
Strove not her steps to reach my side
  Down all the echoing stair?)

'I wish that he were come to me,
  For he will come,' she said.
'Have I not prayed in Heaven?—on earth,
  Lord, Lord, has he not pray'd?
Are not two prayers a perfect strength?
  And shall I feel afraid?

'When round his head the aureole clings,
  And he is clothed in white,
I'll take his hand and go with him
  To the deep wells of light;

---

1   See Job 38.7.

We will step down as to a stream,
   And bathe there in God's sight.

'We two will stand beside that shrine,
   Occult, withheld, untrod,
Whose lamps are stirred continually
   With prayer sent up to God;
And see our old prayers, granted, melt
   Each like a little cloud.

'We two will lie i' the shadow of
   That living mystic tree[1]
Within whose secret growth the Dove[2]
   Is sometimes felt to be,
While every leaf that His plumes touch
   Saith His Name audibly.

'And I myself will teach to him,
   I myself, lying so,
The songs I sing here, which his voice
   Shall pause in, hushed and slow,
And find some knowledge at each pause,
   Or some new thing to know.'

(Alas! We two, we two, thou say'st!
   Yea, one wast thou with me
That once of old. But shall God lift
   To endless unity
The soul whose likeness with thy soul
   Was but its love for thee?)

'We two,' she said, 'will seek the groves
   Where the lady Mary is,
With her five handmaidens, whose names
   Are five sweet symphonies,
Cecily, Gertrude, Magdalen,
   Margaret and Rosalys.

'Circlewise sit they, with bound locks
   And foreheads garlanded;
Into the fine cloth white like flame
   Weaving the golden thread,
To fashion the birth-robes for them
   Who are just born, being dead.

---

1   the tree of life, mentioned in Revelations 22.2
2   a traditional symbol of the Holy Ghost

'He shall fear, haply, and be dumb:
　　Then will I lay my cheek
To his, and tell about our love,
　　Not once abashed or weak:
And the dear Mother will approve
　　My pride, and let me speak.

'Herself shall bring us, hand in hand,
　　To Him round whom all souls
Kneel, the clear-ranged unnumbered heads
　　Bowed with their aureoles:
And angels meeting us shall sing
　　To their citherns and citoles.[1]

'There will I ask of Christ the Lord
　　Thus much for him and me:—
Only to live as once on earth
　　With Love,—only to be,
As then awhile, for ever now
　　Together, I and he.'

She gazed and listened and then said,
　　Less sad of speech than mild,—
'All this is when he comes.' She ceased.
　　The light thrilled towards her, fill'd
With angels in strong level flight.
　　Her eyes prayed, and she smil'd.

(I saw her smile.) But soon their path
　　Was vague in distant spheres:
And then she cast her arms along
　　The golden barriers,
And laid her face between her hands,
　　And wept. (I heard her tears.)

The Card-dealer[2]

Could you not drink her gaze like wine?
　　Yet though its splendour swoon
Into the silence languidly
　　As a tune into a tune,
Those eyes unravel the coiled night
　　And know the stars at noon.

1　stringed instruments
2　Originally sub-titled "Vingt-et-un. From a picture."

The gold that's heaped beside her hand,
    In truth rich prize it were;
And rich the dreams that wreathe her brows
    With magic stillness there;
And he were rich who should unwind
    That woven golden hair.

Around her, where she sits, the dance
    Now breathes its eager heat;
And not more lightly or more true
    Fall there the dancers' feet
Than fall her cards on the bright board
    As 'twere an heart that beat.

Her fingers let them softly through,
    Smooth polished silent things;
And each one as it falls reflects
    In swift light-shadowings,
Blood-red and purple, green and blue,
    The great eyes of her rings.

Whom plays she with? With thee, who lov'st
    Those gems upon her hand;
With me, who search her secret brows;
    With all men, bless'd or bann'd.
We play together, she and we,
    Within a vain strange land:

A land without any order,—
    Day even as night, (one saith,)—
Where who lieth down ariseth not
    Nor the sleeper awakeneth;
A land of darkness as darkness itself
    And of the shadow of death.[1]

What be her cards, you ask? Even these:—
    The heart, that doth but crave
More, having fed; the diamond,
    Skilled to make base seem brave;
The club, for smiting in the dark;
    The spade, to dig a grave.

And do you ask what game she plays?
    With me 'tis lost or won;
With thee it is playing still; with him
    It is not well begun;

---

1   from Job 10.22

But 'tis a game she plays with all
    Beneath the sway o' the sun.

Thou seest the card that falls,—she knows
    The card that followeth:
Her game in thy tongue is called Life,
    As ebbs thy daily breath:
When she shall speak, thou'lt learn her tongue
And knows she calls it Death.

from: *The House of Life*

Sonnet

A Sonnet is a moment's monument,—
    Memorial from the Soul's eternity
    To one dead deathless hour. Look that it be
Whether for lustral[1] rite or dire portent
Of its own arduous fullness reverent:
    Carve it in ivory or in ebony,
    As Day or Night may rule; and let Time see
Its flowering crest impearled and orient.

A Sonnet is a coin: its face reveals
    The soul—its converse, to what Power 'tis due:
Whether for tribute to the august appeals
    Of Life, or dower in Love's high retinue,
It serve; or, 'mid the dark wharf's cavernous breath,
In Charon's palm it pay the toll to Death.[2]

Silent Noon

Your hands lie open in the long fresh grass,—
    The finger-points look through like rosy blooms:
    Your eyes smile peace. The pasture gleams and glooms
'Neath billowing skies that scatter and amass.
All round our nest, far as the eye can pass,
    Are golden kingcup-fields with silver edge
    Where the cow-parsley skirts the hawthorn-hedge.
'Tis visible silence, still as the hour-glass.

Deep in the sun-searched growths the dragon-fly
Hangs like a blue thread loosened from the sky:—

---

1   purificatory
2   For a silver coin, Charon would ferry the dead across the river Styx to Hades.

So this wing'd hour is dropt to us from above.
Oh! clasp we to our hearts, for deathless dower,
This close-companioned inarticulate hour
    When twofold silence was the song of love.

A Superscription

Look in my face; my name is Might-have-been;
    I am also called No-more, Too-late, Farewell;
    Unto thine ear I hold the dead-sea shell
Cast up thy Life's foam-fretted feet between;
Unto thine eyes the glass[1] where that is seen
    Which had Life's form and Love's, but by my spell
    Is now a shaken shadow intolerable,
Of ultimate things unuttered the frail screen.

Mark me, how still I am! But should there dart
    One moment through thy soul the soft surprise
    Of that winged Peace which lulls the breath of sighs,—
Then shalt thou see me smile, and turn apart
Thy visage to mine ambush at thy heart
    Sleepless with cold commemorative eyes.

The One Hope

When vain desire at last and vain regret
    Go hand in hand to death, and all is vain,
    What shall assuage the unforgotten pain
And teach the unforgetful to forget?
Shall Peace be still a sunk stream long unmet,—
    Or may the soul at once in a green plain
    Stoop through the spray of some sweet life-fountain
And cull the dew-drenched flowering amulet?

Ah! When the wan soul in that golden air
    Between the scriptured petals softly blown
    Peers breathless for the gift of grace unknown,—
Ah! let none other alien spell soe'er
But only the one Hope's one name be there,—
    Not less nor more, but even that word alone.

* * *

---

1   mirror

Emily Dickinson

(1830–1866)

214: I taste a liquor never brewed

I taste a liquor never brewed— a Consonance rhyme
From Tankards scooped in Pearl— b
Not all the Frankfort Berries[1] c
Yield such an Alcohol! b

Inebriate of Air—am I—
And Debauchee of Dew—
Reeling—thro endless summer days—
From inns of Molten Blue—

When "Landlords" turn the drunken Bee
Out of the Foxglove's door—
When Butterfies—renounce their "drams" —
I shall but drink the more!

Till Seraphs swing their snowy Hats— a
And Saints—to windows run— b
To see the little Tippler c
From Manzanilla[2] come! b   run] aseonanee
                                come] rhyme

241: I like a look of Agony

I like a look of Agony
Because I know it's true—
Men do not sham Convulsion
Nor simulate, a Throe—

The Eyes glaze once—and that is Death— a
Impossible to feign b
The Beads upon the Forehead c   ) just a
By homely Anguish strung. b   ) ghost of
                                  rhyme

258: There's a certain Slant of light

There's a certain Slant of light,
Winter Afternoons—
That oppresses, like the Heft
Of Cathedral Tunes—

Heavenly Hurt, it gives us—

---

1   wine grapes from the Frankfort region of the Rhine, in Germany
2   name of a Spanish sherry

Many of her finest poems were on death, as represented in this book.

We can find no scar,
But internal difference,
Where the Meanings, are—

unique for her age in her meter

None may teach it—Any—
'Tis the Seal Despair—
An imperial affliction
Sent us of the Air—

Know as Common or hymn meter / ballad | abcb rhyme

When it comes, the Landscape listens—
Shadows—hold their breath—
When it goes, 'tis like the Distance
On the look of Death—

tetrameter/trimeter tetrameter/trimeter alternation

303: The Soul selects her own Society

The Soul selects her own Society—
Then—shuts the Door—
To her divine Majority—
Present no more—

Unmoved—she notes the Chariots—pausing—
At her low Gate—
Unmoved—an Emperor be kneeling
Upon her Mat—

I've known her—from an ample nation—
Choose One—
Then—close the Valves of her attention—
Like Stone—

341: After great pain, a formal feeling comes

After great pain, a formal feeling comes—
The Nerves sit ceremonious, like Tombs—
The stiff Heart questions was it He, that bore,
And Yesterday, or Centuries before?

The Feet, mechanical, go round—
Of Ground, or Air, or Ought[1]—
A Wooden way
Regardless grown,
A Quartz contentment, like a stone—

---

1   nothing

[handwritten: She really liked Keats + Eliza. Bar. Browning]

This is the Hour of Lead—
Remembered, if outlived,
As Freezing persons, recollect the Snow—
First—Chill—then Stupor—then the letting go—

449: I died for Beauty

I died for Beauty—but was scarce
Adjusted in the Tomb
When One who died for Truth, was lain
In an adjoining Room—

He questioned softly "Why I failed"?
"For Beauty", I replied— *[handwritten: made up her own word]*
"And I—for Truth—Themself are One—
We Bretheren, are", He said—

[handwritten: conversation (almost) b/n Keats + her → Ode to a Grecian Urn]

And so, as Kinsmen, met a Night—
We talked between the Rooms—
Until the Moss had reached our lips—
And covered up—our names—

465: I heard a Fly buzz– when I died

[handwritten: The very moment of death– the speaker is actually dead]

I heard a Fly buzz—when I died—
The Stillness in the Room
Was like the Stillness in the Air—
Between the Heaves of Storm—

The Eyes around—had wrung them dry—
And Breaths were gathering firm
For that last Onset—when the King
Be witnessed—in the Room—

[handwritten: her will]

I willed my Keepsakes—Signed away
What portion of me be
Assignable—and then it was
There interposed a Fly—

With Blue—uncertain stumbling Buzz— *[handwritten: A blue fly]*
Between the light—and me—
And then the Windows failed—and then
I could not see to see—

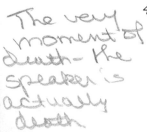
[handwritten: physical sight → (eyes windows into the soul) or the light coming from the windows dims.]

585: I like to see it lap the Miles

I like to see it lap the Miles—
And lick the Valleys up—
And stop to feed itself at Tanks—
And then—prodigious step

Around a Pile of Mountains—
And supercilious peer
In Shanties—by the sides of Roads—
And then a Quarry pare

To fit it's sides
And crawl between
Complaining all the while
In horrid—hooting stanza—
Then chase itself down Hill—

And neigh like Boanerges[1]—
Then—prompter than a Star
Stop—docile and omnipotent
At it's own stable door—

712: Because I could not stop for Death

[handwritten: Death + the Maiden → old subject beautiful poem girl + death he comes for her]

Because I could not stop for Death—
He kindly stopped for me—
The Carriage held but just Ourselves—
And Immortality.

We slowly drove—He knew no haste
And I had put away
My labor and my leisure too,
For His Civility— *[handwritten: & She doesn't seem to quite understand where they're going]*

We passed the School, where Children strove
At Recess—in the Ring—
We passed the Fields of Gazing Grain—
We passed the Setting Sun—

Or rather—He passed Us—
The Dews drew quivering and chill—
For only Gossamer, my Gown— *[handwritten: & represents times bridal wear]*
My Tippet[2]—only Tulle—

---

1 "sons of thunder," the name given by Christ to James and John (Mark 3.17)
2 a woman's short cloak or cape

[handwritten annotation left margin: As if he (a suitor?) is taking her somewhere for them to dwell.]

We paused before a House that seemed *[handwritten: — the House is a tomb in the ground]*
A Swelling of the Ground—
The Roof was scarcely visible—
The Cornice—in the Ground—

Since then—'tis Centuries—and yet *[handwritten: I've been dead for centuries but the longest moment I've ever lived was the moment I realized that I was heading for immortality/her death.]*
Feels shorter than the Day
I first surmised the Horses Heads
Were toward Eternity—

986: A narrow Fellow in the Grass

A narrow Fellow in the Grass
Occasionally rides—
You may have met Him—did you not
His notice sudden is—

The Grass divides as with a Comb—
A spotted shaft is seen—
And then it closes at your feet
And opens further on—

He likes a Boggy Acre
A Floor too cool for Corn—
Yet when a Boy, and Barefoot—
I more than once at Noon
Have passed, I thought, a Whip lash
Unbraiding in the Sun
When stooping to secure it
It wrinkled, and was gone—

Several of Nature's People
I know, and they know me—
I feel for them a transport
Of cordiality—

But never met this Fellow
Attended, or alone
Without a tighter breathing
And Zero at the Bone—

1227: *My triumph lasted till the Drums*

My Triumph lasted till the Drums
Had left the Dead alone
And then I dropped my Victory
And chastened stole along
To where the finished Faces
Conclusion turned on me
And then I hated Glory
And wished myself were They.

What is to be is best descried
When it has also been—
Could Prospect taste of Retrospect
The tyrannies of Men
Were Tenderer—diviner
The Transitive toward.
A Bayonet's contrition
Is nothing to the Dead.

Christina Georgina Rossetti

(1830–1894)

Goblin Market

Morning and evening
Maids heard the goblins cry
"Come buy our orchard fruits,
Come buy, come buy:
Apples and quinces,
Lemons and oranges,
Plump unpecked cherries,
Melons and raspberries,
Bloom-down-cheeked peaches,
Swart-headed mulberries,
Wild free-born cranberries,
Crab-apples, dewberries,
Pine-apples, blackberries,
Apricots, strawberries;—
All ripe together
In summer weather,—
Morns that pass by,
Fair eves that fly;
Come buy, come buy:
Our grapes fresh from the vine,
Pomegranates full and fine,
Dates and sharp bullaces,
Rare pears and greengages,
Damsons and bilberries,
Taste them and try:
Currants and gooseberries,
Bright-fire-like barberries,
Figs to fill your mouth,
Citrons from the South,
Sweet to tongue and sound to eye;
Come buy, come buy."

Evening by evening
Among the brookside rushes,
Laura bowed her head to hear,
Lizzie veiled her blushes:
Crouching close together
In the cooling weather,
With clasping arms and cautioning lips,
With tingling cheeks and finger tips.
"Lie close," Laura said,
Pricking up her golden head:
"We must not look at goblin men,
We must not buy their fruits:
Who knows upon what soil they fed
Their hungry thirsty roots?"
"Come buy," call the goblins

Hobbling down the glen.
"Oh," cried Lizzie, "Laura, Laura,
You should not peep at goblin men."
Lizzie covered up her eyes,
Covered close lest they should look;
Laura reared her glossy head,
And whispered like the restless brook:
"Look, Lizzie, look, Lizzie,
Down the glen tramp little men.
One hauls a basket,
One bears a plate,
One lugs a golden dish
Of many pounds weight.
How fair the vine must grow
Whose grapes are so luscious;
How warm the wind must blow
Thro' those fruit bushes."
"No," said Lizzie: "No, no, no;
Their offers should not charm us,
Their evil gifts would harm us."
She thrust a dimpled finger
In each ear, shut eyes and ran:
Curious Laura chose to linger
Wondering at each merchant man.
One had a cat's face,
One whisked a tail,
One tramped at a rat's pace,
One crawled like a snail,
One like a wombat prowled obtuse and furry,
One like a ratel[1] tumbled hurry skurry.
She heard a voice like voice of doves
Cooing all together:
They sounded kind and full of loves
In the pleasant weather.

Laura stretched her gleaming neck
Like a rush-imbedded swan,
Like a lily from the beck,[2]
Like a moonlit poplar branch.
Like a vessel at the launch
When its last restraint is gone.

Backwards up the mossy glen
Turned and trooped the goblin men,
With their shrill repeated cry,
"Come buy, come buy."

---

1   a nocturnal carnivore related to the badger, found in South Africa and India
2   small stream

When they reached where Laura was
They stood stock still upon the moss,
Leering at each other,
Brother with queer brother;
Signalling each other,
Brother with sly brother.
One set his basket down,
One reared his plate;
One began to weave a crown
Of tendrils, leaves, and rough nuts brown
(Men sell not such in any town);
One heaved the golden weight
Of dish and fruit to offer her:
"Come buy, come buy," was still their cry.

Laura stared but did not stir,
Longed but had no money:
The whisk-tailed merchant bade her taste
In tones as smooth as honey,
The cat-faced purr'd,
The rat-paced spoke a word
Of welcome, and the snail-paced even was heard;
One parrot-voiced and jolly
Cried 'Pretty Goblin' still for 'Pretty Polly;'—
One whistled like a bird.

But sweet-tooth Laura spoke in haste:
"Good folk, I have no coin;
To take were to purloin:
I have no copper in my purse,
I have no silver either,
And all my gold is on the furze
That shakes in windy weather
Above the rusty heather."
"You have much gold upon your head,"
They answered all together:
"Buy from us with a golden curl."
She clipped a precious golden lock,
She dropped a tear more rare than pearl,
Then sucked their fruit globes fair or red:
Sweeter than honey from the rock,
Stronger than man-rejoicing wine,
Clearer than water flowed that juice;
She never tasted such before,
How should it cloy with length of use?
She sucked and sucked and sucked the more
Fruits which that unknown orchard bore;
She sucked until her lips were sore;
Then flung the emptied rinds away
But gathered up one kernel-stone,

And knew not was it night or day
As she turned home alone.

Lizzie met her at the gate
Full of wise upbraidings:
"Dear, you should not stay so late,
Twilight is not good for maidens;
Should not loiter in the glen
In the haunts of goblin men.
Do you not remember Jeanie,
How she met them in the moonlight,
Took their gifts both choice and many,
Ate their fruits and wore their flowers
Plucked from bowers
Where summer ripens at all hours?
But ever in the noonlight
She pined and pined away;
Sought them by night and day,
Found them no more, but dwindled and grew grey;
Then fell with the first snow,
While to this day no grass will grow
Where she lies low:
I planted daisies there a year ago
That never blow.
You should not loiter so."
"Nay, hush," said Laura:
"Nay, hush, my sister:
I ate and ate my fill,
Yet my mouth waters still;
To-morrow night I will
Buy more:" and kissed her:
"Have done with sorrow;
I'll bring you plums to-morrow
Fresh on their mother twigs,
Cherries worth getting;
You cannot think what figs
My teeth have met in,
What melons icy-cold
Piled on a dish of gold
Too huge for me to hold,
What peaches with a velvet nap,
Pellucid grapes without one seed:
Odorous indeed must be the mead
Whereon they grow, and pure the wave they drink
With lilies at the brink,
And sugar-sweet their sap."

Golden head by golden head,
Like two pigeons in one nest
Folded in each other's wings,
They lay down in their curtained bed:

Like two blossoms on one stem,
Like two flakes of new-fall'n snow,
Like two wands of ivory
Tipped with gold for awful[1] kings.
Moon and stars gazed in at them,
Wind sang to them lullaby,
Lumbering owls forbore to fly,
Not a bat flapped to and fro
Round their rest:
Cheek to cheek and breast to breast
Locked together in one nest.

Early in the morning
When the first cock crowed his warning,
Neat like bees, as sweet and busy,
Laura rose with Lizzie:
Fetched in honey, milked the cows,
Aired and set to rights the house,
Kneaded cakes of whitest wheat,
Cakes for dainty mouths to eat,
Next churned butter, whipped up cream,
Fed their poultry, sat and sewed;
Talked as modest maidens should:
Lizzie with an open heart,
Laura in an absent dream,
One content, one sick in part;
One warbling for the mere bright day's delight,
One longing for the night.

At length slow evening came:
They went with pitchers to the reedy brook;
Lizzie most placid in her look,
Laura most like a leaping flame.
They drew the gurgling water from its deep;
Lizzie plucked purple and rich golden flags,
Then turning homeward said: "The sunset flushes
Those furthest loftiest crags;
Come, Laura, not another maiden lags,
No wilful squirrel wags,
The beasts and birds are fast asleep."
But Laura loitered still among the rushes
And said the bank was steep.

And said the hour was early still,
The dew not fall'n, the wind not chill;
Listening ever, but not catching

---

1   awe-inspiring

The customary cry,
"Come buy, come buy,"
With its iterated jingle
Of sugar-baited words:
Not for all her watching
Once discerning even one goblin
Racing, whisking, tumbling, hobbling;
Let alone the herds
That used to tramp along the glen,
In groups or single,
Of brisk fruit-merchant men.
Till Lizzie urged, "O Laura, come;
I hear the fruit-call, but I dare not look:
You should not loiter longer at this brook:
Come with me home.
The stars rise, the moon bends her arc,
Each glowworm winks her spark,
Let us get home before the night grows dark:
For clouds may gather
Tho' this is summer weather,
Put out the lights and drench us thro';
Then if we lost our way what should we do?"

Laura turned cold as stone
To find her sister heard that cry alone,
That goblin cry,
"Come buy our fruits, come buy."
Must she then buy no more such dainty fruit?
Must she no more such succous[1] pasture find,
Gone deaf and blind?
Her tree of life drooped from the root:
She said not one word in her heart's sore ache;
But peering thro' the dimness, nought discerning,
Trudged home, her pitcher dripping all the way;
So crept to bed, and lay
Silent till Lizzie slept;
Then sat up in a passionate yearning,
And gnashed her teeth for baulked desire, and wept
As if her heart would break.

Day after day, night after night,
Laura kept watch in vain
In sullen silence of exceeding pain.
She never caught again the goblin cry:
"Come buy, come buy;"—
She never spied the goblin men

---

1   juicy

Hawking their fruits along the glen:
But when the noon waxed bright
Her hair grew thin and grey;
She dwindled, as the fair full moon doth turn
To swift decay and burn
Her fire away.

One day remembering her kernel-stone
She set it by a wall that faced the south;
Dewed it with tears, hoped for a root.
Watched for a waxing shoot,
But there came none;
It never saw the sun,
It never felt the trickling moisture run:
While with sunk eyes and faded mouth
She dreamed of melons, as a traveller sees
False waves in desert drouth
With shade of leaf-crowned trees,
And burns the thirstier in the sandful breeze.

She no more swept the house,
Tended the fowls or cows,
Fetched honey, kneaded cakes of wheat,
Brought water from the brook:
But sat down listless in the chimney-nook

And would not eat.
Tender Lizzie could not bear
To watch her sister's cankerous care
Yet not to share.
She night and morning
Caught the goblins' cry:
"Come buy our orchard fruits,
Come buy, come buy:"—
Beside the brook, along the glen,
She heard the tramp of goblin men,
The voice and stir
Poor Laura could not hear;
Longed to buy fruit to comfort her,
But feared to pay too dear.
She thought of Jeanie in her grave,
Who should have been a bride;
But who for joys brides hope to have
Fell sick and died
In her gay prime,
In earliest Winter time,
With the first glazing rime,
With the first snow-fall of crisp Winter time.

Till Laura dwindling
Seemed knocking at Death's door:

Then Lizzie weighed no more
Better and worse;
But put a silver penny in her purse,
Kissed Laura, crossed the heath with clumps of furze
At twilight, halted by the brook:
And for the first time in her life
Began to listen and look.

Laughed every goblin
When they spied her peeping:
Came towards her hobbling,
Flying, running, leaping,
Puffing and blowing,
Chuckling, clapping, crowing,
Clucking and gobbling,
Mopping and mowing,[1]
Full of airs and graces,
Pulling wry faces,
Demure grimaces,
Cat-like and rat-like,
Ratel- and wombat-like,
Snail-paced in a hurry,
Parrot-voiced and whistler,
Helter skelter, hurry skurry,
Chattering like magpies,
Fluttering like pigeons,
Gliding like fishes,—
Hugged her and kissed her:
Squeezed and caressed her:
Stretched up their dishes,
Panniers, and plates:
"Look at our apples
Russet and dun,
Bob at our cherries,
Bite at our peaches,
Citrons and dates,
Grapes for the asking,
Pears red with basking
Out in the sun,
Plums on their twigs;
Pluck them and suck them,
Pomegranates, figs."—

"Good folk," said Lizzie,
Mindful of Jeanie:
"Give me much and many:"—

---

1   grimacing, making faces

Held out her apron,
Tossed them her penny.
"Nay, take a seat with us,
Honour and eat with us,"
They answered grinning:
"Our feast is but beginning,
Night yet is early,
Warm and dew pearly,
Wakeful and starry:
Such fruits as these
No man can carry;
Half their bloom would fly,
Half their dew would dry,
Half their flavour would pass by.
Sit down and feast with us,
Be welcome guest with us,
Cheer you and rest with us."—
"Thank you," said Lizzie: "But one waits
At home alone for me:
So without further parleying,
If you will not sell me any
Of your fruits tho' much and many,
Give me back my silver penny
I tossed you for a fee."—
They began to scratch their pates,
No longer wagging, purring,
But visibly demurring,
Grunting and snarling.
One called her proud,
Cross-grained, uncivil;
Their tones waxed loud,
Their looks were evil.
Lashing their tails
They trod and hustled her,
Elbowed and jostled her,
Clawed with their nails,
Barking, mewing, hissing, mocking,
Tore her gown and soiled her stocking,
Twitched her hair out by the roots,
Stamped upon her tender feet,
Held her hands and squeezed their fruits
Against her mouth to make her eat.

White and golden Lizzie stood,
Like a lily in a flood,—
Like a rock of blue-veined stone
Lashed by tides obstreperously,—
Like a beacon left alone
In a hoary roaring sea
Sending up a golden fire,—
Like a fruit-crowned orange-tree

White with blossoms honey-sweet
Sore beset by wasp and bee,—
Like a royal virgin town
Topped with gilded dome and spire
Close beleaguered by a fleet
Mad to tug her standard down.

One may lead a horse to water
Twenty cannot make him drink.
Tho' the goblins cuffed and caught her,
Coaxed and fought her,
Bullied and besought her,
Scratched her, pinched her black as ink,
Kicked and knocked her,
Mauled and mocked her,
Lizzie uttered not a word;
Would not open lip from lip
Lest they should cram a mouthful in:
But laughed in heart to feel the drip
Of juice that syrupped all her face,
And lodged in dimples of her chin,
And streaked her neck which quaked like curd.
At last the evil people,
Worn out by her resistance,
Flung back her penny, kicked their fruit
Along whichever road they took,
Not leaving root or stone or shoot;
Some writhed into the ground,
Some dived into the brook
With ring and ripple,
Some scudded on the gale without a sound,
Some vanished in the distance.

In a smart, ache, tingle,
Lizzie went her way;
Knew not was it night or day;
Sprang up the bank, tore thro' the furze,
Threaded copse and dingle,
And heard her penny jingle
Bouncing in her purse,—
Its bounce was music to her ear.
She ran and ran
As if she feared some goblin man
Dogged her with gibe or curse
Or something worse:
But not one goblin skurried after,
Nor was she pricked by fear;
The kind heart made her windy-paced
That urged her home quite out of breath with haste
And inward laughter.

She cried, "Laura," up the garden,
"Did you miss me?
Come and kiss me.
Never mind my bruises,
Hug me, kiss me, suck my juices
Squeezed from goblin fruits for you,
Goblin pulp and goblin dew.
Eat me, drink me, love me;
Laura, make much of me;
For your sake I have braved the glen
And had to do with goblin merchant men."

Laura started from her chair,
Flung her arms up in the air,
Clutched her hair:
"Lizzie, Lizzie, have you tasted
For my sake the fruit forbidden?
Must your light like mine be hidden,
Your young life like mine be wasted,
Undone in mine undoing,
And ruined in my ruin,
Thirsty, cankered, goblin-ridden?"—
She clung about her sister,
Kissed and kissed and kissed her:
Tears once again
Refreshed her shrunken eyes,
Dropping like rain
After long sultry drouth;[1]
Shaking with aguish fear, and pain,
She kissed and kissed her with a hungry mouth.

Her lips began to scorch,
That juice was wormwood to her tongue,
She loathed the feast:
Writhing as one possessed she leaped and sung,
Rent all her robe, and wrung
Her hands in lamentable haste,
And beat her breast.
Her locks streamed like the torch
Borne by a racer at full speed,
Or like the mane of horses in their flight,
Or like an eagle when she stems the light[2]
Straight toward the sun,
Or like a caged thing freed,
Or like a flying flag when armies run.

---

1   drought
2   makes headway against the light, like a ship against a current

Swift fire spread thro' her veins, knocked at her heart,
Met the fire smouldering there
And overbore its lesser flame;
She gorged on bitterness without a name:
Ah! fool, to choose such part
Of soul-consuming care!
Sense failed in the mortal strife:
Like the watch-tower of a town
Which an earthquake shatters down,
Like a lightning-stricken mast,
Like a wind-uprooted tree
Spun about,
Like a foam-topped waterspout
Cast down headlong in the sea,
She fell at last;
Pleasure past and anguish past,
Is it death or is it life?

Life out of death.
That night long Lizzie watched by her,
Counted her pulse's flagging stir,
Felt for her breath,
Held water to her lips, and cooled her face
With tears and fanning leaves:
But when the first birds chirped about their eaves,
And early reapers plodded to the place
Of golden sheaves,
And dew-wet grass
Bowed in the morning winds so brisk to pass,
And new buds with new day
Opened of cup-like lilies on the stream,
Laura awoke as from a dream,
Laughed in the innocent old way,
Hugged Lizzie but not twice or thrice;
Her gleaming locks showed not one thread of grey,
Her breath was sweet as May
And light danced in her eyes.

Days, weeks, months, years
Afterwards, when both were wives
With children of their own;
Their mother-hearts beset with fears,
Their lives bound up in tender lives;
Laura would call the little ones
And tell them of her early prime,
Those pleasant days long gone
Of not-returning time:
Would talk about the haunted glen,
The wicked, quaint fruit-merchant men,
Their fruits like honey to the throat
But poison in the blood;

(Men sell not such in any town:)
Would tell them how her sister stood
In deadly peril to do her good,
And win the fiery antidote:
Then joining hands to little hands
Would bid them cling together,
"For there is no friend like a sister
In calm or stormy weather;
To cheer one on the tedious way,
To fetch one if one goes astray,
To lift one if one totters down,
To strengthen whilst one stands."

Lewis Carroll

(1832–1898)

Jabberwocky[1]

'Twas brillig, and the slithy toves
   Did gyre and gimble in the wabe;
All mimsy were the borogoves,
   And the mome raths outgrabe.

'Beware the Jabberwock, my son!
   The jaws that bite, the claws that catch!
Beware the Jubjub bird, and shun
   The frumious Bandersnatch!'

He took his vorpal sword in hand;
   Long time the manxome foe he sought—
So rested he by the Tumtum tree,
   And stood awhile in thought.

And, as in uffish thought he stood,
   The Jabberwock, with eyes of flame,
Came whiffling through the tulgey wood,
   And burbled as it came!

One, two! One, two! And through and through
   The vorpal blade went snicker-snack!
He left it dead, and with its head
   He went galumphing back.

'And hast thou slain the Jabberwock?
   Come to my arms, my beamish boy
O frabjous day! Callooh! Callay!'
   He chortled in his joy.

'Twas brillig, and the slithy toves
   Did gyre and gimble in the wabe;
All mimsy were the borogoves,
   And the mome raths outgrabe.

---

1   from *Through the Looking-Glass* (1871), ch.1. 44

The White Knight's Song[1]

Haddock's Eyes or The Aged Aged Man
or Ways and Means or A-Sitting On A Gate

I'll tell thee everything I can;
    There's little to relate.
I saw an aged, aged man,
    A-sitting on a gate.
'Who are you, aged man?' I said.
    'And how is it you live?'
And his answer trickled through my head
    Like water through a sieve.

He said 'I look for butterflies
    That sleep among the wheat;
I make them into mutton-pies,
    And sell them in the street.
I sell them unto men,' he said,
    'Who sail on stormy seas;
And that's the way I get my bread—
    A trifle, if you please.'

But I was thinking of a plan
    To dye one's whiskers green,
And always use so large a fan
    That it could not be seen.
So, having no reply to give
    To what the old man said,
I cried, 'Come, tell me how you live!'
    And thumped him on the head.

His accents mild took up the tale;
    He said, 'I go my ways,
And when I find a mountain-rill,
    I set it in a blaze;
And thence they make a stuff they call
    Rowland's Macassar Oil[2]—
Yet twopence-halfpenny is all
    They give me for my toil.'

But I was thinking of a way
    To feed oneself on batter,
And so go on from day to day

---

1   from *Through the Looking-Glass* (1871), ch.8. The poem parodies Wordsworth's poem
"Resolution and Independence."
2   a hair oil, originally made from ingredients obtained in Makassar, in the East Indies.
Rowland and Son were the manufacturers.

Getting a little fatter.
I shook him well from side to side,
　　Until his face was blue; .
'Come, tell me how you live,' I cried
　　'And what it is you do!'

He said, 'I hunt for haddocks' eyes
　　Among the heather bright,
And work them into waistcoat-buttons
　　In the silent night.
And these I do not sell for gold
　　Or coin of silvery shine,
But for a copper halfpenny,
　　And that will purchase nine.

'I sometimes dig for buttered rolls,
　　Or set limed twigs[1] for crabs;
I sometimes search the grassy knolls
　　For wheels of hansom-cabs.
And that's the way' (he gave a wink)
　　'By which I get my wealth—
And very gladly will I drink
　　Your Honour's noble health.'

I heard him then, for I had just
　　Completed my design
To keep the Menai bridge[2] from rust
　　By boiling it in wine.
I thanked him much for telling me
　　The way he got his wealth,
But chiefly for his wish that he
　　Might drink my noble health.

And now, if e'er by chance I put
　　My fingers into glue,
Or madly squeeze a right-hand foot
　　Into a left-hand shoe,
Or if I drop upon my toe
　　A very heavy weight,
I weep, for it reminds me so
Of that old man I used to know—
Whose look was mild, whose speech was slow
Whose hair was whiter than the snow,
Whose face was very like a crow,
With eyes, like cinders, all aglow,
Who seemed distracted with his woe

1　twigs spread with birdlime, or any sticky substance, to catch birds
2　a railway bridge in north Wales, completed in 1850

Who rocked his body to and fro,
And muttered mumblingly and low,
As if his mouth were full of dough,
Who snorted like a buffalo—
That summer evening long ago
  A-sitting on a gate.

Thomas Hardy

(1840–1928)

Hap

If but some vengeful god would call to me
From up the sky, and laugh: 'Thou suffering thing,
Know that thy sorrow is my ecstasy,
That thy love's loss is my hate's profiting!'

Then would I bear it, clench myself, and die,
Steeled by the sense of ire unmerited;
Half-eased in that a Powerfuller than I
Had willed and meted[1] me the tears I shed.

But not so. How arrives it joy lies slain,
And why unblooms the best hope ever sown?
—Crass Casualty obstructs the sun and rain,
And dicing Time for gladness casts a moan. . . .
These purblind Doomsters[2] had as readily strown
Blisses about my pilgrimage as pain.

Nature's Questioning

When I look forth at dawning, pool,
    Field, flock, and lonely tree,
    All seem to gaze at me
Like chastened children sitting silent in a school;

    Their faces dulled, constrained, and worn,
        As though the master's way
        Through the long teaching day
Had cowed them till their early zest was overborne.

    Upon them stirs in lippings mere
        (As if once clear in call,
        But now scarce breathed at all)—
'We wonder, ever wonder, why we find us here!

    'Has some Vast Imbecility,
        Mighty to build and blend,

---

1   allotted
2   dimly-sighted, half-blind judges

But impotent to tend,
Framed us in jest, and left us now to hazardry?

'Or come we of an Automaton
　　Unconscious of our pains? . . .
　　Or are we live remains
Of Godhead dying downwards, brain and eye now gone?

'Or is it that some high Plan betides,
　　As yet not understood,
　　Of Evil stormed by Good,
We the Forlorn Hope over which Achievement strides?'

Thus things around. No answerer I. . . .
　　Meanwhile the winds, and rains,
　　And Earth's old glooms and pains
Are still the same, and Life and Death are neighbours nigh.

Drummer Hodge[1]

I

They throw in Drummer Hodge, to rest
　　Uncoffined—just as found:
His landmark is a kopje-crest[2]
　　That breaks the veldt around;
And foreign constellations west[3]
　　Each night above his mound.

II

Young Hodge the Drummer never knew—
　　Fresh from his Wessex home—
The meaning of the broad Karoo,[4]
　　The Bush, the dusty loam,
And why uprose to nightly view
　　Strange stars amid the gloom.[5]

III

Yet portion of that unknown plain
　　Will Hodge for ever be;

1　Hodge is a soldier killed in the Boer War between the British and the Boer colonists in
　　South Africa (1899-1902).
2　small hill (Afrikaans)
3　used here as a verb, meaning to set in the west
4　a dry plateau or tableland in South Africa
5　twilight

His homely Northern breast and brain
　　Grow to some Southern tree,
And strange-eyed constellations reign
　　His stars eternally.

The Darkling Thrush

I leant upon a coppice gate
　　When Frost was spectre-grey,
And Winter's dregs made desolate
　　The weakening eye of day.
The tangled bine-stems scored the sky
　　Like strings of broken lyres,
And all mankind that haunted nigh
　　Had sought their household fires.

The land's sharp features seemed to be
　　The Century's corpse outleant,[1]
His crypt the cloudy canopy,
　　The wind his death-lament.
The ancient pulse of germ and birth
　　Was shrunken hard and dry,
And every spirit upon earth
　　Seemed fervourless as I.

At once a voice arose among
　　The bleak twigs overhead
In a full-hearted evensong
　　Of joy illimited;
An aged thrush, frail, gaunt, and small,
　　In blast-beruffled plume,
Had chosen thus to fling his soul
　　Upon the growing gloom.

So little cause for carolings
　　Of such ecstatic sound
Was written on terrestrial things
　　Afar or nigh around,
That I could think there trembled through
　　His happy good-night air
Some blessèd Hope, whereof he knew
　　And I was unaware.

1　The poem was written on 31 December, 1900. Hardy images the past century as a corpse
spread out ("outleant") before him.

The Convergence of the Twain

(Lines on the loss of the 'Titanic')[1]

I

In a solitude of the sea
Deep from human vanity,
And the Pride of Life that planned her, stilly couches she.

II

Steel chambers, late the pyres
Of her salamandrine[2] fires,
Cold currents thrid,[3] and turn to rhythmic tidal lyres.

III

Over the mirrors meant
To glass the opulent
The sea-worm crawls—grotesque, slimed, dumb, indifferent.

IV

Jewels in joy designed
To ravish the sensuous mind
Lie lightless, all their sparkles bleared and black and blind.

V

Dim moon-eyed fishes near
Gaze at the gilded gear
And query: 'What does this vaingloriousness down here?' . . .

VI

Well: while was fashioning
This creature of cleaving wing,
The Immanent Will[4] that stirs and urges everything

---

1   the large luxury liner that was proclaimed unsinkable, but collided with an iceberg and sank on its maiden voyage on 15 April 1912
2   Salamanders were mythical lizards said to be able to live in fire.
3   thread through
4   the blind and indifferent force that, in Hardy's view, determines human destiny

VII

Prepared a sinister mate
For her—so gaily great—
A Shape of Ice, for the time far and dissociate.

VIII

And as the smart ship grew
In stature, grace, and hue,
In shadowy silent distance grew the Iceberg too.

IX

Alien they seemed to be:
No mortal eye could see
The intimate welding of their later history,

X

Or sign that they were bent
By paths coincident
On being anon twin halves of one august event,

XI

Till the Spinner of the Years
Said 'Now!' And each one hears,
And consummation comes, and jars two hemispheres.

Channel Firing[1]

That night your great guns, unawares,
Shook all our coffins as we lay,
And broke the chancel window-squares.
We thought it was the Judgment-day

And sat upright. While drearisome
Arose the howl of wakened hounds:
The mouse let fall the altar-crumb,
The worms drew back into the mounds,

The glebe[2] cow drooled. Till God called, 'No;
It's gunnery practice out at sea

---

1 a reference to gunnery practice by British and German warships in the English Channel.
   The poem was written in April 1914; four months later, the first World War broke out.
2 a field belonging to the church

Just as before you went below;
The world is as it used to be:

All nations striving strong to make
Red war yet redder. Mad as hatters
They do no more for Christés sake
Than you who are helpless in such matters.

That this is not the judgment-hour
For some of them's a blessed thing,
For if it were they'd have to scour
Hell's floor for so much threatening. . . .

Ha, ha. It will be warmer when
I blow the trumpet (if indeed
I ever do; for you are men,
And rest eternal sorely need).'

So down we lay again. 'I wonder,
Will the world ever saner be,'
Said one, 'than when He sent us under
In our indifferent century!'

And many a skeleton shook his head.
'Instead of preaching forty year,'
My neighbour Parson Thirdly said,
'I wish I had stuck to pipes and beer.'

Again the guns disturbed the hour,
Roaring their readiness to avenge,
As far inland as Stourton Tower,[1]
And Camelot, and starlit Stonehenge.

In Time of 'The Breaking of Nations'[2]

I

Only a man harrowing clods
    In a slow silent walk
With an old horse that stumbles and nods
    Half asleep as they stalk.

---

1   a tower in Dorset commemmorating Alfred's victory over the Danes in 879 A.D.
2   Written during the first World War. The title alludes to Jeremiah 51.20.

II

Only thin smoke without flame
　From the heaps of couch-grass;
Yet this will go onward the same
　Though Dynasties pass.

III

Yonder a maid and her wight[1]
　Come whispering by:
War's annals will cloud into night
　Ere their story die.

Transformations

Portion of this yew
Is a man my grandsire knew,
Bosomed here at its foot:
This branch may be his wife,
A ruddy human life
Now turned to a green shoot.

These grasses must be made
Of her who often prayed,
Last century, for repose;
And the fair girl long ago
Whom I vainly tried to know
May be entering this rose.

So, they are not underground,
But as nerves and veins abound
In the growths of upper air,
And they feel the sun and rain,
And the energy again
That made them what they were!

1　man

Gerard Manley Hopkins

(1844–1889)

God's Grandeur

The world is charged with the grandeur of God.
　It will flame out, like shining from shook foil;

　It gathers to a greatness, like the ooze of oil
Crushed. Why do men then now not reck his rod?
Generations have trod, have trod, have trod;
　And all is seared with trade; bleared, smeared, with toil;
　And wears man's smudge and shares man's smell: the soil
Is bare now, nor can foot feel, being shod.

And, for all this, nature is never spent;
　There lives the dearest freshness deep down things;
And though the last lights off the black West went
　Oh, morning, at the brown brink eastward, springs—
Because the Holy Ghost over the bent
　World broods with warm breast and with ah! bright wings.

Spring

Nothing is so beautiful as Spring—
　When weeds, in wheels, shoot long and lovely and lush;
　Thrush's eggs look little low heavens, and thrush
Through the echoing timber does so rinse and wring
The ear, it strikes like lightnings to hear him sing;
　The glassy peartree leaves and blooms, they brush
　The descending blue; that blue is all in a rush
With richness; the racing lambs too have fair their fling.

What is all this juice and all this joy?
　A strain of the earth's sweet being in the beginning
In Eden garden.—Have, get, before it cloy,

　Before it cloud, Christ, lord and sour with sinning,
Innocent mind and Mayday in girl and boy,
　Most, O maid's child,[1] thy choice and worthy the winning.

1　Christ, son of Mary

The Windhover:[1]

to Christ our Lord

I caught this morning morning's minion,[2] king-
  dom of daylight's dauphin,[3] dapple-dawn-drawn Falcon, in his
    riding
Of the rolling level underneath him steady air, and striding
High there, how he rung upon the rein of a wimpling[4] wing
In his ecstasy! then off, off forth on swing,
  As a skate's heel sweeps smooth on a bow-bend: the hurl and
    gliding
  Rebuffed the big wind. My heart in hiding
Stirred for a bird,—the achieve of, the mastery of the thing!

Brute beauty and valour and act, oh, air, pride, plume, here
  Buckle! AND the fire that breaks from thee then, a billion
Times told lovelier, more dangerous, O my chevalier![5]

No wonder of it: sheer plod makes plough down sillion[6]
Shine, and blue-bleak embers, ah my dear,
  Fall, gall themselves, and gash gold-vermilion.

Pied Beauty

  Glory be to God for dappled things—
    For skies of couple-colour as a brinded[7] cow;
      For rose-moles all in stipple upon trout that swim;
Fresh-firecoal chestnut-falls; finches' wings;
    Landscape plotted and pieced—fold, fallow, and plough;
    And all trades, their gear and tackle and trim.

All things counter, original, spare, strange;
    Whatever is fickle, freckled (who knows how?)
      With swift, slow; sweet, sour; adazzle, dim;
He fathers-forth whose beauty is past change:
                  Praise him.

---

1   a kestrel, a European falcon
2   favourite or darling
3   heir to the French throne
4   rippling
5   knight
6   selion, the ridge between two furrows in a ploughed field
7   tawny or grayish with irregular streaks

Spring and Fall:

to a Young Child

Margaret, are you grieving
Over Goldengrove unleaving?
Leaves, like the things of man, you
With your fresh thoughts care for, can you?
Ah! as the heart grows older
It will come to such sights colder
By and by, nor spare a sigh
Though worlds of wanwood leafmeal[1] lie;
And yet you *will* weep and know why.
Now no matter, child, the name:
Sorrow's springs are the same.
Nor mouth had, no nor mind, expressed
What heart heard of, ghost guessed:
It is the blight man was born for,
It is Margaret you mourn for.

I wake and feel the fell of dark, not day.

I wake and feel the fell[2] of dark, not day.
What hours, O what black hours we have spent
This night! what sights you, heart, saw, ways you went!
And more must, in yet longer light's delay.
With witness I speak this. But where I say
Hours I mean years, mean life. And my lament
Is cries countless, cries like dead letters[3] sent
To dearest him that lives alas! away.
I am gall, I am heartburn. God's most deep decree
Bitter would have me taste: my taste was me;
Bones built in me, flesh filled, blood brimmed the curse.
Selfyeast of spirit a dull dough sours. I see
The lost are like this, and their scourge to be
As I am mine, their sweating selves; but worse.

No worst, there is none.

No worst, there is none. Pitched past pitch of grief,
More pangs will, schooled at forepangs, wilder wring.
Comforter, where, where is your comforting?
Mary, mother of us, where is your relief?

---

1   a word coined by Hopkins, on analogy with "piecemeal"
2   bitterness
3   unclaimed or undelivered letters remaining at the post office

My cries heave, herds-long; huddle in a main, a chief-
Woe, world-sorrow; on an age-old anvil wince and sing—
Then lull, then leave off. Fury had shrieked 'No ling-
Ering! Let me be fell:[1] force[2] I must be brief'.
O the mind, mind has mountains; cliffs of fall
Frightful, sheer, no-man-fathomed. Hold them cheap
May who ne'er hung there. Nor does long our small
Durance[3] deal with that steep or deep. Here! creep,
Wretch, under a comfort serves in a whirlwind: all
Life death does end and each day dies with sleep.

Carrion Comfort

Not, I'll not, carrion comfort, Despair, not feast on thee;
Not untwist—slack they may be—these last strands of man
In me or, most weary, cry *I can no more*. I can;
Can something, hope, wish day come, not choose not to be.
But ah, but O thou terrible, why wouldst thou rude on me
Thy wring-world right foot rock? lay a lionlimb against me? scan
With darksome devouring eyes my bruised bones? and fan,
O in turns of tempest, me heaped there; me frantic to avoid thee and
    flee?
Why? That my chaff might fly; my grain lie, sheer and clear.
Nay in all that toil, that coil, since (seems) I kissed the rod,
Hand rather, my heart lo! lapped strength, stole joy, would laugh,
    cheer.
Cheer whom though? The hero whose heaven-handling flung me,
    foot trod
Me? or me that fought him? O which one? is it each one? That night,
    that year
Of now done darkness I wretch lay wrestling with (my God!) my God.

---

1   fierce, ruthless
2   perforce, of necessity
3   endurance

Thou art indeed just, Lord

Thou art indeed just, Lord, if I contend
With thee; but, sir, so what I plead is just.
Why do sinners' ways prosper? and why must
Disappointment all I endeavour end?
Wert thou my enemy, O thou my friend,
How wouldst thou worse, I wonder, than thou dost
Defeat, thwart me? Oh, the sots and thralls of lust
Do in spare hours more thrive than I that spend,

Sir, life Upon thy cause. See, banks and brakes[1]
Now, leaved how thick ! laced they are again
With fretty chervil[2], look, and fresh wind shakes

Them; birds build—but not I build; no, but strain,
Time's eunuch, and not breed one work that wakes.
Mine, O thou lord of life, send my roots rain.

---

1   thickets
2   garden herb

Isabella Valancy Crawford

(1850–1887)

The Camp of Souls

My white canoe, like the silvery air
   O'er the River of Death that darkly rolls
When the moons of the world are round and fair,
   I paddle back from the "Camp of Souls."
When the wishton-wish[1] in the low swamp grieves
Come the dark plumes of red "Singing Leaves."

Two hundred times have the moons of spring
   Rolled over the bright bay's azure breath
Since they decked me with plumes of an eagle's wing,
   And painted my face with the "paint of death,"
And from their pipes o'er my corpse there broke
The solemn rings of the blue "last smoke."

Two hundred times have the wintry moons
   Wrapped the dead earth in a blanket white;
Two hundred times have the wild sky loons
   Shrieked in the flush of the golden light
Of the first sweet dawn, when the summer weaves
Her dusky wigwam of perfect leaves.

Two hundred moons of the falling leaf
   Since they laid my bow in my dead right hand
And chanted above me the "song of grief"
   As I took my way to the spirit land;
Yet when the swallow the blue air cleaves
Come the dark plumes of red "Singing Leaves."

White are the wigwams in that far camp,
   And the star-eyed deer on the plains are found;
No bitter marshes or tangled swamp
   In the Manitou's[2] happy hunting-ground!
And the moon of summer forever rolls
Above the red men in their "Camp of Souls."

Blue are its lakes as the wild dove's breast,
   And their murmurs soft as her gentle note;
As the calm, large stars in the deep sky rest,
   The yellow lilies upon them float;
And canoes, like flakes of the silvery snow,
Thro' the tall, rustling rice-beds come and go.

---

1   the whippoorwill, a bird common to eastern North America
2   The Manitou is the Algonquian personification of the all-powerful spirit guiding life and nature.

Green are its forests; no warrior wind
   Rushes on war trail the dusk grove through,
With leaf-scalps of tall trees mourning behind;
   But South Wind, heart friend of Great Manitou,
When ferns and leaves with cool dews are wet,
Blows flowery breaths from his red calumet.[1]

Never upon them the white frosts lie,
   Nor glow their green boughs with the "paint of death";
Manitou smiles in the crystal sky,
   Close breathing above them His life-strong breath;
And He speaks no more in fierce thunder sound,
So near is His happy hunting-ground.

Yet often I love, in my white canoe,
   To come to the forests and camps of earth:
'Twas there death's black arrow pierced me through;
   'Twas there my red-browed mother gave me birth;
There I, in the light of a young man's dawn,
Won the lily heart of dusk "Springing Fawn."

And love is a cord woven out of life,
   And dyed in the red of the living heart;
And time is the hunter's rusty knife,
   That cannot cut the red strands apart:
And I sail from the spirit shore to scan
Where the weaving of that strong cord began.

But I may not come with a giftless hand,
   So richly I pile, in my white canoe,
Flowers that bloom in the spirit land,
   Immortal smiles of Great Manitou.
When I paddle back to the shores of earth
I scatter them over the white man's hearth.

For love is the breath of the soul set free;
   So I cross the river that darkly rolls,
That my spirit may whisper soft to thee
   Of *thine* who wait in the "Camp of Souls."
When the bright day laughs, or the wan night grieves,
Come the dusky plumes of red "Singing Leaves."

---

1   pipe of peace

The Dark Stag

A startled stag, the blue-grey Night,
  Leaps down beyond black pines.
Behind—a length of yellow light—
  The hunter's arrow shines:
His moccasins are stained with red,
  He bends upon his knee,
From covering peaks his shafts are sped,
The blue mists plume his mighty head,—
  Well may the swift Night flee!

The pale, pale Moon, a snow-white doe,
  Bounds by his dappled flank:
They beat the stars down as they go,
  Like wood-bells growing rank.
The winds lift dewlaps from the ground,
  Leap from the quaking reeds;
Their hoarse bays shake the forests round,
With keen cries on the track they bound,—
  Swift, swift the dark stag speeds!

Away! his white doe, far behind,
  Lies wounded on the plain;
Yells at his flank the nimblest wind,
  His large tears fall in rain;
Like lily-pads, small clouds grow white
  About his darkling way;
From his bald nest upon the height
The red-eyed eagle sees his flight;
He falters, turns, the antlered Night,—
  The dark stag stands at bay!

His feet are in the waves of space;
  His antlers broad and dun
He lowers; he turns his velvet face
  To front the hunter, Sun;
He stamps the lilied clouds, and high
  His branches fill the west.
The lean stork sails across the sky,
The shy loon shrieks to see him die,
  The winds leap at his breast.

Roar the rent lakes as thro' the wave
  Their silver warriors plunge,
As vaults from core of crystal cave
  The strong, fierce muskallunge;
Red torches of the sumach glare,
  Fall's council-fires are lit;
The bittern, squaw-like, scolds the air;

The wild duck splashes loudly where
   The rustling rice-spears knit.

Shaft after shaft the red Sun speeds:
   Rent the stag's dappled side,
His breast, fanged by the shrill winds, bleeds,
   He staggers on the tide;
He feels the hungry waves of space
   Rush at him high and blue;
Their white spray smites his dusky face,
Swifter the Sun's fierce arrows race
   And pierce his stout heart thro'.

His antlers fall; once more he spurns
   The hoarse hounds of the day;
His blood upon the crisp blue burns,
   Reddens the mounting spray;
His branches smite the wave—with cries
   The loud winds pause and flag—
He sinks in space—red glow the skies,
The brown earth crimsons as he dies,
   The strong and dusky stag.

The City Tree

I stand within the stony, arid town,
   I gaze forever on the narrow street,
I hear forever passing up and down
   The ceaseless tramp of feet.

I know no brotherhood with far-locked woods,
   Where branches bourgeon from a kindred sap,
Where o'er mossed roots, in cool, green solitudes,
   Small silver brooklets lap.

No emerald vines creep wistfully to me
   And lay their tender fingers on my bark;
High may I toss my boughs, yet never see
   Dawn's first most glorious spark.

When to and fro my branches wave and sway,
   Answ'ring the feeble wind that faintly calls,
They kiss no kindred boughs, but touch alway
   The stones of climbing walls.

My heart is never pierced with song of bird;
   My leaves know nothing of that glad unrest
Which makes a flutter in the still woods heard
   When wild birds build a nest.

There never glance the eyes of violets up,
  Blue into the deep splendour of my green;
Nor falls the sunlight to the primrose cup
  My quivering leaves between.

Not mine, not mine to turn from soft delight
  Of woodbine breathings, honey sweet and warm;
With kin embattled rear my glorious height
  To greet the coming storm!

Not mine to watch across the free, broad plains
  The whirl of stormy cohorts sweeping fast,
The level silver lances of great rains
  Blown onward by the blast!

Not mine the clamouring tempest to defy,
  Tossing the proud crest of my dusky leaves—
Defender of small flowers that trembling lie
  Against my barky greaves!

Not mine to watch the wild swan drift above,
  Balanced on wings that could not choose between
The wooing sky, blue as the eye of love,
  And my own tender green!

And yet my branches spread, a kingly sight,
  In the close prison of the drooping air:
When sun-vexed noons are at their fiery height
  My shade is broad, and there

Come city toilers, who their hour of ease
  Weave out to precious seconds as they lie
Pillowed on horny hands, to hear the breeze
  Through my great branches die.

I see no flowers, but as the children race
  With noise and clamour through the dusty street,
I see the bud of many an angel face,
  I hear their merry feet.

No violets look up, but, shy and grave,
  The children pause and lift their crystal eyes
To where my emerald branches call and wave
  As to the mystic skies.

A. E. Housman

(1859–1936)

Loveliest of trees, the cherry now

Loveliest of trees, the cherry now
Is hung with bloom along the bough,
And stands about the woodland ride
Wearing white for Eastertide.

Now, of my threescore years and ten,
Twenty will not come again,
And take from seventy springs a score,
It only leaves me fifty more.

And since to look at things in bloom
Fifty springs are little room,
About the woodlands I will go
To see the cherry hung with snow.

To an Athlete Dying Young

The time you won your town the race
We chaired you through the market-place;
Man and boy stood cheering by,
And home we brought you shoulder-high.

To-day, the road all runners come,
Shoulder-high we bring you home,
And set you at your threshold down,
Townsman of a stiller town.

Smart lad, to slip betimes away
From fields where glory does not stay
And early though the laurel grows
It withers quicker than the rose.

Eyes the shady night has shut
Cannot see the record cut,
And silence sounds no worse than cheers
After earth has stopped the ears:

Now you will not swell the rout
Of lads that wore their honours out,
Runners whom renown outran
And the name died before the man.

So set, before its echoes fade,
The fleet foot on the sill of shade,
And hold to the low lintel up
The still-defended challenge-cup.

And round that early-laurelled head
Will flock to gaze the strengthless dead,
And find unwithered on its curls
The garland briefer than a girl's.

Is my team ploughing

'Is my team ploughing,
  That I was used to drive
And hear the harness jingle
  When I was man alive?'

Ay, the horses trample,
  The harness jingles now;
No change though you lie under
  The land you used to plough.

'Is football playing
  Along the river shore,
With lads to chase the leather,
  Now I stand up no more?'

Ay, the ball is flying,
  The lads play heart and soul;
The goal stands up, the keeper
  Stands up to keep the goal.

'Is my girl happy,
  That I thought hard to leave,
And has she tired of weeping
  As she lies down at eve?'

Ay, she lies down lightly,
  She lies not down to weep:
Your girl is well contented.
  Be still, my lad, and sleep.

'Is my friend hearty,
  Now I am thin and pine,
And has he found to sleep in
  A better bed than mine?'

Yes, lad, I lie easy,
  I lie as lads would choose;
I cheer a dead man's sweetheart,
  Never ask me whose.

On Wenlock Edge[1] the wood's in trouble

On Wenlock Edge the wood's in trouble;
    His forest fleece the Wrekin[2] heaves;
The gale, it plies the saplings double,
    And thick on Severn snow the leaves.

'Twould blow like this through holt and hanger[3]
    When Uricon[4] the city stood:
'Tis the old wind in the old anger,
    But then it threshed another wood.

Then, 'twas before my time, the Roman
    At yonder heaving hill would stare:
The blood that warms an English yeoman,
    The thoughts that hurt him, they were there.

There, like the wind through woods in riot,
    Through him the gale of life blew high;
The tree of man was never quiet:
    Then 'twas the Roman, now 'tis I.

The gale, it plies the saplings double,
    It blows so hard, 'twill soon be gone:
To-day the Roman and his trouble
    Are ashes under Uricon.

Terence, this is stupid stuff[5]

'Terence, this is stupid stuff:
You eat your victuals fast enough;
There can't be much amiss, 'tis clear,
To see the rate you drink your beer.
But oh, good Lord, the verse you make,
It gives a chap the belly-ache.
The cow, the old cow, she is dead;
It sleeps well, the horned head:
We poor lads, 'tis our turn now
To hear such tunes as killed the cow.
Pretty friendship 'tis to rhyme
Your friends to death before their time
Moping melancholy mad:

---

1   a range of hills in Shropshire
2   a hill in Shropshire, near the river Severn
3   both "holt" and "hanger" describe woods on the sides of hills
4   the Roman city of Uriconium, near Shrewsbury in Shropshire
5   Housman had originally intended to call the volume in which this poem appears "The Poems of Terence Hearsay."

Come, pipe a tune to dance to, lad.'

Why, if 'tis dancing you would be,
There's brisker pipes than poetry.
Say, for what were hop-yards meant,
Or why was Burton built on Trent?[1]
Oh many a peer of England brews
Livelier liquor than the Muse,
And malt does more than Milton can
To justify God's ways to man[2].
Ale, man, ale's the stuff to drink
For fellows whom it hurts to think:
Look into the pewter pot
To see the world as the world's not.
And faith, 'tis pleasant till 'tis past:
The mischief is that 'twill not last.
Oh I have been to Ludlow[3] fair
And left my necktie God knows where,
And carried half-way home, or near,
Pints and quarts of Ludlow beer:
Then the world seemed none so bad,
And I myself a sterling lad;
And down in lovely muck I've lain,
Happy till I woke again.
Then I saw the morning sky:
Heigho, the tale was all a lie;
The world, it was the old world yet,
I was I, my things were wet,
And nothing now remained to do
But begin the game anew.

Therefore, since the world has still
Much good, but much less good than ill,
And while the sun and moon endure
Luck's a chance, but trouble's sure,
I'd face it as a wise man would,
And train for ill and not for good.
'Tis true, the stuff I bring for sale
Is not so brisk a brew as ale:
Out of a stem that scored the hand
I wrung it in a weary land.
But take it: if the smack is sour,
The better for the embittered hour;
It should do good to heart and head
When your soul is in my soul's stead;

---

1   Burton-on-Trent, in Staffordshire, known for its breweries
2   An echo of *Paradise Lost*, 1.26
3   a town in Shropshire

And I will friend you, if I may,
In the dark and cloudy day.

There was a king reigned in the East:
There, when kings will sit to feast,
They get their fill before they think
With poisoned meat and poisoned drink.
He gathered all that springs to birth
From the many-venomed earth;
First a little, thence to more,
He sampled all her killing store;
And easy, smiling, seasoned sound,
Sate the king when healths went round.
They put arsenic in his meat
And stared aghast to watch him eat;
They poured strychnine in his cup
And shook to see him drink it up:
They shook, they stared as white's their shirt:
Them it was their poison hurt.
— I tell the tale that I heard told.
Mithridates,[1] he died old.

The chestnut casts his flambeaux[2]

The chestnut casts his flambeaux, and the flowers
   Stream from the hawthorn on the wind away,
The doors clap to, the pane is blind with showers.
   Pass me the can, lad; there's an end of May.

There's one spoilt spring to scant our mortal lot,
   One season ruined of our little store.
May will be fine next year as like as not:
   Oh ay, but then we shall be twenty-four.

We for a certainty are not the first
   Have sat in taverns while the tempest hurled
Their hopeful plans to emptiness, and cursed
   Whatever brute and blackguard made the world.

It is in truth iniquity on high
   To cheat our sentenced souls of aught they crave,
And mar the merriment as you and I
   Fare on our long fool's-errand to the grave.
Iniquity it is; but pass the can.

---

1   Mithridates VI (131-63 B.C.), King of Pontus in Asia Minor, was said to have rendered himself proof against poisons by taking them in small doses.
2   A flambeau is a burning torch.

My lad, no pair of kings our mothers bore;
Our only portion is the estate of man:
We want the moon, but we shall get no more.

If here to-day the cloud of thunder lours
To-morrow it will hie on far behests;
The flesh will grieve on other bones than ours
Soon, and the soul will mourn in other breasts.

The troubles of our proud and angry dust
Are from eternity, and shall not fail.
Bear them we can, and if we can we must.
Shoulder the sky, my lad, and drink your ale.

The night is freezing fast

The night is freezing fast,
To-morrow comes December;
And winterfalls of old
Are with me from the past;
And chiefly I remember
How Dick would hate the cold.

Fall, winter, fall; for he,
Prompt hand and headpiece clever,
Has woven a winter robe,
And made of earth and sea
His overcoat for ever,
And wears the turning globe.

Charles G. D. Roberts

(1860–1943)

Tantramar Revisited[1]

Summers and summers have come, and gone with the flight of the
    swallow;
Sunshine and thunder have been, storm, and winter, and frost;
Many and many a sorrow has all but died from remembrance,
Many a dream of joy fall'n in the shadow of pain.
Hands of chance and change have marred, or moulded, or broken,
Busy with spirit or flesh, all I most have adored;
Even the bosom of Earth is strewn with heavier shadows,—
Only in these green hills, aslant to the sea, no change!
Here where the road that has climbed from the inland valleys and
    woodlands,
Dips from the hill-tops down, straight to the base of the hills,—
Here, from my vantage-ground, I can see the scattering houses,
Stained with time, set warm in orchards, meadows, and wheat,
Dotting the broad bright slopes outspread to southward and
    eastward,
Wind-swept all day long, blown by the south-east wind.

Skirting the sunbright uplands stretches a riband of meadow,
Shorn of the labouring grass, bulwarked well from the sea,
Fenced on its seaward border with long clay dykes from the turbid
Surge and flow of the tides vexing the Westmoreland shores.
Yonder, toward the left, lie broad the Westmoreland marshes,—
Miles on miles they extend, level, and grassy, and dim,
Clear from the long red sweep of flats to the sky in the distance,
Save for the outlying heights, green-rampired[2] Cumberland Point;
Miles on miles outrolled, and the river channels divide them,—
Miles on miles of green, barred by the hurtling gusts.

Miles on miles beyond the tawny bay is Minudie.[3]
There are the low blue hills; villages gleam at their feet.
Nearer a white sail shines across the water, and nearer
Still are the slim, grey masts of fishing boats dry on the flats.
Ah, how well I remember those wide red flats, above tide-mark
Pale with scurf of the salt, seamed and baked in the sun!
Well I remember the piles of blocks and ropes, and the net-reels
Wound with the beaded nets, dripping and dark from the sea!
Now at this season the nets are unwound; they hang from the rafters
Over the fresh-stowed hay in upland barns, and the wind
Blows all day through the chinks, with the streaks of sunlight,

---

1   The Tantramar River, the Westmoreland marshes, and Cumberland Point are all in the area
       of eastern New Brunswick where Roberts spent his childhood.
2   fortified, bulwarked
3   a village in Nova Scotia, on the Bay of Fundy

and sways them
Softly at will; or they lie heaped in the gloom of a loft.

Now at this season the reels are empty and idle; I see them
Over the lines of the dykes, over the gossiping grass,
Now at this season they swing in the long strong wind, thro'
    the lonesome
Golden afternoon, shunned by the foraging gulls.
Near about sunset the crane will journey homeward above them;
Round them, under the moon, all the calm night long,
Winnowing soft grey wings of marsh-owls wander and wander,
Now to the broad, lit marsh, now to the dusk of the dike.
Soon, thro' their dew-wet frames, in the live keen freshness of
    morning,
Out of the teeth of the dawn blows back the awakening wind.
Then, as the blue day mounts, and the low-shot shafts of the sunlight
Glance from the tide to the shore, gossamers jewelled with dew
Sparkle and wave, where late sea-spoiling fathoms of drift-net
Myriad-meshed, uploomed sombrely over the land.

Well I remember it all. The salt, raw scent of the margin;
While, with men at the windlass, groaned each reel, and the net
Surging in ponderous lengths, uprose and coiled in its station;
Then each man to his home, — well I remember it all!

Yet, as I sit and watch, this present peace of the landscape,—
Stranded boats, these reels empty and idle, the hush,
One grey hawk slow-wheeling above yon cluster of haystacks,—
More than the old-time stir this stillness welcomes me home.
Ah, the old-time stir, how once it stung me with rapture,—
Old-time sweetness, the winds freighted with honey and salt!
Yet will I stay my steps and not go down to the marshland,—
Muse and recall far off, rather remember than see,—
Lest on too close sight I miss the darling illusion,
Spy at their task even here the hands of chance and change.

The Potato Harvest

A high bare field, brown from the plough, and borne
Aslant from sunset; amber wastes of sky
Washing the ridge; a clamour of crows that fly
In from the wide flats where the spent tides mourn
To yon their rocking roosts in pines wind-torn;
A line of grey snake-fence, that zigzags by
A pond and cattle; from the homestead nigh
The long deep summonings of the supper horn.

Black on the ridge, against that lonely flush,
A cart, and stoop-necked oxen; ranged beside,
Some barrels; and the day-worn harvest-folk,

Here, emptying their baskets, jar the hush
With hollow thunders. Down the dusk hillside
Lumbers the wain; and day fades out like smoke.

The Solitary Woodsman

When the grey lake-water rushes
Past the dripping alder-bushes,
    And the bodeful autumn wind
In the fir-tree weeps and hushes,—

When the air is sharply damp
Round the solitary camp,
    And the moose-bush[1] in the thicket
Glimmers like a scarlet lamp,—

When the birches twinkle yellow,
And the cornel[2] bunches mellow,
    And the owl across the twilight
Trumpets to his downy fellow,—

When the nut-fed chipmunks romp
Through the maples' crimson pomp,
    And the slim viburnum flushes
In the darkness of the swamp,—

When the blueberries are dead,
When the rowan clusters red,
    And the shy bear, summer-sleekened,
In the bracken makes his bed,—

On a day there comes once more
To the latched and lonely door,
    Down the wood-road striding silent,
One who has been here before.

Green spruce branches for his head,
Here he makes his simple bed,
    Couching with the sun, and rising
When the dawn is frosty red.

All day long he wanders wide
With the grey moss for his guide,

---

1   a shrub or small tree related to the viburnum, bearing bright red berries and deep scarlet
     foliage in the autumn
2   a type of shrub or small tree of the dogwood family

And his lonely axe-stroke startles
The expectant forest-side.

Toward the quiet close of day
Back to camp he takes his way,
    And about his sober footsteps
Unafraid the squirrels play.

On his roof the red leaf falls,
At his door the bluejay calls,
    And he hears the wood-mice hurry
Up and down his rough log walls;

Hears the laughter of the loon
Thrill the dying afternoon;
    Hears the calling of the moose
Echo to the early moon.

And he hears the partridge drumming,
The belated hornet humming,—
    All the faint, prophetic sounds
That foretell the winter's coming.

And the wind about his eaves
Through the chilly night-wet grieves,
    And the earth's dumb patience fills him,
Fellow to the falling leaves.

The Sower

A brown, sad-coloured hillside, where the soil
    Fresh from the frequent harrow, deep and fine,
    Lies bare; no break in the remote sky-line,
Save where a flock of pigeons streams aloft,
Startled from feed in some low-lying croft,
    Or far-off spires with yellow of sunset shine;
    And here the Sower, unwittingly divine,
Exerts the silent forethought of his toil.

Alone he treads the glebe,[1] his measured stride
    Dumb in the yielding soil; and though small joy
    Dwell in his heavy face, as spreads the blind
Pale grain from his dispensing palm aside,
    This plodding churl grows great in his employ;—
    God-like, he makes provision for mankind.

---

1   land, earth

The Winter Fields

Winds here, and sleet, and frost that bites like steel.
　　The low bleak hill rounds under the low sky.
　　Naked of flock and fold the fallows lie,
Thin streaked with meagre drift. The gusts reveal
By fits the dim grey snakes of fence, that steal
　　Through the white dusk. The hill-foot poplars sigh,
　　While storm and death with winter trample by,
And the iron fields ring sharp, and blind lights reel.
Yet in the lonely ridges, wrenched with pain,
　　Harsh solitary hillocks, bound and dumb,
Grave glebes close-lipped beneath the scourge and chain,
　　Lurks hid the germ of ecstasy—the sum
Of life that waits on summer, till the rain
　　Whisper in April and the crocus come.

The Skater

My glad feet shod with the glittering steel
I was the god of the wingéd heel.[1]

The hills in the far white sky were lost;
The world lay still in the wide white frost;

And the woods hung hushed in their long white dream
By the ghostly, glimmering, ice-blue stream.

Here was a pathway, smooth like glass,
Where I and the wandering wind might pass

To the far-off palaces, drifted deep,
Where Winter's retinue rests in sleep.

I followed the lure, I fled like a bird,
Till the startled hollows awoke and heard

A spinning whisper, a sibilant twang,
As the stroke of the steel on the tense ice rang;

And the wandering wind was left behind
As faster, faster I followed my mind;

Till the blood sang high in my eager brain,
And the joy of my flight was almost pain.

1　in Greek mythology, Hermes, who was messenger of the gods

Then I stayed the rush of my eager speed
And silently went as a drifting seed,—

Slowly, furtively, till my eyes
Grew big with the awe of a dim surmise,

And the hair of my neck began to creep
At hearing the wilderness talk in sleep.

Shapes in the fir-gloom drifted near.
In the deep of my heart I heard my fear.

And I turned and fled, like a soul pursued,
From the white, inviolate solitude.

Bliss Carman

(1861–1929)

Vestigia[1]

I took a day to search for God,
And found Him not. But as I trod
By rocky ledge, through woods untamed,
Just where one scarlet lily flamed,
I saw His footprint in the sod.

Then suddenly all unaware,
Far off in the deep shadows, where
A solitary hermit thrush
Sang through the holy twilight hush—
I heard His voice upon the air.

And even as I marvelled how
God gives us Heaven here and now,
In a stir of wind that hardly shook
The poplar leaves beside the brook—
His hand was light upon my brow.

At last with evening as I turned
Homeward, and thought what I had learned
And all that there was still to probe—
I caught the glory of His robe
Where the last fires of sunset burned.

Back to the world with quickening start
I looked and longed for any part
In making saving Beauty be . . .
And from that kindling ecstasy
I knew God dwelt within my heart.

Low Tide on Grand Pré [2]

The sun goes down, and over all
    These barren reaches by the tide
Such unelusive glories fall,
    I almost dream they yet will bide
    Until the coming of the tide.

And yet I know that not for us,
    By any ecstasy of dream,
He lingers to keep luminous

---

1   from the Latin word "vestigium," meaning foot-step, track
2   Grand Pré ("great meadow") lies on the shores of the Minas Basin in Nova Scotia.

A little while the grievous stream,
    Which frets, uncomforted of dream—

A grievous stream, that to and fro
    Athrough the fields of Acadie[1]
Goes wandering, as if to know
    Why one beloved face[2] should be
    So long from home and Acadie.

Was it a year or lives ago
    We took the grasses in our hands,
And caught the summer flying low
    Over the waving meadow lands,
    And held it there between our hands?

The while the river at our feet—
    A drowsy inland meadow stream—
At set of sun the after-heat
    Made running gold, and in the gleam,
    We freed our birch upon the stream.

There down along the elms at dusk
    We lifted dripping blade to drift,
Through twilight scented fine like musk,
    Where night and gloom awhile uplift,
    Nor sunder soul and soul adrift.

And that we took into our hands
    Spirit of life or subtler thing—
Breathed on us there, and loosed the bands
    Of death, and taught us, whispering,
    The secret of some wonder-thing.

Then all your face grew light, and seemed
    To hold the shadow of the sun;
The evening faltered, and I deemed
    That time was ripe, and years had done
    Their wheeling underneath the sun.

So all desire and all regret,
    And fear and memory, were naught;
One to remember or forget
    The keen delight our hands had caught;
    Morrow and yesterday were naught.

---

1   It was from the Grand Pré region of Nova Scotia that the Acadians were expelled in
    1755.
2   possibly a reference to someone with whom Carman had experienced an unhappy love
    affair

The night has fallen, and the tide . . .
    Now and again comes drifting home,
Across these aching barrens wide,
    A sigh like driven wind or foam:
    In grief the flood is bursting home.

A Northern Vigil

Here by the gray north sea,
    In the wintry heart of the wild,
Comes the old dream of thee,
    Guendolen, mistress and child.

The heart of the forest grieves
    In the drift against my door;
A voice is under the eaves,
    A footfall on the floor.

Threshold, mirror and hall,
    Vacant and strangely aware,
Wait for their soul's recall
    With the dumb expectant air.

Here when the smouldering west
    Burns down into the sea,
I take no heed of rest
    And keep the watch for thee.

I sit by the fire and hear
    The restless wind go by,
On the long dirge and drear,
    Under the low bleak sky.

When day puts out to sea
    And night makes in for land,
There is no lock for thee,
    Each door awaits thy hand!

When night goes over the hill
    And dawn comes down the dale,
It's O for the wild sweet will
    That shall no more prevail!

When the zenith moon is round,
    And snow-wraiths gather and run,
And there is set no bound
    To love beneath the sun,

O wayward will, come near
   The old mad wilful way,
The soft mouth at my ear
   With words too sweet to say!

Come, for the night is cold,
   The ghostly moonlight fills
Hollow and rift and fold
   Of the eerie Ardise hills!

The windows of my room
   Are dark with bitter frost,
The stillness aches with doom
   Of something loved and lost.

Outside, the great blue star
   Burns in the ghostland pale,
Where giant Algebar[1]
   Holds on the endless trail.

Come, for the years are long,
   And silence keeps the door,
Where shapes with the shadows throng
   The firelit chamber floor.

Come, for thy kiss was warm,
   With the red embers' glare
Across thy folding arm
   And dark tumultuous hair!

And though thy coming rouse
   The sleep-cry of no bird,
The keepers of the house[2]
   Shall tremble at thy word.

Come, for the soul is free!
   In all the vast dreamland
There is no lock for thee,
   Each door awaits thy hand.

Ah, not in dreams at all,
   Fleering,[3] perishing, dim,
But thy old self, supple and tall,
   Mistress and child of whim!

---

1   the constellation Orion; also used as a name for Rigel, the brightest star in that
     constellation
2   See Ecclesiastes 12.3.
3   laughing mockingly

The proud imperious guise,
  Impetuous and serene,
The sad mysterious eyes,
  And dignity of mien!

Yea, wilt thou not return,
  When the late hill-winds veer,
And the bright hill-flowers burn
  With the reviving year?

When April comes, and the sea
  Sparkles as if it smiled,
Will they restore to me
  My dark Love, empress and child?

The curtains seem to part;
  A sound is on the stair,
As if at the last . . . I start;
  Only the wind is there.

Lo, now far on the hills
  The crimson fumes uncurled,
Where the caldron mantles and spills
  Another dawn on the world!

The Eavesdropper

In a still room at hush of dawn,
  My Love and I lay side by side
And heard the roaming forest wind
  Stir in the paling autumn-tide.

I watched her earth-brown eyes grow glad
  Because the round day was so fair;
While memories of reluctant night
  Lurked in the blue dusk of her hair.

Outside, a yellow maple tree,
  Shifting upon the silvery blue
With tiny multitudinous sound,
  Rustled to let the sunlight through.

The livelong day the elvish leaves
  Danced with their shadows on the floor;
And the lost children of the wind
  Went straying homeward by our door.

And all the swarthy afternoon
  We watched the great deliberate sun

Walk through the crimsoned hazy world,
  Counting his hilltops one by one.

Then as the purple twilight came
  And touched the vines along our eaves,
Another Shadow stood without
  And gloomed the dancing of the leaves.

The silence fell on my Love's lips;
  Her great brown eyes were veiled and sad
With pondering some maze of dream,
  Though all the splendid year was glad.

Restless and vague as a gray wind
  Her heart had grown, she knew not why.
But hurrying to the open door,
  Against the verge of western sky

I saw retreating on the hills,
  Looming and sinister and black,
The stealthy figure swift and huge
  Of One who strode and looked not back.

The World Voice

I heard the summer sea
Murmuring to the shore
Some endless story of a wrong
The whole world must deplore.

I heard the mountain wind
Conversing with the trees
Of an old sorrow of the hills,
Mysterious as the sea's.

And all that haunted day
It seemed that I could hear
The echo of an ancient speech
Ring in my listening ear.

And then it came to me,
That all that I had heard
Was my own heart in the sea's voice
And the wind's lonely word.

Archibald Lampman

(1861–1899)

The Frogs

I

Breathers of wisdom won without a quest,
   Quaint uncouth dreamers, voices high and strange;
   Flutists of lands where beauty hath no change,
And wintry grief is a forgotten guest,
Sweet murmurers of everlasting rest,
   For whom glad days have ever yet to run,
   And moments are as aeons, and the sun
But ever sunken half-way toward the west.

Often to me who heard you in your day,
   With close rapt ears, it could not choose but seem
That earth, our mother, searching in what way
   Men's hearts might know her spirit's inmost dream;
      Ever at rest beneath life's change and stir,
      Made you her soul, and bade you pipe for her.

II

In those mute days when spring was in her glee,
   And hope was strong, we knew not why or how,
   And earth, the mother, dreamed with brooding brow,
Musing on life, and what the hours might be,
When love should ripen to maternity,
   Then like high flutes in silvery interchange
   Ye piped with voices still and sweet and strange,
And ever as ye piped, on every tree

The great buds swelled; among the pensive woods
   The spirits of first flowers awoke and flung
From buried faces the close-fitting hoods,
   And listened to your piping till they fell,
   The frail spring-beauty[1] with her perfumed bell,
The wind-flower,[2] and the spotted adder-tongue.[3]

III

All the day long, wherever pools might be
   Among the golden meadows, where the air
   Stood in a dream, as it were moorèd there

---

1   the claytonia, a perennial wild flower with white or pinkish blossoms
2   the wood anemone
3   a name applied to various flowering plants, such as the dog-tooth violet

For ever in a noon-tide reverie,
Or where the birds made riot of their glee
  In the still woods, and the hot sun shone down,
  Crossed with warm lucent shadows on the brown
Leaf-paven pools, that bubbled dreamily,

Or far away in whispering river meads
  And watery marshes where the brooding noon,
  Full with the wonder of its own sweet boon,
Nestled and slept among the noiseless reeds,
  Ye sat and murmured, motionless as they,
  With eyes that dreamed beyond the night and day.

IV

And when day passed and over heaven's height,
  Thin with the many stars and cool with dew,
  The fingers of the deep hours slowly drew
The wonder of the ever-healing night,
No grief or loneliness or rapt delight
  Or weight of silence ever brought to you
  Slumber or rest; only your voices grew
More high and solemn; slowly with hushed flight

Ye saw the echoing hours go by, long-drawn,
  Nor ever stirred, watching with fathomless eyes,
  And with your countless clear antiphonies
Filling the earth and heaven, even till dawn,
  Last-risen, found you with its first pale gleam,
  Still with soft throats unaltered in your dream.

V

And slowly as we heard you, day by day,
  The stillness of enchanted reveries
  Bound brain and spirit and half-closèd eyes,
In some divine sweet wonder-dream astray;
To us no sorrow or upreared dismay
  Nor any discord came, but evermore
  The voices of mankind, the outer roar,
Grew strange and murmurous, faint and far away.

Morning and noon and midnight exquisitely,
  Rapt with your voices, this alone we knew,
Cities might change and fall, and men might die,
  Secure were we, content to dream with you
     That change and pain are shadows faint and fleet,
     And dreams are real, and life is only sweet.

Heat

From plains that reel to southward, dim,
    The road runs by me white and bare;
Up the steep hill it seems to swim
    Beyond, and melt into the glare.
Upward half-way, or it may be
    Nearer the summit, slowly steals
A hay-cart, moving dustily
    With idly clacking wheels.

By his cart's side the wagoner
    Is slouching slowly at his ease,
Half-hidden in the windless blur
    Of white dust puffing to his knees.
This wagon on the height above,
    From sky to sky on either hand,
Is the sole thing that seems to move
    In all the heat-held land.

Beyond me in the fields the sun
    Soaks in the grass and hath his will;
I count the marguerites one by one;
    Even the buttercups are still.
On the brook yonder not a breath
    Disturbs the spider or the midge.
The water-bugs draw close beneath
    The cool gloom of the bridge.

Where the far elm-tree shadows flood
    Dark patches in the burning grass,
The cows, each with her peaceful cud,
    Lie waiting for the heat to pass.
From somewhere on the slope near by
    Into the pale depth of the noon
A wandering thrush slides leisurely
    His thin revolving tune.

In intervals of dreams I hear
    The cricket from the droughty ground;
The grasshoppers spin into mine ear
    A small innumerable sound.
I lift mine eyes sometimes to gaze:
    The burning sky-line blinds my sight:
The woods far off are blue with haze:
    The hills are drenched in light.

And yet to me not this or that
    Is always sharp or always sweet;
In the sloped shadow of my hat
    I lean at rest, and drain the heat;

Nay more, I think some blessèd power
  Hath brought me wandering idly here:
In the full furnace of this hour
  My thoughts grow keen and clear.

Morning on the Lièvre[1]

Far above us where a jay
Screams his matins to the day,
Capped with gold and amethyst,
Like a vapour from the forge
Of a giant somewhere hid,
Out of hearing of the clang
Of his hammer, skirts of mist
Slowly up the woody gorge
Lift and hang.

Softly as a cloud we go,
Sky above and sky below,
Down the river; and the dip
Of the paddles scarcely breaks,
With the little silvery drip
Of the water as it shakes
From the blades, the crystal deep
Of the silence of the morn,
Of the forest yet asleep;
And the river reaches borne
In a mirror, purple gray,
Sheer away
To the misty line of light,
Where the forest and the stream
In the shadow meet and plight,
Like a dream.

From amid a stretch of reeds,
Where the lazy river sucks
All the water as it bleeds
From a little curling creek,
And the muskrats peer and sneak
In around the sunken wrecks
Of a tree that swept the skies
Long ago,
On a sudden seven ducks
With a splashy rustle rise,
Stretching out their seven necks,

---

1   The River Lièvre is a tributary of the Ottawa River.

One before, and two behind,
And the others all arow,
And as steady as the wind
With a swiveling whistle go,
Through the purple shadow led,
Till we only hear their whir
In behind a rocky spur,
Just ahead.

The City of the End of Things

Beside the pounding cataracts
Of midnight streams unknown to us
'Tis builded in the leafless tracts
And valleys huge of Tartarus.[1]
Lurid and lofty and vast it seems;
It hath no rounded name that rings,
But I have heard it called in dreams
The City of the End of Things.

Its roofs and iron towers have grown
None knoweth how high within the night,
But in its murky streets far down
A flaming terrible and bright
Shakes all the stalking shadows there,
Across the walls, across the floors,
And shifts upon the upper air
From out a thousand furnace doors;
And all the while an awful sound
Keeps roaring on continually,
And crashes in the ceaseless round
Of a gigantic harmony.
Through its grim depths re-echoing
And all its weary height of walls,
With measured roar and iron ring,
The inhuman music lifts and falls.
Where no thing rests and no man is,
And only fire and night hold sway;
The beat, the thunder and the hiss
Cease not, and change not, night nor day.
And moving at unheard commands,
The abysses and vast fires between,
Flit figures that with clanking hands
Obey a hideous routine;
They are not flesh, they are not bone,

---

1   a region in Hades where the wicked are punished for their misdeeds on earth

They see not with the human eye,
And from their iron lips is blown
A dreadful and monotonous cry;
And whoso of our mortal race
Should find that city unaware,
Lean Death would smite him face to face,
And blanch him with its venomed air:
Or caught by the terrific spell,
Each thread of memory snapt and cut,
His soul would shrivel and its shell
Go rattling like an empty nut.

It was not always so, but once,
In days that no man thinks upon,
Fair voices echoed from its stones,
The light above it leaped and shone:
Once there were multitudes of men,
That built that city in their pride,
Until its might was made, and then
They withered age by age and died.
But now of that prodigious race,
Three only in an iron tower,
Set like carved idols face to face,
Remain the masters of its power;
And at the city gate a fourth,
Gigantic and with dreadful eyes,
Sits looking toward the lightless north,
Beyond the reach of memories;
Fast rooted to the lurid floor,
A bulk that never moves a jot,
In his pale body dwells no more,
Or mind or soul,—an idiot!
But sometime in the end those three
Shall perish and their hands be still,
And with the master's touch shall flee
Their incommunicable skill.
A stillness absolute as death
Along the slacking wheels shall lie,
And, flagging at a single breath,
The fires that moulder out and die.
The roar shall vanish at its height,
And over that tremendous town
The silence of eternal night
Shall gather close and settle down.
All its grim grandeur, tower and hall,
Shall be abandoned utterly,
And into rust and dust shall fall
From century to century;
Nor ever living thing shall grow,
Nor trunk of tree, nor blade of grass;
No drop shall fall, no wind shall blow,

Nor sound of any foot shall pass:
Alone of its accursèd state,
One thing the hand of Time shall spare,
For the grim Idiot at the gate
Is deathless and eternal there.

Winter Evening

To-night the very horses springing by
Toss gold from whitened nostrils. In a dream
The streets that narrow to the westward gleam
Like rows of golden palaces; and high
From all the crowded chimneys tower and die
A thousand aureoles. Down in the west
The brimming plains beneath the sunset rest,
One burning sea of gold. Soon, soon shall fly
The glorious vision, and the hours shall feel
A mightier master; soon from height to height,
With silence and the sharp unpitying stars,
Stern creeping frosts, and winds that touch like steel,
Out of the depth beyond the eastern bars,
Glittering and still shall come the awful night.

Duncan Campbell Scott

(1862–1947)

The Onondaga Madonna[1]

She stands full-throated and with careless pose,
This woman of a weird and waning race,
The tragic savage lurking in her face,
Where all her pagan passion burns and glows;
Her blood is mingled with her ancient foes,
And thrills with war and wildness in her veins;
Her rebel lips are dabbled with the stains
Of feuds and forays and her father's woes.

And closer in the shawl about her breast,
The latest promise of her nation's doom,
Paler than she her baby clings and lies,
The primal warrior gleaming from his eyes;
He sulks, and burdened with his infant gloom,
He draws his heavy brows and will not rest.

Watkwenies[2]

Vengeance was once her nation's lore and law:
When the tired sentry stooped above the rill,
Her long knife flashed, and hissed, and drank its fill;
Dimly below her dripping wrist she saw,
One wild hand, pale as death and weak as straw,
Clutch at the ripple in the pool; while shrill
Sprang through the dreaming hamlet on the hill,
The war-cry of the triumphant Iroquois.[3]

Now clothed with many an ancient flap and fold,
And wrinkled like an apple kept till May,
She weighs the interest-money[4] in her palm,
And, when the Agent calls her valiant name,
Hears, like the war-whoops of her perished day,
The lads playing snow-snake[5] in the stinging cold.

---

1 The Onondagas are one of the tribes in the Iroquoian federation known as the Six Nations.
2 an Indian name meaning "Woman who conquers"
3 the confederacy of Indian tribes including the Mohawks, the Oneidas, the Onondagas, the Cayugas, the Senecas, and the Tuscaroras
4 treaty money, paid by an agent representing the government
5 an Indian game in which a long staff with a head shaped like that of a snake is hurled along the snow

[383]

On The Way To The Mission

They dogged him all one afternoon,
Through the bright snow,
Two whitemen servants of greed;
He knew that they were there,
But he turned not his head;
He was an Indian trapper;
He planted his snow-shoes firmly,
He dragged the long toboggan
Without rest.

The three figures drifted
Like shadows in the mind of a seer;
The snow-shoes were whisperers
On the threshold of awe;
The toboggan made the sound of wings,
A wood-pigeon sloping to her nest.

The Indian's face was calm.
He strode with the sorrow of fore-knowledge,
But his eyes were jewels of content
Set in circles of peace.

They would have shot him;
But momently in the deep forest,
They saw something flit by his side:
Their hearts stopped with fear.
Then the moon rose.
They would have left him to the spirit,

But they saw the long toboggan
Rounded well with furs,
With many a silver fox-skin,
With the pelts of mink and of otter.
They were the servants of greed;
When the moon grew brighter
And the spruces were dark with sleep,
They shot him.
When he fell on a shield of moonlight
One of his arms clung to his burden;
The snow was not melted:
The spirit passed away.
Then the servants of greed
Tore off the cover to count their gains;
They shuddered away into the shadows,
Hearing each the loud heart of the other.
Silence was born.

There in the tender moonlight,
As sweet as they were in life,

Glimmered the ivory features,
Of the Indian's wife.

In the manner of Montagnais[1] women
Her hair was rolled with braid;
Under her waxen fingers
A crucifix was laid.

He was drawing her down to the Mission,
To bury her there in spring,
When the bloodroot comes and the windflower[2]
To silver everything.

But as a gift of plunder
Side by side were they laid,
The moon went on to her setting
And covered them with shade.

The Forsaken

Once in the winter
Out on a lake
In the heart of the north-land,
Far from the Fort
And far from the hunters,
A Chippewa[3] woman
With her sick baby,
Crouched in the last hours
Of a great storm.
Frozen and hungry,
She fished through the ice
With a line of the twisted
Bark of the cedar,
And a rabbit-bone hook
Polished and barbed;
Fished with the bare hook
All through the wild day,
Fished and caught nothing;
While the young chieftain
Tugged at her breasts,
Or slept in the lacings
Of the warm *tikanagan*.[4]

1   a member of an Algonquian-speaking Native people from Quebec and Labrador
2   The bloodroot and the windflower (a wood anemone) are both wild-flowers with pale blossoms that bloom early in the spring.
3   a Native people of Algonquian stock, also known as Ojibway, from the region around Lake Superior
4   a thin rectangular board to which a moss-bag is attached, in which an infant is carried

All the lake-surface
Streamed with the hissing
Of millions of iceflakes
Hurled by the wind;
Behind her the round
Of a lonely island
Roared like a fire
With the voice of the storm
In the deeps of the cedars.
Valiant, unshaken,
She took of her own flesh,
Baited the fish-hook,
Drew in a grey-trout,
Drew in his fellows,
Heaped them beside her,
Dead in the snow.
Valiant, unshaken,
She faced the long distance,
Wolf-haunted and lonely,
Sure of her goal
And the life of her dear one:
Tramped for two days,
On the third in the morning,
Saw the strong bulk
Of the Fort by the river,
Saw the wood-smoke
Hang soft in the spruces,
Heard the keen yelp
Of the ravenous huskies
Fighting for whitefish:
Then she had rest.

Years and years after,
When she was old and withered,
When her son was an old man
And his children filled with vigour,
They came in their northern tour on the verge of winter,
To an island in a lonely lake.
There one night they camped, and on the morrow
Gathered their kettles and birch-bark[1]
Their rabbit-skin robes and their mink-traps,
Launched their canoes and slunk away through the islands,
Left her alone forever,
Without a word of farewell,
Because she was old and useless,
Like a paddle broken and warped,

---

on its mother's back
1   birch-bark "rogans," small bowls made of birchbark

Or a pole that was splintered
Then, without a sigh,
Valiant, unshaken,
She smoothed her dark locks under her kerchief,
Composed her shawl in state,
Then folded her hands ridged with sinews and corded
    with veins,
Folded them across her breasts spent with the nourishing
    of children,
Gazed at the sky past the tops of the cedars,
Saw two spangled nights arise out of the twilight,
Saw two days go by filled with the tranquil sunshine,
Saw, without pain, or dread. or even a moment of longing:
Then on the third great night there came thronging and
    thronging
Millions of snowflakes out of a windless cloud;
They covered her close with a beautiful crystal shroud.
Covered her deep and silent
But in the frost of the dawn
Up from the life below.
Rose a column of breath
Through a tiny cleft in the snow
Fragile, delicately drawn.
Wavering with its own weakness,
In the wilderness a sign of the spirit,
Persisting still in the sight of the sun
Till day was done.
Then all light was gathered up by the hand of God and
    hid in His breast,
Then there was born a silence deeper than silence,
Then she had rest.

At Gull Lake: August, 1810[1]

Gull Lake set in the rolling prairie
Still there are reeds on the shore,
As of old the poplars shimmer
As summer passes;
Winter freezes the shallow lake to the core;
Storm passes,
Heat parches the sedges and grasses,
Night comes with moon-glimmer,
Dawn with the morning-star;
All proceeds in the flow of Time
As a hundred years ago.

---

1   based on an incident recorded in the journal of Alexander Henry the Younger (d.1814),
    a fur trader in the service of the North West Company

Then two camps were pitched on the shore,
The clustered teepees
Of Tabashaw Chief of the Saulteaux;[1]
And on a knoll tufted with poplars
Two grey tents of a trader—
Nairne of the Orkneys.[2]
Before his tents under the shade of the poplars
Sat Keejigo, third of the wives
Of Tabashaw Chief of the Saulteaux;
Clad in the skins of antelopes
Broidered with porcupine quills
Coloured with vivid dyes,
Vermilion here and there
In the roots of her hair,
A half-moon of powder-blue
On her brow, her cheeks
Scored with light ochre streaks.
Keejigo daughter of Launay
The Normandy hunter
And Oshawan of the Saulteaux,
Troubled by fugitive visions
In the smoke of the camp-fires,
In the close dark of the teepee,
Flutterings of colour
Along the flow of the prairie,
Spangles of flower tints
Caught in the wonder of dawn,
Dreams of sounds unheard—
The echoes of echo,
Star she was named for
Keejigo, star of the morning,
Voices of storm—
Wind-rush and lightning—
The beauty of terror;
The twilight moon
Coloured like a prairie lily,
The round moon of pure snow,
The beauty of peace;
Premonitions of love and of beauty
Vague as shadows cast by a shadow.
Now she had found her hero,
And offered her body and spirit
With abject unreasoning passion,
As Earth abandons herself
To the sun and the thrust of the lightning.

---

1   a tribe of Ojibway Indians, originally from the area around Sault Ste. Marie
2   islands off the north coast of Scotland

Quiet were all the leaves of the poplars,
Breathless the air under their shadow,
As Keejigo spoke of these things to her heart
In the beautiful speech of the Saulteaux.

The flower lives on the prairie,
The wind in the sky,
I am here my beloved;
The wind and the flower.

The crane hides in the sand-hills,
Where does the wolverine hide?
I am here my beloved,
Heart's-blood on the feathers
The foot caught in the trap.

Take the flower in your hand,
The wind in your nostrils;
I am here my beloved;
Release the captive,
Heal the wound under the feathers.

A storm-cloud was marching
Vast on the prairie,
Scored with livid ropes of hail,
Quick with nervous vines of lightning—
Twice had Nairne turned her away
Afraid of the venom of Tabashaw,
Twice had the Chief fired at his tents
And now when two bullets
Whistled above the encampment
He yelled "Drive this bitch to her master."

Keejigo went down a path by the lake;
Thick at the tangled edges,
The reeds and the sedges
Were grey as ashes
Against the death-black water;
The lightning scored with double flashes
The dark lake-mirror and loud
Came the instant thunder.
Her lips still moved to the words of her music,
"Release the captive,
Heal the wound under the feathers."

At the top of the bank
The old wives caught her and cast her down
Where Tabashaw crouched by his camp-fire.
He snatched a live brand from the embers,
Seared her cheeks,
Blinded her eyes,

Destroyed her beauty with fire,
Screaming, "Take that face to your lover."
Keejigo held her face to the fury
And made no sound.
The old wives dragged her away
And threw her over the bank
like a dead dog.

Then burst the storm—
The Indians' screams and the howls of the dogs
Lost in the crash of hail
That smashed the sedges and reeds,
Stripped the poplars of leaves,
Tore and blazed onwards,
Wasting itself with riot and tumult—
Supreme in the beauty of terror.

The setting sun struck the retreating cloud
With a rainbow, not an arc but a column
Built with the glory of seven metals;
Beyond in the purple deeps of the vortex
Fell the quivering vines of the lightning.
The wind withdrew the veil from the shrine of the moon,
She rose changing her dusky shade for the glow
Of the prairie lily, till free of all blemish of colour
She came to her zenith without a cloud or a star,
A lovely perfection, snow-pure in the heaven of midnight.
After the beauty of terror the beauty of peace.

But Keejigo came no more to the camps of her people;
Only the midnight moon knew where she felt her way,
Only the leaves of autumn, the snows of winter
Knew where she lay.

Rudyard Kipling

(1865–1936)

Cities and Thrones and Powers

Cities and Thrones and Powers
  Stand in Time's eye,
Almost as long as flowers,
  Which daily die:
But, as new buds put forth
  To glad new men,
Out of the spent and unconsidered Earth
  The Cities rise again.

This season's Daffodil
  She never hears
What change, what chance,[1] what chill,
  Cut down last year's;
But with bold countenance,
  And knowledge small,
Esteems her seven days' continuance
  To be perpetual.

So Time that is o'erkind
  To all that be,
Ordains us e'en as blind,
  As bold as she:
That in our very death,
  And burial sure,
Shadow to shadow, well persuaded, saith,
  'See how our works endure!'

The Way through the Woods

They shut the road through the woods
Seventy years ago.
Weather and rain have undone it again,
And now you would never know
There was once a road through the woods
Before they planted the trees.
It is underneath the coppice and heath
And the thin anemones.
Only the keeper sees
That, where the ring-dove broods,
And the badgers roll at ease,
There was once a road through the woods.

---

1   an echo of "the changes and chances of this mortal life," from the Communion Service
in the Book of Common Prayer

Yet, if you enter the woods
Of a summer evening late,
When the night-air cools on the trout-ringed pools
Where the otter whistles his mate,
(They fear not men in the woods,
Because they see so few.)
You will hear the beat of a horse's feet,
And the swish of a skirt in the dew,
Steadily cantering through
The misty solitudes,
As though they perfectly knew
The old lost road through the woods. . . .
But there is no road through the woods.

Recessional[1]

1897

God of our fathers, known of old,
   Lord of our far-flung battle-line,
Beneath whose awful Hand we hold
   Dominion over palm and pine—
Lord God of Hosts, be with us yet,
Lest we forget—lest we forget!

The tumult and the shouting dies;
   The Captains and the Kings depart:
Still stands Thine ancient sacrifice,
   An humble and a contrite heart.
Lord God of Hosts, be with us yet,
Lest we forget—lest we forget!

Far-called, our navies melt away;
   On dune and headland sinks the fire:[2]
Lo, all our pomp of yesterday
   Is one with Nineveh and Tyre![3]
Judge of the Nations, spare us yet,
Lest we forget—lest we forget!

If, drunk with sight of power, we loose
   Wild tongues that have not Thee in awe,
Such boastings as the Gentiles use,

---

1   a hymn sung as the choir or clergy leave the chancel after a service. The poem was
     written on the occasion of the celebrations for Queen Victoria's Diamond Jubilee in 1897.
2   Kipling alludes to the bonfires lit all across the kingdom on the night of the Jubilee.
3   once great cities at the centre of long fallen empires in Assyria and Phoenicia

Or lesser breeds without the Law—
Lord God of Hosts, be with us yet,
Lest we forget—lest we forget!

For heathen heart that puts her trust
  In reeking tube and iron shard,
All valiant dust that builds on dust,
  And guarding, calls not Thee to guard,
For frantic boast and foolish word—
Thy mercy on Thy People, Lord!

The Hyaenas

After the burial-parties leave
  And the baffled kites have fled;
The wise hyaenas come out at eve
  To take account of our dead.

How he died and why he died
  Troubles them not a whit.
They snout the bushes and stones aside
  And dig till they come to it.

They are only resolute they shall eat
  That they and their mates may thrive,
And they know that the dead are safer meat
  Than the weakest thing alive.

(For a goat may butt, and a worm may sting,
  And a child will sometimes stand;
But a poor dead soldier of the King
  Can never lift a hand.)

They whoop and halloo and scatter the dirt
  Until their tushes[1] white
Take good hold in the army shirt,
  And tug the corpse to light,

And the pitiful face is shewn again
  For an instant ere they close;
But it is not discovered to living men—
  Only to God and to those

---

1   canine teeth

Who, being soulless, are free from shame,
  Whatever meat they may find.
Nor do they defile the dead man's name—
  That is reserved for his kind.

References to Helen + Troy;
biographical references;
Maud Gonne
Most of his best
poetry written out of his frustration
One of his favorite
Subj's is
unrequited love.

begins as an obsessed romantic; fond of Keats, known as last romantic poet eventually decided he needed to transform his style. Big on remaking himself. Moved to a harder, tougher style.

William Butler Yeats

(1865–1939)

The Sorrow of Love

The brawling of a sparrow in the eaves, *a*
The brilliant moon and all the milky sky, *b*
And all that famous harmony of leaves, *a*
Had blotted out man's image and his cry. *b*

A girl arose that had red mournful lips *c*
And seemed the greatness of the world in tears, *d*
Doomed like Odysseus[1] and the labouring ships *c*
And proud as Priam[2] murdered with his peers; *d*

Arose, and on the instant clamorous eaves, *a*
A climbing moon upon an empty sky, *b*
And all that lamentation of the leaves, *a*
Could but compose man's image and his cry. *b*

When You Are Old *Melancholy mood*

When you are old and grey and full of sleep, *a*
And nodding by the fire, take down this book, *b*
And slowly read, and dream of the soft look *b*
Your eyes had once, and of their shadows deep; *a*

How many loved your moments of glad grace, *c*
And loved your beauty with love false or true, *d*
But one man loved the pilgrim soul in you, *d*
And loved the sorrows of your changing face; *c*

And bending down beside the glowing bars, *e*
Murmur, a little sadly, how Love fled *f*
And paced upon the mountains overhead *f*
And hid his face amid a crowd of stars. *e*

1 hero of Homer's *Odyssey*, which describes his ten year journey home after the Trojan War
2 King of Troy

*Maud Gonne's
husband shot in 1916.*

Easter 1916[1]

I have met them at close of day
Coming with vivid faces
From counter or desk among grey
Eighteenth-century houses.
I have passed with a nod of the head
Or polite meaningless words,
Or have lingered awhile and said
Polite meaningless words,
And thought before I had done
Of a mocking tale or a gibe
To please a companion
Around the fire at the club,
Being certain that they and I
But lived where motley is worn:
All changed, changed utterly:
A terrible beauty is born.

That woman's days were spent
In ignorant good-will,
Her nights in argument
Until her voice grew shrill.[2]
What voice more sweet than hers
When, young and beautiful,
She rode to harriers?
This man had kept a school[3]
And rode our wingèd horse;[4]
This other his helper and friend
Was coming into his force;
He might have won fame in the end,
So sensitive his nature seemed,
So daring and sweet his thought.
This other man I had dreamed
A drunken, vainglorious lout.[5]
He had done most bitter wrong
To some who are near my heart,
Yet I number him in the song;
He, too, has resigned his part
In the casual comedy;

---

1 On Easter Monday, 1916, a group of Irish nationalists led an abortive uprising against the ruling British. The leaders of the rebellion, named in Yeats's poem, were captured and executed.
2 Constance Gore-Booth, later Countess Markiewicz, an ardent Irish nationalist. Her death sentence was commuted.
3 Patrick Pearse, a poet and schoolteacher, who had been prominent in the fighting. "This other his helper" was Thomas MacDonagh, a poet.
4 Pegasus, the winged horse associated with poetic inspiration
5 Major John MacBride, who had married Maude Gonne, Yeats's early love. They were separated after only two years.

He, too, has been changed in his turn,
Transformed utterly:
A terrible beauty is born.

Hearts with one purpose alone
Through summer and winter seem
Enchanted to a stone
To trouble the living stream.
The horse that comes from the road,
The rider, the birds that range
From cloud to tumbling cloud,
Minute by minute they change;
A shadow of cloud on the stream
Changes minute by minute;
A horse-hoof slides on the brim,
And a horse plashes within it;
The long-legged moor-hens dive,
And hens to moor-cocks call;
Minute by minute they live:
The stone's in the midst of all.

Too long a sacrifice
Can make a stone of the heart.
O when may it suffice?
That is Heaven's part, our part
To murmur name upon name,
As a mother names her child
When sleep at last has come
On limbs that had run wild.
What is it but nightfall?
No, no, not night but death;
Was it needless death after all?
For England may keep faith
For all that is done and said.
We know their dream; enough
To know they dreamed and are dead;
And what if excess of love
Bewildered them till they died?
I write it out in a verse—
MacDonagh and MacBride
And Connolly[1] and Pearse
Now and in time to be,
Wherever green is worn,
Are changed, changed utterly:
A terrible beauty is born.

---

1   James Connolly, another leader of the uprising

An Irish Airman Foresees His Death

I know that I shall meet my fate
Somewhere among the clouds above;
Those that I fight I do not hate,
Those that I guard I do not love;
My country is Kiltartan Cross,
My countrymen Kiltartan's poor,
No likely end could bring them loss
Or leave them happier than before.
Nor law, nor duty bade me fight,
Nor public men, nor cheering crowds,
A lonely impulse of delight
Drove to this tumult in the clouds;
I balanced all, brought all to mind,
The years to come seemed waste of breath,
A waste of breath the years behind
In balance with this life, this death.

1 of most quoted poems of all time

The Second Coming

Innocence is being destroyed

Turning and turning in the widening gyre[1]
The falcon cannot hear the falconer;
Things fall apart; the centre cannot hold;
Mere[2] anarchy is loosed upon the world,
The blood-dimmed tide is loosed, and everywhere
The ceremony of innocence is drowned;
The best lack all conviction, while the worst
Are full of passionate intensity.

We live in a world where the falcon can't hear the falconer.

The best people do not stand up, the worst are passionate in their evil

What's coming next is not the return of Christ but of something violent, chaotic

Surely some revelation is at hand;
Surely the Second Coming is at hand.
The Second Coming! Hardly are those words out
When a vast image out of *Spiritus Mundi*[3]
Troubles my sight: somewhere in sands of the desert
A shape with lion body and the head of a man,
A gaze blank and pitiless as the sun,
Is moving its slow thighs, while all about it
Reel shadows of the indignant desert birds.
The darkness drops again; but now I know
That twenty centuries of stony sleep
Were vexed to nightmare by a rocking cradle,[4]

- the sphinx

where is the world going

---

1 a circular or spiral movement. Yeats applies the term to cycles of history, and here sees one great movement, the Christian era, coming to an end.
2 used in the obsolete sense of absolute, unqualified
3 the spirit or soul of the universe, in which are stored the memories of the human race
4 i.e., the birth of Christ

And what rough beast, its hour come round at last,
Slouches towards Bethlehem to be born?

Doesn't deny that Christ will, but what will happen in the meantime

A *Prayer For My Daughter*[1]

Once more the storm is howling, and half hid
Under this cradle-hood and coverlid
My child sleeps on. There is no obstacle
But Gregory's wood and one bare hill
Whereby the haystack- and roof-levelling wind,
Bred on the Atlantic, can be stayed;
And for an hour I have walked and prayed
Because of the great gloom that is in my mind.

I have walked and prayed for this young child an hour
And heard the sea-wind scream upon the tower,
And under the arches of the bridge, and scream
In the elms above the flooded stream;
Imagining in excited reverie
That the future years had come,
Dancing to a frenzied drum,
Out of the murderous innocence of the sea.

May she be granted beauty and yet not
Beauty to make a stranger's eye distraught,
Or hers before a looking-glass, for such,
Being made beautiful overmuch,
Consider beauty a sufficient end,
Lose natural kindness and maybe
The heart-revealing intimacy
That chooses right, and never find a friend.

Helen being chosen found life flat and dull
And later had much trouble from a fool,[2]
While that great Queen, that rose out of the spray,[3]
Being fatherless could have her way
Yet chose a bandy-leggèd smith for man.
It's certain that fine women eat
A crazy salad with their meat
Whereby the Horn of Plenty is undone.

In courtesy I'd have her chiefly learned;
Hearts are not had as a gift but hearts are earned
By those that are not entirely beautiful;

---

1   Anne Butler, born 26 February 1919 in Galway
2   Helen was married to the Greek king Menelaus, whom she left to live with Paris.
3   Venus, who sprang from the foam of the sea, was married to Vulcan.

Yet many, that have played the fool
For beauty's very self, has charm made wise,
And many a poor man that has roved,
Loved and thought himself beloved,
From a glad kindness cannot take his eyes.

May she become a flourishing hidden tree
That all her thoughts may like the linnet[1] be,
And have no business but dispensing round
Their magnanimities of sound,
Nor but in merriment begin a chase,
Nor but in merriment a quarrel.
O may she live like some green laurel
Rooted in one dear perpetual place.

My mind, because the minds that I have loved,
The sort of beauty that I have approved,
Prosper but little, has dried up of late,
Yet knows that to be choked with hate
May well be of all evil chances chief.
If there's no hatred in a mind
Assault and battery of the wind
Can never tear the linnet from the leaf.

An intellectual hatred is the worst,
So let her think opinions are accursed.
Have I not seen the loveliest woman born[2]
Out of the mouth of Plenty's horn,
Because of her opinionated mind
Barter that horn and every good
By quiet natures understood
For an old bellows full of angry wind?
Considering that, all hatred driven hence,

The soul recovers radical innocence
And learns at last that it is self-delighting,
Self-appeasing, self-affrighting,
And that its own sweet will is Heaven's will;
She can, though every face should scowl
And every windy quarter howl
Or every bellows burst, be happy still.

And may her bridegroom bring her to a house
Where all's accustomed, ceremonious;
For arrogance and hatred are the wares

---

1   a small song-bird
2   Maud Gonne, who was loved by Yeats but who had married Major John MacBride in
    1903

Peddled in the thoroughfares.
How but in custom and in ceremony
Are innocence and beauty born?
Ceremony's a name for the rich horn,
And custom for the spreading laurel tree.

Leda and the Swan[1]

A sudden blow: the great wings beating still
Above the staggering girl, her thighs caressed
By the dark webs, her nape caught in his bill,
He holds her helpless breast upon his breast.

How can those terrified vague fingers push
The feathered glory from her loosening thighs?
And how can body, laid in that white rush,
But feel the strange heart beating where it lies?

A shudder in the loins engenders there
The broken wall, the burning roof and tower[2]
And Agamemnon dead.[3]
                        Being so caught up,
So mastered by the brute blood of the air,
Did she put on his knowledge with his power
Before the indifferent beak could let her drop?

Sailing to Byzantium[4]

I

That is no country for old men. The young
In one another's arms, birds in the trees
—Those dying generations—at their song,
The salmon-falls, the mackerel-crowded seas,
Fish, flesh, or fowl, commend all summer long
Whatever is begotten, born, and dies.
Caught in that sensual music all neglect
Monuments of unageing intellect.

---

1   In Greek mythology, Leda was visited by Zeus in the form of a swan, and from their
    union were born Helen and Clytemnestra. To Yeats this was a kind of "violent
    annunciation," signalling the beginning of Greek civilization.
2   the destruction of Troy, caused by the love of Helen and Paris
3   Clytemnestra murdered Agamemnon, her husband.
4   Later Constantinople, now Istanbul. To Yeats the Byzantium of antiquity represented a
    perfect union of "religious, aesthetic, and practical life."

[401]

II

An aged man is but a paltry thing,
A tattered coat upon a stick, unless
Soul clap its hands and sing, and louder sing
For every tatter in its mortal dress,
Nor is there singing school but studying
Monuments of its own magnificence;
And therefore I have sailed the seas and come
To the holy city of Byzantium.

III

O sages standing in God's holy fire
As in the gold mosaic of a wall,
Come from the holy fire, perne in a gyre,[1]
And be the singing-masters of my soul.
Consume my heart away; sick with desire
And fastened to a dying animal
It knows not what it is; and gather me
Into the artifice of eternity.

IV

Once out of nature I shall never take
My bodily form from any natural thing,
But such a form as Grecian goldsmiths make
Of hammered gold and gold enamelling
To keep a drowsy Emperor awake;
Or set upon a golden bough[2] to sing
To lords and ladies of Byzantium
Of what is past, or passing, or to come.

Among School Children

I

I walk through the long schoolroom questioning;
A kind old nun in a white hood replies;
The children learn to cipher and to sing,
To study reading-books and history,
To cut and sew, be neat in everything
In the best modern way—the children's eyes
In momentary wonder stare upon

---

1   spin or whirl in a spiral motion
2   Yeats notes that somewhere he had read "that in the Emperor's palace at Byzantium was a tree made of gold and silver, and artificial birds that sang."

A sixty-year-old smiling public man.

II

I dream of a Ledaean¹ body, bent
Above a sinking fire, a tale that she
Told of a harsh reproof, or trivial event
That changed some childish day to tragedy—
Told, and it seemed that our two natures blent
Into a sphere from youthful sympathy,
Or else, to alter Plato's parable,²
Into the yolk and white of the one shell.

III

And thinking of that fit of grief or rage
I look upon one child or t'other there
And wonder if she stood so at that age—
For even daughters of the swan can share
Something of every paddler's heritage—
And had that colour upon cheek or hair,
And thereupon my heart is driven wild:
She stands before me as a living child.

IV

Her present image floats into the mind—
Did Quattrocento³ finger fashion it
Hollow of cheek as though it drank the wind
And took a mess of shadows for its meat?
And I though never of Ledaean kind
Had pretty plumage once—enough of that,
Better to smile on all that smile, and show
There is a comfortable kind of old scarecrow.

V

What youthful mother, a shape upon her lap
Honey of generation⁴ had betrayed,
And that must sleep, shriek, struggle to escape
As recollection or the drug decide,
Would think her son, did she but see that shape
With sixty or more winters on its head,

---

1 like Leda
2 In the *Symposium*, Plato explains love by propounding that primeval man was divided into two, and that love is the search for reunion of those two halves.
3 a reference to the artists of fifteenth-century Italy
4 a drug that blots out the infant's memories of pre-natal happiness, and that "betrays" it into this world

A compensation for the pang of his birth,
Or the uncertainty of his setting forth?

VI

Plato thought nature but a spume that plays
Upon a ghostly paradigm of things;[1]
Solider Aristotle[2] played the taws
Upon the bottom of a king of kings;
World-famous golden-thighed Pythagoras[3]
Fingered upon a fiddle-stick or strings
What a star sang and careless Muses heard:
Old clothes upon old sticks to scare a bird.

VII

Both nuns and mothers worship images,
But those the candles light are not as those
That animate a mother's reveries,
But keep a marble or a bronze repose.
And yet they too break hearts—O Presences
That passion, piety or affection knows,
And that all heavenly glory symbolise—
O self-born mockers of man's enterprise;

VIII

Labour is blossoming or dancing where
The body is not bruised to pleasure soul,
Nor beauty born out of its own despair,
Nor blear-eyed wisdom out of midnight oil.
O chestnut-tree, great-rooted blossomer,
Are you the leaf, the blossom or the bole?
O body swayed to music, O brightening glance,
How can we know the dancer from the dance?

---

1   Plato saw nature as merely appearance, veiling the ultimate reality.
2   "Solider" because unlike Plato, he did believe in the reality of matter. He was tutor to
Alexander the Great, whom he disciplined with the "taws," or strap.
3   Greek philosopher of the sixth century B.C. who applied the mathematical principles of
music to the workings of the universe. According to legend, he had a golden thigh.

Lapis Lazuli[1]

(For Harry Clifton)

I have heard that hysterical women say
They are sick of the palette and fiddle-bow,
Of poets that are always gay,
For everybody knows or else should know
That if nothing drastic is done
Aeroplane and Zeppelin will come out,
Pitch like King Billy[2] bomb-balls in
Until the town lie beaten flat.

All perform their tragic play,
There struts Hamlet, there is Lear,
That's Ophelia, that Cordelia;
Yet they, should the last scene be there,
The great stage curtain about to drop,
If worthy their prominent part in the play,
Do not break up their lines to weep.
They know that Hamlet and Lear are gay;
Gaiety transfiguring all that dread.
All men have aimed at, found and lost;
Black out; Heaven blazing into the head:
Tragedy wrought to its uttermost.
Though Hamlet rambles and Lear rages,
And all the drop-scenes drop at once
Upon a hundred thousand stages,
It cannot grow by an inch or an ounce.

On their own feet they came, or on shipboard,
Camel-back, horse-back, ass-back, mule-back,
Old civilisations put to the sword.
Then they and their wisdom went to rack:
No handiwork of Callimachus,[3]
Who handled marble as if it were bronze,
Made draperies that seemed to rise
When sea-wind swept the corner, stands;
His long lamp-chimney shaped like the stem
Of a slender palm, stood but a day;
All things fall and are built again,
And those that build them again are gay.

Two Chinamen, behind them a third,
Are carved in lapis lazuli,

---

1   a dark blue stone
2   William III, who defeated the army of James II at the Battle of the Boyne in 1690
3   Greek sculptor of the fifth century B.C.

Over them flies a long-legged bird,
A symbol of longevity;
The third, doubtless a serving-man,
Carries a musical instrument.

Every discoloration of the stone,
Every accidental crack or dent,
Seems a water-course or an avalanche,
Or lofty slope where it still snows
Though doubtless plum or cherry-branch
Sweetens the little half-way house
Those Chinamen climb towards, and I
Delight to imagine them seated there;
There, on the mountain and the sky,
On all the tragic scene they stare.
One asks for mournful melodies;
Accomplished fingers begin to play.
Their eyes mid many wrinkles, their eyes,
Their ancient, glittering eyes, are gay.

The Circus Animals' Desertion

I

I sought a theme and sought for it in vain,
I sought it daily for six weeks or so.
Maybe at last, being but a broken man,
I must be satisfied with my heart, although
Winter and summer till old age began
My circus animals were all on show,
Those stilted boys, that burnished chariot,
Lion and woman and the Lord knows what.

II

What can I but enumerate old themes?
First that sea-rider Oisín[1] led by the nose
Through three enchanted islands, allegorical dreams,
Vain gaiety, vain battle, vain repose,
Themes of the embittered heart, or so it seems,
That might adorn old songs or courtly shows;
But what cared I that set him on to ride,
I, starved for the bosom of his faery bride?

And then a counter-truth filled out its play,

---

1 legendary Irish hero, about whom Yeats wrote in his first book, *The Wanderings of Oisín and Other Poems* (1889)

The Countess Cathleen[1] was the name I gave it;
She, pity-crazed, had given her soul away,
But masterful Heaven had intervened to save it.
I thought my dear[2] must her own soul destroy,
So did fanaticism and hate enslave it,
And this brought forth a dream and soon enough
This dream itself had all my thought and love.

And when the Fool and Blind Man stole the bread
Cuchulain[3] fought the ungovernable sea;
Heart-mysteries there, and yet when all is said
It was the dream itself enchanted me:
Character isolated by a deed
To engross the present and dominate memory.
Players and painted stage took all my love,
And not those things that they were emblems of.

III

Those masterful images because complete
Grew in pure mind, but out of what began?
A mound of refuse or the sweepings of a street,
Old kettles, old bottles, and a broken can,
Old iron, old bones, old rags, that raving slut
Who keeps the till. Now that my ladder's gone,
I must lie down where all the ladders start,
In the foul rag-and-bone shop of the heart.

---

1   an early play by Yeats about an Irish countess who sells her soul to the devil to get food
    for the peasants
2   Maud Gonne
3   a legendary Irish hero, who appears in Yeats's play *On Baile's Strand*

Robert Frost

(1874–1963)

Mending Wall

Something there is that doesn't love a wall,
That sends the frozen-ground-swell under it
And spills the upper boulders in the sun,
And makes gaps even two can pass abreast.
The work of hunters is another thing:
I have come after them and made repair
Where they have left not one stone on a stone,
But they would have the rabbit out of hiding,
To please the yelping dogs. The gaps I mean,
No one has seen them made or heard them made,
But at spring mending-time we find them there.
I let my neighbor know beyond the hill;
And on a day we meet to walk the line
And set the wall between us once again.
We keep the wall between us as we go.
To each the boulders that have fallen to each.
And some are loaves and some so nearly balls
We have to use a spell to make them balance:
"Stay where you are until our backs are turned!"
We wear our fingers rough with handling them.
Oh, just another kind of outdoor game,
One on a side. It comes to little more:
There where it is we do not need the wall:
He is all pine and I am apple orchard.
My apple trees will never get across
And eat the cones under his pines, I tell him.
He only says, "Good fences make good neighbors."
Spring is the mischief in me, and I wonder
If I could put a notion in his head:
"*Why* do they make good neighbors? Isn't it
Where there are cows? But here there are no cows.
Before I built a wall I'd ask to know
What I was walling in or walling out,
And to whom I was like to give offense.
Something there is that doesn't love a wall,
That wants it down." I could say "Elves" to him,
But it's not elves exactly, and I'd rather
He said it for himself. I see him there,
Bringing a stone grasped firmly by the top
In each hand, like an old-stone savage armed.
He moves in darkness as it seems to me,
Not of woods only and the shade of trees.
He will not go behind his father's saying,
And he likes having thought of it so well
He says again, "Good fences make good neighbors."

After Apple-Picking

My long two-pointed ladder's sticking through a tree
Toward heaven still,
And there's a barrel that I didn't fill
Beside it, and there may be two or three
Apples I didn't pick upon some bough.
But I am done with apple-picking now.
Essence of winter sleep is on the night,
The scent of apples: I am drowsing off.
I cannot rub the strangeness from my sight
I got from looking through a pane of glass
I skimmed this morning from the drinking trough
And held against the world of hoary grass.
It melted, and I let it fall and break.
But I was well
Upon my way to sleep before it fell,
And I could tell
What form my dreaming was about to take.
Magnified apples appear and disappear,
Stem end and blossom end,
And every fleck of russet showing clear.
My instep arch not only keeps the ache,
It keeps the pressure of a ladder-round.
I feel the ladder sway as the boughs bend.
And I keep hearing from the cellar bin
The rumbling sound
Of load on load of apples coming in.
For I have had too much
Of apple-picking: I am overtired
Of the great harvest I myself desired.
There were ten thousand thousand fruit to touch,
Cherish in hand, lift down, and not let fall.
For all
That struck the earth,
No matter if not bruised or spiked with stubble,
Went surely to the cider-apple heap
As of no worth.
One can see what will trouble
This sleep of mine, whatever sleep it is.
Were he not gone,
The woodchuck could say whether it's like his
Long sleep, as I describe its coming on,
Or just some human sleep.

The Road Not Taken

Two roads diverged in a yellow wood,
And sorry I could not travel both
And be one traveler, long I stood

And looked down one as far as I could
To where it bent in the undergrowth;

Then took the other, as just as fair,
And having perhaps the better claim,
Because it was grassy and wanted wear;
Though as for that, the passing there
Had worn them really about the same,

And both that morning equally lay
In leaves no step had trodden black.
Oh, I kept the first for another day!
Yet knowing how way leads on to way,
I doubted if I should ever come back.

I shall be telling this with a sigh
Somewhere ages and ages hence:
Two roads diverged in a wood, and I—
I took the one less traveled by,
And that has made all the difference.

Birches

When I see birches bend to left and right
Across the lines of straighter darker trees,
I like to think some boy's been swinging them.
But swinging doesn't bend them down to stay
As ice storms do. Often you must have seen them
Loaded with ice a sunny winter morning
After a rain. They click upon themselves
As the breeze rises, and turn many-colored
As the stir cracks and crazes their enamel.
Soon the sun's warmth makes them shed crystal shells
Shattering and avalanching on the snow crust—
Such heaps of broken glass to sweep away
You'd think the inner dome of heaven had fallen.
They are dragged to the withered bracken by the load,
And they seem not to break; though once they are bowed
So low for long, they never right themselves:
You may see their trunks arching in the woods
Years afterwards, trailing their leaves on the ground
Like girls on hands and knees that throw their hair
Before them over their heads to dry in the sun.
But I was going to say when Truth broke in
With all her matter of fact about the ice storm,
I should prefer to have some boy bend them
As he went out and in to fetch the cows—
Some boy too far from town to learn baseball,
Whose only play was what he found himself,
Summer or winter, and could play alone.

One by one he subdued his father's trees
By riding them down over and over again
Until he took the stiffness out of them,
And not one but hung limp, not one was left
For him to conquer. He learned all there was
To learn about not launching out too soon
And so not carrying the tree away
Clear to the ground. He always kept his poise
To the top branches, climbing carefully
With the same pains you use to fill a cup
Up to the brim, and even above the brim.
Then he flung outward, feet first, with a swish,
Kicking his way down through the air to the ground.
So was I once myself a swinger of birches.
And so I dream of going back to be.
It's when I'm weary of considerations,
And life is too much like a pathless wood
Where your face burns and tickles with the cobwebs
Broken across it, and one eye is weeping
From a twig's having lashed across it open.
I'd like to get away from earth awhile.
And then come back to it and begin over.
May no fate willfully misunderstand me
And half grant what I wish and snatch me away
Not to return. Earth's the right place for love:
I don't know where it's likely to go better.
I'd like to go by climbing a birch tree,
And climb black branches up a snow-white trunk
Toward heaven, till the tree could bear no more,
But dipped its top and set me down again.
That would be good both going and coming back.
One could do worse than be a swinger of birches.

Fire and Ice

Some say the world will end in fire,
Some say in ice.
From what I've tasted of desire
I hold with those who favor fire.
But if it had to perish twice,
I think I know enough of hate
To say that for destruction ice
Is also great
And would suffice.

Stopping by Woods on a Snowy Evening

Whose woods these are I think I know.
His house is in the village, though;
He will not see me stopping here
To watch his woods fill up with snow.

My little horse must think it queer
To stop without a farmhouse near
Between the woods and frozen lake
The darkest evening of the year.

He gives his harness bells a shake
To ask if there is some mistake.
The only other sound's the sweep
Of easy wind and downy flake.

The woods are lovely, dark, and deep,
But I have promises to keep,
And miles to go before I sleep,
And miles to go before I sleep.

Acquainted with the Night

I have been one acquainted with the night.
I have walked out in rain—and back in rain.
I have outwalked the furthest city light.

I have looked down the saddest city lane.
I have passed by the watchman on his beat
And dropped my eyes, unwilling to explain.

I have stood still and stopped the sound of feet
When far away an interrupted cry
Came over houses from another street,

But not to call me back or say good-by;
And further still at an unearthly height
One luminary clock against the sky
Proclaimed the time was neither wrong nor right.
I have been one acquainted with the night.

Desert Places

Snow falling and night falling fast, oh, fast
In a field I looked into going past,
And the ground almost covered smooth in snow,
But a few weeds and stubble showing last.

The woods around it have it—it is theirs.
All animals are smothered in their lairs.
I am too absent-spirited to count;
The loneliness includes me unawares.

And lonely as it is, that loneliness
Will be more lonely ere it will be less—
A blanker whiteness of benighted snow
With no expression, nothing to express.

They cannot scare me with their empty spaces
Between stars—on stars where no human race is.
I have it in me so much nearer home
To scare myself with my own desert places.

Neither Out Far Nor In Deep

The people along the sand
All turn and look one way.
They turn their back on the land.
They look at the sea all day.

As long as it takes to pass
A ship keeps raising its hull;
The wetter ground like glass
Reflects a standing gull.

The land may vary more;
But wherever the truth may be—
The water comes ashore,
And the people look at the sea.

They cannot look out far.
They cannot look in deep.
But when was that ever a bar
To any watch they keep?

He uses common poetic strategy describing H + using it to convey some further message

begins similar to It. Sonnet

Design

a flower, usually blue, so it's a mutation

I found a dimpled spider, fat and white, a
On a white heal-all, holding up a moth b
Like a white piece of rigid satin cloth— a
Assorted characters of death and blight b
Mixed ready to begin the morning right, a
Like the ingredients of a witches' broth— b
A snow-drop spider, a flower like a froth, b
And dead wings carried like a paper kite. a

pos. image - bride, bed coll. imimus

simile

simile

What had that flower to do with being white, a
The wayside blue and innocent heal-all? c
What brought the kindred spider to that height, b
Then steered the white moth thither in the night? b
What but design of darkness to appall?— a c
If design govern in a thing so small.

The Silken Tent

English Sonnet

Quite Delicate love Poem, add. ... to his wife

I very long sentence →

I long extended elaborate metaphor

Even the commitment is a gentle bond

She is as in a field a silken tent a
At midday when a sunny summer breeze b
Has dried the dew and all its ropes relent, a
So that in guys it gently sways at ease, b
And its supporting central cedar pole, c
That is its pinnacle to heavenward d
And signifies the sureness of the soul, c
Seems to owe naught to any single cord, d
But strictly held by none, is loosely bound e
By countless silken ties of love and thought f
To everything on earth the compass round, e
And only by one's going slightly taut f
In the capriciousness of summer air g
Is of the slightest bondage made aware. g

/ x - stressed

I found / a dimpled spider, fat / + white

Robert Service

(1874–1958)

The Shooting of Dan Mcgrew

A bunch of the boys were whooping it up in the Malamute saloon;
The kid that handles the music-box was hitting a jag-time tune;
Back of the bar, in a solo game, sat Dangerous Dan McGrew,
And watching his luck was his light-o'-love, the lady that's known
      as Lou.

When out of the night, which was fifty below, and into the din
      and the glare,
There stumbled a miner fresh from the creeks, dog dirty and
      loaded for bear.
He looked like a man with a foot in the grave and scarcely the strength
      of a louse,
Yet he tilted a poke of dust[1] on the bar, and he called for drinks for
      the house.
There was none could place the stranger's face, though we searched
      ourselves for a clue;
But we drank his health, and the last to drink was Dangerous
      Dan McGrew.

There's men that somehow just grip your eyes, and hold them hard
      like a spell;
And such was he, and he looked to me like a man who had lived in
      hell;
With a face most hair, and the dreary stare of a dog whose day is done,
As he watered the green stuff in his glass, and the drops fell one
      by one.
Then I got to figgering who he was, and wondering what he'd do,
And I turned my head—and there watching him was the lady that's
      known as Lou.

His eyes went rubbering round the room, and he seemed in a kind of
      daze,
Till at last that old piano fell in the way of his wandering gaze.
The rag-time kid was having a drink; there was no one else on the
      stool,
So the stranger stumbles across the room, and flops down there like
      a fool.
In a buckskin shirt that was glazed with dirt he sat, and I saw him sway;
Then he clutched the keys with his talon hands—my God! but that man
      could play.

Were you ever out in the Great Alone, when the moon was awful clear,

---

1   a small bag of gold-dust

And the icy mountains hemmed you in with a silence you most could
      hear;
With only the howl of a timber wolf, and you camped there in the
      cold,
A half-dead thing in a stark, dead world, clean mad for the muck called
      gold;
While high overhead, green, yellow and red, the North Lights swept in
      bars?—
Then you've a hunch what the music meant . . . hunger and night and
      the stars.

And hunger not of the belly kind, that's banished with bacon and beans,
But the gnawing hunger of lonely men for a home and all that it means;
For a fireside far from the cares that are, four walls and a roof above;
But oh! so cramful of cosy joy, and crowned with a woman's love—
A woman dearer than all the world, and true as Heaven is true—
(God! how ghastly she looks through her rouge,—the lady that's known
      as Lou.)

Then on a sudden the music changed, so soft that you scarce could
      hear;
But you felt that your life had been looted clean of all that it once held
      dear;
That someone had stolen the woman you loved; that her love was a
      devil's lie;
That your guts were gone, and the best for you was to crawl away and
      die.
'Twas the crowning cry of a heart's despair, and it thrilled you through
      and through—
"I guess I'll make it a spread misere,[1]" said Dangerous Dan McGrew.

The music almost died away . . . then it burst like a pent-up flood;
And it seemed to say, "Repay, repay," and my eyes were blind with
      blood.
The thought came back of an ancient wrong, and it stung like a frozen
      lash,
And the lust awoke to kill, to kill . . . then the music stopped with a
      crash,
And the stranger turned, and his eyes they burned in a most peculiar
      way;
In a buckskin shirt that was glazed with dirt he sat, and I saw him
      sway;
Then his lips went in in a kind of grin, and he spoke, and his voice
      was calm,
And "Boys," says he, "you don't know me, and none of you care a
      damn;

---

1   a hand in the card-game of whist in which the caller undertakes not to win a single trick

But I want to state, and my words are straight, and I'll bet my poke
      they're true,
That one of you is a hound of hell . . . and that one is Dan McGrew."

Then I ducked my head, and the lights went out, and two guns blazed
      in the dark,
And a woman screamed, and the lights went up, and two men lay stiff
      and stark.
Pitched on his head, and pumped full of lead, was Dangerous Dan
      McGrew,
While the man from the creeks lay clutched to the breast of the lady
      that's known as Lou.

These are the simple facts of the case, and I guess I ought to know.
They say that the stranger was crazed with "hooch," and I'm not denying
      it's so.
I'm not so wise as the lawyer guys, but strictly between us two—
The woman that kissed him and—pinched his poke—was the lady that's
      known as Lou.

Only a Boche[1]

We brought him in from between the lines: we'd better have
      let him lie;
For what's the use of risking one's skin for a *tyke* that's
      going to die?
What's the use of tearing him loose under a gruelling fire,
When he's shot in the head, and worse than dead, and all
      messed up on the wire?

However, I say, we brought him in. *Diable!* The mud was bad;
The trench was crooked and greasy and high, and oh, what a
      time we had!
And often we slipped, and often we tripped, but never he
      made a moan;
And how we were wet with blood and with sweat! but we
      carried him in like our own.

Now there he lies in the dug-out dim, awaiting the ambulance,
And the doctor shrugs his shoulders at him, and remarks, "He
      hasn't a chance."
And we squat and smoke at our game of bridge on the
      glistening, straw-packed floor,
And above our oaths we can hear his breath deep-drawn in a
      kind of snore.

---

1   French name for a German soldier

For the dressing station is long and low, and the candles gutter
    dim,
And the mean light falls on the cold clay walls and our faces
    bristly and grim;
And we flap our cards on the lousy straw, and we laugh and
    jibe as we play,
And you'd never know that the cursed foe was less than a
    mile away.
As we con our cards in the rancid gloom, oppressed by that
    snoring breath,
You'd never dream that our broad roof-beam was swept by the
    broom of death.

Heigh-ho! My turn for the dummy hand; I rise and I stretch
    a bit;
The fetid air is making me yawn, and my cigarette's unlit,
So I go to the nearest candle flame, and the man we brought
    is there,
And his face is white in the shabby light, and I stand at his feet
    and stare.
Stand for a while, and quietly stare: for strange though it seems
    to be,
The dying Boche on the stretcher there has a queer
    resemblance to me.

It gives one a kind of a turn, you know, to come on a thing
    like that.
It's just as if I were lying there, with a turban of blood for a hat,
Lying there in a coat grey-green instead of a coat grey-blue,
With one of my eyes all shot away, and my brain half tumbling
    through;
Lying there with a chest that heaves like a bellows up and down,
And a cheek as white as snow on a grave, and lips that are
    coffee brown.

And confound him, too! He wears, like me, on his finger
    a wedding ring,
And around his neck, as around my own, by a greasy bit
    of string,
A locket hangs with a woman's face, and I turn it about to see:
Just as I thought . . . on the other side the faces of children
    three;
Clustered together cherub-like, three little laughing girls,
With the usual tiny rosebud mouths and the usual silken curls.
"Zut!" I say. "He has beaten me; for me, I have only two,"
And I push the locket beneath his shirt, feeling a little blue.

Oh, it isn't cheerful to see a man, the marvellous work of God,
Crushed in the mutilation mill, crushed to a smeary clod;
Oh, it isn't cheerful to hear him moan; but it isn't that I mind,

It isn't the anguish that goes with him, it's the anguish he leaves
    behind.
For his going opens a tragic door that gives on a world of pain,
And the death he dies, those who live and love, will die again
    and again.

So here I am at my cards once more, but it's kind of spoiling
    my play,
Thinking of those three brats of his so many a mile away.
War is war, and he's only a Boche, and we all of us take our
    chance;
But all the same I'll be mighty glad when I'm hearing the
    ambulance.
One foe the less, but all the same I'm heartily glad I'm not
The man who gave him his broken head, the sniper who fired
    the shot.

No trumps you make it, I think you said? You'll pardon me if
    I err;
For a moment I thought of other things . . . *Mon Dieu! Quelle
vache de guerre.*[1]

---

1   My God, what a lousy war.

Wallace Stevens

(1879-1955)

The Emperor of Ice-Cream

Call the roller of big cigars,
The muscular one, and bid him whip
In kitchen cups concupiscent curds.
Let the wenches dawdle in such dress
As they are used to wear, and let the boys
Bring flowers in last month's newspapers.
Let be be finale of seem.[1]
The only emperor is the emperor of ice-cream.

Take from the dresser of deal,
Lacking the three glass knobs, that sheet
On which she embroidered fantails once
And spread it so as to cover her face.
If her horny feet protrude, they come
To show how cold she is, and dumb.
Let the lamp affix its beam.
The only emperor is the emperor of ice-cream.

Anecdote of the Jar

I placed a jar in Tennessee,
And round it was, upon a hill.
It made the slovenly wilderness
Surround that hill.

The wilderness rose up to it,
And sprawled around, no longer wild.
The jar was round upon the ground
And tall and of a port in air.

It took dominion everywhere.
The jar was gray and bare.
It did not give of bird or bush,
Like nothing else in Tennessee.

---

1   Stevens wrote that this line means "let being become the conclusion or denouement of appearing to be: in short, ice cream is an absolute good. The poem is obviously not about ice cream, but about being as distinguished from seeming to be" (*Letters* 341).

Thirteen Ways of Looking at a Blackbird[1]

I

Among twenty snowy mountains,
The only moving thing
Was the eye of the blackbird.

II

I was of three minds,
Like a tree
In which there are three blackbirds.

III

The blackbird whirled in the autumn winds.
It was a small part of the pantomime.

IV

A man and a woman
Are one.
A man and a woman and a blackbird
Are one.

V

I do not know which to prefer,
The beauty of inflections
Or the beauty of innuendoes,
The blackbird whistling
Or just after.

VI

Icicles filled the long window
With barbaric glass.
The shadow of the blackbird
Crossed it, to and fro.
The mood
Traced in the shadow
An indecipherable cause.

---

1   "This group of poems is not meant to be a collection of epigrams or of ideas, but of
sensations" (Stevens, *Letters* 251).

VII

O thin men of Haddam,[1]
Why do you imagine golden birds?
Do you not see how the blackbird
Walks around the feet
Of the women about you?

VIII

I know noble accents
And lucid, inescapable rhythms;
But I know, too,
That the blackbird is involved
In what I know.

IX

When the blackbird flew out of sight,
It marked the edge
Of one of many circles.

X

At the sight of blackbirds
Flying in a green light,
Even the bawds of euphony
Would cry out sharply.

XI

He rode over Connecticut
In a glass coach.
Once, a fear pierced him,
In that he mistook
The shadow of his equipage
For blackbirds.

XII

The river is moving.
The blackbird must be flying.

---

1   a town in Connecticut

XIII

It was evening all afternoon.
It was snowing
And it was going to snow.
The blackbird sat
In the cedar-limbs.

The Idea of Order at Key West[1]

She sang beyond the genius of the sea.
The water never formed to mind or voice,
Like a body wholly body, fluttering
Its empty sleeves; and yet its mimic motion
Made constant cry, caused constantly a cry,
That was not ours although we understood,
Inhuman, of the veritable ocean.

The sea was not a mask. No more was she.
The song and water were not medleyed sound
Even if what she sang was what she heard,
Since what she sang was uttered word by word.
It may be that in all her phrases stirred
The grinding water and the gasping wind;
But it was she and not the sea we heard.

For she was the maker of the song she sang.
The ever-hooded, tragic-gestured sea
Was merely a place by which she walked to sing.
Whose spirit is this? we said, because we knew
It was the spirit that we sought and knew
That we should ask this often as she sang.

If it was only the dark voice of the sea
That rose, or even colored by many waves;
If it was only the outer voice of sky
And cloud, of the sunken coral water-walled,
However clear, it would have been deep air,
The heaving speech of air, a summer sound
Repeated in a summer without end
And sound alone. But it was more than that,
More even than her voice, and ours, among
The meaningless plungings of water and the wind,
Theatrical distances, bronze shadows heaped
On high horizons, mountainous atmospheres

---

1   Key West is the most southerly of the coral islands that comprise the Florida Keys, south
of Miami.

Of sky and sea.
                    It was her voice that made
The sky acutest at its vanishing.
She measured to the hour its solitude.
She was the single artificer of the world
In which she sang. And when she sang, the sea,
Whatever self it had, became the self
That was her song, for she was the maker. Then we,
As we beheld her striding there alone,
Knew that there never was a world for her
Except the one she sang and, singing, made.

Ramon Fernandez,[1] tell me, if you know,
Why, when the singing ended and we turned
Toward the town, tell why the glassy lights,
The lights in the fishing boats at anchor there,
As the night descended, tilting in the air,
Mastered the night and portioned out the sea,
Fixing emblazoned zones and fiery poles,
Arranging, deepening, enchanting night.

Oh! Blessed rage for order, pale Ramon,
The maker's rage to order words of the sea,
Words of the fragrant portals, dimly-starred,
And of ourselves and of our origins,
In ghostlier demarcations, keener sounds.

The Motive for Metaphor

You like it under the trees in autumn,
Because everything is half dead.
The wind moves like a cripple among the leaves
And repeats words without meaning.

In the same way, you were happy in spring,
With the half colors of quarter-things,
The slightly brighter sky, the melting clouds,
The single bird, the obscure moon—

The obscure moon lighting an obscure world
Of things that would never be quite expressed,
Where you yourself were never quite yourself
And did not want nor have to be,

---

1   Although there was a French literary critic called Ramon Fernandez (1894-1944), Stevens
     indicated that "Ramon Fernandez was not intended to be anyone at all" (*Letters* 798).

Desiring the exhilarations of changes:
The motive for metaphor, shrinking from
The weight of primary noon,
The A B C of being,

The ruddy temper, the hammer
Of red and blue, the hard sound—
Steel against intimation—the sharp flash,
The vital, arrogant, fatal, dominant X.

E. J. Pratt

(1882–1964)

The Shark

He seemed to know the harbour,
So leisurely he swam;
His fin,
Like a piece of sheet-iron,
Three-cornered,
And with knife-edge,
Stirred not a bubble
As it moved
With its base-line on the water.

His body was tubular
And tapered
And smoke-blue,
And as he passed the wharf
He turned,
And snapped at a flat-fish
That was dead and floating.
And I saw the flash of a white throat,
And a double row of white teeth,
And eyes of metallic grey,
Hard and narrow and slit.

Then out of the harbour,
With that three-cornered fin
Shearing without a bubble the water
Lithely,
Leisurely,
He swam—
That strange fish,
Tubular, tapered, smoke-blue,
Part vulture, part wolf,
Part neither—for his blood was cold.

From Stone to Steel

From stone to bronze, from bronze to steel
Along the road-dust of the sun,
Two revolutions of the wheel
From Java to Geneva¹ run.

---

1 "Java Man" (pithecanthropus) is one of the oldest known fossils of human remains. Geneva was from 1920 to 1946 the home of the League of Nations, the predecessor of the United Nations.

The snarl Neanderthal is worn
Close to the smiling Aryan[1] lips,
The civil polish of the horn
Gleams from our praying finger tips.

The evolution of desire
Has but matured a toxic wine,
Drunk long before its heady fire
Reddened Euphrates[2] or the Rhine.

Between the temple and the cave
The boundary lies tissue thin:
The yearlings still the altars crave
As satisfaction for a sin.

The road goes up, the road goes down—
Let Java or Geneva be—
But whether to the cross or crown,
The path lies through Gethsemane.[3]

The Prize Cat

Pure blood domestic, guaranteed,
Soft-mannered, musical in purr,
The ribbon had declared the breed,
Gentility was in the fur.

Such feline culture in the gads
No anger ever arched her back—
What distance since those velvet pads
Departed from the leopard's track!

And when I mused how Time had thinned
The jungle strains within the cells,
How human hands had disciplined
Those prowling optic parallels;

I saw the generations pass
Along the reflex of a spring,
A bird had rustled in the grass,
The tab had caught it on the wing:

---

1 In Nazi ideology, the Aryan race—people of Caucasian, especially Nordic, stock—
represented a superior form of human development.
2 the river that flows from Turkey to the Persian Gulf
3 the garden outside Jerusalem where Christ was betrayed and apprehended; see Matthew
26.36-56.

Behind the leap so furtive-wild
Was such ignition in the gleam,
I thought an Abyssinian[1] child
Had cried out in the whitethroat's scream.

The Highway

What aeons passed without a count or name,
Before the cosmic seneschal,
Succeeding with a plan
Of weaving stellar patterns from a flame,
Announced at his high carnival
An orbit—with Aldebaran![2]

And when the drifting years had sighted land,
And hills and plains declared their birth
Amid volcanic throes,
What was the lapse before the marshal's hand
Had found a garden on the earth,
And led forth June with her first rose?

And what the gulf between that and the hour,
Late in the simian-human day,
When Nature kept her tryst
With the unfoldment of the star and flower—
When in her sacrificial way
Judaea blossomed with her Christ!

But what made *our* feet miss the road that brought
The world to such a golden trove,
In our so brief a span?
How may we grasp again the hand that wrought
Such light, such fragrance, and such love,
O star! O rose! O Son of Man!

---

1   Italy, led by Mussolini, invaded Abyssinia (later Ethiopia) in 1935.
2   a red star of the first magnitude in the constellation of Taurus

from: *Towards the Last Spike*[1]

(*The last gap in the mountains–between the Selkirks and Savona's Ferry–is closed*)

The Road itself was like a stream that men
Had coaxed and teased or bullied out of Nature.
As if watching for weak spots in her codes,
It sought for levels like the watercourses.
It sinuously took the bends, rejoiced
In plains and easy grades, found gaps, poured through them,
But hating steep descents avoided them.
Unlike the rivers which in full rebellion
Against the canyons' hydrophobic slaver
Went to the limit of their argument:
Unlike again, the stream of steel had found
A way to climb, became a mountaineer.
From the Alberta plains it reached the Summit,
And where it could not climb, it cut and curved,
Till from the Rockies to the Coastal Range
It had accomplished what the Rivers had,
Making a hundred clean Caesarian cuts,
And bringing to delivery in their time
Their smoky, lusty-screaming locomotives.

The Spike

Silver or gold? Van Horne had rumbled 'Iron.'
No flags or bands announced this ceremony,
No Morse in circulation through the world,
And though the vital words like Eagle Pass,
Craigellachie, were trembling in their belfries,
No hands were at the ropes. The air was taut
With silences as rigid as the spruces
Forming the background in November mist.
More casual than camera-wise, the men
Could have been properties upon a stage,
Except for road maps furrowing their faces.

Rogers,[2] his both feet planted on a tie,
Stood motionless as ballast. In the rear,
Covering the scene with spirit-level eyes,

---

1   Pratt's poem tells the story of the building of the Canadian Pacific Railway, which climaxes
     in the driving of the "Last Spike" at Craigellachie in Eagle Pass, B.C., on 7 November
     1885. The principal actor in Pratt's vivid account is William Van Horne (1843-1915), a
     native of Illinois and the general manager of the CPR, whose energy and determination
     ensured the success of the project.
2   A. B. Rogers (1829-1889), the surveyor who found the route through the mountains that
     the railway would follow

Predestination on his chin, was Fleming.[1]
The only one groomed for the ritual
From smooth silk hat and well-cut square-rig beard
Down through his Caledonian longitude,
He was outstaturing others by a foot,
And upright as the mainmast of a brig.
Beside him, barely reaching to his waist,
A water-boy had wormed his way in front
To touch this last rail with his foot, his face
Upturned to see the cheek-bone crags of Rogers.
The other side of Fleming, hands in pockets,
Eyes leaden-lidded under square-crowned hat,
And puncheon-bellied under overcoat,
Unsmiling at the focused lens — Van Horne.
Whatever ecstasy played round that rail
Did not leap to his face. Five years had passed,
Less than five years — so well within the pledge.
The job was done. Was this the slouch of rest?
Not to the men he drove through walls of granite.
The embers from the past were in his soul,
Banked for the moment at the rail and smoking,
Just waiting for the future to be blown.

At last the spike and Donald[2] with the hammer!
His hair like frozen moss from Labrador
Poked out under his hat, ran down his face
To merge with streaks of rust in a white cloud.
What made him fumble the first stroke? Not age:
The snow belied his middle sixties. Was
It lapse of caution or his sense of thrift,
That elemental stuff which through his life
Never pockmarked his daring but had made
The man the canniest trader of his time,
Who never missed a rat-count, never failed
To gauge the size and texture of a pelt?
Now here he was caught by the camera,
Back bent, head bowed, and staring at a sledge,
Outwitted by an idiotic nail.
Though from the crowd no laughter, yet the spike
With its slewed neck was grinning up at Smith.
Wrenched out, it was replaced. This time the hammer
Gave a first tap as with apology,
Another one, another, till the spike
Was safely stationed in the tie and then
The Scot, invoking his ancestral clan,

---

1   Sandford Fleming (1827-1915), a leading railway engineer and surveyor
2   Donald Smith (1830-1914), an executive with the Hudson's Bay Company and the Bank
      of Montreal, was one of the principal financiers of the CPR.

Using the hammer like a battle-axe,
His eyes bloodshot with memories of Flodden,[1]
Descended on it, rammed it to its home.

. . . . .

The stroke released a trigger for a burst
Of sound that stretched the gamut of the air.
The shouts of engineers and dynamiters,
Of locomotive-workers and explorers,
Flanking the rails, were but a tuning-up
For a massed continental chorus. Led
By Moberly (of the Eagles and *this* Pass)
And Rogers (of *his own*), followed by Wilson,
And Ross (charged with the Rocky Mountain Section),
By Egan (general of the Western Lines),
Cambie and Marcus Smith, Harris of Boston,
The roar was deepened by the bass of Fleming,
And heightened by the laryngeal fifes
Of Dug McKenzie and John H. McTavish.
It ended when Van Horne spat out some phlegm
To ratify the tumult with 'Well Done'
Tied in a knot of monosyllables.

Merely the tuning up! For on the morrow
The last blow on the spike would stir the mould
Under the drumming of the prairie wheels,
And make the whistles from the steam out-crow
The Fraser. Like a gavel it would close
Debate, making Macdonald's 'sea to sea'[2]
Pour through two oceanic megaphones —
Three thousand miles of *Hail* from port to port;
And somewhere in the middle of the line
Of steel, even the lizard heard the stroke.
The breed had triumphed after all. To drown
The traffic chorus, she must blend the sound
With those inaugural, narcotic notes
Of storm and thunder which would send her back
Deeper than ever in Laurentian sleep.

* * *

1   At the battle of Flodden in 1513, the English defeated the Scots.
2   the phrase adopted in 1867 as the motto of Canada ("A mari usque ad mare"); it is taken
    from Psalms 72.8.

William Carlos Williams

(1883–1963)

The Red Wheelbarrow

so much depends
upon

a red wheel
barrow

glazed with rain
water

beside the white
chickens

Queen-Anne's-Lace

Her body is not so white as
anemone petals nor so smooth—nor
so remote a thing. It is a field
of the wild carrot taking
the field by force; the grass
does not raise above it.
Here is no question of whiteness,
white as can be, with a purple mole
at the center of each flower.
Each flower is a hand's span
of her whiteness. Wherever
his hand has lain there is
a tiny purple blemish. Each part
is a blossom under his touch
to which the fibres of her being
stem one by one, each to its end,
until the whole field is a
white desire, empty, a single stem,
a cluster, flower by flower,
a pious wish to whiteness gone over—
or nothing.

This Is Just To Say

I have eaten
the plums
that were in
the icebox

and which
you were probably
saving
for breakfast

Forgive me
they were delicious
so sweet
and so cold

At the Ball Game

The crowd at the ball game
is moved uniformly

by a spirit of uselessness
which delights them—

all the exciting detail
of the chase

and the escape, the error
the flash of genius—

all to no end save beauty
the eternal—

So in detail they, the crowd,
are beautiful

for this
to be warned against

saluted and defied—
It is alive, venomous

it smiles grimly
its words cut—

The flashy female with her
mother, gets it—

The Jew gets it straight—it

is deadly, terrifying—

It is the Inquisition,[1] the
Revolution

It is beauty itself
that lives

day by day in them
idly—

This is
the power of their faces

It is summer, it is the solstice
the crowd is

cheering, the crowd is laughing
in detail

permanently, seriously
without thought

The Yachts

contend in a sea which the land partly encloses
shielding them from the too-heavy blows
of an ungoverned ocean which when it chooses

tortures the biggest hulls, the best man knows
to pit against its beatings, and sinks them pitilessly.
Mothlike in mists, scintillant in the minute

brilliance of cloudless days, with broad bellying sails
they glide to the wind tossing green water
from their sharp prows while over them the crew crawls

ant-like, solicitously grooming them, releasing,
making fast as they turn, lean far over and having
caught the wind again, side by side, head for the mark.[2]

In a well guarded arena of open water surrounded by
lesser and greater craft which, sycophant, lumbering
and flittering follow them, they appear youthful, rare

---

1   the Roman Catholic court established to identify and punish heretics; the Spanish
Inquisition of the fifteenth century was particularly harsh in its treatment of Jews.
2   the starting point

as the light of a happy eye, live with the grace
of all that in the mind is fleckless, free and
naturally to be desired. Now the sea which holds them

is moody, lapping their glossy sides, as if feeling
for some slightest flaw but fails completely.
Today no race. Then the wind comes again. The yachts

move, jockeying for a start, the signal is set and they
are off. Now the waves strike at them but they are too
well made, they slip through, though they take in canvas.

Arms with hands grasping seek to clutch at the prows.
Bodies thrown recklessly in the way are cut aside.
It is a sea of faces about them in agony, in despair

until the horror of the race dawns staggering the mind,
the whole sea become an entanglement of watery bodies
lost to the world bearing what they cannot hold. Broken,

beaten, desolate, reaching from the dead to be taken up
they cry out, failing, failing! their cries rising
in waves still as the skillful yachts pass over.

The Dance

In Brueghel's great picture, The Kermess,[1]
the dancers go round, they go round and
around, the squeal and the blare and the
tweedle of bagpipes, a bugle and fiddles
tipping their bellies (round as the thick-
sided glasses whose wash they impound)
their hips and their bellies off balance
to turn them. Kicking and rolling about
the Fair Grounds, swinging their butts, those
shanks must be sound to bear up under such
rollicking measures, prance as they dance
in Brueghel's great picture, The Kermess.

---

1   Pieter Brueghel the Elder (c.1520-1569), Flemish painter. A kermess was originally an outdoor church festival in the Low Countries, with much feasting, sports, and games.

Landscape With The Fall of Icarus[1]

According to Brueghel
when Icarus fell
it was spring

a farmer was ploughing
his field
the whole pageantry

of the year was
awake tingling
near

the edge of the sea
concerned
with itself

sweating in the sun
that melted
the wings' wax

unsignificantly
off the coast
there was

a splash quite unnoticed
this was
Icarus drowning

---

1   A painting by Pieter Brueghel the Elder (c.1520-1569). Wearing wings made by his father
Daedalus, Icarus flew too close to the sun; the wax on the wings melted, and Icarus fell
to his death.

D. H. Lawrence

(1885–1930)

Piano

Softly, in the dusk, a woman is singing to me;
Taking me back down the vista of years, till I see
A child sitting under the piano, in the boom of the tingling strings
And pressing the small, poised feet of a mother who smiles as she
      sings.

In spite of myself, the insidious mastery of song
Betrays me back, till the heart of me weeps to belong
To the old Sunday evenings at home, with winter outside
And hymns in the cozy parlour, the tinkling piano our guide.

So now it is vain for the singer to burst into clamour
With the great black piano appassionato. The glamour
Of childish days is upon me, my manhood is cast
Down in the flood of remembrance, I weep like a child for the past.

Snake

A snake came to my water-trough
On a hot, hot day, and I in pyjamas for the heat,
To drink there.

In the deep, strange-scented shade of the great dark carob tree
I came down the steps with my pitcher
And must wait, must stand and wait, for there he was at the trough
      before me.

He reached down from a fissure in the earth-wall in the gloom
And trailed his yellow-brown slackness soft-bellied down, over the edge
      of the stone trough
And rested his throat upon the stone bottom,
And where the water had dripped from the tap, in a small clearness,
He sipped with his straight mouth,
Softly drank through his straight gums, into his slack long body,
Silently.

Someone was before me at my water-trough,
And I, like a second comer, waiting.

He lifted his head from his drinking, as cattle do,
And looked at me vaguely, as drinking cattle do,
And flickered his two-forked tongue from his lips, and mused a moment,
And stooped and drank a little more,
Being earth-brown, earth-golden from the burning bowels of the earth
On the day of Sicilian July, with Etna smoking.

The voice of my education said to me
He must be killed,
For in Sicily the black, black snakes are innocent, the gold are venomous.

And voices in me said, if you were a man
You would take a stick and break him now, and finish him off.

But must I confess how I liked him,
How glad I was he had come like a guest in quiet, to drink at my
              water-trough
And depart peaceful, pacified, and thankless,
Into the burning bowels of this earth?

Was it cowardice, that I dared not kill him?
Was it perversity, that I longed to talk to him?
Was it humility, to feel so honoured?
I felt so honoured.

And yet those voices:
If you were not afraid, you would kill him!

And truly I was afraid, I was most afraid,
But even so, honoured still more
That he should seek my hospitality
From out the dark door of the secret earth.

He drank enough
And lifted his head, dreamily, as one who has drunken,
And flickered his tongue like a forked night on the air, so black,
Seeming to lick his lips,
And looking around like a god, unseeing, into the air,
And slowly turned his head,
And slowly, very slowly, as if thrice adream,
Proceeded to draw his slow length curving round
And climb again the broken bank of my wall-face.

And as he put his head into that dreadful hole,
And as he slowly drew up, snake-easing his shoulders, and entered farther,
A sort of horror, a sort of protest against his withdrawing into that
              horrid black hole,
Deliberately going into the blackness, and slowly drawing himself after,
Overcame me now his back was turned.
I looked round, I put down my pitcher,
I picked up a clumsy log
And threw it at the water-trough with a clatter.

I think I did not hit him,
But suddenly that part of him that was left behind convulsed in
              undignified haste,
Writhed like lightning, and was gone
Into the black hole, the earth-lipped fissure in the wall-front,

At which, in the intense still noon, I stared with fascination.

And immediately I regretted it.
I thought how paltry, how vulgar, what a mean act!
I despised myself and the voices of my accursed human education.

And I thought of the albatross,[1]
And I wished he would come back, my snake.

For he seemed to me again like a king,
Like a king in exile, uncrowned in the underworld,
Now due to be crowned again.

And so, I missed my chance with one of the lords
Of life.
And I have something to expiate;
A pettiness.

How Beastly the Bourgeois Is

How beastly the bourgeois is
especially the male of the species—

Presentable, eminently presentable—
shall I make you a present of him?

Isn't he handsome? isn't he healthy? isn't he a fine specimen?
doesn't he look the fresh clean englishman, outside?
Isn't it god's own image? tramping his thirty miles a day
after partridges, or a little rubber ball?
wouldn't you like to be like that, well off, and quite the thing?

Oh, but wait!
Let him meet a new emotion, let him be faced with another
        man's need,
let him come home to a bit of moral difficulty, let life face
        him with a new demand on his understanding
and then watch him go soggy, like a wet meringue.
Watch him turn into a mess; either a fool or a bully.
Just watch the display of him, confronted with a new demand
        on his intelligence,
a new life-demand.
How beastly the bourgeois is
especially the male of the species—

---

1   the bird slaughtered by the Ancient Mariner in Coleridge's *Rime of the Ancient Mariner*

Nicely groomed, like a mushroom
standing there so sleek and erect and eyeable—
and like a fungus, living on the remains of bygone life
sucking his life out of the dead leaves of greater life than his
      own.

And even so, he's stale, he's been there too long.
Touch him, and you'll find he's all gone inside
just like an old mushroom, all wormy inside, and hollow
under a smooth skin and an upright appearance.

Full of seething, wormy, hollow feelings
rather nasty—
How beastly the bourgeois is!

Standing in their thousands, these appearances, in damp Eng-
      land
what a pity they can't all be kicked over
like sickening toadstools, and left to melt back, swiftly
into the soil of England.

Bavarian Gentians

Not every man has gentians in his house
In soft September, at slow, sad Michaelmas.[1]

Bavarian gentians, big and dark, only dark
Darkening the day-time torch-like with the smoking blueness of
      Pluto's[2] gloom,
Ribbed and torch-like with their blaze of darkness spread blue
Down flattening into points, flattened under the sweep of white
      day
Torch-flower of the blue-smoking darkness, Pluto's dark-blue
      daze,
Black lamps from the halls of Dis, burning dark blue,
Giving off darkness, blue darkness, as Demeter's pale lamps give
      off light,
Lead me then, lead me the way.

Reach me a gentian, give me a torch
Let me guide myself with the blue, forked torch of this flower
Down the darker and darker stairs, where blue is darkened on
      blueness,

---

1   29 September
2   Pluto, also known as Dis, was the god of the underworld who abducted Persephone,
      daughter of the corn goddess Demeter. Persephone was allowed to return to earth each
      spring, but had to rejoin Pluto in Hades each autumn.

Even where Persephone goes, just now, from the frosted
        September
To the sightless realm where darkness is awake upon the dark
And Persephone herself is but a voice
Or a darkness invisible enfolded in the deeper dark
Of the arms Plutonic, and pierced with the passion of
        dense gloom,
Among the splendour of torches of darkness, shedding
        darkness on the lost bride and her groom.

After The Opera

Down the stone stairs
Girls with their large eyes wide with tragedy
Lift looks of shocked and momentous emotion up at me.
And I smile.

Ladies
Stepping like birds with their bright and pointed feet
Peer anxiously forth, as if for a boat to carry them out of the
        wreckage;
And among the wreck of the theatre crowd
I stand and smile.
They take tragedy so becomingly;
Which pleases me.

But when I meet the weary eyes
The reddened, aching eyes of the bar-man with thin arms,
I am glad to go back to where I came from.

The Ship of Death[1]

I

Now it is autumn and the falling fruit
and the long journey towards oblivion.

The apples falling like great drops of dew
to bruise themselves an exit from themselves.

And it is time to go, to bid farewell
to one's own self, and find an exit
from the fallen self.

---

1   In *Etruscan Places,* Lawrence describes the Etruscan tombs in which would be laid little
bronze ships to bear the souls of the dead over to the other world.

II

Have you built your ship of death, O have you?
O build your ship of death, for you will need it.

The grim forest is at hand, when the apples will fall
thick, almost thundrous, on the hardened earth.

And death is on the air like a smell of ashes!
Ah! can't you smell it?
And in the bruised body, the frightened soul
finds itself shrinking, wincing from the cold
that blows upon it through the orifices.

III

And can a man his own quietus make
with a bare bodkin?[1]

With daggers, bodkins, bullets, man can make
a bruise or break of exit for his life;
but is that a quietus, O tell me, is it quietus?

Surely not so! for how could murder, even self-murder
ever a quietus make?

IV

O let us talk of quiet that we know,
that we can know, the deep and lovely quiet
of a strong heart at peace!

How can we this, our own quietus, make?

V

Build then the ship of death, for you must take
the longest journey, to oblivion.

And die the death, the long and painful death
that lies between the old self and the new.

Already our bodies are fallen, bruised, badly bruised,
already our souls are oozing through the exit
of the cruel bruise.

---

1   See *Hamlet* III. i. 75-76

Already the dark and endless ocean of the end
is washing in through the breaches of our wounds,
already the flood is upon us.

O build your ship of death, your little ark
and furnish it with food, with little cakes, and wine
for the dark flight down oblivion.

VI

Piecemeal the body dies, and the timid soul
has her footing washed away, as the dark flood rises.

We are dying, we are dying, we are all of us dying
and nothing will stay the death-flood rising within us
and soon it will rise on the world, on the outside world.

We are dying, we are dying, piecemeal our bodies are dying
and our strength leaves us,
and our soul cowers naked in the dark rain over the flood,
cowering in the last branches of the tree of our life.

VII

We are dying, we are dying, so all we can do
is now to be willing to die, and to build the ship
of death to carry the soul on the longest journey.

A little ship, with oars and food
and little dishes, and all accoutrements
fitting and ready for the departing soul.

Now launch the small ship, now as the body dies
and life departs, launch out, the fragile soul
in the fragile ship of courage, the ark of faith
with its store of food and little cooking pans
and change of clothes,
upon the flood's black waste
upon the waters of the end
upon the sea of death, where still we sail
darkly, for we cannot steer, and have no port.

There is no port, there is nowhere to go
only the deepening blackness darkening still
blacker upon the soundless, ungurgling flood
darkness at one with darkness, up and down
and sideways utterly dark, so there is no direction any more
and the little ship is there; yet she is gone.
She is not seen, for there is nothing to see her by.
She is gone! gone! and yet

somewhere she is there.
Nowhere!

VIII

And everything is gone, the body is gone
completely under, gone, entirely gone.
The upper darkness is heavy as the lower,
between them the little ship
is gone

It is the end, it is oblivion.

IX

And yet out of eternity a thread
separates itself on the blackness,
a horizontal thread
that fumes a little with pallor upon the dark.

Is it illusion? or does the pallor fume
a little higher?
Ah wait, wait, for there's the dawn,
the cruel dawn of coming back to life
out of oblivion.

Wait, wait, the little ship
drifting, beneath the deathly ashy grey
of a flood-dawn.

Wait, wait! even so, a flush of yellow
and strangely, O chilled wan soul, a flush of rose.

A flush of rose, and the whole thing starts again.

X

The flood subsides, and the body, like a worn sea-shell
emerges strange and lovely.
And the little ship wings home, faltering and lapsing
on the pink flood,
and the frail soul steps out, into the house again
filling the heart with peace.

Swings the heart renewed with peace
even of oblivion.

Oh build your ship of death. Oh build it!
for you will need it.
For the voyage of oblivion awaits you.

Ezra Pound

(1885-1972)

Portrait d'une Femme

Your mind and you are our Sargasso Sea,[1]
London has swept about you this score years
And bright ships left you this or that in fee:
Ideas, old gossip, oddments of all things,
Strange spars of knowledge and dimmed wares of price.
Great minds have sought you—lacking someone else.
You have been second always. Tragical?
No. You preferred it to the usual thing:
One dull man, dulling and uxorious,
One average mind—with one thought less, each year.
Oh, you are patient, I have seen you sit
Hours, where something might have floated up.
And now you pay one. Yes, you richly pay.
You are a person of some interest, one comes to you
And takes strange gain away:
Trophies fished up; some curious suggestion;
Fact that leads nowhere; and a tale or two,
Pregnant with mandrakes,[2] or with something else
That might prove useful and yet never proves,
That never fits a corner or shows use,
Or finds its hour upon the loom of days:
The tarnished, gaudy, wonderful old work;
Idols and ambergris and rare inlays,
These are your riches, your great store; and yet
For all this sea-hoard of deciduous things,
Strange woods half sodden, and new brighter stuff:
In the slow float of different light and deep,
No! there is nothing! In the whole and all,
Nothing that's quite your own.
      Yet this is you.

The River-Merchant's Wife: A Letter[3]

While my hair was still cut straight across my forehead
I played about the front gate, pulling flowers.
You came by on bamboo stilts, playing horse,
You walked about my seat, playing with blue plums.
And we went on living in the village of Chōkan:

---

1   a part of the North Atlantic known for its calm waters and its masses of floating seaweed
2   a plant of the nightshade family with narcotic properties, supposed to give a cry when
     pulled out
3   Pound's adaptation of a poem by the Chinese poet Li Po (701-62), whose name is given
     in its Japanese form ("Rihaku") at the end of the poem

Two small people, without dislike or suspicion.

At fourteen I married My Lord you.
I never laughed, being bashful.
Lowering my head, I looked at the wall.
Called to, a thousand times, I never looked back.

At fifteen I stopped scowling,
I desired my dust to be mingled with yours
Forever and forever and forever.
Why should I climb the look out?

At sixteen you departed,
You went into far Ku-tō-en, by the river of swirling eddies,
And you have been gone five months.
The monkeys make sorrowful noise overhead.

You dragged your feet when you went out.
By the gate now, the moss is grown, the different mosses,
Too deep to clear them away!
The leaves fall early this autumn, in wind.
The paired butterflies are already yellow with August
Over the grass in the West garden;
They hurt me. I grow older.
If you are coming down through the narrows of the river Kiang,
Please let me know beforehand,
And I will come out to meet you
            As far as Chō-fū-Sā.

                                                    Rihaku

In a Station of the Metro

The apparition of these faces in the crowd;
Petals on a wet, black bough.

Commission

Go, my songs, to the lonely and the unsatisfied,
Go also to the nerve-racked, go to the enslaved-by-
            convention,
Bear to them my contempt for their oppressors.
Go as a great wave of cool water,
Bear my contempt of oppressors.

Speak against unconscious oppression,
Speak against the tyranny of the unimaginative,
Speak against bonds.
Go to the bourgeoise who is dying of her ennuis,
Go to the women in suburbs.

Go to the hideously wedded,
Go to them whose failure is concealed,
Go to the unluckily mated,
Go to the bought wife,
Go to the woman entailed.

Go to those who have delicate lust,
Go to those whose delicate desires are thwarted,
Go like a blight upon the dulness of the world;
Go with your edge against this,
Strengthen the subtle cords,
Bring confidence upon the algae and the tentacles of the soul.

Go in a friendly manner,
Go with an open speech.
Be eager to find new evils and new good,
Be against all forms of oppression.
Go to those who are thickened with middle age,
To those who have lost interest.

Go to the adolescent who are smothered in family—
Oh how hideous it is
To see three generations of one house gathered together!
It is like an old tree with shoots,
And with some branches rotted and falling.
Go out and defy opinion,
Go against this vegetable bondage of the blood.
Be against all sorts of mortmain.

The Garden

En robe de parade.[1]
Samain

Like a skein of loose silk blown against a wall
She walks by the railing of a path in Kensington Gardens,[2]
And she is dying piece-meal
    of a sort of emotional anaemia.

And round about there is a rabble
Of the filthy, sturdy, unkillable infants of the very poor.
They shall inherit the earth.

In her is the end of breeding.

---

1   "In court attire; dressed for a state occasion." The phrase is taken from a poem by the French poet Albert Samain (1858-1900).
2   a public garden in London, close to Hyde Park and Kensington Palace

Her boredom is exquisite and excessive.
She would like some one to speak to her,
And is almost afraid that I
    will commit that indiscretion.

Canto I[1]

And then went down to the ship,
Set keel to breakers, forth on the godly sea, and
We set up mast and sail on that swart ship,
Bore sheep aboard her, and our bodies also
Heavy with weeping, and winds from sternward
Bore us out onward with bellying canvas,
Circe's[2] this craft, the trim-coifed goddess.
Then sat we amidships, wind jamming the tiller,
Thus with stretched sail, we went over sea till day's end.
Sun to his slumber, shadows o'er all the ocean,
Came we then to the bounds of deepest water,
To the Kimmerian[3] lands, and peopled cities
Covered with close-webbed mist, unpierced ever
With glitter of sun-rays
Nor with stars stretched, nor looking back from heaven
Swartest night stretched over wretched men there.
The ocean flowing backward, came we then to the place
Aforesaid by Circe.
Here did they rites, Perimedes and Eurylochus,[4]
And drawing sword from my hip
I dug the ell-square pitkin;[5]
Poured we libations unto each the dead,
First mead and then sweet wine, water mixed with white flour.
Then prayed I many a prayer to the sickly death's-heads;
As set in Ithaca, sterile bulls of the best
For sacrifice, heaping the pyre with goods,
A sheep to Tiresias only, black and a bell-sheep.[6]
Dark blood flowed in the fosse,[7]
Souls out of Erebus,[8] cadaverous dead, of brides
Of youths and of the old who had borne much;
Souls stained with recent tears, girls tender,
Men many, mauled with bronze lance heads,

---

1   an adaptation, based on a sixteenth-century Latin translation, of Book XI of Homer's
    Odyssey, which describes Odysseus's visit to the underworld
2   Circe was the island enchantress on whose advice Odysseus went to Hades in search of
    the prophet Tiresias.
3   The Cimmerians lived in a land of mist and darkness on the edge of the known world.
4   two of Odysseus's companions
5   a small pit, one "ell" (45 inches) on each side
6   the sheep that leads the flock
7   trench
8   Hades, land of the dead

Battle spoil, bearing yet dreory[1] arms,
These many crowded about me; with shouting,
Pallor upon me, cried to my men for more beasts;
Slaughtered the herds, sheep slain of bronze;
Poured ointment, cried to the gods,
To Pluto the strong, and praised Proserpine;[2]
Unsheathed the narrow sword,
I sat to keep off the impetuous impotent dead,
Till I should hear Tiresias.
But first Elpenor[3] came, our friend Elpenor,
Unburied, cast on the wide earth,
Limbs that we left in the house of Circe,
Unwept, unwrapped in sepulchre, since toils urged other.
Pitiful spirit. And I cried in hurried speech:
"Elpenor, how art thou come to this dark coast?
Cam'st thou afoot, outstripping seamen?"

      And he in heavy speech:
"Ill fate and abundant wine. I slept in Circe's ingle.[4]
Going down the long ladder unguarded,
I fell against the buttress,
Shattered the nape-nerve, the soul sought Avernus.[5]
But thou, O King, I bid remember me, unwept, unburied,
Heap up mine arms, be tomb by sea-bord, and inscribed:
A man of no fortune, and with a name to come.
And set my oar up, that I swung mid fellows."

And Anticlea[6] came, whom I beat off, and then Tiresias Theban,
Holding his golden wand, knew me, and spoke first:
"A second time?[7] why? man of ill star,
Facing the sunless dead and this joyless region?
Stand from the fosse, leave me my bloody bever[8]
For soothsay."
      And I stepped back,
And he strong with the blood, said then: "Odysseus
Shalt return through spiteful Neptune,[9] over dark seas,
Lose all companions." And then Anticlea came.

---

1   bloody (Old English "dreor," gore)
2   the god of the underworld, and his queen, the daughter of Demeter
3   a companion of Odysseus who had died on Circe's island and had been left unburied
4   a fire, or open hearth
5   a lake near Naples, believed to be the entrance to Hades
6   Odysseus's mother
7   An error in Pound's source: in fact, Odysseus had not been to the underworld, or met
    Tiresias, before.
8   drink; the libation of blood brought by Odysseus
9   god of the sea, who would raise a storm to delay Odysseus's passage

Lie quiet Divus. I mean, that is Andreas Divus,[1]
In officina Wecheli, 1538, out of Homer.
And he sailed, by Sirens[2] and thence outward and away
And unto Circe.
        Venerandam,[3]
In the Cretan's phrase, with the golden crown, Aphrodite,
Cypri munimenta sortita est,[4] mirthful, oricalchi, with golden
Girdles and breast bands, thou with dark eyelids
Bearing the golden bough of Argicida.[5] So that:

---

1   the Italian translator, who had produced the translation used by Pound "in the workshop
    of [Chretien] Wechel, 1538"
2   the sea-nymphs who sought to lure Odysseus and his companions to their doom by
    singing to them
3   "Worthy of worship," a phrase applied to Aphrodite, goddess of love, by Georgius Dartona
    Cretensis, in his translation of one of the Homeric hymns contained in the same volume
    as Divus' translation of Homer.
4   "The fortifications of Cyprus she obtained as her realm," from another of the Homeric
    hymns translated by Georgius Dartona Cretensis. From the same source comes "oricalchi",
    meaning of brass or copper.
5   This may refer to the wand of Hermes, slayer of the many-eyed herdsman Argus. However,
    some editors read "Argicida" to mean "slayer of the Argi," an epithet that might be
    applied to Aphrodite as one who slew Greeks in the Trojan War.

Siegfried Sassoon

(1886–1967)

A Night Attack

The rank stench of those bodies haunts me still,
And I remember things I'd best forget.
For now we've marched to a green, trenchless land
Twelve miles from battering guns: along the grass
Brown lines of tents are hives for snoring men;
Wide, radiant water sways the floating sky
Below dark, shivering trees. And living-clean
Comes back with thoughts of home and hours of sleep.

To-night I smell the battle; miles away
Gun-thunder leaps and thuds along the ridge;
The spouting shells dig pits in fields of death,
And wounded men are moaning in the woods.
If any friend be there whom I have loved,
God speed him safe to England with a gash.

It's sundown in the camp; some youngster laughs,
Lifting his mug and drinking health to all
Who come unscathed from that unpitying waste.
(Terror and ruin lurk behind his gaze.)
Another sits with tranquil, musing face,
Puffing his pipe and dreaming of the girl
Whose last scrawled letter lies upon his knee.
The sunlight falls, low-ruddy from the west,
Upon their heads; last week they might have died;
And now they stretch their limbs in tired content.

One says "The bloody Bosche¹ has got the knock;
And soon they'll crumple up and chuck their games.
We've got the beggars on the run at last!"
Then I remembered someone that I'd seen
Dead in a squalid, miserable ditch,
Heedless of toiling feet that trod him down.
He was a Prussian with a decent face,
Young, fresh, and pleasant, so I dare to say.
No doubt he loathed the war and longed for peace,
And cursed our souls because we'd killed his friends.

One night he yawned along a half-dug trench
Midnight; and then the British guns began
With heavy shrapnel bursting low, and "hows"²
Whistling to cut the wire with blinding din.

---

1   the name given by the French to German soldiers
2   howitzer shells

He didn't move; the digging still went on;
Men stooped and shovelled; someone gave a grunt,
And moaned and died with agony in the sludge.
Then the long hiss of shells lifted and stopped.

He stared into the gloom; a rocket curved,
And rifles rattled angrily on the left
Down by the wood, and there was noise of bombs.
Then the damned English loomed in scrambling haste
Out of the dark and struggled through the wire,
And there were shouts and curses; someone screamed
And men began to blunder down the trench
Without their rifles. It was time to go:
He grabbed his coat; stood up, gulping some bread;
Then clutched his head and fell.
                              I found him there
In the gray morning when the place was held.
His face was in the mud; one arm flung out
As when he crumpled up; his sturdy legs
Were bent beneath his trunk; heels to the sky.

Conscripts

'Fall in, that awkward squad,[1] and strike no more
Attractive attitudes! Dress by the right!
The luminous rich colours that you wore
Have changed to hueless khaki in the night.
Magic? What's magic got to do with you?
There's no such thing! Blood's red, and skies are blue.'

They gasped and sweated, marching up and down.
I drilled them till they cursed my raucous shout.
Love chucked his lute away and dropped his crown.
Rhyme got sore heels and wanted to fall out.
'Left, right! Press on your butts!' They looked at me
Reproachful; how I longed to set them free!

I gave them lectures on Defence, Attack;
They fidgeted and shuffled, yawned and sighed,
And boggled at my questions. Joy was slack,
And Wisdom gnawed his fingers, gloomy-eyed.
Young Fancy—how I loved him all the while—
Stared at his note-book with a rueful smile.

---

1   a military term for a group of recruits at drill

Their training done, I shipped them all to France,
Where most of those I'd loved too well got killed.
Rapture and pale Enchantment and Romance,
And many a sickly, slender lord who'd filled
My soul long since with lutanies[1] of sin,
Went home, because they couldn't stand the din.

But the kind, common ones that I despised
(Hardly a man of them I'd count as friend),
What stubborn-hearted virtues they disguised!
They stood and played the hero to the end,
Won gold and silver medals bright with bars,
And marched resplendent home with crowns and stars.

Base Details

If I were fierce, and bald, and short of breath,
    I'd live with scarlet Majors at the Base,
And speed glum heroes up the line to death.
    You'd see me with my puffy petulant face,
Guzzling and gulping in the best hotel,
    Reading the Roll of Honour. 'Poor young chap,'
I'd say—'I used to know his father well;
    Yes, we've lost heavily in this last scrap.'
And when the war is done and youth stone dead,
    I'd toddle safely home and die—in bed.

---

1   lute music; with a play on "litanies"

H. D. (Hilda Doolittle)

(1886–1961)

Oread[1]

Whirl up, sea—
whirl your pointed pines,
splash your great pines
on our rocks,
hurl your green over us,
cover us with your pools of fir.

Leda

Where the slow river
meets the tide,
a red swan lifts red wings
and darker beak,
and underneath the purple down
of his soft breast
uncurls his coral feet.

Through the deep purple
of the dying heat
of sun and mist,
the level ray of sun-beam
has caressed
the lily with dark breast,
and flecked with richer gold
its golden crest.

Where the slow lifting
of the tide,
floats into the river
and slowly drifts
among the reeds,
and lifts the yellow flags,
he floats
where tide and river meet.

Ah kingly kiss—
no more regret
nor old deep memories
to mar the bliss;
where the low sedge is thick,
the gold day-lily

---

1   a mountain nymph

outspreads and rests
beneath soft fluttering
of red swan wings
and the warm quivering
of the red swan's breast.

Helen

All Greece hates
the still eyes in the white face,
the lustre as of olives
where she stands,
and the white hands.

All Greece reviles
the wan face when she smiles,
hating it deeper still
when it grows wan and white,
remembering past enchantments
and past ills.

Greece sees unmoved,
God's daughter,[1] born of love,
the beauty of cool feet
and slenderest knees,
could love indeed the maid,
only if she were laid,
white ash amid funereal cypresses.

---

1   Helen was the daughter of Leda and Zeus (see Yeats's poem "Leda and the Swan").
Married to Menelaus, King of Sparta, she was carried off by Paris to Troy. Her abduction
led to the Trojan War; after the fall of Troy, she returned with her husband to Sparta.

Fragment Thirty-six

I know not what to do:
my mind is divided.—SAPPHO.[1]

I know not what to do,
my mind is reft:
is song's gift best?
is love's gift loveliest?
I know not what to do,
now sleep has pressed
weight on your eyelids.

Shall I break your rest,
devouring, eager?
is love's gift best?
nay, song's the loveliest:
yet were you lost,
what rapture
could I take from song?
what song were left?
I know not what to do:
to turn and slake
the rage that burns,
with my breath burn
and trouble your cool breath?
so shall I turn and take
snow in my arms?
(is love's gift best?)
yet flake on flake
of snow were comfortless,
did you lie wondering,
wakened yet unawake.

Shall I turn and take
comfortless snow within my arms?
press lips to lips
that answer not,
press lips to flesh
that shudders not nor breaks?

Is love's gift best?
shall I turn and slake
all the wild longing?
O I am eager for you!
as the Pleiads[2] shake

---

1   Greek poet born on the island of Lesbos in the seventh century B.C.; only fragments of her work remain.

white light in whiter water
so shall I take you?

My mind is quite divided,
my minds hesitate,
so perfect matched,
I know not what to do:
each strives with each
as two white wrestlers
standing for a match,
ready to turn and clutch
yet never shake muscle nor nerve nor tendon;
so my mind waits
to grapple with my mind,
yet I lie quiet,
I would seem at rest.

I know not what to do:
strain upon strain,
sound surging upon sound
makes my brain blind;
as a wave-line may wait to fall
yet (waiting for its falling)
still the wind may take
from off its crest,
white flake on flake of foam,
that rises,
seeming to dart and pulse
and rend the light,
so my mind hesitates
above the passion
quivering yet to break,
so my mind hesitates
above my mind,
listening to song's delight.

I know not what to do:
will the sound break,
rending the night
with rift on rift of rose
and scattered light?

will the sound break at last
as the wave hesitant,
or will the whole night pass
and I lie listening awake?

---

2   The Pleiades are a group of stars in the constellation Taurus.

Fragment Forty

Love . . . bitter-sweet.—SAPPHO.

1

Keep love and he wings,
with his bow,[1]
up, mocking us,
keep love and he taunts us
and escapes.

Keep love and he sways apart
in another world,
outdistancing us.

Keep love and he mocks,
ah, bitter and sweet,
your sweetness is more cruel
than your hurt.

Honey and salt,
fire burst from the rocks
to meet fire
spilt from Hesperus.

Fire darted aloft and met fire:
in that moment
love entered us.

2

Could Eros be kept?
he were prisoned long since
and sick with imprisonment;
could Eros be kept?
others would have broken
and crushed out his life.
Could Eros be kept?
we too sinning, by Kypris,[2]
might have prisoned him outright.

Could Eros be kept?
nay, thank him and the bright goddess
that he left us.

---

1   Eros, the son of Aphrodite, is traditionally represented as a winged archer.
2   Cyprus

3

Ah, love is bitter and sweet,
but which is more sweet,
the sweetness
or the bitterness?
none has spoken it.

Love is bitter,
but can salt taint sea-flowers,
grief, happiness?

Is it bitter to give back
love to your lover
if he crave it?

Is it bitter to give back
love to your lover
if he wish it
for a new favourite?
who can say,
or is it sweet?

Is it sweet
to possess utterly?
or is it bitter,
bitter as ash?

4

I had thought myself frail;
a petal,
with light equal
on leaf and under-leaf.

I had thought myself frail;
a lamp,
shell, ivory or crust of pearl,
about to fall shattered,
with flame spent.

I cried:
"I must perish,
I am deserted,
an outcast, desperate
in this darkness,"

(such fire rent me with Hesperus,[1])
then the day broke.

5

What need of a lamp
when day lightens us,
what need to bind love
when love stands
with such radiant wings
over us?

What need—
yet to sing love,
love must first shatter us.

---

1   the evening star, the planet Venus

Marianne Moore

(1887–1972)

Poetry

I, too, dislike it: there are things that are important beyond all this fiddle.
  Reading it, however, with a perfect contempt for it, one discovers in
  it after all, a place for the genuine.
      Hands that can grasp, eyes
      that can dilate, hair that can rise
        if it must, these things are important not because a

high-sounding interpretation can be put upon them but because they are
  useful. When they become so derivative as to become unintelligible,
  the same thing may be said for all of us, that we
      do not admire what
      we cannot understand: the bat
        holding on upside down or in quest of something to

eat, elephants pushing, a wild horse taking a roll, a tireless wolf under
  a tree, the immovable critic twitching his skin like a horse that feels
        a flea, the base-
  ball fan, the statistician—
      nor is it valid
        to discriminate against "business documents and

schoolbooks";[1] all these phenomena are important. One must make a
        distinction
  however: when dragged into prominence by half poets, the result is
        not poetry,
  nor till the poets among us can be
    "literalists of
    the imagination"[2]—above
      insolence and triviality and can present

for inspection, "imaginary gardens with real toads in them," shall we have
  it. In the meantime, if you demand on the one hand,
  the raw material of poetry in
      all its rawness and
      that which is on the other hand
        genuine, then you are interested in poetry.

---

1   Moore's note quotes from the *Diaries of Tolstoy* (1917), in which Tolstoy considers the
     boundary between poetry and prose: "Poetry is verse: prose is not verse. Or else poetry is
     everything with the exception of business documents and school books."
2   In *Ideas of Good and Evil* (1903), W. B. Yeats had called Blake "a too literal realist of
     imagination as others are of nature."

Poetry *(Revised version)*

I, too, dislike it.
   Reading it, however, with a perfect contempt for it, one dis-
      covers in
   it, after all, a place for the genuine.

The Fish

   wade
   through black jade.
      Of the crow-blue mussel shells, one keeps
      adjusting the ash heaps;
         opening and shutting itself like

   an
   injured fan.
      The barnacles which encrust the side
      of the wave, cannot hide
         there for the submerged shafts of the

   sun,
   split like spun
      glass, move themselves with spotlight swiftness
      into the crevices—
         in and out, illuminating

   the
   turquoise sea
      of bodies. The water drives a wedge
      of iron through the iron edge
         of the cliff; whereupon the stars,

   pink
   rice-grains, ink-
      bespattered jellyfish, crabs like green
      lilies, and submarine
         toadstools, slide each on the other.

   All
   external
      marks of abuse are present on this
      defiant edifice—
         all the physical features of

ac-
cident—lack
     of cornice, dynamite grooves, burns, and
     hatchet strokes, these things stand
          out on it; the chasm side is

dead.
Repeated
     evidence has proved that it can live
     on what can not revive
          its youth. The sea grows old in it.

Critics and Connoisseurs

There is a great amount of poetry in unconscious
     fastidiousness. Certain Ming
          products, imperial floor coverings of coach-
     wheel yellow, are well enough in their way but I have seen
                                                            something
               that I like better—a
          mere childish attempt to make an imperfectly bal-
          lasted animal stand up,
               similar determination to make a pup
                    eat his meat from the plate.

I remember a swan under the willows in Oxford,
     with flamingo-colored, maple-
          leaflike feet. It reconnoitered like a battle-
     ship. Disbelief and conscious fastidiousness were
          ingredients in its
               disinclination to move. Finally its hardihood was
                    not proof against its
               proclivity to more fully appraise such bits
                    of food as the stream

bore counter to it; it made away with what I gave it
     to eat. I have seen this swan and
          I have seen you; I have seen ambition without
     understanding in a variety of forms. Happening to stand
               by an ant-hill, I have
                    seen a fastidious ant carrying a stick north, south,
                         east, west, till it turned on
                    itself, struck out from the flower-bed into the lawn,
                         and returned to the point

from which it had started. Then abandoning the stick as
  useless and overtaxing its
    jaws with a particle of whitewash—pill-like but
heavy, it again went through the same course of procedure.
      What is
    there in being able
      to say that one has dominated the stream in an attitude
            of self-defense;
      in proving that one has had the experience
        of carrying a stick?

No Swan So Fine

"No water so still as the
    dead fountains of Versailles.[1]" No swan,
with swart blind look askance
and gondoliering legs, so fine
    as the chintz china one with fawn-
brown eyes and toothed gold
collar on to show whose bird it was.

Lodged in the Louis Fifteenth
    candelabrum-tree[2] of cockscomb-
tinted[3] buttons, dahlias,
sea urchins, and everlastings,[4]
    it perches on the branching foam
of polished sculptured
flowers—at ease and tall. The king is dead.

---

1   The palace of the French king Louis XIV, near Paris. The phrase cited by Moore comes from
     an article by Percy Philips in the *New York Times Magazine*, 10 May 1931.
2   The reference is to "A pair of Louis XV candelabra with Dresden figures of swans belonging
     to Lord Balfour" (Moore's note).
3   Coxcombs are plants with bright red or yellow flowers.
4   plants of the aster family, whose flowers keep their form and colour when dried

Edith Sitwell

(1887–1964)

The Swans

In the green light of water, like the day
Under green boughs, the spray
And air-pale petals of the foam seem flowers,—
Dark-leaved arbutus blooms with wax-pale bells
And their faint honey-smells,
The velvety syringa with smooth leaves,
Gloxinia with a green shade in the snow,
Jasmine and moon-clear orange-blossoms and green
     blooms
Of the wild strawberries from the shade of woods.
Their showers
Pelt the white women under the green trees,
Venusia, Cosmopolita, Pistillarine—
White solar statues, white rose-trees in snow
Flowering for ever, child-women, half stars
Half flowers, waves of the sea, born of a dream.

Their laughter flying through the trees like doves,
These angels come to watch their whiter ghosts
In the air-pale water, archipelagos
Of stars and young thin moons from great wings falling
As ripples widen.
These are their ghosts, their own white angels these!
O great wings spreading—
Your bones are made of amber, smooth and thin
Grown from the amber dust that was a rose
Or nymph in swan-smooth waters.
                But Time's winter falls
With snows as soft, as soundless. . . . Then, who knows
Rose-footed swan from snow, or girl from rose?

Still Falls the Rain

The Raids, 1940. Night and Dawn[1]

Still falls the Rain—
Dark as the world of man, black as our loss—
Blind as the nineteen hundred and forty nails
Upon the Cross.

Still falls the Rain

---

1   The raids on Britain by German bombers began in earnest in September 1940.

With a sound like the pulse of the heart that is changed to
      the hammer-beat
In the Potter's Field,[1] and the sound of the impious feet

On the Tomb:
          Still falls the Rain
In the Field of Blood where the small hopes breed and
      the human brain
Nurtures its greed, that worm with the brow of Cain.[2]

Still falls the Rain
At the feet of the Starved Man hung upon the Cross.
Christ that each day, each night, nails there, have mercy
      on us—
On Dives and on Lazarus[3]:
Under the Rain the sore and the gold are as one.

Still falls the Rain—
Still falls the Blood from the Starved Man's wounded Side:
He bears in His Heart all wounds,—those of the light
      that died,
The last faint spark
In the self-murdered heart, the wounds of the sad un-
    comprehending dark,
The wounds of the baited bear,—
The blind and weeping bear whom the keepers beat
On his helpless flesh . . . the tears of the hunted hare.

Still falls the Rain—
Then—O Ile leape up to my God: who pulles me
      doune—[4]
See, see where Christ's blood streames in the firmament:
It flows from the Brow we nailed upon the tree
Deep to the dying, to the thirsting heart
That holds the fires of the world,—dark-smirched with
      pain
As Caesar's laurel crown.

Then sounds the voice of One who like the heart of man
Was once a child who among beasts has lain—
'Still do I love, still shed my innocent light, my Blood,
      for thee.'

---

1   When Judas repented his betrayal of Christ, he returned the 30 pieces of silver he had
      been given; the chief priests then used the money to buy a potter's field to bury strangers
      in, "Wherefore that field was called, The field of blood, unto this day" (Matthew 27.3-8).
2   the first murderer
3   the parable of the rich man and the beggar, told in Luke 16.19-31
4   the words of Faustus when he realizes that he must finally be damned, in Christopher
      Marlowe's play *The Tragical History of Doctor Faustus* (1604)

Two Songs of Queen Anne Boleyn

To Natalie Payley

I

The King of Nowhere said to me,
Nodding his wintry crown
That seemed an ass's crown of ears
Or a broken town,

'Young girl, your love begs, "Give to me
Your body, for your soul
Is only an illusion." But,'
Said the winter air
(The aged King of Nowhere),

'You must lay your body by,
As other women may lay bare
Their bodies to the foolish air
That they call "Love"; Nowhere, alone,
Shall then be Lovers' Town;

Though you have little shelter there
From Truth that is the winter air,
Yet you will share my crown.'
That old King grey as olive-trees
Sighed in the withering winter wind.

'If,' said the nodding King of Nothing,
'Your body be the stepping-stone
For your love's path to Heaven from Hell,
Young girl, you must beware.

For stone when fretted upon stone
In the body's death-ghosted despair
May breed the all-devouring fire—
The lovers' Judgment-noon.

Then the heart that was the Burning-Bush
May change to a Nessus-robe of flame
That wraps not only its true love
But all the gibbering ghosts that came.
That flame then dies to a winter candle,
Lightless, guttering down.
And the soul that was the root of Being
Changes to Nothing-town.'

II

At Cockcrow

As I lay in my love's low bed
That is the primal clay
From which the night and day arise,
My love said, 'It is day.

That red glare on the window-panes
Is from the rising sun. . . .
Fear not it is the Judgment Day
Or Blood from the Crucified's Veins.

Shall I not feel your kiss again—
Its red light on my brow?'
'I only know that kiss will change
Into the brand of Cain.'

I sleepy sighed, 'What is that sound?'
'The world turns in its sleep
From good to ill, from ill to good
On what was once God's ground.'

You'll hear my bone clack on your heart—
Your heart clack on my bone.
That sound once seemed the first sunrise:
Now I must sleep alone.

The cock crowed thrice[1] and men arise
To earn two pence or thirty pence[2]
That on the last day nothing buys
Excepting dark for the Dead,

Weighing their eyelids down. . . . But I
Must have a dark more deep—
Lest when I hear the cock crow thrice
I turn like the world in my sleep

And know that red blare (three cock-cries)
Heralds the lovers' dawn—
The first kiss and last sound we hear
When we (alone) lie on the bier
With the two pence and the thirty pence
And the sins of the world on our eyes.

---

1   On the night of his betrayal, Jesus told Peter that "this night before the cock crow, thou
     shalt deny me thrice" (Matthew 26.34).
2   Judas received 30 pieces of silver for his betrayal of Christ (Matthew 26.15).

The Poet Laments the Coming of Old Age

I see the children running out of school;
They are taught that Goodness means a blinding hood
Or is heaped by Time like the hump on an agèd back,
And that Evil can be cast like an old rag
And Wisdom caught like a hare and held in the golden
    sack
Of the heart. . . . But I am one who must bring back
    sight to the blind.

Yet there was a planet dancing in my mind
With a gold seed of Folly . . . long ago . . . .
And where is that grain of Folly? . . . with the hare-
    wild wind
Of my spring it has gone from one who must bring back
    sight to the blind.

For I, the fool, was once like the philosopher
Sun who laughs at evil and at good:
I saw great things mirrored in littleness,
Who now see only that great Venus wears Time's filthy
    dress—
A toothless crone who once had the Lion's mouth.

The Gold Appearances from Nothing[1] rise
In sleep, by day . . . two thousand years ago
There was a man who had the Lion's leap,
Like the Sun's, to take the worlds and loves he would,
But (laughed the philosopher Sun, and I, the fool)

Great golden Alexander[2] and his thunder-store
Are now no more
Than the armoured knight who buzzed on the window-
    pane
And the first drops of rain.

He lies in sleep. . . . But still beneath a thatch
Of hair like sunburnt grass, the thieving sweet thoughts
    move
Toward the honey-hive. . . . And another sweet-tooth
    Alexander runs
Out of the giant shade that is his school,
To take the dark knight's world, the honeycomb.

---

1   a reference to a passage in Plato's dialogue "The Sophists" which considers the difference
    between a thing's name and its existence
2   Alexander the Great (356-323 B.C.)

The Sun's simulacrum, the gold-sinewed man
Lies under a hump of grass, as once I thought to wear
With patience, Goodness like a hump on my agèd back.
. . . But Goodness grew not with age, although my heart
     must bear
The weight of all Time's filth, and Wisdom is not a hare
     in the golden sack

Of the heart . . . . It can never be caught. Though I
     bring back sight to the blind
My seed of Folly has gone, that could teach me to bear
That the gold-sinewed body that had the blood of all the
     earth in its veins
Has changed to an old rag of the outworn world
And the great heart that the first Morning made
Should wear all Time's destruction for a dress.

John Crowe Ransom

(1888–1974)

Bells for John Whiteside's Daughter

There was such speed in her little body,
And such lightness in her footfall,
It is no wonder her brown study[1]
Astonishes us all.

Her wars were bruited in our high window.
We looked among orchard trees and beyond,
Where she took arms against her shadow,
Or harried unto the pond

The lazy geese, like a snow cloud
Dripping their snow on the green grass,
Tricking and stopping, sleepy and proud,
Who cried in goose, Alas,

For the tireless heart within the little
Lady with rod that made them rise
From their noon apple-dreams and scuttle
Goose-fashion under the skies!

But now go the bells, and we are ready,
In one house we are sternly stopped
To say we are vexed at her brown study,
Lying so primly propped.

Blue Girls

Twirling your blue skirts, travelling the sward
Under the towers of your seminary,
Go listen to your teachers old and contrary
Without believing a word.

Tie the white fillets then about your hair
And think no more of what will come to pass
Than bluebirds that go walking on the grass
And chattering on the air.

Practise your beauty, blue girls, before it fail;
And I will cry with my loud lips and publish
Beauty which all our power shall never establish,
It is so frail.

---

1   reverie, daydream

For I could tell you a story which is true;
I know a woman with a terrible tongue,
Blear eyes fallen from blue,
All her perfections tarnished—yet it is not long
Since she was lovelier than any of you.

Jack's Letter

Do not imagine that Jack and Rose apart
Can thrive much, for they cannot lie together
Under the same roof or the same weather.
These are the moons of absence grieving the heart.

If I knew any gods upon the hill,
I'd ask the kindest: Wet your lips and bless
The little ones that die of separateness,
Absent and impotent and unspoken still.

But Jack has wits which he would put to use;
He would convey to Rose his pent-up love
And duly receive acknowledgement thereof.
A letter is his proper and pure excuse.

Too cold and dry he finds the paper sheet,
And atrabilious[1] and sour is ink;
He'd set his matter forth but stops to think
His passion must in transit lose its heat;

So plants on four sides of the folio
Himself in bulbs of cunning charactery,[2]
But Rose must guess the cipher, seeing she
Must water him with tears if he would grow.

The glade is not so green now, Jack says there;
The fish have all gone down the dwindling stream;
The birds have scattered and become a dream;
Himself works with his flowers and goes nowhere.

Here then lies Jack beneath a penny seal.
The dainty lady of the superscription
If she have very delicate perception
With eyes may see and with nice fingers feel.

---

[1]   melancholy
[2]   letters

The post is gone, and the event will tell.
If only she will hug it to her bosom
Her parcel soon will thicken to a blossom
Which will be soft to hold and sweet to smell.

T. S. Eliot

(1888–1965)

The Love Song of J. Alfred Prufrock

*S'io credessi che mia risposta fosse
A persona che mai tornasse al mondo,
Questa fiamma staria senza più scosse.
Ma per ciò che giammai di questo fondo
Non tornò vivo alcun, s'i'odo il vero,
Senza tema d'infamia ti rispondo.*[1]

Let us go then, you and I,
When the evening is spread out against the sky
Like a patient etherised upon a table;
Let us go, through certain half-deserted streets,
The muttering retreats
Of restless nights in one-night cheap hotels
And sawdust restaurants with oyster-shells:
Streets that follow like a tedious argument
Of insidious intent
To lead you to an overwhelming question . . .
Oh, do not ask, 'What is it?'
Let us go and make our visit.

In the room the women come and go
Talking of Michelangelo.

The yellow fog that rubs its back upon the window-panes,
The yellow smoke that rubs its muzzle on the window-panes,
Licked its tongue into the corners of the evening,
Lingered upon the pools that stand in drains,
Let fall upon its back the soot that falls from chimneys,
Slipped by the terrace, made a sudden leap,
And seeing that it was a soft October night,
Curled once about the house, and fell asleep.

And indeed there will be time
For the yellow smoke that slides along the street
Rubbing its back upon the window-panes;
There will be time, there will be time
To prepare a face to meet the faces that you meet;
There will be time to murder and create,
And time for all the works and days[2] of hands

---

1   "If I thought that my answer were being given to one who would ever return to the
world, this flame would cease to move; but since from this abyss none has returned alive,
if what I hear is true, without fear of infamy I answer you" (Dante, *Inferno*, XXVII.61-66)

2   an echo of *Works and Days*, the title of a poetic treatise on agricultural life by the Greek
poet Hesiod (eighth century B.C.).

That lift and drop a question on your plate;
Time for you and time for me,
And time yet for a hundred indecisions,
And for a hundred visions and revisions,
Before the taking of a toast and tea.

In the room the women come and go
Talking of Michelangelo.

And indeed there will be time
To wonder, 'Do I dare?' and, 'Do I dare?'
Time to turn back and descend the stair,
With a bald spot in the middle of my hair—
(They will say: 'How his hair is growing thin!')
My morning coat, my collar mounting firmly to the chin,
My necktie rich and modest, but asserted by a simple pin—
(They will say: 'But how his arms and legs are thin!')
Do I dare
Disturb the universe?
In a minute there is time
For decisions and revisions which a minute will reverse.

For I have known them all already, known them all—
Have known the evenings, mornings, afternoons,
I have measured out my life with coffee spoons;
I know the voices dying with a dying fall[1]
Beneath the music from a farther room.
    So how should I presume?

And I have known the eyes already, known them all—
The eyes that fix you in a formulated phrase,
And when I am formulated, sprawling on a pin,
When I am pinned and wriggling on the wall,
Then how should I begin
To spit out all the butt-ends of my days and ways?
    And how should I presume?

And I have known the arms already, known them all—
Arms that are braceleted and white and bare
(But in the lamplight, downed with light brown hair!)
Is it perfume from a dress
That makes me so digress?
Arms that lie along a table, or wrap about a shawl.
    And should I then presume?
    And how should I begin?

---

1   See *Twelfth Night* I.i.4.

. . . . .

Shall I say, I have gone at dusk through narrow streets
And watched the smoke that rises from the pipes
Of lonely men in shirt-sleeves, leaning out of windows? . . .

I should have been a pair of ragged claws
Scuttling across the floors of silent seas.

. . . . .

And the afternoon, the evening, sleeps so peacefully!
Smoothed by long fingers,
Asleep . . . tired . . . or it malingers,
Stretched on the floor, here beside you and me.
Should I, after tea and cakes and ices,
Have the strength to force the moment to its crisis?
But though I have wept and fasted, wept and prayed,
Though I have seen my head (grown slightly bald) brought in
        upon a platter,[1]
I am no prophet—and here's no great matter;
I have seen the moment of my greatness flicker,
And I have seen the eternal Footman hold my coat, and snicker,
And in short, I was afraid.

And would it have been worth it, after all,
After the cups, the marmalade, the tea,
Among the porcelain, among some talk of you and me,
Would it have been worth while,
To have bitten off the matter with a smile,
To have squeezed the universe into a ball
To roll it towards some overwhelming question,
To say: 'I am Lazarus,[2] come from the dead,
Come back to tell you all, I shall tell you all'—
If one, settling a pillow by her head,
        Should say: 'That is not what I meant at all.
        That is not it, at all.'

And would it have been worth it, after all,
Would it have been worth while,
After the sunsets and the dooryards and the sprinkled streets,
After the novels, after the teacups, after the skirts that trail along
        the floor—
And this, and so much more?—
It is impossible to say just what I mean!
But as if a magic lantern threw the nerves in patterns on a

---

1 Like John the Baptist: see Matthew 14.3-11, Mark 6.17-28.
2 See John 11.1-44.

    screen:
Would it have been worth while
If one, settling a pillow or throwing off a shawl,
And turning toward the window, should say:
    'That is not it at all,
    That is not what I meant, at all.'

        . . . . .

No! I am not Prince Hamlet, nor was meant to be;
—Am an attendant lord, one that will do
To swell a progress,[1] start a scene or two,
Advise the prince; no doubt, an easy tool,
Deferential, glad to be of use,
Politic, cautious, and meticulous;
Full of high sentence, but a bit obtuse;
At times, indeed, almost ridiculous—
Almost, at times, the Fool.

I grow old . . . I grow old . . .
I shall wear the bottoms of my trousers rolled.

Shall I part my hair behind? Do I dare to eat a peach?
I shall wear white flannel trousers, and walk upon the beach.
I have heard the mermaids singing, each to each.

I do not think that they will sing to me.

I have seen them riding seaward on the waves
Combing the white hair of the waves blown back
When the wind blows the water white and black.

We have lingered in the chambers of the sea
By sea-girls wreathed with seaweed red and brown
Till human voices wake us, and we drown.

Preludes

I

    The winter evening settles down
    With smell of steaks in passageways.
    Six o'clock.
    The burnt-out ends of smoky days.
    And now a gusty shower wraps

---

1   fill out a stage procession

The grimy scraps
Of withered leaves about your feet
And newspapers from vacant lots;
The showers beat
On broken blinds and chimney-pots,
And at the corner of the street
A lonely cab-horse steams and stamps.
And then the lighting of the lamps.

II

The morning comes to consciousness
Of faint stale smells of beer
From the sawdust-trampled street
With all its muddy feet that press
To early coffee-stands.
With the other masquerades
That time resumes,
One thinks of all the hands
That are raising dingy shades
In a thousand furnished rooms.

III

You tossed a blanket from the bed,
You lay upon your back, and waited;
You dozed, and watched the night revealing
The thousand sordid images
Of which your soul was constituted;
They flickered against the ceiling.
And when all the world came back
And the light crept up between the shutters
And you heard the sparrows in the gutters,
You had such a vision of the street
As the street hardly understands;
Sitting along the bed's edge, where
You curled the papers from your hair,
Or clasped the yellow soles of feet
In the palms of both soiled hands.

IV

His soul stretched tight across the skies
That fade behind a city block,
Or trampled by insistent feet
At four and five and six o'clock;
And short square fingers stuffing pipes,
And evening newspapers, and eyes
Assured of certain certainties,
The conscience of a blackened street
Impatient to assume the world.

I am moved by fancies that are curled
Around these images, and cling:
The notion of some infinitely gentle
Infinitely suffering thing.

Wipe your hand across your mouth, and laugh;
The worlds revolve like ancient women
Gathering fuel in vacant lots.

Sweeney Among the Nightingales

ωμοι πεπληνμαι καιριαν πληγην εσω[1]

Apeneck Sweeney spreads his knees
Letting his arms hang down to laugh,
The zebra stripes along his jaw
Swelling to maculate[2] giraffe.

The circles of the stormy moon
Slide westward toward the River Plate,[3]
Death and the Raven[4] drift above
And Sweeney guards the hornèd gate.[5]

Gloomy Orion and the Dog[6]
Are veiled; and hushed the shrunken seas;
The person in the Spanish cape
Tries to sit on Sweeney's knees

Slips and pulls the table cloth
Overturns a coffee-cup,
Reorganised upon the floor
She yawns and draws a stocking up;

The silent man in mocha brown
Sprawls at the window-sill and gapes;
The waiter brings in oranges
Bananas figs and hothouse grapes;

---

1   The epigraph reads, "Alas, I have been struck a mortal blow within," the words of Aeschylus when he is murdered by his wife Clytemnestra, in Aeschylus's *Agamemnon*.
2   stained, spotted
3   the estuary between Argentina and Uruguay
4   the southern constellation Corvus
5   The gates of horn in Hades, from which issue forth true dreams; from the other gates, made of iron, come false visions (Virgil, *Aeneid* 879-901).
6   the constellation of Orion, and the Dog Star, Sirius

The silent vertebrate in brown
Contracts and concentrates, withdraws;
Rachel *née* Rabinovitch
Tears at the grapes with murderous paws;

She and the lady in the cape
Are suspect, thought to be in league;
Therefore the man with heavy eyes
Declines the gambit, shows fatigue,

Leaves the room and reappears
Outside the window, leaning in,
Branches of wistaria
Circumscribe a golden grin;

The host with someone indistinct
Converses at the door apart,
The nightingales are singing near
The Convent of the Sacred Heart,

And sang within the bloody wood
When Agamemnon cried aloud
And let their liquid siftings fall
To stain the stiff dishonoured shroud.

The Hollow Men

Mistah Kurtz—he dead[1]

A penny for the Old Guy[2]

I

We are the hollow men
We are the stuffed men
Leaning together
Headpiece filled with straw. Alas!
Our dried voices, when
We whisper together
Are quiet and meaningless
As wind in dry grass
Or rats' feet over broken glass
In our dry cellar

---

1 The words announcing the death of the company agent in Conrad's *Heart of Darkness*.
2 The cry of English children each 5 November, asking for money for their straw effigies of Guy Fawkes, the Catholic conspirator detected in the act of trying to blow up the English Parliament on 5 November 1605.

Shape without form, shade without colour,
Paralysed force, gesture without motion;

Those who have crossed
With direct eyes, to death's other Kingdom
Remember us—if at all—not as lost
Violent souls, but only
As the hollow men
The stuffed men.

II

Eyes I dare not meet in dreams
In death's dream kingdom
These do not appear:
There, the eyes are
Sunlight on a broken column
There, is a tree swinging
And voices are
In the wind's singing
More distant and more solemn
Than a fading star.

Let me be no nearer
In death's dream kingdom
Let me also wear
Such deliberate disguises
Rat's coat, crowskin, crossed staves
In a field
Behaving as the wind behaves
No nearer—

Not that final meeting
In the twilight kingdom

III

This is the dead land
This is cactus land
Here the stone images
Are raised, here they receive
The supplication of a dead man's hand
Under the twinkle of a fading star.

Is it like this
In death's other kingdom
Waking alone
At the hour when we are
Trembling with tenderness

Lips that would kiss
Form prayers to broken stone.

IV

The eyes are not here
There are no eyes here
In this valley of dying stars
In this hollow valley
This broken jaw of our lost kingdoms

In this last of meeting places
We grope together
And avoid speech
Gathered on this beach of the tumid river[1]

Sightless, unless
The eyes reappear
As the perpetual star
Multifoliate rose[2]
Of death's twilight kingdom
The hope only
Of empty men.

V

Here we go round the prickly pear
Prickly pear prickly pear
Here we go round the prickly pear
At five o'clock in the morning.

Between the idea
And the reality
Between the motion
And the act
Falls the Shadow

      For Thine is the Kingdom

Between the conception
And the creation
Between the emotion
And the response
Falls the Shadow

       Life is very long

---

1 See Dante's *Inferno*, III, where the damned are seen to gather by the river Acheron to be taken into Hell.

2 a many-petaled rose; the image used by Dante to show Christ triumphant, in the *Paradiso* section of his *Divine Comedy*

Between the desire
And the spasm
Between the potency
And the existence
Between the essence
And the descent
Falls the Shadow

For Thine is the Kingdom

For Thine is
Life is
For Thine is the

This is the way the world ends
This is the way the world ends
This is the way the world ends
Not with a bang but a whimper.

Journey of the Magi[1]

'A cold coming we had of it,
Just the worst time of the year
For a journey, and such a long journey:
The ways deep and the weather sharp,
The very dead of winter.'[2]
And the camels galled, sore-footed, refractory,
Lying down in the melting snow.
There were times we regretted
The summer palaces on slopes, the terraces,
And the silken girls bringing sherbet.
Then the camel men cursing and grumbling
And running away, and wanting their liquor and women,
And the night-fires going out, and the lack of shelters,
And the cities hostile and the towns unfriendly
And the villages dirty and charging high prices:
A hard time we had of it.
At the end we preferred to travel all night,
Sleeping in snatches,
With the voices singing in our ears, saying
That this was all folly.

Then at dawn we came down to a temperate valley,

---

1   the Wise Men who go to Bethlehem to witness the birth of Christ: Matthew 2.1-12
2   The first five lines of the poem are adapted from the sermon preached by Bishop Lancelot
     Andrewes at Christmas, 1622.

Wet, below the snow line, smelling of vegetation,
With a running stream and a water-mill beating the darkness,
And three trees on the low sky,
And an old white horse galloped away in the meadow.
Then we came to a tavern with vine-leaves over the lintel,
Six hands at an open door dicing for pieces of silver,
And feet kicking the empty wine-skins.
But there was no information, and so we continued
And arrived at evening, not a moment too soon
Finding the place; it was (you may say) satisfactory.

All this was a long time ago, I remember,
And I would do it again, but set down
This set down
This: were we led all that way for
Birth or Death? There was a Birth, certainly,
We had evidence and no doubt. I had seen birth and death,
But had thought they were different; this Birth was
Hard and bitter agony for us, like Death, our death.
We returned to our places, these Kingdoms,
But no longer at ease here, in the old dispensation,
With an alien people clutching their gods.
I should be glad of another death.

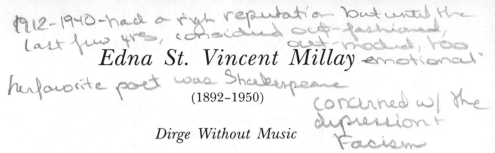

1912-1940 - had a high reputation but until the last few yrs, considered old-fashioned, out-moded, too emotional.

Edna St. Vincent Millay

(1892-1950)

her favorite poet was Shakespeare

concerned w/ the depression + facism

Dirge Without Music

I am not resigned to the shutting away of loving hearts in the
  hard ground.
So it is, and so it will be, for so it has been, time out of mind:
Into the darkness they go, the wise and the lovely. Crowned
With lilies and with laurel they go; but I am not resigned. *outmoded*

Lovers and thinkers, into the earth with you. *style - her*
Be one with the dull, the indiscriminate dust. *poetry still*
A fragment of what you felt, of what you knew, *contains poetic*
A formula, a phrase remains,—but the best is lost. *diction. (traces of)*

The answers quick and keen, the honest look, the laughter, the
  love,—
They are gone. They are gone to feed the roses. Elegant and
  curled
Is the blossom. Fragrant is the blossom. I know. But I do not
  approve.
More precious was the light in your eyes than all the roses in the
  world.

Down, down, down into the darkness of the grave
Gently they go, the beautiful, the tender, the kind;
Quietly they go, the intelligent, the witty, the brave.
I know. But I do not approve. And I am not resigned.

Journey
archaic old-fashioned

Ah, could I lay me down in this long grass
And close my eyes, and let the quiet wind
Blow over me—I am so tired, so tired
Of passing pleasant places ! All my life,
Following Care along the dusty road,
Have I looked back at loveliness and sighed;
Yet at my hand an unrelenting hand
Tugged ever, and I passed. All my life long
Over my shoulder have I looked at peace;
And now I fain would lie in this long grass
And close my eyes.

inclination to do so

archaic diction

            Yet onward!
                    Cat-birds call
Through the long afternoon, and creeks at dusk

[485]

Are guttural. Whip-poor-wills[1] wake and cry,
Drawing the twilight close about their throats.
Only my heart makes answer. Eager vines
Go up the rocks and wait; flushed apple-trees
Pause in their dance and break the ring for me;
Dim, shady wood-roads, redolent of fern
And bayberry, that through sweet bevies thread
Of round-faced roses, pink and petulant,
Look back and beckon ere they disappear.
Only my heart, only my heart responds.

Yet, ah, my path is sweet on either side
All through the dragging day,—sharp underfoot
And hot, and like dead mist the dry dust hangs—
But far, oh, far as passionate eye can reach,
And long, ah, long as rapturous eye can cling,
The world is mine: blue hill, still silver lake,
Broad field, bright flower, and the long white road;
A gateless garden, and an open path;
My feet to follow, and my heart to hold.

Elegy Before Death

There will be rose and rhododendron
    When you are dead and under ground;
Still will be heard from white syringas[2]
    Heavy with bees, a sunny sound;

Still will the tamaracks be raining
    After the rain has ceased, and still
Will there be robins in the stubble,
    Grey sheep upon the warm green hill.

Spring will not ail nor autumn falter;
    Nothing will know that you are gone,—
Saving alone some sullen plough-land
    None but yourself sets foot upon;

Saving the may-weed and the pig-weed
    Nothing will know that you are dead,—
These, and perhaps a useless wagon
    Standing beside some tumbled shed.

Oh, there will pass with your great passing
    Little of beauty not your own,—

---

1   small nocturnal birds, common to eastern North America
2   lilacs

EDNA ST. VINCENT MILLAY

last stanza -
Shift in thought

These things
will pass
away

sentimentality
was being
overused, she
takes a tongue-
in-cheek love poem

Only the light from common water,
    Only the grace from simple stone!

Love is not necessary
for everyday life
yet it is still important

Trad. ENG.
sonnet

Love is Not All

Love is not all: it is not meat nor drink a
Nor slumber nor a roof against the rain; b
Nor yet a floating spar to men that sink a
And rise and sink and rise and sink again; b
Love can not fill the thickened lung with breath, c
Nor clean the blood, nor set the fractured bone; d
Yet many a man is making friends with death e
Even as I speak, for lack of love alone. d
It well may be that in a difficult hour, e
Pinned down by pain and moaning for release, f
Or nagged by want past resolution's power, e
I might be driven to sell your love for peace, f
Or trade the memory of this night for food. g
It well may be. I do not think I would. g

basic
iambic
(sort of) but
not penta-
meter
syllables
vary

explait our
memory

Turn -
almost sounds
like a sonnet
but it still goes on

I can see that I
might do this
(exploit our love, write about it, sell it)

Prob. 1st poem on this
subj.
bad case of PMS -
interesting

Menses[1]

(He speaks, but to himself, being aware how it is with her)

Kind of monologue
that
she
does this

Think not I have not heard.
Well-fanged the double word
And well-directed flew.

from the man's point
of view. He's witnessing
her mood swings.
What happens
in the
relationship

I felt it. Down my side
Innocent as oil I see the ugly venom slide:
Poison enough to stiffen us both, and all our friends;
But I am not pierced, so there the mischief ends.

There is more to be said; I see it coiling;
The impact will be pain.
Yet coil; yet strike again.
You cannot riddle the stout mail I wove
Long since, of wit and love.

armour (chainmail)

Trying to
understand how the
man reacts
Quite touching

As for my answer . . . stupid in the sun
He lies, his fangs drawn:
I will not war with you.

She's trying to
understand this from
the man's view

---

1   menstruation

[487]

You know how wild you are. You are willing to be turned
To other matters; you would be grateful, even.
You watch me shyly. I (for I have learned
More things than one in our few years together)
Chafe at the churlish wind, the unseasonable weather.

"Unseasonable?" you cry, with harsher scorn
Than the theme warrants; "Every year it is the same!
'Unseasonable!' they whine, these stupid peasants!—and never
    since they were born
Have they known a spring less wintry! Lord, the shame,
The crying shame of seeing a man no wiser than the beasts he
    feeds—
His skull as empty as a shell!"

("Go to. You are unwell.")- *didn't actually say out loud*

Such is my thought, but such are not my words.

"What is the name," I ask, "of those big birds
With yellow breast and low and heavy flight,
That make such mournful whistling?"

                                    "Meadowlarks,"
You answer primly, not a little cheered.
"Some people shoot them." Suddenly your eyes are wet
And your chin trembles. On my breast you lean,
And sob most pitifully for all the lovely things that are not and
    have been.

"How silly I am!—and I *know* how silly I am!"
You say; "You are very patient. You are very kind.
I shall be better soon. Just Heaven consign and damn
To tedious Hell this body with its muddy feet in my mind!"

*I hate having this body
in/between my mind,*

Hugh MacDiarmid

(1892–1978)

In the Children's Hospital

Does it matter? – losing your legs? . . .
                    –Siegfried Sassoon

Now let the legless boy show the great lady
How well he can manage his crutches.
It doesn't matter though the Sister objects,
'He's not used to them yet,' when such is
The will of the Princess. Come, Tommy,
Try a few desperate steps through the ward.
Then the hand of Royalty will pat your head
And life suddenly cease to be hard.
For a couple of legs are surely no miss
When the loss leads to such an honour as this!
One knows, when one sees how jealous the rest
Of the children are, it's been all for the best! —
But would the sound of your sticks on the floor
Thundered in her skull for evermore!

We must look at the harebell

We must look at the harebell as if
We had never seen it before.
Remembrance gives an accumulation of satisfaction
Yet the desire for change is very strong in us
And change is in itself a recreation.
To those who take any pleasure
In flowers, plants, birds, and the rest
An ecological change is recreative.
(Come. Climb with me. Even the sheep are different
And of new importance.
The coarse-fleeced, hardy Herdwick,
The Hampshire Down, artificially fed almost from birth,
And butcher-fat from the day it is weaned,
The Lincoln-Longwool, the biggest breed in England,
With the longest fleece, and the Southdown
Almost the smallest—and between them thirty other breeds,
Some whitefaced, some black,
Some with horns and some without,
Some long-wooled, some short-wooled,
In England where the men, and women too,
Are almost as interesting as the sheep.)
Everything is different, everything changes,
Except for the white bedstraw which climbs all the way
Up from the valleys to the tops of the high passes
The flowers are all different and more precious
Demanding more search and particularity of vision.

Look ! Here and there a pinguicula[1] eloquent of the Alps
Still keeps a purple-blue flower
On the top of its straight and slender stem.
Bog-asphodel, deep-gold, and comely in form,
The queer, almost diabolical, sundew,
And when you leave the bog for the stag moors and the rocks
The parsley fern — a lovelier plant
Than even the proud Osmunda Regalis[2]—
Flourishes in abundance
Showing off oddly contrasted fronds
From the cracks of the lichened stones.
It is pleasant to find the books
Describing it as 'very local.'
Here is a change indeed!
The universal is the particular.

In Memoriam Dylan Thomas[3]

I rejoiced when from Wales once again
Came the ffff-putt of a triple-feathered arrow
Which looked as if it had never moved.[4]

But now the bowman has fitted one more nock[5]
To his string, and discharged the arrow straight up into the air
Partly as a gesture of farewell, partly of triumph,
And beautiful! — I watched the arrow go up.
The sun was already westing[6] towards evening
So, as the arrow topped the trees
And climbed into sunlight,
It began to burn against the evening like the sun itself.
Up and up it went, not weaving as it would have done
With a snatching loose, but soaring, swimming,
Aspiring towards heaven, steady, golden and superb.

Just as it had spent its force,
Just as its ambition had been dimmed by destiny
And it was preparing to faint, to turn over,
To pour back into the bosom of its mother earth,
A terrible portent happened.
A gore[7] crow came flapping wearily

---

1 insect catching plant with thick greasy leaves
2 a flowering fern
3 Dylan Thomas died on 9 November 1953.
4 "With acknowledgements to T. H. White, *The Sword in the Stone*. The reference here is to the author's friend, Dylan Thomas" (McDiarmid's note).
5 the notch at the butt-end of an arrow, to fit it to the bowstring
6 setting in the west
7 dirty, bloody

Before the approaching night.
It came, it did not waver, it took the arrow,
It flew away, heavy and hoisting,
With the arrow in its beak. I was furious.
I had loved the arrow's movement,
Its burning ambition in the sunlight,
And it was such a splendid arrow,
Perfectly-balanced, sharp, tight-feathered,
Clean-nocked, and neither warped nor scraped.

I was furious but I was frightened.
It is a very old and recurring portent in our history.
We remember the story of Valerius Corvus[1]
(Ah, would my bowman had been saved like Valerius
By a crow which hid him from the foe with its wings!)
And the famous episode in the great Irish epic of Ulster,
The *Táin Bó Chuailgné*,[2]
In which the goddess Morrigu attacks Cuchulainn,
Who scorned her love,
In the form of a crow.
(A like episode is depicted on one of the decorated faces
Of an Etruscan[3] alabaster vase in the Florence Museum,
Among scenes of the Trojan War).
The crow is not a mere flight of fancy.
It is the creature which stands for battle
And the gods and goddesses of war.

But the crow cannot quench the light
With its outstretched wings forever
Nor break the law of gravity
Nor swallow the arrow.
We shall get it back. Never fear!
And how I shall rejoice when the War is over
And there comes from Wales once again
The fff-putt of a triple-feathered arrow
Which looks as if it had never moved!

---

1   Marcus Valerius Corvus (c.370-270) was helped by a raven which flew into his enemy's
     face during combat. (Latin "corvus" means raven.)
2   "The Cattle Raid of Cooley," a story about the mythological Irish hero Cuchulainn,
     translated by Lady Gregory as "Cuchulainn of Muirthemne."
3   from Etruria, an ancient country of west central Italy

Archibald Macleish

(1892–1982)

The Silent Slain

for Kenneth MacLeish, 1894-1918[1]

We too, we too, descending once again
The hills of our own land, we too have heard
Far off—Ah, que ce cor a longue haleine[2]—.
The horn of Roland in the passages of Spain,
The first, the second blast, the failing third,
And with the third turned back and climbed once more
The steep road southward, and heard faint the sound
Of swords, of horses, the disastrous war,
And crossed the dark defile at last, and found
At Roncevaux upon the darkening plain
The dead against the dead and on the silent ground
The silent slain—

The End of the World

Quite unexpectedly as Vasserot
The armless ambidextrian was lighting
A match between his great and second toe
And Ralph the lion was engaged in biting
The neck of Madame Sossman while the drum
Pointed, and Teeny was about to cough
In waltz-time swinging Jocko by the thumb—
Quite unexpectedly the top blew off:

And there, there overhead, there, there, hung over
Those thousands of white faces, those dazed eyes,
There in the starless dark the poise, the hover,
There with vast wings across the canceled skies,
There in the sudden blackness the black pall
Of nothing, nothing, nothing—nothing at all.

---

1   the poet's brother, killed while flying a mission in Belgium in World War I
2   (French) "How long this trumpet sounds"; from the 12th-century epic *Chanson de Roland*,
which tells how Roland, the great knight of Charlemagne, sounds the horn to call for
help, but too late to save himself or his men from the Saracens in the battle at Roncevaux.

Ars Poetica

A poem should be palpable and mute
As a globed fruit,

Dumb
As old medallions to the thumb,

Silent as the sleeve-worn stone
Of casement ledges where the moss has grown—

A poem should be wordless
As the flight of birds.

*

A poem should be motionless in time
As the moon climbs,

Leaving, as the moon releases
Twig by twig the night-entangled trees,

Leaving, as the moon behind the winter leaves,
Memory by memory the mind—

A poem should be motionless in time
As the moon climbs.

*

A poem should be equal to:
Not true.

For all the history of grief
An empty doorway and a maple leaf.

For love
The leaning grasses and two lights above the sea—

A poem should not mean
But be.

You, Andrew Marvell[1]

And here face down beneath the sun
And here upon earth's noonward height
To feel the always coming on
The always rising of the night:

To feel creep up the curving east
The earthy chill of dusk and slow
Upon those under lands the vast
And ever climbing shadow grow

And strange at Ecbatan[2] the trees
Take leaf by leaf the evening strange
The flooding dark about their knees
The mountains over Persia change

And now at Kermanshah[3] the gate
Dark empty and the withered grass
And through the twilight now the late
Few travelers in the westward pass

And Baghdad darken and the bridge
Across the silent river gone
And through Arabia the edge
Of evening widen and steal on

And deepen on Palmyra's[4] street
The wheel rut in the ruined stone
And Lebanon fade out and Crete
High through the clouds and overblown

And over Sicily the air
Still flashing with the landward gulls
And loom and slowly disappear
The sails above the shadowy hulls

And Spain go under and the shore
Of Africa the gilded sand
And evening vanish and no more
The low pale light across that land

Nor now the long light on the sea:

---

1   Compare Marvell's "To His Coy Mistress," p.81 above.
2   the ancient capital of the Medes (now the city of Hamadan in modern Iran)
3   a city and district in Iran
4   a once-great city in Syria, now in ruins

And here face downward in the sun
To feel how swift how secretly
The shadow of the night comes on . . .

"Dover Beach" – A Note to that Poem[1]

The wave withdrawing
Withers with seaward rustle of flimsy water
Sucking the sand down, dragging at empty shells.
The roil after it settling, too smooth, smothered . . .

After forty a man's a fool to wait in the
Sea's face for the full force and the roaring of
Surf to come over him: droves of careening water.
After forty the tug's out and the salt and the
Sea follow it: less sound and violence.
Nevertheless the ebb has its own beauty—
Shells sand and all and the whispering rustle.
There's earth in it then and the bubbles of foam gone.

Moreover—and this too has its lovely uses—
It's the outward wave that spills the inward forward
Tripping the proud piled mute virginal
Mountain of water in wallowing welter of light and
Sound enough—thunder for miles back. It's a fine and a
Wild smother to vanish in: pulling down—
Tripping with outward ebb the urgent inward.

Speaking alone for myself it's the steep hill and the
Toppling lift of the young men I am toward now,
Waiting for that as the wave for the next wave.
Let them go over us all I say with the thunder of
What's to be next in the world. It's we will be under it!

---

1   See "Dover Beach," by Matthew Arnold.

Wilfred Owen

(1893-1918)

Arms and the Boy[1]

Let the boy try along this bayonet-blade
How cold steel is, and keen with hunger of blood;
Blue with all malice, like a madman's flash;
And thinly drawn with famishing for flesh.

Lend him to stroke these blind, blunt bullet-heads
Which long to nuzzle in the hearts of lads,
Or give him cartridges of fine zinc teeth,
Sharp with the sharpness of grief and death.

For his teeth seem for laughing round an apple.
There lurk no claws behind his fingers supple;
And God will grow no talons at his heels,
Nor antlers through the thickness of his curls.

Insensibility

I

Happy are men who yet before they are killed
Can let their veins run cold.
Whom no compassion fleers
Or makes their feet
Sore on the alleys cobbled with their brothers.
The front line withers,
But they are troops who fade, not flowers
For poets' tearful fooling:
Men, gaps for filling:
Losses who might have fought
Longer; but no one bothers.

II

And some cease feeling
Even themselves or for themselves.
Dullness best solves
The tease and doubt of shelling,
And Chance's strange arithmetic
Comes simpler than the reckoning of their shilling.
They keep no check on armies' decimation.

---

1   a play on the opening of Virgil's *Aeneid*, "Arms and the man I sing..."

III

Happy are these who lose imagination:
They have enough to carry with ammunition.
Their spirit drags no pack,
Their old wounds save with cold can not more ache.
Having seen all things red,
Their eyes are rid
Of the hurt of the colour of blood for ever.
And terror's first constriction over,
Their hearts remain small-drawn.
Their senses in some scorching cautery of battle
Now long since ironed,
Can laugh among the dying, unconcerned.

IV

Happy the soldier home, with not a notion
How somewhere, every dawn, some men attack,
And many sighs are drained.
Happy the lad whose mind was never trained:
His days are worth forgetting more than not.
He sings along the march
Which we march taciturn, because of dusk,
The long, forlorn, relentless trend
From larger day to huger night.

V

We wise, who with a thought besmirch
Blood over all our soul,
How should we see our task
But through his blunt and lashless eyes?
Alive, he is not vital overmuch;
Dying, not mortal overmuch;
Nor sad, nor proud,
Nor curious at all.
He cannot tell
Old men's placidity from his.

VI

But cursed are dullards whom no cannon stuns,
That they should be as stones;
Wretched are they, and mean
With paucity that never was simplicity.
By choice they made themselves immune
To pity and whatever moans in man
Before the last sea and the hapless stars;

Whatever mourns when many leave these shores;
Whatever shares
The eternal reciprocity of tears.

Dulce et Decorum Est

Bent double, like old beggars under sacks,
Knock-kneed, coughing like hags, we cursed through sludge,
Till on the haunting flares we turned our backs,
And towards our distant rest began to trudge.
Men marched asleep. Many had lost their boots,
But limped on, blood-shod. All went lame, all blind;
Drunk with fatigue; deaf even to the hoots
Of gas-shells dropping softly behind.

Gas! GAS! Quick, boys!—An ecstasy of fumbling,
Fitting the clumsy helmets just in time,
But someone still was yelling out and stumbling
And flound'ring like a man in fire or lime—
Dim, through the misty panes[1] and thick green light,
As under a green sea, I saw him drowning.

In all my dreams before my helpless sight
He plunges at me, guttering, choking, drowning.

If in some smothering dreams, you too could pace
Behind the wagon that we flung him in,
And watch the white eyes writhing in his face,
His hanging face, like a devil's sick of sin;
If you could hear, at every jolt, the blood
Come gargling from the froth-corrupted lungs,
Bitter as the cud
Of vile, incurable sores on innocent tongues,—
My friend,[2] you would not tell with such high zest
To children ardent for some desperate glory,
The old Lie: Dulce et decorum est
Pro patria mori.[3]

---

1   the transparent celluloid visors in the gas masks
2   The poem was originally to have been dedicated to Jessie Pope, a writer of patriotic
    verses for children.
3   "Sweet and fitting it is to die for one's country" (Horace, *Odes*)

Anthem for Doomed Youth

What passing-bells for these who die as cattle?
Only the monstrous anger of the guns.
Only the stuttering rifles' rapid rattle
Can patter out their hasty orisons.
No mockeries for them from prayers or bells,
Nor any voice of mourning save the choirs,—
The shrill, demented choirs of wailing shells;
And bugles calling for them from sad shires.

What candles may be held to speed them all?
Not in the hands of boys, but in their eyes
Shall shine the holy glimmers of good-byes.
The pallor of girls' brows shall be their pall;
Their flowers the tenderness of silent minds,
And each slow dusk a drawing-down of blinds.

Strange Meeting[1]

It seemed that out of battle I escaped
Down some profound dull tunnel, long since scooped
Through granites which titanic wars had groined.
Yet also there encumbered sleepers groaned,
Too fast in thought or death to be bestirred.
Then, as I probed them, one sprang up, and stared
With piteous recognition in fixed eyes,
Lifting distressful hands as if to bless.
And by his smile, I knew that sullen hall,
By his dead smile I knew we stood in Hell.
With a thousand pains that vision's face was grained;
Yet no blood reached there from the upper ground,
And no guns thumped, or down the flues made moan.
'Strange friend,' I said, 'here is no cause to mourn.'
'None,' said the other, 'save the undone years,
The hopelessness. Whatever hope is yours,
Was my life also; I went hunting wild
After the wildest beauty in the world,
Which lies not calm in eyes, or braided hair,
But mocks the steady running of the hour,
And if it grieves, grieves richlier than here.
For of my glee might many men have laughed,
And of my weeping something had been left,

---

1   "And one whose spear had pierced me, leaned beside,/ With quivering lips and humid
     eyes;—and all / Seemed like some brothers on a journey wide / Gone forth, whom now
     strange meeting did befall / In a strange land" (Shelley, *The Revolt of Islam* (1818),
     1828-32).

Which must die now. I mean the truth untold,
The pity of war, the pity war distilled.[1]
Now men will go content with what we spoiled.
Or, discontent, boil bloody, and be spilled.
They will be swift with swiftness of the tigress,
None will break ranks, though nations trek from progress.
Courage was mine, and I had mystery,
Wisdom was mine, and I had mastery;
To miss the march of this retreating world
Into vain citadels that are not walled.
Then, when much blood had clogged their chariot-wheels,
I would go up and wash them from sweet wells,
Even with truths that lie too deep for taint.
I would have poured my spirit without stint
But not through wounds; not on the cess of war.
Foreheads of men have bled where no wounds were.
I am the enemy you killed, my friend.
I knew you in this dark; for so you frowned
Yesterday through me as you jabbed and killed.
I parried; but my hands were loath and cold.
Let us sleep now. . . . '

---

1   In a draft preface for his poems, Owen wrote: "My Subject is War, and the pity of War.
The Poetry is in the pity."

Dorothy Parker

(1893–1967)

Bohemia[1]

Authors and actors and artists and such
Never know nothing, and never know much.
Sculptors and singers and those of their kidney
Tell their affairs from Seattle to Sydney.
Playwrights and poets and such horses' necks
Start off from anywhere, end up at sex.
Diarists, critics, and similar roe
Never say nothing, and never say no.
People Who Do Things exceed my endurance;
God, for a man that solicits insurance!

A Pig's-Eye View of Literature

The lives and times of John Keats, Percy Bysshe Shelley, and George Gordon Noel, Lord Byron

Byron and Shelley and Keats
Were a trio of lyrical treats.
The forehead of Shelley was cluttered with curls,
And Keats never was a descendant of earls,
And Byron walked out with a number of girls,
   But it didn't impair the poetical feats
      Of Byron and Shelley,
      Of Byron and Shelley,
   Of Byron and Shelley and Keats.

Oscar Wilde[2]

If, with the literate, I am
Impelled to try an epigram,
I never seek to take the credit;
We all assume that Oscar said it.

---

1   A term descriptive of the society of artists, actors, and writers, who seem to lead lives as free and unconventional as those of the gypsies, who at one time were thought to have originated in Bohemia.
2   Oscar Wilde (1854-1900), English playwright and man of letters, renowned for his epigrammatic wit

Harriet Beecher Stowe[1]

The pure and worthy Mrs. Stowe
Is one we all are proud to know
As mother, wife, and authoress—
Thank God, I am content with less!

D. G. Rossetti[2]

Dante Gabriel Rossetti
Buried all of his *libretti,*
Thought the matter over—then
Went and dug them up again.

Thomas Carlyle[3]

Carlyle combined the lit'ry life
With throwing teacups at his wife,
Remarking, rather testily,
"Oh, stop your dodging, Mrs. C.!"

Charles Dickens

Who call him spurious and shoddy
Shall do it o'er my lifeless body.
I heartily invite such birds
To come outside and say those words!

Alexandre Dumas and his Son[4]

Although I work, and seldom cease,
At Dumas *père* and Dumas *fils,*
Alas, I cannot make me care
For Dumas *fils* and Dumas *père.*

Alfred, Lord Tennyson

Should Heaven send me any son,
I hope he's not like Tennyson.
I'd rather have him play a fiddle
Than rise and bow and speak an idyll.

---

1   Harriet Beecher Stowe (1811-1896), American novelist, author of *Uncle Tom's Cabin* (1852)
2   D. G. Rossetti (1828-82), English poet and painter. At his wife's death in 1862 he buried
     with her the manuscript of some of his poems, which he later disinterred and published.
3   Thomas Carlyle (1795-1881), English essayist and historian, whose marriage to Jane Welsh
     was marred by his irascibility and inconsiderateness towards her.
4   "Dumas père" (1802-70), wrote historical novels such as *The Three Musketeers*; his son,
     "Dumas fils" (1824-95), was a dramatist, his best-known play being *The Lady of the Camelias.*

George Gissing[1]

When I admit neglect of Gissing,
They say I don't know what I'm missing.
Until their arguments are subtler,
I think I'll stick to Samuel Butler.[2]

Walter Savage Landor[3]

Upon the work of Walter Landor
I am unfit to write with candor.
If you can read it, well and good;
But as for me, I never could.

George Sand[4]

What time the gifted lady took
Away from paper, pen, and book,
She spent in amorous dalliance
(They do those things so well in France).

* * *

On Being a Woman

Why is it, when I am in Rome,
I'd give an eye to be at home,
But when on native earth I be,
My soul is sick for Italy?

And why with you, my love, my lord,
Am I spectacularly bored,
Yet do you up and leave me—then
I scream to have you back again?

---

1   George Gissing (1857-1903), English author of realist novels
2   Samuel Butler (1835-1902), English essayist, author of the satirical romance *Erewhon* (1872)
3   Walter Savage Landor (1775-1864), English poet and essayist, author of *Imaginary Conversations* (1824-1829)
4   George Sand (1804-1876), a French novelist, who acquired some notoriety for her affairs with the poet Alfred de Musset and the composer Frederic Chopin

Sonnet For the End of a Sequence

So take my vows and scatter them to sea;
Who swears the sweetest is no more than human.
And say no kinder words than these of me:
"Ever she longed for peace, but was a woman!
And thus they are, whose silly female dust
Needs little enough to clutter it and bind it,
Who meet a slanted gaze, and ever must
Go build themselves a soul to dwell behind it."

For now I am my own again, my friend!
This scar but points the whiteness of my breast;
This frenzy, like its betters, spins an end,
And now I am my own. And that is best.
Therefore, I am immeasurably grateful
To you, for proving shallow, false, and hateful.

e. e. cummings

(1894–1962)

the Cambridge ladies who live in furnished souls

the Cambridge ladies who live in furnished souls
are unbeautiful and have comfortable minds
(also, with the church's protestant blessings
daughters, unscented shapeless spirited)
they believe in Christ and Longfellow, both dead,
are invariably interested in so many things—
at the present writing one still finds
delighted fingers knitting for the is it Poles?
perhaps. While permanent faces coyly bandy
scandal of Mrs. N and Professor D
. . . . the Cambridge ladies do not care, above
Cambridge if sometimes in its box of
sky lavender and cornerless, the
moon rattles like a fragment of angry candy

goodby Betty, don't remember me

goodby Betty, don't remember me
pencil your eyes dear and have a good time
with the tall tight boys at Tabari'
s, keep your teeth snowy, stick to beer and lime,
wear dark, and where your meeting breasts are round
have roses darling, it's all i ask of you—
but that when light fails and this sweet profound
Paris moves with lovers, two and two
bound for themselves, when passionately dusk
brings softly down the perfume of the world
(and just as smaller stars begin to husk
heaven) you, you exactly paled and curled

with mystic lips take twilight where i know:
proving to Death that Love is so and so.

somewhere i have never travelled, gladly beyond

somewhere i have never travelled,gladly beyond
any experience,your eyes have their silence:
in your most frail gesture are things which enclose me,
or which i cannot touch because they are too near

your slightest look easily will unclose me
though i have closed myself as fingers,
you open always petal by petal myself as Spring opens
(touching skilfully,mysteriously)her first rose

or if your wish be to close me,i and
my life will shut very beautifully,suddenly,
as when the heart of this flower imagines
the snow carefully everywhere descending;

nothing which we are to perceive in this world equals
the power of your intense fragility:whose texture
compels me with the colour of its countries,
rendering death and forever with each breathing

(i do not know what it is about you that closes
and opens;only something in me understands
the voice of your eyes is deeper than all roses)
nobody,not even the rain,has such small hands

anyone lived in a pretty how town

anyone lived in a pretty how town
(with up so floating many bells down)
spring summer autumn winter
he sang his didn't he danced his did.

Women and men(both little and small)
cared for anyone not at all
they sowed their isn't they reaped their same
sun moon stars rain

children guessed(but only a few
and down they forgot as up they grew
autumn winter spring summer)
that noone loved him more by more

when by now and tree by leaf
she laughed his joy she cried his grief
bird by snow and stir by still
anyone's any was all to her

someones married their everyones
laughed their cryings and did their dance
(sleep wake hope and then)they
said their nevers they slept their dream

stars rain sun moon
(and only the snow can begin to explain
how children are apt to forget to remember
with up so floating many bells down)

one day anyone died i guess
(and noone stooped to kiss his face)

busy folk buried them side by side
little by little and was by was

all by all and deep by deep
and more by more they dream their sleep
noone and anyone earth by april
wish by spirit and if by yes.

Women and men(both dong and ding)
summer autumn winter spring
reaped their sowing and went their came
sun moon stars rain

i sing of Olaf glad and big

i sing of Olaf glad and big
whose warmest heart recoiled at war:
a conscientious object-or

his wellbelovéd colonel(trig[1]
westpointer most succinctly bred)
took erring Olaf soon in hand;
but—though an host of overjoyed
noncoms(first knocking on the head
him)do through icy waters roll
that helplessness which others stroke
with brushes recently employed
anent this muddy toiletbowl,
while kindred intellects evoke
allegiance per blunt instruments—
Olaf(being to all intents
a corpse and wanting any rag
upon what God unto him gave)
responds,without getting annoyed
"I will not kiss your f.ing flag"

straightway the silver bird[2] looked grave
(departing hurriedly to shave)

but—though all kinds of officers
(a yearning nation's blueeyed pride)
their passive prey did kick and curse
until for wear their clarion
voices and boots were much the worse,
and egged the firstclassprivates on

---

1   primly neat
2   insignia of an army colonel

his rectum wickedly to tease
by means of skilfully applied
bayonets roasted hot with heat—
Olaf(upon what were once knees)
does almost ceaselessly repeat
"there is some s. I will not eat"
our president,being of which
assertions duly notified
threw the yellowsonofabitch
into a dungeon,where he died

Christ(of His mercy infinite)
i pray to see;and Olaf,too

preponderatingly because
unless statistics lie he was
more brave than me:more blond than you.

i thank You God for most this amazing day

i thank You God for most this amazing
day:for the leaping greenly spirits of trees
and a blue true dream of sky;and for everything
which is natural which is infinite which is yes

(i who have died am alive again today,
and this is the sun's birthday;this is the birth
day of life and of love and wings:and of the gay
great happening illimitably earth)

how should tasting touching hearing seeing
breathing any—lifted from the no
of all nothing—human merely being
doubt unimaginable You?

(now the ears of my ears awake and
now the eyes of my eyes are opened)

Robert Graves

(1895–1985)

Down

Downstairs a clock had chimed, two o'clock only.
Then outside from the hen-roost crowing came.
Why should the shift-wing call against the clock,
Three hours from dawn? Now shutters click and knock,
And he remembers a sad superstition
Unfitting for the sick-bed. . . . Turn aside,
Distract, divide, ponder the simple tales
That puzzled childhood; riddles, turn them over—
Half-riddles, answerless, the more intense.
Lost bars of music tinkling with no sense
Recur, drowning uneasy superstition.

Mouth open he was lying, this sick man,
And sinking all the while; how had he come
To sink? On better nights his dream went flying,
Dipping, sailing the pasture of his sleep,
But now (since clock and cock) had sunk him down
Through mattress, bed, floor, floors beneath, stairs, cellars,
Through deep foundations of the manse;[1] still sinking
Through unturned earth. How had he magicked space
With inadvertent motion or word uttered
Of too-close-packed intelligence (such there are),
That he should penetrate with sliding ease
Dense earth, compound of ages, granite ribs
And groins? Consider: there was some word uttered,
Some abracadabra—then, like a stage-ghost,
Funereally with weeping, down, drowned, lost!

Oh, to be a child once more, sprawling at ease
On smooth turf of a ruined castle court!
Once he had dropped a stone between the slabs
That masked an ancient well, mysteriously
Plunging his mind down with it. Hear it go
Rattling and rocketing into secret void!
Count slowly: one, two, three! and echoes come
Fainter and fainter, merged in the general hum
Of bees and flies; only a thin draught rises
To chill the drowsy air. There he had lain
As if unborn, until life floated back
From the deep waters.
                          Oh, to renew now
That bliss of repossession, kindly sun

---

1   clergyman's house

Forfeit for ever, and the towering sky!

Falling, falling! Day closed up behind him.
Now stunned by the violent subterrene flow
Of rivers, whirling down to hiss below
On the flame-axis of this terrible earth;
Toppling upon their waterfall, O spirit. . . .

The Cool Web

Children are dumb to say how hot the day is,
How hot the scent is of the summer rose,
How dreadful the black wastes of evening sky,
How dreadful the tall soldiers drumming by.

But we have speech, to chill the angry day,
And speech, to dull the rose's cruel scent.
We spell away the overhanging night,
We spell away the soldiers and the fright.

There's a cool web of language winds us in,
Retreat from too much joy or too much fear:
We grow sea-green at last and coldly die
In brininess and volubility.

But if we let our tongues lose self-possession,
Throwing off language and its watery clasp
Before our death, instead of when death comes,
Facing the wide glare of the children's day,
Facing the rose, the dark sky and the drums,
We shall go mad no doubt and die that way.

Recalling War

Entrance and exit wounds are silvered clean,
The track aches only when the rain reminds.
The one-legged man forgets his leg of wood,
The one-armed man his jointed wooden arm.
The blinded man sees with his ears and hands
As much or more than once with both his eyes.
Their war was fought these twenty years ago
And now assumes the nature-look of time,
As when the morning traveller turns and views
His wild night-stumbling carved into a hill.

What, then, was war? No mere discord of flags
But an infection of the common sky
That sagged ominously upon the earth
Even when the season was the airiest May.

Down pressed the sky, and we, oppressed, thrust out
Boastful tongue, clenched fist and valiant yard.
Natural infirmities were out of mode,
For Death was young again: patron alone
Of healthy dying, premature fate-spasm.

Fear made fine bed-fellows. Sick with delight
At life's discovered transitoriness,
Our youth became all-flesh and waived the mind.
Never was such antiqueness of romance,
Such tasty honey oozing from the heart.
And old importances came swimming back—
Wine, meat, log-fires, a roof over the head,
A weapon at the thigh, surgeons at call.
Even there was a use again for God—
A word of rage in lack of meat, wine, fire,
In ache of wounds beyond all surgeoning.

War was return of earth to ugly earth,
War was foundering of sublimities,
Extinction of each happy art and faith
By which the world had still kept head in air,
Protesting logic or protesting love,
Until the unendurable moment struck—
The inward scream, the duty to run mad.

And we recall the merry ways of guns—
Nibbling the walls of factory and church
Like a child, piecrust; felling groves of trees
Like a child, dandelions with a switch.
Machine-guns rattle toy-like from a hill,
Down in a row the brave tin-soldiers fall:
A sight to be recalled in elder days
When learnedly the future we devote
To yet more boastful visions of despair.

Down, Wanton, Down!

Down, wanton, down! Have you no shame
That at the whisper of Love's name,
Or Beauty's, presto! up you raise
Your angry head and stand at gaze?

Poor bombard-captain, sworn to reach
The ravelin[1] and effect a breach—

---

1   A bombard captain is an officer in charge of a cannon; a ravelin is a projecting part of
a castle wall.

Indifferent what you storm or why,
So be that in the breach you die!

Love may be blind, but Love at least
Knows what is man and what mere beast;
Or Beauty wayward, but requires
More delicacy from her squires.

Tell me, my witless, whose one boast
Could be your staunchness at the post,
When were you made a man of parts
To think fine and profess the arts?

Will many-gifted Beauty come
Bowing to your bald rule of thumb,
Or Love swear loyalty to your crown?
Be gone, have done! Down, wanton, down!

A Slice of Wedding Cake

Why have such scores of lovely, gifted girls
    Married impossible men?
Simple self-sacrifice may be ruled out,
    And missionary endeavour, nine times out of ten.

Repeat 'impossible men': not merely rustic,
    Foul-tempered or depraved
(Dramatic foils chosen to show the world
    How well women behave, and always have behaved).

Impossible men: idle, illiterate,
    Self-pitying, dirty, sly,
For whose appearance even in City parks
    Excuses must be made to casual passers-by.

Has God's supply of tolerable husbands
    Fallen, in fact, so low?
Or do I always over-value woman
    At the expense of man?
                    Do I?
                        It might be so.

F. R. Scott

(1899–1984)

The Canadian Authors Meet[1]

Expansive puppets percolate self-unction
Beneath a portrait of the Prince of Wales.
Miss Crotchet's muse has somehow failed to function,
Yet she's a poetess. Beaming, she sails

From group to chattering group, with such a dear
Victorian saintliness, as is her fashion,
Greeting the other unknowns with a cheer—
Virgins of sixty who still write of passion.

The air is heavy with Canadian topics,
And Carman, Lampman, Roberts, Campbell, Scott,[2]
Are measured for their faith and philanthropics,
Their zeal for God and King, their earnest thought.

The cakes are sweet, but sweeter is the feeling
That one is mixing with the *literati;*[3]
It warms the old, and melts the most congealing.
Really, it is a most delightful party.

Shall we go round the mulberry bush, or shall
We gather at the river,[4] or shall we
Appoint a Poet Laureate[5] this fall,
Or shall we have another cup of tea?

O Canada, O Canada, O can
A day go by without new authors springing
To paint the native maple, and to plan
More ways to set the selfsame welkin ringing?

Lakeshore

The lake is sharp along the shore
Trimming the bevelled edge of land
To level curves; the fretted sands
Go slanting down through liquid air

---

1   The Canadian Authors' Association was founded in 1921. An early version of this poem appeared in 1927.
2   Canadian poets active at the turn of the century, and all represented in this anthology, with the exception of William Wilfred Campbell (1858-1918)
3   men and women of letters
4   words from a gospel song
5   in England, the post of official poet of the realm, charged with writing verses to commemorate state occasions

Till stones below shift here and there
Floating upon their broken sky
All netted by the prism wave
And rippled where the currents are.

I stare through windows at this cave
Where fish, like planes, slow-motioned, fly.
Poised in a still of gravity
The narrow minnow, flicking fin,
Hangs in a paler, ochre sun,
His doorways open everywhere.

And I am a tall frond that waves
Its head below its rooted feet
Seeking the light that draws it down
To forest floors beyond its reach
Vivid with gloom and eerie dreams.

The water's deepest colonnades
Contract the blood, and to this home
That stirs the dark amphibian
With me the naked swimmers come
Drawn to their prehistoric womb.

They too are liquid as they fall
Like tumbled water loosed above
Until they lie, diagonal,
Within the cool and sheltered grove
Stroked by the fingertips of love.

Silent, our sport is drowned in fact
Too virginal for speech or sound
And each is personal and laned
Along his private aqueduct.

Too soon the tether of the lungs
Is taut and straining, and we rise
Upon our undeveloped wings
Toward the prison of our ground
A secret anguish in our thighs
And mermaids in our memories.

This is our talent, to have grown
Upright in posture, false-erect,
A landed gentry, circumspect,
Tied to a horizontal soil
The floor and ceiling of the soul;
Striving, with cold and fishy care
To make an ocean of the air.

Sometimes, upon a crowded street,
I feel the sudden rain come down
And in the old, magnetic sound
I hear the opening of a gate
That loosens all the seven seas.
Watching the whole creation drown
I muse, alone, on Ararat.[1]

Laurentian Shield[2]

Hidden in wonder and snow, or sudden with summer,
This land stares at the sun in a huge silence
Endlessly repeating something we cannot hear.
Inarticulate, arctic,
Not written on by history, empty as paper,
It leans away from the world with songs in its lakes
Older than love, and lost in the miles.

This waiting is wanting.
It will choose its language
When it has chosen its technic,
A tongue to shape the vowels of its productivity.

A language of flesh and roses.

Now there are pre-words,
Cabin syllables,
Nouns of settlement
Slowly forming, with steel syntax,
The long sentence of its exploitation.

The first cry was the hunter, hungry for fur,
And the digger for gold, nomad, no-man, a particle;
Then the bold commands of monopolies, big with machines,
Carving their kingdoms out of the public wealth;
And now the drone of the plane, scouting the ice,
Fills all the emptiness with neighbourhood
And links our future over the vanished pole.

But a deeper note is sounding, heard in the mines,
The scattered camps and the mills, a language of life,
And what will be written in the full culture of occupation
Will come, presently, tomorrow,
From millions whose hands can turn this rock into children.

---

1   the mountain in Turkey where Noah's ark is said to have come to rest (Genesis 8.4)
2   the great mass of ancient granite that surrounds Hudson's Bay and covers half of Canada

Trans Canada

Pulled from our ruts by the made-to-order gale
We sprang upward into a wider prairie
And dropped Regina below like a pile of bones.[1]
Sky tumbled upon us in waterfalls,
But we were smarter than a Skeena salmon[2]
And shot our silver body over the lip of air
To rest in a pool of space
On the top storey of our adventure.

A solar peace
And a six-way choice.

Clouds, now, are the solid substance,
A floor of wool roughed by the wind
Standing in waves that halt in their fall.
A still of troughs.

The plane, our planet,
Travels on roads that are not seen or laid
But sound in instruments on pilots' ears,
While underneath
The sure wings
Are the everlasting arms of science.

Man, the lofty worm, tunnels his latest clay,
And bores his new career.

This frontier, too, is ours.
This everywhere whose life can only be led
At the pace of a rocket
Is common to man and man.
And every country below is an I land.[3]

The sun sets on its top shelf,
And stars seem farther from our nearer grasp.

I have sat by night beside a cold lake
And touched things smoother than moonlight on still water,
But the moon on this cloud sea is not human,
And here is no shore, no intimacy,
Only the start of space, the road to suns.

---

1   Until 1882, Regina was known as Pile of Bones, because of the slaughter of buffalo that
    had taken place in that region.
2   The Skeena is a river in British Columbia, near Prince Rupert.
3   an echo of Donne's words, "No man is an *Iland*, intire of it selfe" (*Devotions* XVII)

Last Rites

Within his tent of pain and oxygen
This man is dying; grave, he mutters prayers,
Stares at the bedside altar through the screens,
Lies still for invocation and for hands.
Priest takes his symbols from a leather bag.
Surplice and stole, the pyx[1] and marks of faith,
And makes a chancel in the ether air.
Nurse too is minister. Tall cylinders,
Her altar-boys, press out rich draughts for lungs
The fluid slowly fills. The trick device
Keeps the worn heart from failing, and bright dials
Flicker their needles as the pressures change,
Like eyelids on his eyes. Priest moves in peace,
Part of his other world. Nurse prays with skills,
Serving her Lord with rites and acts of love.
Both acolytes are uniformed in white
And wear a holy look, for both are near
The very point and purpose of their art.
Nurse is precise and careful. She will fail
In the end, and lose her battle. Death will block
The channels of her aid, and brush aside
All her exact inventions, leaving priest
Triumphant on his ground. But nurse will stare
This evil in the face, will not accept,
Will come with stranger and more cunning tools
To other bedsides, adding skill to skill,
Till death is driven slowly farther back.
How far? She does not ask.
                                        Priest does not fight.
He lives through death and death is proof of him.
In the perpetual, unanswerable why
Are born the symbol and the sacrifice.
The warring creeds run past the boundary
And stake their claims to heaven; science drives
The boundary back, and claims the living land,
A revelation growing, piece by piece,
Wonder and mystery as true as God.
And I who watch this rightness and these rites,
I see my father in the dying man,
I am his son who dwells upon the earth,
There is a holy spirit in this room,
And straight toward me from both sides of time
Endless the known and unknown roadways run.

---

1   the casket which holds the Eucharistic bread or wafer

W. L. M. K. [1]

How shall we speak of Canada,
Mackenzie King dead?
The Mother's boy in the lonely room
With his dog, his medium and his ruins?

He blunted us.

We had no shape
Because he never took sides,
And no sides
Because he never allowed them to take shape.

He skilfully avoided what was wrong
Without saying what was right,
And never let his on the one hand
Know what his on the other hand was doing.

The height of his ambition
Was to pile a Parliamentary Committee on a Royal Commission,
To have "conscription if necessary
But not necessarily conscription," [2]
To let Parliament decide—
Later.

Postpone, postpone, abstain.

Only one thread was certain:
After World War I
Business as usual,
After World War II
Orderly decontrol.
Always he led us back to where we were before.

He seemed to be in the centre
Because we had no centre,
No vision
To pierce the smoke-screen of his politics.

Truly he will be remembered
Wherever men honour ingenuity,
Ambiguity, inactivity, and political longevity.

---

1   William Lyon Mackenzie King (1874-1950), Prime Minister of Canada 1921-1926, 1926-
    1930, 1935-1948. King was a spiritualist, keeping in touch with his dead mother by means
    of the occult. He was also a collector of architectural ruins.
2   Mackenzie's slogan during the bitter debates about conscription in 1942

Let us raise up a temple
To the cult of mediocrity,
Do nothing by halves
Which can be done by quarters.

Basil Bunting

(1900–1985)

Personal Column

. . . As to my heart, that may as well be forgotten
or labelled: Owner will dispose of same
to a good home, refs. exchgd., h.&c.,
previous experience desired but not essential
or let on a short lease to suit convenience.

What the Chairman Told Tom

Poetry? It's a hobby.
I run model trains.
Mr Shaw there breeds pigeons.

It's not work. You don't sweat.
Nobody pays for it.
You *could* advertise soap.

Art, that's opera; or repertory—
The Desert Song.
Nancy was in the chorus.

But to ask for twelve pounds a week—
married, aren't you?—
you've got a nerve.

How could I look a bus conductor
in the face
if I paid you twelve pounds?

Who says it's poetry, anyhow?
My ten year old
can do it *and* rhyme.

I get three thousand and expenses,
a car, vouchers,
but I'm an accountant.

They do what I tell them,
my company.
What do *you* do?

Nasty little words, nasty long words,
it's unhealthy.
I want to wash when I meet a poet.

They're Reds, addicts,
all delinquents.
What you write is rot.

Mr Hines says so, and he's a schoolteacher,
he ought to know.
Go and find *work*

I am agog for foam

To Peggy Mullett

I am agog for foam. Tumultuous come
with teeming sweetness to the bitter shore
tidelong unrinsed and midday parched and numb
with expectation. If the bright sky bore
with endless utterance of a single blue
unphrased, its restless immobility
infects the soul, which must decline into
an anguished and exact sterility
and waste away: then how much more the sea
trembling with alteration must perfect
our loneliness by its hostility.
The dear companionship of its elect
deepens our envy. Its indifference
haunts us to suicide. Strong memories
of sprayblown days exasperate impatience
to brief rebellion and emphasise
the casual impotence we sicken of.
But when mad waves spring, braceletted with foam,
towards us in the angriness of love
crying a strange name, tossing as they come
repeated invitations in the gay
exuberance of unexplained desire,
we can forget the sad splendour and play
at wilfulness until the gods require
renewed inevitable hopeless calm
and the foam dies and we again subside
into our catalepsy, dreaming foam,
while the dry shore awaits another tide.

Nothing

Nothing
substance utters or time
stills and restrains
joins design and

supple measure deftly
as thought's intricate polyphonic
score dovetails with the tread
sensuous things
keep in our consciousness.

Celebrate man's craft
and the word spoken in shapeless night, the
sharp tool paring away
waste and the forms
cut out of mystery!

When taut string's note
passes ears' reach or red rays or violet
fade, strong over unseen
forces the word
ranks and enumerates . . .

mimes clouds condensed
and hewn hills and bristling forests,
steadfast corn in its season
and the seasons
in their due array,

life of man's own body
and death . . .
                    The sound thins into melody,
discourse narrowing, craft
failing, design
petering out.

Ears heavy to breeze of speech and
thud of the ictus.[1]

---

1   rhythmical or metrical stress

Kenneth Slessor

(1901–1971)

Wild Grapes

The old orchard, full of smoking air,
Full of sour marsh and broken boughs, is there,
But kept no more by vanished Mulligans,
Or Hartigans, long drowned in earth themselves,
Who gave this bitter fruit their care.

Here's where the cherries grew that birds forgot,
And apples bright as dogstars;[1] now there is not
An apple or a cherry; only grapes,
But wild ones, Isabella grapes they're called,
Small, pointed, black, like boughs of musket-shot.

Eating their flesh, half-savage with black fur,
Acid and gipsy-sweet, I thought of her,
Isabella, the dead girl, who has lingered on
Defiantly when all have gone away,
In an old orchard where swallows never stir.

Isabella grapes, outlaws of a strange bough,
That in their harsh sweetness remind me somehow
Of dark hair swinging and silver pins,
A girl half-fierce, half-melting, as these grapes,
Kissed here — or killed here — but who remembers now?

Five Bells[2]

Time that is moved by little fidget wheels
Is not my Time, the flood that does not flow.
Between the double and the single bell
Of a ship's hour, between a round of bells
From the dark warship riding there below,
I have lived many lives, and this one life
Of Joe,[3] long dead, who lives between five bells.

Deep and dissolving verticals of light
Ferry the falls of moonshine down. Five bells
Coldly rung out in a machine's voice. Night and water

---

1   stars in the Greater or Lesser Dog constellations, the brightest being Sirius, also known
    as the Dog Star
2   The passing of time in a watch at sea is marked by the sounding of a bell each half hour;
    thus in a four-hour watch, "five bells" would indicate the fifth half-hour since the
    beginning of the watch.
3   The poem commemorates Joe Lynch, a friend who drowned in Sydney Harbour in the
    1930s.

Pour to one rip of darkness, the Harbour floats
In air, the Cross[1] hangs upside-down in water.

Why do I think of you, dead man, why thieve
These profitless lodgings from the flukes of thought
Anchored in Time? You have gone from earth,
Gone even from the meaning of a name;
Yet something's there, yet something forms its lips
And hits and cries against the ports of space,
Beating their sides to make its fury heard.

Are you shouting at me, dead man, squeezing your face
In agonies of speech on speechless panes?
Cry louder, beat the windows, bawl your name!

But I hear nothing, nothing . . . only bells,
Five bells, the bumpkin calculus of Time.
Your echoes die, your voice is dowsed by Life,
There's not a mouth can fly the pygmy strait—
Nothing except the memory of some bones
Long shoved away, and sucked away, in mud;
And unimportant things you might have done,
Or once I thought you did; but you forgot,
And all have now forgotten—looks and words
And slops of beer; your coat with buttons off,
Your gaunt chin and pricked eye, and raging tales
Of Irish kings and English perfidy,
And dirtier perfidy of publicans
Groaning to God from Darlinghurst.

Five bells.

Then I saw the road, I heard the thunder
Tumble, and felt the talons of the rain
The night we came to Moorebank in slab-dark,
So dark you bore no body, had no face,
But a sheer voice that rattled out of air
(As now you'd cry if I could break the glass),
A voice that spoke beside me in the bush,
Loud for a breath or bitten off by wind,
Of Milton, melons, and the Rights of Man,[2]
And blowing flutes, and how Tahitian girls
Are brown and angry-tongued, and Sydney girls
Are white and angry-tongued, or so you'd found.
But all I heard was words that didn't join

---

1   the Southern Cross, a constellation with four bright stars in the shape of a cross, visible
    only in the southern hemisphere
2   title of a political treatise by Thomas Paine, published in 1791-92

So Milton became melons, melons girls,
And fifty mouths, it seemed, were out that night,
And in each tree an Ear was bending down,
Or something had just run, gone behind grass,
When, blank and bone-white, like a maniac's thought,
The naphtha-flash of lightning slit the sky,
Knifing the dark with deathly photographs.
There's not so many with so poor a purse
Or fierce a need, must fare by night like that,
Five miles in darkness on a country track,
But when you do, that's what you think.

Five bells.

In Melbourne, your appetite had gone,
Your angers too; they had been leechcd away
By the soft archery of summer rains
And the sponge-paws of wetness, the slow damp
That stuck the leaves of living, snailed the mind,
And showed your bones, that had been sharp with rage,
The sodden ecstasies of rectitude.
I thought of what you'd written in faint ink,
Your journal with the sawn-off lock, that stayed behind
With other things you left, all without use,
All without meaning now, except a sign
That someone had been living who now was dead:
'At Labassa. Room 6 x 8
On top of the tower; because of this, very dark
And cold in winter. Everything has been stowed
Into this room—500 books all shapes
And colours, dealt across the floor
And over sills and on the laps of chairs;
Guns, photoes of many differant things
And differant curioes that I obtained. . . .'
In Sydney, by the spent aquarium-flare
Of penny gaslight on pink wallpaper,
We argued about blowing up the world,
But you were living backward, so each night
You crept a moment closer to the breast,
And they were living, all of them, those frames
And shapes of flesh that had perplexed your youth,
And most your father, the old man gone blind,
With fingers always round a fiddle's neck,
That graveyard mason whose fair monuments
And tablets cut with dreams of piety
Rest on the bosoms of a thousand men
Staked bone by bone, in quiet astonishment
At cargoes they had never thought to bear,
These funeral-cakes of sweet and sculptured stone.

Where have you gone? The tide is over you,
The turn of midnight water's over you,

As Time is over you, and mystery,
And memory, the flood that does not flow.
You have no suburb, like those easier dead
In private berths of dissolution laid—
The tide goes over, the waves ride over you
And let their shadows down like shining hair,
But they are Water; and the sea-pinks bend
Like lilies in your teeth, but they are Weed;
And you are only part of an Idea.
I felt the wet push its black thumb-balls in,
The night you died, I felt your eardrums crack,
And the short agony, the longer dream,
The Nothing that was neither long nor short;
But I was bound, and could not go that way,
But I was blind, and could not feel your hand.
If I could find an answer, could only find
Your meaning, or could say why you were here
Who now are gone, what purpose gave you breath
Or seized it back, might I not hear your voice?

I looked out of my window in the dark
At waves with diamond quills and combs of light
That arched their mackerel-backs and smacked the sand
In the moon's drench, that straight enormous glaze,
And ships far off asleep, and Harbour-buoys
Tossing their fireballs wearily each to each,
And tried to hear your voice, but all I heard
Was a boat's whistle, and the scraping squeal
Of seabirds' voices far away, and bells,
Five bells. Five bells coldly ringing out.

Five bells.

Beach Burial

Softly and humbly to the Gulf of Arabs
The convoys of dead sailors come;
At night they sway and wander in the waters far under,
But morning rolls them in the foam.

Between the sob and clubbing of the gunfire
Someone, it seems, has time for this,
To pluck them from the shallows and bury them in burrows
And tread the sand upon their nakedness;

And each cross, the driven stake of tidewood,
Bears the last signature of men,
Written with such perplexity, with such bewildered pity,
The words choke as they begin—

"Unknown seaman"—the ghostly pencil
Wavers and fades, the purple drips,
The breath of the wet season has washed their inscriptions
As blue as drowned men's lips,

Dead seamen, gone in search of the same landfall,
Whether as enemies they fought,
Or fought with us, or neither; the sand joins them together,
Enlisted on the other front.

El Alamein[1]

---

1   in northern Egypt, site of a British victory over Axis forces in 1942

Langston Hughes

(1902–1967)

The Weary Blues

Droning a drowsy syncopated tune,
Rocking back and forth to a mellow croon,
    I heard a Negro play.
Down on Lenox Avenue[1] the other night
By the pale dull pallor of an old gas light
    He did a lazy sway. . . .
    He did a lazy sway. . . .
To the tune o' those Weary Blues.
With his ebony hands on each ivory key
He made that poor piano moan with melody.
    O Blues!
Swaying to and fro on his rickety stool
He played that sad raggy tune like a musical fool.
    Sweet Blues!
Coming from a black man's soul.
    O Blues!
In a deep song voice with a melancholy tone
I heard that Negro sing, that old piano moan—
    "Ain't got nobody in all this world,
    Ain't got nobody but ma self.
    I's gwine to quit ma frownin'
    And put ma troubles on the shelf."
Thump, thump, thump, went his foot on the floor.
He played a few chords then he sang some more—
    "I got the Weary Blues
    And I can't be satisfied.
    Got the Weary Blues
    And can't be satisfied—
    I ain't happy no mo'
    And I wish that I had died."
And far into the night he crooned that tune.
The stars went out and so did the moon.
The singer stopped playing and went to bed
While the Weary Blues echoed through his head
He slept like a rock or a man that's dead.

---

1   in Harlem

Trumpet Player

The Negro
With the trumpet at his lips
Has dark moons of weariness
Beneath his eyes
Where the smoldering memory
Of slave ships
Blazed to the crack of whips
About his thighs.

The Negro
With the trumpet at his lips
Has a head of vibrant hair
Tamed down,
Patent-leathered now
Until it gleams
Like jet—
Were jet a crown.

The music
From the trumpet at his lips
Is honey
Mixed with liquid fire.
The rhythm
From the trumpet at his lips
Is ecstasy
Distilled from old desire—

Desire
That is longing for the moon
Where the moonlight's but a spotlight
In his eyes,
Desire
That is longing for the sea
Where the sea's a bar-glass
Sucker size.

The Negro
With the trumpet at his lips
Whose jacket
Has a *fine* one-button roll,
Does not know
Upon what riff the music slips
Its hypodermic needle
To his soul—

But softly
As the tune comes from his throat
Trouble
Mellows to a golden note.

Harlem

What happens to a dream deferred?

Does it dry up
like a raisin in the sun?
Or fester like a sore—
And then run?
Does it stink like rotten meat?
Or crust and sugar over—
like a syrupy sweet?

Maybe it just sags
like a heavy load.

Or does it explode?

A. J. M. Smith

(1902–1980)

The Lonely Land

Cedar and jagged fir
uplift sharp barbs
against the gray
and cloud-piled sky;
and in the bay
blown spume and windrift
and thin, bitter spray
snap
at the whirling sky;
and the pine trees
lean one way.

A wild duck calls
to her mate,
and the ragged
and passionate tones
stagger and fall,
and recover,
and stagger and fall,
on these stones—
are lost
in the lapping of water
on smooth, flat stones.

This is a beauty
of dissonance,
this resonance
of stony strand,
this smoky cry
curled over a black pine
like a broken
and wind-battered branch
when the wind
bends the tops of the pines
and curdles the sky
from the north.

This is the beauty
of strength
broken by strength
and still strong.

News of the Phoenix[1]

They say the Phoenix is dying, some say dead.
Dead without issue is what one message said,
But that has been suppressed, officially denied.

I think myself the man who sent it lied.
In any case, I'm told, he has been shot,
As a precautionary measure, whether he did or not.

Prothalamium[2]

Here in this narrow room there is no light;
The dead tree sings against the window pane;
Sand shifts a little, easily; the wall
Responds a little, inchmeal, slowly, down.

My sister, whom my dust shall marry, sleeps
Alone, yet knows what bitter root it is
That stirs within her; see, it splits the heart—
Warm hands grown cold, grown nerveless as a fin,
And lips enamelled to a hardness—
Consummation ushered in
By wind in sundry corners.

This holy sacrament was solemnized
In harsh poetics a good while ago—
At Malfy[3] and the Danish battlements,[4]
And by that preacher from a cloud in Paul's.[5]

No matter: each must read the truth himself,
Or, reading it, reads nothing to the point.
Now these are me, whose thought is mine, and hers,
Who are alone here in this narrow room—
Tree fumbling pane, bell tolling,
Ceiling dripping and the plaster falling,
And Death, the voluptuous, calling.

---

1   The Phoenix is a mythical bird said to perish every thousand years, and to rise renewed
    from the ashes of its funeral pyre.
2   a song before a wedding
3   a reference to *The Duchess of Malfi* (1623), a tragedy by John Webster
4   an allusion to *Hamlet*
5   St. Paul's Cathedral in London, where John Donne, as Dean from 1621-1631, gave many
    sermons

The Archer

Bend back thy bow, O Archer, till the string
Is level with thine ear, thy body taut,
Its nature art, thyself thy statue wrought
Of marble blood, thy weapon the poised wing
Of coiled and aquiline Fate. Then, loosening, fling
The hissing arrow like a burning thought
Into the empty sky that smokes as the hot
Shaft plunges to the bullseye's quenching ring.

So for a moment, motionless, serene,
Fixed between time and time, I aim and wait;
Nothing remains for breath now but to waive
His prior claim and let the barb fly clean
Into the heart of what I know and hate—
That central black, the ringed and targeted grave.

Stevie Smith

(1902–1971)

The River God

I may be smelly, and I may be old,
Rough in my pebbles, reedy in my pools,
But where my fish float by I bless their swimming
And I like the people to bathe in me, especially women.
But I can drown the fools
Who bathe too close to the weir, contrary to rules.
And they take a long time drowning
As I throw them up now and then in a spirit of clowning.
Hi yih, yippity-yap, merrily I flow,
O I may be an old foul river but I have plenty of go.
Once there was a lady who was too bold
She bathed in me by the tall black cliff where the water runs
    cold,
So I brought her down here
To be my beautiful dear.
Oh will she stay with me will she stay
This beautiful lady, or will she go away?
She lies in my beautiful deep river bed with many a weed
To hold her, and many a waving reed.
Oh who would guess what a beautiful white face lies there
Waiting for me to smooth and wash away the fear
She looks at me with. Hi yih, do not let her
Go. There is no one on earth who does not forget her
Now. They say I am a foolish old smelly river
But they do not know of my wide original bed
Where the lady waits, with her golden sleepy head.
If she wishes to go I will not forgive her.

Away, Melancholy

Away, melancholy,
Away with it, let it go.

Are not the trees green,
The earth as green?
Does not the wind blow,
Fire leap and the rivers flow?
Away melancholy.

The ant is busy
He carrieth his meat,
All things hurry
To be eaten or eat.
Away, melancholy.

Man, too, hurries,
Eats, couples, buries,
He is an animal also
With a hey ho melancholy,
Away with it, let it go.

Man of all creatures
Is superlative
(Away melancholy)
He of all creatures alone
Raiseth a stone
(Away melancholy)
Into the stone, the god
Pours what he knows of good
Calling, good, God.
Away melancholy, let it go.

Speak not to me of tears,
Tyranny, pox, wars,
Saying, Can God
Stone of man's thought, be good?

Say rather it is enough
That the stuffed
Stone of man's good, growing,
By man's called God.
Away, melancholy, let it go.

Man aspires
To good,
To love
Sighs;

Beaten, corrupted, dying
In his own blood lying
Yet heaves up an eye above
Cries, Love, love.
It is his virtue needs explaining,
Not his failing.

Away, melancholy,
Away with it, let it go.

Mother, Among the Dustbins

Mother, among the dustbins and the manure
I feel the measure of my humanity, an allure
As of the presence of God. I am sure

In the dustbins, in the manure, in the cat at play,
Is the presence of God, in a sure way
He moves there. Mother, what do you say?

I too have felt the presence of God in the broom
I hold, in the cobwebs in the room,
But most of all in the silence of the tomb.

Ah! but that thought that informs the hope of our kind
Is but an empty thing, what lies behind?—
Naught but the vanity of a protesting mind

That would not die. This is the thought that bounces
Within a conceited head and trounces
Inquiry. Man is most frivolous when he pronounces.

Well Mother, I shall continue to feel as I do,
And I think you would be wise to do so too,
Can you question the folly of man in the creation of God?
    Who are you?

The Blue from Heaven

A legend of King Arthur of Britain.

King Arthur rode in another world
And his twelve knights rode behind him
And Guinevere was there
Crying: Arthur, where are you dear?

Why is the King so blue
Why is he this blue colour?
It is because the sun is shining
And he rides under the blue cornflowers.

High wave the cornflowers
That shed the pale blue light
And under the tall cornflowers
Rides King Arthur and his twelve knights.

And Guinevere is there
Crying: Arthur, where are you dear?

First there were twelve knights riding
And then there was only one
And King Arthur said to the one knight,
Be gone.

All I wish for now, said Arthur,
Is the beautiful colour blue

And to ride in the blue sunshine
And Guinevere I do not wish for you.

Oh Lord, said Guinevere
I do not see the colour blue
And I wish to ride where our knights rode,
After you.

Go back, go back, Guinevere,
Go back to the palace, said the King.
So she went back to the palace
And her grief did not seem to her a small thing.

The Queen has returned to the palace
Crying: Arthur, where are you dear?
And every day she speaks of Arthur's grandeur
To the knights who are there.

That Arthur has fallen from the grandeur
Of his powers all agree
And the falling off of Arthur
Becomes their theme presently.

As if it were only temporarily
And it was not for ever
They speak, but the Queen knows
He will come back never.

Yes, Arthur has passed away
Gladly he has laid down his reigning powers
He has gone to ride in the blue light
Of the peculiar towering cornflowers.

Not Waving but Drowning

Nobody heard him, the dead man,
But still he lay moaning:
I was much further out than you thought
And not waving but drowning.

Poor chap, he always loved larking
And now he's dead
It must have been too cold for him his heart gave way,
They said.

Oh, no no no, it was too cold always
(Still the dead one lay moaning)
I was much too far out all my life
And not waving but drowning.

Countee Cullen

(1903-1946)

Yet Do I Marvel

I doubt not God is good, well-meaning, kind,
And did He stoop to quibble could tell why
The little buried mole continues blind,
Why flesh that mirrors Him must some day die,
Make plain the reason tortured Tantalus[1]
Is baited by the fickle fruit, declare
If merely brute caprice dooms Sisyphus[2]
To struggle up a never-ending stair.
Inscrutable His ways are, and immune
To catechism by a mind too strewn
With petty cares to slightly understand
What awful brain compels His awful hand.
Yet do I marvel at this curious thing:
To make a poet black, and bid him sing!

To John Keats, Poet, At Spring Time

(For Carl Van Vechten)

I cannot hold my peace, John Keats;
There never was a spring like this;
It is an echo, that repeats
My last year's song and next year's bliss.
I know, in spite of all men say
Of Beauty, you have felt her most.
Yea, even in your grave her way
Is laid. Poor, troubled, lyric ghost,
Spring never was so fair and dear
As Beauty makes her seem this year.

I cannot hold my peace, John Keats,
I am as helpless in the toil
Of Spring as any lamb that bleats
To feel the solid earth recoil
Beneath his puny legs. Spring beats
Her tocsin[3] call to those who love her,
And lo! the dogwood petals cover
Her breast with drifts of snow, and sleek

---

1   In Greek mythology, a Lydian king tortured in Hades by being forced to stand in water
       that receded when he tried to drink, and under a tree with fruit he could not reach.
2   The legendary king of Corinth was condemned in Hades to roll a large stone to the top
       of a hill, whence it would roll down again, requiring him to repeat the task in perpetuity.
3   a signal sounded on a bell

White gulls fly screaming to her, and hover
About her shoulders, and kiss her cheek,
While white and purple lilacs muster
A strength that bears them to a cluster
Of color and odor; for her sake
All things that slept are now awake.

And you and I, shall we lie still,
John Keats, while Beauty summons us?
Somehow I feel your sensitive will
Is pulsing up some tremulous
Sap road of a maple tree, whose leaves
Grow music as they grow, since your
Wild voice is in them, a harp that grieves
For life that opens death's dark door.
Though dust, your fingers still can push
The Vision Splendid to a birth,
Though now they work as grass in the hush
Of the night on the broad sweet page of the earth.

"John Keats is dead," they say, but I
Who hear your full insistent cry
In bud and blossom, leaf and tree,
Know John Keats still writes poetry.
And while my head is earthward bowed
To read new life sprung from your shroud,
Folks seeing me must think it strange
That merely spring should so derange
My mind. They do not know that you,
John Keats, keep revel with me, too.

From the Dark Tower

(To Charles S. Johnson)

We shall not always plant while others reap
The golden increment of bursting fruit,
Not always countenance, abject and mute,
That lesser men should hold their brothers cheap;
Not everlastingly while others sleep
Shall we beguile their limbs with mellow flute,
Not always bend to some more subtle brute;
We were not made eternally to weep.

The night whose sable breast relieves the stark,
White stars is no less lovely being dark,
And there are buds that cannot bloom at all
In light, but crumple, piteous, and fall;
So in the dark we hide the heart that bleeds,
And wait, and tend our agonizing seeds.

Richard Eberhart

(b. 1904)

The Groundhog

In June, amid the golden fields,
I saw a groundhog lying dead.
Dead lay he; my senses shook,
And mind outshot our naked frailty.
There lowly in the vigorous summer
His form began its senseless change,
And made my senses waver dim
Seeing nature ferocious in him.
Inspecting close his maggots' might
And seething cauldron of his being,
Half with loathing, half with a strange love,
I poked him with an angry stick.
The fever arose, became a flame
And Vigour circumscribed the skies,
Immense energy in the sun,
And through my frame a sunless trembling.
My stick had done nor good nor harm.
Then stood I silent in the day
Watching the object, as before;
And kept my reverence for knowledge
Trying for control, to be still,
To quell the passion of the blood;
Until I had bent down on my knees
Praying for joy in the sight of decay.
And so I left; and I returned
In Autumn strict of eye, to see
The sap gone out of the groundhog,
But the bony sodden hulk remained.
But the year had lost its meaning,
And in intellectual chains
I lost both love and loathing,
Mured up in the wall of wisdom.
Another summer took the fields again
Massive and burning, full of life,
But when I chanced upon the spot
There was only a little hair left,
And bones bleaching in the sunlight
Beautiful as architecture;
I watched them like a geometer,[1]
And cut a walking stick from a birch.
It has been three years, now.
There is no sign of the groundhog.

---

1 One who is skilled in geometry; the word is also applied to a class of caterpillar.

I stood there in the whirling summer,
My hand capped a withered heart,
And thought of China and of Greece,
Of Alexander[1] in his tent;
Of Montaigne[2] in his tower,
Of Saint Theresa[3] in her wild lament.

The Fury of Aerial Bombardment

You would think the fury of aerial bombardment
Would rouse God to relent; the infinite spaces
Are still silent. He looks on shock-pried faces.
History, even, does not know what is meant.

You would feel that after so many centuries
God would give man to repent; yet he can kill
As Cain could, but with multitudinous will,
No farther advanced than in his ancient furies.

Was man made stupid to see his own stupidity?
Is God by definition indifferent, beyond us all?
Is the eternal truth man's fighting soul
Wherein the Beast ravens in its own avidity?

Of Van Wettering I speak, and Averill,
Names on a list,[4] whose faces I do not recall
But they are gone to early death, who late in school
Distinguished the belt feed lever from the belt holding pawl.[5]

---

1   Alexander the Great (356-323 B.C.), king of Macedon and conqueror of the Persian
    Empire
2   Montaigne (1533-1592) was a French philosopher and essayist.
3   Saint Theresa (1515-1582), known as St. Theresa of Avila, was a Spanish nun renowned
    for her piety and her work with the Carmelite Order.
4   As a gunnery instructor in World War II, Eberhart often saw the names of past students
    on the casualty lists.
5   parts of the .50 calibre Browning machine gun, mounted in American aircraft in World
    War II

Earle Birney

(1904–1991)

Vancouver Lights

About me the night   moonless   wimples the mountains
wraps ocean   land   air   and mounting
sucks at the stars   The city   throbbing below
webs the sable peninsula   The golden
strands overleap the seajet   by bridge and buoy
vault the shears of the inlet   climb the woods
toward me   falter   and halt   Across to the firefly
haze of a ship on the gulf's erased horizon
roll the lambent spokes of a lighthouse

Through the feckless years we have come to the time
when to look on this quilt of lamps is a troubling delight
Welling from Europe's bog   through Africa flowing
and Asia   drowning the lonely lumes[1] on the oceans
tiding up over Halifax   now to this winking
outpost comes flooding the primal ink

On this mountain's brutish forehead with terror of space
I stir   of the changeless night and the stark ranges
of nothing   pulsing down from beyond and between
the fragile planets   We are a spark beleaguered
by darkness   this twinkle we make in a corner of emptiness
how shall we utter our fear that the black Experimentress
will never in the range of her microscope find it?   Our Phoebus[2]
himself is a bubble that dries on Her slide   while the Nubian[3]
wears for an evening's whim a necklace of nebulae

Yet we must speak   we the unique glowworms
Out of the waters and rocks of our little world
we conjured these flames   hooped these sparks
by our will   From blankness and cold we fashioned stars
to our size   and signalled Aldebaran[4]
This must we say   whoever may be to hear us
if murk devour   and none weave again in gossamer:

These rays were ours
we made and unmade them   Not the shudder of continents
doused us   the moon's passion   nor crash of comets
In the fathomless heat of our dwarfdom   our dream's combustion

---

1   variant form of dialect "leam," meaning light or ray.
2   an epithet of Apollo, god of the sun; here, the sun itself
3   a member of the Black tribes formerly ruling the territory between Egypt and Abyssinia (Ethiopia)
4   a red star of the first magnitude, in the constellation of Taurus

we contrived the power the blast that snuffed us
No one bound Prometheus[1] Himself he chained
and consumed his own bright liver O stranger
Plutonian descendant or beast in the stretching night—
there was light

Anglosaxon Street[2]

Dawndrizzle ended dampness steams from
blotching brick and blank plasterwaste
Faded housepatterns hoary and finicky
unfold stuttering stick like a phonograph

Here is a ghetto gotten for goyim[3]
O with care denuded of nigger and kike[4]
No coonsmell rankles reeks only cellarrot
attar of carexhaust catcorpse and cookinggrease
Imperial hearts heave in this haven
Cracks across windows are welded with slogans
There'll Always Be An England enhances geraniums
and V's for Victory vanquish the housefly

Ho! with climbing sun march the bleached beldames
festooned with shopping bags farded[5] flatarched
bigthewed Saxonwives stepping over buttrivers
waddling back wienerladen to suckle smallfry

Hoy! with sunslope shrieking over hydrants
flood from learninghall the lean fingerlings
Nordic nobblecheeked not all clean of nose
leaping Commandowise into leprous lanes

What! after whistleblow! spewed from wheelboat
after daylong doughtiness dire handplay
in sewertrench or sandpit come Saxonthegns[6]
Junebrown Jutekings[7] jawslack for meat

Sit after supper on smeared doorsteps

---

1 In Greek myth, the Titan who stole fire from Heaven to give to humankind, for which he was punished by being chained to a rock while an eagle devoured his liver each day.
2 Birney here imitates the strong-stress metre of Anglo-Saxon poetry, with four heavy stresses to the line (regardless of the number of intervening light syllables), a pause or *caesura* at mid-line, and emphatic use of alliteration.
3 a Yiddish word meaning non-Jews
4 a derogatory term for Jew
5 painted (i.e., with make-up)
6 Saxon knights, warriors
7 The Jutes were one of the Germanic tribes that settled in Britain in the fifth and sixth centuries.

not humbly swearing   hatedeeds on Huns
profiteers politicians   pacifists Jews

Then by twobit magic   to muse in movie
unlock picturehoard   or lope to alehall
soaking bleakly   in beer skittleless

Home again to hotbox   and humid husbandhood
in slumbertrough adding   sleepily to Anglekin
Alongside in lanenooks   carling and leman[1]
caterwaul and clip   careless of Saxonry
with moonglow and haste   and a higher heartbeat

Slumbers now slumtrack   unstinks cooling
waiting brief for milkmaid   mornstar and worldrise

From the Hazel Bough

I met a lady
   on a lazy street
hazel eyes
   and little plush feet

her legs swam by
   like lovely trout
eyes were trees
   where boys leant out

hands in the dark and
   a river side
round breasts rising
   with the finger's tide

she was plump as a finch
   and live as a salmon
gay as silk and
   proud as a Brahmin[2]

we winked when we met
   and laughed when we parted
never took time
   to be brokenhearted

but no man sees
   where the trout lie now

---

1   a woman and her sweetheart
2   a member of the highest Hindu caste

or what leans out
   from the hazel bough

Bushed

He invented a rainbow but lightning struck it
shattered it into the lake-lap of a mountain
so big his mind slowed when he looked at it

Yet he built a shack on the shore
learned to roast porcupine belly and
wore the quills on his hatband

At first he was out with the dawn
whether it yellowed bright as wood-columbine
or was only a fuzzed moth in a flannel of storm
But he found the mountain was clearly alive
sent messages whizzing down every hot morning
boomed proclamations at noon and spread out
a white guard of goat
before falling asleep on its feet at sundown

When he tried his eyes on the lake   ospreys
would fall like valkyries[1]
choosing the cut-throat[2]
He took then to waiting
till the night smoke rose from the boil of the sunset

But the moon carved unknown totems
out of the lakeshore
owls in the beardusky woods derided him
moosehorned cedars circled his swamps and tossed
their antlers up to the stars
then he knew   though the mountain slept   the winds
were shaping its peak to an arrowhead
poised

And now he could only
bar himself in and wait
for the great flint to come singing into his heart

---

1   in Norse mythology, one of the handmaids of Odin who would slay the heroes chosen to
die in battle, then conduct them to Valhalla
2   trout

The Bear on the Delhi Road

Unreal   tall as a myth
by the road the Himalayan bear
is beating the brilliant air
with his crooked arms
About him two men   bare
spindly as locusts   leap

One pulls on a ring
in the great soft nose   His mate
flicks   flicks with a stick
up at the rolling eyes

They have not led him here
down from the fabulous hills
to this bald alien plain
and the clamorous world   to kill
but simply to teach him to dance

They are peaceful both   these spare
men of Kashmir   and the bear
alive is their living   too
If   far on the Delhi way
around him galvanic they dance
it is merely to wear   wear
from his shaggy body the tranced
wish forever to stay
only an ambling bear
four-footed in berries

It is no more joyous for them
in this hot dust to prance
out of reach of the praying claws
sharpened to paw for ants
in the shadows of deodars[1]
It is not easy to free
myth from reality
or rear this fellow up
to lurch   lurch with them
in the tranced dancing of men

---

1   East Indian cedars

El Greco: Espolio[1]

The carpenter is intent on the pressure of his hand
on the awl   and the trick of pinpointing his strength
through the awl to the wood   which is tough
He has no effort to spare for despoilings
or to worry if he'll be cut in on the dice
His skill is vital to the scene   and the safety of the state
Anyone can perform the indignities   It's his hard arms
and craft that hold the eyes of the convict's women
There is the problem of getting the holes exact
(in the middle of this elbowing crowd)
and deep enough to hold the spikes
after they've sunk through those bared feet
and inadequate wrists he knows are waiting behind him

He doesn't sense perhaps that one of the hands
is held in a curious gesture over him—
giving   or asking   forgiveness?—
but he'd scarcely take time to be puzzled by poses
Criminals come in all sorts   as anyone knows who makes crosses
are as mad or sane as those who decide on their killings
Our one at least has been quiet so far
though they say he talked himself into this trouble
a carpenter's son who got notions of preaching

Well here's a carpenter's son who'll have carpenter sons
God willing   and build what's wanted temples or tables
mangers or crosses   and shape them decently
working alone in that firm and profound abstraction
which blots out the bawling of rag-snatchers
To construct with hands   knee-weight   braced thigh
keeps the back turned from death

But it's too late now for the other carpenter's boy
to return to this peace before the nails are hammered

---

1   A painting ("The Disrobing of Christ") by El Greco (c.1541-1614), a Greek painter active in
Spain.

John Betjeman

(1906–1984)

The Cottage Hospital[1]

At the end of a long-walled garden
    in a red provincial town,
A brick path led to a mulberry—
    scanty grass at its feet.
I lay under blackening branches
    where the mulberry leaves hung down
Sheltering ruby fruit globes
    from a Sunday-tea-time heat.
Apple and plum espaliers
    basked upon bricks of brown;
The air was swimming with insects,
    and children played in the street.

Out of this bright intentness
    into the mulberry shade
Musca domestica (housefly)
    swung from the August light
Slap into slithery rigging
    by the waiting spider made
Which spun the lithe elastic
    till the fly was shrouded tight.
Down came the hairy talons
    and horrible poison blade
And none of the garden noticed
    that fizzing, hopeless fight.

Say in what Cottage Hospital
    whose pale green walls resound
With the tap upon polished parquet
    of inflexible nurses' feet
Shall I myself be lying
    when they range the screens around?
And say shall I groan in dying,
    as I twist the sweaty sheet?
Or gasp for breath uncrying,
    as I feel my senses drown'd
While the air is swimming with insects
    and children play in the street?

---

1   a small country hospital in England

Late-Flowering Lust

My head is bald, my breath is bad,
  Unshaven is my chin,
I have not now the joys I had
  When I was young in sin.

I run my fingers down your dress
  With brandy-certain aim
And you respond to my caress
  And maybe feel the same.

But I've a picture of my own
  On this reunion night,
Wherein two skeletons are shewn
  To hold each other tight;

Dark sockets look on emptiness
  Which once was loving-eyed,
The mouth that opens for a kiss
  Has got no tongue inside.

I cling to you inflamed with fear
  As now you cling to me,
I feel how frail you are my dear
  And wonder what will be—

A week? or twenty years remain?
  And then—what kind of death?
A losing fight with frightful pain
  Or a gasping fight for breath?

Too long we let our bodies cling,
  We cannot hide disgust
At all the thoughts that in us spring
  From this late-flowering lust.

A Subaltern's Love-song

Miss J. Hunter Dunn, Miss J. Hunter Dunn,
Furnish'd and burnish'd by Aldershot[1] sun,
What strenuous singles we played after tea,
We in the tournament—you against me!

Love-thirty, love-forty, oh! weakness of joy,
The speed of a swallow, the grace of a boy,
With carefullest carelessness, gaily you won,
I am weak from your loveliness, Joan Hunter Dunn.

Miss Joan Hunter Dunn, Miss Joan Hunter Dunn,
How mad I am, sad I am, glad that you won.
The warm-handled racket is back in its press,
But my shock-headed victor, she loves me no less.

Her father's euonymus[2] shines as we walk,
And swing past the summer-house, buried in talk,
And cool the verandah that welcomes us in
To the six-o'clock news and a lime-juice and gin.

The scent of the conifers, sound of the bath,
The view from my bedroom of moss-dappled path,
As I struggle with double-end evening tie,
For we dance at the Golf Club, my victor and I.

On the floor of her bedroom lie blazer and shorts
And the cream-coloured walls are be-trophied with sports,
And westering, questioning settles the sun
On your low-leaded window, Miss Joan Hunter Dunn.

The Hillman[3] is waiting, the light's in the hall,
The pictures of Egypt are bright on the wall,
My sweet, I am standing beside the oak stair
And there on the landing's the light on your hair.

By roads "not adopted[4]", by woodlanded ways,
She drove to the club in the late summer haze,
Into nine-o'clock Camberley,[5] heavy with bells
And mushroomy, pine-woody, evergreen smells.

---

1   a town in southern England, the site of a military barracks
2   a type of shrub or small tree
3   a make of automobile; similarly the later reference to "Rovers and Austins"
4   i.e., unincorporated by any local authority
5   a small town south-west of London

Miss Joan Hunter Dunn, Miss Joan Hunter Dunn,
I can hear from the car-park the dance has begun.
Oh! full Surrey twilight! importunate band!
Oh! strongly adorable tennis-girl's hand!

Around us are Rovers and Austins afar,
Above us, the intimate roof of the car,
And here on my right is the girl of my choice,
With the tilt of her nose and the chime of her voice,

And the scent of her wrap, and the words never said,
And the ominous, ominous dancing ahead.
We sat in the car park till twenty to one
And now I'm engaged to Miss Joan Hunter Dunn.

W. H. Auden

1907–1973

Lay your sleeping head, my love,

Lay your sleeping head, my love,
Human on my faithless arm;
Time and fevers burn away
Individual beauty from
Thoughtful children, and the grave
Proves the child ephemeral:
But in my arms till break of day
Let the living creature lie,
Mortal, guilty, but to me
The entirely beautiful.

Soul and body have no bounds:
To lovers as they lie upon
Her tolerant enchanted slope
In their ordinary swoon,
Grave the vision Venus sends
Of supernatural sympathy,
Universal love and hope;
While an abstract insight wakes
Among the glaciers and the rocks
The hermit's sensual ecstasy.

Certainty, fidelity
On the stroke of midnight pass
Like vibrations of a bell,
And fashionable madmen raise
Their pedantic boring cry:
Every farthing of the cost,
All the dreaded cards foretell,
Shall be paid, but from this night
Not a whisper, not a thought,
Not a kiss nor look be lost.

Beauty, midnight, vision dies:
Let the winds of dawn that blow
Softly round your dreaming head
Such a day of sweetness show
Eye and knocking heart may bless,
Find the mortal world enough;
Noons of dryness see you fed
By the involuntary powers,
Nights of insult let you pass
Watched by every human love.

Musée des Beaux Arts

About suffering they were never wrong,
The Old Masters: how well they understood
Its human position; how it takes place
While someone else is eating or opening a window or just
    walking dully along;
How, when the aged are reverently, passionately waiting
For the miraculous birth, there always must be
Children who did not specially want it to happen, skating
On a pond at the edge of the wood:
They never forgot
That even the dreadful martyrdom must run its course
Anyhow in a corner, some untidy spot
Where the dogs go on with their doggy life and the
    torturer's horse
Scratches its innocent behind on a tree.

In Brueghel's *Icarus*,[1] for instance: how everything turns away
Quite leisurely from the disaster; the ploughman may
Have heard the splash, the forsaken cry,
But for him it was not an important failure; the sun shone
As it had to on the white legs disappearing into the green
Water; and the expensive delicate ship that must have seen
Something amazing, a boy falling out of the sky,[2]
Had somewhere to get to and sailed calmly on.

In Memory of W. B. Yeats[3]

(d. Jan. 1939)

1

He disappeared in the dead of winter:
The brooks were frozen, the airports almost deserted,
And snow disfigured the public statues;
The mercury sank in the mouth of the dying day.
O all the instruments agree
The day of his death was a dark cold day.

Far from his illness
The wolves ran on through the evergreen forests,

---

1   *The Fall of Icarus*, by Pieter Brueghel the Elder (c.1520-1569) hangs in the Palace of the
    Royal Museums of Painting and Sculpture in Brussels. The detail of the horse in the
    previous lines is taken from *The Massacre of the Innocents*, another painting by Breughel.
2   Using wings of feathers and wax, Daedalus and his son Icarus tried to make their way
    from Crete to Sicily; but Icarus flew too high, the wax melted, and he drowned.
3   Yeats died in France on 29 January 1939.

The peasant river was untempted by the fashionable quays;
By mourning tongues
The death of the poet was kept from his poems.

But for him it was his last afternoon as himself,
An afternoon of nurses and rumours;
The provinces of his body revolted,
The squares of his mind were empty,
Silence invaded the suburbs,
The current of his feeling failed: he became his admirers.

Now he is scattered among a hundred cities
And wholly given over to unfamiliar affections;
To find his happiness in another kind of wood[1]
And be punished under a foreign code of conscience.
The words of a dead man
Are modified in the guts of the living.

But in the importance and noise of tomorrow
When the brokers are roaring like beasts on the floor of
    the Bourse, [2]
And the poor have the sufferings to which they are
    fairly accustomed,
And each in the cell of himself is almost convinced of
    his freedom;
A few thousand will think of this day
As one thinks of a day when one did something slightly unusual.
O all the instruments agree
The day of his death was a dark cold day.

2

You were silly like us: your gift survived it all;
The parish of rich women, physical decay,
Yourself; mad Ireland hurt you into poetry.
Now Ireland has her madness and her weather still,
For poetry makes nothing happen: it survives
In the valley of its saying where executives
Would never want to tamper; it flows south
From ranches of isolation and the busy griefs,
Raw towns that we believe and die in; it survives,
A way of happening, a mouth.

---

1   At the beginning of the *Inferno*, Dante has strayed from the road and finds himself "in a dark wood."
2   the stock exchange in Paris

3

Earth, receive an honoured guest;
William Yeats is laid to rest:
Let the Irish vessel lie
Emptied of its poetry.

Time that is intolerant[1]
Of the brave and innocent,
And indifferent in a week
To a beautiful physique,

Worships language and forgives
Everyone by whom it lives;
Pardons cowardice, conceit,
Lays its honours at their feet.

Time that with this strange excuse
Pardoned Kipling[2] and his views,
And will pardon Paul Claudel,[3]
Pardons him[4] for writing well.

In the nightmare of the dark
All the dogs of Europe bark,
And the living nations wait,[5]
Each sequestered in its hate;

Intellectual disgrace
Stares from every human face,
And the seas of pity lie
Locked and frozen in each eye.

Follow, poet, follow right
To the bottom of the night,
With your unconstraining voice
Still persuade us to rejoice;

With the farming of a verse
Make a vineyard of the curse,
Sing of human unsuccess
In a rapture of distress;

---

1   Auden removed this stanza and the two following in the 1966 edition of his *Collected Shorter Poems*.
2   Rudyard Kipling (1865-1936), English novelist and poet, was a staunch supporter of British imperialism.
3   Claudel (1868-1955) was a French writer and diplomat with extremely conservative views.
4   i.e., Yeats, whose anti-democratic views were not shared by Auden.
5   The poem was written in February 1939, six months before the outbreak of World War II.

In the deserts of the heart
Let the healing fountain start,
In the prison of his days
Teach the free man how to praise.

The Unknown Citizen

*(To JS/07/M/378
This Marble Monument
Is Erected by the State)*

He was found by the Bureau of Statistics to be
One against whom there was no official complaint,
And all the reports on his conduct agree
That, in the modern sense of an old-fashioned word, he
    was a saint,
For in everything he did he served the Greater Community.
Except for the War till the day he retired
He worked in a factory and never got fired,
But satisfied his employers, Fudge Motors Inc.
Yet he wasn't a scab or odd in his views,
For his Union reports that he paid his dues,
(Our report on his Union shows it was sound)
And our Social Psychology workers found
That he was popular with his mates and liked a drink.
The Press are convinced that he bought a paper every day
And that his reactions to advertisements were normal in
      every way.
Policies taken out in his name prove that he was fully insured,
And his Health-card shows he was once in hospital but left
      it cured.
Both Producers Research and High-Grade Living declare
He was fully sensible to the advantages of the Instalment Plan
And had everything necessary to the Modern Man,
A phonograph, a radio, a car and a frigidaire.
Our researchers into Public Opinion are content
That he held the proper opinions for the time of year;
When there was peace, he was for peace; when there was war,
    he went.
He was married and added five children to the population,
Which our Eugenist[1] says was the right number for a parent of
      his generation,
And our teachers report that he never interfered with
      their education.

---

1   one who studies the development of physically or mentally improved human beings
through selective breeding

Was he free? Was he happy? The question is absurd:
Had anything been wrong, we should certainly have heard.

Our Bias

The hour-glass whispers to the lion's paw,
The clock-towers tell the gardens day and night,
How many errors Time has patience for,
How wrong they are in being always right.

Yet Time, however loud its chimes or deep,
However fast its falling torrent flows,
Has never put the lion off his leap
Nor shaken the assurance of the rose.

For they, it seems, care only for success:
While we choose words according to their sound
And judge a problem by its awkwardness;

And Time with us was always popular.
When have we not preferred some going round
To going straight to where we are?

September 1, 1939[1]

I sit in one of the dives
On Fifty-second Street
Uncertain and afraid
As the clever hopes expire
Of a low dishonest decade:
Waves of anger and fear
Circulate over the bright
And darkened lands of the earth,
Obsessing our private lives;
The unmentionable odour of death
Offends the September night.

Accurate scholarship can
Unearth the whole offence
From Luther[2] until now
That has driven a culture mad,

---

1 World War II broke out in Europe on 3 September 1939. Auden had left England to
   take up residence in the United States in January 1939.
2 Martin Luther (1483-1546), the German religious leader whose attacks on ecclesiastical
   corruption began the Protestant Reformation in Europe

Find what occurred at Linz,[1]
What huge imago made
A psychopathic god:
I and the public know
What all schoolchildren learn,
Those to whom evil is done
Do evil in return.

Exiled Thucydides[2] knew
All that a speech can say
About Democracy,
And what dictators do,
The elderly rubbish they talk
To an apathetic grave;
Analysed all in his book,
The enlightenment driven away,
The habit-forming pain,
Mismanagement and grief:
We must suffer them all again.

Into this neutral air
Where blind skyscrapers use
Their full height to proclaim
The strength of Collective Man,
Each language pours its vain
Competitive excuse:
But who can live for long
In an euphoric dream;
Out of the mirror they stare,
Imperialism's face
And the international wrong.

Faces along the bar
Cling to their average day:
The lights must never go out,
The music must always play,
All the conventions conspire
To make this fort assume
The furniture of home;
Lest we should see where we are,
Lost in a haunted wood,
Children afraid of the night
Who have never been happy or good.

---

1   the capital of upper Austria, on the River Danube, where the German dictator Adolf
     Hitler (1889-1945) spent his boyhood
2   Athenian historian (c.460-c.395 B.C.), whose failure as a naval commander led to his
     twenty-year exile

The windiest militant trash
Important Persons shout
Is not so crude as our wish:
What mad Nijinsky[1] wrote
About Diaghilev
Is true of the normal heart;
For the error bred in the bone
Of each woman and each man
Craves what it cannot have,
Not universal love
But to be loved alone.

From the conservative dark
Into the ethical life
The dense commuters come,
Repeating their morning vow;
"I *will* be true to the wife,
I'll concentrate more on my work,"
And helpless governors wake
To resume their compulsory game:
Who can release them now,
Who can reach the deaf,
Who can speak for the dumb?

Defenceless under the night
Our world in stupor lies;
Yet, dotted everywhere,
Ironic points of light
Flash out wherever the Just
Exchange their messages:
May I, composed like them
Of Eros and of dust,
Beleaguered by the same
Negation and despair,
Show an affirming flame.

---

1 Vaslav Nijinsky (1890-1950), Russian ballet dancer and choreographer, worked with the
Russian ballet producer Sergei Diaghilev (1872-1929) until their falling-out in 1913. In
1917 Nijinsky's mental instability forced him into permanent retirement. In his diary,
published in 1937, Nijinsky wrote: "Some politicians are hypocrites like Diaghilev, who
does not want universal love, but to be loved alone. I want universal love."

Song

As I walked out one evening,
　Walking down Bristol Street,
The crowds upon the pavement
　Were fields of harvest wheat.

And down by the brimming river
　I heard a lover sing
Under an arch of the railway:
　'Love has no ending.

I'll love you, dear, I'll love you
　Till China and Africa meet
And the river jumps over the mountain
　And the salmon sing in the street.

I'll love you till the ocean
　Is folded and hung up to dry
And the seven stars[1] go squawking
　Like geese about the sky.

The years shall run like rabbits
　For in my arms I hold
The Flower of the Ages
　And the first love of the world.'

But all the clocks in the city
　Began to whirr and chime:
'O let not Time deceive you,
　You cannot conquer Time.

In the burrows of the Nightmare
　Where Justice naked is,
Time watches from the shadow
　And coughs when you would kiss.

In headaches and in worry
　Vaguely life leaks away,
And Time will have his fancy
　To-morrow or to-day.

Into many a green valley
　Drifts the appalling snow;
Time breaks the threaded dances
　And the diver's brilliant bow.

1　the group of stars known as the Pleiades

O plunge your hands in water,
    Plunge them in up to the wrist;
Stare, stare in the basin
    And wonder what you've missed.

The glacier knocks in the cupboard,
    The desert sighs in the bed,

And the crack in the tea-cup opens
    A lane to the land of the dead.

Where the beggars raffle the banknotes
    And the Giant is enchanting to Jack,
And the Lily-white Boy is a Roarer
    And Jill goes down on her back.[1]

O look, look in the mirror,
    O look in your distress;
Life remains a blessing
    Although you cannot bless.

O stand, stand at the window
    As the tears scald and start;
You shall love your crooked neighbour
    With your crooked heart.'

It was late, late in the evening,
    The lovers they were gone;
The clocks had ceased their chiming
    And the deep river ran on.

---

1   These references—to the fairy tale about Jack the Giant-Killer, the song "Green Grow the Rushes," and the nursery rhyme "Jack and Jill"—suggest a world in which the natural order is subverted.

Louis MacNeice

(b. 1907)

Bagpipe music

It's no go[1] the merrygoround, it's no go the rickshaw,
All we want is a limousine and a ticket for the peepshow.
Their knickers are made of crêpe-de-chine, their shoes are made of
      python,
Their halls are lined with tiger rugs and their walls with heads of
      bison.

John MacDonald found a corpse, put it under the sofa,
Waited till it came to life and hit it with a poker,
Sold its eyes for souvenirs, sold its blood for whisky,
Kept its bones for dumb-bells to use when he was fifty.

It's no go the Yogi-Man,[2] it's no go Blavatsky,[3]
All we want is a bank balance and a bit of skirt in a taxi.

Annie MacDougall went to milk, caught her foot in the heather,
Woke to hear a dance record playing of Old Vienna.
It's no go your maidenheads, it's no go your culture,
All we want is a Dunlop tyre and the devil mend the puncture.

The Laird o' Phelps spent Hogmanay declaring he was sober,
Counted his feet to prove the fact and found he had one foot over.
Mrs. Carmichael had her fifth, looked at the job with repulsion,
Said to the midwife 'Take it away; I'm through with over-
      production'.

It's no go the gossip column, it's no go the ceilidh,[4]
All we want is a mother's help and a sugar-stick for the baby.

Willie Murray cut his thumb, couldn't count the damage,
Took the hide of an Ayrshire cow and used it for a bandage.
His brother caught three hundred cran[5] when the seas were lavish,
Threw the bleeders back in the sea and went upon the parish.[6]

It's no go the Herring Board,[7] it's no go the Bible,
All we want is a packet of fags[8] when our hands are idle.

---

1   i.e., the attempt is hopeless; the keynote in this picture of Scotland during the years of
     the Depression
2   a devotee of yoga
3   Madame Helena Blavatsky (1831-1891), founder of the Theosophical Society, which
     promoted a contemplative religion similar in some respects to Buddhism.
4   a convivial musical gathering
5   "Cran" is a Scots term for a measure of herring (about 750 fish).
6   sought charitable relief
7   a government body that sought to control herring stocks in the seas around Britain
8   British slang for cigarettes

It's no go the picture palace, it's no go the stadium,
It's no go the country cot with a pot of pink geraniums,
It's no go the Government grants, it's no go the elections,
Sit on your arse for fifty years and hang your hat on a pension.

It's no go my honey love, it's no go my poppet;
Work your hands from day to day, the winds will blow the profit.
The glass is falling hour by hour, the glass will fall for ever,
But if you break the bloody glass you won't hold up the weather.

The British Museum Reading Room

Under the hive-like dome the stooping haunted readers
Go up and down the alleys, tap the cells of knowledge—
    Honey and wax, the accumulation of years—
Some on commission, some for the love of learning,
Some because they have nothing better to do
Or because they hope these walls of books will deaden
    The drumming of the demon in their ears.

Cranks, hacks, poverty-stricken scholars,
In pince-nez, period hats or romantic beards
    And cherishing their hobby or their doom
Some are too much alive and some are asleep
Hanging like bats in a world of inverted values,
Folded up in themselves in a world which is safe and silent:
    This is the British Museum Reading Room.

Out on the steps in the sun the pigeons are courting,
Puffing their ruffs and sweeping their tails or taking
    A sun-bath at their ease
And under the totem poles—the ancient terror—
Between the enormous fluted Ionic columns
There seeps from heavily jowled or hawk-like foreign faces
    The guttural sorrow of the refugees.

Thalassa[1]

    Run out the boat, my broken comrades;
    Let the old seaweed crack, the surge
    Burgeon oblivious of the last
    Embarkation of feckless men,
    Let every adverse force converge—

---

1   (Greek) the sea

Here we must needs embark again.

Run up the sail, my heartsick comrades;
Let each horizon tilt and lurch—
You know the worst: your wills are fickle,
Your values blurred, your hearts impure
And your past life a ruined church—
But let your poison be your cure.

Put out to sea, ignoble comrades,
Whose record shall be noble yet;
Butting through scarps of moving marble
The narwhal dares us to be free;
By a high star our course is set,
Our end is Life. Put out to sea.

Theodore Roethke

(1908-1963)

My Papa's Waltz

The whiskey on your breath
Could make a small boy dizzy;
But I hung on like death:
Such waltzing was not easy.

We romped until the pans
Slid from the kitchen shelf;
My mother's countenance
Could not unfrown itself.

The hand that held my wrist
Was battered on one knuckle;
At every step you missed
My right ear scraped a buckle.

You beat time on my head
With a palm caked hard by dirt,
Then waltzed me off to bed
Still clinging to your shirt.

The Waking

I wake to sleep, and take my waking slow.
I feel my fate in what I cannot fear.
I learn by going where I have to go.

We think by feeling. What is there to know?
I hear my being dance from ear to ear.
I wake to sleep, and take my waking slow.

Of those so close beside me, which are you?
God bless the Ground! I shall walk softly there,
And learn by going where I have to go.

Light takes the Tree; but who can tell us how?
The lowly worm climbs up a winding stair,
I wake to sleep, and take my waking slow.

Great Nature has another thing to do
To you and me; so take the lively air,
And, lovely, learn by going where to go.

This shaking keeps me steady. I should know.
What falls away is always. And is near.
I wake to sleep, and take my waking slow.
I learn by going where I have to go.

Elegy for Jane

My Student, Thrown by a Horse

I remember the neckcurls, limp and damp as tendrils;
And her quick look, a sidelong pickerel smile;
And how, once startled into talk, the light syllables leaped for her,
And she balanced in the delight of her thought,
A wren, happy, tail into the wind,
Her song trembling the twigs and small branches.
The shade sang with her;
The leaves, their whispers turned to kissing;
And the mold sang in the bleached valleys under the rose.

Oh, when she was sad, she cast herself down into such a pure
    depth,
Even a father could not find her:
Scraping her cheek against straw;
Stirring the clearest water.

My sparrow, you are not here,
Waiting like a fern, making a spiny shadow.
The sides of wet stones cannot console me,
Nor the moss, wound with the last light.

If only I could nudge you from this sleep,
My maimed darling, my skittery pigeon.
Over this damp grave I speak the words of my love:
I, with no rights in this matter,
Neither father nor lover.

I Knew a Woman

I knew a woman, lovely in her bones,
When small birds sighed, she would sigh back at them;
Ah, when she moved, she moved more ways than one:
The shapes a bright container can contain!
Of her choice virtues only gods should speak,
Or English poets who grew up on Greek
(I'd have them sing in chorus, cheek to cheek).

How well her wishes went! She stroked my chin,
She taught me Turn, and Counter-turn, and Stand;[1]
She taught me Touch, that undulant white skin;
I nibbled meekly from her proffered hand;

---

1   parts of the Pindaric ode (strophe, anti-strophe, and epode)

She was the sickle; I, poor I, the rake,
Coming behind her for her pretty sake
(But what prodigious mowing we did make).

Love likes a gander, and adores a goose:
Her full lips pursed, the errant note to seize;
She played it quick, she played it light and loose;
My eyes, they dazzled at her flowing knees;
Her several parts could keep a pure repose,
Or one hip quiver with a mobile nose
(She moved in circles, and those circles moved).

Let seed be grass, and grass turn into hay:
I'm martyr to a motion not my own;
What's freedom for? To know eternity.
I swear she cast a shadow white as stone.
But who would count eternity in days?
These old bones live to learn her wanton ways:
(I measure time by how a body sways).

Dolor

I have known the inexorable sadness of pencils,
Neat in their boxes, dolor of pad and paper-weight,
All the misery of manilla folders and mucilage,
Desolation in immaculate public places,
Lonely reception room, lavatory, switchboard,
The unalterable pathos of basin and pitcher,
Ritual of multigraph,[1] paper-clip, comma,
Endless duplication of lives and objects.
And I have seen dust from the walls of institutions,
Finer than flour, alive, more dangerous than silica,
Sift, almost invisible, through long afternoons of tedium,
Dropping a fine film on nails and delicate eyebrows,
Glazing the pale hair, the duplicate grey standard faces.

---

1   a kind of office duplicating machine

A. D. Hope

(b. 1907)

Imperial Adam

Imperial Adam, naked in the dew,
Felt his brown flanks and found the rib was gone.
Puzzled he turned and saw where, two and two,
The mighty spoor of Jahweh[1] marked the lawn.

Then he remembered through mysterious sleep
The surgeon fingers probing at the bone,
The voice so far away, so rich and deep:
"It is not good for him to live alone."

Turning once more he found Man's counterpart
In tender parody breathing at his side.
He knew her at first sight, he knew by heart
Her allegory of sense unsatisfied.

The pawpaw drooped its golden breasts above
Less generous than the honey of her flesh;
The innocent sunlight showed the place of love;
The dew on its dark hairs winked crisp and fresh.

This plump gourd severed from his virile root,
She promised on the turf of Paradise
Delicious pulp of the forbidden fruit;
Sly as the snake she loosed her sinuous thighs,

And waking, smiled up at him from the grass;
Her breasts rose softly and he heard her sigh—
From all the beasts whose pleasant task it was
In Eden to increase and multiply

Adam had learned the jolly deed of kind[2]:
He took her in his arms and there and then,
Like the clean beasts, embracing from behind,
Began in joy to found the breed of men.

Then from the spurt of seed within her broke
Her terrible and triumphant female cry,
Split upward by the sexual lightning stroke.
It was the beasts now who stood watching by:

The gravid elephant, the calving hind,
The breeding bitch, the she-ape big with young

---

1   the name of the God of Israel in the Old Testament
2   nature

Were the first gentle midwives of mankind;
The teeming lioness rasped her with her tongue;

The proud vicuña nuzzled her as she slept
Lax on the grass; and Adam watching too
Saw how her dumb breasts at their ripening wept,
The great pod of her belly swelled and grew,

And saw its water break, and saw, in fear,
Its quaking muscles in the act of birth,
Between her legs a pigmy face appear,
And the first murderer lay upon the earth.

Australia

A Nation of trees, drab green and desolate grey
In the field uniform of modern wars,
Darkens her hills, those endless, outstretched paws
Of Sphinx demolished or stone lion worn away.

They call her a young country, but they lie:
She is the last of lands, the emptiest,
A woman beyond her change of life, a breast
Still tender but within the womb is dry.

Without songs, architecture, history:
The emotions and superstitions of younger lands,
Her rivers of water drown among inland sands,
The river of her immense stupidity

Floods her monotonous tribes from Cairns to Perth.
In them at last the ultimate men arrive
Whose boast is not: "we live" but "we survive",
A type who will inhabit the dying earth.

And her five cities, like five teeming sores,
Each drains her: a vast parasite robber-state
Where second-hand Europeans pullulate
Timidly on the edge of alien shores.

Yet there are some like me turn gladly home
From the lush jungle of modern thought, to find
The Arabian desert of the human mind,
Hoping, if still from the deserts the prophets come,

Such savage and scarlet as no green hills dare
Springs in that waste, some spirit which escapes
The learned doubt, the chatter of cultured apes
Which is called civilization over there.

The Return of Persephone[1]

Gliding through the still air, he made no sound;
Wing-shod and deft, dropped almost at her feet,
And searched the ghostly regiments and found
The living eyes, the tremor of breath, the beat
Of blood in all that bodiless underground.

She left her majesty; she loosed the zone
Of darkness and put by the rod of dread.
Standing, she turned her back upon the throne
Where, well she knew, the Ruler of the Dead,
Lord of her body and being, sat like stone;

Stared with his ravenous eyes to see her shake
The midnight drifting from her loosened hair,
The girl once more in all her actions wake,
The blush of colour in her cheeks appear
Lost with her flowers that day beside the lake.

The summer flowers scattering, the shout,
The black manes plunging down to the black pit—
Memory or dream? She stood awhile in doubt,
Then touched the Traveller God's[2] brown arm and met
His cool, bright glance and heard his words ring out:

"Queen of the Dead and Mistress of the Year!"
—His voice was the ripe ripple of the corn;
The touch of dew, the rush of morning air—
"Remember now the world where you were born;
The month of your return at last is here."

And still she did not speak, but turned again
Looking for answer, for anger, for command:
The eyes of Dis were shut upon their pain;
Calm as his marble brow, the marble hand
Slept on his knee. Insuperable disdain

Foreknowing all bounds of passion, of power, of art,
Mastered but could not mask his deep despair.
Even as she turned with Hermes to depart,
Looking her last on her grim ravisher
For the first time she loved him from her heart.

---

1   Persephone (the Greek name of Proserpine) was abducted by Dis (Pluto), god of the underworld, while she was gathering flowers. Responding to the entreaties of her mother, Demeter, Zeus allowed Persephone to spend six months of each year on the earth.

2   Hermes, the messenger of the gods and patron of travellers, who conducted the souls of the dead to the infernal regions

Parabola

Year after year the princess lies asleep
Until the hundred years foretold are done,
Easily drawing her enchanted breath.
Caught on the monstrous thorns around the keep,
Bones of the youths who sought her, one by one
Rot loose and rattle to the ground beneath.

But when the Destined Lover at last shall come,
For whom alone Fortune reserves the prize,
The thorns give way; he mounts the cobwebbed stair;
Unerring he finds the tower, the door, the room,
The bed where, waking at his kiss she lies
Smiling in the loose fragrance of her hair.

That night, embracing on the bed of state,
He ravishes her century of sleep
And she repays the debt of that long dream;
Future and Past compose their vast debate;
His seed now sown, her harvest ripe to reap
Enact a variation on the theme.

For in her womb another princess waits,
A sleeping cell, a globule of bright dew.
Jostling their way up that mysterious stair,
A horde of lovers bursts between the gates,
All doomed but one, the destined suitor, who
By luck first reaches her and takes her there.

A parable of all we are or do!
The life of Nature is a formal dance
In which each step is ruled by what has been
And yet the pattern emerges always new
The marriage of linked cause and random chance
Gives birth perpetually to the unforeseen.

One parable for the body and the mind:
With science and heredity to thank,
The heart is quite predictable as a pump,
But, let love change its beat, the choice is blind.
'Now' is a cross-roads where all maps prove blank,
And no one knows which way the cat will jump.

So here stand I, by birth a cross between
Determined pattern and incredible chance,
Each with an equal share in what I am.
Though I should read the code stored in the gene,
Yet the blind lottery of circumstance
Mocks all solutions to its cryptogram.

As in my flesh, so in my spirit stand I
When does *this* hundred years draw to its close?
The hedge of thorns before me gives no clue.
My predecessor's carcass, shrunk and dry,
Stares at me through the spikes. Oh well, here goes!
I have this thing, and only this, to do.

The Pleasure of Princes

What pleasures have great princes? These: to know
Themselves reputed mad with pride or power;
To speak few words—few words and short bring low
This ancient house, that city with flame devour;

To make old men, their father's enemies,
Drunk on the vintage of the former age;
To have great painters show their mistresses
Naked to the succeeding time; engage

The cunning of able, treacherous ministers
To serve, despite themselves, the cause they hate,
And leave a prosperous kingdom to their heirs
Nursed by the caterpillars of the state;

To keep their spies in good men's hearts; to read
The malice of the wise, and act betimes;
To hear the Grand Remonstrances of greed,
Led by the pure; cheat justice of her crimes;

To beget worthless sons and, being old,
By starlight climb the battlements, and while
The pacing sentry hugs himself for cold,
Keep vigil like a lover, muse and smile,

And think, to see from the grim castle steep
The midnight city below rejoice and shine:
"There my great demon grumbles in his sleep
And dreams of his destruction, and of mine."

Meditation on a Bone

A piece of bone, found at Trondhjem[1] in 1901, with the following runic inscription (about A.D. 1050) cut on it: *I loved her as a maiden; I will not trouble Erlend's detestable wife; better she should be a widow.*

Words scored upon a bone,
Scratched in despair or rage—
Nine hundred years have gone;
Now, in another age,
They burn with passion on
A scholar's tranquil page.

The scholar takes his pen
And turns the bone about,
And writes those words again.
Once more they seethe and shout,
And through a human brain
Undying hate rings out.

"I loved her when a maid;
I loathe and love the wife
That warms another's bed:
Let him beware his life!"
The scholar's hand is stayed;
His pen becomes a knife

To grave in living bone
The fierce archaic cry.
He sits and reads his own
Dull sum of misery.
A thousand years have flown
Before that ink is dry.

And, in a foreign tongue,
A man, who is not he,
Reads and his heart is wrung
This ancient grief to see,
And thinks: When I am dung,
What bone shall speak for me?

---

1   Trondheim, a city in Norway

Stephen Spender

(b. 1909)

The Express

After the first powerful, plain manifesto
The black statement of pistons, without more fuss
But gliding like a queen, she leaves the station.
Without bowing and with restrained unconcern
She passes the houses which humbly crowd outside,
The gasworks, and at last the heavy page
Of death, printed by gravestones in the cemetery.
Beyond the town, there lies the open country
Where, gathering speed, she acquires mystery,
The luminous self-possession of ships on ocean.
It is now she begins to sing—at first quite low
Then loud, and at last with a jazzy madness—
The song of her whistle screaming at curves,
Of deafening tunnels, brakes, innumerable bolts.
And always light, aerial, underneath,
Retreats the elate metre of her wheels.
Steaming through metal landscape on her lines,
She plunges new eras of white happiness,
Where speed throws up strange shapes, broad curves
And parallels clean like trajectories from guns.
At last, further than Edinburgh or Rome,
Beyond the crest of the world, she reaches night
Where only a low stream-line brightness
Of phosphorus on the tossing hills is light.
Ah, like a comet through flame, she moves entranced,
Wrapt in her music no bird song, no, nor bough
Breaking with honey buds, shall ever equal.

The Pylons

The secret of these hills was stone, and cottages
Of that stone made,
And crumbling roads
That turned on sudden hidden villages.

Now over these small hills, they have built the concrete
That trails black wire;
Pylons, those pillars
Bare like nude giant girls that have no secret.

The valley with its gilt and evening look
And the green chestnut
Of customary root,
Are mocked dry like the parched bed of a brook.

But far above and far as sight endures
Like whips of anger
With lightning's danger
There runs the quick perspective of the future.

This dwarfs our emerald country by its trek
So tall with prophecy:
Dreaming of cities
Where often clouds shall lean their swan-white neck.

A. M. Klein

(1909–1972)

Psalm VI: A Psalm of Abraham,
Concerning That Which He Beheld Upon
The Heavenly Scarp

And on that day, upon the heavenly scarp,
The hosannahs ceased, the hallelujahs died,
And music trembled on the silenced harp.
An angel, doffing his seraphic pride,
Wept; and his tears so bitter were, and sharp,
That where they fell, the blossoms shrivelled and died.

Another with such voice intoned the psalm
It sang forth blasphemy against the Lord.
Oh, that was a very imp in angeldom
Who, thinking evil, said no evil word—
But only pointed, at each *Te Deum*[1]
Down to the earth, and its unspeakable horde.

The Lord looked down, and saw the cattle-cars:[2]
Men ululating to a frozen land.
He saw a man tear at his flogged scars,
And saw a babe look for its blown-off hand.
Scholars, he saw, sniffing their bottled wars,
And doctors who had geniuses unmanned.[3]

The gentle violinist whose fingers played
Such godly music, washing a pavement, with lye,
He saw. He heard the priest who called His aid.
He heard the agnostic's undirected cry.
Unto Him came the odour Hunger made,
And the odour of blood before it is quite dry.

The angel who wept looked into the eyes of God.
The angel who sang ceased pointing to the earth.
A little cherub who'd spied the earthly sod
Went mad, and flapped his wings in crazy mirth.
And the good Lord said nothing, but with a nod
Summoned the angels of Sodom[4] down to earth.

---

1 opening of a Latin prayer of thanksgiving ("Te Deum laudamus," Thee God we praise)
2 the railway cars used by the Nazis to transport prisoners to concentration camps
3 "a reference to the German procedure of sterilization" (from a letter by Klein)
4 See Genesis 18 and 19, which describe the destruction of the corrupt cities of Sodom
   and and Gomorrah.

For the Sisters of the Hotel Dieu

In pairs,
as if to illustrate their sisterhood,
the sisters pace the hospital garden walks.
In their robes black and white immaculate hoods
they are like birds,
the safe domestic fowl of the House of God.

O biblic birds,
who fluttered to me in my childhood illnesses
—me little, afraid, ill, not of your race,—
the cool wing for my fever, the hovering solace,
the sense of angels—
be thanked, O plumage of paradise, be praised.

Autobiographical

Out of the ghetto streets where a Jewboy
Dreamed pavement into pleasant Bible-land,
Out of the Yiddish slums where childhood met
The friendly beard, the loutish Sabbath-goy,[1]
Or followed, proud, the Torah-escorting[2] band,
Out of the jargoning city I regret,
Rise memories, like sparrows rising from
The gutter-scattered oats,
Like sadness sweet of synagogal hum,
Like Hebrew violins
Sobbing delight upon their Eastern notes.

Again they ring their little bells, those doors[3]
Deemed by the tender-year'd, magnificent:
Old Ashkenazi's[4] cellar, sharp with spice;
The widows' double-parloured candy-stores
And nuggets sweet bought for one sweaty cent;
The warm fresh-smelling bakery, its pies,
Its cakes, its navel'd bellies of black bread;
The lintels candy-poled
Of barber-shop, bright-bottled, green, blue, red;
And fruit-stall piled, exotic,
And the big synagogue door, with letters of gold.

---

1   the non-Jew employed to do work forbidden to Orthodox Jews on the Sabbath, such as lighting fires
2   The Torah is the scroll containing the Mosaic laws.
3   Klein is recalling the little groceries of his neighbourhood, which had bells on their doors.
4   a common surname for Jews from central Europe

Again my kindergarten home is full—
Saturday night—with kin and compatriot:
My brothers playing Russian card-games; my
Mirroring sisters looking beautiful,
Humming the evening's imminent fox-trot;
My uncle Mayer, of blessed memory,
Still murmuring *maariv*,[1] counting holy words;
And the two strangers, come
Fiery from Volhynia's[2] murderous hordes—
The cards and humming stop.
And I too swear revenge for that pogrom.

Occasions dear: the four-legged *aleph*[3] named
And angel pennies[4] dropping on my book;
The rabbi patting a coming scholar-head;
My mother, blessing candles, Sabbath-flamed,
Queenly in her Warsovian perruque;[5]
My father pickabacking me to bed
To tell tall tales about the Baal Shem Tov[6]—
Letting me curl his beard.
Oh memory of unsurpassing love,
Love leading a brave child
Through childhood's ogred corridors, unfear'd!

The week in the country at my brother's—(May
He own fat cattle in the fields of heaven!)
Its picking of strawberries from grassy ditch,
Its odour of dogrose and of yellowing hay—
Dusty, adventurous, sunny days, all seven!—
Still follow me, still warm me, still are rich
With the cow-tinkling peace of pastureland.
The meadow'd memory
Is sodded with its clover, and is spanned
By that same pillow'd sky
A boy on his back one day watched enviously.

And paved again the street: the shouting boys,
Oblivious of mothers on the stoops,
Playing the robust robbers and police,
The corncob battle—all high-spirited noise
Competitive among the lot-drawn groups.
Another day, of shaken apple trees

---

1   the evening prayer
2   a region of Poland
3   The character for Aleph, the first letter in the Hebrew alphabet, has four "legs."
4   Klein's father would reward him for knowing his lessons by surreptitiously dropping
    pennies on his book and claiming they had been left there by angels.
5   It was the custom for Orthodox Jewish women from Poland to wear wigs.
6   an 18th-century rabbi who founded the Chassidic movement

In the rich suburbs, and a furious dog,
And guilty boys in flight;
Hazelnut games, and games in the synagogue—
The burrs,[1] the Haman rattle,[2]
The Torah dance on Simchas Torah night.[3]

Immortal days of the picture calendar
Dear to me always with the virgin joy
Of the first flowering of senses five,
Discovering birds, or textures, or a star,
Or tastes sweet, sour, acid, those that cloy;
And perfumes. Never was I more alive.
All days thereafter are a dying off,
A wandering away
From home and the familiar. The years doff
Their innocence.
No other day is ever like that day.

I am no old man fatuously intent
On memories, but in memory I seek
The strength and vividness of nonage days,
Not tranquil recollection of event.
It is a fabled city that I seek;
It stands in Space's vapours and Time's haze;
Thence comes my sadness in remembered joy
Constrictive of the throat;
Thence do I hear, as heard by a Jewboy,
The Hebrew violins,
Delighting in the sobbed Oriental note.

---

1   Klein is recalling the custom of throwing burrs and thistles at the elders of the synagogue
    on the anniversary of the destruction of the Temple in Jerusalem by the Romans in
    A.D.70.
2   A rattle sounded during the Purim service each time the name of Haman is mentioned;
    Haman sought the destruction of the Jews, but was foiled by Queen Esther (see the Book
    of Esther, 3-7).
3   a festival celebrating the conclusion of the year's reading from the Torah

Montreal

O city metropole, isle riverain!¹
Your ancient pavages and sainted routs
Traverse my spirit's conjured avenues!
Splendour erablic² of your promenades
Foliates there, and there your maisonry
Of pendant balcon and escalier'd march,³
Unique midst English habitat,
Is vivid Normandy!

You populate the pupils of my eyes:
Thus, does the Indian, plumed, furtivate
Still through your painted autumns, Ville-Marie⁴!
Though palisades have passed, though calumet⁵
With tabac of your peace enfumes the air,
Still do I spy the phantom, aquiline,
Genuflect, moccasin'd, behind
His statue⁶ in the square!

Thus, costumed images before me pass,
Haunting your archives architectural:
*Coureur de bois*⁷, in posts where pelts were portaged;
Seigneur⁸ within his candled manoir; Scot
Ambulant through his bank, pillar'd and vast.
Within your chapels, voyaged mariners
Still pray, and personage departed,
All present from your past!

Grand port of navigations, multiple
The lexicons uncargo'd at your quays,
Sonnant though strange to me; but chiefest, I,
Auditor of your music, cherish the
Joined double-melodied vocabulaire
Where English vocable and roll Ecossic,⁹
Mollified by the parle of French
Bilinguefact your air!

---

1   Like many of the words in this poem, this is a kind of "Franglais" that plays on English
    and French meanings. In French, "riverain" means riverside. Zailig Pollock, Klein's editor,
    also suggests a pun on "riverrun," the first word of James Joyces's novel *Finnegan's Wake*.
2   from French "érable," maple
3   from French "escalier," staircase, and "marche," step
4   the mission settlement established in 1642, that became Montreal
5   pipe of peace
6   the figure of a native Indian, part of a statue commemmorating the explorer Maisonneuve
    in the Place d'Armes in Montreal
7   the earliest trappers and fur traders in French Canada
8   the owner of a "seigneury," land in French Canada granted by the King of France
9   from French "ecossais," Scottish

Such your suaver voice, hushed Hochelaga[1]!
But for me also sound your potencies,
Fortissimos of sirens fluvial,
Bruit of manufactory, and thunder
From foundry issuant, all puissant tone
Implenishing your hebdomad;[2] and then
Sanct silence, and your argent belfries
Clamant in orison!

You are a part of me, O all your quartiers—
And of dire pauvrete and of richesse—
To finished time my homage loyal claim;
You are locale of infancy, milieu
Vital of institutes that formed my fate;
And you above the city, scintillant,
Mount Royal, are my spirit's mother,
Almative, poitrinate!
Never do I sojourn in alien place
But I do languish for your scenes and sounds,
City of reverie, nostalgic isle,
Pendant most brilliant on Laurentian cord![3]
The coigns of your boulevards—my signiory—
Your suburbs are my exile's verdure fresh,
Your parks, your fountain'd parks—
Pasture of memory!

City, O city, you are vision'd as
A parchemin roll of saecular exploit
Inked with the script of eterne souvenir!
You are in sound, chanson and instrument!
Mental, you rest forever edified
With tower and dome; and in these beating valves,
Here in these beating valves, you will
For all my mortal time reside!

The Rocking Chair

It seconds the crickets of the province. Heard
in the clean lamplit farmhouses of Quebec,—
wooden,—it is no less a national bird;
and rivals, in its cage, the mere stuttering clock.
To its time, the evenings are rolled away;
and in its peace the pensive mother knits

---

1   the Indian village that was to become Montreal
2   filling up your week
3   the Laurentian, or Canadian, Shield, the Pre-Cambrian plateau covering much of eastern
    Canada

contentment to be worn by her family,
grown-up, but still cradled by the chair in which she sits.

It is also the old man's pet, pair to his pipe,
the two aids of his arithmetic and plans,
plans rocking and puffing into market-shape;
and it is the toddler's game and dangerous dance.
Moved to the verandah, on summer Sundays, it is,
among the hanging plants, the girls, the boy-friends,
sabbatical and clumsy, like the white haloes
dangling above the blue serge suits of the young men.

It has a personality of its own;
is a character (like that old drunk Lacoste,
exhaling amber, and toppling on his pins);
it is alive; individual; and no less
an identity than those about it. And
it is tradition. Centuries have been flicked
from its arcs, alternately flicked and pinned.
It rolls with the gait of St. Malo.[1] It is act

and symbol, symbol of this static folk
which moves in segments, and returns to base,—
a sunken pendulum: *invoke, revoke;*
loosed yon, leashed hither, motion on no space.
O, like some Anjou ballad, all refrain,
which turns about its longing, and seems to move
to make a pleasure out of repeated pain,
its music moves, as if always back to a first love.

Political Meeting

For Camillien Houde[2]

On the school platform, draping the folding seats,
they wait the chairman's praise and glass of water.
Upon the wall the agonized Y initials their faith.

Here all are laic; the skirted brothers have gone.
Still, their equivocal absence is felt, like a breeze
that gives curtains the sounds of surplices.

The hall is yellow with light, and jocular;

---

1   The birthplace of Jacques Cartier, the French explorer who discovered the St. Lawrence
     River in 1535
2   Houde, the Mayor of Montreal, was an outspoken opponent of conscription in Quebec
     during World War II, and was interned for his views.

suddenly some one lets loose upon the air
the ritual bird[1] which the crowd in snares of singing

catches and plucks, throat, wings, and little limbs.
Fall the feathers of sound, like *alouette's*.
The chairman, now, is charming, full of asides and wit,

building his orators, and chipping off
the heckling gargoyles popping in the hall.
(Outside, in the dark, the street is body-tall,

flowered with faces intent on the scarecrow thing
that shouts to thousands the echoing
of their own wishes.) The Orator has risen!

Worshipped and loved, their favourite visitor,
a country uncle with sunflower seeds in his pockets,
full of wonderful moods, tricks, imitative talk,

he is their idol: like themselves, not handsome,
not snobbish, not of the *Grande Allée!*[2] *Un homme!*
Intimate, informal, he makes bear's compliments

to the ladies; is gallant; and grins;
goes for the balloon, his opposition, with pins;
jokes also on himself, speaks of himself

in the third person, slings slang, and winks with folklore;
and knows now that he has them, kith and kin.
Calmly, therefore, he begins to speak of war,

praises the virtue of being *Canadien*,
of being at peace, of faith, of family,
and suddenly his other voice: *Where are your sons?*

He is tearful, choking tears; but not he
would blame the clever English; in their place
he'd do the same; maybe.

Where *are* your sons?
                          The whole street wears one face,
shadowed and grim; and in the darkness rises
the body-odour of race.

---

1   i.e., the French-Canadian song *Alouette*
2   the street on which the rich lived in Quebec City

Dorothy Livesay

(b. 1909)

used to teach at UofA
came from a priviledged family
for some yrs was a communist (father a liberal writer)
30's - enormous
reforming for the world; stressed; fought for

The Difference

from 1920's style
graceful

sonnet in every way but one — doesn't have a sonnet rhyme scheme, suggested rhymes

Your way of loving is too slow for me.
For you, I think, must know a tree by heart
Four seasons through, and note each single leaf
With microscopic glance before it falls—
And after watching soberly the turn
Of autumn into winter and the slow
Awakening again, the rise of sap
Then only will you cry: "I love this tree!"

As if the beauty of the thing could be
Made lovelier or marred by any mood
Of wind, or by the sun's caprice; as if
All beauty had not sprung up with the seed—
With such slow ways you find no time to love
A falling flame, a flower's brevity.

rhythms very jagged
incredible action, not smooth
vigorous exploration

Bartok and the Geranium[1]

never comes to a rest

He is unrelenting + there is the serenity of the geranium.

She lifts her green umbrellas
Towards the pane
Seeking her fill of sunlight
Or of rain;
Whatever falls
She has no commentary
Accepts, extends,
Blows out her furbelows,
Her bustling boughs;

2 distinct + diff. personalities can exist together

geranium looks like this piece of clothing. Pleat or gathering in a garment

And all the while he whirls
Explodes in space,
Never content with this small room:
Not even can he be
Confined to sky
But must speed high and higher still
From galaxy to galaxy,
Wrench from the stars their momentary notes
Steal music from the moon.

contrast + yet similarity in the two. Geranium's are intensive (colour, smell) individual, r. like Bartok,

often seems as if its written about sex — trad. roles of sexual male vs female

She's daylight
He is dark
She's heaven-held breath

not all people like them.

---

1   Béla Bartók (1881-1945), Hungarian composer

[584]

He storms and crackles
Spits with hell's own spark.

*one of her great subj's
is that of male + female*

Yet in this room, this moment now
These together breathe and be:
She, essence of serenity,
He in a mad intensity
Soars beyond sight
Then hurls, lost Lucifer[1]
From Heaven's height.

*Some unusual
rhymes*

And when he's done, he's out:
She leans a lip against the glass
And preens herself in light.

*all women who had
to struggle in 1 way
or another*

The Three Emilys[2]

*3 models of
inspiration*

These women crying in my head
Walk alone, uncomforted:
The Emilys, these three
Cry to be set free—
And others whom I will not name
Each different, each the same.

Yet they had liberty!
Their kingdom was the sky:
They batted clouds with easy hand,
Found a mountain for their stand;
From wandering lonely they could catch
The inner magic of a heath—
A lake their palette, any tree
Their brush could be.

heath in N. Eng
Brontë wrote about the
Emily Carr painted
trees

*Em Dickinson
wrote about*

And still they cry to me
As in reproach—
I, born to hear their inner storm
Of separate man in woman's form,
I yet possess another kingdom, barred
To them, these three, this Emily.
I move as mother in a frame,
My arteries
Flow the immemorial way
Towards the child, the man;
And only for brief span

*She thinks of
their loneliness*

*1 way she is
diff from them,
Livesay is married
+ has a child.*

---

1   See Isaiah 14.12: "How art thou fallen from heaven, O Lucifer, son of the morning!"
2   Emily Brontë (1818-1848), English novelist; Emily Dickinson (1830-1886), American poet; Emily Carr (1871-1945), Canadian artist and writer

Am I an Emily on mountain snows
And one of these.

And so the whole that I possess
Is still much less—
They move triumphant through my head:
I am the one
Uncomforted.

Lament

for J.F.B.L.[1]

What moved me, was the way your hand
Lay in my hand, not withering,
But warm, like a hand cooled in a stream
And purling still; or a bird caught in a snare
Wings folded stiff, eyes in a stare,
But still alive with the fear,
Heart hoarse with hope—
So your hand, your dead hand, my dear.

And the veins, still mounting as blue rivers,
Mounting towards the tentative finger-tips,
The delta where four seas come in—
Your fingers promontories into colourless air
Were rosy still—not chalk (like cliffs
You knew in boyhood, Isle of Wight[2]):
But blushed with colour from the sun you sought
And muscular from garden toil;
Stained with the purple of an iris bloom,
Violas grown for a certain room;
Hands seeking faïence, filagree,
Chinese lacquer and ivory—
Brussels lace; and a walnut piece
Carved by a hand now phosphorus.

What moved me, was the way your hand
Held life, although the pulse was gone.
The hand that carpentered a children's chair,
Carved out a stair
Held leash upon a dog in strain
Gripped wheel, swung sail,
Flicked horse's rein
And then again

1 Livesay's father
2 a small island off the southern coast of England

Moved kings and queens meticulous on a board,
Slashed out the cards, cut bread, and poured
A purring cup of tea;

The hand so neat and nimble
Could make a tennis partner tremble,
Write a resounding round
Of sonorous verbs and nouns—
Hand that would not strike a child, and yet
Could ring a bell[1] and send a man to doom.

And now unmoving in this Spartan room
The hand still speaks:
After the brain was fogged
And the tight lips tighter shut,
After the shy appraising eyes
Relinquished fire for the sea's green gaze—
The hand still breathes, fastens its hold on life;
Demands the whole, establishes the strife.

What moved me, was the way your hand
Lay cool in mine, not withering;
As bird still breathes, and stream runs clear—
So your hand; your dead hand, my dear.

On Looking into Henry Moore[2]

i

Sun stun me sustain me
turn me to stone:
Stone goad me gall me
urge me to run.

When I have found
passivity in fire
and fire in stone
female and male
I'll rise alone
self-extending and self-known.

ii

The message of the tree is this:
aloneness is the only bliss

---

1 Presumably a press bell; in the 1920s J.F.B. Livesay was manager of the Canadian Press.
2 English sculptor, b. 1898

Self-adoration is not in it
(Narcissus[1] tried, but could not win it)

Rather, to extend the root
tombwards, be at home with death

But in the upper branches know
a green eternity of fire and snow.

iii

The fire in the farthest hills
is where I'd burn myself to bone:
clad in the armour of the sun
I'd stand anew alone

Take off this flesh   this hasty dress
prepare my half-self for myself:
one unit   as a tree or stone
woman in man   and man in womb.

Not a poem about sex

The Unquiet Bed —1968

The woman I am
is not what you see
I'm not just bones
and crockery

the woman I am
knew love and hate
hating the chains
that parents make

longing that love
might set men free
yet hold them fast
in loyalty

the woman I am
is not what you see
move over love
make room for me

---

1   In Greek mythology, the beautiful youth who thought his own reflection was a beautiful
nymph, and died pining for an unattainable love.

Anne Wilkinson

(1910–1961)

Lens

I

The poet's daily chore
Is my long duty;
To keep and cherish my good lens
For love and war
And wasps about the lilies
And mutiny within.

My woman's eye is weak
And veiled with milk;
My working eye is muscled
With a curious tension,
Stretched and open
As the eyes of children;
Trusting in its vision
Even should it see
The holy holy spirit gambol
Counterheadwise,
Lithe and warm as any animal.

My woman's iris circles
A blind pupil;
The poet's eye is crystal,
Polished to accept the negative,
The contradictions in a proof
And the accidental
Candour of the shadows;
The shutter, oiled and smooth
Clicks on the grace of heroes
Or on some bestial act
When lit with radiance
The afterwords the actors speak
Give depths to violence,

Or if the bull is great
And the matador
And the sword
Itself the metaphor.

II

In my dark room the years
Lie in solution,
Develop film by film.
Slow at first and dim
Their shadows bite

On the fine white pulp of paper.

An early snap of fire
Licking the arms of air
I hold against the light, compare
The details with a prehistoric view
Of land and sea
And cradles of mud that rocked
The wet and sloth of infancy

A stripe of tiger, curled
And sleeping on the ribs of reason
Prints as clear
As Eve and Adam, pearled
With sweat, staring at an apple core;

And death, in black and white
Or politic in green and Easter film,
Lands on steely points, a dancer
Disciplined to the foolscap stage,
The property of poets
Who command his robes, expose
His moving likeness on the page.

In June and Gentle Oven

In June and gentle oven
Summer kingdoms simmer
As they come
And flower and leaf and love
Release
Their sweetest juice.

No wind at all
On the wide green world
Where fields go stroll-
ing by
And in and out
An adder of a stream
Parts the daisies
On a small Ontario farm.

And where, in curve of meadow,
Lovers, touching, lie,
A church of grass stands up
And walls them, holy, in.

Fabulous the insects
Stud the air
Or walk on running water,

Klee-drawn[1] saints
And bright as angels are.
Honeysuckle here
Is more than bees can bear
And time turns pale
And stops to catch its breath
And lovers slip their flesh
And light as pollen
Play on treble water
Till bodies reappear
And a shower of sun
To dry their languor.

Then two in one the lovers lie
And peel the skin of summer
With their teeth
And suck its marrow from a kiss
So charged with grace
The tongue, all knowing
Holds the sap of June
Aloof from seasons, flowing.

My Bones Predict

My bones predict the striking hour of thunder
And water as I huddle under
    The tree the lightning renders

I'm hung with seaweed, winding in its caul
The nightmare of a carp whose blood runs cold,
    A crab who apes my crawl

My lens is grafted from a jungle eye
To focus on the substance of a shadow's
    Shadow on the sky

My forest filtered drum is pitched to hear
The serpent split the grass before the swish
    Is feather in my ear

I've learned from land and sea of every death
Save one, the easy rest, the little catnap
    Tigers know from birth

---

1   Paul Klee (1879-1940), Swiss painter and etcher, known for his stick-like figures

Nature be damned

I

Pray where would lamb and lion be
If they lay down in amity?
Could lamb then nibble living grass?
Lamb and lion both must starve;
Bird and flower, too, must die of love.

II

I go a new dry way, permit no weather
Here, on undertaker's false green sod
Where I sit down beneath my false tin tree.
There's too much danger in a cloud,
In wood or field, or close to moving water.
With my black blood — who can tell?
The dart of one mosquito might be fatal;

Or in the flitting dusk a bat
Might carry away my destiny,
Hang it upside down from a rafter
In a barn unknown to me.

I hide my skin within the barren city
Where artificial moons pull no man's tide,
And so escape my green love till the day
Vine breaks through brick and strangles me.

III

I was witch and I could be
Bird or leaf
Or branch and bark of tree.

In rain and two by two my powers left me;
Instead of curling down as root and worm
My feet walked on the surface of the earth,
And I remember a day of evil sun
When forty green leaves withered on my arm.

And so I damn the font where I was blessed,
Am unbeliever; was deluded lover; never
Bird or leaf or branch and bark of tree.
Each, separate as curds from whey,
Has signature to prove identity.

And yet we're kin in appetite;
Tree, bird in the tree and I.
We feed on dung, a fly, a lamb

And burst with seed
Of tree, of bird, of man,
Till tree is bare
And bird and I are bone
And feaster is reborn
The feast, and feasted on.

IV

Once a year in the smoking bush
A little west of where I sit
I burn my winter caul to a green ash.
This is an annual festival,
Nothing to stun or startle;
A coming together—water and sun
In summer's first communion.

Today again I burned my winter caul
Though senses nodded, dulled by ritual.

One hundred singing orioles
And five old angels wakened me;
Morning sky rained butterflies
And simple fish, bass and perch,
Leapt from the lake in salutation.
St. Francis,[1] drunk among the daisies,
Opened his ecstatic eye.

Then roused from this reality I saw
Nothing, anywhere, but snow.

On a Bench in a Park

On a bench in a park
Where I went walking
A boy and girl,
Their new hearts breaking
Sat side by side
And miles apart
And they wept most bitterly.

'Why do you mourn,'
I asked,
'You, who are barely born?'

---

1   St. Francis of Assisi (c.1181-1226), renowned for his love of nature

'For gold that is gone,'
Said the girl,
'I weep distractedly.'

I turned to the youth,
'And you?'
'For what I have not gained,' he cried,
'Possessing her
I lost myself and died.'

And so we sat, a trio
Tuned to sobs,
And miles to go
And miles and miles apart

Till they, amazed
That one as old as I
Had juice enough for tears,
Dried their streaming eyes
To ask the cause of mine.

I told of the grit I'd found
In a grain of truth,
Mentioned an aching tooth
Decayed with fears
And the sum of all I'd lost
In the increased tax on years.

They yawned and rose
And walked away. I moved
To go but death sat down.
His cunning hand
Explored my skeleton.

Elizabeth Bishop

(1911–1979)

The Fish

I caught a tremendous fish
and held him beside the boat
half out of water, with my hook
fast in a corner of his mouth.
He didn't fight.
He hadn't fought at all.
He hung a grunting weight,
battered and venerable
and homely. Here and there
his brown skin hung in strips
like ancient wallpaper,
and its pattern of darker brown
was like wallpaper:
shapes like full-blown roses
stained and lost through age.
He was speckled with barnacles,
fine rosettes of lime,
and infested
with tiny white sea-lice,
and underneath two or three
rags of green weed hung down.
While his gills were breathing in
the terrible oxygen
—the frightening gills,
fresh and crisp with blood,
that can cut so badly—
I thought of the coarse white flesh
packed in like feathers,
the big bones and the little bones,
the dramatic reds and blacks
of his shiny entrails,
and the pink swim-bladder
like a big peony.
I looked into his eyes
which were far larger than mine
but shallower, and yellowed,
the irises backed and packed
with tarnished tinfoil
seen through the lenses
of old scratched isinglass.
They shifted a little, but not
to return my stare.
—It was more like the tipping
of an object toward the light.
I admired his sullen face,
the mechanism of his jaw,
and then I saw

that from his lower lip
—if you could call it a lip—
grim, wet, and weaponlike,
hung five old pieces of fish-line,
or four and a wire leader
with the swivel still attached,
with all their five big hooks
grown firmly in his mouth.
A green line, frayed at the end
where he broke it, two heavier lines,
and a fine black thread
still crimped from the strain and snap
when it broke and he got away.
Like medals with their ribbons
frayed and wavering,
a five-haired beard of wisdom
trailing from his aching jaw.
I stared and stared
and victory filled up
the little rented boat,
from the pool of bilge
where oil had spread a rainbow
around the rusted engine
to the bailer rusted orange,
the sun-cracked thwarts,
the oarlocks on their strings,
the gunnels—until everything
was rainbow, rainbow, rainbow!
And I let the fish go.

In the Waiting Room

In Worcester, Massachusetts,
I went with Aunt Consuelo
to keep her dentist's appointment
and sat and waited for her
in the dentist's waiting room.
It was winter. It got dark
early. The waiting room
was full of grown-up people,
arctics and overcoats,
lamps and magazines.
My aunt was inside
what seemed like a long time
and while I waited I read
the *National Geographic*
(I could read) and carefully
studied the photographs:
the inside of a volcano,
black, and full of ashes;

then it was spilling over
in rivulets of fire.
Osa and Martin Johnson[1]
dressed in riding breeches,
laced boots, and pith helmets.
A dead man slung on a pole
—"Long Pig," the caption said.
Babies with pointed heads
wound round and round with string;
black, naked women with necks
wound round and round with wire
like the necks of light bulbs.
Their breasts were horrifying.
I read it right straight through.
I was too shy to stop.
And then I looked at the cover:
the yellow margins, the date.
Suddenly, from inside,
came an *oh!* of pain
—Aunt Consuelo's voice—
not very loud or long.
I wasn't at all surprised;
even then I knew she was
a foolish, timid woman.
I might have been embarrassed,
but wasn't. What took me
completely by surprise
was that it was *me:*
my voice, in my mouth.
Without thinking at all
I was my foolish aunt,
I—we—were falling, falling,
our eyes glued to the cover
of the *National Geographic,*
February, 1918.

I said to myself: three days
and you'll be seven years old.
I was saying it to stop
the sensation of falling off
the round, turning world
into cold, blue-black space.
But I felt: you are an *I,*
you are an *Elizabeth,*
you are one of *them.*
Why should you be one, too?

---

1   wife and husband team of explorers

I scarcely dared to look
to see what it was I was.
I gave a sidelong glance
—I couldn't look any higher—
at shadowy gray knees,
trousers and skirts and boots
and different pairs of hands
lying under the lamps.
I knew that nothing stranger
had ever happened, that nothing
stranger could ever happen.
Why should I be my aunt,
or me, or anyone?
What similarities—
boots, hands, the family voice
I felt in my throat, or even
the *National Geographic*
and those awful hanging breasts—
held us all together
or made us all just one?
How—I didn't know any
word for it—how "unlikely". . .
How had I come to be here,
like them, and overhear
a cry of pain that could have
got loud and worse but hadn't?

The waiting room was bright
and too hot. It was sliding
beneath a big black wave,
another, and another.

Then I was back in it.
The War[1] was on. Outside,
in Worcester, Massachusetts,
were night and slush and cold,
and it was still the fifth
of February, 1918.

---

1   World War I

One Art

The art of losing isn't hard to master;
so many things seem filled with the intent
to be lost that their loss is no disaster.

Lose something every day. Accept the fluster
of lost door keys, the hour badly spent.
The art of losing isn't hard to master.

Then practice losing farther, losing faster:
places, and names, and where it was you meant
to travel. None of these will bring disaster.

I lost my mother's watch. And look! my last, or
next-to-last, of three loved houses went.
The art of losing isn't hard to master.

I lost two cities, lovely ones. And, vaster,
some realms I owned, two rivers, a continent.
I miss them, but it wasn't a disaster.

—Even losing you (the joking voice, a gesture
I love) I shan't have lied. It's evident
the art of losing's not too hard to master
though it may look like (*Write* it!) like disaster.

The Armadillo

For Robert Lowell

This is the time of year
when almost every night
the frail, illegal fire balloons appear.
Climbing the mountain height,

rising toward a saint
still honored in these parts,
the paper chambers flush and fill with light
that comes and goes, like hearts.

Once up against the sky it's hard
to tell them from the stars—
planets, that is—the tinted ones:
Venus going down, or Mars,

or the pale green one. With a wind,
they flare and falter, wobble and toss;

but if it's still they steer between
the kite sticks of the Southern Cross,[1]

receding, dwindling, solemnly
and steadily forsaking us,
or, in the downdraft from a peak,
suddenly turning dangerous.

Last night another big one fell.
It splattered like an egg of fire
against the cliff behind the house.
The flame ran down. We saw the pair

of owls who nest there flying up
and up, their whirling black-and-white
stained bright pink underneath, until
they shrieked up out of sight.

The ancient owls' nest must have burned.
Hastily, all alone,
a glistening armadillo left the scene,
rose-flecked, head down, tail down,

and then a baby rabbit jumped out,
short-eared, to our surprise.
So soft!—a handful of intangible ash
with fixed, ignited eyes.

Too pretty, dreamlike mimicry!
O falling fire and piercing cry
and panic, and a weak mailed fist
clenched ignorant against the sky!

Sestina[2]

September rain falls on the house.
In the failing light, the old grandmother
sits in the kitchen with the child
beside the Little Marvel Stove,
reading the jokes from the almanac,
laughing and talking to hide her tears.

---

1   a constellation visible only from the southern hemisphere
2   A poetic form with six unrhymed stanzas, the words ending each line in the first stanza
     appearing in different order in the other five. The poem closes with a three line envoy
     which includes all six end-words.

She thinks that her equinoctial tears
and the rain that beats on the roof of the house
were both foretold by the almanac,
but only known to a grandmother.
The iron kettle sings on the stove.
She cuts some bread and says to the child,

It's time for tea now; but the child
is watching the teakettle's small hard tears
dance like mad on the hot black stove,
the way the rain must dance on the house.
Tidying up, the old grandmother
hangs up the clever almanac

on its string. Birdlike, the almanac
hovers half open above the child,
hovers above the old grandmother
and her teacup full of dark brown tears.
She shivers and says she thinks the house
feels chilly, and puts more wood in the stove.

It was to be, says the Marvel Stove.
I know what l know, says the almanac.
With crayons the child draws a rigid house
and a winding pathway. Then the child
puts in a man with buttons like tears
and shows it proudly to the grandmother.

But secretly, while the grandmother
busies herself about the stove,
the little moons fall down like tears
from between the pages of the almanac
into the flower bed the child
has carefully placed in the front of the house.

Time to plant tears, says the almanac.
The grandmother sings to the marvellous stove
and the child draws another inscrutable house.

Allen Curnow

(b. 1911)

House and Land

Wasn't this the site, asked the historian,
Of the original homestead?
Couldn't tell you, said the cowman;
I just live here, he said,
Working for old Miss Wilson
Since the old man's been dead.

Moping under the bluegums
The dog trailed his chain
From the privy as far as the fowlhouse
And back to the privy again,
Feeling the stagnant afternoon
Quicken with the smell of rain.

There sat old Miss Wilson,
With her pictures on the wall,
The baronet uncle, mother's side,
And one she called The Hall;
Taking tea from a silver pot
For fear the house might fall.

People in the *colonies*, she said,
Can't quite understand . . .
Why, from Waiau¹ to the mountains
It was all father's land.

She's all of eighty said the cowman,
Down at the milking-shed.
I'm leaving here next winter.
Too bloody quiet, he said.

The spirit of exile, wrote the historian,
Is strong in the people still.
He reminds me rather, said Miss Wilson,
Of Harriet's youngest, Will.
The cowman, home from the shed, went drinking
With the rabbiter home from the hill.²

The sensitive nor'west afternoon
Collapsed, and the rain came;
The dog crept into his barrel

---

1   a river in the South Island of New Zealand
2   an echo of Robert Louis Stevenson's poem "Requiem": "Home is the sailor, home from
      sea, / And the hunter home from the hill."

Looking lost and lame.
But you can't attribute to either
Awareness of what great gloom
Stands in a land of settlers
With never a soul at home.

The Unhistoric Story

Whaling for continents coveted deep in the south
The Dutchman[1] envied the unknown, drew bold
Images of market-place, populous river-mouth,
The Land of Beach ignorant of the value of gold:
    Morning in Murderers' Bay,
    Blood drifted away.[2]
    It was something different, something
    Nobody counted on.

Spider, clever and fragile, Cook[3] showed how
To spring a trap for islands, turning from planets
His measuring mission, showed what the musket could do,
Made his Christmas goose of the wild gannets.
    Still as the collier steered
    No continent appeared;
    It was something different, something
    Nobody counted on.

The roving tentacles touched, rested, clutched
Substantial earth, that is, accustomed haven
For the hungry whaler. Some inland, some hutched
Rudely in bays, the shaggy foreshore shaven,
    Lusted, preached as they knew;
    But as the children grew
    It was something different, something
    Nobody counted on.

Green slashed with flags,[4] pipeclay and boots in the bush,
Christ in canoes[5] and the musketed Maori boast;
All a rubble-rattle at Time's glacial push:
Vogel and Seddon[6] howling empire from an empty coast

---

1   Abel Tasman, a captain in the service of the Dutch East Indies Company, was the first
    European to discover New Zealand in 1642.
2   Tasman landed a boat, the crew of which was killed by the Maoris, the aboriginal
    inhabitants of New Zealand.
3   Captain James Cook (1728-1779) mapped the coastline of New Zealand in 1769, and took
    possession for the English Crown.
4   The flags of surveyors and prospectors claiming mineral rights; gold was discovered in
    the 1850s.
5   English missionaries began their work in New Zealand as early as 1814.
6   New Zealand premiers in the last quarter of the 19th century

A vast ocean laughter
Echoed unheard, and after
All it was different, something
Nobody counted on.

The pilgrim dream pricked by a cold dawn died
Among the chemical farmers, the fresh towns; among
Miners, not husbandmen, who piercing the side
Let the land's life, found like all who had so long
  Bloodily or tenderly striven
  To rearrange the given,
  It was something different, something
  Nobody counted on.

After all re-ordering of old elements
Time trips up all but the humblest of heart
Stumbling after the fire, but not in the smoke of events;
For many are called,[1] but many are left at the start,
  And whatever islands may be
  Under or over the sea,
  It is something different, something
  Nobody counted on.

Out of Sleep

Awake but not yet up, too early morning
Brings you like bells in matrix of mist
Noises the mind may finger, but no meaning.
Two blocks away a single car has crossed

Your intersection with the hour; each noise
A cough in the cathedral of your waking—
The cleaners have no souls, no sins—each does
Some job, Christ dying or the day breaking.

This you suppose is what goes on all day.
No one is allowed long to stop and listen,
But takes brief turns at it: now as you lie

Dead calm, a gust in the damp cedar hissing
Will have the mist right off in half a minute.
You will not grasp the meaning, you will be in it.

---

1 "For many are called, but few are chosen" (Matthew 22.14)

The Skeleton of the Great Moa[1] in the
Canterbury Museum, Christchurch

The skeleton of the moa on iron crutches
Broods over no great waste; a private swamp
Was where this tree grew feathers once, that hatches
Its dusty clutch, and guards them from the damp.

Interesting failure to adapt on islands,
Taller but not more fallen than I, who come
Bone to his bone, peculiarly New Zealand's.
The eyes of children flicker round this tomb

Under the skylights, wonder at the huge egg
Found in a thousand pieces, pieced together
But with less patience than the bones that dug
In time deep shelter against ocean weather:

Not I, some child, born in a marvellous year,
Will learn the trick of standing upright here.

---

1   The moa was a giant bird, now extinct, that was native to New Zealand. It was 10-12 ft high.

Irving Layton

(b. 1914)

The Birth of Tragedy[1]

And me happiest when I compose poems.
  Love, power, the huzza of battle
  are something, are much;
yet a poem includes them like a pool
  water and reflection.
In me, nature's divided things—
  tree, mould on tree—
  have their fruition;
I am their core. Let them swap,
bandy, like a flame swerve
I am their mouth; as a mouth I serve.

And I observe how the sensual moths
  big with odour and sunshine
  dart into the perilous shrubbery;
or drop their visiting shadows
  upon the garden I one year made
of flowering stone to be a footstool
  for the perfect gods:
  who, friends to the ascending orders,
sustain all passionate meditations
and call down pardons
for the insurgent blood.

A quiet madman, never far from tears,
  I lie like a slain thing
  under the green air the trees
inhabit, or rest upon a chair
  towards which the inflammable air
tumbles on many robins' wings;
  noting how seasonably
  leaf and blossom uncurl
and living things arrange their death,
while someone from afar off
blows birthday candles for the world.

---

1 an allusion to *The Birth of Tragedy* (1872), a work by the German writer Friedrich Wilhelm
Nietzsche (1844-1900)

Butterfly on Rock

The large yellow wings, black-fringed,
were motionless

They say the soul of a dead person
will settle like that on the still face[1]

But I thought: the rock has borne this;
this butterfly is the rock's grace,
its most obstinate and secret desire
to be a thing alive made manifest

Forgot were the two shattered porcupines
I had seen die in the bleak forest.
Pain is unreal; death, an illusion:
There is no death in all the land,
I heard my voice cry;
And brought my hand down on the butterfly
And felt the rock move beneath my hand.

The Bull Calf

The thing could barely stand. Yet taken
from his mother and the barn smells
he still impressed with his pride,
with the promise of sovereignty in the way
his head moved to take us in.
The fierce sunlight tugging the maize from the ground
licked at his shapely flanks.
He was too young for all that pride.
I thought of the deposed Richard II.[2]

"No money in bull calves," Freeman had said.
The visiting clergyman rubbed the nostrils
now snuffing pathetically at the windless day.
"A pity," he sighed.
My gaze slipped off his hat toward the empty sky
that circled over the black knot of men,
over us and the calf waiting for the first blow.

---

1   alluding to the ancient belief that the soul might be seen fluttering from the mouth of
     the deceased in the form of a moth or butterfly
2   Richard II (1367-1400) was overthrown by Henry Bolingbroke and deposed by Parliament
     in 1399; Layton is doubtless thinking of Shakespeare's portrait of him in the play *Richard
     II.*

Struck,
the bull calf drew in his thin forelegs
as if gathering strength for a mad rush . . .
tottered . . . raised his darkening eyes to us,
and I saw we were at the far end
of his frightened look, growing smaller and smaller
till we were only the ponderous mallet
that flicked his bleeding ear
and pushed him over on his side, stiffly,
like a block of wood.

Below the hill's crest
the river snuffled on the improvised beach.
We dug a deep pit and threw the dead calf into it.
It made a wet sound, a sepulchral gurgle,
as the warm sides bulged and flattened.
Settled, the bull calf lay as if asleep,
one foreleg over the other,
bereft of pride and so beautiful now,
without movement, perfectly still in the cool pit,
I turned away and wept.

The Cold Green Element

At the end of the garden walk
the wind and its satellite wait for me;
their meaning I will not know
          until I go there,
but the black-hatted undertaker

who, passing, saw my heart beating in the grass,
is also going there. Hi, I tell him,
a great squall in the Pacific blew a dead poet
          out of the water,
who now hangs from the city's gates.

Crowds depart daily to see it, and return
with grimaces and incomprehension;
if its limbs twitched in the air
          they would sit at its feet
peeling their oranges.

And turning over I embrace like a lover
the trunk of a tree, one of those
for whom the lightning was too much
          and grew a brilliant
hunchback with a crown of leaves.

The ailments escaped from the labels
of medicine bottles are all fled to the wind;

I've seen myself lately in the eyes
        of old women,
spent streams mourning my manhood,

in whose old pupils the sun became
a bloodsmear on broad catalpa leaves
and hanging from ancient twigs,
        my murdered selves
sparked the air like the muted collisions

of fruit. A black dog howls down my blood,
a black dog with yellow eyes;
he too by someone's inadvertence
        saw the bloodsmear
on the broad catalpa leaves.

But the furies[1] clear a path for me to the worm
who sang for an hour in the throat of a robin,
and misled by the cries of young boys
        I am again
a breathless swimmer in that cold green element.

Cain

Taking the air rifle from my son's hand,
I measured back five paces, the Hebrew
In me, narcissist, father of children,
Laid to rest. From there I took aim and fired.
The silent ball hit the frog's back an inch
Below the head. He jumped at the surprise
Of it, suddenly tickled or startled
(He must have thought) and leaped from the wet sand
Into the surrounding brown water. But
The ball had done its mischief. His next spring
Was a miserable flop, the thrust all gone
Out of his legs. He tried—like Bruce[2]—again,
Throwing out his sensitive pianist's
Hands as a dwarf might or a helpless child.
His splash disturbed the quiet pondwater
And one old frog behind his weedy moat
Blinking, looking self-complacently on.
The lin's surface[3] at once became closing

---

1   possibly the Furies of classical legend, the three avenging goddesses who punished
     wrongdoers
2   An allusion to the legend of Robert Bruce, the 14th century king of Scotland, who learned
     from watching a spider the importance of ceaseless endeavour.
3   A lin, or linn, is a pool.

Eyelids and bubbles like notes of music
Liquid, luminous, dropping from the page
White, white-bearded, a rapid crescendo
Of inaudible sounds and a crones' whispering
Backstage among the reeds and bulrushes
As for an expiring Lear or Oedipus.

But Death makes us all look ridiculous.
Consider this frog (dog, hog, what you will)
Sprawling, his absurd corpse rocked by the tides
That his last vain spring had set in movement.
Like a retired oldster, I couldn't help sneer,
Living off the last of his insurance:
Billows—now crumbling—the premiums paid.
Absurd, how absurd. I wanted to kill
At the mockery of it, kill and kill
Again—the self-infatuate frog, dog, hog,
Anything with the stir of life in it,
Seeing the dead leaper, Chaplin-footed,
Rocked and cradled in this afternoon
Of tranquil water, reeds, and blazing sun,
The hole in his back clearly visible
And the torn skin a blob of shadow
Moving when the quiet poolwater moved.
O Egypt, marbled Greece, resplendent Rome,
Did you also finally perish from a small bore
In your back you could not scratch? And would
Your mouths open ghostily, gasping out
Among the murky reeds, the hidden frogs,
We climb with crushed spines toward the heavens?

When the next morning I came the same way
The frog was on his back, one delicate
Hand on his belly, and his white shirt front
Spotless. He looked as if he might have been
A comic; tapdancer apologizing
For a fall, or an Emcee, his wide grin
Coaxing a laugh from us for an aside
Or perhaps a joke we didn't quite hear.

From Colony to Nation

A dull people,
but the rivers of this country
are wide and beautiful

A dull people
enamoured of childish games,
but food is easily come by
and plentiful

Some with a priest's voice
in their cage of ribs: but
on high mountain-tops and in thunderstorms
the chirping is not heard

Deferring to beadle and censor;
not ashamed for this,
but given over to horseplay,
the making of money

A dull people, without charm
or ideas,
settling into the clean empty look
of a Mountie or dairy farmer
as into a legacy

One can ignore them
(the silences, the vast distances help)
and suppose them at the bottom
of one of the meaner lakes,
their bones not even picked for souvenirs.

Kenneth Mackenzie

(1913–1955)

Shall then another . . .

"C'est vous perdre une seconde fois, que de croire qu'un autre vous possède . . ."[1]

Villarceaux à Ninon de Lenclos.

Shall then another do what I have done—
be with those legs and arms and breasts at one?
Shall the warm silken skin, that I alone knew,
be for another's couching, and shall he own new
gestures of hers—some subtle modification
of that loose drop of the head, of that dilation
amorous yet brutal of her pupils' caverns?
Shall he bait beasts and halt at the white taverns
and scale those purple climaxes, half-sleeping,
knowing not what he's accomplished? Shall the weeping
of that warm womb, the sobbing of its throat
be music to him, till by note by note
it's lost and wasted, as he grows there—too
used and occasion-hardened, and the brew
of love sours in his belly?
How can I think that he between her knees
shall at length find time to think, or hawk, or sneeze,
go over the day's events, yet up and down,
plan for tomorrow, cool above her frown
and tighter arms, as in the pleasure-pain
she parts from beauty, and becomes huge and plain
and draws him deeper—a Demeter's sigh[2]
sealing the spasm. Tell me—how shall I,
who always knew these monstrous movements of her,
dream and know now she has let another love her?
How shall I bear or dare to bring to mind
memory's cheap coin, finding it unrefined
by the heat of mental passions and sharp fires?
Or how, in her importunate desires
being somehow re-embraced, shall I go on,
saying, "These contacts have been, but are gone
into the void of all such", and not fling
back to her, roused to frenzy by the sting
of knowing my own demise was not my end?
There are some women who would have a friend

---

1   "It's losing you a second time, to think that another possesses you." Anne Lenclos, known as Ninon de Lenclos (1620-1705), was a Frenchwoman famous for the number of her lovers, as well as for her wit and beauty.

2   Demeter was the Greek goddess of the corn and agriculture, and mother of Persephone.

out of a vanquished lover; but not she—

"Get off," she said; "you are an enemy."
And so the gate of returning was left unlocked
though closed; however called against and mocked,
the enemy can return, but the friend's bound
by welcome's pleasant-coloured chains, and ground
under the heel of mighty unsuspicion.

This is a murderous and foul condition!
I love the woman. Let me forget my fear
and find a courage such as harlots wear
who stultify the mind till the body looms
merry and dominating in their rooms
and fills out space and squashes memory
by frequent repetition. Let me be
all body, and mindless.

How warm and dry her skin was! It outglowed
the single candle flame whose colour flowed
up to her overleaning face like a flower.
She never made one move to test her power,
but, with a smile as happy as a child's,
blew out the golden light.

Caesura[1]

Sometimes at night when the heart stumbles and stops
a full second endless the endless steps
that lead me on through this time terrain
without edges and beautiful terrible
are gone never to proceed again.

Here is a moment of enormous trouble
when the kaleidoscope sets unalterable
and at once without meaning without motion
like a stalled aeroplane in the middle sky
ready to fall down into a waiting ocean.

Blackness rises. Am I now to die
and feel the steps no more and not see day
break out its answering smile of hail all's well
from east full round to east and hear the bird
whistle all creatures that on earth do dwell[2]?

---

1   In prosody, a break or pause that occurs about the middle of a line of verse.
2   taken from a hymn

Not now. Old heart has stopped to think of a word
as someone in a dream by far too weird
to be unlikely feels a kiss and stops
to praise all heaven stumbling in all his senses . . .
and suddenly hears again the endless steps.

The Snake

Withdrawing from the amorous grasses
from the warm and luscious water
the snake is soul untouched by both
nor does the fire of day through which it passes
mark it or cling. Immaculate navigator
it carries death within its mouth.

Soul is the snake that moves at will
through all the nets of circumstance
like the wind that nothing stops,
immortal movement in a world held still
by rigid anchors of intent or chance
and ropes of fear and stays of hopes.

It is the source of all dispassion
the voiceless life above communion
secret as the spring of wind
nor does it know the shames of self-confession
the weakness that enjoys love's coarse dominion
or the betrayals of the mind.

Soul is the snake the cool viator[1]
sprung from a shadow on the grass
quick and intractable as breath
gone as it came like the everlasting water
reflecting god in immeasurable space—
and in its mouth it carries death.

---

1   traveller, wayfarer

Two Trinities

Are you ready? soul said again
smiling deep in the dark
where mind and I live passionately
grain rasping across grain
in a strangled question-mark
—or so we have lived lately.

I looked through the hollow keyhole
at my wife not young any more
with my signature on her forehead
and her spirit hers and whole
unsigned by me—as before
we knew each other, and wed.

I looked at my grown daughter
cool and contained as a flower
whose bees I shall not be among—
vivid as white spring water
full of womanish power
like the first phrases of a song.

I looked at my son, and wept
in my mouth's cave to see
the seed ready for sowing
and the harvest unready to be reaped—
green fruit shocked from the tree,
the bird killed on the wing.

Well? soul said and I said,
Mind and I are at one
to go with you now—finally
joined now to be led—
for our place here is gone:
we are not among those three.

Soul said, *Now come with me.*

Henry Reed

(1914–1986)

from: *Lessons of the War*

To Alan Michell

Vixi duellis nuper idoneus
Et militavi non sine gloria[1]

I: Naming of Parts

To-day we have naming of parts. Yesterday,
We had daily cleaning. And to-morrow morning,
We shall have what to do after firing. But to-day,
To-day we have naming of parts. Japonica[2]
Glistens like coral in all of the neighbouring gardens,
      And to-day we have naming of parts.

This is the lower sling swivel. And this
Is the upper sling swivel, whose use you will see,
When you are given your slings. And this is the piling swivel,
Which in your case you have not got. The branches
Hold in the gardens their silent, eloquent gestures,
      Which in our case we have not got.

This is the safety-catch, which is always released
With an easy flick of the thumb. And please do not let me
See anyone using his finger. You can do it quite easy
If you have any strength in your thumb. The blossoms
Are fragile and motionless, never letting anyone see
      Any of them using their finger.

And this you can see is the bolt. The purpose of this
Is to open the breech, as you see. We can slide it
Rapidly backwards and forwards: we call this
Easing the spring. And rapidly backwards and forwards
The early bees are assaulting and fumbling the flowers:
      They call it easing the Spring.

They call it easing the Spring: it is perfectly easy
If you have any strength in your thumb: like the bolt,
And the breech, and the cocking-piece, and the point of
                      balance,

---

1   "Lately I have lived among battles, suitably enough, and have served not without glory."
     Reed has taken two lines from Horace's *Odes*, altering only Horace's word "puellis" (girls)
     to "duellis" (battles).
2   an Asian shrub with bright scarlet flowers

Which in our case we have not got; and the almond-blossom
Silent in all of the gardens and the bees going backwards
        and forwards,
  For to-day we have naming of parts.

II: *Judging Distances*

Not only how far away, but the way that you say it
Is very important. Perhaps you may never get
The knack of judging a distance, but at least you know
How to report on a landscape: the central sector,
The right of arc and that, which we had last Tuesday,
  And at least you know

That maps are of time, not place, so far as the army
Happens to be concerned—the reason being,
Is one which need not delay us. Again, you know
There are three kinds of tree, three only, the fir and the poplar,
And those which have bushy tops to; and lastly
  That things only seem to be things.

A barn is not called a barn, to put it more plainly,
Or a field in the distance, where sheep may be safely grazing[1]
You must never be over-sure. You must say, when reporting:
At five o'clock in the central sector is a dozen
Of what appear to be animals; whatever you do,
  Don't call the bleeders *sheep*.

I am sure that's quite clear; and suppose, for the sake of
        example,
The one at the end, asleep, endeavours to tell us
What he sees over there to the west, and how far away,
After first having come to attention. There to the west,
On the fields of summer the sun and the shadows bestow
  Vestments of purple and gold.

The still white dwellings are like a mirage in the heat,
And under the swaying elms a man and a woman
Lie gently together. Which is, perhaps, only to say
That there is a row of houses to the left of arc,
And that under some poplars a pair of what appear to be
        humans
  Appear to be loving.

Well that, for an answer, is what we might rightly call

---

1 an allusion to the Christmas anthem "Sheep May Safely Graze," by J.S.Bach

Moderately satisfactory only, the reason being,
Is that two things have been omitted, and those are important.
The human beings, now: in what direction are they,
And how far away, would you say? And do not forget
      There may be dead ground in between.

There may be dead ground in between; and I may not have got
The knack of judging a distance; I will only venture
A guess that perhaps between me and the apparent lovers,
(Who, incidentally, appear by now to have finished,)
At seven o'clock from the houses, is roughly a distance
      Of about one year and a half.

IV: Unarmed Combat

In due course of course you will all be issued with
Your proper issue; but until tomorrow,
You can hardly be said to need it; and until that time,
We shall have unarmed combat. I shall teach you
The various holds and rolls and throws and breakfalls
   Which you may sometimes meet.

And the various holds and rolls and throws and breakfalls
Do not depend on any sort of weapon,
But only on what I might coin a phrase and call
The ever-important question of human balance,
And the ever-important need to be in a strong
      Position at the start.

There are many kinds of weakness about the body,
Where you would least expect, like the ball of the foot.
But the various holds and rolls and throws and breakfalls
Will always come in useful. And never be frightened
To tackle from behind: it may not be clean to do so,
      But this is global war.

So give them all you have, and always give them
As good as you get; it will always get you somewhere
(You may not know it, but you can tie a Jerry[1]
Up without a rope; it is one of the things I shall teach you).
Nothing will matter if only you are ready for him.
      The readiness is all.[2]

The readiness is all. How can I help but feel
I have been here before? But somehow then,

---

1   World War II slang for a German soldier
2   from *Hamlet* V.ii.236

I was the tied-up one. How to get out
Was always then my problem. And even if I had
A piece of rope I was always the sort of person
　　　Who threw the rope aside.

And in my time I have given them all I had,
Which was never as good as I got, and it got me nowhere.
And the various holds and rolls and throws and breakfalls
Somehow or other I always seemed to put
In the wrong place. And as for war, my wars
　　　Were global from the start.

Perhaps I was never in a strong position,
Or the ball of my foot got hurt, or I had some weakness
Where I had least expected. But I think I see the point:
While awaiting a proper issue, we must learn the lesson
Of the ever-important question of human balance.
　　　It is courage that counts.

Things may be the same again; and we must fight
Not in the hope of winning but rather of keeping
Something alive: so that when we meet our end,
It may be said that we tackled wherever we could,
That battle-fit we lived, and though defeated,
　　　Not without glory fought.

* * *

Randall Jarrell

(1914–1965)

Losses

It was not dying: everybody died.
It was not dying: we had died before
In the routine crashes—and our fields
Called up the papers, wrote home to our folks,
And the rates rose, all because of us.
We died on the wrong page of the almanac,
Scattered on mountains fifty miles away;
Diving on haystacks, fighting with a friend,
We blazed up on the lines we never saw.
We died like aunts or pets or foreigners.
(When we left high school nothing else had died
For us to figure we had died like.)

In our new planes, with our new crews, we bombed
The ranges by the desert or the shore,
Fired at towed targets, waited for our scores—
And turned into replacements and woke up
One morning, over England, operational.
It wasn't different: but if we died
It was not an accident but a mistake
(But an easy one for anyone to make).
We read our mail and counted up our missions—
In bombers named for girls, we burned
The cities we had learned about in school—
Till our lives wore out; our bodies lay among
The people we had killed and never seen.
When we lasted long enough they gave us medals;
When we died they said, "Our casualties were low."
They said, "Here are the maps"; we burned the cities.

It was not dying—no, not ever dying;
But the night I died I dreamed that I was dead,
And the cities said to me: "Why are you dying?
We are satisfied, if you are; but why did I die?"

The Death of the Ball Turret Gunner

From my mother's sleep I fell into the State,
And I hunched in its belly till my wet fur froze.
Six miles from earth, loosed from its dream of life,
I woke to black flak and the nightmare fighters.
When I died they washed me out of the turret with a hose.

The Woman at the Washington Zoo

The saris go by me from the embassies.

Cloth from the moon. Cloth from another planet.
They look back at the leopard like the leopard.

And I . . . .
            this print of mine, that has kept its color
Alive through so many cleanings; this dull null
Navy I wear to work, and wear from work, and so
To my bed, so to my grave, with no
Complaints, no comment: neither from my chief,
The Deputy Chief Assistant, nor his chief—
Only I complain. . . . this serviceable
Body that no sunlight dyes, no hand suffuses
But, dome-shadowed, withering among columns,
Wavy beneath fountains—small, far-off, shining
In the eyes of animals, these beings trapped
As I am trapped but not, themselves, the trap,
Aging, but without knowledge of their age,
Kept safe here, knowing not of death, for death—
Oh, bars of my own body, open, open!

The world goes by my cage and never sees me.
And there come not to me, as come to these,
The wild beasts, sparrows pecking the llamas' grain,
Pigeons settling on the bears' bread, buzzards
Tearing the meat the flies have clouded. . .
            Vulture,
When you come for the white rat that the foxes left,
Take off the red helmet of your head, the black
Wings that have shadowed me, and step to me as man:
The wild brother at whose feet the white wolves fawn,
To whose hand of power the great lioness
Stalks, purring. . . .
            You know what I was,
You see what I am: change me, change me!

William Stafford

(b. 1914)

Traveling through the Dark

Traveling through the dark I found a deer
dead on the edge of the Wilson River road.
It is usually best to roll them into the canyon:
that road is narrow; to swerve might make more dead.

By glow of the tail-light I stumbled back of the car
and stood by the heap, a doe, a recent killing;
she had stiffened already, almost cold.
I dragged her off; she was large in the belly.

My fingers touching her side brought me the reason—
her side was warm; her fawn lay there waiting,
alive, still, never to be born.
Beside that mountain road I hesitated.

The car aimed ahead its lowered parking lights;
under the hood purred the steady engine.
I stood in the glare of the warm exhaust turning red;
around our group I could hear the wilderness listen.

I thought hard for us all—my only swerving—,
then pushed her over the edge into the river.

A Message from the Wanderer

Today outside your prison I stand
and rattle my walking stick: Prisoners, listen;
you have relatives outside. And there are
thousands of ways to escape.

Years ago I bent my skill to keep my
cell locked, had chains smuggled to me in pies,
and shouted my plans to jailers;
but always new plans occurred to me,
or the new heavy locks bent hinges off,
or some stupid jailer would forget
and leave the keys.

Inside, I dreamed of constellations—
those feeding creatures outlined by stars,
their skeletons a darkness between jewels,
heroes that exist only where they are not.

Thus freedom always came nibbling my thought,
just as—often, in light, on the open hills—
you can pass an antelope and not know

and look back, and then—even before you see—
there is something wrong about the grass.
And then you see.

That's the way everything in the world is waiting.

Now—these few more words, and then I'm
gone: Tell everyone just to remember
their names, and remind others, later, when we
find each other. Tell the little ones
to cry and then go to sleep, curled up
where they can. And if any of us get lost,
if any of us cannot come all the way—
remember: there will come a time when
all we have said and all we have hoped
will be all right.

There will be that form in the grass.

At the Un-National Monument Along the Canadian Border

This is the field where the battle did not happen,
where the unknown soldier did not die.
This is the field where grass joined hands,
where no monument stands,
and the only heroic thing is the sky.

Birds fly here without any sound,
unfolding their wings across the open.
No people killed—or were killed—on this ground
hallowed by neglect and an air so tame
that people celebrate it by forgetting its name.

John Berryman

(1914–1972)

A Professor's Song

(. . . rabid or dog-dull.) Let me tell you how
The Eighteenth Century couplet ended. Now
Tell me. Troll me the sources of that Song —
Assigned last week—by Blake. Come, come along,
Gentlemen. (Fidget and huddle, do. Squint soon.)
I want to end these fellows all by noon.

'That deep romantic chasm'[1]—an early use;
The word is from the French, by our abuse
Fished out a bit. (Red all your eyes. O when?)
'A poet is a man speaking to men'[2]:
But I am then a poet, am I not?—
Ha ha. The radiator, please. Well, what?

Alive now—no—Blake would have written prose,
But movement following movement crisply flows,
So much the better, better the much so,
As burbleth Mozart. Twelve. The class can go.
Until I meet you, then, in Upper Hell[3]
Convulsed, foaming immortal blood: farewell.

Desires of Men and Women

Exasperated, worn, you conjure a mansion,
The absolute butlers in the spacious hall,
Old silver, lace, and privacy, a house
Where nothing has for years been out of place,
Neither shoe-horn nor affection been out of place,
Breakfast in summer on the eastern terrace,
All justice and all grace.

At the reception
Most beautifully you conduct yourselves—
Expensive and accustomed, bow, speak French,
That Cinquecento[4] miniature recall
The Duke presented to your great-grandmother—

---

1   from Coleridge's "Kubla Khan" (written 1797-1798)
2   from Wordsworth's Preface to the second edition of the *Lyrical Ballads* (1800)
3   In the *Inferno*, Canto 12, Dante must cross the Phlegethon, a river of boiling blood, in which are immersed tyrants and opressors.
4   of sixteenth-century Italy

And none of us, my dears, would dream of you
The half-lit and lascivious apartments
That are in fact your goal, for which you'd do
Murder if you had not your cowardice
To prop the law; or dream of you the rooms,
Glaring and inconceivably vulgar,
Where now you are, where now you wish for life,
Whence you project your naked fantasies.

from: *The Dream Songs*

14

Life, friends, is boring. We must not say so.
After all, the sky flashes, the great sea yearns,
we ourselves flash and yearn,
and moreover my mother told me as a boy
(repeatedly) 'Ever to confess you're bored
means you have no

Inner Resources.' I conclude now I have no
inner resources, because I am heavy bored.
Peoples bore me,
literature bores me, especially great literature,
Henry bores me, with his plights & gripes
as bad as achilles,[1]

who loves people and valiant art, which bores me.
And the tranquil hills, & gin, look like a drag
and somehow a dog
has taken itself & its tail considerably away
into mountains or sea or sky, leaving
behind: me, wag.

29

There sat down, once, a thing on Henry's heart
só heavy, if he had a hundred years
& more, & weeping, sleepless, in all them time
Henry could not make good.
Starts again always in Henry's ears
the little cough somewhere, an odour, a chime.

---

1   Believing himself ill-used by Agamemnon, Achilles sulked in his tent and refused for a
time to join the Greeks in their battle against the Trojans.

And there is another thing he has in mind
like a grave Sienese[1] face a thousand years
would fail to blur the still profiled reproach of. Ghastly,
with open eyes, he attends, blind.
All the bells say: too late. This is not for tears;
thinking.

But never did Henry, as he thought he did,
end anyone and hacks her body up
and hide the pieces, where they may be found.
He knows: he went over everyone, & nobody's missing.
Often he reckons, in the dawn, them up.
Nobody is ever missing.

384

The marker slants, flowerless, day's almost done,
I stand above my father's grave with rage,
often, often before
I've made this awful pilgrimage to one
who cannot visit me, who tore his page
out: I come back for more,

I spit upon this dreadful banker's grave[2]
who shot his heart out in a Florida dawn
O ho alas alas
When will indifference come, I moan & rave
I'd like to scrabble till I got right down
away down under the grass

and ax the casket open ha to see
just how he's taking it, which he sought so hard
we'll tear apart
the mouldering grave clothes ha & then Henry
will heft the ax once more, his final card,
and fell it on the start.

* * *

---

1   from Siena in Tuscany, a centre of religious art in 13th century Italy
2   Berryman's father, a banker in Florida, shot himself outside his son's window.

Douglas LePan

(b. 1914)

Coureurs de Bois[1]

Thinking of you, I think of the *coureurs de bois*,
Swarthy men grown almost to savage size
Who put their brown wrists through the arras of the woods
And were lost—sometimes for months. Word would come back:
One had been seen at Crêve-coeur, deserted and starving,
One at Sault Sainte Marie shouldering the rapids.
Giant-like, their labours stalked in the streets of Quebec
Though they themselves had dwindled in distance: names only;
Rumours; quicksilvery spies into nature's secrets;
Rivers that seldom ran in the sun. Their resource
Would sparkle and then flow back under clouds of hemlock.

So you should have travelled with them. Or with La Salle.[2]
He could feed his heart with the heart of a continent,
Insatiate, how noble a wounded animal,
Who sought for his wounds the balsam of adventure,
The sap from some deep, secret tree. But now
That the forests are cut down, the rivers charted,
Where can you turn, where can you travel? Unless
Through the desperate wilderness behind your eyes,
So full of falls and glooms and desolations,
Disasters I have glimpsed but few would dream of,
You seek new Easts. The coats of difficult honour,
Bright with brocaded birds and curious flowers,
Stowed so long with vile packs of pemmican,
Futile, weighing you down on slippery portages,
Would flutter at last in the courts of a clement country,
Where the air is silken, the manners easy,
Under a guiltless and reconciling sun.

You hesitate. The trees are entangled with menace.
The voyage is perilous into the dark interior.
But then your hands go to the thwarts. You smile. And so
I watch you vanish in a wood of heroes,
Wild Hamlet with the features of Horatio.

---

1   the unlicensed traders and trappers in early Quebec
2   René-Robert Cavelier, sieur de La Salle (1643-1687). An adventurer and explorer, he
     descended the Mississippi and founded Louisiana in 1682.

A Country Without A Mythology

No monuments or landmarks guide the stranger
Going among this savage people, masks
Taciturn or babbling out an alien jargon
And moody as barbaric skies are moody.

Berries must be his food. Hurriedly
He shakes the bushes, plucks pickerel from the river,
Forgetting every grace and ceremony,
Feeds like an Indian, and is on his way.

And yet, for all his haste, time is worth nothing.
The abbey clock, the dial in the garden,
Fade like saint's days and festivals.
Months, years, are here unbroken virgin forests.

There is no law—even no atmosphere
To smooth the anger of the flagrant sun.
November skies sting, sting like icicles.
The land is open to all violent weathers.

Passion is not more quick. Lightnings in August
Stagger, rocks split, tongues in the forest hiss,
As fire drinks up the lovely sea-dream coolness.
This is the land the passionate man must travel.

Sometimes—perhaps at the tentative fall of twilight—
A belief will settle that waiting around the bend
Are sanctities of childhood, that melting birds
Will sing him into a limpid gracious Presence.

The hills will fall in folds, the wilderness
Will be a garment innocent and lustrous
To wear upon a birthday, under a light
That curls and smiles, a golden-haired Archangel.

And now the channel opens. But nothing alters.
Mile after mile of tangled struggling roots,
Wild-rice, stumps, weeds, that clutch at the canoe,
Wild birds hysterical in tangled trees.

And not a sign, no emblem in the sky
Or boughs to friend him as he goes; for who
Will stop where, clumsily constructed, daubed
With war-paint, teeters some lust-red manitou?[1]

---

1   the personification in Algonquian legend of the spirit governing nature

An Incident

Arrange the scene with only a shade of difference
And he would be a boy in his own native
And fern-fronded providence,
With a map in his hand, searching for a portage overgrown
With brush. Slim he is as a moccasin-flower
With his throat open
To the winds, to the four winds, quivering,
Who alone by the worm-holed flower of the rose-pink house
Bears the weight of this many-ringed, foreign noon,
Shadowless, vast and pitiless.
Notched by the wedge of his frown, it takes no notice.
Light that, alive, would be pungent with resin,
Sapless, now weighs and ponders like limestone.

What is he waiting for
As he studies a map the colour of his youth?
Time stops and whirs in his ear like a hummingbird
As he gazes this way and that
For someone to relieve him
For someone to break through the thicket of his isolation.

In the silence
The grasshoppers crackle and crumble the summer
Between their thin wings
And their singing thighs.
And his head has begun to sing,
To sing with the heat.
Stampeding, his blood butts him like a bull-calf.
How should one so young have learned how to wait?

Ah! there is the relief.
A stray round has caught him at the nape of the neck
And splayed him flat on the earth,
His blood flung wide as a sunburst.

And the pink house, that eavesdropped
Through smoke-blackened holes to each palpitation,
Recovering its reserve,
Sucks in unblemished stillness;
While the wise light with petrified foliage
Having disposed of this awkward animal tremor
Again stands superb as a temple.

Dylan Thomas

(1914-1953)

The Force That Through The Green Fuse
Drives The Flower

The force that through the green fuse drives the flower
Drives my green age; that blasts the roots of trees
Is my destroyer.
And I am dumb to tell the crooked rose
My youth is bent by the same wintry fever.

The force that drives the water through the rocks
Drives my red blood; that dries the mouthing streams
Turns mine to wax.
And I am dumb to mouth unto my veins
How at the mountain spring the same mouth sucks.

The hand that whirls the water in the pool
Stirs the quicksand; that ropes the blowing wind
Hauls my shroud sail.
And I am dumb to tell the hanging man
How of my clay is made the hangman's lime.

The lips of time leech to the fountain head;
Love drips and gathers, but the fallen blood
Shall calm her sores.
And I am dumb to tell a weather's wind
How time has ticked a heaven round the stars.

And I am dumb to tell the lover's tomb
How at my sheet goes the same crooked worm.

And Death Shall Have No Dominion[1]

And death shall have no dominion.
Dead men naked they shall be one
With the man in the wind and the west moon;
When their bones are picked clean and the clean bones gone,
They shall have stars at elbow and foot;
Though they go mad they shall be sane,
Though they sink through the sea they shall rise again;
Though lovers be lost love shall not;
And death shall have no dominion.

---

1   Compare Romans 6.9: "...Christ being raised from the dead dieth no more; death hath
no more dominion over him."

And death shall have no dominion.
Under the windings of the sea
They lying long shall not die windily;
Twisting on racks when sinews give way,
Strapped to a wheel, yet they shall not break;
Faith in their hands shall snap in two,
And the unicorn evils run them through;
Split all ends up they shan't crack;
And death shall have no dominion.

And death shall have no dominion.
No more may gulls cry at their ears
Or waves break loud on the seashores;
Where blew a flower may a flower no more
Lift its head to the blows of the rain;
Though they be mad and dead as nails,
Heads of the characters hammer through daisies;
Break in the sun till the sun breaks down,
And death shall have no dominion.

Do Not Go Gentle Into That Good Night

Do not go gentle into that good night,
Old age should burn and rave at close of day;
Rage, rage against the dying of the light.

Though wise men at their end know dark is right,
Because their words had forked no lightning they
Do not go gentle into that good night.

Good men, the last wave by, crying how bright
Their frail deeds might have danced in a green bay,
Rage, rage against the dying of the light.

Wild men who caught and sang the sun in flight,
And learn, too late, they grieved it on its way,
Do not go gentle into that good night.

Grave men, near death, who see with blinding sight
Blind eyes could blaze like meteors and be gay,
Rage, rage against the dying of the light.

And you, my father, there on the sad height,
Curse, bless, me now with your fierce tears, I pray.
Do not go gentle into that good night.
Rage, rage against the dying of the light.

[631]

Fern Hill[1]

Now as I was young and easy under the apple boughs
About the lilting house and happy as the grass was green,
   The night above the dingle starry,
     Time let me hail and climb
    Golden in the heydays of his eyes,
And honoured among wagons I was prince of the apple towns
And once below a time I lordly had the trees and leaves
    Trail with daisies and barley
   Down the rivers of the windfall light.

And as I was green and carefree, famous among the barns
About the happy yard and singing as the farm was home,
   In the sun that is young once only,
     Time let me play and be
    Golden in the mercy of his means,
And green and golden I was huntsman and herdsman, the
      calves
Sang to my horn, the foxes on the hills barked clear and cold,
    And the sabbath rang slowly
   In the pebbles of the holy streams.

All the sun long it was running, it was lovely, the hay
Fields high as the house, the tunes from the chimneys, it was air
   And playing, lovely and watery
     And fire green as grass.
   And nightly under the simple stars
As I rode to sleep the owls were bearing the farm away,
All the moon long I heard, blessed among stables, the nightjars
   Flying with the ricks, and the horses
    Flashing into the dark.

And then to awake, and the farm, like a wanderer white
With the dew, come back, the cock on his shoulder: it was all
   Shining, it was Adam and maiden,
     The sky gathered again
   And the sun grew round that very day.
So it must have been after the birth of the simple light
In the first, spinning place, the spellbound horses walking warm
   Out of the whinnying green stable
    On to the fields of praise.

And honoured among foxes and pheasants by the gay house
Under the new made clouds and happy as the heart was long,
   In the sun born over and over,

---

1   the farm-house in Wales belonging to Thomas's aunt, Ann Jones, where he spent his
summers as a child

I ran my heedless ways,
My wishes raced through the house high hay
And nothing I cared, at my sky blue trades, that time allows
In all his tuneful turning so few and such morning songs
  Before the children green and golden
    Follow him out of grace,

Nothing I cared, in the lamb white days, that time would take me
Up to the swallow thronged loft by the shadow of my hand,
  In the moon that is always rising,
    Nor that riding to sleep
  I should hear him fly with the high fields
And wake to the farm forever fled from the childless land.
Oh as I was young and easy in the mercy of his means,
    Time held me green and dying
  Though I sang in my chains like the sea.

A Refusal To Mourn The Death, By Fire, Of A Child In London

Never until the mankind making
Bird beast and flower
Fathering and all humbling darkness
Tells with silence the last light breaking
And the still hour
Is come of the sea tumbling in harness

And I must enter again the round
Zion[1] of the water bead
And the synagogue of the ear of corn
Shall I let pray the shadow of a sound
Or sow my salt seed
In the least valley of sackcloth to mourn

The majesty and burning of the child's death.
I shall not murder
The mankind of her going with a grave truth
Nor blaspheme down the stations of the breath
With any further
Elegy of innocence and youth.

Deep with the first dead lies London's daughter,
Robed in the long friends,
The grains beyond age, the dark veins of her mother,

---

1   Heaven, heavenly city

Secret by the unmourning water
Of the riding Thames.
After the first death, there is no other.

In My Craft Or Sullen Art

In my craft or sullen art
Exercised in the still night
When only the moon rages
And the lovers lie abed
With all their griefs in their arms,
I labour by singing light
Not for ambition or bread
Or the strut and trade of charms
On the ivory stages
But for the common wages
Of their most secret heart.

Not for the proud man apart
From the raging moon I write
On these spindrift pages
Nor for the towering dead
With their nightingales and psalms
But for the lovers, their arms
Round the griefs of the ages,
Who pay no praise or wages
Nor heed my craft or art.

After The Funeral

(In memory of Ann Jones[1])

After the funeral, mule praises, brays,
Windshake of sailshaped ears, muffle-toed tap
Tap happily of one peg in the thick
Grave's foot, blinds down the lids, the teeth in black,
The spittled eyes, the salt ponds in the sleeves,
Morning smack of the spade that wakes up sleep,
Shakes a desolate boy who slits his throat
In the dark of the coffin and sheds dry leaves,
That breaks one bone to light with a judgment clout,
After the feast of tear-stuffed time and thistles
In a room with a stuffed fox and a stale fern,
I stand, for this memorial's sake, alone

---

1   Thomas's aunt, who died in 1933

In the snivelling hours with dead, humped Ann
Whose hooded, fountain heart once fell in puddles
Round the parched worlds of Wales and drowned each sun
(Though this for her is a monstrous image blindly
Magnified out of praise; her death was a still drop;
She would not have me sinking in the holy
Flood of her heart's fame; she would lie dumb and deep
And need no druid of her broken body).
But I, Ann's bard on a raised hearth, call all
The seas to service that her wood-tongued virtue
Babble like a bellbuoy over the hymning heads,
Bow down the walls of the ferned and foxy woods
That her love sing and swing through a brown chapel,
Bless her bent spirit with four, crossing birds.
Her flesh was meek as milk, but this skyward statue
With the wild breast and blessed and giant skull
Is carved from her in a room with a wet window
In a fiercely mourning house in a crooked year.
I know her scrubbed and sour humble hands
Lie with religion in their cramp, her threadbare
Whisper in a damp word, her wits drilled hollow,
Her fist of a face died clenched on a round pain;
And sculptured Ann is seventy years of stone.
These cloud-sopped, marble hands, this monumental
Argument of the hewn voice, gesture and psalm,
Storm me forever over her grave until
The stuffed lung of the fox twitch and cry Love
And the strutting fern lay seeds on the black sill.

Judith Wright

(b. 1915)

Song

O where does the dancer dance—[1]
the invisible centre spin—
whose bright periphery holds
the world we wander in?

For it is he we seek—
the source and death of desire;
we blind as blundering moths
around that heart of fire.

Caught between birth and death
we stand alone in the dark
to watch the blazing wheel
on which the earth is a spark,

crying, Where does the dancer dance—
the terrible centre spin,
whose flower will open at last
to let the wanderer in?

The Bull

In the olive darkness of the sally-trees
silently moved the air from night to day.
The summer-grass was thick with honey-daisies
where he, a curled god, a red Jupiter,[2]
heavy with power among his women lay.

But summer's bubble-sound of sweet creek-water
dwindles and is silent; the seeding grasses
grow harsh, and wind and frost in the black sallies
roughen the sleek-haired slopes. Seek him out, then,
the angry god betrayed, whose godhead passes,

and down the hillsides drive him from his mob.
What enemy steals his strength—what rival steals
his mastered cows? His thunders powerless,
the red storm of his body shrunk with fear,
runs the great bull, the dogs upon his heels.

---

1   Compare the last line of Yeats's "Among School Children": "How can we know the dancer
from the dance?"
2   In Greek mythology, Zeus (Roman, Jupiter) took the form of a bull when he came to
Europa.

Woman to Man

The eyeless labourer in the night,
the selfless, shapeless seed I hold,
builds for its resurrection day—
silent and swift and deep from sight
foresees the unimagined light.

This is no child with a child's face;
this has no name to name it by:
yet you and I have known it well.
This is our hunter and our chase,
the third who lay in our embrace.

This is the strength that your arm knows,
the arc of flesh that is my breast,
the precise crystals of our eyes.
This is the blood's wild tree that grows
the intricate and folded rose.

This is the maker and the made;
this is the question and reply;
the blind head butting at the dark,
the blaze of light along the blade.
Oh hold me, for I am afraid.

Woman to Child

You who were darkness warmed my flesh
where out of darkness rose the seed.
Then all a world I made in me;
all the world you hear and see
hung upon my dreaming blood.

There moved the multitudinous stars,
and coloured birds and fishes moved.
There swam the sliding continents.
All time lay rolled in me, and sense,
and love that knew not its beloved.

O node and focus of the world;
I hold you deep within that well
you shall escape and not escape—
that mirrors still your sleeping shape;
that nurtures still your crescent cell.

I wither and you break from me;
yet though you dance in living light
I am the earth, I am the root,

I am the stem that fed the fruit,
the link that joins you to the night.

Request to a Year

If the year is meditating a suitable gift,
I should like it to be the attitude
of my great-great-grandmother,
legendary devotee of the arts,

who, having had eight children
and little opportunity for painting pictures,
sat one day on a high rock
beside a river in Switzerland

and from a difficult distance viewed
her second son, balanced on a small ice-floe,
drift down the current towards a waterfall
that struck rock-bottom eighty feet below,

while her second daughter, impeded,
no doubt, by the petticoats of the day,
stretched out a last-hope alpenstock[1]
(which luckily later caught him on his way).

Nothing, it was evident, could be done;
and with the artist's isolating eye
my great-great-grandmother hastily sketched the scene.
The sketch survives to prove the story by.

Year, if you have no Mother's day present planned;
reach back and bring me the firmness of her hand.

At Cooloola

The blue crane fishing in Cooloola's twilight
has fished there longer than our centuries.
He is the certain heir of lake and evening,
and he will wear their colour till he dies,

but I'm a stranger, come of a conquering people.
I cannot share his calm, who watch his lake,
being unloved by all my eyes delight in,
and made uneasy, for an old murder's sake.

---

1   a long staff used by mountain climbers

Those dark-skinned people who once named Cooloola
knew that no land is lost or won by wars,
for earth is spirit: the invader's feet will tangle
in nets there and his blood be thinned by fears.

Riding at noon and ninety years ago,
my grandfather was beckoned by a ghost—
a black accoutred warrior armed for fighting,
who sank into bare plain, as now into time past.

White shores of sand, plumed reed and paperbark,[1]
clear heavenly levels frequented by crane and swan—
I know that we are justified only by love,
but oppressed by arrogant guilt, have room for none.

And walking on clean sand among the prints
of bird and animal, I am challenged by a driftwood spear
thrust from the water; and, like my grandfather,
must quiet a heart accused by its own fear.

---

1   a tree with a bark consisting of numerous thin layers of a corky material

P. K. Page

(b. 1916)

The Stenographers

After the brief bivouac of Sunday,
their eyes, in the forced march of Monday to Saturday,
hoist the white flag, flutter in the snow-storm of paper,
haul it down and crack in the mid-sun of temper.

In the pause between the first draft and the carbon
they glimpse the smooth hours when they were children—
the ride in the ice-cart, the ice-man's name,
the end of the route and the long walk home;

remember the sea where floats at high tide
were sea marrows growing on the scatter-green vine
or spools of grey toffee, or wasps' nests on water;
remember the sand and the leaves of the country.

Bell rings and they go and the voice draws their pencil
like a sled across snow; when its runners are frozen
rope snaps and the voice then is pulling no burden
but runs like a dog on the winter of paper.

Their climates are winter and summer—no wind
for the kites of their hearts—no wind for a flight;
a breeze at the most, to tumble them over
and leave them like rubbish—the boy-friends of blood.

In the inch of the noon as they move they are stagnant.
The terrible calm of the noon is their anguish;
the lip of the counter, the shapes of the straws
like icicles breaking their tongues, are invaders.

Their beds are their oceans—salt water of weeping
the waves that they know—the tide before sleep;
and fighting to drown they assemble their sheep
in columns and watch them leap desks for their fences
and stare at them with their own mirror-worn faces.

In the felt of the morning the calico-minded,
sufficiently starched, insert papers, hit keys,
efficient and sure as their adding machines;
yet they weep in the vault, they are taut as net curtains
stretched upon frames. In their eyes I have seen
the pin men of madness in marathon trim
race round the track of the stadium pupil.

Young Girls

Nothing, not even fear of punishment
can stop the giggle in a girl.
Oh mothers' trim
shapes on the chesterfield cannot dispel
their lolloping fatness.
Adolescence tumbles about in them
on cinder schoolyard or behind the expensive gates.

See them in class like porpoises *maine animal*
with smiles and tears
loosed from the same subterranean faucet; some
find individual adventure in
the obtuse angle, some in a phrase
that leaps like a smaller fish from a sea of words.
But most, deep in their daze, dawdle and roll,
their little breasts like wounds beneath their clothes.

Conting main image

A shoal of them in a room makes it a pool.
How can one teacher keep the water out,
or, being adult, find the springs and taps
of their tempers and tortures?
Who on a field filled with their female cries
can reel them in on a line of words
or land them neatly in a net?
On the dry ground they goggle, flounder, flap.

Too much weeping in them and unfamiliar blood *Menses*
has set them perilously afloat.
Not divers these—but as if the waters rose in flood—
making them partially amphibious
and always drowning a little and hearing bells;
until the day the shore line wavers less,
and caught and swung on the bright hooks of their sex,
earth becomes home, their natural element.

The Landlady

Through sepia air the boarders come and go,
impersonal as trains. Pass silently
the craving silence swallowing her speech;
click doors like shutters on her camera eye.

Because of her their lives become exact:
their entrances and exits are designed;
phone calls are cryptic. Oh, her ticklish ears
advance and fall back stunned.

Nothing is unprepared. They hold the walls
about them as they weep or laugh. Each face
is dialled to zero publicly. She peers
stippled with curious flesh;

pads on the patient landing like a pulse,
unlocks their keyholes with the wire of sight,
searches their rooms for clues when they are out,
pricks when they come home late.

Wonders when they are quiet, jumps when they move,
dreams that they dope or drink, trembles to know
the traffic of their brains, jaywalks their street
in clumsy shoes.

Yet knows them better than their closest friends:
their cupboards and the secrets of their drawers,
their books, their private mail, their photographs
are theirs and hers.

Knows when they wash, how frequently their clothes
go to the cleaners, what they like to eat,
their curvature of health, but even so
is not content.

And like a lover must know all, all, all.
Prays she may catch them unprepared at last
and palm the dreadful riddle of their skulls—
hoping the worst.

Social comment about tourists in life those world

The Permanent Tourists

Somnolent through landscapes and by trees
nondescript, almost anonymous,
they alter as they enter foreign cities—
the terrible tourists with their empty eyes
longing to be filled with monuments.

Verge upon statues in the public squares
remembering the promise of memorials
yet never enter the entire event
as dogs, abroad in any kind of weather,
move perfectly within their rainy climate.

Lock themselves into snapshots on the steps
of monolithic bronze as if suspecting
the subtle mourning of the photograph
might later conjure in the memory
all they are now incapable of feeling.

And search all heroes out: the boy who gave
his life to save a town; the stolid queen;
forgotten politicians minus names
and the plunging war dead, permanently brave,
forever and ever going down to death.

Look, you can see them nude in any café
reading their histories from the bill of fare,
creating futures from a foreign teacup.
Philosophies like ferns bloom from the fable
that travel is broadening at the café table.

Yet somehow beautiful, they stamp the plaza.
Classic in their anxiety they call
all sculptured immemorial stone
into their passive eyes, as rivers
draw ruined columns to their placid glass.

T-bar

Relentless, black on white, the cable runs
through metal arches up the mountain side.
At intervals giant pickaxes are hung
on long hydraulic springs. The skiers ride
propped by the axehead, twin automatons
supported by its handle, one each side.

In twos they move slow motion up the steep
incision in the mountain. Climb. Climb.
Somnambulists, bolt upright in their sleep
their phantom poles swung lazily behind,
while to the right, the empty T-bars keep
in mute descent, slow monstrous jigging time.

Captive the skiers now and innocent,
wards of eternity, each pair alone.
They mount the easy vertical ascent,
pass through successive arches, bride and groom,
as through successive naves, are newly wed
participants in some recurring dream.

So do they move forever. Clocks are broken.
In zones of silence they grow tall and slow,
inanimate dreamers, mild and gentle-spoken
blood-brothers of the haemophilic snow
until the summit breaks and they awaken
imagos from the stricture of the tow.

Jerked from her chrysalis the sleeping bride
suffers too sudden freedom like a pain.

The dreaming bridegroom severed from her side
singles her out, the old wound aches again.
Uncertain, lost, upon a wintry height
these two, not separate, but no longer one.

Now clocks begin to peck and sing. The slow
extended minute like a rubber band
contracts to catapult them through the snow
in tandem trajectory while behind
etching the sky-line, obdurate and slow
the spastic T-bars pivot and descend.

Stories of Snow

Those in the vegetable rain retain
an area behind their sprouting eyes
held soft and rounded with the dream of snow
precious and reminiscent as those globes—
souvenir of some never-nether land—
which hold their snow-storms circular, complete,
high in a tall and teakwood cabinet.

In countries where the leaves are large as hands
where flowers protrude their fleshy chins
and call their colours,
an imaginary snow-storm sometimes falls
among the lilies.
And in the early morning one will waken
to think the glowing linen of his pillow
a northern drift, will find himself mistaken
and lie back weeping.
And there the story shifts from head to head,
of how in Holland, from their feather beds
hunters arise and part the flakes and go
forth to the frozen lakes in search of swans—
the snow-light falling white along their guns,
their breath in plumes.
While tethered in the wind like sleeping gulls
ice-boats wait the raising of their wings
to skim the electric ice at such a speed
they leap jet strips of naked water,
and how these flying, sailing hunters feel
air in their mouths as terrible as ether.
And on the story runs that even drinks
in that white landscape dare to be no colour;
how flasked and water clear, the liquor slips
silver against the hunters' moving hips.
And of the swan in death these dreamers tell
of its last flight and how it falls, a plummet,
pierced by the freezing bullet

and how three feathers, loosened by the shot,
descend like snow upon it.
While hunters plunge their fingers in its down
deep as a drift, and dive their hands
up to the neck of the wrist
in that warm metamorphosis of snow
as gentle as the sort that woodsmen know
who, lost in the white circle, fall at last
and dream their way to death.

And stories of this kind are often told
in countries where great flowers bar the roads
with reds and blues which seal the route to snow—
as if, in telling, raconteurs unlock
the colour with its complement and go
through to the area behind the eyes
where silent, unrefractive whiteness lies.

intent visual experience

After Rain

The good goes out into the garden, everything has been covered into green lace. The snails have taken over + nibbled everything

The snails have made a garden of green lace:
broderie anglaise[1] from the cabbages,
chantilly[2] from the choux-fleurs,[3] tiny veils—
I see already that I lift the blind
upon a woman's wardrobe of the mind.

Such female whimsy floats about me like
a kind of tulle, a flimsy mesh,
while feet in gum boots pace the rectangles—
garden abstracted, geometry awash—
an unknown theorem argued in green ink,
dropped in the bath.
Euclid[4] in glorious chlorophyll, half drunk.

I none too sober slipping in the mud
where rigged with guys of rain
the clothes-reel gauche
as the rangey skeleton of some
gaunt delicate spidery mute
is pitched as if
listening;
while hung from one thin rib

---

1   open embroidery on white linen or cambric
2   Chantilly is a fine French lace, named for the town where it is made.
3   cauliflowers
4   the Greek mathematician of the 3rd century B.C. who developed the principles of
geometry

a silver web—
its infant, skeletal, diminutive,
now sagged with sequins, pulled ellipsoid,
glistening.

I suffer shame in all these images.
The garden is primeval, Giovanni
in soggy denim squelches by my hub
over his ruin,
shakes a doleful head.
But he so beautiful and diademmed,
his long Italian hands so wrung with rain
I find his ache exists beyond my rim
and almost weep to see a broken man
made subject to my whim.

O choir him, birds, and let him come to rest
within this beauty as one rests in love,
till pears upon the bough
encrusted with
small snails as pale as pearls
hang golden in
a heart that knows tears are a part of love.

And choir me too to keep my heart a size
larger than seeing, unseduced by each
bright glimpse of beauty striking like a bell,
so that the whole may toll,
its meaning shine
clear of the myriad images that still—
do what I will—encumber its pure line.

The Selves

Every other day I am an invalid.
Lie back among the pillows and white sheets
lackadaisical O lackadaisical.
Brush my hair out like a silver fan.
Allow myself to be wheeled into the sun.
Calves' foot jelly, a mid-morning glass of port,
these I accept and rare azaleas in pots.

The nurses humour me. They call me 'dear'.
I am pilled and pillowed into another sphere
and there my illness rules us like a queen,
is absolute monarch, wears a giddy crown
and I, its humble servant at all times, am its least
serf on occasion and excluded from the feast.

Every other *other* day I am as fit
as planets circling.
I brush my hair into a golden sun,
strike roses from a bush,
rare plants in pots
blossom within the green of my eyes, I am
enviable O I am enviable.

Somewhere in between the two, a third
wishes to speak, cannot make itself heard,
stands unmoving, mute, invisible,
a bolt of lightning in its naked hand.

Robert Lowell

(1917–1977)

As a Plane Tree by the Water[1]

Darkness has called to darkness, and disgrace
Elbows about our windows in this planned
Babel[2] of Boston where our money talks
And multiplies the darkness of a land
Of preparation where the Virgin walks
And roses spiral her enamelled face
Or fall to splinters on unwatered streets.
Our Lady of Babylon,[3] go by, go by,
I was once the apple of your eye;
Flies, flies are on the plane tree, on the streets.

The flies, the flies, the flies of Babylon
Buzz in my ear-drums while the devil's long
Dirge of the people detonates the hour
For floating cities where his golden tongue
Enchants the masons of the Babel Tower
To raise tomorrow's city to the sun
That never sets upon these hell-fire streets
Of Boston, where the sunlight is a sword
Striking at the withholder of the Lord:
Flies, flies are on the plane tree, on the streets.

Flies strike the miraculous waters of the iced
Atlantic and the eyes of Bernadette[4]
Who saw Our Lady standing in the cave
At Massabielle, saw her so squarely that
Her vision put out reason's eyes. The grave
Is open-mouthed and swallowed up in Christ.
O walls of Jericho![5] And all the streets
To our Atlantic wall are singing: "Sing,
Sing for the resurrection of the King."
Flies, flies are on the plane tree, on the streets.

---

1   from Ecclesiasticus 24.14
2   The place where people planned to build a tower reaching heaven, but were prevented
    when God confounded human language, so that people should no longer understand
    one another (Genesis 11).
3   the Assyrian city associated with decadence and corruption
4   St. Bernadette (1844-1879) at 14 years of age had visions of the Virgin Mary, who appeared
    to her in a cave at Massabielle, near Lourdes, France.
5   See the Book of Joshua 6.

Skunk Hour

(*For Elizabeth Bishop*)[1]

Nautilus Island's hermit
heiress still lives through winter in her Spartan cottage;
her sheep still graze above the sea.
Her son's a bishop. Her farmer
is first selectman in our village;
she's in her dotage.

Thirsting for
the hierarchic privacy
of Queen Victoria's century,
she buys up all
the eyesores facing her shore,
and lets them fall.

The season's ill—
we've lost our summer millionaire,
who seemed to leap from an L. L. Bean[2]
catalogue. His nine-knot yawl
was auctioned off to lobstermen.
A red fox stain covers Blue Hill.[3]

And now our fairy
decorator brightens his shop for fall;
his fishnet's filled with orange cork,
orange, his cobbler's bench and awl;
there is no money in his work,
he'd rather marry.

One dark night,
my Tudor Ford climbed the hill's skull;
I watched for love-cars. Lights turned down,
they lay together, hull to hull,
where the graveyard shelves on the town. . .
My mind's not right.

A car radio bleats,
"Love, O careless Love[4]. . . ." I hear
my ill-spirit sob in each blood cell,
as if my hand were at its throat. . . .

---

1 Lowell has stated that the form of his poem was indebted to Elizabeth Bishop's "The
  Armadillo" (see p. 599)
2 a mail-order company in Maine specializing in outdoor clothes
3 a mountain in Maine near where Lowell was living
4 a popular song of the 1950s.

I myself am hell;[1]
nobody's here—

only skunks, that search
in the moonlight for a bite to eat.
They march on their soles up Main Street:
white stripes, moonstruck eyes' red fire
under the chalk-dry and spar spire
of the Trinitarian Church.

I stand on top
of our back steps and breathe the rich air—
a mother skunk with her column of kittens swills the garbage
  pail.
She jabs her wedge-head in a cup
of sour cream, drops her ostrich tail,
and will not scare.

For the Union Dead

"Relinquunt Omnia Servare Rem Publicam."[2]

The old South Boston Aquarium stands
in a Sahara of snow now. Its broken windows are boarded.
The bronze weathervane cod has lost half its scales.
The airy tanks are dry.

Once my nose crawled like a snail on the glass;
my hand tingled
to burst the bubbles
drifting from the noses of the cowed, compliant fish.

My hand draws back. I often sigh still
for the dark downward and vegetating kingdom
of the fish and reptile. One morning last March,
I pressed against the new barbed and galvanized

fence on the Boston Common.[3] Behind their cage,
yellow dinosaur steamshovels were grunting
as they cropped up tons of mush and grass
to gouge their underworld garage.

Parking spaces luxuriate like civic

---

1   an echo of Satan in *Paradise Lost* IV.75: "Which way I fly is Hell; myself am Hell."
2   (Latin) "They give up all to serve the republic."
3   a public park in the centre of Boston, on one side of which stands the Massachusetts State House

sandpiles in the heart of Boston.
A girdle of orange, Puritan-pumpkin colored girders
braces the tingling Statehouse,

shaking over the excavations, as it faces Colonel Shaw[1]
and his bell-cheeked Negro infantry
on St. Gaudens' shaking Civil War relief,
propped by a plank splint against the garage's earthquake.

Two months after marching through Boston,
half the regiment was dead;
at the dedication,
William James[2] could almost hear the bronze Negroes breathe.

Their monument sticks like a fishbone
in the city's throat.
Its Colonel is as lean
as a compass-needle.

He has an angry wrenlike vigilance,
a greyhound's gentle tautness;
he seems to wince at pleasure,
and suffocate for privacy.

He is out of bounds now. He rejoices in man's lovely,
peculiar power to choose life and die—
when he leads his black soldiers to death,
he cannot bend his back.

On a thousand small town New England greens,
the old white churches hold their air
of sparse, sincere rebellion; frayed flags
quilt the graveyards of the Grand Army of the Republic.

The stone statues of the abstract Union Soldier
grow slimmer and younger each year—
wasp-waisted, they doze over muskets
and muse through their sideburns . . .

Shaw's father wanted no monument
except the ditch,
where his son's body was thrown
and lost with his "niggers."

---

1   Robert Gould Shaw (1837-1863) led the first Black regiment in the North during the
     American Civil War, and was killed with many of his troops in an attack on the
     Confederate position at Fort Wagner, South Carolina. A bronze memorial by Augustus
     Saint-Gaudens, dedicated in 1897, stands on Boston Common facing the State House.
2   American philosopher and psychologist (1842-1910), brother of novelist Henry James.

The ditch is nearer.
There are no statues for the last war[1] here;
on Boylston Street, a commercial photograph
shows Hiroshima boiling

over a Mosler Safe, the "Rock of Ages"
that survived the blast. Space is nearer.
When I crouch to my television set,
the drained faces of Negro school-children rise like balloons.

Colonel Shaw
is riding on his bubble,
he waits
for the blessèd break.

The Aquarium is gone. Everywhere,
giant finned cars nose forward like fish;
a savage servility
slides by on grease.

The Public Garden

Burnished, burned-out, still burning as the year
you lead me to our stamping ground.
The city and its cruising cars surround
the Public Garden. All's alive—
the children crowding home from school at five,
punting a football in the bricky air,
the sailors and their pick-ups under trees
with Latin labels. And the jaded flock
of swanboats paddles to its dock.
The park is drying.
Dead leaves thicken to a ball
inside the basin of a fountain, where
the heads of four stone lions stare
and suck on empty fawcets. Night
deepens. From the arched bridge, we see
the shedding park-bound mallards, how they keep
circling and diving in the lanternlight,
searching for something hidden in the muck.
And now the moon, earth's friend, that cared so much
for us, and cared so little, comes again—
always a stranger! As we walk,
it lies like chalk

---

1   World War II

over the waters. Everything's aground.
Remember summer? Bubbles filled
the fountain, and we splashed. We drowned
in Eden, while Jehovah's grass-green lyre
was rustling all about us in the leaves
that gurgled by us, turning upside down . . .
The fountain's failing waters flash around
the garden. Nothing catches fire.

Miriam Waddington

(b. 1917)

Thou Didst Say Me

Late as last summer
Thou didst say me, love
I choose you, you, only you.
oh the delicate del-
icate serpent of your lips
the golden lie bedazzled
me with wish and flash
of joy and I was fool.

I was fool, bemused
bedazed by summer, still
bewitched and wandering
in murmur hush in green-
ly sketched-in fields
I was, I was, so sweet
I was, so honied with
your gold of love and love
and still again more love.

late as last autumn
thou didst say me, dear
my doxy,[1] I choose you and
always you, thou didst pledge
me love and through the red-
plumed weeks and soberly
I danced upon your words
and garlanded these
tender dangers.

year curves to ending now
and thou dost say me, wife
I choose another love, and oh
the delicate del-
icate serpent of your mouth
stings deep, and bitter
iron cuts and shapes
my death, I was so fool

---

1   archaic term for wench, sweetheart

Sea Bells

Five fathoms deep my father lies,
and of his bones are my bones made,
this is his blindness in my eyes,[1]
his limping paced my grave.

Oh daughter toll the sea-green bell .
and shake the coral from your hair,
the sea was once your bed of birth,
your given name your knell

My body was your sepulchre,
the wide world was your cell,
my hand has written in your blood
what time and tide will tell.

The tide has since cast up its scroll
and told what time could tell;
five fathoms deep my father lies
his daughter deeper fell

To see the seeing of his eyes
and take what pearls might have to give;
five fathoms deep in sleep he lies
whose death waked me to live.

Ten Years and More

When my husband
lay dying a mountain
a lake three
cities ten years
and more
lay between us:

There were our
sons my wounds
and theirs,
despair loneliness,
handfuls of un-
hammered nails
pictures never
hung all

---

1   The first three lines echo the song "Full fathom five thy father lies" in Shakespeare's *The Tempest* I.ii.394.

The uneaten
meals and unslept
sleep; there was
retirement, and
worst of all
a green umbrella
he can never
take back.

I wrote him a
letter but all
I could think of
to say was: do you
remember Severn[1]
River, the red canoe
with the sail
and lee-boards?

I was really saying
for the sake of our
youth and our love
I forgave him for
everything
and I was asking him
to forgive me too.

---

1   a river in Ontario

Margaret Avison

(b. 1918)

The Butterfly

An uproar,
a spruce-green sky, bound in iron,
the murky sea running a sulphur scum:
I saw a butterfly suddenly;
it clung between the ribs of the storm, wavering
and flung against the battering bone-wind.
I remember it, glued to the grit of that rain-strewn beach
that glowered around it, swallowed its startled design
in the larger irridescence of unstrung dark.

That wild, sour air, the miles of crouching forest, those wings,
when all-enveloping air is a
thinglass globe, swirling with storm,
tempt one to the abyss.

The butterfly's meaning, even though smashed.
Imprisoned in endless cycle? No. The meaning!
Can't we stab that one angle
into the curve of space that sweeps beyond
our farthest knowing, out into light's
place of invisibility?

Voluptuaries and Others

That Eureka of Archimedes[1] out of his bath
Is the kind of story that kills what it conveys;
Yet the banality is right for that story, since it is not a communicable
        one
But just a particular instance of
The kind of lighting up of the terrain
That leaves aside the whole terrain, really,
But signalizes, and compels, an advance in it.
Such an advance through a be-it-what-it-may but
        take-it-not-quite-as-given locale:
Probably that is the core of being alive.
The speculation is not a concession
To limited imaginations. Neither is it
A constrained voiding of the quality of immanent death.
Such near values cannot be measured in values
Just because the measuring

---

1   The Greek philosopher and mathematician Archimedes (c.287-212 B.C.) is said to have
    cried "Eureka!" (I have found it!) when he discovered the principle that a body displaces
    its own bulk of water when immersed.

Consists in that other kind of lighting up
That shows the terrain comprehended, as also its containing space,
And wipes out adjectives, and all shadows
     (or, perhaps, all but shadows).

The Russians made a movie of a dog's head
Kept alive by blood controlled by physics, chemistry, equipment,
     and
Russian women scientists in cotton gowns with writing tablets.
The heart lay on a slab midway in the apparatus
And went phluff, phluff.
Like the first kind of illumination, that successful experiment
Cannot be assessed either as conquest or as defeat.
But it is living, creating the chasm of creation,
Contriving to cast only man to brood in it, further.
History makes the spontaneous jubilation at such moments less and
     less likely though,
And that story about Archimedes does get into public school
     textbooks.

The Swimmer's Moment

For everyone
The swimmer's moment at the whirlpool comes,
But many at that moment will not say
"This is the whirlpool, then."
By their refusal they are saved
From the black pit, and also from contesting
The deadly rapids, and emerging in
The mysterious, and more ample, further waters.
And so their bland-blank faces turn and turn
Pale and forever on the rim of suction
They will not recognize.
Of those who dare the knowledge
Many are whirled into the ominous centre
That, gaping vertical, seals up
For them an eternal boon of privacy,
So that we turn away from their defeat
With a despair, not from their deaths, but for
Ourselves, who cannot penetrate their secret
Nor even guess at the anonymous breadth
Where one or two have won:
(The silver reaches of the estuary).

Butterfly Bones OR Sonnet Against Sonnets

The cyanide jar seals life, as sonnets move
Towards final stiffness. Cased in a white glare
These specimens stare for peering boys, to prove
Strange certainties. Plane, dogsled and safari
Assure continuing range. The sweep-net skill,
The patience, learning, leave all living stranger.
Insect—or poem—waits for the fix, the frill
Precision can effect, brilliant with danger.
What law and wonder the museum spectres
Bespeak is cryptic for the shivery wings,
The world cut-diamond-eyed, those eyes' reflectors,
Or herbal grass, sunned motes, fierce listening.
Might sheened and rigid trophies strike men blind
Like Adam's lexicon locked in the mind?

The Dumbfounding

When you walked here,
took skin, muscle, hair,
eyes, larynx, we
withheld all honour: "His house is clay,
how can he tell us of his far country?"

Your not-familiar pace
in flesh, across the waves,
woke only our distrust.
Twice-torn we cried "A ghost"
and only on our planks counted you fast.

Dust wet with your spittle
cleared mortal trouble.
We called you a blasphemer,
a devil-tamer.

The evening you spoke of going away
we could not stay.
All legions massed. You had to wash, and rise,
alone, and face
out of the light, for us.

You died.
We said,
"The worst is true, our bliss
has come to this."

When you were seen by men
in holy flesh again

we hoped so despairingly for such report
we closed their windpipes for it.

Now you have sought
and seek, in all our ways, all thoughts,
streets, musics—and we make of these a din
trying to lock you out, or in,
to be intent. And dying.

Yet you are
constant and sure,
the all-lovely, all-men's-way
to that far country.

Winning one, you again
all ways would begin
life: to make new
flesh, to empower
the weak in nature
to restore
or stay the sufferer;

lead through the garden to
trash, rubble, hill,
where, the outcast's outcast, you
sound dark's uttermost, strangely light-brimming, until
time be full.

A Nameless One

Hot in June a narrow winged
long-elbowed-thread-legged
living insect lived
and died within
the lodgers' second-floor bathroom here.

At 6 A.M.
wafting ceilingward,
no breeze but what it living made there;

at noon standing
still as a constellation of spruce needles
before the moment of
making it, whirling;

at four a
wilted flotsam, cornsilk, on the linoleum:

now that it is
over, I

look with new eyes
upon this room
adequate for one to
be, in.

Its insect-day
has threaded a needle
for me for my eyes dimming
over rips and tears and
thin places.

New Year's Poem

The Christmas twigs crispen and needles rattle
Along the windowledge.
    A solitary pearl
Shed from the necklace spilled at last week's party
Lies in the suety, snow-luminous plainness
Of morning, on the windowledge beside them.
And all the furniture that circled stately
And hospitable when these rooms were brimmed
With perfumes, furs, and black-and-silver
Crisscross of seasonal conversation, lapses
Into its previous largeness.
    I remember
Anne's rose-sweet gravity, and the stiff grave
Where cold so little can contain;
I mark the queer delightful skull and crossbones
Starlings and sparrows left, taking the crust,
And the long loop of winter wind
Smoothing its arc from dark Arcturus[1] down
To the bricked corner of the drifted courtyard,
And the still windowledge.
    Gentle and just pleasure
It is, being human, to have won from space
This unchill, habitable interior
Which mirrors quietly the light
Of the snow, and the new year.

---

1   an orange-red star in the constellation Botes

tremendous range
remarkable beauty + dignity to comic, absurd
extraordinary
Very Canadian poet in his subj matter

Al Purdy

(b. 1918)

Remains of an Indian Village

Underfoot rotten boards, forest rubble, bones. . .
Animals were here after the plague,
after smallpox to make another ending:
for the tutelary gods of decay
acknowledge aid from any quarter. . .

the sprouts
of the plant)
seedling

Here the charging cotyledons of spring
press green forefingers
on femurs, vertebrae, and delicate
belled skulls of children;
the moon's waylaid light does not shrink
from bone relics and other beauties of nature . . .

Death is certainly absent now,
at least in the overwhelming sense
that it once walked at night in the village
and howled thru the mouths of dogs—
But everything fades
and wavers into something else,
the seasonal cycle and the planet's rhythm
vary imperceptibly into the other;
spirits of the dead are vanished,
only great trees remain,
and the birth certificate of cedars *quite figurative*
specifies no memory of a village . . . *somewhat*
frivolous yet charming

now a
personal
reference,
not that
relevant to
the poem

(And I have seen myself fade
from a woman's eyes
while I was standing there,
and the earth was aware of
me no longer—)
But I come here as part of the process
In the pale morning light,
thinking what has been thought by no one
for years of their absence,
in some way continuing them—
And I observe the children's shadows
running in this green light from
        a distant star
into the near forest—
wood violets and trilliums of
a hundred years ago
blooming and vanishing—
the villages of the brown people
toppling and returning—
What moves and lives
    occupying the same space,

elegiac poet

what touches what touched them
            owes them.. .

Standing knee-deep in the joined earth
of their weightless bones,
in the archaeological sunlight,
the trembling voltage of summer,
in the sunken reservoirs of rain,
standing waist-deep in the criss-cross
rivers of shadows,
in the village of nightfall,
the hunters silent and women
bending over dark fires,
I hear their broken consonants . . .

The Cariboo Horses

little sexist;
thinks a lot
about sex

At 100 Mile House[1] the cowboys ride in rolling
stagey cigarettes with one hand reining
half-tame bronco rebels on a morning grey as stone
—so much like riding dangerous women
            with whiskey coloured eyes—   *sexual collapse*
such women as once fell dead with their lovers
with fire in their heads and slippery froth on thighs
—Beaver or Carrier[2] women maybe or
            Blackfoot[3] squaws far past the edge of this valley
on the other side of those two toy mountain ranges
            from the sunfierce plains beyond

But only horses
                        waiting in stables
hitched at taverns
                        standing at dawn
pastured outside the town with
jeeps and fords and chevys and
busy muttering stake trucks rushing
importantly over roads of man's devising
over the safe known roads of the ranchers
families and merchants of the town
                        On the high prairie
are only horse and rider
                        wind in dry grass
clopping in silence under the toy mountains
dropping sometimes and

elegiac poem

---

1   a small town in the Cariboo region of central British Columbia
2   Athapaskan-speaking Indian bands living in British Columbia
3   Blackfoot Indians belong to the Algonquian peoples living in Alberta and Montana.

lost in the dry grass
golden oranges of dung

Only horses
no stopwatch memories or palace ancestors
not Kiangs[1] hauling undressed stone in the Nile Valley
and having stubborn Egyptian tantrums or
Onagers[2] racing thru Hither Asia and
the last Quagga[3] screaming in African highlands
lost relatives of these
whose hooves were thunder
the ghosts of horses battering thru the wind
whose names were the wind's common usage
whose life was the sun's
arriving here at chilly noon
in the gasoline smell of the
dust and waiting 15 minutes
at the grocer's

The Country North of Belleville

Bush land scrub land—
Cashel Township and Wollaston[4]
Elzevir McClure and Dungannon
green lands of Weslemkoon Lake
where a man might have some
opinion of what beauty
is and none deny him
for miles

Yet this is the country of defeat
where Sisyphus[5] rolls a big stone
year after year up the ancient hills
picnicking glaciers have left strewn
with centuries' rubble
backbreaking days
in the sun and rain
when realization seeps slow in the mind
without grandeur or self-deception in
noble struggle
of being a fool—

---

1   wild asses of eastern Asia
2   wild asses from central Asia
3   a South African equine mammal, now extinct
4   In these and other names, Purdy is referring to pioneer settlements in southern Ontario.
5   in Greek mythology, the man whose punishment in Hades was to roll a huge stone to
    the top of a hill, whence it would roll down and he would have to begin again

A country of quiescence and still distance
a lean land
                not like the fat south
with inches of black soil on
                earth's round belly
And where the farms are
                it's as if a man stuck
both thumbs in the stony earth and pulled

                it apart
                to make room
enough between the trees
for a wife
                and maybe some cows and
                room for some
of the more easily kept illusions—
And where the farms have gone back
to forest
                are only soft outlines
                shadowy differences—
Old fences drift vaguely among the trees
                a pile of moss-covered stones
gathered for some ghost purpose
has lost meaning under the meaningless sky
                —they are like cities under water
and the undulating green waves of time
                are laid on them— *grief over any human*
                                        endeavour that ended
                                        in defeat /abandonment

This is the country of our defeat
                and yet
during the fall plowing a man
might stop and stand in a brown valley of the furrows
                and shade his eyes to watch for the same
                red patch mixed with gold
                that appears on the same
                spot in the hills
                year after year
                and grow old .
plowing and plowing a ten-acre field until
the convolutions run parallel with his own brain—
And this is a country where the young
                                leave quickly
unwilling to know what their fathers know
or think the words their mothers do not say—

Herschel Monteagle and Faraday
lakeland rockland and hill country
a little adjacent to where the world is
a little north of where the cities are and
sometime
we may go back there

to the country of our defeat
Wollaston Elzevir and Dungannon
and Weslemkoon lake land
where the high townships of Cashel
McClure and Marmora once were—
But it's been a long time since
and we must enquire the way
of strangers— *Purdy loved the dark*

Wilderness Gothic

Across Roblin Lake, two shores away,
they are sheathing the church spire
with new metal. Someone hangs in the sky
over there from a piece of rope,
hammering and fitting God's belly-scratcher, *common term for a church steeple*
working his way up along the spire
until there's nothing left to nail on—

Perhaps the workman's faith reaches beyond:
touches intangibles, wrestles with Jacob,[1]
replacing rotten timber with pine thews,
pounds hard in the blue cave of the sky,
contends heroically with difficult problems of
gravity, sky navigation and mythopoeia,
his volunteer time and labour donated to God,
minus sick benefits of course on a non-union job—

Fields around are yellowing into harvest,
nestling and fingerling are sky and water borne,
death is yodelling quiet in green woodlots,
and bodies of three young birds have disappeared
in the sub-surface of the new county highway—

That picture is incomplete, part left out
that might alter the whole Dürer[2] landscape:
gothic ancestors peer from medieval sky,
dour faces trapped in photograph albums escaping
to clop down iron roads with matched greys:
work-sodden wives groping inside their flesh
for what keeps moving and changing and flashing
beyond and past the long frozen Victorian day.
A sign of fire and brimstone? A two-headed calf
born in the barn last night? A sharp female agony?
An age and a faith moving into transition,

1   As Jacob wrestled with the angel: see Genesis 32.24-32
2   Albrecht Dürer (1471-1528), German painter and engraver

the dinner cold and new-baked bread a failure,
deep woods shiver and water drops hang pendant,
double-yolked eggs and the house creaks a little—
Something is about to happen. Leaves are still.
Two shores away, a man hammering in the sky.
Perhaps he will fall.

Lament For the Dorsets

(Eskimos extinct in the 14th century AD)

Animal bones and some mossy tent rings
scrapers and spearheads   carved ivory swans
all that remains of the Dorset giants
who drove the Vikings back to their long ships
talked to spirits of earth and water
—a picture of terrifying old men
so large they broke the backs of bears
so small they lurk behind bone rafters
in the brain of modern hunters
among good thoughts and warm things
and come out at night
to spit on the stars

The big men with clever fingers
who had no dogs and hauled their sleds
over the frozen northern oceans
awkward giants
                killers of seal
they couldn't compete with little men
who came from the west with dogs
Or else in a warm climatic cycle
the seals went back to cold waters
and the puzzled Dorsets scratched their heads
with hairy thumbs around 1350 A.D.
—couldn't figure it out
went around saying to each other plaintively
            "What's wrong? What happened?
            Where are the seals gone?"
And died

Twentieth-century people
apartment dwellers
executives of neon death
warmakers with things that explode
—they have never imagined us in their future
how could we imagine them in the past
squatting among the moving glaciers
six hundred years ago
with glowing lamps?

[667]

As remote or nearly
as the trilobites and swamps
when coal became
or the last great reptile hissed
at a mammal the size of a mouse
that squeaked and fled

Did they ever realize at all
what was happening to them?
Some old hunter with one lame leg
a bear had chewed
sitting in a caribou-skin tent
—the last Dorset?
Let's say his name was Kudluk
and watch him sitting there
carving 2-inch ivory swans
for a dead grand-daughter
taking them out of his mind
the places in his mind
where pictures are
He selects a sharp stone tool
to gouge a parallel pattern of lines
on both sides of the swan
holding it with his left hand
bearing down and transmitting
his body's weight
from brain to arm and right hand
and one of his thoughts
turns to ivory
The carving is laid aside
in beginning darkness
at the end of hunger
and after a while wind
blows down the tent and snow
begins to cover him

After 600 years
the ivory thought
is still warm

(handwritten margin notes:)
extinct class of anithropoid

Going from a more abstract study to deal w/ it from a personal view – trying to understand another human

Creating a person an individual w/ a personality trying to humanize the situation There were people

back to present

On the Decipherment of "Linear B"[1]

(By Michael Ventris and associates)

Grammatic structure first, then phonetic values:
Ventris mailing progress reports to philologists
for comment (by air across the Atlantic):
the endgame—all the dusty Cretan sibilants
hissing delightedly back to life on scholar tongues,
whispering possible gossip to the co-translators
—that turned out to be inventories,
amphorae in warehouses, wine long vanished,
dried to red dust in the guts of Mycenaean[2] warriors;
listings of clergy reserves, military property:
"Horse vehicle, painted red, supplied with reins";
words, preserved like nothing machines make,
perfect, unflawed, the same.

We see them (dramatic as hell), the code-breakers,
in shirt sleeves, drinking gallons of coffee:
gowned Oxford dons, real estate brokers,
American academics—a linguistic orgy,
broken by twitterings of girlish excitement,
punctuated with cries of discovery.

It turns out Minos[3] was maybe an expatriate
Greek, who said to hell with hiero-
glyphic symbols: brought in the smith Daedalus
(a bad mistake re Pasiphae's morals)
to promote Greek investment, Linear B and stud poker—
Well anyway, Ventris figured it out,
and anyone can sit down after work reading
comic books or Agamemnon's[4] diaries now.

But Knossos[5] did burn, its flaming windows
signalled the stars 3,000 years ago:
when men died foetal, rolled into blackened balls,
and women, abandoned by children and lovers,
fled to the palace upper rooms with skirts on fire:
and over the island a south wind blowing—

*Again,
burning*

---

1 Linear B was one of two scripts found at Knossus on the island of Crete. It was deciphered in 1952 by the young English architect Michael Ventris.
2 The Linear B script was a form of writing associated principally with the mainland city of Mycenae rather than the island of Crete.
3 The legendary king of Crete. He angered the god Poseidon, who made his wife Pasiphae fall in love with a bull; the offspring was a monster called the Minotaur, which was kept in a labyrinth devised by the Athenian craftsman Daedalus.
4 King of Mycenae, and leader of the Greek armies in the Trojan War
5 the palace of the Minoan kings on Crete, which suffered sudden destruction by fire in about 1400 B.C.

Richard Wilbur

(b. 1921)

Digging For China

"Far enough down is China," somebody said.
"Dig deep enough and you might see the sky
As clear as at the bottom of a well.
Except it would be real—a different sky.
Then you could burrow down until you came
To China! Oh, it's nothing like New Jersey.
There's people, trees, and houses, and all that,
But much, much different. Nothing looks the same."

I went and got the trowel out of the shed
And sweated like a coolie all that morning,
Digging a hole beside the lilac-bush,
Down on my hands and knees. It was a sort
Of praying, I suspect. I watched my hand
Dig deep and darker, and I tried and tried
To dream a place where nothing was the same.
The trowel never did break through to blue.

Before the dream could weary of itself
My eyes were tired of looking into darkness,
My sunbaked head of hanging down a hole.
I stood up in a place I had forgotten,
Blinking and staggering while the earth went round
And showed me silver barns, the fields dozing
In palls of brightness, patens growing and gone
In the tides of leaves, and the whole sky china blue.
Until I got my balance back again
All that I saw was China, China, China.

The Pardon

My dog lay dead five days without a grave
In the thick of summer, hid in a clump of pine
And a jungle of grass and honeysuckle-vine.
I who had loved him while he kept alive

Went only close enough to where he was
To sniff the heavy honeysuckle-smell
Twined with another odor heavier still
And hear the flies' intolerable buzz.

Well, I was ten and very much afraid.
In my kind world the dead were out of range
And I could not forgive the sad or strange
In beast or man. My father took the spade

And buried him. Last night I saw the grass
Slowly divide (it was the same scene
But now it glowed a fierce and mortal green)
And saw the dog emerging. I confess

I felt afraid again, but still he came
In the carnal sun, clothed in a hymn of flies,
And death was breeding in his lively eyes.
I started in to cry and call his name,

Asking forgiveness of his tongueless head.
. . . I dreamt the past was never past redeeming:
But whether this was false or honest dreaming
I beg death's pardon now. And mourn the dead.

The Death of a Toad

A toad the power mower caught,
Chewed and clipped of a leg, with a hobbling hop has got
  To the garden verge, and sanctuaried him
  Under the cineraria[1] leaves, in the shade
    Of the ashen heartshaped leaves, in a dim,
      Low, and a final glade.

The rare original heartsblood goes,
Spends on the earthen hide, in the folds and wizenings, flows
  In the gutters of the banked and staring eyes. He lies
  As still as if he would return to stone,
    And soundlessly attending, dies
      Toward some deep monotone,

Toward misted and ebullient seas
And cooling shores, toward lost Amphibia's emperies.[2]
  Day dwindles, drowning, and at length is gone
  In the wide and antique eyes, which still appear
    To watch, across the castrate lawn,
      The haggard daylight steer.

---

1   an ornamental plant with heart-shaped leaves. From the same Latin root comes the word
     "cinerarium," a place for keeping the ashes of a cremated body.
2   "Amphibia" is derived from "amphibian," the class of vertebrates to which the toad
     belongs. "Emperies": realms, domains.

Love Calls Us to the Things of This World[1]

The eyes open to a cry of pulleys,
And spirited from sleep, the astounded soul
Hangs for a moment bodiless and simple
As false dawn.
               Outside the open window
The morning air is all awash with angels.

    Some are in bed-sheets, some are in blouses,
Some are in smocks: but truly there they are.
Now they are rising together in calm swells
Of halcyon feeling, filling whatever they wear
With the deep joy of their impersonal breathing;

    Now they are flying in place, conveying
The terrible speed of their omnipresence, moving
And staying like white water; and now of a sudden
They swoon down into so rapt a quiet
That nobody seems to be there.
                     The soul shrinks

    From all that it is about to remember,
From the punctual rape of every blessèd day,
And cries,
      "Oh, let there be nothing on earth but laundry,
Nothing but rosy hands in the rising steam
And clear dances done in the sight of heaven."

    Yet, as the sun acknowledges
With a warm look the world's hunks and colors,
The soul descends once more in bitter love
To accept the waking body, saying now
In a changed voice as the man yawns and rises,

    "Bring them down from their ruddy gallows;
Let there be clean linen for the backs of thieves;
Let lovers go fresh and sweet to be undone,
And the heaviest nuns walk in a pure floating
Of dark habits,
            keeping their difficult balance."

---

1   quotation from the writings of St. Augustine

Beasts

Beasts in their major freedom
Slumber in peace tonight. The gull on his ledge
Dreams in the guts of himself the moon-plucked waves below,
And the sunfish leans on a stone, slept
By the lyric water,

In which the spotless feet
Of deer make dulcet splashes, and to which
The ripped mouse, safe in the owl's talon, cries
Concordance. Here there is no such harm
And no such darkness

As the selfsame moon observes
Where, warped in window-glass, it sponsors now
The werewolf's painful change. Turning his head away
On the sweaty bolster, he tries to remember
The mood of manhood,

But lies at last, as always,
Letting it happen, the fierce fur soft to his face,
Hearing with sharper ears the wind's exciting minors,
The leaves' panic, and the degradation
Of the heavy streams.

Meantime, at high windows
Far from thicket and pad-fall, suitors of excellence
Sigh and turn from their work to construe again the painful
Beauty of heaven, the lucid moon
And the risen hunter,

Making such dreams for men
As told will break their hearts as always, bringing
Monsters into the city, crows on the public statues,
Navies fed to the fish in the dark
Unbridled waters.

A Late Aubade

You could be sitting now in a carrel
Turning some liver-spotted page,
Or rising in an elevator-cage
Toward Ladies' Apparel.

You could be planting a raucous bed
Of salvia, in rubber gloves,
Or lunching through a screed of someone's loves
With pitying head,

Or making some unhappy setter
Heel, or listening to a bleak
Lecture on Schoenberg's[1] serial technique.
Isn't this better?

Think of all the time you are not
Wasting, and would not care to waste,
Such things, thank God, not being to your taste.
Think what a lot

Of time, by woman's reckoning,
You've saved, and so may spend on this,
You who had rather lie in bed and kiss
Than anything.

It's almost noon, you say? If so,
Time flies, and I need not rehearse
The rosebuds-theme of centuries of verse.
If you *must* go,

Wait for a while, then slip downstairs
And bring us up some chilled white wine,
And some blue cheese, and crackers, and some fine
Ruddy-skinned pears.

---

1   Arnold Schoenberg (1874-1951), German-American composer noted for his use of a
twelve-tone series in his compositions

Raymond Souster

(b. 1921)

Young Girls

With night full of spring and stars we stand
here in this dark doorway and watch the young
girls pass, two, three together, hand in hand.
They are like flowers whose fragrance hasn't sprung
or awakened, whose bodies now dimly feel
the flooding, upward welling of the trees;
whose senses, caressed by the wind's soft fingers, reel
with a mild delirium that makes them ill at ease.

They lie awake at night, unable to sleep,
then walk the streets, kindled by strange desires;
they steal lightning glances at us, unable to keep
control upon those subterranean fires.
We whistle after them, then laugh, for they
stiffen, not knowing what to do or say.

Memory of Bathurst Street[1]

"Where are you, boy?"
my Aunt Maggie's calling,
but I can't hear her
in my attic eyrie,
where I watch the heat
swirl up from the tar roofs,
waiting for the cry
of the bearded rag-picker
down the lane from Ulster Street.

"Where are you, boy?"
my Uncle Jim's calling,
but I can't hear him
for the cooing of birds
inside this pigeon-coop
at the back of the garden,
where I scrape up the droppings
to earn my allowance.

"Where are you, boy?"
my Aunt Lizzie's calling,
but I can't hear her
from the upstairs sitting-room,

---

1   in Toronto

as I turn the pages
of my favourite book
where the Highlanders lie
in the blood of their death
on green Spion Kop.[1]

Queen Anne's Lace

It's a kind of flower
that if you didn't know it
you'd pass by the rest of your life.

But once it's pointed out
you'll look for it always,
even in places
where you know it can't possibly be.

You will never tire
of bending over to examine,
to marvel at this,
shyest filigree of wonder
born among grasses.

You will imagine poems
as brief, as spare,
so natural with themselves
as to take breath away.

Words Before a Statue of Champlain[2]

Couchiching Park, Orillia[3]

Whether or not he wore spurs
(which bothers my father
once in the cavalry)
is a moot question,
but well in keeping
with the high-flowing plume
the broad-brimmed hat
the sword in scabbard
his loose-flowing robes.

---

1   the site of a British defeat by the Boers on 24 January 1900 in the South African war
2   Samuel de Champlain (1567-1635), French explorer and founder of Quebec
3   Orillia is in southern Ontario.

The sculptor, no Rodin,[1]
has at least caught
the look of vision
in the man's eyes,
the gleam of unrest
(slow flame burning
beneath the brow):

the other figures cluttering
the statue's base
garbage,
thrown in for good measure
to give the town
its money's worth—
the crazy-eyed Jesuit
the cowering Indians—
Samuel should run them through
two at a time right now
for defiling this moment
of history:
"Samuel de Champlain
with fifteen companions
arrived in these parts
Summer 1615,
and spent the winter
at Cahiagué,
chief village of the Hurons
near this place."

This Easter Sunday
the sun strong
the wind warm with spring,
but the ice core still solid
far as eye can see
on Lake Couchiching,
as if refusing
to believe in its death
foretold on the front page
of the local daily:

George Creagh,
Coldwater Road,
retired minister:
"I think April 24th
would be a good day
for the ice to go out"

---

1   Auguste Rodin (1840-1917), French sculptor

(the town's favourite guessing game):

but standing here now
on Government Wharf,
looking down at the ice-slabs
still four feet thick,
the 24th looks
very optimistic indeed

As for Samuel—
what would he say
looking at us here
in this April?

The boy and girl
strolling up the road,
arms around each other
as only lovers twine them,
the kids playing baseball
on the bumpy diamond,
one winding up to throw
the way you'd expect
a Canadian to do it,
much strength, no finesse;

me with my weak eyes
so slapped by the ice glare
I have to turn away,
with a small boy making mud-pies
down at the water's edge
with what must be ice-water:

otherwise the lake
not that much different
when he scanned it then
wondering what lay beyond.

But the rest of it,
these times, this town,
these people he never knew,
all different, changed,
torn up, confused,
turned inward, buried under.

The town of course
Leacock's still[1]
(the Stephen Leacock Hotel,
TV in every room),
the many signs,
his summer house
out old Brewery Bay,

Sunshine Sketches
of a Little Town
with its old houses
on quiet tree-heavy
streets still beautiful
and hiding well
what twisted lives
what family skeletons,

but as solid still
as the red-grained rock
the highway going north
to Gravenhurst, Bracebridge
cuts harshly through;

yet curiously stiff,
out of joint,
like the top face carved
on the curious, miniature
totem-pole over yonder—
not a real totem-pole
but like so much
in this faked-over world
a joke, a caricature
(not really intended)
of a lost people,
Indian:

(a word people say
with the self-same love
they spit phlegm from the throat.
Indian.
Furtive, poorly dressed,
in the back-water streets
of this town,
sun-bronzed faces
of the past and no future)

---

1   Stephen Leacock (1869-1944), Canadian humorist and historian, had his summer home
in Orillia, and used the town as his model for "Mariposa" in *Sunshine Sketches of a Little
Town* (1912)

but once allies,
fellow warriors,
of this man cast in bronze,
man with comic-opera clothes,
sword dragging the ground,
man with vision obsolete
as these sixteen-pounders
dated 1810
they've dragged from the lake,

man with that spirit
of an age we deny,
still defiling the destiny
these ancestors charted

passed to barren hands.

Lagoons, Hanlan's Point

Mornings
before the sun's liquid
spilled gradually, flooding
the island's cool cellar,
there was the boat
and the still lagoons,
with the sound of my oars
the only intrusion
over cries of birds
in the marshy shallows,
or the loud thrashing
of the startled crane
rushing the air.

And in one strange
dark, tree-hung entrance,
I followed the sound
of my heart all the way
to the reed-blocked ending,
with the pads of the lily
thick as green-shining film
covering the water.

And in another
where the sun came
to probe the depths
through a shaft of branches,
I saw the skeletons
of brown ships rotting
far below in their burial-ground,

and wondered what strange fish
with what strange colours
swam through these palaces
under the water. . . .

A small boy
with a flat-bottomed punt
and an old pair of oars
moving with wonder
through the antechamber
of a waking world.

Philip Larkin

(1922–1985)

Poetry of Departures

Sometimes you hear, fifth-hand,
As epitaph:
He chucked up everything
And just cleared off,
And always the voice will sound
Certain you approve
This audacious, purifying,
Elemental move.

And they are right, I think.
We all hate home
And having to be there:
I detest my room,
Its specially-chosen junk,
The good books, the good bed,
And my life, in perfect order:
So to hear it said

He walked out on the whole crowd
Leaves me flushed and stirred,
Like *Then she undid her dress*
Or *Take that you bastard;*
Surely I can, if he did?
And that helps me stay
Sober and industrious.
But I'd go today,

Yes, swagger the nut-strewn roads,
Crouch in the fo'c'sle[1]
Stubbly with goodness, if
It weren't so artificial,
Such a deliberate step backwards
To create an object:
Books; china; a life
Reprehensibly perfect.

---

1   the phonetic spelling of "forecastle," the front part of a merchant ship containing the
sailors' living quarters

Church Going

Once I am sure there's nothing going on
I step inside, letting the door thud shut.
Another church: matting, seats, and stone,
And little books; sprawlings of flowers, cut
For Sunday, brownish now; some brass and stuff
Up at the holy end; the small neat organ;
And a tense, musty, unignorable silence,
Brewed God knows how long. Hatless, I take off
My cycle-clips in awkward reverence,

Move forward, run my hand around the font.
From where I stand, the roof looks almost new—
Cleaned, or restored? Someone would know: I don't.
Mounting the lectern, I peruse a few
Hectoring large-scale verses, and pronounce
'Here endeth' much more loudly than I'd meant.
The echoes snigger briefly. Back at the door
I sign the book, donate an Irish sixpence,[1]
Reflect the place was not worth stopping for.

Yet stop I did: in fact I often do,
And always end much at a loss like this,
Wondering what to look for; wondering, too,
When churches fall completely out of use
What we shall turn them into, if we shall keep
A few cathedrals chronically on show,
Their parchment, plate and pyx[2] in locked cases,
And let the rest rent-free to rain and sheep.
Shall we avoid them as unlucky places?

Or, after dark, will dubious women come
To make their children touch a particular stone;
Pick simples[3] for a cancer; or on some
Advised night see walking a dead one?
Power of some sort or other will go on
In games, in riddles, seemingly at random;
But superstition, like belief, must die,
And what remains when disbelief has gone?
Grass, weedy pavement, brambles, buttress, sky,

A shape less recognisable each week,
A purpose more obscure. I wonder who

---

1 Though it looked like its English counterpart, the Irish sixpence was not legal tender in
   England.
2 the casket containing the communion wafers
3 an archaic term for medicinal plants

Will be the last, the very last, to seek
This place for what it was; one of the crew
That tap and jot and know what rood-lofts[1] were?
Some ruin-bibber, randy for antique,
Or Christmas-addict, counting on a whiff
Of gown-and-bands[2] and organ-pipes and myrrh?
Or will he be my representative,

Bored, uninformed, knowing the ghostly silt
Dispersed, yet tending to this cross of ground
Through suburb scrub because it held unspilt
So long and equably what since is found
Only in separation—marriage, and birth,
And death, and thoughts of these—for which was built
This special shell? For, though I've no idea
What this accoutred frowsty barn is worth,
It pleases me to stand in silence here;

A serious house on serious earth it is,
In whose blent air all our compulsions meet,
Are recognised, and robed as destinies.
And that much never can be obsolete,
Since someone will forever be surprising
A hunger in himself to be more serious,
And gravitating with it to this ground,
Which, he once heard, was proper to grow wise in,
If only that so many dead lie round.

Lines on a Young Lady's Photograph Album

At last you yielded up the album, which,
Once open, sent me distracted. All your ages
Matt and glossy on the thick black pages!
Too much confectionery, too rich:
I choke on such nutritious images.

My swivel eye hungers from pose to pose—
In pigtails, clutching a reluctant cat;
Or furred yourself, a sweet girl-graduate;
Or lifting a heavy-headed rose
Beneath a trellis, or in a trilby hat[3]

---

1   The rood is a crucifix raised on the middle of a rood screen, a screen separating the
nave and the choir; over this sits a gallery or platform known as the rood loft.

2   i.e., clergyman's attire; the bands are two linen strips that hang down the front of the
clergyman's gown

3   a soft felt hat with a narrow brim and an indented crown, named after *Trilby* (1894), a
popular novel by George du Maurier

(Faintly disturbing, that, in several ways)—
From every side you strike at my control,
Not least through these disquieting chaps who loll
At ease about your earlier days:
Not quite your class, I'd say, dear, on the whole.

But o, photography! as no art is,
Faithful and disappointing! that records
Dull days as dull, and hold-it smiles as frauds,
And will not censor blemishes
Like washing-lines, and Hall's-Distemper boards,[1]

But shows the cat as disinclined, and shades
A chin as doubled when it is, what grace
Your candour thus confers upon her face!
How overwhelmingly persuades
That this is a real girl in a real place,

In every sense empirically true!
Or is it just *the past*? Those flowers, that gate,
These misty parks and motors, lacerate
Simply by being over; you
Contract my heart by looking out of date.

Yes, true; but in the end, surely, we cry
Not only at exclusion, but because
It leaves us free to cry. We know *what was*
Won't call on us to justify
Our grief, however hard we yowl across

The gap from eye to page. So I am left
To mourn (without a chance of consequence)
You, balanced on a bike against a fence;
To wonder if you'd spot the theft
Of this one of you bathing; to condense,

In short, a past that no one now can share,
No matter whose your future; calm and dry,
It holds you like a heaven, and you lie
Unvariably lovely there,
Smaller and clearer as the years go by.

---

1   advertisements for a brand of paint

Ambulances

Closed like confessionals, they thread
Loud noons of cities, giving back
None of the glances they absorb.
Light glossy grey, arms on a plaque,[1]
They come to rest at any kerb:
All streets in time are visited.

Then children strewn on steps or road,
Or women coming from the shops
Past smells of different dinners, see
A wild white face that overtops
Red stretcher-blankets momently
As it is carried in and stowed,

And sense the solving emptiness
That lies just under all we do,
And for a second get it whole,
So permanent and blank and true.
The fastened doors recede. *Poor soul,*
They whisper at their own distress;

For borne away in deadened air
May go the sudden shut of loss
Round something nearly at an end,
And what cohered in it across
The years, the unique random blend
Of families and fashions, there

At last begin to loosen. Far
From the exchange of love to lie
Unreachable inside a room
The traffic parts to let go by
Brings closer what is left to come,
And dulls to distance all we are.

---

1   the coat-of-arms of a city or local authority, displayed on a plaque attached to the vehicle

Sad Steps[1]

Groping back to bed after a piss
I part thick curtains, and am startled by
The rapid clouds, the moon's cleanliness.

Four o'clock: wedge-shadowed gardens lie
Under a cavernous, a wind-picked sky.
There's something laughable about this,

The way the moon dashes through clouds that blow
Loosely as cannon-smoke to stand apart
(Stone-coloured light sharpening the roofs below)

High and preposterous and separate—
Lozenge of love! Medallion of art!
O wolves of memory! Immensements! No,

One shivers slightly, looking up there.
The hardness and the brightness and the plain
Far-reaching singleness of that wide stare

Is a reminder of the strength and pain
Of being young; that it can't come again,
But is for others undiminished somewhere.

An Arundel Tomb[2]

Side by side, their faces blurred,
The earl and countess lie in stone,
Their proper habits vaguely shown
As jointed armour, stiffened pleat,
And that faint hint of the absurd—
The little dogs under their feet.

Such plainness of the pre-baroque
Hardly involves the eye, until
It meets his left-hand gauntlet, still
Clasped empty in the other; and
One sees, with a sharp tender shock,
His hand withdrawn, holding her hand.

They would not think to lie so long.
Such faithfulness in effigy

---

1 An allusion to Sidney's poem "With how sad steps, oh moon, thou climbst the skies"
   (see p.27 above).
2 Arundel is a small town in Sussex; Arundel Castle is the seat of the Dukes of Norfolk.

Was just a detail friends would see:
A sculptor's sweet commissioned grace
Thrown off in helping to prolong
The Latin names around the base.

They would not guess how early in
Their supine stationary voyage
The air would change to soundless damage,
Turn the old tenantry away;
How soon succeeding eyes begin
To look, not read. Rigidly they

Persisted, linked, through lengths and breadths
Of time. Snow fell, undated. Light
Each summer thronged the glass. A bright
Litter of birdcalls strewed the same
Bone-riddled ground. And up the paths
The endless altered people came,

Washing at their identity.
Now, helpless in the hollow of
An unarmorial age, a trough
Of smoke in slow suspended skeins
Above their scrap of history,
Only an attitude remains:

Time has transfigured them into
Untruth. The stone fidelity
They hardly meant has come to be
Their final blazon, and to prove
Our almost-instinct almost true:
What will survive of us is love.

The Explosion

On the day of the explosion
Shadows pointed towards the pithead:
In the sun the slagheap slept.

Down the lane came men in pitboots
Coughing oath-edged talk and pipe-smoke,
Shouldering off the freshened silence.

One chased after rabbits; lost them;
Came back with a nest of lark's eggs;
Showed them; lodged them in the grasses.

So they passed in beards and moleskins,
Fathers, brothers, nicknames, laughter,
Through the tall gates standing open.

At noon, there came a tremor; cows
Stopped chewing for a second; sun,
Scarfed as in a heat-haze, dimmed.

The dead go on before us, they
Are sitting in God's house in comfort,
We shall see them face to face—

Plain as lettering in the chapels
It was said, and for a second
Wives saw men of the explosion

Larger than in life they managed—
Gold as on a coin, or walking
Somehow from the sun towards them,

One showing the eggs unbroken.

Aubade[1]

I work all day, and get half-drunk at night.
Waking at four to soundless dark, I stare.
In time the curtain-edges will grow light.
Till then I see what's really always there:
Unresting death, a whole day nearer now,
Making all thought impossible but how
And where and when I shall myself die.
Arid interrogation: yet the dread
Of dying, and being dead,
Flashes afresh to hold and horrify.

The mind blanks at the glare. Not in remorse
— The good not done, the love not given, time
Torn off unused — nor wretchedly because
An only life can take so long to climb
Clear of its wrong beginnings, and may never;
But at the total emptiness for ever,
The sure extinction that we travel to
And shall be lost in always. Not to be here,
Not to be anywhere,
And soon; nothing more terrible, nothing more true.

This is a special way of being afraid
No trick dispels. Religion used to try,

---

1 a song announcing or welcoming the coming of dawn

That vast moth-eaten musical brocade
Created to pretend we never die,
And specious stuff that says *No rational being*
Can fear a thing it will not feel, not seeing
That this is what we fear—no sight, no sound,
No touch or taste or smell, nothing to think with,
Nothing to love or link with,
The anaesthetic from which none come round.

And so it stays just on the edge of vision,
A small unfocused blur, a standing chill
That slows each impulse down to indecision.
Most things may never happen: this one will,
And realisation of it rages out
In furnace-fear when we are caught without
People or drink. Courage is no good:
It means not scaring others. Being brave
Lets no one off the grave.
Death is no different whined at than withstood.

Slowly light strengthens, and the room takes shape.
It stands plain as a wardrobe, what we know,
Have always known, know that we can't escape,
Yet can't accept. One side will have to go.
Meanwhile telephones crouch, getting ready to ring
In locked-up offices, and all the uncaring
Intricate rented world begins to rouse.
The sky is white as clay, with no sun.
Work has to be done.
Postmen like doctors go from house to house.

Denise Levertov

(b. 1923)

Laying the Dust

What a sweet smell rises
when you lay the dust—
bucket after bucket of water thrown
on the yellow grass.
The water

flashes
each time you
make it leap—
arching its glittering back.
The sound of
more water
pouring into the pail
almost quenches my thirst.
Surely when flowers
grow here, they'll not
smell sweeter than this
wet ground, suddenly black.

The Jacob's Ladder[1]

The stairway is not
a thing of gleaming strands
a radiant evanescence
for angels' feet that only glance in their tread, and need not
touch the stone.

It is of stone.
A rosy stone that takes
a glowing tone of softness
only because behind it the sky is a doubtful, a doubting
night gray.

A stairway of sharp
angles, solidly built.
One sees that the angels must spring
down from one step to the next, giving a little
lift of the wings:

and a man climbing
must scrape his knees, and bring

---

1   In a dream, Jacob saw a ladder extending from earth to heaven, with angels ascending
    and descending; see Genesis 28.12.

the grip of his hands into play. The cut stone
consoles his groping feet. Wings brush past him.
The poem ascends.

The Dog of Art

That dog with daisies for eyes
who flashes forth
flame of his very self at every bark
is the Dog of Art.
Worked in wool, his blind eyes
look inward to caverns and jewels
which they see perfectly,
and his voice
measures forth the treasure
in music sharp and loud,
sharp and bright,
bright flaming barks,
and growling smoky soft, the Dog
of Art turns to the world
the quietness of his eyes.

Matins[1]

i

The authentic! Shadows of it
sweep past in dreams, one could say imprecisely,
evoking the almost-silent
ripping apart of giant
sheets of cellophane. No.
It thrusts up close. Exactly in dreams
it has you off-guard, you
recognize it before you have time.
For a second before waking
the alarm bell is a red conical hat, it
takes form.

ii

The authentic! I said
rising from the toilet seat.
The radiator in rhythmic knockings
spoke of the rising steam.

---

1   morning prayers

The authentic, I said
breaking the handle of my hairbrush as I
brushed my hair in
rhythmic strokes: That's it,
that's joy, it's always
a recognition, the known
appearing fully itself, and
more itself than one knew.

iii

The new day rises
as heat rises,
knocking in the pipes
with rhythms it seizes for its own
to speak of its invention—
the real, the new-laid
egg whose speckled shell
the poet fondles and must break
if he will be nourished.

iv

A shadow painted where
yes, a shadow must fall.
The cow's breath
not forgotten in the mist, in the
words. Yes,
verisimilitude draws up
heat in us, zest
to follow through,
follow through,
follow
transformations of day
in its turning, in its becoming.

v

Stir the holy grains, set
the bowls on the table and
call the child to eat.

While we eat we think,
as we think an undercurrent
of dream runs through us
faster than thought
towards recognition.

Call the child to eat,
send him off, his mouth
tasting of toothpaste, to go down

into the ground, into a roaring train
and to school.

His cheeks are pink
his black eyes hold his dreams, he has left
forgetting his glasses.

Follow down the stairs at a clatter
to give them to him and save
his clear sight.

Cold air
comes in at the street door.

vi

The authentic! It rolls
just out of reach, beyond
running feet and
stretching fingers, down
the green slope and into
the black waves of the sea.
Speak to me, little horse, beloved,
tell me
how to follow the iron ball,
how to follow through to the country
beneath the waves
to the place where I must kill you and you step out
of your bones and flystrewn meat
tall, smiling, renewed,
formed in your own likeness

vii

Marvelous Truth, confront us
at every turn,
in every guise, iron ball,
egg, dark horse, shadow,
cloud
of breath on the air,

dwell
in our crowded hearts
our steaming bathrooms, kitchens full of
things to be done, the
ordinary streets.

Thrust close your smile
that we know you, terrible joy.

The Novel

A wind is blowing. The book being written
shifts, halts, pages
yellow and white drawing apart
and inching together in
new tries. A single white half sheet
skims out under the door.

And cramped in their not yet
halfwritten lives, a man and a woman
grimace in pain. Their cat
yawning its animal secret,
stirs in the monstrous limbo of erasure.
They live (when they live) in fear

of blinding, of burning, of choking under a
mushroom cloud in the year of the roach.
And they want (like us) the eternity
of today, they want this fear to be
struck out at once by a thick black
magic marker, everywhere, every page,

the whole sheets of it crushed, crackling,
and tossed in the fire
            and when they were fine ashes
            the stove would cool and be cleaned
            and a jar of flowers would be put to stand
            on top of the stove in the spring light.

Meanwhile from page to page they
buy things, acquiring the look of a
full life; they argue, make silence bitter,
plan journeys, move house, implant
despair in each other
and then in the nick of time

they save one another with tears,
remorse, tenderness—
hooked on those wonder-drugs.
Yet they do have—
don't they—like us—
their days of grace, they

halt, stretch, a vision
breaks in on the cramped grimace,

inscape[1] of transformation.
Something sundered begins to knit.
By scene, by sentence, something is rendered
back into life, back to the gods.

Caedmon[2]

All others talked as if
talk were a dance.
Clodhopper I, with clumsy feet
would break the gliding ring.
Early I learned to
hunch myself
close by the door:
then when the talk began
I'd wipe my
mouth and wend
unnoticed back to the barn
to be with the warm beasts,
dumb among body sounds
of the simple ones.
I'd see by a twist
of lit rush the motes
of gold moving
from shadow to shadow
slow in the wake
of deep untroubled sighs.
The cows
munched or stirred or were still. I
was at home and lonely,
both in good measure. Until
the sudden angel affrighted me—light effacing
my feeble beam,
a forest of torches, feathers of flame, sparks upflying:
but the cows as before
were calm, and nothing was burning,
      nothing but I, as that hand of fire
touched my lips and scorched my tongue
and pulled my voice
        into the ring of the dance.

---

1   a term coined by the English poet Gerard Manley Hopkins (1844-1889) to mean the individual or essential quality of something

2   An unlettered herdsman of the 7th century who, according to the historian Bede, received the power of song in a vision, entered a monastery, and wrote poetry based on translations of the scriptures.

The Day the Audience Walked Out on Me, and Why

(May 8th, 1970, Goucher College, Maryland)

Like this it happened:
after the antiphonal reading from the psalms
and the dance of lamentation before the altar,
and the two poems, 'Life at War' and
                                        'What Were They Like?'[1]
I began my rap,
and said:
Yes, it is well that we have gathered
in this chapel to remember
the students shot at Kent State,[2]

but let us be sure we know
our gathering is a mockery unless
we remember also
the black students shot at Orangeburg[3] two years ago,
and Fred Hampton[4] murdered in his bed
by the police only months ago.

And while I spoke the people
—girls, older women, a few men—
began to rise and turn
their backs to the altar and leave.

And I went on and said,
Yes, it is well that we remember
all of these, but let us be sure
we know it is hypocrisy
to think of them unless
we make our actions their memorial,
actions of militant resistance.

By then the pews were almost empty
and I returned to my seat and a man stood up
in the back of the quiet chapel
(near the wide-open doors through which
the green of May showed, and the long shadows
                          of late afternoon)
and said my words
desecrated a holy place.

---

1 "Life at War" and "What Were They Like?" are two poems by Levertov, protesting the
   war in Vietnam.
2 the university in Ohio where four students were killed and nine wounded by National
   Guard units during an anti-war demonstraion on 4 May 1970
3 in South Carolina
4 Fred Hampton was killed by police in December 1969.

And a few days later
when some more students (black) were shot
at Jackson, Mississippi,
no one desecrated the white folks' chapel,
because no memorial service was held.

Nissim Ezekiel

(b. 1924)

The Company I Keep

No greater curse
than a minor talent
in the verse-ring bull-ring, yet
millions revel in it
and I am counted
one among them, mixing
metaphors and platitudes—
sailing in the same boat.
Damn all you sensitive poets,
seducers of experience,
self-worshippers and publishers,
editors of small magazines,
broadcasters of small-weather woes,
victims of your own spontaneous fraud.
You are in hell
and do not know it.
When did you last write
a real poem? Never mind,
there are the book reviews
as compensation, and I too
was once in advertising.
We shall never learn
the secrets of singularity.
Our fate is to stir up
a variety of disasters,
but our main contribution to scandal
is the unspeakable line.
Young and old, men and women,
our only achievement
is monumentality
of vanity.
The only art we master
is the art of economising
in intelligence and skill,
with a rhyme or two to show
we can still do it, our self-release
a trail of smoke
to tickle the nostrils of gullible folk.

Poet, Lover, Birdwatcher

To force the pace and never to be still
Is not the way of those who study birds
Or women. The best poets wait for words.
The hunt is not an exercise of will
But patient love relaxing on a hill
To note the movement of a timid wing;
Until the one who knows that she is loved
No longer waits but risks surrendering—
In this the poet finds his moral proved,
Who never spoke before his spirit moved.

The slow movement seems, somehow, to say much more.
To watch the rarer birds, you have to go
Along deserted lanes and where the rivers flow
In silence near the source, or by a shore
Remote and thorny like the heart's dark floor.
And there the women slowly turn around,
Not only flesh and bone but myths of light
With darkness at the core, and sense is found
By poets lost in crooked, restless flight,
The deaf can hear, the blind recover sight.

In India

I

Always, in the sun's eye,
Here among the beggars,
Hawkers, pavement sleepers,
Hutment dwellers, slums,
Dead souls of men and gods,
Burnt-out mothers, frightened
Virgins, wasted child
And tortured animal,
All in noisy silence
Suffering the place and time,
I ride my elephant of thought,
A Cézanne[1] slung around my neck.

II

The Roman Catholic Goan[2] boys
The whitewashed Anglo-lndian boys

---

1   Paul Cézanne (1839-1906), French painter
2   from Goa, a region on the west coast of India, formerly administered by Portugal

The musclebound Islamic boys
Were earnest in their prayers.

They copied, bullied, stole in pairs
They bragged about their love affairs
They carved the table broke the chairs
But never missed their prayers.

The Roman Catholic Goan boys
Confessed their solitary joys
Confessed their games with high-heeled toys
And hastened to the prayers.

The Anglo-Indian gentlemen
Drank whisky in some Jewish den
With Muslims slowly creeping in
Before or after prayers.

III

To celebrate the year's end:
men in grey or black,
women, bosom semi-bare,
twenty-three of us in all,
six nations represented.

The wives of India sit apart.
They do not drink,
they do not talk,
of course, they do not kiss.
The men are quite at home
among the foreign styles
(what fun the flirting is!)
I myself, decorously,
press a thigh or two in sly innocence.
The party is a great success.

Then someone says: we can't
enjoy it, somehow, don't you think?
The atmosphere corrupt,
and look at our wooden wives . . . .
I take him out to get some air.

IV

This, she said to herself
As she sat at table
With the English boss,
Is IT. This is the promise:
The long evenings
In the large apartment

With cold beer and Western music,
Lucid talk of art and literature,
And of all 'the changes India needs'.
At the second meeting
In the large apartment
After cold beer and the music on,
She sat in disarray.

The struggle had been hard
And not altogether successful.
Certainly the blouse
Would not be used again.
But with true British courtesy
He lent her a safety pin
Before she took the elevator down.

Night of the Scorpion

I remember the night my mother
was stung by a scorpion. Ten hours
of steady rain had driven him
to crawl beneath a sack of rice.
Parting with his poison—flash
of diabolic tail in the dark room—
he risked the rain again.
The peasants came like swarms of flies
and buzzed the Name of God a hundred times
to paralyse the Evil One.
With candles and with lanterns
throwing giant scorpion shadows
on the sun-baked walls
they searched for him: he was not found.
They clicked their tongues.
With every movement that the scorpion made
his poison moved in Mother's blood, they said.
May he sit still, they said.
May the sins of your previous birth
be burned away tonight, they said.
May your suffering decrease
the misfortunes of your next birth, they said.
May the sum of evil
balanced in this unreal world
against the sum of good
become diminished by your pain.
May the poison purify your flesh
of desire, and your spirit of ambition,
they said, and they sat around
on the floor with my mother in the centre,
the peace of understanding on each face.
More candles, more lanterns, more neighbours,

more insects, and the endless rain.
My mother twisted through and through
groaning on a mat.
My father, sceptic, rationalist,
trying every curse and blessing,
powder, mixture, herb and hybrid.
He even poured a little paraffin
upon the bitten toe and put a match to it.
I watched the flame feeding on my mother.
I watched the holy man perform his rites
to tame the poison with an incantation.
After twenty hours
it lost its sting.
My mother only said:
Thank God the scorpion picked on me
and spared my children.

In The Garden

It seemed to me so much like you,
To find the planning of the garden
Faulty, and the birds too few.

Your walk was slow, informal there
Among the trees whose names you knew,
And flowers commonplace or rare.

The elephant of broken stone
Deserved, you said, a closer view
Than animals of flesh and bone.

The spacious lawns with sand defined
Where children shouted, breezes blew,
Or water like a lucid mind

Negotiates obstructive rocks;
And bridges modestly designed;
Were better than the tower of clocks,

And hedges ruining every view—
At which I felt your kindness harden:
It seemed to me so much like you.

Carolyn Kizer

(b. 1925)

from: *Pro Femina*

Three

I will speak about women of letters, for I'm in the racket.
Our biggest successes to date? Old maids to a woman.
And our saddest conspicuous failures? The married spinsters
On loan to the husbands they treated like surrogate fathers.
Think of that crew of self-pitiers, not-very-distant,
Who carried the torch for themselves and got first-degree burns.
Or the sad sonneteers, toast-and-teasdales[1] we loved at thirteen;
Middle-aged virgins seducing the puerile anthologists
Through lust-of-the-mind; barbiturate-drenched Camilles[2]
With continuous periods, murmuring softly on sofas
When poetry wasn't a craft but a sickly effluvium,
The air thick with incense, musk, and emotional blackmail.

I suppose they reacted from an earlier womanly modesty
When too many girls were scabs to their stricken sisterhood,
Impugning our sex to stay in good with the men,
Commencing their insecure bluster. How they must have swaggered
When women themselves endorsed their own inferiority !
Vestals, vassals and vessels, rolled into several,
They took notes in rolling syllabics, in careful journals,
Aiming to please a posterity that despises them.
But we'll always have traitors who swear that a woman surrenders
Her Supreme Function, by equating Art with aggression
And failure with Femininity. Still, it's just as unfair
To equate Art with Femininity, like a prettily-packaged commodity
When we are the custodians of the world's best-kept secret:
Merely the private lives of one-half of humanity.

But even with masculine dominance, we mares and mistresses
Produced some sleek saboteuses, making their cracks
Which the porridge-brained males of the day were too thick to perceive,
Mistaking young hornets for perfectly harmless bumblebees.
Being thought innocuous rouses some women to frenzy;
They try to be ugly by aping the ways of the men
And succeed. Swearing, sucking cigars and scorching the bedspread,

Slopping straight shots, eyes blotted, vanity-blown
In the expectation of glory: *she writes like a man!*

---

1   a reference to Sara Teasdale (1884-1933), American poet
2   Camille is the consumptive heroine in the English translation of Alexandre Dumas' play *The Lady of the Camelias* (1852). In the French original, her name is Marguerite Gautier.

This drives other women mad in a mist of chiffon.
(One poetess draped her gauze over red flannels, a practical feminist.)

But we're emerging from all that, more or less,
Except for some lady-like laggards and Quarterly priestesses[1]
Who flog men for fun, and kick women to maim competition.
Now, if we struggle abnormally, we may almost seem normal;
If we submerge our self-pity in disciplined industry;
If we stand up and be hated, and swear not to sleep with editors;
If we regard ourselves formally, respecting our true limitations
Without making an unseemly show of trying to unfreeze our assets;
Keeping our heads and our pride while remaining unmarried;
And if wedded, kill guilt in its tracks when we stack up the dishes
And defect to the typewriter. And if mothers, believe in the luck of
      our children,
Whom we forbid to devour us, whom we shall not devour,
And the luck of our husbands and lovers, who keep free women.

* * *

The Ungrateful Garden

Midas[2] watched the golden crust
That formed over his streaming sores,
Hugged his agues, loved his lust,
But damned to hell the out-of-doors

Where blazing motes of sun impaled
The serried roses, metal-bright.
"Those famous flowers," Midas wailed,
"Have scorched my retina with light."

This gift, he'd thought, would gild his joys,
Silt up the waters of his grief;
His lawns a wilderness of noise,
The heavy clang of leaf on leaf.

Within, the golden cup is good
To heft, to sip the yellow mead.
Outside, in summer's rage, the rude
Gold thorn has made his fingers bleed.

"I strolled my halls in golden shift,
As ruddy as a lion's meat.

---

1   i.e., critics for high-powered academic journals
2   the legendary king of Phrygia whose touch turned everything to gold

Then I rushed out to share my gift,
And golden stubble cut my feet."

Dazzled with wounds, he limped away
To climb into his golden bed.
Roses, roses can betray.
"Nature is evil," Midas said.

The Copulating Gods

Brushing back the curls from your famous brow,
Lingering over the prominent temple vein
Purple as Aegean columns in the dawn,
Calm now, I ponder how self-consciously
The gods must fornicate.
It is that sense of unseen witness:
Those mortals with whom we couple or have coupled,
Clinging to our swan-suits, our bull-skills,[1]
Our masquerades in coin[2] and shrubbery.

We were their religion before they were born.
The spectacle of our carnality
Confused them into spiritual lust.
The headboard of our bed became their altar;
Rare nectar, shared, a common sacrament.
The wet drapery of our sheets, molded
To noble thighs, is made the basis
For a whole new aesthetic:
God is revealed as the first genius.

Men continue to invent our histories,
Deny our equal pleasure in each other.
Club-foot,[3] nymphomanic, they dub us,
Then fabricate the net that God will cast
Over our raptures: we, trussed[4] up like goats,
Paraded past the searchlights of the sky
By God himself, the ringmaster and cuckold,
Amidst a thunderous laughter and applause.

---

1   Zeus, chief among the Greek gods, came to Leda in the form of a swan, and to Europa in the shape of a bull.

2   in architecture, a corner or angle of a building

3   Hephaestus, son of Zeus and Hera, was born lame; he was married to Aphrodite, who bore him Eros.

4   Aphrodite engaged in an amorous affair with Ares (Mars), but the pair were discovered and caught in a net by Aphrodite's husband Hephaestus, then exposed to the ridicule of the assembled gods.

Tracing again the bones of your famous face,
I know we are not their history but our myth.
Heaven prevents time; and our astral raptures
Float buoyant in the universe. Come, kiss!
Come, swoon again, we who invented dying
And the whole alchemy of resurrection.
They will concoct a scripture explaining this.

James Merrill

(b. 1926)

Angel

Above my desk, whirring and self-important
(Though not much larger than a hummingbird)
In finely woven robes, school of Van Eyck,[1]
Hovers an evidently angelic visitor.
He points one index finger out the window
At winter snatching to its heart,
To crystal vacancy, the misty
Exhalations of houses and of people running home
From the cold sun pounding on the sea;
While with the other hand
He indicates the piano
Where the Sarabande No. 1 lies open
At a passage I shall never master
But which has already, and effortlessly, mastered me.
He drops his jaw as if to say, or sing,
'Between the world God made
And this music of Satie,[2]
Each glimpsed through veils, but whole,
Radiant and willed,
Demanding praise, demanding surrender,
How can you sit there with your notebook?
What do you think you are doing?'
However he says nothing—wisely: I could mention
Flaws in God's world, or Satie's; and for that matter
How did he come by *his* taste for Satie?
Half to tease him, I turn back to my page,
Its phrases thus far clotted, unconnected.
The tiny angel shakes his head.
There is no smile on his round, hairless face.
He does not want even these few lines written.

After Greece

Light into the olive entered
And was oil. Rain made the huge pale stones
Shine from within. The moon turned his hair white
Who next stepped from between the columns,
Shielding his eyes. All through
The countryside were old ideas
Found lying open to the elements.

---

1   Hubert Van Eyck (c.1366-1426) and his brother Jan Van Eyck (c.1385-1440), Flemish
     painters, known for the brilliance of their colouring
2   Erik Satie (1866-1925), French composer

Of the gods' houses only
A minor premise here and there
Would be balancing the heaven of fixed stars
Upon a Doric capital. The rest
Lay spilled, their fluted drums half sunk in cyclamen
Or deep in water's biting clarity
Which just barely upheld me
The next week, when I sailed for home.
But where is home—these walls ?
These limbs? The very spaniel underfoot
Races in sleep, toward what?
It is autumn. I did not invite
Those guests, windy and brittle, who drink my liquor.
Returning from a walk I find
The bottles filled with spleen, my room itself
Smeared by reflection onto the far hemlocks.
I some days flee in dream
Back to the exposed porch of the maidens
Only to find my great-great-grandmothers
Erect there, peering
Into a globe of red Bohemian glass.
As it swells and sinks, I call up
Graces, Furies, Fates,[1] removed
To my country's warm, lit halls, with rivets forced
Through drapery, and nothing left to bear.
They seem anxious to know
What holds up heaven nowadays.
I start explaining how in that vast fire
Were other irons—well, Art, Public Spirit,
Ignorance, Economics, Love of Self,
Hatred of Self, a hundred more,
Each burning to be felt, each dedicated
To sparing us the worst; how I distrust them
As I should have done those ladies; how I want
Essentials: salt, wine, olive, the light, the scream—
No! I have scarcely named you,
And look, in a flash you stand full-grown before me,
Row upon row, Essentials,
Dressed like your sister caryatids[2]
Or tombstone angels jealous of their dead,
With undulant coiffures, lips weathered, cracked by grime,
And faultless eyes gone blank beneath the immense
Zinc and gunmetal northern sky . . .
Stay then. Perhaps the system

---

1   In Greek mythology, the Graces were three goddesses who presided over all matters
     relating to social enjoyment and the arts; the Furies pursued and punished those who
     had done wrong; and the three Fates were goddesses who controlled human destiny.
2   in architecture, supporting columns cut in the shape of women in Greek costume

Calls for spirits. This first glass I down
To the last time
I ate and drank in that old world. May I
Also survive its meanings, and my own.

The Broken Home

Crossing the street,
I saw the parents and the child
At their window, gleaming like fruit
With evening's mild gold leaf.

In a room on the floor below,
Sunless, cooler—a brimming
Saucer of wax, marbly and dim—
I have lit what's left of my life.

I have thrown out yesterday's milk
And opened a book of maxims.
The flame quickens. The word stirs.

Tell me, tongue of fire,
That you and I are as real
At least as the people upstairs.

My father, who had flown in World War I,
Might have continued to invest his life
In cloud banks well above Wall Street[1] and wife.
But the race was run below, and the point was to win.

Too late now, I make out in his blue gaze
(Through the smoked glass of being thirty-six)
The soul eclipsed by twin black pupils, sex
And business; time was money in those days.

Each thirteenth year he married. When he died
There were already several chilled wives
In sable orbit—rings, cars, permanent waves.
We'd felt him warming up for a green bride.

He could afford it. He was "in his prime"
At three score ten. But money was not time.
When my parents were younger this was a popular act:
A veiled woman would leap from an electric, wine-dark car
To the steps of no matter what—the Senate or the

---

1   Merrill's father was a founding partner of the investment company of Merrill Lynch.

     Ritz Bar—
And bodily, at newsreel speed, attack

No matter whom—Al Smith[1] or José Maria Sert [2]
Or Clemenceau[3]—veins standing out on her throat
As she yelled *War Mongerer! Pig! Give us the vote!*,
And would have to be hauled away in her hobble skirt.[4]

What had the man done? Oh, made history.
Her business (he had implied) was giving birth,
Tending the house, mending the socks.

Always that same old story —
Father Time and Mother Earth,
A marriage on the rocks.

One afternoon, red, satyr-thighed
Michael, the Irish setter, head
Passionately lowered, led
The child I was to a shut door. Inside,

Blinds beat sun from the bed.
The green-gold room throbbed like a bruise.
Under a sheet, clad in taboos
Lay whom we sought, her hair undone, outspread,

And of a blackness found, if ever now, in old
Engravings where the acid bit.
I must have needed to touch it
Or the whiteness—was she dead?
Her eyes flew open, startled strange and cold.
The dog slumped to the floor. She reached for me. I fled.

Tonight they have stepped out onto the gravel.
The party is over. It's the fall
Of 1931. They love each other still.

She: Charlie, I can't stand the pace.
He: Come on, honey—why, you'll bury us all!

A lead soldier guards my windowsill:
Khaki rifle, uniform, and face.
Something in me grows heavy, silvery, pliable.

---

1   Alfred Smith (1873-1944), a governor of New York
2   Spanish painter (1876-1945), known for his murals
3   Georges Clemenceau (1841-1929), twice prime minister of France, who visited the U.S.
     in the early 1920s
4   a skirt fitting very closely below the knee

How intensely people used to feel!
Like metal poured at the close of a proletarian novel,
Refined and glowing from the crucible,
I see those two hearts, I'm afraid,
Still. Cool here in the graveyard of good and evil,
They are even so to be honored and obeyed.

. . . Obeyed, at least, inversely. Thus
I rarely buy a newspaper, or vote.
To do so, I have learned, is to invite
The tread of a stone guest[1] within my house.

Shooting this rusted bolt, though, against him,
I trust I am no less time's child than some
Who on the heath impersonate Poor Tom[2]
Or on the barricades risk life and limb.

Nor do I try to keep a garden, only
An avocado in a glass of water—
Roots pallid, gemmed with air. And later,

When the small gilt leaves have grown
Fleshy and green, I let them die, yes, yes,
And start another. I am earth's no less.

A child, a red dog roam the corridors,
Still, of the broken home. No sound. The brilliant
Rag runners halt before wide-open doors.
My old room! Its wallpaper—cream, medallioned
With pink and brown—brings back the first nightmares,
Long summer colds, and Emma, sepia-faced,
Perspiring over broth carried upstairs
Aswim with golden fats I could not taste.

The real house became a boarding-school.
Under the ballroom ceiling's allegory
Someone at last may actually be allowed
To learn something; or, from my window, cool
With the unstiflement of the entire story,
Watch a red setter stretch and sink in cloud.

---

1   In the various versions of Don Juan's story, Don Juan jestingly invites to a banquet the statue of a man he killed; whereupon the statue comes, seizes him, and delivers him to devils.

2   In *King Lear,* to escape the wrath of his father the Earl of Gloucester, Edgar disguises himself as the madman "poor Tom," who lives upon a barren heath.

Robert Creeley

(b. 1926)

The Hill

It is some time since I have been
to what it was had once turned me backwards,
and made my head into
a cruel instrument.

It is simple
to confess. Then done,
to walk away, walk away,
to come again.

But that form, I must answer,
is dead in me, completely,
and I will not allow it
to reappear—

Saith perversity, the willful,
the magnanimous cruelty,
which is in me
like a hill.

The Rain

All night the sound had
come back again,
and again falls
this quiet, persistent rain.

What am I to myself
that must be remembered,
insisted upon
so often? Is it

that never the ease,
even the hardness,
of rain falling
will have for me

something other than this,
something not so insistent—
am I to be locked in this
final uneasiness.

Love, if you love me,
lie next to me.
Be for me, like rain,
the getting out

of the tiredness, the fatuousness, the semi-
lust of intentional indifference.
Be wet
with a decent happiness.

The Door

for Robert Duncan

It is hard going to the door
cut so small in the wall where
the vision which echoes loneliness
brings a scent of wild flowers in a wood.

What I understood, I understand.
My mind is sometime torment,
sometimes good and filled with livelihood,
and feels the ground.

But I see the door,
and knew the wall, and wanted the wood,
and would get there if I could
with my feet and hands and mind.

Lady, do not banish me
for digressions. My nature
is a quagmire of unresolved
confessions. Lady, I follow.

I walked away from myself,
I left the room l found the garden,
I knew the woman
in it, together we lay down.

Dead night remembers. In December
we change, not multiplied but dispersed,
sneaked out of childhood,
the ritual of dismemberment.

Mighty magic is a mother,
in her there is another issue
of fixture, repeated form, the race renewal,
the charge of the command.

The garden echoes across the room.
It is fixed in the wall like a mirror
that faces a window behind you
and reflects the shadows.

May I go now?
Am I allowed to bow myself down
in the ridiculous posture of renewal,
of the insistence of which I am the virtue?

Nothing for You is untoward.
Inside You would also be tall,
more tall, more beautiful.
Come toward me from the wall, I want to be with You.

So I screamed to You,
who hears as the wind, and changes
multiply, invariably,
changes in the mind.

Running to the door, I ran down
as a clock runs down. Walked backwards,
stumbled, sat down
hard on the floor near the wall.

Where were You.
How absurd, how vicious.
There is nothing to do but get up.
My knees were iron, I rusted in worship, of You.

For that one sings, one
writes the spring poem, one goes on walking.
The Lady has always moved to the next town
and you stumble on after Her.

The door in the wall leads to the garden
where in the sunlight sit
the Graces in long Victorian dresses,
of which my grandmother had spoken.

History sings in their faces.
They are young, they are obtainable,
and you follow after them also
in the service of God and Truth.

But the Lady is indefinable,
she will be the door in the wall
to the garden in sunlight.
I will go on talking forever.

I will never get there.
Oh Lady, remember me
who in Your service grows older
not wiser, no more than before.

How can I die alone.
Where will I be then who am now alone,
what groans so pathetically
in this room where I am alone?

I will go to the garden.
I will be a romantic. I will sell
myself in hell,
in heaven also I will be.

In my mind I see the door,
I see the sunlight before me across the floor
beckon to me, as the Lady's skirt
moves small beyond it.

W. D. Snodgrass

(b. 1926)

April Inventory

The green catalpa tree has turned
All white; the cherry blooms once more.
In one whole year I haven't learned
A blessed thing they pay you for.
The blossoms snow down in my hair;
The trees and I will soon be bare.

The trees have more than I to spare.
The sleek, expensive girls I teach,
Younger and pinker every year,
Bloom gradually out of reach.
The pear tree lets its petals drop
Like dandruff on a tabletop.

The girls have grown so young by now
I have to nudge myself to stare,
This year they smile and mind me how
My teeth are falling with my hair.
In thirty years I may not get
Younger, shrewder, or out of debt.

The tenth time, just a year ago,
I made myself a little list
Of all the things I'd ought to know,
Then told my parents, analyst,
And everyone who's trusted me
I'd be substantial, presently.

I haven't read one book about
A book or memorized one plot.
Or found a mind I did not doubt.
I learned one date. And then forgot.
And one by one the solid scholars
Get the degrees, the jobs, the dollars.

And smile above their starchy collars.
I taught my classes Whitehead's[1] notions;
One lovely girl, a song of Mahler's.[2]
Lacking a source-book or promotions,
I showed one child the colors of
A luna moth and how to love.

---

1   Alfred North Whitehead (1861-1947), English mathematician and philosopher
2   Gustav Mahler (1860-1911), Austro-Hungarian composer

I taught myself to name my name,
To bark back, loosen love and crying;
To ease my woman so she came,
To ease an old man who was dying.
I have not learned how often I
Can win, can love, but choose to die.

I have not learned there is a lie
Love shall be blonder, slimmer, younger;
That my equivocating eye
Loves only by my body's hunger;
That I have forces, true to feel,
Or that the lovely world is real.

While scholars speak authority
And wear their ulcers on their sleeves,
My eyes in spectacles shall see
These trees procure and spend their leaves.
There is a value underneath
The gold and silver in my teeth.

Though trees turn bare and girls turn wives,
We shall afford our costly seasons;
There is a gentleness survives
That will outspeak and has its reasons.
There is a loveliness exists,
Preserves us, not for specialists.

The Mother

She stands in the dead center like a star;
They form around her like her satellites
Taking her energies, her heat, light
And massive attraction on their paths, however far.

Born of her own flesh; still, she feels them drawn
Into the outer cold by dark forces;
They are in love with suffering and perversion,
With the community of pain. Thinking them gone,

Out of her reach, she is consoled by evil
In neighbors, children, the world she cannot change,
That lightless universe where they range
Out of the comforts of her disapproval.

If evil did not exist, she would create it
To die in righteousness, her martyrdom
To that sweet dominion they have bolted from.
Then, at last, she can think that she is hated

And is content. Things can decay, break,
Spoil themselves; who cares? She'll gather the debris
With loving tenderness to give them; she
Will weave a labyrinth of waste, wreckage

And hocus-pocus; leave free no fault
Or cornerhole outside those lines of force
Where she and only she can thread a course.
All else in her grasp grows clogged and halts.

Till one by one, the areas of her brain
Switch off and she has filled all empty spaces;
Now she hallucinates in their right places
Their after-images, reversed and faint.

And the drawn strands of love, spun in her mind,
Turn dark and cluttered, precariously hung
With the black shapes of her mates, her sapless young,
Where she moves by habit, hungering and blind.

Diplomacy: The Father

Your mission, in any disputed area, is to find
        (as in yourself)
which group, which element among the contending forces
    seems, by nature, most fit to take control.
Stronger perhaps, more driven, gifted with resources—
    no matter: able to bind in a firm goal
the ennervating local passions native to our kind.
        That force, of course, is

your enemy—whom you cannot choose but love.
        As in yourself,
it's this, it's those so loved, that can grow oppressive
    and steal your hard-bought freedom to choose
that you won't love. Act loving, then. Make no aggressive
    move; make friends. Make, though, for future use,
notes on their debts, beliefs, whom they're most fond of—
        their weaknesses. If

anything, appear more loyal—pretend to feel
        as in yourself
you'd truly want to feel: affectionate and admiring.
    Then hate grows, discovering the way such foes enslave
you worst: if you loved them, you'd *feel* free. Conspiring
    to outwit such subtlety, devise and save
good reasons for your hatred; count wounds. Conceal,
        though, this entire ring

of proofs, excuses, wrongs which you maintain
    as in yourself
might harbor some benign, enfeebling growth.
  As for followers, seek those who'll take your aid:
the weak. In doubt who's weaker, finance both.
  Collect the dawdlers, the brilliant but afraid,
the purchasable losers—those who, merely to gain
    some power they can loathe,

would quite as willingly be out of power
    as in. Yourself? —
friend, this is lonely work. Deep cravings will persist
  for true allies, for those you love; you will long
to speak your mind out sometimes, or to assist
    someone who, given that help, might grow strong
and admirable. You've reached your bleakest hour,
    the pitiless test.

But think: why let your own aid diminish you?
    As in yourself,
so in those who take your help, your values or your name,
  you've sought out their best thoughts, their hidden talents
only to buy out, to buy off. Your fixed aim,
    whatever it costs, must still be for a balance
of power in the family, the firm, the whole world through.
    Exactly the same

as a balance of impotence—in any group or nation
    as in yourself.
Suppose some one of them rose up and could succeed
  your foe—he'd *be* your foe. To underlings, dispense
all they can ask, but don't need; give till they need
    your giving. One gift could free them: confidence.
They'd never dare ask. Betray no dedication
    to any creed

or person—talk high ideals; then you'll be known
    as, in yourself,
harmless. Exact no faith from them, no affection;
  suppose they've learned no loyalty to you—
that's one step taken in the right direction.
  Never forbid them. Let no one pay back what's due;
the mere air they breathe should come as a loan
    beyond collection.

Like air, you must be everywhere at once, where-
    as, in your self-
defense, make yourself scarce. Your best disguise
  is to turn gray, spreading yourself so thin
you're one with all unknowns—essential. Vaporize
    into the fog all things that happen, happen in

or fail to happen. In the end, you have to appear
   as unworldly in the eyes

of this whole sanctioned world that your care drained
   as in yours. Self-
sacrifice has borne you, then, through that destruction
  programmed into life; you live on in that loving tension
you leave to those who'll still take your instruction.
   You've built their world; an air of soft suspension
which you survive in, as cradled and sustained
   as in yourself.

The Poet Ridiculed by Hysterical Academics

Is it, then, your opinion
  Women are putty in your hands?
Is this the face[1] to launch upon
  A thousand one night stands?

First, please, would you be so kind
  As to define your contribution
To modern verse, the Western mind
  And human institutions?

Where, where is the long, flowing hair,
  The velvet suit, the broad bow tie;
Where is the other-worldly air,
  Where the abstracted eye?

Describe the influence on your verse
  Of Oscar Mudwarp's mighty line,
The theories of Susan Schmersch
  Or the spondee's decline.

You've labored to present us with
  This mouse-sized volume; shall this equal
The epic glories of Joe Smith?
  He's just brought out a sequel.

Where are the beard, the bongo drums,
  Tattered T-shirt and grubby sandals,
As who, released from Iowa,[2] comes
  To tell of wondrous scandals?

---

1   A play on the lines in Marlowe's play *Doctor Faustus* (1604): "Was this the face that launch'd a thousand ships..." (sc.14).

2   an allusion to the well-known creative writing programme at the University of Iowa

Have you subversive, out of date,
  Or controversial ideas?
And can you really pull your weight
  Among such minds as these?

              Ah, what avails the tenure race,
                Ah, what the Ph.D.,
              When all departments have a place
                For nincompoops like thee?

Allen Ginsberg

(b. 1926)

A Supermarket in California

What thoughts I have of you tonight, Walt Whitman,[1] for I walked down the sidestreets under the trees with a headache self-conscious looking at the full moon.

In my hungry fatigue, and shopping for images, I went into the neon fruit supermarket, dreaming of your enumerations!

What peaches and what penumbras! Whole families shopping at night! Aisles full of husbands! Wives in the avocados, babies in the tomatoes! —and you, García Lorca,[2] what were you doing down by the watermelons?

I saw you, Walt Whitman, childless, lonely old grubber, poking among the meats in the refrigerator and eyeing the grocery boys.

I heard you asking questions of each: Who killed the pork chops? What price bananas? Are you my Angel?

I wandered in and out of the brilliant stacks of cans following you, and followed in my imagination by the store detective.

We strode down the open corridors together in our solitary fancy tasting artichokes, possessing every frozen delicacy, and never passing the cashier.

Where are we going, Walt Whitman? The doors close in an hour. Which way does your beard point tonight?

(I touch your book and dream of our odyssey in the supermarket and feel absurd.)

Will we walk all night through solitary streets? The trees add shade to shade, lights out in the houses, we'll both be lonely.

Will we stroll dreaming of the lost America of love past blue automobiles in driveways, home to our silent cottage?

Ah, dear father, graybeard, lonely old courage-teacher, what America did you have when Charon[3] quit poling his ferry and you got out on a smoking bank and stood watching the boat disappear on the black waters of Lethe?[4]

---

1 Walt Whitman (1819-1892), American poet, author of *Leaves of Grass*
2 García Lorca (1899-1936), Spanish poet and dramatist
3 in Greek mythology, the boatman who ferried the souls of the dead across the river Styx to Hades
4 a river in Hades whose waters brought forgetfulness

My Sad Self

To Frank O'Hara[1]

Sometimes when my eyes are red
I go up on top of the RCA Building
    and gaze at my world, Manhattan—
      my buildings, streets I've done feats in,
        lofts, beds, coldwater flats
—on Fifth Ave below which I also bear in mind,
    its ant cars, little yellow taxis, men
      walking the size of specks of wool—
Panorama of the bridges, sunrise over Brooklyn machine,
    sun go down over New Jersey where I was born
      & Paterson where I played with ants—
my later loves on 15th Street,
    my greater loves of Lower East Side,
      my once fabulous amours in the Bronx
        faraway—
paths crossing in these hidden streets,
    my history summed up, my absences
    and ecstasies in Harlem—
    —sun shining down on all I own
    in one eyeblink to the horizon
      in my last eternity—
             matter is water.

Sad,
    I take the elevator and go
      down, pondering,
and walk on the pavements staring into all man's
        plateglass, faces,
    questioning after who loves,
    and stop, bemused
      in front of an automobile shopwindow
    standing lost in calm thought,
      traffic moving up & down 5th Avenue blocks behind me
        waiting for a moment when . . .

Time to go home & cook supper & listen to
    the romantic war news on the radio

        . . . all movement stops
& I walk in the timeless sadness of existence,
    tenderness flowing thru the buildings,
      my fingertips touching reality's face,

---

1   Frank O'Hara (1926-1966), American poet, active in the art world of New York in the
1950s and 1960s

my own face streaked with tears in the mirror
 of some window—at dusk—
  where I have no desire—
for bonbons—or to own the dresses or Japanese
 lampshades of intellection—

Confused by the spectacle around me,
 Man struggling up the street
  with packages, newspapers,
   ties, beautiful suits
  toward his desire
Man, woman, streaming over the pavements
  red lights clocking hurried watches &
  movements at the curb—

And all these streets leading
 so crosswise, honking, lengthily,
  by avenues
stalked by high buildings or crusted into slums
  thru such halting traffic
   screaming cars and engines
so painfully to this
 countryside, this graveyard
  this stillness
   on deathbed or mountain
 once seen
  never regained or desired
   in the mind to come
where all Manhattan that I've seen must disappear.

James K. Baxter

(1926–1972)

The Bay

On the road to the bay was a lake of rushes
Where we bathed at times and changed in the bamboos.
Now it is rather to stand and say:
How many roads we take that lead to Nowhere,
The alley overgrown, no meaning now but loss:
Not that veritable garden where everything comes easy.

And by the bay itself were cliffs with carved names
And a hut on the shore beside the Maori[1] ovens.
We raced boats from the banks of the pumice creek
Or swam in those autumnal shallows
Growing cold in amber water, riding the logs
Upstream, and waiting for the taniwha.[2]

So now I remember the bay and the little spiders
On driftwood, so poisonous and quick.
The carved cliffs and the great outcrying surf
With currents round the rocks and the birds rising.
A thousand times an hour is torn across
And burned for the sake of going on living.
But I remember the bay that never was
And stand like stone and cannot turn away.

Elegy for an Unknown Soldier

There was a time when I would magnify
His ending; scatter words as if I wept
Tears not my own but man's. There was a time.
But not now so. He died of a common sickness.

Nor did any new star shine
Upon that day when he came crying out
Of fleshy darkness to a world of pain
And waxen eyelids let the daylight enter.

So felt and tasted, found earth good enough.
Later he played with stones and wondered
If there was land beyond the dark sea rim
And where the road led out of the farthest paddock.

---

1   the aboriginal peoples of New Zealand
2   In Maori legend, the taniwha were fabulous monsters, usually in the form of giant lizards
     or fish.

Awkward at school, he could not master sums.
Could you expect him then to understand
The miracle and menace of his body
That grew as mushrooms grow from dusk to dawn?

He had the weight though for a football scrum
And thought it fine to listen to the cheering
And drink beer with the boys, telling them tall
Stories of girls that he had never known.

So when the War came he was glad and sorry,
But soon enlisted. Then his mother cried
A little, and his father boasted how
He'd let him go, though needed for the farm.

Likely in Egypt he would find out something
About himself, if flies and drunkenness
And deadly heat could tell him much—until
In his first battle a shell splinter caught him.

So crown him with memorial bronze among
The older dead, child of a mountainous island.[1]
Wings of a tarnished victory shadow him
Who born of silence has burned back to silence.

The Homecoming

Odysseus has come home, to the gully farm
Where the macrocarpa[2] windbreak shields a house
Heavy with time's reliques—the brown-filmed photographs
Of ghosts more real than he; the mankind-measuring arm
Of a pendulum clock; and true yet to her vows,
His mother, grief's Penelope.[3] At the blind the sea wind laughs.

The siege more long and terrible than Troy's
Begins again. A Love demanding all,
Hypochondriacal, sea-dark and contentless:
This was the sour ground that nurtured a boy's
Dream of freedom; this, in Circe's hall[4]
Drugged him; his homecoming finds this, more relentless.

---

1   i.e., New Zealand
2   an evergreen tree, widely cultivated as a windbreak
3   wife of Odysseus, who waited twenty years for his return from the siege of Troy
4   Circe was the enchantress who used magic potions to keep Odysseus and his men on
     her island; only Odysseus, fortified by a special herb, was able to resist her.

She does not say, 'You have changed'; nor could she imagine any
Otherwise to the quiet maelstrom spinning
In the circle of their days. Still she would wish to carry
Him folded within her, shut from the wild and many
Voices of life's combat, in the cage of beginning;
She counts it natural that he should never marry.

She will cook his meals; complain of the south weather
That wrings her joints. And he—rebels; and yields
To the old covenant— calms the bleating
Ewe in birth travail. The smell of saddle leather
His sacrament; or the sale day drink; yet hears beyond sparse
       fields
On reef and cave the sea's hexameter beating.

My love late walking

My love late walking in the rain's white aisles
I break words for, though many tongues
Of night deride and the moon's boneyard smile

Cuts to the quick our newborn sprig of song.
See and believe, my love, the late yield
Of bright grain, the sparks of harvest wrung

From difficult joy. My heart is an open field.
There you may stray wide or stand at home
Nor dread the giant's bone and broken shield

Or any tendril locked on a thunder stone,
Nor fear, in the forked grain, my hawk who flies
Down to your feathered sleep alone

Striding blood coloured on a wind of sighs.
Let him at the heart of your true dream move,
My love, in the lairs of hope behind your eyes.

I sing, to the rain's harp, of light renewed,
The black tares broken, fresh the phoenix[1] light
I lost among time's rags and burning tombs.

My love walks long in harvest aisles tonight.

---

1   The phoenix was a mythical bird that rose anew every thousand years out of the ashes
     of its own funeral pyre.

Phyllis Webb

(b. 1927)

A Tall Tale

The whale, improbable as lust,
carved out a cave
for the seagirl's rest;
with rest the seagirl, sweet as dust, devised
a manner for the whale
to lie between her thighs.
Like this they lay
within the shadowed cave[1]
under the waters, under the waters wise,
and nested there, and nested there and stayed,
this coldest whale aslant the seagirl's thighs.

Two hundred years perhaps swam by them there
before the cunning waters so distilled the pair
they turned to brutal artifacts of stone
polished, O petrified prisoners of their lair.
And thus, with quiet, submerged in deathly calm.
the two disclosed a future geologic long,
lying cold, whale to thigh revealed
the secret of their comfort
to the marine weeds,
to fish, to shell, sand, sediment and wave,
to the broken, dying sun
which probed their ocean grave.
These, whale and seagirl, stone gods,
stone lust, stone grief,
interred on the sedimented sand
amongst the orange starfish.
these cold and stony mariners
invoked the moral snail
and in sepulchral voice intoned a moral tale:

"Under the waters, under the waters wise,
all loving flesh will quickly meet demise,
the cave, the shadow cave is nowhere wholly safe
and even the oddest couple can scarcely find relief:
appear then to submit to this tide and timing sea,
but secrete a skillful shell and stone and perfect be."

---

1   In the *Republic*, Book VII, Plato describes the men who live in a cavern, and who see
only the shadows of real objects projected by a bright fire on the cavern's inner walls.

Patience

Patience is the wideness of the night
the simple pain of stars
the muffled explosion of velvet
it moves itself generally
through particulars
accepts the telling of time
without day's relativity.

But more than these accommodations
patience is love withdrawn
into the well; immersion into
a deep place where green begins.
It is the slow beat of slanting eyes
down the heart's years,
it is the silencer
and the loving now
involves no word.
Patience is the answer
poised in grief—the knowing—
it is the prose of tears
withheld and the aging,
the history in the heart
and futures where pain
is a lucid cargo.

Marvell's Garden[1]

Marvell's garden, that place of solitude,
is not where I'd choose to live
yet is the fixed sundial
that turns me round
unwillingly
in a hot glade
as closer, closer I come to contradiction,
to the shade green within the green shade.

The garden where Marvell scorned love's solicitude—
that dream—and played instead an arcane solitaire,
shuffling his thoughts like shadowy chance
across the shrubs of ecstasy,
and cast the myths away to flowering hours
as yes, his mind, that sea, caught at green
thoughts shadowing a green infinity.

---

1   Andrew Marvell (1621-1678), author of "The Garden" (see above, p.83). Webb alludes
here to a number of details in Marvell's poem.

And yet Marvell's garden was not Plato's
garden—and yet—he *did* care more for the form
of things than for the thing itself—
ideas and visions,
resemblances and echoes,
things seeming and being
not quite what they were.

That was his garden, a kind of attitude
struck out of an earth too carefully attended,
wanting to be left alone.
And I don't blame him for that.
God knows, too many fences fence us out
and his garden closed in on Paradise.

On Paradise! When I think of his hymning
Puritans in the Bermudas, the bright oranges[1]
lighting up that night! When I recall
his rustling tinsel hopes
beneath the cold decree of steel,
Oh, I have wept for some new convulsion
to tear together this world and his.

But then I saw his luminous plumèd Wings
prepared for flight,
and then I heard him singing glory
in a green tree,
and then I caught the vest he'd laid aside
all blest with fire.

And I have gone walking slowly in
his garden of necessity
leaving brothers, lovers, Christ
outside my walls
where they have wept without
and I within.

Breaking

Give us wholeness, for we are broken.
But who are we asking, and why do we ask?
Destructive element heaves close to home,
our years of work broken against a breakwater.

---

1   The reference here is to Marvell's poem "Bermudas."

Shattered gods, self-iconoclasts,
it is with Lazarus[1] unattended we belong
(the fall of the sparrow is unbroken song).
The crucifix has clattered to the ground,
the living Christ has spent a year in Paris,
travelled on the Metro, fallen in the Seine.
We would not raise our silly gods again.
Stigmata sting, they suddenly appear
on every blessed person everywhere.
If there is agitation there is cause.

Ophelia, Hamlet, Othello, Lear,
Kit Smart,[2] William Blake, John Clare.[3]
Van Gogh.[4] Henry IV of Pirandello,[5]
Gerard de Nerval,[6] Antonin Artaud[7]
bear a crown of darkness.
It is better so.

Responsible now each to his own attack,
we are bequeathed their ethos and our death.
Greek marble white and whiter grows
breaking into history of a west.
If we could stand so virtuously white
crumbling in the terrible Grecian light.

There is a justice in destruction.
It isn't "isn't fair".
A madhouse is designed for the insane,
a hospital for wounds that will re-open,
a war is architecture for aggression,
and Christ's stigmata body-minted token.
What are we whole or beautiful or good for but to be absolutely
          broken?

---

1   See John 11 for the story of the death and resurrection of Lazarus.
2   Christopher Smart (1722-1771), an English poet who struggled with bouts of mental illness; author of *Jubilate Agno* (see above, p. 136).
3   English rustic poet (1793-1864), who spent much of his life in a mental asylum.
4   Vincent Van Gogh (1853-1890), Dutch painter, who struggled with poverty and mental illness, and eventually committed suicide.
5   Luigi Pirandello (1867-1936), Italian novelist and dramatist, author of the play *Henri IV* (1922), whose protagonist spends most of his life in a mental asylum.
6   French author of prose and verse (1808-1855), whose death may have been caused by suicide.
7   French actor and director (1896-1948), noted for his promotion of a "Theatre of Cruelty."

Anne Sexton

(1928-1974)

Her Kind

I have gone out, a possessed witch,
haunting the black air, braver at night;
dreaming evil, I have done my hitch
over the plain houses, light by light:
lonely thing, twelve-fingered, out of mind.
A woman like that is not a woman, quite.
I have been her kind.

I have found the warm caves in the woods,
filled them with skillets, carvings, shelves,
closets, silks, innumerable goods;
fixed the suppers for the worms and the elves:
whining, rearranging the disaligned.
A woman like that is misunderstood.
I have been her kind.

I have ridden in your cart, driver,
waved my nude arms at villages going by,
learning the last bright routes, survivor
where your flames still bite my thigh
and my ribs crack where your wheels wind.
A woman like that is not ashamed to die.
I have been her kind.

In the Deep Museum

My God, my God, what queer corner am I in?
Didn't I die, blood running down the post,
lungs gagging for air, die there for the sin
of anyone, my sour mouth giving up the ghost?
Surely my body is done? Surely I died?
And yet, I know, I'm here. What place is this?
Cold and queer, I sting with life. I lied.
Yes, I lied. Or else in some damned cowardice
my body would not give me up. I touch
fine cloth with my hands and my cheeks are cold.
If this is hell, then hell could not be much,
neither as special nor as ugly as I was told.

What's that I hear, snuffling and pawing its way
toward me? Its tongue knocks a pebble out of place
as it slides in, a sovereign. How can I pray?
It is panting; it is an odor with a face
like the skin of a donkey. It laps my sores.
It is hurt, I think, as I touch its little head.
It bleeds. I have forgiven murderers and whores

and now I must wait like old Jonah,[1] not dead
nor alive, stroking a clumsy animal. A rat.
His teeth test me; he waits like a good cook,
knowing his own ground. I forgive him that,
as I forgave my Judas[2] the money he took.

Now I hold his soft red sore to my lips
as his brothers crowd in, hairy angels who take
my gift. My ankles are a flute. I lose hips
and wrists. For three days, for love's sake,
I bless this other death. Oh, not in air—
in dirt. Under the rotting veins of its roots,
under the markets, under the sheep bed where
the hill is food, under the slippery fruits
of the vineyard, I go. Unto the bellies and jaws
of rats I commit my prophecy and fear.
Far below The Cross, I correct its flaws.
We have kept the miracle. I will not be here.

Cinderella

You always read about it:
the plumber with twelve children
who wins the Irish Sweepstakes.
From toilets to riches.
That story.

Or the nursemaid,
some luscious sweet from Denmark
who captures the oldest son's heart.
From diapers to Dior.
That story.

Or a milkman who serves the wealthy,
eggs, cream, butter, yogurt, milk,
the white truck like an ambulance
who goes into real estate
and makes a pile.
From homogenized to martinis at lunch.

Or the charwoman
who is on the bus when it cracks up
and collects enough from the insurance.
From mops to Bonwit Teller.[3]

---

1   See the Book of Jonah 4.
2   the disciple who betrayed Christ to the Romans for 30 pieces of silver; see Matthew 26.15.
3   an expensive women's clothing store in New York City

That story.

Once
the wife of a rich man was on her deathbed
and she said to her daughter Cinderella:
Be devout. Be good. Then I will smile
down from heaven in the seam of a cloud.
The man took another wife who had
two daughters, pretty enough
but with hearts like blackjacks.
Cinderella was their maid.
She slept on the sooty hearth each night
and walked around looking like Al Jolson.[1]
Her father brought presents home from town,
jewels and gowns for the other women
but the twig of a tree for Cinderella.
She planted that twig on her mother's grave
and it grew to a tree where a white dove sat.
Whenever she wished for anything the dove
would drop it like an egg upon the ground.
The bird is important, my dears, so heed him.

Next came the ball, as you all know.
It was a marriage market.
The prince was looking for a wife.
All but Cinderella were preparing
and gussying up for the big event.
Cinderella begged to go too.
Her stepmother threw a dish of lentils
into the cinders and said: Pick them
up in an hour and you shall go.
The white dove brought all his friends;
all the warm wings of the fatherland came,
and picked up the lentils in a jiffy.
No, Cinderella, said the stepmother,
you have no clothes and cannot dance.
That's the way with stepmothers.

Cinderella went to the tree at the grave
and cried forth like a gospel singer:
Mama! Mama! My turtledove,
send me to the prince's ball!
The bird dropped down a golden dress
and delicate little gold slippers.
Rather a large package for a simple bird.
So she went. Which is no surprise.

---

1   Al Jolson (1886-1950), American singer and entertainer best known for his routines in
black-face makeup

Her stepmother and sisters didn't
recognize her without her cinder face
and the prince took her hand on the spot
and danced with no other the whole day.

As nightfall came she thought she'd better
get home. The prince walked her home
and she disappeared into the pigeon house
and although the prince took an axe and broke
it open she was gone. Back to her cinders.
These events repeated themselves for three days.
However on the third day the prince
covered the palace steps with cobbler's wax[1]
and Cinderella's gold shoe stuck upon it.
Now he would find whom the shoe fit
and find his strange dancing girl for keeps.
He went to their house and the two sisters
were delighted because they had lovely feet.
The eldest went into a room to try the slipper on
but her big toe got in the way so she simply
sliced it off and put on the slipper.
The prince rode away with her until the white dove
told him to look at the blood pouring forth.
That is the way with amputations.
They don't just heal up like a wish.
The other sister cut off her heel
but the blood told as blood will.
The prince was getting tired.
He began to feel like a shoe salesman.
But he gave it one last try.
This time Cinderella fit into the shoe
like a love letter into its envelope.

At the wedding ceremony
the two sisters came to curry favor
and the white dove pecked their eyes out.
Two hollow spots were left
like soup spoons.

Cinderella and the prince
lived, they say, happily ever after,
like two dolls in a museum case
never bothered by diapers or dust,
never arguing over the timing of an egg,
never telling the same story twice,
never getting a middle-aged spread,

---

1   a resinous substance used by shoe-makers for rubbing their thread

their darling smiles pasted on for eternity.
Regular Bobbsey Twins.[1]
That story.

---

1   Characters in a series of children's stories by "Laura Lee Hope," the pseudonym of a
collective of American authors, notably Edward L. Stratemeyer (1862-1930).

Maya Angelou

(b. 1928)

Caged Bird

A free bird leaps
on the back of the wind
and floats downstream
till the current ends
and dips his wing
in the orange sun rays
and dares to claim the sky.

But a bird that stalks
down his narrow cage
can seldom see through
his bars of rage
his wings are clipped and
his feet are tied
so he opens his throat to sing.

The caged bird sings
with a fearful trill
of things unknown
but longed for still
and his tune is heard
on the distant hill
for the caged bird
sings of freedom.

The free bird thinks of another breeze
and the trade winds soft through the sighing trees
and the fat worms waiting on a dawn-bright lawn
and he names the sky his own.

But a caged bird stands on the grave of dreams
his shadow shouts on a nightmare scream
his wings are clipped and his feet are tied
so he opens his throat to sing.

The caged bird sings
with a fearful trill
of things unknown
but longed for still
and his tune is heard
on the distant hill
for the caged bird
sings of freedom.

Our Grandmothers

She lay, skin down on the moist dirt,
the canebrake rustling
with the whispers of leaves, and
loud longing of hounds and
the ransack of hunters crackling the near branches.

She muttered, lifting her head a nod toward freedom,
I shall not, I shall not be moved.[1]

She gathered her babies,
their tears slick as oil on black faces,
their young eyes canvassing mornings of madness.
Momma, is Master going to sell you
from us tomorrow?

Yes.
Unless you keep walking more
and talking less.
Yes.
Unless the keeper of our lives
releases me from all commandments.
Yes.
And your lives,
never mine to live,
will be executed upon the killing floor of innocents.
Unless you match my heart and words,
saying with me,

I shall not be moved.

In Virginia tobacco fields,
leaning into the curve
on Steinway
pianos, along Arkansas roads,
in the red hills of Georgia,
into the palms of her chained hands, she
cried against calamity,
You have tried to destroy me
and though I perish daily,

I shall not be moved.

Her universe, often
summarized into one black body

---

1   Psalms 62.6; also the refrain to a well-known gospel song.

falling finally from the tree to her feet,
made her cry each time in a new voice.
All my past hastens to defeat,
and strangers claim the glory of my love,
Iniquity has bound me to his bed,

yet, I must not be moved.

She heard the names,
swirling ribbons in the wind of history:
nigger, nigger bitch, heifer,
mammy, property, creature, ape, baboon,
whore, hot tail, thing, it.
She said, But my description cannot
fit your tongue, for
I have a certain way of being in this world,
and I shall not, I shall not be moved.

No angel stretched protecting wings
above the heads of her children,
fluttering and urging the winds of reason
into the confusion of their lives.
They sprouted like young weeds,
but she could not shield their growth
from the grinding blades of ignorance, nor
shape them into symbolic topiaries.
She sent them away,
underground, overland, in coaches and
shoeless.
When you learn, teach.
When you get, give.
As for me,

I shall not be moved.

She stood in midocean, seeking dry land.
She searched God's face.
Assured,
she placed her fire of service
on the altar, and though
clothed in the finery of faith,
when she appeared at the temple door,
no sign welcomed
Black Grandmother. Enter here.

Into the crashing sound,
into wickedness, she cried,
No one, no, nor no one million
ones dare deny me God. I go forth
alone, and stand as ten thousand.

The Divine upon my right
impels me to pull forever
at the latch on Freedom's gate.

The Holy Spirit upon my left leads my
feet without ceasing into the camp of the
righteous and into the tents of the free.

These momma faces, lemon-yellow, plum-purple,
honey-brown, have grimaced and twisted
down a pyramid of years.
She is Sheba[1] and Sojourner,[2]
        Harriet and Zora,[3]
        Mary Bethune[4] and Angela,[5]
        Annie to Zenobia.[6]

She stands
before the abortion clinic,
confounded by the lack of choices.
In the Welfare line,
reduced to the pity of handouts.
Ordained in the pulpit, shielded
by the mysteries.
In the operating room,
husbanding life.
In the choir loft,
holding God in her throat.
On lonely street corners,
hawking her body.
In the classroom, loving the
children to understanding.

Centered on the world's stage,
she sings to her loves and beloveds,
to her foes and detractors:
However I am perceived and deceived,

---

1 The Queen of Sheba, who visited King Solomon to test his wisdom (I Kings 10).
2 The pseudonym of a Black woman (c.1797-1883) born in New York State of slave parents.
   In 1843, after a period of domestic service, she took the name "Sojourner Truth," and
   entered a career of speaking for Black rights and women's suffrage.
3 Harriet Tubman (c.1820-1913), a former slave, helped set up the "underground railway"
   by means of which slaves might escape to Canada. Zora Neale Hurston (1891-1960) was
   a leading figure in the "Harlem Renaissance," the flowering of Black literature, music,
   and art in the 1920s and 1930s.
4 Mary McLeod Bethune (1875-1955) established the first secondary school for Black
   students, which later became Bethune-Cookman College in Daytona, Florida. Bethune was
   also the first Black woman to serve as a Presidential advisor, during the Roosevelt
   administration.
5 Possibly a reference to Angela Davis, the Black activist known for her work on California
   college campuses in the 1960s.
6 i.e., A to Z

however my ignorance and conceits,
lay aside your fears that I will be undone,

for I shall not be moved.

Adrienne Rich

(b. 1929)

Aunt Jennifer's Tigers

Aunt Jennifer's tigers prance across a screen,
Bright topaz denizens of a world of green.
They do not fear the men beneath the tree;
They pace in sleek chivalric certainty.

Aunt Jennifer's fingers fluttering through her wool
Find even the ivory needle hard to pull.
The massive weight of Uncle's wedding band
Sits heavily upon Aunt Jennifer's hand.

When Aunt is dead, her terrified hands will lie
Still ringed with ordeals she was mastered by.
The tigers in the panel that she made
Will go on prancing, proud and unafraid.

Planetarium

*Thinking of Caroline Herschel (1750–1848)[1]
astronomer, sister of William; and others.*

A woman in the shape of a monster
a monster in the shape of a woman
the skies are full of them

a woman   'in the snow
among the Clocks and instruments
or measuring the ground with poles'

in her 98 years to discover
8 comets

she whom the moon ruled
like us
levitating into the night sky
riding the polished lenses

Galaxies of women, there
doing penance for impetuousness
ribs chilled
in those spaces   of the mind

---

1   Caroline Herschel, usually remembered as sister to the English astronomer William
    Herschel (1738-1822), was an important astronomer in her own right, and published a
    star catalogue in 1848.

An eye,

      'virile, precise and absolutely certain'
from the mad webs of Uranusborg[1]

                                 encountering the NOVA[2]

every impulse of light exploding
from the core
as life flies out of us

      Tycho whispering at last
      'Let me not seem to have lived in vain'

What we see, we see
and seeing is changing

the light that shrivels a mountain
and leaves a man alive

Heartbeat of the pulsar
heart sweating through my body

The radio impulse
pouring in from Taurus[3]

      I am bombarded yet   I stand

I have been standing all my life in the
direct path of a battery of signals
the most accurately transmitted most
untranslatable language in the universe
I am a galactic cloud so deep   so invo-
luted that a light wave could take 15
years to travel through me And has
taken   I am an instrument in the shape
of a woman trying to translate pulsations
into images   for the relief of the body
and the reconstruction of the mind.

---

1   The Danish astronomer Tycho Brahe (1546-1601) built an observatory called Uranienborg
     on Hven Island in Sweden.
2   A new star, discovered by Brahe in 1573. A nova is also a star that suddenly flares up,
     then fades after a few weeks or months.
3   the constellation of the Bull

Orion[1]

Far back when I went zig-zagging
through tamarack pastures
you were my genius, you
my cast-iron Viking, my helmed
lion-heart king in prison.[2]
Years later now you're young

my fierce half-brother, staring
down from that simplified west
your breast open, your belt dragged down
by an oldfashioned thing, a sword
the last bravado you won't give over
though it weighs you down as you stride

and the stars in it are dim
and maybe have stopped burning.
But you burn, and I know it;
as I throw back my head to take you in
an old transfusion happens again:
divine astronomy is nothing to it.

Indoors I bruise and blunder,
break faith, leave ill enough
alone, a dead child born in the dark.
Night cracks up over the chimney,
pieces of time, frozen geodes[3]
come showering down in the grate.

A man reaches behind my eyes
and finds them empty
a woman's head turns away
from my head in the mirror
children are dying my death
and eating crumbs of my life.

Pity is not your forte.
Calmly you ache up there
pinned aloft in your crow's nest,
my speechless pirate!
You take it all for granted
and when I look you back

---

1   The constellation named after the hunter Orion, who is depicted with belt and sword.
2   An allusion to King Richard I of England (1157-1199), known as "Richard the Lion-
       Hearted," who was imprisoned in Austria on his way home from the Crusades.
3   rocks with hollow, crystal-lined centres

it's with a starlike eye
shooting its cold and egotistical spear
where it can do least damage.
Breathe deep! No hurt, no pardon
out here in the cold with you
you with your back to the wall.

A Valediction Forbidding Mourning[1]

My swirling wants. Your frozen lips.
The grammar turned and attacked me.
Themes, written under duress.
Emptiness of the notations.

They gave me a drug that slowed the healing of wounds.
I want you to see this before I leave:
the experience of repetition as death
the failure of criticism to locate the pain
the poster in the bus that said:
my bleeding is under control.

A red plant in a cemetery of plastic wreaths.

A last attempt: the language is a dialect called metaphor.
These images go unglossed: hair, glacier, flashlight.
When I think of a landscape I am thinking of a time.
When I talk of taking a trip I mean forever.
I could say: those mountains have a meaning
but further than that I could not say.

To do something very common, in my own way.

Final Notations

it will not be simple, it will not be long
it will take little time, it will take all your thought
it will take all your heart, it will take all your breath
it will be short, it will not be simple

it will touch through your ribs, it will take all your heart
it will not be long, it will occupy your thought
as a city is occupied, as a bed is occupied
it will take all your flesh, it will not be simple

---

1   The title of a poem by John Donne (see p. 42 above)

You are coming into us who cannot withstand you
you are coming into us who never wanted to withstand you
you are taking parts of us into places never planned
you are going far away with pieces of our lives

it will be short, it will take all your breath
it will not be simple, it will become your will

Peter Porter

(b. 1929)

Sydney Cove, 1788[1]

The Governor[2] loves to go mapping—round and round
The inlets of the Harbour in his pinnace.
He fingers a tree-fern, sniffs the ground

And hymns it with a unison of feet—
We march to church and executions. No one,
Even Banks,[3] could match the flora of our fleet.

Grog from Madeira[4] reminds us most of home,
More than the pork and British weevils[5] do.
On a diet of flour, your hair comes out in your comb.

A seaman who tried to lie with a native girl
Ran off when he smelt her fatty hide.
Some say these oysters are the sort for pearls.

Green shoots of the Governor's wheat have browned.
A box of bibles was washed up today,
The chaplain gave them to two Methodists. Ross found

A convict selling a baby for a jug of rum.
Those black hills which wrestle with
The rain are called Blue Mountains. Come

Genocide or Jesus we can't work this land.
The sun has framed it for our moralists
To dry the bones of forgers in the sand.

We wake in the oven of its cloudless sky,
Already the blood-encircled sun is up.
Mad sharks swim in the convenient sea.

The Governor says we mustn't land a man
Or woman with gonorrhoea. Sound felons only
May leave their bodies in a hangman's land.

Where all is novel, the only rule's explore.
Amelia Levy and Elizabeth Fowles spent the night
With Corporal Plowman and Corporal Winxstead for

---

1 The first British ships with convict settlers arrived in Sydney Cove in 1788.
2 Arthur Phillips, Governor 1788-1792
3 Joseph Banks, who accompanied Captain Cook on his voyage to the South Pacific in
  1768-70, was a scientific observer representing the British Royal Society.
4 rum from Madeira, a group of Portuguese islands west of Morocco
5 small beetles

PETER PORTER

A shirt apiece. These are our home concerns.
The cantor curlew sings the surf asleep.
The moon inducts the lovers in the ferns.

Annotations of Auschwitz[1]

1

When the burnt flesh is finally at rest,
The fires in the asylum grates will come up
And wicks turn down to darkness in the madman's eyes.

2

My suit is hairy, my carpet smells of death,
My toothbrush handle grows a cuticle.
I have six million foulnesses of breath.
Am I mad? The doctor holds my testicles
While the room fills with the zyklon B[2] I cough.

3

On Piccadilly underground I fall asleep—
I shuffle with the naked to the steel door,
Now I am only ten from the front—I wake up—
We are past Gloucester Rd,[3] I am not a Jew,
But scratches web the ceiling of the train.

4

Around staring buildings the pale flowers grow;
The frenetic butterfly, the bee made free by work,
Rouse and rape the pollen pads, the nectar stoops.
The rusting railway ends here. The blind end in Europe's gut.
Touch one piece of unstrung barbed wire—
Let it taste blood: let one man scream in pain,
Death's Botanical Gardens can flower again.

5

A man eating his dressing in the hospital
Is lied to by his stomach. It's a final feast to him

---

1   Auschwitz, a town in south-west Poland, was the site of one of the most notorious Nazi
      death camps during World War II.
2   the poison gas used by the Nazis in murdering concentration-camp prisoners
3   a stop on the Piccadilly Line of the London Underground

Of beef, blood pudding and black bread.
The orderly can't bear to see this mimic face
With its prim accusing picture after death.
On the stiff square a thousand bodies
Dig up useless ground—he hates them all,
These lives ignoble as ungoverned glands.
They fatten in statistics everywhere
And with their sick, unkillable fear of death
They crowd out peace from executioners' sleep.

6

Forty thousand bald men drowning in a stream—
The like of light on all those bobbing skulls
Has never been seen before. Such death, says the painter,
Is worthwhile—it makes a colour never known.
It makes a sight that's unimagined, says the poet.
It's nothing to do with me, says the man who hates
The poet and the painter. Six million deaths can hardly
Occur at once. What do they make? Perhaps
An idiot's normalcy. I need never feel afraid
When I salt the puny snail—cruelty's grown up
And waits for time and men to bring into its hands
The snail's adagio and all the taunting life
Which has not cared about or guessed its tortured scope.

7

London is full of chickens on electric spits,
    Cooking in windows where the public pass.
This, say the chickens, is their Auschwitz,
    And all poultry eaters are psychopaths.

Soliloquy at Potsdam[1]

There are always the poor[2]—
Getting themselves born in crowded houses,
Feeding on the parish,[3] losing their teeth early
And learning to dodge blows, getting
Strong bodies—cases for the warped nut of the mind.
The masterful cat-o'-nine-tails, the merciful
Discipline of the hours of drill[4]—better

---

1   Frederick II of Prussia, known as "Frederick the Great" (1712-1786) built the palace of
     Sans Souci at Potsdam, a small town near Berlin.
2   "For the poor always ye have with you" (John 12.8).
3   i.e., relying on local charity for their food
4   Frederick was a keen soldier.

Than being poor in crowded Europe, the swan-swept
Waters where the faces dredge for bread
And the soggy dead are robbed on their way to the grave.
I can hear it from this window, the musket-drill
On the barrack square. Later today I'll visit
The punishment block. Who else in Europe
Could take these verminous, clutching creatures
And break them into men? What of the shredded back
And the broken pelvis, when the side-drum sounds,
When the uniformed wave tilts and overwhelms
The cheese-trading burghers' world, the aldermanic
Principalities. The reformers sit at my table,
They talk well but they've never seen a battle
Or watched the formed brain in the flogged body
Marching to death on a bellyful of soup and orders.
There has to be misery so there can be discipline.
People will have to die because I cannot bear
Their clinging to life. Why are the best trumpeters
Always French? Watch the west, the watershed
Of revolution. Now back to Quantz.[1] I like to think
That in an afternoon of three sonatas
A hundred regiments have marched more miles
Than lie between here and Vienna and not once
Has a man broken step. Who would be loved
If he could be feared and hated, yet still
Enjoy his lust, eat well and play the flute?

An Australian Garden

for Sally Lehmann

Here we enact the opening of the world
And everything that lives shall have a name
To show its heart; there shall be Migrants,
Old Believers, Sure Retainers; the cold rose
Exclaim perfection to the gangling weeds,
The path lead nowhere—this is like entering
One's self, to find the map of death
Laid out untidily, a satyr's grin
Signalling 'You are here': tomorrow
They are replanting the old court,
Puss may be banished from the sun-warmed stone.

See how our once-lived lives stay on to haunt us,
The flayed beautiful limbs of childhood

---

1   Johann Joachim Quantz (1697-1773), a German composer and flute virtuoso; he was
Frederick's flute teacher, and composed about 300 concertos for him.

In the bole and branches of a great angophora¹—
Here we can climb and sit on memory
And hear the words which death was making ready
From the start. Such talking as the trees attempt
Is a lesson in perfectability. It stuns
The currawongs² along the breaks of blue—
Their lookout cries have guarded Paradise
Since the expulsion of the heart, when man,
Bereft of joy, turned his red hand to gardens.

Spoiled Refugees nestle near Great Natives;
A chorus of winds stirs the pagoda'd stamens:
In this hierarchy of miniatures
Someone is always leaving for the mountains,
Civil servant ants are sure the universe
Stops at the hard hibiscus; the sun is drying
A beleaguered snail and the hydra-headed
Sunflowers wave like lights. If God were to plant
Out all His hopes, He'd have to make two more
Unknown Lovers, ready to find themselves
In innocence, under the weight of His green ban.

In the afternoon we change—an afterthought,
Those deeper greens which join the stalking shadows—
The lighter wattles³ look like men of taste
With a few well-tied leaves to brummel-up⁴
Their poise. Berries dance in a southerly wind
And the garden tide has turned. Dark on dark.
Janus⁵ leaves are opening to the moon
Which makes its own grave roses. Old Man
Camellias root down to keep the sun intact,
The act is canopied with stars. A green sea
Rages through the landscape all the night.

We will not die at once. Nondescript pinks
Survive the death of light and over-refined
Japanese petals bear the weight of dawn's first
Insect. An eye makes damask on the dew.
Time for strangers to accustom themselves
To habitat. What should it be but love?
The transformations have been all to help
Unmagical creatures find their proper skins,
The virgin and the leonine. The past's a warning

1   a tree in eastern Australia, with vase-like fruits
2   magpie-like Australian birds with ringing calls
3   Australian species of acacia plant
4   Australian slang for dress up, probably derived from the name of George "Beau" Brummel
     (1778-1840), a noted English dandy
5   a Roman deity represented with two heads looking in opposite directions

That the force of joy is quite unswervable—
'Out of this wood do not desire to go'.[1]

In the sun, which is the garden's moon, the barefoot
Girl espies her monster, all his lovely specialty
Like hairs about his heart. The dream is always
Midday and the two inheritors are made
Proprietors. They have multiplied the sky.
Where is the water, where the terraces, the Tritons[2]
And the cataracts of moss? This is Australia
And the villas are laid out inside their eyes:
It would be easy to unimagine everything,
Only the pressure made by love and death
Holds up the bodies which this Eden grows.

---

1   from Shakespeare's *A Midsummer Night's Dream* III.i.159
2   sea-gods, sons of Poseidon and Amphitrite, human to the waist with a dolphin's tail below;
     usually shown blowing through a sea-shell

Derek Walcott

(b. 1930)

A Far Cry from Africa

A wind is ruffling the tawny pelt
Of Africa. Kikuyu,[1] quick as flies,
Batten upon the bloodstreams of the veldt.
Corpses are scattered through a paradise.
Only the worm, colonel of carrion, cries:
"Waste no compassion on these separate dead!"
Statistics justify and scholars seize
The salients of colonial policy.
What is that to the white child hacked in bed?
To savages, expendable as Jews?

Threshed out by beaters, the long rushes break
In a white dust of ibises whose cries
Have wheeled since civilization's dawn
From the parched river or beast-teeming plain.
The violence of beast on beast is read
As natural law, but upright man
Seeks his divinity by inflicting pain.
Delirious as these worried beasts, his wars
Dance to the tightened carcass of a drum,
While he calls courage still that native dread
Of the white peace contracted by the dead.

Again brutish necessity wipes its hands
Upon the napkin of a dirty cause, again
A waste of our compassion, as with Spain,[2]
The gorilla wrestles with the superman.
I who am poisoned with the blood of both,
Where shall I turn, divided to the vein?
I who have cursed
The drunken officer of British rule, how choose
Between this Africa and the English tongue I love?
Betray them both, or give back what they give?
How can I face such slaughter and be cool?
How can I turn from Africa and live?

---

1   members of a Bantu tribe of East Africa, who fought against British settlers in Kenya
2   A reference to the Spanish Civil War (1936-39), in which many left-wing idealists from
     Europe and North America fought and died: in vain, as it turned out, since the Fascists
     under Franco defeated the Republicans and took power.

Ruins of a Great House

*though our longest sun sets at right declensions and
makes but winter arches, it cannot be long before we
lie down in darkness, and have our light in ashes . . .*
                    —BROWNE, *Urn Burial*[1]

Stones only, the disjecta membra[2] of this Great House,
Whose moth-like girls are mixed with candledust,
Remain to file the lizard's dragonish claws.
The mouths of those gate cherubs shriek with stain;
Axle and coach wheel silted under the muck
Of cattle droppings.
                    Three crows flap for the trees
And settle, creaking the eucalyptus boughs.
A smell of dead limes quickens in the nose
The leprosy of empire.
                    "Farewell, green fields,
                    Farewell, ye happy groves!"[3]
Marble like Greece, like Faulkner's South[4] in stone,
Deciduous beauty prospered and is gone,
But where the lawn breaks in a rash of trees
A spade below dead leaves will ring the bone
Of some dead animal or human thing
Fallen from evil days, from evil times.[5]

It seems that the original crops were limes
Grown in the silt that clogs the river's skirt;
The imperious rakes[6] are gone, their bright girls gone,
The river flows, obliterating hurt.
I climbed a wall with the grille ironwork
Of exiled craftsmen protecting that great house
From guilt, perhaps, but not from the worm's rent
Nor from the padded cavalry of the mouse.
And when a wind shook in the limes I heard
What Kipling[7] heard, the death of a great empire, the abuse
Of ignorance by Bible and by sword.

A green lawn, broken by low walls of stone,
Dipped to the rivulet, and pacing, I thought next

---

1   In *Urn Burial*, Sir Thomas Browne (1605-1682) treats of funeral cerimonies, death, and
     immortality.
2   (Latin) fragments, scattered remains.
3   Compare "Farewell happy fields / Where joy forever dwells" (*Paradise Lost* I, 249).
4   i.e., the American South created in the novels of William Faulkner (1897-1962)
5   ". . . though fall'n on evil days, / On evil days though fall'n. . . ." (*Paradise Lost*, VII,
     25).
6   dissolute men
7   Rudyard Kipling (1865-1936), English author and poet. See his poem "Recessional," p. 392
     above.

Of men like Hawkins, Walter Raleigh, Drake,[1]
Ancestral murderers and poets, more perplexed
In memory now by every ulcerous crime.
The world's green age then was a rotting lime
Whose stench became the charnel galleon's text.[2]
The rot remains with us, the men are gone.
But, as dead ash is lifted in a wind
That fans the blackening ember of the mind,
My eyes burned from the ashen prose of Donne.

Ablaze with rage I thought,
Some slave is rotting in this manorial lake,
But still the coal of my compassion fought
That Albion[3] too was once
A colony like ours, "part of the continent, piece of the main,"[4]
Nook-shotten, rook o'erblown, deranged
By foaming channels and the vain expense
Of bitter faction.
           All in compassion ends
So differently from what the heart arranged:
"as well as if a manor of thy friend's . . ."

A Letter from Brooklyn

An old lady writes me in a spidery style,
Each character trembling, and I see a veined hand
Pellucid as paper, travelling on a skein
Of such frail thoughts its thread is often broken;
Or else the filament from which a phrase is hung
Dims to my sense, but caught, it shines like steel,
As touch a line and the whole web will feel.
She describes my father, yet I forget her face
More easily than my father's yearly dying;
Of her I remember small, buttoned boots and the place
She kept in our wooden church on those Sundays
Whenever her strength allowed;
Grey-haired, thin-voiced, perpetually bowed.

---

1   Hawkins, Walter Raleigh, and Drake were sixteenth-century British explorers and
     adventurers who, in the name of Queen Elizabeth I, opened the way to British political
     and mercantile conquest in the Caribbean and North America.
2   Many slaves died in the cramped holds of the galleons taking them to captivity.
3   an ancient name for Britain
4   a quotation from John Donne's "Devotions" XVII: "No man is an *Iland*, intire of it selfe;
     every man is a peece of the *Continent*, a part of the *maine*; if a *Clod* bee washed away by
     the Sea, *Europe* is the lesse, as well as if a *Promontorie* were, as well as if a *Mannor* of thy
     friends or of *thine owne* were...."

"I am Mable Rawlins," she writes, "and know both your parents";
He is dead, Miss Rawlins, but God bless your tense:
"Your father was a dutiful, honest,
Faithful, and useful person."
For such plain praise what fame is recompense?
"A horn-painter, he painted delicately on horn,
He used to sit around the table and paint pictures."
The peace of God needs nothing to adorn
It, nor glory nor ambition.
"He is twenty-eight years buried," she writes, "he was called
                                                            home,
And is, I am sure, doing greater work."
The strength of one frail hand in a dim room
Somewhere in Brooklyn, patient and assured,
Restores my sacred duty to the Word.
"Home, home," she can write, with such short time to live,
Alone as she spins the blessings of her years;
Not withered of beauty if she can bring such tears,
Nor withdrawn from the world that breaks its lovers so;
Heaven is to her the place where painters go,
All who bring beauty on frail shell or horn,
There was all made, thence their *lux-mundi*[1] drawn,
Drawn, drawn, till the thread is resilient steel,
Lost though it seems in darkening periods,
And there they return to do work that is God's.

So this old lady writes, and again I believe.
I believe it all, and for no man's death I grieve.

Map of Europe

Like Leonardo's[2] idea
Where landscapes open on a waterdrop
Or dragons crouch in stains,
My flaking wall, in the bright air,
Maps Europe with its veins.

On its limned window ledge
A beer can's gilded rim gleams like
Evening along a Canaletto[3] lake,
Or like that rocky hermitage
Where, in his cell of light, haggard Jerome[4]

---

1   light of the world; see Matthew 5.14, John 8.12
2   Leonardo da Vinci (1452-1519), Florentine painter, sculptor, and architect
3   Giovanni Antonio Canale (1697-1768), also called Canaletto, an Italian painter of landscapes
4   St. Jerome (c.340-420), one of the Latin Church Fathers

Prays that His kingdom come
To the far city.

The light creates its stillness. In its ring
Everything IS. A cracked coffee cup,
A broken loaf, a dented urn become
Themselves, as in Chardin,[1]
Or in beer-bright Vermeer,[2]
Not objects of our pity.

In it is no *lacrimae rerum*,[3]
No art. Only the gift
To see things as they are, halved by a darkness
From which they cannot shift.

The Sea Is History

Where are your monuments, your battles, martyrs?
Where is your tribal memory? Sirs,
in that grey vault. The sea. The sea
has locked them up. The sea is History.

First, there was the heaving oil,
heavy as chaos;
then, like a light at the end of a tunnel,

the lantern of a caravel,
and that was Genesis.
Then there were the packed cries,
the shit, the moaning:

Exodus.
Bone soldered by coral to bone,
mosaics
mantled by the benediction of the shark's shadow,

that was the Ark of the Covenant.[4]
Then came from the plucked wires
of sunlight on the sea floor

the plangent harps of the Babylonian[5] bondage,
as the white cowries clustered like manacles

---

1 Jean-Baptiste Simeon Chardin (1699-1779), a French painter of still-life
2 Jan Vermeer (1632-1675), a Dutch painter of interior scenes
3 (Latin) "the tears for things," tears wept for misfortune; a phrase in Virgil's *Aeneid* I, 462
4 the chest containing the tablets bearing the Ten Commandments
5 The Jews were captives in Babylonia, an ancient empire of Mesopotamia, from 597 B.C.
   until its conquest by Persia in 538 B.C.

on the drowned women,

and those were the ivory bracelets
of the Song of Solomon,
but the ocean kept turning blank pages

looking for History.
Then came the men with eyes heavy as anchors
who sank without tombs,

brigands who barbecued cattle,
leaving their charred ribs like palm leaves on the shore,
then the foaming, rabid maw

of the tidal wave swallowing Port Royal,[1]
and that was Jonah,[2]
but where is your Renaissance?

Sir, it is locked in them sea-sands
out there past the reef's moiling shelf,
where the men-o'-war floated down;

strop on these goggles, I'll guide you there myself.
It's all subtle and submarine,
through colonnades of coral,

past the gothic windows of sea-fans
to where the crusty grouper, onyx-eyed,
blinks, weighted by its jewels, like a bald queen;

and these groined caves with barnacles
pitted like stone
are our cathedrals,

and the furnace before the hurricanes:
Gomorrah.[3] Bones ground by windmills
into marl and cornmeal,

and that was Lamentations—
that was just Lamentations,
it was not History;

then came, like scum on the river's drying lip,

---

1   a town and naval station in Jamaica, destroyed by an earthquake in 1692
2   Jonah was swallowed by a "great fish," which flung him upon dry land three days later;
     see the Book of Jonah.
3   One of the two cities destroyed by God for their corruption and decadence; see Genesis
     18, 19.

the brown reeds of villages
mantling and congealing into towns,

and at evening, the midges' choirs,
and above them, the spires
lancing the side of God

as His son set, and that was the New Testament.

Then came the white sisters clapping
to the waves' progress,
and that was Emancipation—

jubilation, O jubilation—
vanishing swiftly
as the sea's lace dries in the sun,

but that was not History,
that was only faith,
and then each rock broke into its own nation;

then came the synod of flies,
then came the secretarial heron,
then came the bullfrog bellowing for a vote,
fireflies with bright ideas
and bats like jetting ambassadors
and the mantis,[1] like khaki police,

and the furred caterpillars of judges
examining each case closely,
and then in the dark ears of ferns

and in the salt chuckle of rocks
with their sea pools, there was the sound
like a rumour without any echo

of History, really beginning.

---

1   a species of insect

Menelaus[1]

Wood smoke smudges the sea.
A bonfire lowers its gaze.
Soon the sand is circled with ugly
ash. Well, there were days

when, through her smoke-grey
eyes, I saw the white trash that was
Helen: too worn-out to argue
with her Romany[2] ways.

That gypsy constancy,
wiry and hot, is gone;
firm hill and wavering sea
resettle in the sun.

I would not wish her curse
on any: that necks should spurt,
limbs hacked to driftwood, because
a wave hoists its frilled skirt.

I wade clear, chuckling shallows
without armour now, or cause,
and bend, letting the hollows
of cupped palms salt my scars.

Ten years. Wasted in quarrel
for sea-grey eyes. A whore's.
Under me, crusted in coral,
towers pass, and a small sea-horse.

---

1   King of Sparta and husband of Helen, the woman whose flight to Troy with Paris
    precipitated the ten-year Trojan War
2   gypsy

Ted Hughes

(b. 1930)

The Thought-Fox

I imagine this midnight moment's forest:
Something else is alive
Beside the clock's loneliness
And this blank page where my fingers move.

Through the window I see no star:
Something more near
Though deeper within darkness
Is entering the loneliness:

Cold, delicately as the dark snow
A fox's nose touches twig, leaf;
Two eyes serve a movement, that now
And again now, and now, and now

Sets neat prints into the snow
Between trees, and warily a lame
Shadow lags by stump and in hollow
Of a body that is bold to come

Across clearings, an eye,
A widening deepening greenness,
Brilliantly, concentratedly,
Coming about its own business

Till, with a sudden sharp hot stink of fox,
It enters the dark hole of the head.
The window is starless still; the clock ticks,
The page is printed.

Hawk Roosting

I sit in the top of the wood, my eyes closed.
Inaction, no falsifying dream
Between my hooked head and hooked feet:
Or in sleep rehearse perfect kills and eat.

The convenience of the high trees!
The air's buoyancy and the sun's ray
Are of advantage to me;
And the earth's face upward for my inspection.

My feet are locked upon the rough bark.
It took the whole of Creation
To produce my foot, my each feather:
Now I hold Creation in my foot

Or fly up, and revolve it all slowly—
I kill where I please because it is all mine.
There is no sophistry in my body:
My manners are tearing off heads—

The allotment of death.
For the one path of my flight is direct
Through the bones of the living.
No arguments assert my right:

The sun is behind me.
Nothing has changed since I began.
My eye has permitted no change.
I am going to keep things like this.

Pike

Pike, three inches long, perfect
Pike in all parts, green tigering the gold.
Killers from the egg: the malevolent aged grin.
They dance on the surface among the flies.

Or move, stunned by their own grandeur,
Over a bed of emerald, silhouette
Of submarine delicacy and horror.
A hundred feet long in their world.

In ponds, under the heat-struck lily pads—
Gloom of their stillness:
Logged on last year's black leaves, watching upwards.
Or hung in an amber cavern of weeds

The jaws' hooked clamp and fangs
Not to be changed at this date;
A life subdued to its instrument;
The gills kneading quietly, and the pectorals.

Three we kept behind glass,
Jungled in weed: three inches, four,
And four and a half: fed fry to them—
Suddenly there were two. Finally one.

With a sag belly and the grin it was born with.
And indeed they spare nobody.
Two, six pounds each, over two feet long,
High and dry and dead in the willow-herb—

One jammed past its gills down the other's gullet:
The outside eye stared: as a vice locks—

The same iron in this eye
Though its film shrank in death.

A pond I fished, fifty yards across,
Whose lilies and muscular tench
Had outlasted every visible stone
Of the monastery that planted them—

Stilled legendary depth:
It was as deep as England. It held
Pike too immense to stir, so immense and old
That past nightfall I dared not cast

But silently cast and fished
With the hair frozen on my head
For what might move, for what eye might move.
The still splashes on the dark pond,

Owls hushing the floating woods
Frail on my ear against the dream
Darkness beneath night's darkness had freed,
That rose slowly towards me, watching.

The Jaguar

The apes yawn and adore their fleas in the sun.
The parrots shriek as if they were on fire, or strut
Like cheap tarts to attract the stroller with the nut.
Fatigued with indolence, tiger and lion

Lie still as the sun. The boa-constrictor's coil
Is a fossil. Cage after cage seems empty, or
Stinks of sleepers from the breathing straw.
It might be painted on a nursery wall.

But who runs like the rest past these arrives
At a cage where the crowd stands, stares, mesmerized,
As a child at a dream, at a jaguar hurrying enraged
Through prison darkness after the drills of his eyes

On a short fierce fuse. Not in boredom—
The eye satisfied to be blind in fire,
By the bang of blood in the brain deaf the ear—
He spins from the bars, but there's no cage to him

More than to the visionary his cell:
His stride is wildernesses of freedom:
The world rolls under the long thrust of his heel.
Over the cage floor the horizons come.

Second Glance at a Jaguar

Skinful of bowls, he bowls them,
The hip going in and out of joint, dropping the spine
With the urgency of his hurry
Like a cat going along under thrown stones, under cover,
Glancing sideways, running
Under his spine. A terrible, stump-legged waddle
Like a thick Aztec[1] disemboweller,
Club-swinging, trying to grind some square
Socket between his hind legs round,
Carrying his head like a brazier of spilling embers,
And the black bit of his mouth, he takes it
Between his back teeth, he has to wear his skin out,
He swipes a lap at the water-trough as he turns,
Swivelling the ball of his heel on the polished spot,
Showing his belly like a butterfly,
At every stride he has to turn a corner
In himself and correct it. His head
Is like the worn-down stump of another whole jaguar,
His body is just the engine shoving it forward,
Lifting the air up and shoving on under,
The weight of his fangs hanging the mouth open,
Bottom jaw combing the ground. A gorged look,
Gangster, club-tail lumped along behind gracelessly,
He's wearing himself to heavy ovals,
Muttering some mantra,[2] some drum-song of murder
To keep his rage brightening, making his skin
Intolerable, spurred by the rosettes, the cain-brands,
Wearing the spots off from the inside,
Rounding some revenge. Going like a prayer-wheel,[3]
The head dragging forward, the body keeping up,
The hind legs lagging. He coils, he flourishes
The blackjack tail as if looking for a target,
Hurrying through the underworld, soundless.

---

1 The Aztecs, a Central American people destroyed by the Spanish conquest of the 16th century, practiced human sacrifice.
2 Indian prayer or incantation
3 a cylinder with written prayers, used by the Buddhists of Tibet

Wodwo[1]

What am I? Nosing here, turning leaves over
Following a faint stain on the air to the river's edge
I enter water. What am I to split
The glassy grain of water looking upward I see the bed
Of the river above me upside down very clear
What am I doing here in mid-air? Why do I find
this frog so interesting as I inspect its most secret
interior and make it my own? Do these weeds
know me and name me to each other have they
seen me before, do I fit in their world? I seem
separate from the ground and not rooted but dropped
out of nothing casually I've no threads
fastening me to anything I can go anywhere
I seem to have been given the freedom
of this place what am I then? And picking
bits of bark off this rotten stump gives me
no pleasure and it's no use so why do I do it
me and doing that have coincided very queerly
But what shall I be called am I the first
have I an owner what shape am I what
shape am I am I huge if I go
to the end on this way past these trees and past these trees
till I get tired that's touching one wall of me
for the moment if I sit still how everything
stops to watch me I suppose I am the exact centre
but there's all this what is it roots
roots roots roots and here's the water
again very queer but I'll go on looking

---

1   The word is taken from the Middle English poem "Sir Gawain and the Green Knight,"
and means "wild man of the woods."

Edward Kamau Brathwaite

(b. 1930)

Wings of a Dove[1]

1

Brother Man the Rasta[2]
man, beard full of lichens
brain full of lice
watched the mice
come up through the floor-
boards of his down-
town, shanty-town kitchen,
and smiled. Blessed are the poor
in health, he mumbled,
that they should inherit this
wealth. Blessed are the meek
hearted, he grumbled,
for theirs is this stealth.

Brother Man the Rasta
man, hair full of lichens
head hot as ice
watched the mice
walk into his poor
hole, reached for his peace
and the pipe of his ganja
and smiled how the mice
eyes, hot pumice
pieces, glowed into his room
like ruby, like rhinestone
and suddenly startled like
diamond.

And I
Rastafar-I
in Babylon's[3] boom
town, crazed by the moon
and the peace of this chalice, I
prophet and singer, scourge
of the gutter, guardian
Trench Town, the Dungle and Young's
Town, rise and walk through the now silent

---

1   Compare Psalms 55.6: "Oh that I had wings like a dove!"
2   Rastafarians are members of a movement based in Jamaica that worships Hailie Selassie,
     the former Emperor of Ethiopia, and seeks a return to Africa by all black races.
3   Babylon was an ancient city of Mesopotamia, centre of the empire that took the Jews
     captive in the 6th century B.C.

streets of affliction, hawk's eyes
hard with fear, with
affection, and hear my people
cry, my people
shout:

Down down
white
man, con
man, brown
man, down
down full
man, frown-
ing fat
man, that
white black
man that
lives in
the town.

Rise rise
locks-
man,[1] Solo-
man[2] wise
man, rise
rise rise
leh we
laugh
dem, mock
dem, stop
dem, kill
dem an' go
back back
to the black
man lan'
back back
to Af-
rica.

2

Them doan mean it, yuh know,
them cahn help it
but them clean-face browns in
Babylon town is who I most fear

---

1   possibly a reference to the "dreadlocks" worn by Rastafarians
2   perhaps King Solomon, renowned for his judicial wisdom

an' who fears most I.
Watch de vulture dem a-fly-
in', hear de crow a-dem crow
see what them money a-buy?

Caw caw caw caw.
Ol' crow, ol' crow, cruel ol'
ol' crow, that's all them got
to show.

Crow fly flip flop
hip hop
pun de ground; na
feet feel firm

pun de firm stones; na
good pickney[1] born
from de flesh
o' dem bones;

naw naw naw naw.

3

So beat dem drums
dem, spread

dem wings dem,
watch dem fly

dem, soar dem
high dem,

clear in the glory of the Lord.

Watch dem ship dem
come to town dem

full o' silk dem
full o' food dem

an' dem 'plane dem
come to groun' dem

full o' flash dem

1　children

full o' cash dem

silk dem food dem
shoe dem wine dem

that dem drink dem
an' consume dem

praisin' the glory of the Lord.

So beat dem burn
dem, learn

dem that dem
got dem nothin'

but dem
bright bright baubles

that will burst dem
when the flame dem

from on high dem
raze an' roar dem

an' de poor dem
rise an' rage dem

in de glory of the Lord.

Calypso

1

The stone had skidded arc'd and bloomed into islands:
Cuba and San Domingo
Jamaica and Puerto Rico
Grenada Guadeloupe Bonaire

curved stone hissed into reef
wave teeth fanged into clay
white splash flashed into spray
Bathsheba Montego Bay

bloom of the arcing summers . . .

2

The islands roared into green plantations
ruled by silver sugar cane
sweat and profit
cutlass profit
islands ruled by sugar cane

And of course it was a wonderful time
a profitable hospitable well-worth-your-time
when captains carried receipts for rices
letters spices wigs
opera glasses swaggering asses
debtors vices pigs

O it was a wonderful time
an elegant benevolent redolent time—
and young Mrs. P.'s quick irrelevant crime
at four o'clock in the morning . . .

3

But what of black Sam
with the big splayed toes
and the shoe black shiny skin?

He carries bucketfulls of water
'cause his Ma's just had another daughter.

And what of John with the European name
who went to school and dreamt of fame
his boss one day called him a fool
and the boss hadn't even been to school . . .

4

Steel drum steel drum
hit the hot calypso dancing
hot rum hot rum
who goin' stop this bacchanalling?

For we glance the banjo
dance the limbo
grow our crops by maljo

have loose morals
gather corals
father our neighbour's quarrels

perhaps when they come
with their cameras and straw
hats: sacred pink tourists from the frozen Nawth

we should get down to those
white beaches
where if we don't wear breeches

it becomes an island dance
Some people doin' well
while others are catchin' hell

o the boss gave our Johnny the sack
though we beg him please
please to take 'im back

so the boy now nigratin' overseas . . .

Jay Macpherson

(b. 1931)

The Boatman

You might suppose it easy
For a maker[1] not too lazy
To convert the gentle reader to an Ark:
But it takes a willing pupil
To admit both gnat and camel[2]
—Quite an eyeful, all the crew that must embark.

After me when comes the deluge[3]
And you're looking round for refuge
From God's anger pouring down in gush and spout,
Then you take the tender creature
—You remember, that's the reader—
And you pull him through his navel inside out.

That's to get his beasts outside him,
For they've got to come aboard him,
As the best directions have it, two by two.
When you've taken all their tickets
And you've marched them through his sockets,
Let the tempest bust Creation: heed not you.

For you're riding high and mighty
In a gale that's pushing ninety
With a solid bottom under you—that's his.
Fellow flesh affords a rampart,
And you've got along for comfort
All the world there ever shall be, was, and is.

The Fisherman

The world was first a private park
Until the angel, after dark,
Scattered afar to wests and easts
The lovers and the friendly beasts.

And later still a home-made boat
contained Creation set afloat,

---

1 The word here carries both the sense of creator and the archaic meaning of poet (medieval "makar").
2 "Ye blind guides, which strain at a gnat, and swallow a camel" (Matthew 23.24).
3 Compare "Après nous le déluge," a saying popularly attributed to (among others) King Louis XV of France.

No rift nor leak that might betray
The creatures to a hostile day.

But now beside the midnight lake
One single fisher sits awake
And casts and fights and hauls to land
A myriad forms upon the sand.

Old Adam on the naming-day
Blessed each and let it slip away:
The fisher of the fallen mind
Sees no occasion to be kind,

But on his catch proceeds to sup;
Then bends, and at one slurp sucks up
The lake and all that therein is
To slake that hungry gut of his,

Then whistling makes for home and bed
As the last morning breaks in red;
But God the Lord with patient grin
Lets down his hook and hoicks him in.

A Lost Soul

Some are plain lucky—we ourselves among them:
Houses with books, with gardens, all we wanted,
Work we enjoy, with colleagues we feel close to—
        Love we have, even:

True love and candid, faithful, strong as gospel,
Patient, untiring, fond when we are fretful.
Having so much, how is it that we ache for
        Those darker others?

Some days for them we could let slip the whole damn
Soft bed we've made ourselves, our friends in Heaven
Let slip away, buy back with blood our ancient
        Vampires and demons.

First loves and oldest, what names shall I call you?
Older to me than language, old as breathing,
Born with me, in this flesh: by now I know you're
        Greed, pride and envy.

Too long I've shut you out, denied acquaintance,
Favoured less barefaced vices, hoped to pass for
Reasonable, rate with those who more inclined to
        Self-hurt than murder.

You were my soul: in arrogance I banned you.
Now I recant—return, possess me, take my
Hands, bind my eyes, infallibly restore my
    Share in perdition.

The Well

A winter hanging over the dark well,
My back turned to the sky,
To see if in that blackness something stirs,
Or glints, or winks an eye:

Or, from the bottom looking up, I see
Sky's white, my pupil head—
Lying with all that's lost, with all that shines
My winter with the dead:

A well of truth, of images, of words.
Low where Orion[1] lies
I watch the solstice pit become a stair,
The constellations rise.

---

1   a constellation named after the mythical Greek hunter Orion, and associated with stormy
weather

Sylvia Plath

(1932–1963)

The Colossus[1]

I shall never get you put together entirely,
Pieced, glued, and properly jointed.
Mule-bray, pig-grunt and bawdy cackles
Proceed from your great lips.
It's worse than a barnyard.

Perhaps you consider yourself an oracle,
Mouthpiece of the dead, or of some god or other.
Thirty years now I have laboured
To dredge the silt from your throat.
I am none the wiser.

Scaling little ladders with gluepots and pails of lysol
I crawl like an ant in mourning
Over the weedy acres of your brow
To mend the immense skull-plates and clear
The bald, white tumuli of your eyes.

A blue sky out of the Oresteia[2]
Arches above us. O father, all by yourself
You are pithy and historical as the Roman Forum.
I open my lunch on a hill of black cypress.
Your fluted bones and acanthine[3] hair are littered

In their old anarchy to the horizon-line.
It would take more than a lightning-stroke
To create such a ruin.
Nights, I squat in the cornucopia
Of your left ear, out of the wind,

Counting the red stars and those of plum-colour.
The sun rises under the pillar of your tongue.
My hours are married to shadow.
No longer do I listen for the scrape of a keel
On the blank stones of the landing.

---

1   an allusion to the gigantic bronze statue of the sun-god erected at Rhodes c.280 B.C.
2   A trilogy of plays by the Greek dramatist Aeschylus (525-456 B.C.), which tell the story
     of Oreste's search for revenge after the murder of his father Agamemnon by his mother
     Clytemnestra and her lover Aegisthus
3   Acanthus is a plant with large spiny leaves, common in the Mediterranean.

Black Rook in Rainy Weather

On the stiff twig up there
Hunches a wet black rook
Arranging and rearranging its feathers in the rain.
I do not expect a miracle
Or an accident

To set the sight on fire
In my eye, nor seek
Any more in the desultory weather some design,
But let spotted leaves fall as they fall,
Without ceremony, or portent.

Although, I admit, I desire,
Occasionally, some backtalk
From the mute sky, I can't honestly complain:
A certain minor light may still
Lean incandescent

Out of kitchen table or chair
As if a celestial burning took
Possession of the most obtuse objects now and then—
Thus hallowing an interval
Otherwise inconsequent

By bestowing largesse, honor,
One might say love. At any rate, I now walk
Wary (for it could happen
Even in this dull, ruinous landscape); skeptical,
Yet politic; ignorant

Of whatever angel may choose to flare
Suddenly at my elbow. I only know that a rook
Ordering its black feathers can so shine
As to seize my senses, haul
My eyelids up, and grant

A brief respite from fear
Of total neutrality. With luck,
Trekking stubborn through this season
Of fatigue, I shall
Patch together a content

Of sorts. Miracles occur,
If you care to call those spasmodic
Tricks of radiance miracles. The wait's begun again,
The long wait for the angel,
For that rare, random descent.

Crossing the Water

Black lake, black boat, two black, cut-paper people.
Where do the black trees go that drink here?
Their shadows must cover Canada.

A little light is filtering from the water flowers.
Their leaves do not wish us to hurry:
They are round and flat and full of dark advice.

Cold worlds shake from the oar.
The spirit of blackness is in us, it is in the fishes.
A snag is lifting a valedictory, pale hand;

Stars open among the lilies.
Are you not blinded by such expressionless sirens?
This is the silence of astounded souls.

Face Lift

You bring me good news from the clinic,
Whipping off your silk scarf, exhibiting the tight white
Mummy-cloths, smiling: I'm all right.
When I was nine, a lime-green anaesthetist
Fed me banana gas through a frog-mask. The nauseous
        vault
Boomed with bad dreams and the Jovian voices of surgeons.
Then mother swam up, holding a tin basin.
O I was sick.

They've changed all that. Travelling
Nude as Cleopatra in my well-boiled hospital shift,
Fizzy with sedatives and unusually humorous,
I roll to an anteroom where a kind man
Fists my fingers for me. He makes me feel something
        precious
Is leaking from the finger-vents. At the count of two
Darkness wipes me out like chalk on a blackboard . . .
I don't know a thing.

For five days I lie in secret,
Tapped like a cask, the years draining into my pillow.
Even my best friend thinks I'm in the country.
Skin doesn't have roots, it peels away easy as paper.
When I grin, the stitches tauten. I grow backward. I'm
        twenty,
Broody and in long skirts on my first husband's sofa, my
        fingers
Buried in the lambswool of the dead poodle;
I hadn't a cat yet.

Now she's done for, the dewlapped lady
I watched settle, line by line, in my mirror—
Old sock-face, sagged on a darning egg.
They've trapped her in some laboratory jar.
Let her die there, or wither incessantly for the next fifty
    years,
Nodding and rocking and fingering her thin hair.
Mother to myself, I wake swaddled in gauze,
Pink and smooth as a baby.

Last Words

I do not want a plain box, I want a sarcophagus
With tigery stripes, and a face on it
Round as the moon, to stare up.
I want to be looking at them when they come
Picking among the dumb minerals, the roots.
I see them already—the pale, star-distance faces.
Now they are nothing, they are not even babies.
I imagine them without fathers or mothers, like the first gods.
They will wonder if I was important.
I should sugar and preserve my days like fruit!
My mirror is clouding over—
A few more breaths, and it will reflect nothing at all.
The flowers and the faces whiten to a sheet.

I do not trust the spirit. It escapes like steam
In dreams, through mouth-hole or eye-hole. I can't stop it.
One day it won't come back. Things aren't like that.
They stay, their little particular lusters
Warmed by much handling. They almost purr.
When the soles of my feet grow cold,
The blue eye of my turquoise will comfort me.
Let me have my copper cooking pots, let my rouge pots
Bloom about me like night flowers, with a good smell.
They will roll me up in bandages, they will store my heart
Under my feet in a neat parcel.
I shall hardly know myself. It will be dark,
And the shine of these small things sweeter than the face of Ishtar.[1]

---

1   the goddess of love and fertility in Babylonian and Assyrian mythology

Ariel[1]

Stasis in darkness.
Then the substanceless blue
Pour of tor and distances.

God's lioness,
How one we grow,
Pivot of heels and knees!—The furrow

Splits and passes, sister to
The brown arc
Of the neck I cannot catch,

Nigger-eye
Berries cast dark
Hooks—

Black sweet blood mouthfuls,
Shadows.
Something else

Hauls me through air—
Thighs, hair;
Flakes from my heels.

White
Godiva,[2] I unpeel—
Dead hands, dead stringencies.

And now I
Foam to wheat, a glitter of seas.
The child's cry

Melts in the wall.
And I
Am the arrow,

The dew that flies
Suicidal, at one with the drive
Into the red

Eye, the cauldron of morning.

---

1   An airy spirit employed by Prospero in Shakespeare's *The Tempest*. "Ariel" was also the
name Plath gave to her horse.
2   The English woman who, according to legend, fulfilled an agreement with her husband
to ride naked down the streets of Coventry if he would remove oppressive taxes.

[handwritten annotations: suspected she suffered from the Electra Complex (opp of the Oedipus) / her real pain was not a Nazi / Startling / recorded 2 wks before she committed suicide successfully, / rage against her father]

Daddy

You do not do, you do not do
Any more, black shoe
In which I have lived like a foot
For thirty years, poor and white,
Barely daring to breathe or Achoo.

Daddy, I have had to kill you.
You died before I had time—
Marble-heavy, a bag full of God,
Ghastly statue with one grey toe
Big as a Frisco seal

[handwritten: casts terms that her father (Nazi) + me (Jew) → not true]

And a head in the freakish Atlantic
Where it pours bean green over blue
In the waters off beautiful Nauset.
I used to pray to recover you.
Ach, du.[1]

In the German tongue, in the Polish town[2]
Scraped flat by the roller
Of wars, wars, wars.
But the name of the town is common.
My Polack friend

[handwritten: Strong rhythms]

Says there are a dozen or two.
So I never could tell where you
Put your foot, your root,
I never could talk to you.
The tongue stuck in my jaw.

It stuck in a barb wire snare
Ich, ich, ich, ich,[3]
I could hardly speak.
I thought every German was you.
And the language obscene

[handwritten: like the Jews, she was stripped of everything (self-identity) etc.]

An engine, an engine
Chuffing me off like a Jew.
A Jew to Dachau, Auschwitz, Belsen.[4]
I began to talk like a Jew.
I think I may well be a Jew.

[handwritten: Carries a bit too far / she uses horrendous unimaginary suffering to express her suffering]

1   (German) Oh, you.
2   Plath's father, Otto Plath, emigrated to the U.S. from the Polish town of Grabow.
3   (German) I, I, I, I,
4   Dachau, Auschwitz, and Belsen were sites of Nazi concentration camps during World War II.

The snows of the Tyrol, the clear beer of Vienna
Are not very pure or true.
With my gypsy ancestress and my weird luck
And my Taroc pack[1] and my Taroc pack
I may be a bit of a Jew.

I have always been scared of *you*,
With your Luftwaffe, your gobbledygoo.
And your neat moustache
And your Aryan eye, bright blue.
Panzer-man,[2] panzer-man, O You—

Not God but a swastika
So black no sky could squeak through.
Every woman adores a Fascist,
The boot in the face, the brute
Brute heart of a brute like you.

You stand at the blackboard,[3] daddy,
In the picture I have of you,
A cleft in your chin instead of your foot
But no less a devil for that, no not
Any less the black man who

Bit my pretty red heart in two.
I was ten when they buried you.
At twenty I tried to die
And get back, back, back to you.
I thought even the bones would do.

But they pulled me out of the sack,
And they stuck me together with glue. *psychoanalysis*
And then I knew what to do.
I made a model of you,
A man in black with a Meinkampf[4] look

And a love of the rack and the screw.
And I said I do, I do. *marriage*
So daddy, I'm finally through. *Now she's got another horrible*
The black telephone's off at the root,
The voices just can't worm through.

---

1   the Tarot cards that are used for fortune telling
2   "Panzers" were German armoured divisions, notably those equipped with tanks.
3   Otto Plath taught biology and German at Boston University.
4   *Mein Kampf* (1924) is the title of the book by Adolf Hitler outlining his political philosophy.

[handwritten annotation: blames all her mental problems on her father; agressively explores also her anger at him; focus/fixation; her rage, suicide the final resolution]

If I've killed one man, I've killed two—
[handwritten: husband] The vampire who said he was you
And drank my blood for a year,
[handwritten: her married yrs] Seven years, if you want to know.
Daddy, you can lie back now.

There's a stake in your fat black heart
And the villagers never liked you.
They are dancing and stamping on you.
They always *knew* it was you.
Daddy, daddy, you bastard, I'm through.

Edge[1]

The woman is perfected.
Her dead

Body wears the smile of accomplishment,
The illusion of a Greek necessity

Flows in the scrolls of her toga,
Her bare

Feet seem to be saying:
We have come so far, it is over.

Each dead child coiled, a white serpent,
One at each little

Pitcher of milk, now empty.
She has folded

Them back into her body as petals
Of a rose close when the garden

Stiffens and odours bleed
From the sweet, deep throats of the night flower.

The moon has nothing to be sad about,
Staring from her hood of bone.

She is used to this sort of thing.
Her blacks crackle and drag.

---

1   According to Ted Hughes, Plath's husband, "Edge" was written a week before Plath
    committed suicide on 11 February 1963.

Alden Nowlan

(1933–1983)

Warren Pryor

When every pencil meant a sacrifice
his parents boarded him at school in town,
slaving to free him from the stony fields,
the meagre acreage that bore them down.

They blushed with pride when, at his graduation,
they watched him picking up the slender scroll,
his passport from the years of brutal toil
and lonely patience in a barren hole.

When he went in the Bank their cups ran over.
They marvelled how he wore a milk-white shirt
work days and jeans on Sundays. He was saved
from their thistle-strewn farm and its red dirt.

And he said nothing. Hard and serious
like a young bear inside his teller's cage,
his axe-hewn hands upon the paper bills
aching with empty strength and throttled rage.

The Bull Moose

Down from the purple mist of trees on the mountain,
lurching through forests of white spruce and cedar,
stumbling through tamarack swamps,
came the bull moose
to be stopped at last by a pole-fenced pasture.

Too tired to turn or, perhaps, aware
there was no place left to go, he stood with the cattle.
They, scenting the musk of death, seeing his great head
like the ritual mask of a blood god, moved to the other end
of the field, and waited.

The neighbours heard of it, and by afternoon
cars lined the road. The children teased him
with alder switches and he gazed at them
like an old, tolerant collie. The women asked
if he could have escaped from a Fair.

The oldest man in the parish remembered seeing
a gelded moose yoked with an ox for plowing.
The young men snickered and tried to pour beer
down his throat, while their girl friends took their pictures.

And the bull moose let them stroke his tick-ravaged flanks,
let them pry open his jaws with bottles, let a giggling girl
plant a little purple cap
of thistles on his head.

When the wardens came, everyone agreed it was a shame
to shoot anything so shaggy and cuddlesome.
He looked like the kind of pet
women put to bed with their sons.

So they held their fire. But just as the sun dropped in the river
the bull moose gathered his strength
like a scaffolded king, straightened and lifted his horns
so that even the wardens backed away as they raised their rifles.
When he roared, people ran to their cars. All the young men
leaned on their automobile horns as he toppled.

The Execution

On the night of the execution
a man at the door
mistook me for the coroner.
"Press", I said.

But he didn't understand. He led me
into the wrong room
where the sheriff greeted me:
"You're late, Padre".

"You're wrong", I told him. "I'm Press".
"Yes, of course, Reverend Press".
We went down a stairway.

"Ah, Mr. Ellis", said the Deputy.
"Press!" I shouted. But he shoved me
through a black curtain.
The lights were so bright
I couldn't see the faces
of the men sitting
opposite. But, thank God, I thought
they can see me!

"Look!", I cried. "Look at my face!
Doesn't anybody know me?"

Then a hood covered my head.
"Don't make it harder for us", the hangman whispered.

I, Icarus[1]

There was a time when I could fly. I swear it.
Perhaps, if I think hard for a moment, I can even tell you the
      year.
My room was on the ground floor at the rear of the house.
My bed faced a window.
Night after night I lay on my bed and willed myself to fly.
It was hard work, I can tell you.
Sometimes I lay perfectly still for an hour before I felt
      my body rising from the bed.
I rose slowly, slowly until I floated three or four feet
      above the floor.
Then, with a kind of swimming motion, I propelled myself
      toward the window.
Outside, I rose higher and higher, above the pasture fence,
      above the clothesline, above the dark, haunted trees
      beyond the pasture.
And, all the time, I heard the music of flutes.
It seemed the wind made this music.
And sometimes there were voices singing.

In Those Old Wars

In those old wars
where generals wore yellow ringlets
and sucked lemons at their prayers,
other things being equal
the lost causes were the best.

Lee[2] rode out of history
on his gray horse, Traveller,
so perfect a hero
had he not existed
it would have been necessary to invent him—
war stinks without gallantry.

An aide, one of the few who survived,
told him,
Country be damned, general,
for six months these men
have had no country but you.

---

1   In Greek mythology, Icarus and his father Daedalus sought to fly from Crete to Sicily
     using wings made of feathers and wax; Icarus ventured too close to the sun, causing the
     wax to melt, and he fell to his death in the sea.
2   Robert E. Lee, general of the Confederate Army during the American Civil War (1861-
     1865).

They fought barefoot
and drank blueberryleaf tea.

The politicians
strung up Grant[1]
like a carrot,
made him a Merovingian.[2]
They stole everything,
even the coppers from Lincoln's dead eyes.

In those days, the vanquished
surrendered their swords like gentlemen,
the victors alone
surrendered their illusions.
The easiest thing to do for a Cause
is to die for it.

The Word

Though I have the gift of tongues
and can move mountains,
my words are nothing
compared with yours,
though you only
look up from my arms
and whisper my name.

This is not pride
because I know
it is not
my name that you whisper
but a sign
between us,
like the word
that was spoken
at the beginning
of the world
and will be spoken again
only when the world ends.

This is not that word
but the other
that must be spoken

---

1   Ulysses S. Grant (1822-1885), commander of the Union armies during the American Civil
      War. He served two terms as President, from 1869-1877.
2   The name of the first dynasty of Frankish kings, which was founded in the fifth century,
      and lasted until the middle of the eighth.

over and over
while the world lasts.

Tears,
laughter,
a lifetime!
All in one word!

The word you whisper
when you look up
from my arms
and seem to say
my name.

Leonard Cohen

(b. 1934)

Elegy

Do not look for him
In brittle mountain streams:
They are too cold for any god;
And do not examine the angry rivers
For shreds of his soft body
Or turn the shore stones for his blood;
But in the warm salt ocean
He is descending through cliffs
Of slow green water
And the hovering coloured fish
Kiss his snow-bruised body
And build their secret nests
In his fluttering winding-sheet.

You Have the Lovers

[handwritten: a ritual]
[handwritten: ghost of love in the past]
[handwritten: situation doesn't occur in the real world]

You have the lovers,
they are nameless, their histories only for each other, *[handwritten: somehow in]*
and you have the room, the bed and the windows. *[handwritten: the house, the]*
Pretend it is a ritual. *[handwritten: lovers who]*
Unfurl the bed, bury the lovers, blacken the windows, *[handwritten: had lived there]*
let them live in that house for a generation or two. *[handwritten: before are not]*
No one dares disturb them. *[handwritten: dead, you can]*
Visitors in the corridor tiptoe past the long closed door, *[handwritten: still feel]*
they listen for sounds, for a moan, for a song: *[handwritten: their presence]*
nothing is heard, not even breathing. *[handwritten: not a wild experience,]*
You know they are not dead,
you can feel the presence of their intense love. *[handwritten: Garden of Ed]*
Your children grow up, they leave you, *[handwritten: Adam + Eve have no]*
they have become soldiers and riders. *[handwritten: clothes.]*
Your mate dies after a life of service. *[handwritten: Garden inhabited]*
Who knows you? Who remembers you? *[handwritten: This ideal]*
But in your house a ritual is in progress: *[handwritten: these special]*
it is not finished: it needs more people. *[handwritten: human]*
One day the door is opened to the lover's chamber. *[handwritten: beings]*
The room has become a dense garden,
full of colours, smells, sounds you have never known.
The bed is smooth as a wafer of sunlight,
in the midst of the garden it stands alone. *[handwritten: suggests G of Eden]*
In the bed the lovers, slowly and deliberately and silently,
perform the act of love.
Their eyes are closed,
as tightly as if heavy coins of flesh lay on them.
Their lips are bruised with new and old bruises.
Her hair and his beard are hopelessly tangled.
When he puts his mouth against her shoulder

[handwritten left margin: user addressed is a hypothetical human people discovering the reality of sex in old age speaker in the position of an eavesdropping child]

sex, solumn
not a wild party somewhere
'a kind of Dionysian
infinitely suggestive experience

so united they no longer separate 1 from another

she is uncertain whether her shoulder
has given or received the kiss.
All her flesh is like a mouth.
He carries his fingers along her waist
and feels his own waist caressed.
She holds him closer and his own arms tighten around her.
She kisses the hand beside her mouth.
It is his hand or her hand, it hardly matters,
there are so many more kisses.
You stand beside the bed, weeping with happiness,
you carefully peel away the sheets
from the slow-moving bodies.
Your eyes are filled with tears, you barely make out the
     lovers.
As you undress you sing out, and your voice is magnificent
because now you believe it is the first human voice
heard in that room.
The garments you let fall grow into vines.
You climb into bed and recover the flesh.
You close your eyes and allow them to be sewn shut.
You create an embrace and fall into it.
There is only one moment of pain or doubt
as you wonder how many multitudes are lying beside your
     body,
but a mouth kisses and a hand soothes the moment away.

loves interplay of victim + victimizer

A Kite is a Victim

loved image of control + mastery poem about writing poetry

A kite is a victim you are sure of.
You love it because it pulls
gentle enough to call you master,
strong enough to call you fool;
because it lives
like a desperate trained falcon
in the high sweet air,
and you can always haul it down
to tame it in your drawer.

A kite is a fish you have already caught
in a pool where no fish come,
so you play him carefully and long,
and hope he won't give up,
or the wind die down.

A kite is the last poem you've written,
so you give it to the wind,
but you don't let it go
until someone finds you
something else to do.

A kite is a contract of glory
that must be made with the sun,
so you make friends with the field
the river and the wind,
then you pray the whole cold night before,
under the travelling cordless moon,
to make you worthy and lyric and pure.

trying to discover a
I Have Not Lingered In European Monasteries *Zen joy*
in the
everyday
experience

I have not lingered in European monasteries
and discovered among the tall grasses tombs of knights
who fell as beautifully as their ballads tell;
I have not parted the grasses
or purposefully left them thatched.

I have not released my mind to wander and wait
in those great distances
between the snowy mountains and the fishermen,
like a moon,
or a shell beneath the moving water.

I have not held my breath
so that I might hear the breathing of God,
or tamed my heartbeat with an exercise,
or starved for visions. *(re. Native American)*
Although I have watched him often
I have not become the heron,
leaving my body on the shore,
and I have not become the luminous trout,
leaving my body in the air.

I have not worshipped wounds and relics,
or combs of iron,
or bodies wrapped and burnt in scrolls.

I have not been unhappy for ten thousand years.
During the day I laugh and during the night I sleep.
My favourite cooks prepare my meals,
my body cleans and repairs itself,
and all my work goes well.

prof. most famous work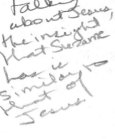

Suzanne Takes You Down

Suzanne takes you down
to her place near the river,
you can hear the boats go by
you can stay the night beside her.
And you know that she's half crazy
but that's why you want to be there
and she feeds you tea and oranges
that come all the way from China.
Just when you mean to tell her
that you have no gifts to give her,
she gets you on her wave-length
and she lets the river answer
that you've always been her lover.
　　　And you want to travel with her,
　　　you want to travel blind
　　　and you know that she can trust you
　　　because you've touched her perfect body
　　　with your mind.

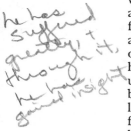

Jesus was a sailor
when he walked upon the water[1]
and he spent a long time watching
from a lonely wooden tower
and when he knew for certain
only drowning men could see him
he said All men will be sailors then
until the sea shall free them,
but he himself was broken
long before the sky would open,
forsaken, almost human,
he sank beneath your wisdom like a stone.
　　　And you want to travel with him,
　　　you want to travel blind
　　　and you think maybe you'll trust him
　　　because he touched your perfect body
　　　with his mind.

Suzanne takes your hand
and she leads you to the river,
she is wearing rags and feathers
from Salvation Army counters.
The sun pours down like honey
on our lady of the harbour
as she shows you where to look

1　See Matthew 14.23-33.

among the garbage and the flowers,
there are heroes in the seaweed
there are children in the morning,
they are leaning out for love
they will lean that way forever
while Suzanne she holds the mirror.
    And you want to travel with her
    and you want to travel blind
    and you're sure that she can find you
    because she's touched her perfect body
    with her mind.

Imamu Amiri Baraka (LeRoi Jones)

(b. 1934)

Three Modes of History and Culture

Chalk mark sex of the nation, on walls we drummers
know
as cathedrals. Cathedra, in a churning meat milk.

Women glide through looking for telephones. Maps
weep
and are mothers and their daughters listening to

music teachers. From heavy beginnings. Plantations,
learning
America, as speech, and a common emptiness. Songs knocking

inside old women's faces. Knocking through cardboard trunks.
Trains
leaning north, catching hellfire in windows, passing through

the first ignoble cities of missouri, to illinois, and the panting
Chicago.
And then all ways, we go where flesh is cheap. Where factories

sit open, burning the chiefs. Make your way! Up through fog and
history
Make your way, and swing the general, that it come flash open

and spill the innards of that sweet thing we heard, and gave theory
to.
Breech, bridge, and reach, to where all talk is energy. And there's

enough, for anything singular. All our lean prophets and rhythms.
Entire
we arrive and set up shacks, hole cards, Western hearts at the edge

of saying. Thriving to balance the meanness of particular skies.
Race
of madmen and giants.

Brick songs. Shoe songs. Chants of open weariness.
Knife wiggle early evenings of the wet mouth. Tongue
dance midnight, any season shakes our house. Don't
tear my clothes! To doubt the balance of misery
ripping meat hug shuffle fuck. The Party of Insane
Hope. I've come from there too. Where the dead told lies
about clever social justice. Burning coffins voted

and staggered through cold white streets listening
to Willkie or Wallace or Dewey[1] through the dead face
of Lincoln.[2] Come from there, and belched it out.

I think about a time when I will be relaxed.
When flames and non-specific passion wear themselves
away. And my eyes and hands and mind can turn
and soften, and my songs will be softer
and lightly weight the air.

I Substitute For The Dead Lecturer

*What is most precious, because
it is lost. What is lost,
because it is most
precious.*

They have turned, and say that I am dying. That
I have thrown
my life
away. They
have left me alone, where
there is no one, nothing
save who I am. Not a note
nor a word.

        Cold air batters
the poor (and their minds
turn open
like sores). What kindness
What wealth
can I offer? Except
what is, for me,
ugliest. What is
for me, shadows, shrieking
phantoms. Except
they have need
of life. Flesh
at least,
        should be theirs.

---

1   All three were politicians who ran for President and lost: Willkie in 1940, Wallace in
1948, and Dewey in 1944 and 1948.
2   Abraham Lincoln (1809-1865), sixth President of the United States, abolished slavery in 1862
and was assassinated three years later.

The Lord has saved me
to do this. The Lord
has made me strong. I
am as I must have
myself. Against all
thought, all music, all
my soft loves.

For all these wan roads
I am pushed to follow, are
my own conceit. A simple muttering
elegance, slipped in my head
pressed on my soul, is my heart's
worth. And I am frightened
that the flame of my sickness
will burn off my face. And leave
the bones, my stewed black skull,
an empty cage of failure.

Ostriches & Grandmothers!

All meet here with us, finally: the
uptown, way-west, den of inconstant
moralities.
Faces up: all
my faces turned up
to the sun.

1

Summer's mist nods against the trees
till distance grows in my head
like an antique armada
dangled motionless from the horizon.

Unbelievable changes. Restorations.
Each day like my niña's[1] fan
tweaking the flat air
back and forth till the room
is a blur of flowers.

Intimacy takes on human form . . .
& sheds it like a hide.
               Lips, eyes,
tiny lace coughs

---

1   Spanish word for grandmother

reflected on night's stealth.

                        2

Tonight, one star.
eye of the dragon.
                    The Void
signaling.
Reminding someone
it's still there.

                        3

It's these empty seconds
I fill with myself. Each
a recognition. A complete
utterance.

Here, it is color; motion;
the feeling of dazzling beauty
Flight.

As
the trapeze rider
leans
with arms spread

wondering at the bar's
delay

Audre Lorde

(1934–1992)

Outside

In the center of a harsh and spectrumed city
all things natural are strange.
I grew up in a genuine confusion
between grass and weeds and flowers
and what colored meant
except for clothes you couldn't bleach
and nobody called me nigger
until I was thirteen.
Nobody lynched my momma
but what she'd never been
had bleached her face of everything
but very private furies
and made the other children
call me yellow snot at school.

And how many times have I called myself back
through my bones confusion
black
like marrow meaning meat
and how many times have you cut me
and run in the streets
my own blood
who do you think me to be
that you are terrified of becoming
or what do you see in my face
you have not already discarded
in your own mirror
what face do you see in my eyes
that you will someday
come to
acknowledge your own?
Who shall I curse that I grew up
believing in my mother's face
or that I lived in fear of potent darkness
wearing my father's shape
they have both marked me
with their blind and terrible love
and I am lustful now for my own name.

Between the canyons of their mighty silences
mother bright and father brown
I seek my own shapes now
for they never spoke of me
except as theirs
and the pieces I stumble and fall over
I still record as proof
that I am beautiful

twice
blessed with the images
of who they were
and who I thought them once to be
of what I move
toward and through
and what I need
to leave behind me
most of all
I am blessed within my selves
who are come to make our shattered faces
whole.

Stations

Some women love
to wait
for life   for a ring
in the June light   for a touch
of the sun to heal them   for another
woman's voice   to make them whole
to untie their hands
put words in their mouths
form to their passages   sound
to their screams   for some other sleeper
to remember   their future   their past.

Some women wait for their right
train   in the wrong station
in the alleys of morning
for the noon to holler
the night come down.

Some women wait for love
to rise up
the child of their promise
to gather from earth
what they do not plant
to claim pain for labor
to become
the tip of an arrow   to aim
at the heart of now
but it never stays.

Some women wait for visions
that do not return
where they were not welcome
naked
for invitations to places
they always wanted

to visit
to be repeated.

Some women wait for themselves
around the next corner
and call the empty spot peace
but the opposite of living
is only not living
and the stars do not care.

Some women wait for something
to change   and nothing
does change
so they change
themselves.

The Art of Response

The first answer was incorrect
the second was
sorry   the third trimmed its toenails
on the Vatican steps
the fourth went mad
the fifth
nursed a grudge until it bore twins
that drank poisoned grape juice in Jonestown[1]
the sixth   wrote a book about it
the seventh
argued a case before the Supreme Court
against taxation on Girl Scout Cookies
the eighth held a news conference
while four Black babies
and one other   picketed New York City
for a hospital bed to die in
the ninth and tenth swore
Revenge on the Opposition
and the eleventh dug their graves
next to Eternal Truth
the twelfth
processed funds from a Third World country
that provides doctors for Central Harlem
the thirteenth
refused
the fourteenth sold cocaine and shamrocks

---

1   a settlement located in Guyana, named for Jim Jones, self-appointed religious leader. In
November 1978 Jones persuaded nearly a thousand members of his sect to drink poisoned
juice: an act of mass suicide commonly known as the Jonestown Massacre.

near a toilet in the Big Apple circus
the fifteenth
changed the question.

Hanging Fire

I am fourteen
and my skin has betrayed me
the boy I cannot live without
still sucks his thumb
in secret
how come my knees are
always so ashy
what if I die
before morning
and momma's in the bedroom
with the door closed.

I have to learn how to dance
in time for the next party
my room is too small for me
suppose I die before graduation
they will sing sad melodies
but finally
tell the truth about me
There is nothing I want to do
and too much
that has to be done
and momma's in the bedroom
with the door closed.

Nobody even stops to think
about my side of it
I should have been on Math Team
my marks were better than his
why do I have to be
the one
wearing braces
I have nothing to wear tomorrow
will I live long enough
to grow up
and momma's in the bedroom
with the door closed.

Fleur Adcock

(b. 1934)

Wife to Husband

From anger into the pit of sleep
You go with a sudden skid. On me
Stillness falls gradually, a soft
Snowfall, a light cover to keep
Numb for a time the twitching nerves.

Your head on the pillow is turned away;
My face is hidden. But under snow
Shoots uncurl, the green thread curves
Instinctively upwards. Do not doubt
That sense of purpose in mindless flesh:
Between our bodies a warmth grows;
Under the blankets hands move out,
Your back touches my breast, our thighs
Turn to find their accustomed place.

Your mouth is moving over my face:
Do we dare, now, to open our eyes?

Unexpected Visit

I have nothing to say about this garden.
I do not want to be here, I can't explain
What happened. I merely opened a usual door
And found this. The rain

Has just stopped, and the gravel paths are trickling
With water. Stone lions, on each side,
Gleam like wet seals, and the green birds
Are stiff with dripping pride.

Not my kind of country. The gracious vistas,
The rose-gardens and terraces, are all wrong—
As comfortless as the weather. But here I am.
I cannot tell how long

I have stood gazing at grass too wet to sit on,
Under a sky so dull I cannot read
The sundial, staring along the curving walks
And wondering where they lead;

Not really hoping, though, to be enlightened.
It must be morning, I think, but there is no
Horizon behind the trees, no sun as clock
Or compass. I shall go

And find, somewhere among the formal hedges
Or hidden behind a trellis, a toolshed. There
I can sit on a box and wait. Whatever happens
May happen anywhere,

And better, perhaps, among the rakes and flowerpots
And sacks of bulbs than under this pallid sky:
Having chosen nothing else, I can at least
Choose to be warm and dry.

Leaving the Tate[1]

Coming out with your clutch of postcards
in a Tate Gallery bag and another clutch
of images packed into your head you pause
on the steps to look across the river

and there's a new one: light bright buildings,
a streak of brown water, and such a sky
you wonder who painted it—Constable?[2] No:
too brilliant. Crome?[3] No: too ecstatic—

a madly pure Pre-Raphaelite[4] sky,
perhaps, sheer blue apart from the white plumes
rushing up it (today, that is,
April. Another day would be different

but it wouldn't matter. All skies work.)
Cut to the lower right for a detail:
seagulls pecking on mud, below
two office blocks and a Georgian terrace.[5]

Now swing to the left, and take in plane-trees
bobbled with seeds, and that brick building,
and a red bus . . . Cut it off just there,
by the lamp-post. Leave the scaffolding in.

That's your next one. Curious how
these outdoor pictures didn't exist
before you'd looked at the indoor pictures,
the ones on the walls. But here they are now,

---

1   the Tate Gallery: an art gallery in London, England
2   John Constable (1776-1837), English artist, especially noted for his landscape paintings.
3   John Crome (1768-1821), English landscape painter and etcher.
4   The Pre-Raphaelite Brotherhood, founded in 1848 by a group of young artists and writers,
     called for artists to reject modern conventions and return to the simpler, more natural
     styles supposedly characteristic of art before the time of Raphael.
5   row of houses built during the reign of the first four Georges in England (1714-1830)

marching out of their panorama
and queuing up for the viewfinder
your eye s become. You can isolate them
by holding your optic muscles still.

You can zoom in on figure studies
(that boy with the rucksack), or still lives,
abstracts, townscapes. No one made them.
The light painted them. You're in charge

of the hanging committee. Put what space
you like around the ones you fix on,
and gloat. Art multiplies itself.
Art's whatever you choose to frame.

Below Loughrigg

The power speaks only out of sleep and blackness
no use looking for the sun
what is not present cannot be illumined

Katherine's lungs, remember, eaten by disease
but Mary's fingers too
devoured and she goes on writing

The water speaks from the rocks, the cavern speaks
where water halloos through it
this happens also in darkness

A steep bit here, up from the valley
to the terraces, the path eroded by water
Now listen for the voice

These things wane with the vital forces
he said, little having waned in him
except faith, and anger had replaced it

One force can be as good as another
we may not think so; but channelled
in ways it has eaten out; issuing

into neither a pool nor the sea
but a shapely lake afloat with wooded islands
a real water and multiplied on maps

which can be read in the sunlight; for the sun
will not be stopped from visiting
and the lake exists and the winds sing over it.

Kofi Awoonor

(b. 1935)

On the Way to Durham, N.C.

So my heart flutters
little tiny flurries of Long Island snow
showers last February, I sit
waiting for a resolution
of this knot
for the untying moment
of this monster that sits upon the hill
risen once like the ark above the hill
after the flood.
I heard the bells of the small church
above the old man's evening call
for the poor of my land to gather
for the sharing moment.

News came today of violence
of army brutality against unarmed students
and I hurt in the privacy of my lonely bed
the miracle of the iron fired on our anvil
branding here on this body our history our race
I am the grandfather for whom there's no recognition
whom they arrested in Memphis my soul in the streets
for indecency. I remember the dance
of salmons on my shore
the lovely smile of the oyster
in conversation with the blue claw crab
the dome shell king strutting sideways
the ritual dancer of the village lane
and the sprat singing in the wail of the Christmas wind

We've begun the descent
the smell of tarmac paraffin
over the white clouds of North Carolina
the land is visible
the green land cascades through hills
and byways on the one percent inhabitable spot
where the drink is spilled
and we are home.
water miraculous comrade of time
and birth; a drink of the land
    oh, our land

The First Circle

1

the flat end of sorrow here
two crows fighting over New Year's Party
leftovers. From my cell, I see a cold
hard world.

2

So this is the abcess that
hurts the nation—
jails, torture, blood
and hunger.
One day it will burst;
it must burst.

3

When I heard you were taken
we speculated, those of us at large
where you would be
in what nightmare will you star?
That night I heard the moans
wondering whose child could now
be lost in the cellars of oppression.
Then you emerged, tall, and bloody-eyed.

It was the first time
I wept.

4

The long nights I dread most
the voices from behind the bars
the early glow of dawn before
the guard's steps wake me up,
the desire to leap and stretch
and yawn in anticipation
of another dark home-coming day
only to find that
I cannot.
riding the car into town,
hemmed in between them
their guns poking me in the ribs,
I never had known that my people
wore such sad faces, so sad
they were, on New Year's Eve,
so very sad.

I Rejoice

At departure time the family came
my mother silent as ever
my sister organized like an avenging army
her husband is petty gambler and thief
the wives and their hypocritical relays
telling their woes and the misconduct of their children
and my father, I think I see my father
dead now these six years.
I've still to plaster the grave and
erect a marble head
and work out an inscription my sister says
with fitting quotes from the holy book
"Lord in Thy Gracious Keeping
Leave we now thy servant sleeping"
or words to that effect.
I know he sleeps not
torments my fitful sleep of midage
promises a fruitful turn in his failed field.

sparrows abound in our town
brown dunghill birds chirpers
unafraid of funeral gatherings and the
coming rain.

George Bowering

(b. 1935)

Grandfather

Grandfather
        Jabez Harry Bowering
strode across the Canadian prairie
hacking down trees
           and building churches
delivering personal baptist sermons in them
leading Holy holy holy lord god almighty songs in them
red haired man squared off in the pulpit
reading Saul on the road to Damascus[1] at them

Left home
        big walled Bristol town
at age eight
        to make a living
buried his stubby fingers in root snarled earth
for a suit of clothes and seven hundred gruelly meals a year
taking an anabaptist[2] cane across the back every day
for four years till he was whipped out of England

Twelve years old
        and across the ocean alone
to apocalyptic Canada
           Ontario of bone bending child labor
six years on the road to Damascus till his eyes were blinded
with the blast of Christ and he wandered west
to Brandon among wheat kings and heathen Saturday nights
young red haired Bristol boy shoveling coal
in the basement of Brandon college five in the morning

Then built his first wooden church and married
a sick girl who bore two live children and died
leaving several pitiful letters and the Manitoba night

He moved west with another wife and built children and
        churches
Saskatchewan Alberta British Columbia Holy holy holy[3]
lord god almighty
           struck his labored bones with pain
and left him a postmaster prodding grandchildren with crutches

---

1   Saul, afterwards called Paul, persecuted Christians until he experienced a revelation while
     on the way to Damascus (Acts 9.1-9).
2   member of a sect rejecting infant baptism and limiting membership to adults baptised
     after a confession of faith
3   from Revelations 4.8

another dead wife and a glass bowl of photographs
and holy books unopened save the bible by the bed

Till he died the day before his eighty fifth birthday
in a Catholic hospital of sheets white as his hair

The Swing[1]

Renoir's people
seem to stand
on a forest floor
of blossoms.

The girl on the swing
could be fifteen, her dress
of new flowers.

She leans coyly
or thoughtfully away
from the two men
with straw hats.

They are artists
on a Sunday afternoon
warm in loose clothing,

some kind of wonder
for the child who
makes the fourth figure.

She is clasping her empty hands
in front of her, her head up,
her eyes the only ones
looking outward.

---

1   the title of a painting by the French artist Pierre Auguste Renoir (1841-1919)

My Father in New Zealand

Everyone agrees,
when you visit New Zealand
you are back in the Fifties.

The Fifties! My father is still alive!
I looked around for him on the long main street of Wellington.[1]
I kept turning on Cuba Street to see if he was behind me.
I listened for his quiet voice in the Auckland airport.
I lifted brims of bent sheepmen's hats, looking for his face.

He was there somewhere, I had no right
to wander both islands without talking with him.

I rued the hours I spent in the wrong places,
the Vibrations disco in Christchurch, the Maori bars,
the poetry reading at the library. He
would never show up in such a place, and my time
was running out.

Every time I watched a flashing leg
instead of seeking his dear old frame
I was suffused with guilt, a true Canadian abroad.

Dear Ewart, if they are right you are there somewhere,
& I have twenty years to find you
before you are gone again, maybe to some other country.

But how many years do I have left, whose frame
looks so much like yours? Can I wait twenty years,
hoping you move to a closer country?

Are you in New Zealand, looking for me too?
I am a lot older now, I look more like you.
Call me by the secret name we had when I was a child,
the name we never spoke. I'll hear you if I can get there.

Dancing Bones

Dancing bones on reason's day,
artful frame of reference,
very nearly scape the eye
in rimes that leap the outer fence,
dodging realists on their way.

---

1   The capital of New Zealand, on the North Island; Auckland is also on the North Island;
Christchurch is on the South Island.

Young in flesh and young in ear,
older than this land in wit,
under walls he passes by
napping old thematic crit,
garrison of lazy fear.

Leaves Flipping

The leaves flipping green and silver in the wind

Moon eye daughters bend necks, looking at
the leaves flipping green and silver in the wind

Moon eye daughters bend necks, looking at
the leaves flipping green and silver in the wind
just this side of South Dakota, 1948

Say welcome great baseball season, give us all
moon eye daughters bending necks, looking at
the leaves flipping green and silver in the wind
just this side of South Dakota, 1948

Say welcome great baseball season, give us please
moon-daughters, bend necks, looking at
the leaves flipping green and silver in the wind
just this side of South Dakota, 1948,
a peaceful objective, a family gathering, rain barrel

She sits carelessly in a white painted iron chair,
says welcome great baseball season, give us all
moon daughters, bend long necks, looking at
the leaves flipping green and silver in the wind
just this side of South Dakota, 1948,
a peaceful objective, a family gathering, rain barrel

She sits carelessly in the white painted iron chair,
says welcome great baseball season, give us both
moon daughters, bend long necks, looking at
the leaves nipping green and silver in the wind
just this side of South Dakota, 1948,
a peaceful objective, a family gathering, rain barrel,
dust rising behind a coupé getting larger as it arrives.

The Kingdome¹ 1974

We got seats high behind home plate,
Dwight and Paul and I, looked down
at a big green pinball machine!

The ball should boing off the shortstop,
Boeing!² 50,000 points, five free games
Here in the Great North West, rain

outside the grey concrete roof, sea full of perch
beyond the Ocean Isles in the fog, Mariners
an expansion ball team forever.

Dwight catches a foul ball
but he has to drop his beer to get it.
What is the American League doing in the rain forest?

Is coming to Seattle really coming to the USA?
Old coots with caulked boots crack peanuts and jokes,
nice working class slim fellows in the bleachers;

they're kind of Canadians, kind of too hip
to be Canadians, baseball's been in the North West
as long as the railroad.

But they used to play between rainfalls; now
it's pinball, colours flashing, now Dwight and Paul
and I stomp our feet hard for a rally against the Yanks

and the whole place shuts down dark
except for the simple scoreboard lights
that spell TILT, game over, good night.

---

1   a domed stadium in Seattle, home to the Seattle Mariners baseball team
2   Seattle is the major manufacturing centre for Boeing Aircraft.

Marge Piercy

(b. 1936)

The secretary chant

My hips are a desk.
From my ears hang
chains of paper clips.
Rubber bands form my hair.
My breasts are wells of mimeograph ink.
My feet bear casters.
Buzz. Click.
My head is a badly organized file.
My head is a switchboard
where crossed lines crackle.
Press my fingers
and in my eyes appear
credit and debit.
Zing. Tinkle.
My navel is a reject button.
From my mouth issue canceled reams.
Swollen, heavy, rectangular
I am about to be delivered
of a baby
Xerox machine.
File me under W
because I wonce
was
a woman.

I will not be your sickness

Opening like a marigold
crop of sun and dry soil
acrid, bright, sturdy.

Spreading its cancer
through the conduits of the body,
a slow damp murder.

Breathing like the sea
glowing with foam and plankton.
Rigid as an iron post

driven between my breasts.
Will you lift your hands
and shape this love

into a thing of goodness?
Will you permit me to live
when you are not looking?

Will you let me ask questions
with my mouth open?
I will not pretend any longer

to be a wind or a mood.
Even with our eyes closed
we are walking on someone's map.

The cat's song

Mine, says the cat, putting out his paw of darkness.
My lover, my friend, my slave, my toy, says
the cat making on your chest his gesture of drawing
milk from his mother's forgotten breasts.

Let us walk in the woods, says the cat.
I'll teach you to read the tabloid of scents,
to fade into shadow, wait like a trap, to hunt.
Now I lay this plump warm mouse on your mat.

You feed me, I try to feed you, we are friends,
says the cat, although I am more equal than you.
Can you leap twenty times the height of your body?
Can you run up and down trees? Jump between roofs?

Let us rub our bodies together and talk of touch.
My emotions are pure as salt crystals and as hard.
My lusts glow like my eyes. I sing to you in the mornings
walking round and round your bed and into your face.

Come I will teach you to dance as naturally
as falling asleep and waking and stretching long, long.
I speak greed with my paws and fear with my whiskers.
Envy lashes my tail. Love speaks me entire, a word

of fur. I will teach you to be still as an egg
and to slip like the ghost of wind through the grass.

Barbie Doll

This girlchild was born as usual
and presented dolls that did pee-pee
and miniature GE stoves and irons
and wee lipsticks the color of cherry candy.
Then in the magic of puberty, a classmate said:
You have a great big nose and fat legs.

She was healthy, tested intelligent,
possessed strong arms and back,
abundant sexual drive and manual dexterity.
She went to and fro apologizing.
Everyone saw a fat nose on thick legs.

She was advised to play coy,
exhorted to come on hearty,
exercise, diet, smile and wheedle.
Her good nature wore out
like a fan belt.
So she cut off her nose and her legs
and offered them up.

In the casket displayed on satin she lay
with the undertaker's cosmetics painted on,
a turned-up putty nose,
dressed in a pink and white nightie.
Doesn't she look pretty? everyone said.
Consummation at last.
To every woman a happy ending.

Daryl Hine

(b. 1936)

Northwest Passages

Here low tide and morning coincide
When ocean's underside, as if a veil
Were twitched aside, denuded by the tide,
Emerges flat, unprofitable, stale.[1]
Here pubescent forests fail to hide
The five-o'clock shadow on the mountainside
Close shaven to make newsprint and junk mail.
Here civilization, predominantly male,
Perpetrates unnatural matricide.

Snooty, aloof, polluted mountaintops,
Stuck-up, their heads forever in the clouds
While they cold-shoulder low-brow tourist traps
Strike forbidding, lofty attitudes
Against a breathless sky, sublimely iced.
How isolated and exclusive are
These uninhabitable altitudes
Domesticated by the calendar,
The picturesque prohibitively priced.

Stark on the covers of slick magazines
Where landscapes look too beautiful for words
The wilderness excels at making scenes.
Its present rate of defloration means
That travel nowadays is for the birds.
The home of mobile homes away from home,
Once the haunt of cormorants and cranes,
Of eagle and of seagull, has become
The realm of Burger Kings and Dairy Queens.

Tabula Rasa?[2]

For John Hollander

Titivate: cosmetic task
like cleaning up   a cluttered desk
to disinter   a dud decade
too undecided   to decode.

---

1   "How weary, stale, flat, and unprofitable / seem to me all the uses of this world" (*Hamlet*, I.ii.133-4)

2   a clean slate (Latin: "a scraped tablet")

Drifted drafts   of dry leaves make
decomposition   run amuck:
iffy *ifs*   and *buts* and *ands*,
abandoned means   aborted ends.
Legible leftover   language litters
the blankety-blank   embarrassed blotter's
doodles, indelible   dead letters
dictated but   not signed indeed
by the effete   influential dead
whose symptoms I   cannot deny:
Tennyson's elbow   Housman's knee.

Tabula rasa: trash the past?
scrap these screwed-up   scribbled post
scripts, pathetic   unpaid bills,
parodies   or parables?
Beg the question   and begin
anew and ever   more again,
ex nihilo?[1]   perhaps not quite
now every *bon mot*[2]   is a quote.
For plagiarists   and staircase wits
taste's wastebasket   always waits.

Point Grey[3]

Brought up as I was to ask of the weather
Whether it was fair or overcast,
Here, at least, it is a pretty morning,
The first fine day as I am told in months.
I took a path that led down to the beach,
Reflecting as I went on landscape, sex and weather.

I met a welcome wonderful enough
To exorcise the educated ghost
Within me. No, this country is not haunted,
Only the rain makes spectres of the mountains.

There they are, and there somehow is the problem
Not exactly of freedom or of generation
But just of living and the pain it causes.
Sometimes I think the air we breathe is mortal
And dies, trapped, in our unfeeling lungs.

---

1   (Latin) out of nothing
2   (French) clever saying
3   the peninsula on the west side of Vancouver, B.C.

Not too distant the mountains and the morning
Dropped their dim approval on the gesture
With which enthralled I greeted all this grandeur.
Beside the path, half buried in the bracken,
Stood a long-abandoned concrete bunker,
A little temple of lust, its rough walls covered
With religious frieze and votary inscription.

Personally I know no one who doesn't suffer
Some sore of guilt, and mostly bedsores, too,
Those that come from scratching where it itches
And that dangerous sympathy called prurience.
But all about release and absolution
Lie, in the waves that lap the dirty shingle
And the mountains that rise at hand above the rain.
Though I had forgotten that it could be so simple,
A beauty of sorts is nearly always within reach.

Judith Rodriguez

(b. 1936)

Eskimo occasion

I am in my Eskimo-hunting-song mood,
Aha!
The lawn is tundra   the car will not start
the sunlight is an avalanche   we are avalanche-struck at our
    breakfast
struck with sunlight through glass   me and my spoonfed
    daughters
out of this world in our kitchen.

I will sing the song of my daughter-hunting,
Oho!
The waves lay down   the ice grew strong
I sang the song   of dark water under ice
the song of winter fishing   the magic for seal rising
among the ancestor-masks.

I waited by water to dream new spirits,
Hoo!
The water spoke   the ice shouted
the sea opened   the sun made young shadows
they breathed my breathing   I took them from deep water
I brought them fur-warmed home.

I am dancing the years of the two great hunts,
Ya-hay!
It was I who waited   cold in the wind-break
I stamp like the bear   I call like the wind of the thaw
I leap like the sea spring-running.   My sunstruck daughters
    splutter
and chuckle and bang their spoons:

Mummy is singing at breakfast and dancing!
So big!

A lifetime devoted to literature

In your twenties you knew with elegiac certainty
you would die young. Your father's heart attack
tallied, a verification.

Thirty was your worst year: the thirties fatal to genius,
and genius undeclared by the would-be oracles.
You gave thought to publication;

then a news item — friend dropped dead in the street —
coeval, a get-up-and-go editorial
viceroy at thirty-four —

cheered you somehow. You planned aloud and in detail,
publishers ventured for you, reviews came your way
as you learned to joke and your hair thinned,

and several thromboses onward you inhabit unruffled
an active advisory presence: a sitter on Boards
preparing to live for ever.

Rebeca in a mirror

Our little tantrum, flushed and misery-hollow,
sits having it out
in a mirror; drawn stiff as it
till her joke of a body, from flat,
flaps with the spasms of crying.
The small eyes frighten
the small eyes clutching
out of such puffed intensity of rage.
She will not look at people about, or follow
a dangled toy. No-one can budge her huge
fury of refusal; being accustomed
to orchards of encouraging faces rolled in her lap,
cloud-bursts of ministering teats and spoons
and the pair of deft pin-welding scavengers
that keep her clean,
she is appalled by her own lonely image.
And we, that she's into
this share of knowledge,
and is ridiculously
comic in her self-feeding anger,
her frantic
blindness by now to the refuge
of a dozen anchoring shoulders and outheld hands,
vassals,
her multitudes . . .

Yet who can be more alone, months walled
in her cot's white straw,
the family hushed
and hovering, afraid to touch
so small
a trigger of uproar;
or so much as flutter
one of her million or more
petulant rufflers spoiling for noise and action
around the nerve-end flares that signal ruction?

And think, she has not long come
through a year of twilight time in one gradual place
further and faster
than death, or the endless relays
of causeless disaster;
frail-cauled,[1] a hero, past perils vaster than space
she has come—
and can never re-enter
the unasked bodily friendship
of her first home.

---

1   The caul is that part of the amniotic sac that sometimes envelops an infant's head at
birth.

Seamus Heaney

(b.1939)

Personal Helicon[1]

For Michael Longley

As a child, they could not keep me from wells
And old pumps with buckets and windlasses.
I loved the dark drop, the trapped sky, the smells
Of waterweed, fungus and dank moss.

One, in a brickyard, with a rotted board top.
I savoured the rich crash when a bucket
Plummeted down at the end of a rope.
So deep you saw no reflection in it.

A shallow one under a dry stone ditch
Fructified like any aquarium.
When you dragged out long roots from the soft mulch
A white face hovered over the bottom.

Others had echoes, gave back your own call
With a clean new music in it. And one
Was scaresome for there, out of ferns and tall
Foxgloves, a rat slapped across my reflection.

Now, to pry into roots, to finger slime,
To stare, big-eyed Narcissus,[2] into some spring
Is beneath all adult dignity. I rhyme
To see myself, to set the darkness echoing.

Poor Women in a City Church

The small wax candles melt to light,
Flicker in marble, reflect bright
Asterisks on brass candlesticks:
At the Virgin's altar on the right
Blue flames are jerking on wicks.

Old dough-faced women with black shawls
Drawn down tight kneel in the stalls.
Cold yellow candle-tongues, blue flame

---

1   In Greek mythology, Mount Helicon was the site of the fountain of Hippocrene, sacred
     to the Muses.
2   a lovely youth who mistook his own reflection for a beautiful nymph, and pined away
     for love of this image

Mince and caper as whispered calls
Take wing up to the Holy Name.

Thus each day in the sacred place
They kneel. Golden shrines, altar lace,
Marble columns and cool shadows
Still them. In the gloom you cannot trace
A wrinkle on their beeswax brows.

Docker

There, in the corner, staring at his drink.
The cap juts like a gantry's crossbeam,
Cowling plated forehead and sledgehead jaw.
Speech is clamped in the lips' vice.

That fist would drop a hammer on a Catholic—
Oh yes, that kind of thing could start again;
The only Roman collar he tolerates
Smiles all round his sleek pint of porter.

Mosaic[1] imperatives bang home like rivets;
God is a foreman with certain definite views
Who orders life in shifts of work and leisure.
A factory horn will blare the Resurrection.

He sits, strong and blunt as a Celtic cross,[2]
Clearly used to silence and an armchair:
Tonight the wife and children will be quiet
At slammed door and smoker's cough in the hall.

The Grauballe Man[3]

As if he had been poured
in tar, he lies
on a pillow of turf
and seems to weep

the black river of himself.
The grain of his wrists
is like bog oak,
the ball of his heel

---

1   like the laws of Moses
2   an upright cross with a circle behind the cross-beam
3   One of a number of men and women from Iron Age times, whose bodies were preserved
     in Danish bogs. They were evidently the victims of ritual sacrifice.

like a basalt egg.
His instep has shrunk
cold as a swan's foot
or a wet swamp root.

His hips are the ridge
and purse of a mussel,
his spine an eel arrested
under a glisten of mud.

The head lifts,
the chin is a visor
raised above the vent
of his slashed throat

that has tanned and toughened.
The cured wound
opens inwards to a dark
elderberry place.

Who will say 'corpse'
to his vivid cast?
Who will say 'body'
to his opaque repose?

And his rusted hair,
a mat unlikely
as a foetus's.
I first saw his twisted face

in a photograph,
a head and shoulder
out of the peat,
bruised like a forceps baby,

but now he lies
perfected in my memory,
down to the red horn
of his nails,

hung in the scales
with beauty and atrocity:
with the Dying Gaul[1]
too strictly compassed

---

1   a famous statue, also known as "The Dying Gladiator," in the Capitoline Museum in
Rome

on his shield,
with the actual weight
of each hooded victim,
slashed and dumped.

The Railway Children

When we climbed the slopes of the cutting
We were eye-level with the white cups
Of the telegraph poles and the sizzling wires.

Like lovely freehand they curved for miles
East and miles west beyond us, sagging
Under their burden of swallows.

We were small and thought we knew nothing
Worth knowing. We thought words travelled the wires
In the shiny pouches of raindrops,

Each one seeded full with the light
Of the sky, the gleam of the lines, and ourselves
So infinitesimally scaled

We could stream through the eye of a needle.

From the Frontier of Writing

The tightness and the nilness round that space
when the car stops in the road, the troops inspect
its make and number and, as one bends his face

towards your window, you catch sight of more
on a hill beyond, eyeing with intent
down cradled guns that hold you under cover

and everything is pure interrogation
until a rifle motions and you move
with guarded unconcerned acceleration—

a little emptier, a little spent
as always by that quiver in the self,
subjugated, yes, and obedient.

So you drive on to the frontier of writing
where it happens again. The guns on tripods;
the sergeant with his on-off mike repeating

data about you, waiting for the squawk
of clearance; the marksman training down
out of the sun upon you like a hawk.

And suddenly you're through, arraigned yet freed,
as if you'd passed from behind a waterfall
on the black current of a tarmac road

past armour-plated vehicles, out between
the posted soldiers flowing and receding
like tree shadows into the polished windscreen.

Margaret Atwood

(b. 1939)

This Is a Photograph of Me

It was taken some time ago.
At first it seems to be
a smeared
print: blurred lines and grey flecks
blended with the paper;

then, as you scan
it, you see in the left-hand corner
a thing that is like a branch: part of a tree
(balsam or spruce) emerging
and, to the right, halfway up
what ought to be a gentle
slope, a small frame house.

In the background there is a lake,
and beyond that, some low hills.

(The photograph was taken
the day after I drowned.

I am in the lake, in the center
of the picture, just under the surface.

It is difficult to say where
precisely, or to say
how large or small I am:
the effect of water
on light is a distortion

but if you look long enough,
eventually
you will be able to see me.)

Journey to the Interior

There are similarities
I notice: that the hills
which the eyes make flat as a wall, welded
together, open as I move
to let me through; become
endless as prairies; that the trees
grow spindly, have their roots
often in swamps; that this is a poor country;
that a cliff is not known
as rough except by hand, and is
therefore inaccessible. Mostly

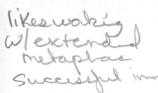

that travel is not the easy going
from point to point, a dotted
line on a map, location
plotted on a square surface
but that I move surrounded by a tangle
of branches, a net of air and alternate
light and dark, at all times;
that there are no destinations
apart from this.

There are differences
of course: the lack of reliable charts;
more important, the distraction of small details:
your shoe among the brambles under the chair
where it shouldn't be; lucent
white mushrooms and a paring knife
on the kitchen table; a sentence
crossing my path, sodden as a fallen log
I'm sure I passed yesterday

       (have I been
walking in circles again?)

but mostly the danger:
many have been here, but only
some have returned safely.

A compass is useless; also
trying to take directions
from the movements of the sun,
which are erratic;
and words here are as pointless
as calling in a vacant
wilderness.

     Whatever I do I must
keep my head. I know
it is easier for me to lose my way
forever here, than in other landscapes

Can,

At the Tourist Centre in Boston

There is my country under glass,
a white relief-
map with red dots for the cities,
reduced to the size of a wall

Seeing her country
reduced to a
series of photos

and beside it 10 blownup snapshots
one for each province,
in purple-browns and odd reds,
the green of the trees dulled;
all blues however

of an assertive purity.

Mountains and lakes and more lakes
(though Quebec is a restaurant and Ontario the empty
interior of the parliament buildings),
with nobody climbing the trails and hauling out
the fish and splashing in the water

but arrangements of grinning tourists—
look here, Saskatchewan
is a flat lake, some convenient rocks
where two children pose with a father
and the mother is cooking something
in immaculate slacks by a smokeless fire,
her teeth white as detergent.

Whose dream is this, I would like to know:
is this a manufactured
hallucination, a cynical fiction, a lure
for export only?

we have people not just nature

I seem to remember people,
at least in the cities, also slush,
machines and assorted garbage. Perhaps
that was my private mirage

which will just evaporate
when I go back. Or the citizens will be gone,
run off to the peculiarly-
green forests
to wait among the brownish mountains
for the platoons of tourists
and plan their odd red massacres.

Unsuspecting
window lady, I ask you:

Do you see nothing
watching you from under the water?

Was the sky ever that blue?

Who really lives there?

*early phase of
the Canada
as a subj.*

[handwritten: bushed—to go mad out in the wilderness]

MARGARET ATWOOD

[handwritten: very interested in Relationships b/h man + the land]

Progressive Insanities of a Pioneer

i

He stood, a point
on a sheet of green paper
proclaiming himself the centre,

[handwritten: Theme—the overwhelming power, the earth is beyond man's capabilities]

with no walls, no borders
anywhere; the sky no height
above him, totally un-
enclosed
and shouted:

Let me out!

ii

He dug the soil in rows,
imposed himself with shovels
He asserted
into the furrows, I
am not random.

The ground
replied with aphorisms:

a tree-sprout, a nameless
weed, words
he couldn't understand.

iii

The house pitched
the plot staked
in the middle of nowhere.

At night the mind
inside, in the middle
of nowhere.

The idea of an animal
patters across the roof.

In the darkness the fields
defend themselves with fences
in vain:
            everything
            is getting in.

pioneer thinks he controls the land. doesn't understand the nature of the land he dealing w/

iv

By daylight he resisted.
He said, disgusted
with the swamp's clamourings and the outbursts
of rocks,

        This is not order
        but the absence
        of order.

He was wrong, the unanswering
forest implied:

        It was
        an ordered absence — *an absence of human beings & human patterns, not necess. an absence of order*

v

For many years
he fished for a great vision,
dangling the hooks of sown
roots under the surface
of the shallow earth.
It was like
enticing whales with a bent
pin. Besides he thought

allusion to Job

God demonstrates his enormous power to this egotistical cocky insignificant human being.

in that country
only the worms were biting.

vi

If he had known unstructured
space is a deluge
and stocked his log house-
boat with all the animals

allusion w/ Noah's ark

even the wolves,

he might have floated.

He might have been OK if he had invited nature + appreciated her intimate nature

But obstinate he
stated, The land is solid
and stamped,

oddity

watching his foot sink
down through stone
up to the knee.

He denies her importance + power

I am not an obj. of your Knowledge

vii

The earth won't let itself be ruled

Things
refused to name themselves; refused
to let him name them. *E our name, not theirs*

The wolves hunted
outside.

On his beaches, his clearings,
by the surf of under-
growth breaking
at his feet, he foresaw
disintegration
                    and in the end
through eyes
made ragged by his
effort, the tension
between subject and object,

the green   *nature breaks in*
vision, the unnamed   *on him + (we assume)*
whale invaded.   *takes over —*
                         an overpowering experience

from: *The Journals of Susanna Moodie*[1]

Further Arrivals

After we had crossed the long illness
that was the ocean, we sailed up-river *— St. Lawrence*

On the first island *Irish*
the immigrants threw off their clothes[2]
and danced like sandflies

We left behind one by one
the cities rotting with cholera,
one by one our civilized
distinctions

and entered a large darkness.

1805– 1885

---

1   Susanna Moodie was an Englishwoman who settled with her husband in rural Ontario in
    1832, and published a graphic account of their experiences in *Roughing It In the Bush*
    (1852), from which Atwood has re-created these monologues.
2   The shedding of clothes is described in chapter One of *Roughing It in the Bush*.

great writer of ambivalence *(handwritten)*

MARGARET ATWOOD (has mixed feelings)

in this poem tries to discuss the mixed feelings *(handwritten)*

It was our own Canadian Love about *(Canadian, Love, about — handwritten insertions)*
ignorance we entered. this country. *(handwritten)*

I have not come out yet

My brain gropes nervous
tentacles in the night, sends out
fears hairy as bears,
demands lamps; or waiting

for my shadowy husband, hears
malice in the trees' whispers.

I need wolf's eyes to see
the truth.

I refuse to look in a mirror.

Whether the wilderness is
real or not
depends on who lives there.

One of Moodie's children died *(handwritten)*

Death of a Young Son by Drowning

He, who navigated with success
the dangerous river of his own birth
once more set forth

on a voyage of discovery
into the land I floated on
but could not touch to claim.

His feet slid on the bank,
the currents took him;
he swirled with ice and trees in the swollen water

and plunged into distant regions,
his head a bathysphere;[1]
through his eyes' thin glass bubbles
he looked out, reckless adventurer
on a landscape stranger than Uranus
we have all been to and some remember.

There was an accident; the air locked,
he was hung in the river like a heart.

---

1   a spherical diving-bell for deep-sea observation

They retrieved the swamped body,

cairn of my plans and future charts,
with poles and hooks
from among the nudging logs.

It was spring, the sun kept shining, the new grass
lept to solidity;
my hands glistened with details.

After the long trip I was tired of waves.
My foot hit rock. The dreamed sails
collapsed, ragged.

I planted him in this country
like a flag.

Dream 1: The Bush Garden

I stood once more in that garden
sold, deserted and
gone to seed

In the dream I could
see down through the earth, could see
the potatoes curled
like pale grubs in the soil
the radishes thrusting down
their fleshy snouts, the beets
pulsing like slow amphibian hearts

Around my feet
the strawberries were surging, huge
and shining

When I bent
to pick, my hands
came away red and wet

In the dream I said
I should have known
anything planted here
would come up blood

Thoughts From Underground

When I first reached this country
I hated it
and I hated it more each year:

in summer the light a
violent blur, the heat
thick as a swamp,
the green things fiercely
shoving themselves upwards, the
eyelids bitten by insects

In winter our teeth were brittle
with cold. We fed on squirrels.
At night the house cracked.
In the mornings, we thawed
the bad bread over the stove.

Then we were made successful
and I felt I ought to love
this country.
              I said I loved it
and my mind saw double.

I began to forget myself
in the middle
of sentences. Events
were split apart

I fought. I constructed
desperate paragraphs of praise, everyone
ought to love it because

and set them up at intervals

        due to natural resources, native industry, superior
        penitentiaries
        we will all be rich and powerful

flat as highway billboards

        who can doubt it, look how
        fast Belleville[1] is growing

(though it is still no place for an english gentleman)

* * *

---

1   a town in southern Ontario where the Moodies eventually settled

Narcissus Echo

Tricks With Mirrors

i

It's no coincidence
this is a used
furniture warehouse.

I enter with you
and become a mirror.

Mirrors
are the perfect lovers,

that's it, carry me up the stairs
by the edges, don't drop me,

that would be bad luck,
throw me on the bed

reflecting side up,
fall into me,

it will be your own
mouth you hit, firm and glassy,

your own eyes you find you
are up against   closed   closed

ii

There is more to a mirror
than you looking at

your full-length body
flawless but reversed,

there is more than this dead blue
oblong eye turned outwards to you.

Think about the frame.
The frame is carved, it is important,

it exists, it does not reflect you,
it does not recede and recede, it has limits

and reflections of its own.
There's a nail in the back

to hang it with; there are several nails,
think about the nails,

pay attention to the nail
marks in the wood,

they are important too.

iii

Don't assume it is passive
or easy, this clarity

with which I give you yourself.
Consider what restraint it

takes: breath withheld, no anger
or joy disturbing the surface

of the ice.
You are suspended in me

beautiful and frozen, I
preserve you, in me you are safe.

It is not a trick either,
it is a craft:

mirrors are crafty.

iv

I wanted to stop this,
this life flattened against the wall,

mute and devoid of colour,
built of pure light,

this life of vision only, split
and remote, a lucid impasse.

I confess: this is not a mirror,
it is a door

I am trapped behind.
I wanted you to see me here,

say the releasing word, whatever
that may be, open the wall.

V

Instead you stand in front of me
combing your hair.

You don't like these metaphors.
All right:

Perhaps I am not a mirror.
Perhaps I am a pool.
Think about pools.

IS / NOT

i

Love is not a profession
genteel or otherwise

sex is not dentistry
the slick filling of aches and cavities

you are not my doctor
you are not my cure,

nobody has that
power, you are merely a fellow/traveller.

Give up this medical concern,
buttoned, attentive,

permit yourself anger
and permit me mine

which needs neither
your approval nor your surprise

which does not need to be made legal
which is not against a disease

but against you,
which does not need to be understood

or washed or cauterized,
which needs instead

to be said and said.
Permit me the present tense.

[handwritten annotation in right margin: language doesn't seem all that powerful / lots of negation, when she starts / pos. it's on the expression of anger / that doesn't rely on imagery or figures of speech]

I am not a saint or a cripple,
I am not a wound; now I will see
whether I am a coward.

I dispose of my good manners,
you don't have to kiss my wrists.

This is a journey, not a war,
there is no outcome,
I renounce predictions

and aspirins, I resign the future
as I would resign an expired passport:
picture and signature are gone
along with holidays and safe returns.

We're stuck here
on this side of the border
in this country of thumbed streets and stale buildings

where there is nothing spectacular
to see and the weather is ordinary

where *love* occurs in its pure form only
on the cheaper of the souvenirs

where we must walk slowly,
where we may not get anywhere

or anything, where we keep going,
fighting our ways, our way
not out but through.

Dennis Lee

(b. 1939)

from: *Civil Elegies*

1

Often I sit in the sun and brooding over the city, always
in airborne shapes among the pollution I hear them, returning;
pouring across the square[1]
in fetid descent, they darken the towers
and the wind-swept place of meeting and whenever
the thick air clogs my breathing it teems with their presence.
Many were born in Canada, and living unlived lives they died
of course but died truncated, stunted, never at
home in native space and not yet
citizens of a human body of kind. And it is Canada
that specialized in this deprivation. Therefore the spectres arrive,
        congregating in bitter droves, thick in the April sunlight,
accusing us and we are no different, though you would not expect
the furies[2] assembled in hogtown[3] and ring me round, invisible, demanding
what time of our lives we wait for till we shall start to be.
Until they come the wide square stretches out
serene and singly by moments it takes us in, each one for now
a passionate civil man, until it
sends us back to the acres of gutted intentions,
back to the concrete debris, to parking scars and the four-square tiers
of squat and righteous lives. And here
once more, I watch the homing furies' arrival.

I sat one morning by the Moore,[4] off to the west
ten yards and saw though diffident my city nailed against the sky
in ordinary glory.
It is not much to ask. A place, a making,
two towers, a teeming, a genesis, a city.
And the men and women moved in their own space,
performing their daily lives, and their presence occurred
in time as it occurred, patricians in
muddy York[5] and made their compact together against the gangs of the new.
And as that crumpled before the shambling onset, again the
lives we had not lived in phalanx invisibly staining
the square and vistas, casting back I saw
regeneration twirl its blood and the rebels riding
riderless down Yonge Street, plain men much

---

1   Nathan Phillips Square, in front of Toronto's New City Hall
2   in Greek mythology, the avenging deities Allecto, Megaera, and Tisiphone, who punished
     wrongdoers
3   a slang name for Toronto
4   an abstract sculpture called "The Archer" by the English sculptor Henry Moore (b.1898)
5   an early name for Toronto, from 1793-1834

goaded by privilege—our other origin, and cried
"Mackenzie[1] knows a word, Mackenzie
knows a meaning!" but it was not true. Eight hundred-odd steely Canadians
turned tail at the cabbage patch when a couple of bullets fizzed
and the loyalists, scared skinny by the sound of their own gunfire,
gawked and bolted south to the fort like rabbits,
the rebels for their part bolting north to the pub: the first
spontaneous mutual retreat in the history of warfare.
Canadians, in flight.

Buildings oppress me, and the sky-concealing wires
bunch zigzag through the air. I know
the dead persist in
buildings, by-laws, porticos—the city I live in
is clogged with their presence; they
dawdle about in our lives and form a destiny, still
incomplete, still dead weight, still
demanding whether Canada will be.

But the mad bomber, Chartier[2] of Major Street, Chartier
said it: that if a country has no past,
neither is it a country and promptly
blew himself to bits in the parliament john, leaving as civil testament
assorted chunks of prophet, twitching and
bobbing to rest in the flush.
And what can anyone do in this country, baffled and
making our penance for ancestors, what did they leave us? Indian-swindlers,
stewards of unclaimed earth and rootless what does it matter if they, our
forebears' flesh and bone were often
good men, good men do not matter to history.
And what can we do here now, for at last we have no notion
of what we might have come to be in America, alternative, and how make public
a presence which is not sold out utterly to the modern? utterly? to the
savage inflictions of what is for real, it pays off, it is only
accidentally less than human?

In the city I long for, green trees still
asphyxiate. The crowds emerge at five from jobs
that rankle and lag. Heavy developers
pay off aldermen still; the craft of neighbourhood,
its whichway streets and generations
anger the planners, they go on jamming their maps
with asphalt panaceas; single men
still eke out evenings courting, in parks, alone.

---

1   In 1837, William Lyon Mackenzie, the first mayor of Toronto, led a rebellion against British
      rule which foundered when the rebels were driven out of their stronghold in Montgomery's
      Tavern on Yonge Street.
2   Paul Chartier, who tried to blow up the Canadian House of Commons in Ottawa in 1966.

A man could spend a lifetime looking for
peace in that city. And the lives give way around him—marriages
founder, the neighbourhoods sag—until
the emptiness comes down on him to stay.
But in the city I long for men complete
their origins. Among the tangle of
hydro, hydrants, second mortgages, amid
the itch for new debentures, greater expressways,
in sober alarm they jam their works of progress, asking where in truth
they come from and to whom they must belong.
And thus they clear a space in which
the full desires of those that begot them, great animating desires
that shrank and grew hectic as the land pre-empted their lives
might still take root, which eddy now and
drift in the square, being neither alive nor dead.
And the people accept a flawed inheritance
and they give it a place in their midst, forfeiting progress, forfeiting
dollars, forfeiting yankee visions of cities that in time it might grow
whole at last in their lives, they might
belong once more to their forebears, becoming their own men.

To be our own men! in dread to live
the land, our own harsh country, beloved, the prairie, the foothills—
and for me it is lake by rapids by stream-fed lake, threading
north through the terminal vistas of black spruce, in a
bitter, cherished land it is farm after
farm in the waste of the continental outcrop—
for me it is Shield[1] but wherever terrain informs our lives and claims us;
and then, no longer haunted by
unlived presence, to live the cities:
to furnish, out of the traffic and smog and the shambles of dead precursors,
a civil habitation that is
human, and our own.

The spectres drift across the square in rows.
How empire permeates! And we sit down
in Nathan Phillips Square, among the sun,
as if our lives were real.
Lacunae.[2] Parking lots. Regenerations.
Newsstand euphorics and Revell's[3] sign, that not
one countryman has learned, that
men and women live that
they may make that
life worth dying. Living. Hey,
the dead ones! Gentlemen, generations of

---

1   the Laurentian Shield
2   blank or empty spaces
3   Revell was the Finnish designer of Toronto's New City Hall.

acquiescent spectres gawk at the chrome
on American cars on Queen Street, gawk and slump and retreat.
And over the square where I sit, congregating above the Archer
they crowd in a dense baffled throng and the sun does not shine through.

* * *

Patrick Lane

(b. 1939)

Pissaro's Tomb[1]

On broad hills, the broken backs of mountains
and the cracks where earth has split from earth
high walls and viaducts, canals and temples
stand rooted in grey stone. But do not speak.
Only the living eye breeds language
where no language is. The words conjured
are only images. The memory of something
in the race that is unknown.

Pissaro stood by these walls
who now lies dried and shrunken
in his tomb beside the sea
The great cathedral shelters him
where priests walk hooded
beside God. And Pissaro died
who broke an empire into dust.
So it is told in our histories.
And so it was. But the dead do not speak.
Only the living eye breeds language
out of dust. It is what holds this empire
still. This lust for history.

On broken hills the monolithic stones
that once were mountains stand.
Men move upon the land. Pissaro
lies in the capital he built.
The men who were his enemies are gone,
their history unknown, their language lost
as ancient times are lost
though they come and go in me
and will until what now I speak
men know as silence.

Winter 6

The guests have arrived at last. The old
woman in rags who pushes a steel cage
filled with her life, and the man with dogs,
the two pit bulls who whine with eagerness
at the end of their tethers. The young boy
with the burns on his face and shoulders

---

1   Francisco Pizarro (c.1471-1541), Spanish conqueror of Peru, died in Lima by an assassin's
     hand.

stands by the piano where the girl with no legs
plays early Mozart, one of the pieces
full of promise composed when he was still
a child. There is wine and fruit and fine brandy.
Everything is ready to begin.

The host is sitting in his study, staring
at a painting from the Ming Dynasty.[1]
Soon he will go down the long white stairs
and join them, but for now he is simply happy,
the painting one of winter, so much
like the porcelain of the period, pale,
with only the faintest of green
buried beneath the pure hard surface.

Winter 9

Each day the time grows less, the hours
shorter by a few minutes, the sun
farther away. He remembers the Inca,
the way they would tie
a rope to the sun and hitch it to stone
out of fear it would never return.
How strange to think of their songs,
the supplications, the hearts torn out,
the blood on the altars. What wonder
must they have known as they lay
their bodies on stone? How simple
their desire, the priests chanting,
the sun drifting farther and farther
north. But not now. For him it is winter
and for them the sun is returning.
He sees them singing on the terraces
as they plant the young corn,
their children waiting for the season
when they are chosen, the one that begins
when everything starts to end.

How beautiful, he thinks, gazing
from his window at the night, this darkness
gathering in the blue snow.

---

1   the ruling dynasty in China from 1368 to 1643, a period of great artistic achievement

Winter 40

She is a northern woman, barely more
than a child, one who has walked through the drifts
to find her dream vision. Her eyes are
covered by a blade of bone, a thin slit
cut in it so the light does not blind her.
The man she has found is not one of the four
possibilities: father, brother, lover, son.
He is the dream man, given to her by the snow.

He has wandered far from the sea,
his crew dead, his ship broken in the ice.
If there were someone there to translate his song
it would start with the words: *At last.*
But only she is there.
As he sings she cuts off his fingers,
only these small bones and the twenty-six
teeth for her necklace.

They will be her medicine, something
to shake over the bellies of women
in childbirth, the heads of men
who have returned empty from hunting,
their minds become snow.

How like a real man he is, she thinks.
How real this dream, the blood on the ice.
How thin he is, how much like the snow is his flesh.

Gwendolyn MacEwen

(1941–1990)

Eden, Eden

it is the thunder is
the vocal monument
to the death-wished rain,
or obelisk in a granite sky
that roars a jawed epitaph
through cut cloud.

in the morning
thunder is the reared stone elephant,
        the grown element of grey;
its trunk is vertical and thick as thunder;
the elephant stubs down the wrenched lightning,
funnelling a coughed verse
for the suicidal rain
in the morning.

the stormed man is heavy with rain
and mumbles beneath the elephant gargle
and his jaw locks human in the rain,
and under the unlocked jaw of the cut sky
and under the bullets of the elephant's trunk

he is thinking of a thunder garden.

behind sense he is thinking of a warped tree
with heavy fruit falling,
peaked rock fighting the ragged fern
in the other storm's centre,
a monolithic thunder tree
and a man and woman naked and green with rain
above its carved roots, genesis

Inside the Great Pyramid[1]

all day the narrow shaft
received us; everyone
came out sweating and
gasping for air, and one
old man collapsed
upon a stair;
      I thought:

---

1   The Great Pyramid at Giza in Egypt covered 13 acres, and originally rose to a height of 481 feet; it was built by the pharoah Cheops in c.2650 B.C.

the fact that it has stood
so long
is no guarantee
it will stand today,
but went in anyway
and heard when I was
halfway up a long
low rumbling like
the echo of ancient stones
first straining to their place;
        I thought:
we have made this, we
have made *this.*
I scrambled out into
the scandalous sun and saw
the desert was an hourglass
we had forgotten to invert,
a tasselled camel falling
to his knees, the River
filling the great waterclock
of earth.

The Discovery

do not imagine that the exploration
ends, that she has yielded all her mystery
or that the map you hold
cancels further discovery

I tell you her uncovering takes years,
takes centuries, and when you find her naked
look again,
admit there is something else you cannot name,
a veil, a coating just above the flesh
which you cannot remove by your mere wish

when you see the land naked, look again
(burn your maps, that is not what I mean),
I mean the moment when it seems most plain
is the moment when you must begin again

Dark Pines Under Water

This land like a mirror turns you inward
And you become a forest in a furtive lake;
The dark pines of your mind reach downward,
You dream in the green of your time,
Your memory is a row of sinking pines.

Explorer, you tell yourself this is not what you came for
Although it is good here, and green;
You had meant to move with a kind of largeness,
You had planned a heavy grace, an anguished dream.

But the dark pines of your mind dip deeper
And you are sinking, sinking, sleeper
In an elementary world;
There is something down there and you want it told.

The Child Dancing

there's no way I'm going to write about
the child dancing in the Warsaw ghetto
in his body of rags

there were only two corpses
on the pavement that day
and the child I will not write about
had a face as pale and trusting
as the moon

(so did
the boy with a green belly full of dirt
lying by the roadside
in a novel of Kazantzakis[1]
and the small girl T. E. Lawrence[2] wrote about
who they found after the Turkish massacre
with one shoulder chopped off, crying:
"don't *hurt* me, Baba!")

I don't feel like slandering them with poetry.

the child who danced
in the Warsaw ghetto
to some music no one else could hear
had moon-eyes, no
green horror and no fear
but something worse

a simple desire to please
the people who stayed

---

1 Nikos Kazantzakis (1883-1957), Greek author of *Zorba the Greek* (1943) and *The Last Temptation of Christ* (1951).
2 Thomas Edward Lawrence (1885-1937), an English archeologist, writer, and soldier, was also known as Lawrence of Arabia. During the British campaign in the Near East in 1915-1916, he led a successful Arab revolt against the occupying Turks.

to watch him shuffle back and forth,
his feet wrapped in the newspapers
of another ordinary day

Letter to a Future Generation

we did not anticipate you, you bright ones
though some of us saw you kneeling behind our bombs,
we did not fervently grow towards you
for most of us grew backwards
sowing our seed in the black fields of history

avoid monuments, engrave our names beneath your own
for you have consumed our ashes by now
for you have one quiet mighty language by now

do not excavate our cities
to catalogue the objects of our doom
but burn all you find to make yourselves room
you have no need of archaeology,
your faces are your total history

for us it was necessary to invent a darkness,
to subtract light in order to see,
for us it was certain death to know our names
as they were written in the black books of history

I stand with an animal at my left hand
and a warm, breathing ghost at my right
saying, Remember that this letter was made
for you to burn, that its meaning lies
only in your burning it,
that its lines await your cleansing fire—
understand it only insofar
as that warm ghost at my right hand breathed
down my blood and for a moment wrote the lines
while guns sounded out from a mythical city
and destroyed the times

Jeni Couzyn

(b. 1942)

House of Changes

My body is a wide house
a commune
of bickering women, hearing
their own breathing
denying each other.

Nearest the door
ready in her black leather
is *Vulnerable*. She lives in the hall
her face painted with care
her black boots reaching her crotch
her black hair shining
her skin milky and soft as butter.
If you should ring the doorbell
she would answer
and a wound would open across her eyes
as she touched your hand.

On the stairs, glossy and determined
is *Mindful*. She's the boss, handing out
punishments and rations and examination
papers with precise
justice. She keeps her perceptions in a huge
album under her arm
her debts in the garden with the weedkill
friends in a card-index
on the windowsill of the sittingroom
and a tape-recording of the world
on earphones
which she plays to herself over and over
assessing her life
writing summaries.

In the kitchen is *Commendable*.
The only lady in the house who
dresses in florals
she is always busy, always doing something
for someone she has
a lot of friends. Her hands are quick and
cunning as blackbirds
her pantry is stuffed with loaves and fishes
she knows the times of trains and
mends fuses and makes
a lot of noise with the vacuum cleaner.
In her linen cupboard, new-ironed and neatly
folded, she keeps her resentments like
wedding presents—each week

takes them out for counting not to
lose any but would never think of
using any being a lady.

Upstairs in a white room is
my favourite. She is *Equivocal*
has no flesh on her bones
that are changeable as yarrow stalks.
She hears her green plants talking
watches the bad dreams under the world
unfolding
spends all her days and nights
arranging her symbols
never sleeps
never eats hamburgers
never lets anyone into her room
never asks for anything.

In the basement is *Harmful.*
She is the keeper of weapons
the watchdog. Keeps intruders at bay
but the others keep her
locked up in the daytime and when she escapes
she comes out screaming
smoke streaming from her nostrils
flames on her tongue
razor-blades for fingernails
skewers for eyes.

I am *Imminent*
live out in the street
watching them. I lodge myself in other people's
heads with a sleeping bag
strapped to my back.
One day I'll perhaps get to like them enough
those rough, truthful women
to move in. One by one
I'm making friends with them all
unobtrusively, slow and steady
slow and steady.

Spell for Jealousy

Be loved, my beloved.
Be sweetened, sour one.
Be filled, empty one.

Bring all the thief has given home to our house
Bring all the thief has given home to our bed
Bring all the thief has given home to our love
Bring all the thief has given home to me.

Light of her brighten me
Spite of her strengthen me
Joy of her gladden me.

Lady as candle is to the full sun of noon
As toad is to the great whale of the ocean
As leaf is to the mighty forest of the mountain
Are you now to me and my loved one.

Let the wind take you
Let the water take you
Let the rain take you.

You are burr in his sock
You are grain in his shoe
Now he will forget you.

Spell to Soften the Hard Heart of a Woman

The almond has trapped herself in a cage of bone,
The chestnut in bristle is hidden,
The gnarled old man still trembles like a boy at the
    sound of your name.

Your hurt be in the ground,
Your fear be in the wind,
Your pain be in the stone.

The cords of your heart are untied,
The envious thorn is drawn from your eye,
The scaly armour falls from you making you young.

By this flame, holy,
By this water, holy,
By earth, holy,
By air, holy.

The spiteful shadow is trimmed from your heel,
The nine wounds from your mother's whip
      are washed from your blood,
Your dark of father is filled with father love.

    Be blessed by gardenia,
    By hyacinth, blessed,
    By honeysuckle, blessed,

    By this star, holy,
    By night, holy,
    By laughter, holy,
    By this kiss, holy.

Daphne Marlatt

(b. 1942)

from: *Steveston*

Ghost

oily ring shimmering, scintillating round the stern
of the boat you have just painted, *Elma K,* all your ties to shore,
your daughters, wife. Candy cache for the littlest grandchild
peering, short-frocked, over the pen where you, below water level,
fork up out of the deep—hooked, iced, dressed in slimey
death rendered visible—salmon.

"Nobody talks about them
anymore," the ghosts that used to rise when you, a child, crossing
the dyke from BC Packers,[1] night, saw, Out of the dark this strange
white light, or covering someone's rooftop, invisible to all but
strangers, this blue light telling of death.

(methane? invisible organic rot? We only know the extinction
of open marsh by concrete; the burial of burial ground by corporate
property.

But *then* there were places, you say, Chinaman's Hat,
where you couldn't sleep at night, fresh flower in your cabin, for
the host of restless souls' unburied hands outstretcht, returning,
claim their link with the decomposing earth

(ancestral: fertile as
death: hello briar rose, blackberry & trumpet flower. All their faces
lucent & warmlipt shining before your eyes: teachers, cabaret girls,
longlegged American army wives you chauffered, cared for, daughters,
friends of your daughters, down thru the water smiles of easy girls,
caught, kore, in the black hole of your eye, yourself a ghost now
of the natural world.

Were you fined? Did you cross the border inad-
verdently? Did chart & compass, all direction, fail? Interned,
your people confined to a small space where rebirth, will,
push you out thru the rings of material prosperity at war's
end fixed, finally, as citizens of an exploited earth:
you drive your own car, construct your own house, create your
registered place at Packers' camp, walk the fine (concrete)
line of private property.

---

1   the largest fish-packers and processors in British Columbia

But still, at night, tied up in some dark harbour,
it's the cries of women in orgasm you hear echoing, with the slap of
water against your hull, coming in, coming in, from far reaches
of the infinite world. And still, at sea, boundaries give way:
white women, white bellies of salmon thieved by powerful boats.

There are no territories. And the ghosts of landlocked camps are
all behind you. Only the blip of depth sounder & fish finder,
harmonic of bells warning a taut line, & the endless hand over
hand flip of the fish into silver pen—successive, infinite—

What do the charts say? Return, return. Return of what doesn't
die. Violence in mute form. Walking a fine line.

Only, always to dream of erotic ghosts of the flowering earth;
to return to a decomposed ground choked by refuse, profit, & the
concrete of private property; to find yourself disinherited from
your claim to the earth.

* * *

from: *Touch to My Tongue*

in the dark of the coast

there is fern and frost, a gathering of small birds melting song in the under-
brush. close, you talk to one. there is the cedar slant of your hair as it falls
gold over your shoulder, over your naked, dearly known skin — its smell, its answering touch to my tongue. fondant, font, found, all that melts, pours. the
dark rain of our being together at last. and the cold wind, curled-up fronds of
tree fern wanting touch, our fingers separate and stiff. we haven't mourned
enough, you say, for our parting, lost to each other the last time through. in
the dark of this place, its fire touch, not fern but frost, just one of the houses
we pass through in the endless constellation of our being, close, and away from
each other, torn and apart. i didn't know your hair, i didn't know your skin
when you beckoned to me in that last place. but i knew your eyes, blue, as
soon as you came around the small hill, knew your tongue. come, you said, we
slid together in the spring, blue, of a place we'd been. terra incognita[1] known,
geysa, gush, upwelling in the hidden Norse we found, we feel it thrust as waters
part for us, hot, through fern, frost, volcanic thrust. it's all there, love, we part
each other coming to, geyser, spouting pool, hidden in and under separate skin
we make for each other through.

* * *

---

1   (Latin) unknown land or region.

Arthur Nortje

(1942-1970)

Letter from Pretoria Central Prison[1]

The bell wakes me at 6 in the pale spring dawn
with the familiar rumble of the guts negotiating
murky corridors that smell of bodies. My eyes
find salutary the insurgent light of distances.
Waterdrops rain crystal cold, my wet face in
ascent from an iron basin
greets its rifled shadow in the doorway.

They walk us to the workshop. I am eminent,
the blacksmith of the block; these active hours
fly like sparks in the furnace, I hammer metals
with zest letting the sweating muscles
forge a forgetfulness of worlds more magnetic.
The heart being at rest, life peaceable,
your words filter softly through my fibres.

Taken care of, in no way am I unhappy,
being changed to neutral. You must decide
today, tomorrow, bear responsibility,
take gaps in pavement crowds, refine ideas.
Our food we get on time. Most evenings
I read books, Jane Austen
for elegance, agreeableness (Persuasion[2]).

Trees are green beyond the wall, leaves through the mesh
are cool in sunshine
among the monastic white flowers of spring that floats
prematurely across the exercise yard, a square
of the cleanest stone I have ever walked on.
Sentinels smoke in their boxes, the wisps
curling lovely through the barbed wire.

Also music and cinema, yesterday double feature.
At 4 p.m. it's back to the cell, don't laugh
to hear how accustomed one becomes. You spoke
of hospital treatment—I see the smart nurses
bringing you grapefruit and tea—good
luck to the troublesome kidney.
Sorry there's no more space. But date your reply.

---

1   Pretoria is the administrative capital of the Republic of South Africa. Among its inmates,
    the Central Prison includes high-risk political prisoners.
2   the title of one of Jane Austen's novels (1818)

Immigrant

Don't travel beyond
Acton at noon in the intimate summer light
of England

to Tuskaloosa, Medicine Hat, preparing
for flight

dismissing the blond aura of the past
at Durban or Johannesburg
no more chewing roots or brewing riots

Bitter[1] costs exorbitantly at London
airport in the neon heat
waiting for the gates to open

Big boy breaking out of the masturbatory
era goes
like eros[2] over atlantis[3] (sunk
in the time-repeating seas, admire our
tenacity)
jetting into the bulldozer civilization
of Fraser and Mackenzie[4]
which is the furthest west that man has gone

A maple leaf is in my pocket.
X-rayed, doctored at Immigration
weighed in at the Embassy
measured as to passport, smallpox, visa
at last the efficient official informs me
I am an acceptable soldier of fortune, don't

tell the Commissioner
I have Oxford poetry in the satchel
propped between my army surplus boots
for as I consider Western Arrow's
pumpkin pancake buttered peas and chicken canadian style

in my mind's customs office
questions fester that turn the menu
into a visceral whirlpool. You can see
that sick bags are supplied.

---

1   a kind of beer in Britain
2   the winged god of love
3   the mythical kingdom flooded by the Atlantic Ocean
4   Simon Fraser (1776-1862) and Alexander Mackenzie (1764-1820), explorers of western
     and northern Canada

Out portholes beyond the invisible propellers
snow mantles the ground peaks over Greenland.
What ice island of the heart has weaned
you away from the known white kingdom
first encountered at Giant's Castle?[1]
You walked through the proteas[2] nooked in the sun rocks
I approached you under the silver trees.
I was cauterized in the granite glare
on the slopes of Table Mountain,[3] I was baffled
by the gold dumps of the vast Witwatersrand[4]
when you dredged me from the sea like a recent fossil.

Where are the mineworkers, the compound Africans,
your Zulu ancestors, where are
the root-eating, bead-charmed Bushmen, the Hottentot sufferers?[5]
Where are the governors and sailors of the
Dutch East India Company,[6] where are
Eva[7] and the women who laboured in the castle?[8]
You are required as an explanation.

Glaciers sprawl in their jagged valleys,
cool in the heights, there are mountains and mountains.
My prairie beloved, you whose eyes are
less forgetful, whose fingers are less oblivious
must write out chits for the physiotherapy customers
must fill out forms for federal tax.

Consolatory, the air whiskies my veins.
The metal engines beetle on to further destinations.
Pilot's voice reports over Saskatchewan
the safety of this route, the use of exits,

facility of gas masks, Western Arrow's
miraculous record. The flat sea washes
in Vancouver bay. As we taxi in
I find I can read the road signs.

Maybe she is like you, maybe most women

---

1   a mountain in the Drakensberg range in Natal, South Africa
2   a large orange flower, the national flower of South Africa
3   a flat-topped mountain near Cape Town, South Africa
4   a gold-rich region near Johannesburg, South Africa
5   The Hottentot tribes were devastated by smallpox epidemics in the 18th century.
6   In 1652 the Dutch East India Company established a settlement at the Cape of Good
     Hope, as a fuelling station on the route to the East Indies.
7   a celebrated Hottentot woman (c.1642-1674) who worked for the first Dutch settlers as
     a translator
8   Begun in 1666, the Castle in Cape Town was the residence of the governors-general at
     the Cape.

deeply resemble you, all of them are
all things to all poets: the cigarette girl
in velvet with mink nipples, fishnet thighs,
whose womb is full of tobacco.
Have a B.C. apple in the A.D. city of the saviour,
and sing the centennial song.[1]

Native's letter

Habitable planets are unknown or too
far away from us to be
of consequence. To be of
value to his homeland must the wanderer
not weep by northern waters, but love
his own bitter clay
roaming through the hard cities, tough
himself as coffin nails.
Harping on the nettles of his melancholy,
keening on the blue strings of the blood,
he will delve into mythologies perhaps
call up spirits through the night.

Or carry memories apocryphal
of Tshaka, Hendrik, Witbooi, Adam Kok,[2]
of the Xhosa nation's dream[3]
as he moonlights in another country:

but he shall also have
cycles of history
outnumbering the guns of supremacy.

Now and wherever he arrives
extending feelers into foreign scenes
exploring times and lives,
equally may he stand and laugh,
explode with a paper bag of poems,

---

1   The poem was written in 1967, the year of Canada's centennial, which was marked by
     (among many other things) a popular song.
2   Tshaka was the powerful Zulu leader who united the Zulu tribes into a major force in
     southern Africa. Hendrik Potgieter was a Dutch settler who, unhappy with British
     administration of the Cape, led other settlers on a great trek to the Transvaal and the
     Orange Free State, 1836-1838. Adam Kok III (1811-1875) led the Griqua nation to its
     home in what became Griqualand. Hendrik Witbooi (c.1840-1905) was a noted leader of
     the Nama tribes in South-West Africa.
3   In 1856, a 14-year-old Xhosa girl called Nongquawuse claimed to have had a dream that,
     if the Xhosa people rid themselves of all their wealth and possessions by a particular
     date, the white settlers would be driven from their land forever. The Xhosa people
     followed her instructions, with catastrophic consequences: over the next year, some 25,000
     people died because they had no means of supporting themselves.

burst upon a million televisions
with a face as in a Karsh[1] photograph,
slave voluntarily in some siberia
to earn the salt of victory.

Darksome, whoever dies
in the malaise of my dear land
remember me at swim,
the moving waters spilling through my eyes:
and let no amnesia
attack at fire hour:
for some of us must storm the castles
some define the happening.

---

1   Yousuf Karsh, well-known Canadian photographer

Michael Ondaatje

(b. 1943)

Henri Rousseau and Friends[1]

for Bill Muysson

In his clean vegetation
the parrot, judicious,
poses on a branch.
The narrator of the scene,
aware of the perfect fruits,
the white and blue flowers,
the snake with an ear for music;
he presides.

The apes
hold their oranges like skulls,
like chalices.
They are below the parrot
above the oranges—
a jungle serfdom which
with this order
reposes.

They are the ideals of dreams.
Among the exactness,
the symmetrical petals,
the efficiently flying angels,
there is complete liberation.
The parrot is interchangeable;
tomorrow in its place
a waltzing man and tiger,
brash legs of a bird.

Greatness achieved
they loll among textbook flowers

and in this pose hang
scattered like pearls
in just as intense a society.
On Miss Adelaide Milton de Groot's walls,
with Lillie P. Bliss in New York.

And there too
in spangled wrists and elbows
and grand façades of cocktails

---

1   Henri Rousseau (1844-1910), a French painter known for the striking clarity and odd
    juxtapositions of his pictures of wild nature

are vulgarly beautiful parrots, appalled lions,
the beautiful and the forceful locked in suns,
and the slight, careful stepping birds.

Dates

Another page of the imagination

It becomes apparent that I miss great occasions.
My birth[1] was heralded by nothing
but the anniversary of Winston Churchill's marriage.
No monuments bled, no instruments[2]
agreed on a specific weather.
It was a seasonal insignificance.

imagine himself in the mother's womb as Stevens arrange his sentences

I console myself with my mother's eighth month.
While she sweated out her pregnancy in Ceylon
a servant ambling over the lawn
with a tray of iced drinks,
a few friends visiting her
to placate her shape, and I
drinking the life lines,
Wallace Stevens[3] sat down in Connecticut
a glass of orange juice at his table
so hot he wore only shorts
and on the back of a letter
began to write 'The Well Dressed Man with a Beard'.

That night while my mother slept
her significant belly cooled
by the bedroom fan
Stevens put words together
that grew to sentences
and shaved them clean and
shaped them, the page suddenly
becoming thought where nothing had been,
his head making his hand
move where he wanted
and he saw his hand was saying
the mind is never finished, no, never
and I in my mother's stomach was growing
as were the flowers outside the Connecticut windows.

---

1   On 12 September 1943. Churchill married Clemintine Hozier on the same date in 1908.
2   an allusion to the opening of W. H. Auden's poem "In Memory of W. B. Yeats"
3   American poet (1879-1955)

appears undramatic
extremely conventional

King Kong meets Wallace Stevens — *1 of the last romantic poet*

Take two photographs—   *Ondatji must have seen him*
Wallace Stevens and King Kong   *as 'an opposite; but they*
(Is it significant that I eat bananas as I write this?)   *did share an*
                                desire to explore the
                                human imagination

Stevens is portly, benign, a white brush cut
striped tie. Businessman but
for the dark thick hands, the naked brain
the thought in him.

Kong is staggering
lost in New York streets again
a spawn of annoyed cars at his toes.
The mind is nowhere.
Fingers are plastic, electric under the skin.
He's at the call of Metro-Goldwyn-Mayer.

Meanwhile W. S. in his suit
is thinking chaos is thinking fences.
In his head the seeds of fresh pain
his exorcising,
the bellow of locked blood.

The hands drain from his jacket,
pose in the murderer's shadow.

very conversational & casual. Almost as if he's
writing a letter to someone discussing his father,
explaining the situation with his father to us

Letters & Other Worlds

metaphors of his father

*"for there was no more darkness for him and, no doubt like Adam
before the fall, he could see in the dark"*

My father's body was a globe of fear
His body was a town we never knew
He hid that he had been where we were going
His letters were a room he seldom lived in
In them the logic of his love could grow

My father's body was a town of fear
He was the only witness to its fear dance
He hid where he had been that we might lose him
His letters were a room his body scared

He came to death with his mind drowning.
On the last day he enclosed himself
in a room with two bottles of gin, later
fell the length of his body
so that brain blood moved
to new compartments
that never knew the wash of fluid

MICHAEL ONDAATJE

and he died in minutes of a new equilibrium.

His early life was a terrifying comedy
and my mother divorced him again and again.
He would rush into tunnels magnetized
by the white eye of trains
and once, gaining instant fame,
managed to stop a Perahara[1] in Ceylon
—the whole procession of elephants dancers
local dignitaries—by falling
dead drunk onto the street.

As a semi-official, and semi-white at that,
the act was seen as a crucial
turning point in the Home Rule Movement
and led to Ceylon's independence in 1948.

(My mother had done her share too—
her driving so bad
she was stoned by villagers
whenever her car was recognized)

For 14 years of marriage
each of them claimed he or she
was the injured party.
Once on the Colombo[2] docks
saying goodbye to a recently married couple
my father, jealous
at my mother's articulate emotion,
dove into the waters of the harbour
and swam after the ship waving farewell.
My mother pretending no affiliation
mingled with the crowd back to the hotel.

Once again he made the papers
though this time my mother
with a note to the editor
corrected the report—saying he was drunk
rather than broken hearted at the parting of friends.
The married couple received both editions
of *The Ceylon Times* when their ship reached Aden.[3]

And then in his last years
he was the silent drinker,

---

1 an annual festival in honour of the Hindu god Vishnu, marked by processions with elephants
2 the capital city of Sri Lanka (formerly Ceylon)
3 a port city in South Yemen, near the entrance to the Red Sea; a former British Colony.

the man who once a week
disappeared into his room with bottles
and stayed there until he was drunk
and until he was sober.

There speeches, head dreams, apologies,
the gentle letters, were composed.
With the clarity of architects
he would write of the row of blue flowers
his new wife had planted,
the plans for electricity in the house,
how my half-sister fell near a snake
and it had awakened and not touched her.
Letters in a clear hand of the most complete empathy
his heart widening and widening and widening
to all manner of change in his children and friends
while he himself edged
into the terrible acute hatred
of his own privacy
till he balanced and fell
the length of his body
the blood screaming in
the empty reservoir of bones
the blood searching in his head without metaphor

The Agatha Christie Books By The Window

In the long open Vancouver Island room
sitting by the indoor avocados
where indoor spring light
falls on the half covered bulbs

and down the long room light falling
onto the dwarf orange tree
vines from south america
the agatha christie books by the window

Nameless morning
solution of grain and colour

There is this amazing light,
colourless, which falls on the warm
stretching brain of the bulb
that is dreaming avocado

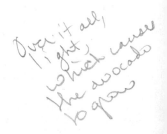

[handwritten annotation top right: living in Hawaii, at this time getting a divorce]

from: *Tin Roof*

Oh Rilke,[1] I want to sit down calm like you
or pace the castle, avoiding the path of the cook, Carlo,[2]
who believes down to his turnip soup
that you speak the voice of the devil.
I want the long lines my friend spoke of
that bamboo which sways muttering
like wooden teeth in the slim volume I have
with its childlike drawing of Duino Castle.

[handwritten annotation: referring to a poem written by a friend]

I have circled your book for years
like a wave combing
the green hair of the sea
kept it with me, your name
a password in the alley.
I always wanted poetry to be that
but this solitude brings no wisdom
just two day old food in the fridge,
certain habits you would not approve of. *[handwritten: → ex. smoking]*
If I said all of your name now
it would be the movement
of the tide you soared over
so your private angel
could become part of a map.
I am too often busy with things
I wish to get away from, and I want
the line to move slowly now, slow
-ly like a careful drunk across the street
no cars in the vicinity
but in his fearful imagination.
How can I link your flowing name
to geckoes or a slice of octopus? *[handwritten: lizard]*
Though there are Rainier[3] beer cans *[handwritten: horrible pun]*
magically, on the windowsill.
And still your lovely letters
January 1912 near Trieste.
The car you were driven in
'at a snail's pace'
through Provence. Wanting
'to go into chrysalis . . .
to live by the heart and nothing else.'[4]
Or your guilt—
            'I howl at the moon

---

1   Rainer Maria Rilke (1875-1926), Austrian poet, author of *The Duino Elegies* (1923), written
    at the Castle of Duino near Trieste on the Adriatic.
2   Carlo was the manservant at the castle; the cook was a woman.
3   a beer company in Seattle
4   from a letter by Rilke of 14 December 1911

with all my heart
and put the blame
on the dogs'[1]

I can see you sitting down
the suspicious cook asleep
so it is just you
and the machinery of the night
that foul beast that sucks and drains
leaping over us sweeping our determination
away with its tail. Us and the coffee,
all the small charms we invade it with.

As at midnight we remember the colour
of the dogwood flower growing
like a woman's sex outside the window.
I wanted poetry to be walnuts
in their green cases
but now it is the sea
and we let it drown us,
and we fly to it released
by giant catapults
of pain loneliness deceit and vanity

---

1   from Rilke's letter of 30 December 1911 to his patroness the Princess Marie von Thurn
und Taxis-Hohenlohe

Tom Wayman

(b. 1945)

Long Beach Suite

i The Washerwoman

Wind
and the sound
the surf makes

also the drumming
of the surf
on distant rocks

and the faint
whisper
at the edge of the foam
moving in along the sand

on a day in late summer,
kelp
and seaweed
left on the lines of the tide
or scattered across the beach

in the afternoon light,
the beach
and the furious
washerwoman
throwing out
pail after pail:
the washerwoman

ii Schooner Trail

At the beginning of the rain,
white logs
up at the shoreline
the rain makes:
salmonberry
high as a man
over the wood planking
at the start of the trail
into the forest
—salal
and bog laurel,
cedar and hemlock
and the hush
of rain falling on the leaves

iii   The Cave of the Rain

Damp
air
and the odor of wet woods,
inland
at the Cave of the Rain:
a hole in the earth beside the trail
under a huge stump
of a snag, steady rain
from the overcast
dripping through fir and cedar above,
descending through air and then
trickling down bark and
broken, rotted roots
to small pools on the earth
beside ferns
and the tangle of fallen logs and branches
like a corpse of something
face down on the sodden ground,
flesh now half decaying wood
and half wet soil,
shoots of fresh green growth
rising from its back,
and fir needles
everywhere on the earth
by the Cave
in the dark-dappled air,
heavy rain.

iv   Night Sky

Smoke drifting
along the beach
in the grey day,
from fires
at the tents pitched
in this cove, plus mist
from the downpour, sea-fog
that thins towards evening
as the rain lightens
and stops
in the dark.

A first star. And then one other.
An onshore wind
brings the swell of the waves closer:
the Pacific
coming in. And out over the blackness,

half a sea of stars.

I start to recognize
constellations I know.
The short flare
of a meteorite passes:
burning in the fragile shell
that through chance
in this solar system
formed
and keeps us alive.
Above the breeze,
the Milky Way
swarms out from horizon to horizon.
So many stars. And the nearest
so distant.

The roaring pulse
of the high tide. I stare at the night sky
in a universe nearly empty,
on a planet mostly sea,
where we live on a shore or margin
that whatever men say
is all we have of the Earth.

A single drop of water
blown on the sea-wind
against my face.

v The Sea

A hot morning; vapor rising
from the wet sand, shouts,
dogs barking, the tide lower
but the waves still white-capped
from yesterday's storm.

Each morning here
a few of the dozens of tents
are collapsed and folded, their owners
shrug into metal packframes,
the bright red and yellow nylon packs
travelling slowly past
and into the woods, while others
appear where the trail ends on the beach, to look
far down the curve of light sand,
forest, and the white rim of the surf
and then closer
at the tents and plastic canopies
placed amid the bleached logs
at the edge of the trees.

Today
my companion and I

hike west from the campsite,
she searching for marine life
along the tideline.
Around one rocky point,
the next large bay
is almost deserted: a couple of distant figures
and then none. In the sunlight
we climb the hill of an island
connected at this tide to the sand.
Near the top, we find a ledge of moss and shoregrass.
We sit, facing the sea.

The line of the horizon. And the salt spray
flung up by the rocks at the foot
of this hill, as the surf
pounds in.

The ocean. The hot day.
As we watch, I remember one theory
of the end of the sea—when a star dies
it explodes, blazing more fiercely: this vast ocean
will boil away.

Like myself
it has its existence, its fate.
But it does not know: the ocean
takes its time,
its time alive. Its surface rolling in
touches other places this day—
despite the names
these men or those give it
this is the one Sea:
largest living thing
on this planet,
here meeting a shore,
an extensive beach,
usually under rain.

If there was no one on this sand, or
on the planet,
it would roll in the same:
gulls and herons,
oystercatchers and crows
in the air, salmon and the grey whales
offshore.

Where a drum-seiner[1]
now works across the horizon
under the cooling sun. And on the beach,
at the foam's edge
the shrill *peep-peep* of the shorebirds,
sandpipers, quickly picking their way
through the tiny refuse
turned up by the last of the ocean's water.

vi   The Crows

And in camp, early next morning
the harsh cry of the crows
heard through canvas: the birds tearing at
garbage

and then flapping away
to roost on the trees overlooking the beach;
someone in swimming
under clearing skies, by noon the clouds lift
to the southeast, revealing mountains

vii   The Praise

Washerwoman   water-giver
crone of rebirth
planet-sharer   lonely and mortal

on this shore
we meet
alive

human being and sea

End and beginning

---

1   fishing-boat with hanging vertical nets wound over a drum

Sharon Thesen

(b. 1946)

Mean Drunk Poem

Backward & down into inbetween as Vicki says. Or as Robin teaches
the gap, from which all things emerge. A left
handed compliment. Bats, houses of parliament, giants, stones.
What woman, witness to such Thought, does not feel
so described & so impotent

she thinks
she must speak. 'I will take your linguistic prick & you
will take my linguistic prick & together we will gap
this imagined earth together.' She has the feeling,
all her life, that she never makes sense. There is something
else, big & dark, at the edge of what she knows, she cannot
say. She always has the feeling she is translating into
Broken english. Language all her life is a second language,
the first is mute & exists. I get drunk

to lubricate my brain & all that comes out
of my Gap
is more bloody writing. No wonder we cook dinner. Have another
kid. Write poetry about the Beloved & kiss ass.
Who cares, as Eleanor says,
who beats whose door down yelling Truth.

The door is only &
always an entrance.

Sing Om[1] as you take the sausage rolls out of the oven.
The Gap is real & there is no such thing as
female intelligence. We're dumber than hell.

---

1   a Buddhist chant

Hello Goodbye[1]

The quiet of a silver afternoon
quickens, a magnet scattering
of books under lampshades
& in the gentle, eerie music
the skyline of Toronto. Helpless,
I yearn for this one or that one
happy in their houses or unhappy
as the case may be. This wasn't
supposed to happen, yet I miss
you all. The music holds me

& won't let go. I grow small,
diminished by all the goodnatured
goodbyes, the 747's taking off,
the daily effort to solve
the puzzled heart. I miss you all
& believe and don't believe
the twisted appearance of completion
as things keep ending. The music

remembers. It hath a soft
& dying fall.[2] God knows
the sentimental beast has spoken
& I wish you were here
anyway. In the lateness
of it all enchantment is not
a dim luxury surrounded by fools.
In the lateness of it all
a numbing silence & the rhythm
of another word written,
and another.

---

1 title of a popular song by the Beatles
2 adapted from *Twelfth Night* I.i.4.

Wanda Coleman

(b. 1950)

Coffee

steam rises over my nose
against this night
cold empty room as wide as my throat; eases/flows
river a mocha memory from aunt ora's
kitchen. she made it in the
big tin percolator and poured the brew into thick
white fist-sized mugs and
put lots of sugar and milk in it for me and
the other kids who loved it better than chocolate
and the neighbor woman used to tell her and us
it wasn't good for young colored children
to drink. it made you get blacker
and blacker

Three Trees

lemon:

we could never
climb you
standing like an
impossible challenge
with prickly limbs to tear
black flesh

peach:

whenever mama wanted a switch
to beat us with
she went to you
shaggy you who belongs to us
black folk now
who used to belong to the white
man named Castro and his boy
who drew pictures of cannibals on
the garage wall
before we integrated the
neighborhood

fig:

we used to climb you
and play peter pan
i would be wendy and the
little white boy up the street
was peter
the neighborhood changed and more blacks came
we used to climb you

and throw rocks at the
ratty little bastards and some of your
fruit also

be quiet. go away

Voices

i hear voices. i hear them often. i've heard them
since childhood. soft persistences
shapeless. they come unexpected. hover on my sleep
pierce and distract my study
speaking in rainbow they discuss me as if i'm
the ghost. say wrong things about me. tell me
i'm different i don't belong
i hear them. the voices. the noise of lies & analyses
threatening to follow me into life

Wanda Why Aren't You Dead

wanda when are you gonna wear your hair down
wanda. that's a whore's name
wanda why ain't you rich
wanda you know no man in his right mind want a
        ready-made family
why don't you lose weight
wanda why are you so angry
how come your feet are so goddamn big
can't you afford to move out of this hell hole
if i were you were you were you
wanda what is it like being black
i hear you don't like black men
tell me you're ac/dc. tell me you're a nympho. tell me you're
        into chains
wanda i don't think you really mean that
you're joking. girl, you crazy
wanda *what* makes you so angry
wanda i think you need this
wanda you have no humor in you you too serious
wanda i didn't know i was hurting you
that was an accident
wanda i know what you're thinking
wanda i don't think they'll take that off of you

wanda why are you so angry

i'm sorry i didn't remember that that that
that that that was so important to you

wanda you're ALWAYS on the attack

wanda wanda wanda i wonder

why ain't you dead

Maxine Tynes

(b. 1950)

Womanskin

women
we keepers and sharers of ancient secrets
of loving
and making homes of houses
of loving
and making love
of loving
and making life
of loving
and making our men whole
of loving
and being women, wives, mothers, sisters, daughters, lovers,
strong, aunts, free, grandmothers, constant, nieces,
women, and Black
we women of colour
distant daughters of
the Nile, the Sahara, Kenya, Zaire, Sudan
the Serengeti[1]
we dance the body-music of light and shadow
we share the palette spectrum
the obsidian sunshade
burnished blue-black brown tantan sepia
coffeecoffee cream ebony
delight of womanskin
strong in
alive in
free in
loving in
working in
laughing in
sharing in
mothering in
growing in
aging in
this skin
this night shade of many shades
this womanskin
we women
keepers and sharers of ancient secrets.

---

1   a great plain in Tanzania, near Lake Victoria

Susan Musgrave

(b. 1951)

At Nootka Sound[1]

Along the river
trees are stranded
bare as witches
and dark as the woman
who never learned to love one man.

(In the north
a woman can learn
to live with too much sadness.
Finding *anything* could be hard.)

The river is haunted
with the slippery black eyes
of drowned pika[2]—
you fish for something quite improbable
expecting those thin dead eyes
to begin to see.

Sometimes along the way
the water cracks
and Indians must mend the river
after every other net—
men with fat dog's eyes
and humps
who cast themselves
toward fish in stone.

What could only be one lifetime
(who can go on pretending forever?)
is when the ground turns cold
and the night is so still
you can't remember having anything to hear.
You lose yourself
and off into the distance
the last birds are throbbing
black and enormous
down towards the sea.

---

1   an inlet on the west coast of Vancouver Island
2   various small harelike mammals without tails

Equinox

Sometimes under the night
I hear whales
trapped at the
sand edges
breathing their
dead sound.

I go out into the rain
and see,
my face
wrinkled like
moonlight
and long nights hard
under the wind's eye.

The stones lie
closer than water,
floating from darkness
like separate tides
to the same sea.

I watch you
with your shadow
come down over the sand:
your knife is
glutted,
your cold hand
has drawn blood out of
fire.
I hear whales
pressing the blind
shore, netted
till I wake binding
weed with water—

how long were you
pinned down
unable to reach
or split the sound?

I hear whales ringing bells
invisible as silence

I hear whales with birds' tongues
and slippery arctic eyes.

How long
did you look

before their eyes knew you?

Do you remember
the colour of their blood?

Lure

Earth place
Water place

Deep
Red
Overhanging mountain

Old fish-slaughter at
Root-Baking Place.

Half-fish
Land-locked salmon

Drift pile
Green
Gravelly river.

Cracked rocks in the
Old fishe-cache.

Earth place
Other place

The fish die
The water is too deep.

Blood
Dark
Falling-Away Mountain

Fish-eye feeds the
White bird

Lay bones around his heart.

Dionne Brand

(b. 1953)

Canto I

ashes head to toes
juju[1] belt
guinea eyes unfolded impossible
squint a sun since drenched
breasts beaded of raised skin
naked woman speaks
syllables come in dust's pace
dried, caked rim of desert mouth
naked woman speaks
run mouth, tell.
when the whites come they were dead men
we did not want to touch them
we did not want to interfere in their business
after the disappearances
many times there were dead men among us
and we cursed them
and we gave them food
when the whites came they were dead men
five men died in our great battles before
guns gave us more heads of our enemies
and those who disappeared were dead men
and the dead take care of their own
for things come and they leave
enemies were dead men and whites were
    dead men
and our city and our people flourished
and died also,
naked woman speak
syllables come in water's pace
long river mouth, tell.

for the skulls of our enemies
were the walls of our wealth
and we filled them with food
and palm wine for our ancestors
and everywhere there were skulls
white of beaten iron and guns and
white with the ancestors' praise and
white with the breath of the whites on our land
white as of eyes on sand on humid vastness
white as the tune of fingers, brisk on dry skin
not even pursed hungry lips were as white

---

1   Originating in West Africa, juju is a fetish or talisman imbued with magical powers.

and not even the sorghum[1] was as white as this
not even the dust of the goat's grounded horn
and each night became different from the next
and we stood by our fires
and left the places outside our compound
to the skulls and the disappeared and the whites
and the skulls stood on their sticks
and no one was born on the nights after
and no one joined their age mates
the disappeared stayed away and did not
help us to kill our enemies
and we ground our breasts and our teeth to powder
belly roped in ashes as the sky falters on the rainbow
naked woman speaks
syllables come in palm wine's pace
run mouth, dry.

Canto II

ancestor dirt
ancestor snake
ancestor lice
ancestor whip
ancestor fish
ancestor slime
ancestor sea
ancestor stick
ancestor iron
ancestor bush
ancestor ship
ancestor old woman, old bead
let me feel your skin
old muscle, old stick
where are my bells?
my rattles
my condiments
my things
to fill houses and minutes,
the fete is starting
where are my things?
my mixtures
my bones
my decorations
old bead! old tamerind[2] switch!

---

1   a kind of stout tropical grass, like cane, which produces a sweet juice and is also used
    for cattle fodder
2   a tropical tree with hard yellow wood

will you bathe me in oils,
will you tie me in white cloth?
call me by my praise name
sing me Oshun¹ song
against this clamor,
ancestor old woman
send my things after me
one moment old lady
more questions
what happened to the ocean in your leap
the boatswain, did he scan
the passage's terrible wet face
the navigator, did he blink or steer the ship
through your screaming night
the captain, did he lash two slaves to the rigging
for example?
lady, my things
water leaden
my maps, my compass
after all, what is the political
position of stars?
drop your crusted cough
where you want,
my hands make precious things
out of phlegm
ancestor wood
ancestor dog
ancestor knife
ancestor old man
dry stick
moustache
skin and cheekbone
why didn't you remember,
why didn't you remember
the name of our tribe
why didn't you tell me
before you died
old horse
you made the white man
ride you
you shot off your leg for him
old man
the name of our tribe is all i wanted
instead you went
to the swamps and bush
and rice paddies

---

1   the Oshun River in southwestern Nigeria, an area originally settled by the Yoruba peoples;
also the goddess Oshun, personification of the river

for the Trading Company
and they buried you in water
crocodile tears!
it would have been better
to remember the name of our tribe
now mosquito dance a ballet
over your grave
the old woman buried with you
wants to leave.

Patricia Young

(b. 1954)

Three Point Five Nine

The minute I was born
Roger Bannister ran the miracle mile.[1]
My mother tells me this
all these years later.
How the priest breezed in
to congratulate her, glibly announced
that she and Roger had both

come through. She cursed
that priest out of the room, screaming,
it *was* a miracle, a bloody miracle
she survived at all—ankles
strapped down in stirrups,
doped like an animal.
But I am not interested

in early forms of female torture.
Ask why she's never told me before
that I was swimming
into the world against
gravity and all good sense,
while somewhere a man tore
round a track defying the limits

of human performance.
How to explain the kinship.
The igniting of my birth.
Despite my mother's bruised
ankles and slurred speech

it seems to me now
a sweet and rare miracle.
This stranger and I,
like two separate thoughts,

blazing through the barriers of some vast,
inscrutable brain.

---

1   Roger Bannister, a British athlete, ran the first sub-four-minute mile at Iffley Road Track,
     Oxford on 6 May 1954. His time was 3 minutes, 59.4 seconds. The term "miracle mile"
     was the title given by the press to a later race held in Vancouver, B.C. on 7 August 1954,
     when both Bannister and John Landy beat four minutes.

The Third Sex

I want to belong to the third sex,
the one which copulates
in the minds of the disheartened,
those weary of the other
inglorious choices. Neither male
nor female, I want to escape
through my left ear.
No longer to bear down
and plunder the wills of our children.
Unbodied! Free of the hopeless
negotiations and load of our bones.
To observe from a distance.
Shaking my head I'll say,
isn't it sad about the humans?
As though they were locusts
or cows, alive
with the blood of a frog.
Oh to celebrate
the beloved without small
thoughts or fear of reproducing
more of the same. No longer
to plague the earth with cockroach
insistence. Not *above,*
but *beside,* not orangutan
or swallow. Futureless, I want to be
a good idea. To glide
from the rooms in which we couple
like dragonflies. Up the sidewalk,
straight into the arms of the ocean.
Unveiling my newborn face
I'll shrug and say,
who can ever
understand what they do?

Photograph, 1958

My father and I play checkers
in profile. He sits on the couch,
leans forward on his elbow, there's
a low coffee table between us.
I am four, sit opposite on a hassock.
He concentrates on the board,
I am watching him, who
is winning?
I no longer know
the rules or object of the game.
Checkers on the board and off,
an open cigarette package, box of matches.

My father wears a loose white
shirt, work pants, my hair
is badly cut, these
are the details. Beyond the barely
furnished room I guess snow:
banked against the front
and back doors. Years later
we'll live in another city.
In an old farmhouse
rock at the green edge
of a golf course. My father
will pull a stove out of a wall
and hurl it across a kitchen
on my account. Boiling lobsters
will fly like wet birds.
In this photograph my face
tilts up toward his. I wait
for him to make his move
and I would gladly wait forever,
deaf to the screams, the scarlet tails
that will one day scatter.

Reading Poetry

WHAT IS A POEM?

Most of us know what a poem is when we see one. Still, poets themselves find it difficult to define a poem, or poetry. When the English poet A. E. Housman was asked to do so, he replied that he could "no more define poetry than a terrier can define a rat"; however, "we both recognised the object by the symptoms which it provokes in us." Housman knew he was in the presence of poetry if he experienced a shiver down the spine, or "a constriction of the throat and a precipitation of water to the eyes." Implicit in Housman's response is a recognition that we have to go beyond mere formal characteristics—stanzas, rhymes, rhythms—if we want to know what poetry is, or why it differs from prose. Poetry both represents and *creates* emotions in a highly condensed way. Therefore, any definition of the genre needs to consider, as much as possible, the impact of poetry on us as readers.

For some readers, poetry is, in Wordsworth's phrase, "the breath and finer spirit of all knowledge." They look to poetry for insights into the nature of human experience, and expect elevated thought in carefully wrought language. In contrast, other readers distrust poetry that seems moralistic or didactic. "We hate poetry that has a palpable design upon us," wrote Keats to his friend Reynolds; rather, poetry should be "great & unobtrusive, a thing which enters into one's soul, and does not startle it or amaze it with itself but with its subject." The American poet Archibald MacLeish took Keats's idea a step further: in his poem "Ars Poetica" (page 493) he suggested that "A poem should not mean / But be." MacLeish was not suggesting that a poem should lack meaning, but rather that meaning should inhere in the poem's expressive and sensuous qualities, not in some explicit statement or versified idea.

Whatever we look for in a poem, the infinitude of forms, styles, and subjects that make up the body of literature we call "poetry" is, in the end, impossible to capture in a definition that would satisfy all readers. All we can do, perhaps, is to agree that a poem is a discourse that is characterized by a heightened attention to language, form, and rhythm, by an expressiveness that works through figurative rather than literal modes, and by a capacity to stimulate our imagination and arouse our feelings.

THE LANGUAGE OF POETRY

To speak of "the language of poetry" implies that poets make use of a vocabulary that is somehow different from the language of everyday life. In fact, all language has the capacity to be "poetic," if by poetry we understand a use of language to which some special importance is attached. The ritualistic utterances of religious ceremonies sometimes have this force; so do the skipping rhymes of children in the schoolyard. We can distinguish such uses of language from the kind of writing we find in, say, a computer user's manual: the author of the manual can describe a given function in a variety of ways, whereas the magic of the skipping rhyme can be invoked only by getting the right words in the right order. So with the poet: he or she chooses particular words in a particular order; the *way* the poet speaks is as important to our understanding as what is said. This doesn't mean that an instruction manual couldn't have poetic qualities—indeed, modern poets have created "found" poems from even less likely materials—but it does mean that in poetry there is an intimate relation among language, form, and meaning, and that the writer deliberately structures and manipulates language to achieve very particular ends.

The best words in the best order

Wordsworth provides us with a useful example of the way that poetry can invest quite ordinary words with a high emotional charge:

> No motion has she now, no force,
> She neither hears nor sees;
> Rolled round in earth's diurnal course
> With rocks, and stones, and trees.

To paraphrase the content of this stanza from "A Slumber Did My Spirit Seal" (page 172), "she" is dead and buried. But the language and structures used here give this prosaic idea great impact. For example, the regular iambic metre of the two last lines conveys something of the inexorable motion of the earth and of Lucy embedded in it; the monosyllabic last line is a grim reminder of her oneness with objects in nature; the repeated negatives in the first two lines drive home the irreparable destructiveness of death; the alliteration in the third and fourth lines gives a tangible suggestion of roundness, circularity, repetition in terms of the earth's shape and motion, suggesting a cycle in which death is perhaps followed by renewal. Even the unusual word "diurnal" (which would not have seemed so unusual to Wordsworth's readers) seems "right" in this context; it lends more weight to the notion of the earth's perpetual movement than its mundane synonym "daily" (which, besides, would not scan here). It is difficult to imagine a change of any kind to these lines; they exemplify another attempted definition of poetry, this one by Coleridge: "the best words in the best order."

Poetic diction and the elevated style

Wordsworth's diction in the "Lucy" poem cited above is a model of clarity; he has chosen language that, in its simplicity and bluntness, conveys the strength of the speaker's feelings far more strongly than an elaborate description of grief in more conventionally "poetic" language might have done. Wordsworth, disturbed by what he felt was a deadness and artificiality in the poetry of his day, sought to "choose incidents and situations from common life" and to describe them in "a selection of language really used by men" (Preface to *Lyrical Ballads*, 2nd. ed., 1800). His plan might seem an implicit reproach of the "raised" style, the elevated diction of epic poetry we associate with Milton's *Paradise Lost*:

> Anon out of the earth a fabric huge
> Rose like an exhalation, with the sound
> Of dulcet symphonies and voices sweet,
> Built like a temple, where pilasters round
> Were set, and Doric pillars overlaid
> With golden architrave; nor did there want
> Cornice or frieze, with bossy sculptures graven;
> The roof was fretted gold.

> (*Paradise Lost* I, 710-17)

At first glance this passage, with its Latinate vocabulary and convoluted syntax, might seem guilty of inflated language and pretentiousness. However, Milton's description of the devils' palace in Hell deliberately seeks to distance us from its subject in order to emphasize the scale and sublimity of the spectacle, far removed from ordinary human experience. In other words, language and style in *Paradise Lost* are well adapted to suit a particular purpose, just as they are in "A Slumber Did My Spirit Seal," though on a wholly different scale. Wordsworth criticized the poetry of his day, not because of its elevation, but because the raised style was too often out of touch with its subject; in his view, the words did not bear any significant relation to the "truths" they were attempting to depict.

"Plain" language in poetry

Since Wordsworth's time, writers have been conscious of a need to narrow the apparent gap between "poetic" language and the language of everyday life. In much of the poetry of the past century, especially free verse, we can observe a growing approximation to speech—even to conversation—in the diction and rhythms of poetry. This may have something to do with the changed role of the poet, who in the twentieth century has discarded the mantle of teacher or prophet that was assumed by poets of earlier times, and who is ready to admit all fields of experience and endeavour as appropriate for poetry. The modern poet looks squarely at life, and can find a provoking beauty in even the meanest of objects:

> Things, things unmentionable
> the sink with the waste farina in it and
> lumps of rancid meat, milk-bottle tops: have
> here a still tranquillity and loveliness
> Have here (in his thoughts)
> a complement tranquil and chaste.

> (from William Carlos Williams, *Paterson*, Book I)

However, we should not assume that a greater concern with the "ordinary," with simplicity, naturalness, and clarity, means a reduction in complexity or suggestiveness. A piece like Williams' "This is Just to Say" (page 433), for all its casual and playful domesticity, skilfully evokes a range of emotions and sense impressions defying simple paraphrase.

IMAGERY, SYMBOLISM, AND FIGURES OF SPEECH

The language of poetry is grounded in the objects and phenomena that create sensory impressions. Sometimes the poet renders these impressions quite literally, in a series of *images* that seek to recreate a scene in the reader's mind:

> Only a man harrowing clods
>   In a slow silent walk
> With an old horse that stumbles and nods
>   Half asleep as they stalk.

> Only thin smoke without flame
>   From the heaps of couch-grass;

Yet this will go onward the same
  Though Dynasties pass.

Yonder a maid and her wight
  Come whispering by:
War's annals will cloud into night
  Ere their story die.

(Hardy, "In Time of 'The Breaking of Nations'")

Here, the objects of everyday life are re-created with sensory details designed to evoke in us the sensations or responses felt by the poet. At the same time, the writer invests the objects with such significance that the poem's meaning extends beyond the literal to the symbolic: that is, the images come to stand for something much larger than the objects they represent. Hardy's poem moves from the presentation of stark images of rural life to a sense of their timelessness. By the last stanza we see the ploughman, the burning grass, the maid and her companion, as symbols of recurring human actions and motives that defy the struggles and conflicts of history.

A similar example of movement from the literal to the symbolic is provided by "The Road Not Taken" (page 409) in which Robert Frost describes how a traveller comes to a spot where "two roads diverged in a yellow wood." The speaker hesitates between the two, noting the degree to which each seems to have been used, as well as the covering of leaves on both. Finally he chooses "the one less travelled by," a choice he concludes "that has made all the difference." Until the last stanza the description presents a series of visual images, re-creating the speaker's indecision as he tries to make a choice. By the last stanza, however, we understand that the divergent roads are more than roads: they represent choices that the speaker has made in life, and that have determined for better or worse all his subsequent experiences.

Imagism

The juxtaposition of clear, forceful images is associated particularly with the *Imagist movement* that flourished at the beginning of the twentieth century. Its chief representative was Ezra Pound, who defined an image as "that which represents an intellectual and emotional complex in an instant of time." Pound's two-line poem "In a Station of the Metro" provides a good example of the Imagists' goal of representing emotions or impressions through the use of concentrated images:

The apparition of these faces in the crowd,
  Petals on a wet, black bough.

The writer uses sharp, clear, concrete details to evoke both a sensory impression and the emotion or the atmosphere of the scene. Though the Imagist movement itself lasted only a short time (from about 1912 to 1917), it had a far-reaching influence on other modern poets such as H.D., T. S. Eliot, and William Carlos Williams.

Figures of Speech

Imagery often works together with figurative expression to extend and deepen the meaning or impact of a poem. "Figurative" language means language that is metaphorical, not literal or referential. Through "figures of speech" such as metaphor and simile, metonymy, synechoche, and personification, the writer may alter the ordinary, denotative meanings of words in order to convey greater force and vividness to ideas or impressions, often by showing likenesses between unlike things.

With *simile*, the poet makes an explicit comparison between the subject (called the *tenor*) and another object or idea (known as the *vehicle*), using "as" or "like":

> It is a beauteous evening, calm and free,
> The holy time is quiet as a Nun
> Breathless with adoration. . . .

In this opening to a sonnet, Wordsworth uses a visual image of a nun in devout prayer to convey in concrete terms the less tangible idea of evening as a "holy time." The comparison also introduces an emotional dimension, conveying something of the feeling that the scene induces in the poet. The simile can thus illuminate and expand meaning in a compact way. The poet may also extend the simile to elaborate at length on any points of likeness: see, for example, Robert Frost's "The Silken Tent" (page 414) in which only the first two words ("She is...") refer to the tenor, leaving the rest of the poem to describe a tent, the vehicle of the comparison.

In *metaphor*, the comparison between tenor and vehicle is implied: connectives such as "like" are omitted, and a kind of identity is created between the subject and the term with which it is being compared. Thus in "The Good-Morrow" (page 39), Donne's lover asserts the endless joy that he and his beloved find in each other:

> My face in thine eye, thine in mine appears,
>   And true plain hearts do in the faces rest;
> Where can we find two better hemispheres,
>   Without sharp north, without declining west?

Here the lovers are transformed into "hemispheres," each of them a half of the world not subject to the usual natural phenomena of wintry cold ("sharp north") or the coming of night ("declining west"). Thus, they form a perfect world in balance, in which the normal processes of decay or decline have been arrested. Donne renders the abstract idea of a love that defies change in pictorial and physical terms, making it more real and accessible to us. The images here are all the more arresting for the degree of concentration involved; it is not merely the absence of "like" or "as" that gives the metaphor such direct power, but the fusion of distinct images and emotions into a new idea.

Personification is the figure of speech in which the writer endows abstract ideas, inanimate objects, or animals with human characteristics. In other words, it is a type of implied metaphorical comparison in which aspects of the subject are compared to the feelings, appearance, or actions of a human being. In the second stanza of his ode "To Autumn" (page 228) Keats personifies the concept of autumnal harvesting in the form of a woman, "sitting careless on a granary floor, / Thy hair soft-lifted by the winnowing wind." Emily Dickinson personifies death as a kind gentleman who stops his carriage to give her a ride ("Because I could not stop for Death," page 321). Personification may also help to create a mood, as when Thomas Gray attributes human feelings to a hooting owl; using such words as "moping" and "complain", Gray invests the bird's cries with the quality of human melancholy:

> . . . from yonder ivy-mantled tow'r
> The moping owl does to the moon complain
> Of such, as wand'ring near her secret bow'r,
> Molest her ancient solitary reign.

(from *Elegy Written in a Country Church-Yard*)

The English critic John Ruskin criticized such attribution of human feelings to objects in nature. Calling this device the *pathetic fallacy*, he objected to what he saw as the distortion and falsification of reality. Modern critics tend to use Ruskin's term as a neutral label, simply to describe instances of extended personification of natural objects.

Apostrophe, which is closely related to personification, has the speaker directly addressing a non-human object or idea as if it were a sentient human listener. Anne Bradstreet's "To my Book", Blake's "The Sick Rose," Shelley's "Ode to the West Wind" and his ode "To a Sky-Lark" all employ apostrophe, personifying the object addressed. Keats's "Ode on a Grecian Urn" (page 226) begins by apostrophizing the urn ("Thou still unravish'd bride of quietness"), then addresses it in a series of questions and reflections through which the speaker attempts to unravel the urn's mysteries.

Apostrophe also appeals to or addresses a person who is absent or dead. W. H. Auden's lament "In Memory of W. B. Yeats" (page 553) apostrophizes both the earth in which Yeats is to be buried ("Earth, receive an honoured guest") and the dead poet himself ("Follow, poet, follow right / To the bottom of the night . . ."). Religious prayers offer an illustration of the workings of apostrophe, since they are direct appeals from an earth-bound supplicant to an invisible god. The suggestion of strong emotion associated with such appeals is a common feature of apostrophe in poetry also, especially poetry with a religious theme, like Donne's Holy Sonnets (e.g., "Batter My Heart, Three-Person'd God," page 45) or Margaret Avison's "The Dumbfounding" (page 659).

Metonymy and *synechdoche* are two closely related figures of speech that further illustrate the power of metaphorical language to convey meaning more intensely and vividly than is possible with prosaic statement. *Metonymy* (from the Greek, meaning "change of name") involves referring to an object or concept by substituting the name of another object or concept with which it is usually associated: for example, we might speak of "the Crown" when we mean the monarch, or describe the U.S. federal government as "the White House." When the writer uses only part of something to signify the whole, or an individual to represent a class, we have an instance of *synecdoche*: T. S. Eliot provides an example in "The Love Song of J. Alfred Prufrock" (page 474) when a crab is described as "a pair of ragged claws." Similarly, synecdoche is present in Milton's contemptous term "blind mouths" to describe the "corrupted clergy" he attacks in "Lycidas" (page xx.).

Dylan Thomas employs both metonymy and synecdoche in his poem "The Hand That Signed the Paper":

The hand that signed the paper felled a city;
Five sovereign fingers taxed the breath,
Doubled the globe of dead and halved a country;
These five kings did a king to death.

The mighty hand leads to a sloping shoulder,
The finger joints are cramped with chalk;
A goose's quill has put an end to murder
That put an end to talk.

The hand that signed the treaty bred a fever,
And famine grew, and locusts came;
Great is the hand that holds dominion over
Man by a scribbled name.

The five kings count the dead but do not soften
The crusted wound nor stroke the brow;
A hand rules pity as a hand rules heaven;
Hands have no tears to flow.

The "hand" of the poem is evidently a synecdoche for a great ruler who enters into treaties with friends and foes to wage wars, conquer kingdoms, and extend his personal power—all at the expense of his suffering subjects. The "goose quill" of the second stanza is a metonymy, standing for the pen used to sign the treaty bringing the war to an end.

Thomas's poem is an excellent example of the power of figurative language, which, by its vividness and concentrated force, can add layers of meaning to a poem, make abstract ideas concrete, and intensify the poem's emotional impact.

THE POEM AS PERFORMANCE: WRITER AND PERSONA

Poetry is always dramatic. Sometimes the drama is explicit, as in Robert Browning's monologues, in which we hear the voice of a participant in a dialogue; in "My Last Duchess" (page 278) we are present as the Duke reflects on the portrait of his late wife for the benefit of a visitor who has come to negotiate on behalf of the woman who is to become his next wife. Or we listen with amusement and pity as the dying Bishop addresses his venal and unsympathetic sons and tries to bargain with them for a fine burial ("The Bishop Orders His Tomb...," page 279). In such poems the notion of a speaking voice is paramount: the speaker is a personage in a play, and the poem a means of conveying plot and character.

Sometimes the drama is less apparent, and takes the form of a plea, or a compliment, or an argument addressed to a silent listener. In Donne's "The Flea" (page 41) we can infer from the poem the situation that has called it forth: a lover's advances are being rejected by his beloved, and his poem is an argument intended to overcome her reluctance by means of wit and logic. We can see a similar example in Marvell's "To His Coy Mistress" (page 81): here the very shape of the poem, its three-paragraph structure, underlines the stages of the speaker's argument as he presents an apparently irrefutable line of reasoning. Much love poetry has this kind of background as its inspiration; the yearnings or lamentations of the lover are part of an imagined scene, not merely versified reflections about an abstraction called "love".

Meditative or reflective poetry can be dramatic too. Donne's Holy Sonnets are pleas from a tormented soul struggling to find its god; Tennyson's "In Memoriam" follows the agonized workings of a mind tracing a path from grief and anger to acceptance and renewed hope (see pages 45 and 267).

We should never assume that the speaker is simply a "voice" for the writer's own views. The speaker in W. H. Auden's "To an Unknown Citizen" (page 556), presenting a summary of the dead citizen's life, appears to be an official spokesperson for the society which the citizen served ("Our report on his union"; "Our researchers..." etc.). The speaker's words are laudatory, yet we perceive immediately that Auden's own views of this society are anything but approving. The speaker seems satisfied with the highly regimented nature of his society, one in which every aspect of the individual's life is under scrutiny and subject to correction. The only things necessary to the happiness of the "Modern Man," it seems, are "A phonograph, a radio, a car, and a frigidaire." The tone here is subtly ironic, an irony created by the gap between the imagined speaker's perception and the real feelings of the writer.

Performance poetry

Poetry began as an oral art, passed on in the form of chants, myths, ballads, and legends recited to an audience of listeners rather than readers. Even today, the dramatic qualities of a poem may extend beyond written text. "Performance poets" combine poetry and stagecraft in presenting their work to live audiences. Dramatic uses of voice, rhythm, body movement, music, and sometimes other visual effects make the "text" of the poem multi-dimensional. For example, Edith Sitwell's poem-sequence *Façade* (1922) was originally set to music: Sitwell read from behind a screen, while a live orchestra played. This performance was designed to enhance the verbal and rhythmic qualities of her poetry:

Beneath the flat and paper sky
The sun, a demon's eye
Glowed through the air, that mask of glass;
All wand'ring sounds that pass

Seemed out of tune, as if the light
Were fiddle-strings pulled tight.
The market-square with spire and bell
Clanged out the hour in Hell.

(from *Façade*)

By performing their poetry, writers can also convey cultural values and traditions. The cultural aspect of performance is central to Black poetry, which originates in a highly oral tradition of folklore and storytelling. From its roots in Africa, this oral tradition has been manifested in the songs and stories of slaves, in spirituals, in the jazz rythmns of the Twenties and the Harlem Renaissance, and most recently, in the rebelliousness of street-rap. Even when it remains "on the page," much Black poetry written in the oral tradition has a compelling rhythmic quality. These stanzas from Langston Hughes' "Dream Boogie" blur the line between spoken poetry and song:

Good morning, daddy!
Ain't you heard
The boogie-woogie rumble
Of a dream deferred?

Listen closely:
You'll hear their feet
Beating and beating out a—

> *You think*
> *It's a happy beat?. . .*

(from "Montage of a Dream Deferred")

Maxine Tynes' "Womanskin" (page 879), with its constant repetitions, digs deeply into the roots of African song and chant. Its performance qualities become clearer when the poem is read aloud:

women
we keepers and sharers of ancient secrets
of loving
and making homes of houses
of loving
and making love
of loving
and making life
of loving
and making our men whole . . .

To perform a poem is one way to see and hear poetry as multi-dimensional, cultural, historical, and even political. Performance is also another way to discover how poetic "meaning" can be constructed in the dynamic relation between speaker and listener.

Tone: the speaker's attitude

In understanding poetry, it is helpful to imagine a poem as having a "voice." The voice may be close to the poet's own, or that of an imagined character, a *persona* adopted by the poet. The tone of the voice will reveal the speaker's attitude to the subject, thus helping to shape our understanding and response. In speech we can indicate our feelings by raising or lowering our voices, and we can accompany words with physical actions. In writing, we must try to convey the tonal inflections of the speaking voice through devices of language and rhythm, through imagery and figures of speech, and through allusions and contrasts.

The ironic tone

Housman's poem "Terence, This Is Stupid Stuff" (page 360) offers a useful example of ways in which manipulating tone can reinforce meaning. When Housman, presenting himself in the poem as "Terence", imagines himself to be criticized for writing gloomy poems, his response to his critics takes the form of an ironic alternative — perhaps they should stick to drinking ale:

> Oh, many a peer of England brews
> Livelier liquor than the Muse,
> And malt does more than Milton can
> To justify God's ways to man.

The tone here is one of heavy scorn. The speaker is impatient with those who refuse to look at the realities of life and death, and who prefer to take refuge in simple-minded pleasure. The ludicrous comparisons, first between the unnamed "peers of England" and the classical Muse of poetry, then between malt and Milton, create a sense of disproportion and ironic tension; the explicit allusion to *Paradise Lost* ("To justify God's ways to man") helps to drive home the poet's bitter recognition that his auditors are part of that fallen world depicted by Milton, yet unable or unwilling to acknowledge their harsh condition. The three couplets that follow offer a series of contrasts: in each case, the first line sets up a pleasant expectation and the second dashes it with a blunt reminder of reality:

> Ale, man, ale's the stuff to drink
> For fellows whom it hurts to think:
> Look into the pewter pot
> To see the world as the world's not.
> And faith, 'tis pleasant till 'tis past:
> The mischief is that 'twill not last.

These are all jabs at the "sterling lads" who would prefer to lie in "lovely muck" and not think about the way the world is. Housman's sardonic advice is all the more pointed for its sharp and ironic tone.

POETIC FORMS

In poetry, language is intimately related to form, which is the structuring of words within identifiable patterns. In prose we speak of phrases, sentences, and paragraphs; in poetry, we identify structures by lines, stanzas, or complete forms such as the sonnet or the ode. Rightly handled, the form enhances expression and meaning, just as a frame can define and enhance a painting or photograph. Unlike the photo frame, however, form in poetry is an integral part of the whole work. At one end of the scale, the term "form" may describe the *epic*, the lengthy narrative governed by such conventions as division into books, a lofty style, and the interplay between human and supernatural characters. At the other end lies the *epigram*, a witty and pointed saying whose distinguishing characteristic is its brevity, as in Alexander Pope's famous couplet,

> I am his Highness' dog at Kew;
> Pray tell me sir, whose dog are you?

Between the epic and the epigram lie many other poetic forms, such as the *sonnet*, the *ballad*, or the *ode*. "Form" may also describe stanzaic patterns like *couplets* and *quatrains*.

The Sonnet

The best-known poetic form is probably the sonnet, the fourteen- line poem inherited from Italy (the word itself is from the Italian *sonetto*, little song or sound). Within those fourteen lines, whether the poet chooses the "Petrarchan" rhyme scheme or the "English" form (see below in the section on "Rhyme"), the challenge is to develop an idea or situation that must find its statement and its resolution within the strict confines of the sonnet frame. Typically, there is a *turn* in the thought that takes the reader by surprise, or that casts the situation in an unexpected light. Thus in Sonnet 130, "My Mistress' Eyes Are Nothing Like the Sun" (page 34), Shakespeare spends the first three quatrains disparaging his lover in a series of unfavourable comparisons—"If snow be white, why then her breasts are dun"— but in the closing couplet his point becomes clear:

> And yet, by heaven, I think my love as rare
> As any she belied with false compare.

In other words, the speaker's disparaging comparisons have really been parodies of sentimental clichés which falsify reality; his mistress has no need of the exaggerations or distortions of conventional love poetry.

Stanzaic forms

Recurring formal groupings of lines within a poem are usually described as "stanzas." A stanza is identified by the number of lines and the patterns of rhyme repeated in each grouping. One of the simpler traditional forms is the *ballad stanza*, with its alternating four and three-foot lines and its *abcb* rhyme scheme. Drawing on its association with medieval ballads and legends, Keats produces the eerie mystery of "La Belle Dame Sans Merci" (page 221):

> I saw pale kings and princes too,
>   Pale warriors, death-pale were they all;
> They cried—"La Belle Dame sans Merci
>   Hath thee in thrall!"

Such imitations are a form of literary allusion; Keats uses a traditional form to remind us of poems like "Sir Patrick Spens" or "Barbara Allen" to dramatize the painful thralldom of love by placing it within a well-known tradition of ballad narratives with similar themes.

The four-line stanza, or *quatrain*, may be used for a variety of effects: from the elegiac solemnity of Gray's "Elegy Written in a Country Churchyard" (page 131) to the apparent lightness and simplicity of some of Emily Dickinson's poems. Tennyson used a rhyming quatrain to such good effect in *In Memoriam* (page 267) that the form he employed (four lines of iambic tetrameter rhyming *abba*) is known as the "In Memoriam stanza".

Other commonly used forms of stanza include the *rhyming couplet, terza rima, ottava rima, rhyme royal,* and the *Spenserian stanza.* Each of these is a rhetorical unit within a longer whole, rather like a paragraph within an essay. The poet's choice among such forms is dictated, at least in part, by the effects that each may produce. Thus the *rhyming couplet* often expresses a complete statement within two lines, creating a sense of density of thought, of coherence and closure; it is particularly effective where the writer wishes to set up contrasts, or to achieve the witty compactness of epigram:

> Of all mad creatures, if the learn'd are right,
> It is the slaver kills, and not the bite.
> A fool quite angry is quite innocent:
> Alas! 'tis ten times worse when they repent.

(from Pope, "Epistle to Dr. Arbuthnot")

Ottava rima, as its Italian name implies, is an eight-line stanza with the rhyme scheme *abababcc*. Though much used by Renaissance poets, it is particularly associated with Byron's *Don Juan*, in which the poet exploits to the full its potential for devastating irony and bathos. It is long enough to allow the development of a single thought in some detail and complexity; the concluding couplet can then, sonnet-like, turn that thought upon its head, or cast it in a wholly unexpected light:

> Sagest of women, even of widows, she
> Resolved that Juan should be quite a paragon,
> And worthy of the noblest pedigree
> (His sire was of Castile, his dam from Aragon).
> Then for accomplishments of chivalry,
> In case our lord the king should go to war again,
> He learned the arts of riding, fencing, gunnery,
> And how to scale a fortress—or a nunnery.

(*Don Juan* I, 38)

Free verse

Not all writers want the order and symmetry—some might say the restraints and limitations—of traditional forms, and many have turned to *free verse* as a means of liberating their thoughts and feelings. Deriving its name from the French "vers libre" made popular by the French Symbolistes at the end of the 19th century, free verse is characterized by irregularity of metre, line length, and rhyme. This does not mean that it has no rules; rather, it follows more closely than other forms the unforced rhythms and accents of natural speech, making calculated use of spacing, line breaks, and "cadences," the rhythmic units that govern phrasing in speech. Walt Whitman's "Song of Myself" (page 298) provides a striking example of the rhythmic power of free verse at its best:

> I am the poet of the Body and I am the poet of the Soul,
> The pleasures of heaven are with me and the pains of hell are with me,
> The first I graft and increase upon myself, the latter I translate
>   into a new tongue.

(from Section 21)

In passages such as this, with its balanced and sonorous phrasing, its repetitions and contrasts, Whitman's language has an almost biblical quality, yet it never loses touch with the cadences of ordinary speech.

Free verse is not a modern invention. Milton was an early practitioner, as was Blake; however, it was the great modern writers of free verse—first Whitman, then Pound, Eliot, and William Carlos Williams—who gave this form a fluidity and flexibility that could free the imagination to deal with any kind of feeling or experience. Perhaps because it depends so much more than traditional forms upon the individual intuitions of the poet, it is the form of poetic structure most commonly found today. The best practitioners recognize that free verse, like any other kind of poetry, demands clarity, precision, and a close connection between technique and meaning.

RHYTHM AND SCANSION

When we read poetry, we often become aware of a pattern of rhythm within a line or set of lines. The formal analysis of that rhythmic pattern, or "metre," is called *scansion*. The verb "to scan" may carry different meanings, depending upon the context: if the critic "scans" a line, he or she is attempting to determine the metrical pattern in which it is cast; if the *line* "scans", we are making the observation that the line conforms to particular metrical rules. Whatever the context, the process of scansion is based on the premise that a line of verse is built on a pattern of stresses, a recurring set of more or less regular beats established by the alternation of light and heavy accents in syllables and words. The rhythmic pattern so distinguished in a given poem is said to be the "metre" of that poem. If we find it impossible to identify any metrical pattern, the poem is probably an example of free verse.

Quantitative, syllabic, and accentual-syllabic verse

Although we owe much of our terminology for analyzing or describing poetry to the Greeks and Romans, the foundation of our metrical system is quite different from theirs. They measured a line of verse by the duration of sound ("quantity") in each syllable, and by the combination of short and long syllables. Such poetry is known as *quantitative* verse.

Unlike Greek or Latin, English is a heavily accented language. Thus poetry of the Anglo-Saxon period, such as *Beowulf*, was *accentual*: that is, the lines were based on a fixed number of accents, or stresses, regardless of the number of syllables in the line:

Oft Scyld Scefing sceaþena þreatum

monegum maegþum meodosetla ofteah.

Few modern poets have written in the accentual tradition. A notable exception was Gerard Manley Hopkins, who based his line on a pattern of strong stresses that he called "sprung rhythm." Hopkins experimented with rhythms and stresses that approximate the accentual quality of natural speech; the result is a line that is emphatic, abrupt, even harsh in its forcefulness:

I caught this morning morning's minion, king-

dom of daylight's dauphin, dapple-dawn-drawn Falcon, in

his riding

Of the rolling level underneath him steady air . . . .

(from "The Windhover," page 349)

Under the influence of French poetry, following the Norman invasion of the eleventh century, English writers were introduced to *syllabic* prosody: that is, poetry in which the number of syllables is the determining factor in the length of any line, regardless of the number of stresses or their placement. Some modern writers have successfully produced syllabic poetry. For example, in Marianne Moore's "The Fish" (page 462), lines of varying lengths in one stanza are symmetrically matched with corresponding lines with a similar number of syllables in other stanzas.

However, the accentual patterns of English, in speech as well as in poetry, were too strongly ingrained to disappear. Instead, the native accentual practice combined with the imported syllabic conventions to produce the *accentual-syllabic* line, in which the writer works with combinations of stressed and unstressed syllables in lines of equal syllabic length. Chaucer was the first great writer to employ the accentual-syllabic line in English poetry:

Ther was also a Nonne, a Prioresse,

That of hir smiling was ful simple and coy.

Hir gretteste ooth was but by sainte Loy!

And she was cleped Madame Eglantine.

(from *The Canterbury Tales*)

The fundamental pattern here is the ten-syllable line (although the convention of sounding the final "e" at the end of a line in Middle English verse sometimes produces eleven syllables). Each line contains five stressed syllables alternating with one or two unstressed syllables. This was to become the predominant metre of poetry in English until the present century.

Identifying poetic metre

Conventionally, metre is established by dividing a line into roughly equal parts, based on the rise and fall of the rhythmic beats. Each of these divisions, conventionally marked by a bar, is known as a *foot*, and within the foot there will be a combination of stressed and unstressed syllables, indicated by the prosodic symbols / (stressed) and X (unstressed).

I know | that I | shall meet | my fate

Somewhere | among | the clouds | above...

(from Yeats, "An Irish Airman Foresees His Death", page 398)

To identify the metre used in a poem, we must first determine what kind of foot predominates, and then count the number of feet in each line. To describe the resultant metre we use terminology borrowed from classical prosody. In identifying the principal metres of English verse we apply the following labels:

iambic (x /): a foot with one weak stress followed by one strong stress:

    "Look home | ward, Ang | el, now, | and melt | with ruth")

trochaic (/ x): strong followed by weak:

    "Tyger! | Tyger! | burning | bright"

anapaestic (x x /): two weak stresses, followed by a strong:

    "I have passed | with a nod | of the head"

dactylic (/ x x): strong stress followed by two weak:

    "Hickory | dickory | dock"

spondaic (/ /): two strong stresses:

    "If hate | killed men, | Brother | Lawrence,

    God's blood, | would not | mine kill | you?"

We also use classical terms to describe the number of feet in a line. Thus, a line with one foot is *monometer*; with two feet, *dimeter*; three feet, *trimeter*; four feet, *tetrameter*; five feet, *pentameter*; and six feet, *hexameter*.

Scansion of the two lines from Yeats's "Irish Airman" quoted above shows that the predominant foot is iambic (x /), that there are four feet to each line, and that the poem is therefore written in *iambic tetrameters*. The first foot of the second line, however, may be read as a trochee ("Somewhere"); the variation upon the iambic norm here is an example of *substitution*, a means whereby the writer may avoid the monotony that would result from adhering too closely to a set rhythm. We very quickly build up an expectation about the dominant metre of a poem; the poet will sometimes disturb that expectation by changing the beat, and so create a pleasurable tension in our awareness.

The prevailing meter in English poetry is iambic, since the natural rhythm of the spoken language is decidedly iambic. Nonetheless, poets may employ other rhythms where it suits their purpose. Thus W. H. Auden can create a solemn tone by the use of a trochaic metre (/ x):

    Earth, receive an honoured guest;

    William Yeats is laid to rest:

    Let the Irish vessel lie

    Emptied of its poetry.

The same metre may be much less funereal, as in Jonson's song "To Celia":

/   x / x   / x   /
Come, my Celia, let us prove,

/   x / x   /   x /
While we may, the sports of love.

/   x   / x   / x / x
Time will not be ours forever;

/ x /   x   /   x / x
He, at length, our good will sever.

The sense of greater pace in this last example derives in part from the more staccato phrasing, and also from the greater use of monosyllabic words. A more obviously lilting, dancing effect is obtained from anapaestic rhythm (x x /):

x   /   x x   / x   x   / x x   /
I sprang to the stirrup, and Joris, and he;

x / x   x   / x   x / x   x   /
I galloped, Dirck galloped, we galloped all three.

/   /   x   x   /   x x   /   x   x   /
"Good speed!" cried the watch, as the gatebolts undrew;

/   /   x x   /   x x / x x   /
"Speed!" echoed the wall to us galloping through.

(from Browning,
"How They Brought the Good News from Ghent to Aix")

Coleridge wittily captured the varying effects of different metres in "Metrical Feet: Lesson for a Boy," which the poet wrote for his sons, and in which he marked the stresses himself:

/ x   /   x   /   x   /
Trochee trips from long to short;

From long to long in solemn sort

/   /   /   /   /   /
Slow Spondee stalks; strong foot! yet ill able

/ x x   /   x   x   / x   x / x x
Ever to come up with Dactyl trisyllable.

x /   x   /   x   / x /
Iambics march from short to long:—

x   x /   x x   /   x x / x x   /
With a leap and a bound the swift Anapaests throng. . . .

A metre which often deals with serious themes is unrhymed iambic pentameter, also known as *blank verse*. This is the metre of Shakespeare's plays, notably his great tragedies; it is the metre, too, of Milton's *Paradise Lost*, to which it lends a desired sonority and magnificence; and of Wordsworth's "Lines Composed a Few Miles above Tintern Abbey" (page 166), where the flexibility of the metre allows the writer to move by turns from description, to narration, to philosophical reflection.

RHYME, CONSONANCE, ASSONANCE, AND ALLITERATION

Perhaps the most obvious sign of poetic form is rhyme: that is, the repetition of syllables with the same or similar sounds. If the rhyme words are placed at the end of the line, they are known as *end-rhymes*. The opening stanza of Housman's "To an Athlete Dying Young" (page 358) has two pairs of end-rhymes:

> The time you won your town the *race*
> We chaired you through the market-*place*;
> Man and boy stood cheering *by*,
> And home we brought you shoulder-*high*.

Words rhyming within a line are *internal rhymes*, as in the first and third lines of this stanza from Coleridge's "The Rime of the Ancient Mariner":

> The fair breeze *blew*, the white foam *flew*
> The furrow followed free;
> We were the *first* that ever *burst*
> Into that silent sea.

When, as is usually the case, the rhyme occurs in a stressed syllable, it is known as a *masculine rhyme*; if the rhyming word ends in an unstressed syllable, it is referred to as *feminine*. The difference is apparent in the opening stanzas of Tennyson's poem "The Lady of Shalott" (page 255), where the first stanza establishes the basic iambic metre with strong stresses on the rhyming words:

> On either side the river *lie*
> Long fields of barley and of *rye*,
> That clothe the wold and meet the *sky*;
> And through the field the road runs *by*
> To many-towered Camelot...

In the second stanza Tennyson changes to trochaic lines, ending in unstressed syllables and feminine rhymes:

> Willows whiten, aspens *quiver*,
> Little breezes dusk and *shiver*
> Through the wave that runs *forever*
> By the island in the *river*
> Flowing down to Camelot.

Not only does Tennyson avoid monotony here by his shift to feminine rhymes, he also darkens the mood by using words that imply a contrast with the bright warmth of day—"quiver," "dusk," "shiver"—in preparation for the introduction of the "silent isle" that embowers the Lady.

Near rhymes

Most of the rhymes in "The Lady of Shalott" are exact, or *perfect* rhymes. However, in the lines just quoted, it is evident that "forever" at the end of the third line is not a "perfect" rhyme; rather, it is an instance of *near* or *slant* rhyme. Such "imperfect" rhymes are quite deliberate; indeed, two stanzas later we find the rhyming sequence "early", "barley", "cheerly", and "clearly", followed by the rhymes "weary", "airy", and "fairy". As with the introduction of feminine rhymes, such divergences from one dominant pattern prevent monotony and avoid a too-mechanical sing-song effect.

More importantly, near-rhymes have an oddly unsettling effect, perhaps because they both raise and frustrate our expectation of a perfect rhyme. Their use certainly gives added emphasis to the words at the end of these chilling lines from Wilfred Owen's "Strange Meeting" (page 499):

> For by my glee might many men have laughed,
> And of my weeping something had been left,
> Which must die now. I mean the truth untold,
> The pity of war, the pity war distilled.
> Now men will go content with what we spoiled,
> Or, discontent, boil bloody, and be spilled.

Consonance and assonance

In Owen's poem, the near-rhymes "laughed / left" and "spoiled / spilled" are good examples of *consonance*, which pairs words with similar consonants but different intervening vowels. Other examples from Owen's poem include "groined / groaned", "hall / Hell", "years / yours", and "mystery / mastery".

Related to consonance as a linking device is *assonance*, the echoing of similar vowel sounds in the stressed syllables of words with differing consonants (lane/hail, penitent/reticence). A device favoured particularly by descriptive poets, it appears often in the work of the English Romantics, especially Shelley and Keats, and their great Victorian successor Tennyson, all of whom had a good ear for the musical quality of language. In the following passage, Tennyson makes effective use of repeated "o" and "ow" sounds to suggest the soft moaning of the wind as it spreads the seed of the lotos plant:

> The Lotos blooms below the barren peak,
> The Lotos blows by every winding creek;
> All day the wind breathes low with mellower tone;
> Through every hollow cave and alley lone
> Round and round the spicy downs the yellow Lotos dust is blown.

(from "The Lotos-Eaters," page 259)

Alliteration

Alliteration connects words which have the same initial consonant. Like consonance and rhyme, alliteration adds emphasis, throwing individual words into strong relief, and lending force to rhythm. This is especially evident in the work of Gerard Manley Hopkins, where alliteration works in conjunction with the heavy stresses of *sprung rhythm*:

> Brute beauty and valour and act, oh, air, pride, plume, here
> Buckle! AND the fire that breaks from thee then, a billion
> Times told lovelier, more dangerous, O my chevalier!

(from "The Windhover," page 349)

Like assonance, alliteration is useful in descriptive poetry, reinforcing an impression or mood through repeated sounds:

> Thou on whose stream, 'mid the steep sky's commotion,
> Loose clouds like Earth's decaying leaves are shed,
> Shook from the tangled boughs of Heaven and Ocean....

> (from Shelley, "Ode to the West Wind", page 212)

The repetition of "s" and "sh" sounds conveys the rushing sound of a wind that drives everything before it. This effect is an example of *onomatopoeia*, the figure of speech in which the sound of the words seems to echo the sense.

Rhyme and poetic structure

Rhyme may play a central role in the structure of a poem. This is particularly apparent in the sonnet form, where the expression of the thought is heavily influenced by the poet's choice of rhyme-scheme. The "English" or "Shakespearean" sonnet has three quatrains rhyming *abab, cdcd, efef*, and concludes with a rhyming couplet, *gg*. This pattern lends itself well to the statement and restatement of an idea, as we find, for example, in Shakespeare's sonnet "That time of year thou mayst in me behold" (page 32). Each of the quatrains presents an image of decline or decay—a tree in winter, the coming of night, a dying fire; the closing couplet then relates these images to the thought of an impending separation and attendant feelings of loss.

The organization of the "Italian" or "Petrarchan" sonnet, by contrast, hinges on a rhyme scheme that creates two parts, an eight-line section (the *octave*) typically rhyming *abbaabba*, and a concluding six-line section (the *sestet*) rhyming *cdecde* or some other variation. In the octave, the writer describes a thought or feeling; in the sestet, the writer elaborates upon that thought, or introduces a sudden "turn" or change of direction. Good examples of the Italian form are Donne's "Batter My Heart, Three-Person'd God" (page 45), and Robert Frost's "Design" (page 414).

Other forms with interlocking rhymes

Other forms besides the sonnet depend upon rhyme for their structural integrity. These include the *rondeau*, a thirteen-line poem with only two rhymes; and the *villanelle*, usually a nineteen-line poem divided into five three-line stanzas (tercets) rhyming *aba*, with a concluding quatrain rhyming *abaa*. A modern example of the villanelle, with its interlocking rhymes and its elaborate repetitions, is Dylan Thomas's "Do Not Go Gentle Into That Good Night" (page 631). The linking effect of rhyme is also essential to the three-line stanza called *terza rima*, the form chosen by Shelley for his "Ode to the West Wind" (page 212), where the rhyme scheme (*aba, bcb, cdc* etc.) gives a strong sense of forward movement.

A poet need not be limited to particular forms to use interlocking rhyme schemes: the first three quatrains in Robert Frost's "Stopping by Woods on a Snowy Evening" (page 412) are rhymed *aaba, bbcb, ccdc*, while the concluding stanza has a single rhyme (deep/keep/sleep/sleep) echoing "sweep" in the third stanza.

Finally, one of the most obvious yet important aspects of rhyme is its sound.

It acts as a kind of musical punctuation, lending verse an added resonance and beauty. And as anyone who has ever had to learn poetry by heart will testify, the sound of rhyme is a welcome aid to memorization.

Rhyme and metre are important tools at the poet's disposal, and can be valuable aids in developing thought as well as in creating rhythmic or musical effects. However, the technical skills needed to turn a good line or create metrical complexities should not be confused with the ability to write good poetry. Sir Philip Sidney wryly observed in his *Defence of Poesy* (1593) that "there have been many excellent poets that never versified, and now swarm many versifiers that need never answer to the name of poets. . . . it is not rhyming and versing that maketh a poet, no more than a long gown maketh an advocate."

Glossary: Poetic and Literary Terms

Accent: the natural emphasis (stress) speakers place on a syllable. In *prosody* it refers to the stress required by meaning or rhythm.

Accentual Verse: poetry in which a line is measured only by the number of accents or stresses, not by the number of syllables. See *sprung rhythm* below.

Accentual-Syllabic Verse: the most common metrical system in traditional English verse, in which a line is measured by the number of syllables and by the pattern of light and heavy accents or stresses.

Alexandrine: a line of verse that is 12 syllables long. In English verse, the alexandrine always has six iambic feet.

Allegory: a story or poem with both a literal meaning and a secondary, often symbolic meaning. Allegory frequently employs *personification* to give concrete embodiment to abstract concepts or entities, such as feelings or personal qualities. It may also present one set of characters or events in the guise of another, using implied parallels for the purposes of satire or political comment, as in Dryden's poem *Absalom and Achitophel.*

Alliteration: the grouping of words with the same initial consonant. The repetition of sound acts as a connector. Also see *assonance* and *consonance* below.

Allusion: a reference, often indirect or unidentified, to a person, thing, or event. A reference in one literary work to another literary work, whether to its content or its form, also constitutes an allusion.

Ambiguity: an "opening" of language created by the writer to allow for multiple meanings or differing interpretations. In literature, ambiguity may be deliberately employed by the writer to enrich meaning; this differs from any unintentional, unwanted, ambiguity in non-literary prose.

Analogy: a broad term that refers to our processes of noting similarities among things or events. Specific forms of analogy in poetry include *simile* and *metaphor* (see below).

Anapaest: a metrical *foot* containing two weak stresses followed by one strong stress: X X / (e.g., underneath, intervene).

Antistrophe: from Greek drama, the chorus's countermovement or reply to an initial movement (strophe). See *ode* below.

Apostrophe: a figure of speech (a *trope*; see *figures of speech* below) in which a writer directly addresses an object—or a dead or absent person—as if the imagined audience were actually listening.

Archetype: in literature and mythology, a recurring idea, symbol, motif, character, or place. To some scholars and psychologists, an archetype represents universal human thought-patterns or experiences.

Assonance: the repetition of identical or similar vowel sounds in stressed syllables in which the surrounding consonants are different: for example, "shame" and "fate"; "gale" and "cage"; or the long "i" sounds in "Beside the pumice isle..."

Aubade: a lyric poem which greets or laments the arrival of dawn.

Ballad: a folk song, or a poem originally recited to an audience, which tells a dramatic story based on legend or history.

Ballade: a *fixed form* (see below) most commonly characterized by only three rhymes, with an 8-line stanza rhyming *ababbcbc* and an *envoy* (see below) rhyming *bcbc*. Both Chaucer and Dante Gabriel Rossetti ("Ballad of the Dead Ladies") adopted this form.

Ballad Stanza: a *quatrain* with alternating four-stress and three-stress lines, rhyming *abcb*. A variant is "common measure," in which the alternating lines are strictly iambic, and rhyme *abab*.

Bathos: an anticlimactic effect brought about by a writer's descent from an elevated subject or tone to the ordinary or trivial.

Bombast: inappropriately inflated or grandiose language.

Blank Verse: unrhymed lines written in iambic pentameter, introduced to English verse by Surrey in his translation of parts of Virgil's *Aeneid* in 1547.

Broken Rhyme: in which a multi-syllable word is split at the end of a line and continued onto the next, to allow an end-rhyme with the split syllable.

Caesura: a pause or break in a line of verse occurring where a phrase, clause, or sentence ends, and indicated in scansion by the mark ||. If it occurs in the middle of the line, it is known as a "medial" caesura.

Canto: a sub-section of a book-length (usually *epic*) poem.

Carpe Diem: Latin (from Horace) meaning "seize the day; enjoy the moment"; it is a common theme in Renaissance love poetry. See, for example, Marvell's "To His Coy Mistress."

Catalectic: a line from which unstressed syllables have been left out. In iambic verse it is usually the first syllable of the line that is omitted; in trochaic, the last.

Chiasmus: a figure of speech (a scheme) that reverses word order in successive parallel clauses. If the word order is A-B-C in the first clause, it becomes C-B-A in the second: for example, Donne's line "She is all states, and all princes, I" in "The Sun Rising" incorporates this reversal (though with an *ellipsis*).

Conceit: an unusually elaborate metaphor or simile that extends beyond its original *tenor* and *vehicle*, sometimes becoming a "master"-analogy for the entire poem (see, for example, Donne's "The Flea"). Ingenious or fanciful images and comparisons were especially popular with the *metaphysical poets* of the 17th century, giving rise to the term "metaphysical conceit."

Concrete Poetry: an experimental form, most popular during the 1950s and 60s, in which the printed type itself forms a visual image of the poem's key words or ideas. See also *pattern poetry*.

Connotation: the implied, often unspoken meaning(s) of a given word, as distinct from its denotation, or literal meaning. Connotations may have highly emotional undertones and are usually culturally specific.

Consonance: the pairing of words with similar initial and ending consonants, but with different vowel sounds (live/love, wander/wonder). See also *alliteration*.

Couplet: a pair of rhyming lines, usually in the same metre. If they form a complete unit of thought and are grammatically complete, the lines are known as a *closed couplet*. See also *heroic couplet* below.

Dactyl: a metrical foot containing one strong stress followed by two weak stresses: / X X (e.g., muttering, helplessly).

Denotation: see *connotation* above.

Dimeter: a line containing two metrical feet.

Dirge: a song or poem that mourns someone's death. See also *elegy* and *lament* below.

Dissonance: harsh, unmusical sounds or rhythms which poets may use deliberately to achieve certain effects.

Dramatic Monologue: a lyric poem taking the form of an utterance by a single person addressing a silent listener. The speaker may be an historical personage, as in some of Browning's dramatic monologues, or a figure drawn from myth or legend, as in some of Tennyson's.

Elegy: a poem which formally mourns the death of a particular person (e.g., Tennyson's "In Memoriam") or in which the poet meditates on other serious subjects (e.g., Gray's "Elegy"). See also *dirge*.

Elegiac Stanza: a quatrain of iambic pentameters rhyming *abab*.

Elision: omitting or suppressing a letter or an unstressed syllable at the beginning or end of a word, so that a line of verse may conform to a given metrical scheme. For example, the three syllables at the beginning of Shakespeare's sonnet 129 are reduced to two by the omission of the first vowel: "Th' expense of spirit in a waste of shame." See also *syncope*.

Ellipsis: the omission of a word or words necessary for the complete grammatical construction of a sentence, but not necessary for our understanding of the sentence.

End-Rhyme: see *rhyme*.

End-stopped: a line of poetry is said to be end-stopped when the end of the line coincides with a natural pause in the syntax, such as the conclusion of a sentence. Compare this with *enjambement*.

Enjambement: the "running-on" of the sense from one line of poetry to the next, with no pause created by punctuation or syntax.

Envoy (Envoi): a half-stanza that forms the conclusion of certain French poetic forms, such as the *sestina* or the *ballade*.

Epic: a lengthy narrative poem, often divided into books and sub-divided into *cantos*. It generally celebrates heroic deeds or events, and the style tends to be lofty and grand.

Epic Simile: an elaborate simile, developed at such length that the "vehicle" of the comparison momentarily displaces the primary subject of the poem.

Epigram: a very short poem, sometimes in *closed couplet* form, characterized by pointed wit.

Epigraph: a quotation placed at the beginning of a discourse to indicate or foreshadow the theme.

Epithalamion: a poem celebrating a wedding.

Euphony: pleasant, musical sounds or rhythms—the opposite of dissonance.

Eye-Rhyme: see *rhyme* below.

Feminine Ending: the ending of a line of poetry on an unstressed syllable. See, for example, the first line of Keat's "Ode on a Grecian Urn": "A thing of beauty is a joy forever."

Feminine Rhyme: see *rhyme* below.

Figures of Speech: deliberate, highly concentrated uses of language to achieve particular purposes or effects on an audience. There are two kinds of figures: schemes and tropes. *Schemes* involve changes in word-sound and word-order, such as *alliteration* and *chiasmus*. *Tropes* play on our understandings of words to extend, alter, or transform meaning, as in *metaphor* and *personification*.

Fixed Forms: the term applied to a number of poetic forms and stanzaic patterns, many derived from French models, such as *ballade, rondeau, sestina*, and *villanelle*. Other "fixed forms" include the *sonnet, rhyme royal, haiku*, and *ottava rima*.

Foot: a unit of a line of verse which contains a particular combination of stressed and unstressed syllables. Dividing a line into metrical feet—then counting the number of feet per line—is part of *scansion* (see below).

Free Verse: poetry that does not follow any regular meter, line length, or rhyming scheme. In many respects, though, free verse follows the complex natural "rules" and rhythmic patterns (or cadences) of speech.

Haiku: a Japanese form, using three unrhymed lines of five, seven, and five syllables. Conventionally, it uses precise, concentrated images to suggest states of feeling, and influenced the work of the Imagist poets in the U.S.

Harlem Renaissance: a flowering of Black American literature during the 1920s, associated particularly but not exclusively with writers out of Harlem in New York City. The movement included such writers as Langston Hughes and Countee Cullen.

Heptameter: a line containing seven metrical feet.

Heroic Couplet: a pair of rhymed iambic pentameters, so called because the form was much used in 17th and 18th-century poems and plays on heroic subjects.

Hexameter: a line containing six metrical feet.

Horatian Ode: inspired by the work of the Roman poet Horace, an ode that is usually calm and meditative in tone, and homostrophic (i.e. having regular stanzas) in form. Keats's odes are English examples. Also see *ode*.

Hymn: a song whose theme is usually religious, in praise of divinity. Literary hymns may praise more secular subjects.

Hyperbole: a *figure of speech* (a trope) that deliberately exaggerates word meanings to achieve particular effects, such as irony.

Iamb: the most common metrical foot in English verse, containing one weak stress followed by one strong stress: X / (e.g., between, achieve).

Idyll: traditionally, a short pastoral poem that idealizes country life, conveying impressions of innocence and happiness.

Image: the recreation in words of objects perceived by the senses, sometimes thought of as "pictures," although other senses besides sight are involved. Besides this literal application, the terms also refers more generally to the descriptive effects of figurative language, especially in *metaphor* and *simile*.

Imagism: a poetic movement that was popular mainly in the second decade of the twentieth century. The goal of Imagist poets such as Ezra Pound, H.D., T.S. Eliot, and William Carlos Williams was to represent emotions or impressions through highly concentrated imagery.

Incantation: a chant or recitation of words that are believed to have magical power. A poem can achieve an "incantatory" effect through a compelling rhyme-scheme and other repetitive patterns.

In Memoriam Stanza: a four-line stanza in iambic tetrameter, rhyming *abba*; named for the stanza used by Tennyson in *In Memoriam*.

Internal Rhyme: see *rhyme*.

Irony: a subtle form of humor in which a statement is understood to mean its opposite. A writer achieves this by carefully making sure that the statement occurs in a context which undermines or twists the statement's "literal" meaning. *Hyperbole* and *litotes* are often used for ironic effect.

Lament: a poem which expresses profound regret or grief either because of a death, or because of the loss of a former, happier state.

Litotes: a *figure of speech* (a trope) in which a writer deliberately uses understatement to highlight the importance of an argument, or to convey an ironic attitude.

Lyric: a poem, usually short, expressing the speaker's feelings or private thoughts. Originally a song performed with accompaniment on a lyre, the lyric poem is often noted for musicality of rhyme and rhythm. The lyric genre includes a variety of forms, including the *sonnet*, the *ode*, the *elegy*, the *madrigal*, the *aubade*, the *dramatic monologue*, and the *hymn*.

Madrigal: a lyric poem, usually short and focusing on pastoral or romantic themes. A madrigal is often set to music.

Masculine Ending: a metrical line ending on a stressed syllable.

Masculine Rhyme: see *rhyme*.

Metaphor: a *figure of speech* (in this case, a trope) in which a comparison is made between two unrelated things or actions without the use of "like" or "as." The primary subject is known as the *tenor*; to illuminate its nature, the writer links it to wholly different images, ideas, or actions referred to as the *vehicle*. Unlike a *simile*, which is a direct comparison of two things, a metaphor "fuses" the separate qualities of two things, creating a new idea. For example, Shakespeare's "Let slip the dogs of war" is a metaphorical statement. The tenor, or primary subject, is "war"; the vehicle of the metaphor is the image of hunting dogs released from their leash. The line fuses the idea of war with the qualities of ravening bloodlust associated with hunting dogs.

Metaphysical Poets: a group of 17th-century English poets, notably Donne, Marvell, and Herbert, who employed unusual imagery and *conceits* (see above) in order to develop intellectual and religious themes. The term "metaphysics" itself refers to the study of our own existence and the nature of knowledge.

Metre: the pattern of stresses, syllables, and pauses that constitute the regular rhythm of a line of verse. The metre of a poem written in the English accentual-syllabic tradition is determined by identifying the strong and weak stresses in a line of verse, and grouping them into recurring units known as *feet*. See *accent*, *accentual-syllabic*, *caesura*, *elision*, and *scansion*. For some of the better-known metres, see *iamb*, *trochee*, *dactyl*, *anapaest*, and *spondee*. See also *monometer*, *dimeter*, *trimeter*, *tetrameter*, *pentameter*, and *hexameter*.

Metonymy: a *figure of speech* (a trope), meaning "change of name," in which a writer refers to an object or idea by substituting the name of another object or idea closely associated with it: for example, the substitution of "crown" for monarchy, "the press" for journalism, or "the pen" for writing. *Synecdoche* (see below) is a kind of metonymy.

Mock-heroic: a style applying the elevated diction and vocabulary of epic poetry to low or ridiculous subjects. An example is provided by Pope's "Rape of the Lock."

Monometer: a line containing one metrical foot.

Nonsense Verse: light, humorous poetry which ignores logic, plays with the absurd, and invents words for amusing effects. Lewis Carroll is one of the best-known practitioners of nonsense verse.

Octave: the first eight lines in an Italian/Petrarchan sonnet, rhyming *abbaabba*. See also *sestet* and *sonnet*, below.

Octosyllabic: a line with eight syllables.

Ode: originally a classical poetic form, used by the Greeks and Romans to convey serious themes. English poetry has evolved three main forms: the Pindaric (imitative of the odes of the Greek poet Pindar); the Horatian (modelled on the work of the Roman writer Horace); and the irregular ode. The Pindaric ode has a tripartite structure of "strophe", "antistrophe", and "epode" (meaning turn, counterturn, and stand) modelled on the songs and movements of the Chorus in Greek drama. The Horatian ode is more personal, reflective, and literary, and employs a pattern of repeated stanzas. The irregular ode, as its name implies, lacks a recurrent stanza pattern, and is sometimes irregular in line length also (see, for example, Wordsworth's "Ode: Intimations of Immortality").

Onomatopoeia: a *figure of speech* (a scheme) in which a word "imitates" a sound, or in which the sound of a word seems to reflect its meaning.

Ottava Rima: an 8-line stanza with the rhyme scheme *ababacc*. For an example, see Byron's *Don Juan*.

Oxymoron: a *figure of speech* (a trope) in which two words whose meanings seem contradictory are placed together: for example, "darkness visible."

Paean: a triumphant, celebratory song, often associated with a military victory.

Parody: a close imitation of a particular literary work, or of the well-known style of a particular author, in order to expose or magnify weaknesses. Parody is a form of satire—humor which ridicules and scorns.

Pastiche: a discourse which borrows other writers' characters, forms, or ideas. Unlike a parody, a pastiche is usually intended as a compliment to the original writer.

Pastoral: in general, pertaining to country life; in prose, drama, and poetry, a stylized type of writing that romanticizes the lives and innocence of country people, particularly shepherds and shepherdesses. Also see *idyll*, above.

Pathetic Fallacy: a neutral term describing a form of *personification*, in which inanimate objects are given human emotions: for example, rain clouds "weeping."

Pathos: the emotional quality of a discourse; or the ability of a discourse to appeal to our emotions.

Pattern Poetry: an early predecessor of modern *concrete poetry*, in which the shape of the poem on the page is intended to suggest or imitate an aspect of the poem's subject. George Herbert's "Easter Wings" is a good example of pattern poetry.

Pentameter: a line containing five metrical feet.

Persona: the assumed identity or "speaking voice" that a writer projects in a discourse. The term "persona" literally means "mask." Even when a writer speaks in the first person, we should be aware that the attitudes or opinions we hear may not necessarily be those of the writer in real life.

Personification: a *figure of speech* (a trope), also known as "prosopopoeia," in which a writer refers to inanimate objects, ideas, or animals as if they were human.

Petrarchan: the earliest form of the *sonnet*, also known as the Italian form, with an 8-line *octave* and a 6-line *sestet*. The Petrarchan sonnet traditionally centres on love and descriptions of physical beauty. See also *sonnet*.

Pindaric: see *ode*.

Pre-Raphaelites: originally a group of Victorian artists and writers, formed in 1848. Their goal was to revive what they considered the simpler, fresher, more natural art that existed before Raphael (1483-1520). The poet Dante Gabriel Rossetti was one of the founders of the group.

Prose Poem: a poetic discourse that uses prose formats—e.g., it may have margins rather than line breaks—yet is written with the kind of attention to rhythm and cadence that characterizes free verse.

Prosody: the study and analysis of metre, rhythm, rhyme, stanzaic pattern, and other devices of versification.

Prothalamion: a wedding song; a term coined by the poet Edmund Spenser, adapted from "epithalamion" (see above).

Pun: a play on words, in which a word with two or more distinct meanings, or two words with similar sounds, may create humorous ambiguities. Also known as "paranomasia."

Pyrrhic: a metrical foot containing two weak stresses: X X

Quantitative Meter: a metrical system used by Greek and Roman poets, in which a line of verse was measured by the "quantity," or length of sound of each syllable. A *foot* was measured in terms of syllables classed as long or short.

Quatrain: a four-line stanza, usually rhymed.

Quintet: a five-line stanza.

Refrain: one or more lines repeated at regular points throughout a poem, often at the end of each stanza.

Rhetoric: in classical Greece and Rome, the art of persuasion and public speaking. In the Middle Ages, rhetoric became equated with style, and particularly figures of speech. Today in poetics, the term "rhetoric" may encompass not only figures of speech, but also the persuasive effects of forms, sounds and word choices.

Rhyme: the repetition of identical or similar sounds in pairs, generally at the ends of metrical lines.

> **End-rhyme:** a rhyming word or syllable at the end of a line.
>
> **Eye Rhyme:** rhyming that depends upon words whose spellings are alike but whose pronunciations are different: for example, though/slough.
>
> **Feminine Rhyme:** a two-syllable (also known as "double") rhyme. The first syllable is stressed and the second unstressed: for example, hasty/tasty. See also *triple rhyme* below.
>
> **Internal Rhyme:** the placement of rhyming words within lines so that at least two words in a line rhyme with each other
>
> **Masculine Rhyme:** a rhyme occurring in single stressed syllables at the end of a line, as in grieve/leave.
>
> **Slant Rhyme:** an imperfect or partial rhyme (also known as "near" or "half" rhyme) in which the final consonants of stressed syllables match but the vowel sounds do not. E.g., spoiled / spilled, taint / stint.
>
> **Triple Rhyme:** a three-syllable rhyme in which the first syllable is stressed and the other two unstressed (e.g., lottery / coterie).
>
> **True Rhyme:** a rhyme in which everything but the initial consonant matches perfectly in sound and spelling.

Rhyme Royal: a stanza of seven iambic pentameters, with a rhyme-scheme of *ababbcc*. This is also known as the Chaucerian stanza, as Chaucer was the first English poet to use this form. See also *septet*.

Rhythm: a pattern of sound created by the arrangement of stressed and unstressed syllables in discourse. In song or verse, a regular rhythmic pattern is described as "metre" (see above).

Romanticism: a major social and cultural movement, originating in Europe, that shaped much of Western artistic thought in the 19th century. Opposing the controlled, rational order of the Enlightenment, Romanticism emphasizes the importance of free, spontaneous self-expression, emotions, and personal experience in producing art. In Romanticism, the "natural" is privileged over the conventional or the artificial.

Rondeau: a thirteen-line poem, generally octosyllabic, with only two rhymes throughout its three stanzas, and an unrhymed refrain at the end of the second and third stanzas, taken from the opening line.

Scansion: the formal analysis of patterns of rhythm and rhyme in poetry. Each line of verse will have a certain number of fairly regular "beats" consisting of alternating stressed and unstressed syllables. To "scan" a poem is to count the beats in each line, to mark stressed and unstressed syllables and indicate their combination into "feet", to note pauses, and to identify rhyme schemes with letters of the alphabet.

Scheme: see *figures of speech* above.

Septet: a stanza containing seven lines.

Sestet: a six-line stanza that forms the second grouping of lines in an Italian/Petrarchan sonnet. See *sonnet* and *sestina*.

Sestina: an elaborate unrhymed poem with six 6-line stanzas and a 3-line *envoy*.

Simile: a *figure of speech* (a trope) which makes an explicit comparison between a particular subject and an object or idea. A simile always uses "like" or "as" to signal the connection. Compare with *metaphor* above.

Sonnet: a highly structured lyric poem, which normally has fourteen lines of iambic pentameter. We can distinguish four major variations of the sonnet.

> **Italian/Petrarchan:** named for the 14th-century Italian poet Petrarch, has an *octave* rhyming *abbaabba*, and a *sestet* rhyming *cdecde*, or *cdcdcd* (other arrangements are possible here). Usually, a *turn* in argument takes place between octave and setset.

> **Spenserian:** after Spenser, who developed the form in his sonnet cycle *Amoretti*. This sonnet form has three *quatrains* linked through interlocking rhyme, and a separately rhyming couplet: *abab bcbc cdcd ee*.

> **Shakespearean:** often called the English sonnet, has three quatrains and a couplet. The quatrains rhyme internally but do not interlock: *abab cdcd efef gg*. The *turn* may occur after the second quatrain, but is usually revealed in the final couplet. Shakespeare's sonnets are the finest examples of this form.

> **Miltonic:** developed by Milton and similar to the Petrarchan, but eliminating the turn after the octave, and thus giving greater unity to the poem's structure of thought.

Spenserian Stanza: a nine-line stanza, with eight iambic pentameters and a concluding alexandrine, rhyming *ababbcbcc*.

Spondee: a metrical foot containing two strong stresses: / / (empire, headache).

Sprung Rhythm: a modern variation of accentual verse, created by Gerard Manley Hopkins, in which rhythms are determined by the number of strong stresses in a line, without regard to the number of unstressed syllables. Hopkins felt that sprung rhythm more closely approximated the natural rhythms of speech than did conventional poetry.

Stanza: any lines of verse that are grouped together and separated from other groups by a space. In metrical poetry, stanzas share metrical and rhyming patterns; however, stanzas may also be formed on the basis of thought, as in irregular odes. Conventional stanza forms include the *tercet*, the *quatrain*, *rhyme royal*, *Spenserian stanza*, and *ottava rima*.

Stress: see *accent*.

Strophe: in a Pindaric ode, the first stanza. This is followed by an *antistrophe* (see above), which presents the same metrical pattern and rhyme scheme, and finally by an *epode*, differing in meter from the preceding stanzas. Upon completion of this "triad," the entire sequence can recur. *Strophe* is also a term for a stanza or other subdivision in a poem.

Sublime: a concept, most popular in 18th-century England, of nature as a force that is awesome, grand and immensely powerful. The sublime was thought of as higher and loftier than something that is merely beautiful.

Syllabic Verse: poetry in which the length of a line is measured solely by the number of syllables, regardless of accents.

Symbol: a word, image, or idea that represents something more, or other, than what it at first appears to stand for. Like metaphor, the symbol extends meaning; but while the tenor and vehicle of metaphor are bound in a specific relationship, a symbol may have a range of connotations. For example, the image of a rose may call forth associations of love, passion, transience, fragility, youth and beauty, among others. Though this power of symbolic representation characterizes all language, poetry most particularly endows the concrete imagery evoked through language with a larger meaning. Such meaning is implied rather than explicitly stated; indeed, much of the power of symbolic language lies in the reader's ability to make meaningful sense of it.

Synecdoche: a kind of *metonymy* in which a writer substitutes the name of a part of something to signify the whole: for example, "sail" for ship or "hand" for a member of the ship's crew.

Syncope: in poetry, the dropping of a letter or syllable from the middle of a word, as in "trav'ler." Such a contraction allows a line to stay within a metrical scheme. See also *elision*.

Tercet: a group, or stanza, of three lines, often linked by an interlocking rhyme scheme as in *terza rima*. See also *triplet*.

Terza Rima: an arrangement of *tercets* interlocked by a rhyme scheme of *aba bcb cdc ded*, etc., and ending with a couplet that rhymes with the second-last line of the final tercet. See, for example, Shelley's "Ode to the West Wind."

Tetrameter: a line containing four metrical feet.

Theme: the governing idea of a discourse, conveyed through the development of the subject, and through the recurrence of certain words, sounds, or metrical patterns.

Tone: the writer's attitude toward a given subject or audience, as expressed though an authorial persona or "voice." Tone can be projected in poetry through particular choices of wording, imagery, figures of speech, and rhythmic devices.

Transcendentalism: a philosophical movement that began in Boston in the 1830s. Also a mode of Romantic thought, Trancendentalism places the supernatural and the natural within one great Unity and believes that each individual person embodies aspects of the divine. The poet and essayist Ralph Waldo Emerson was a founder of Transcendentalism.

Trimeter: a line containing three metrical feet.

Triplet: a group of three lines with the same rhyme, much used by 18th-century poets to relieve the monotony of a series of heroic couplets. See also *tercet*.

Trochee: a metrical foot containing one strong stress followed by one weak stress: / X (heaven, lover).

Trope: Any figure of speech which plays on our understandings of words to extend, alter, or transform "literal" meaning. Common tropes include *metaphor, simile, personification, hyperbole, metonymy, synecdoche*, and *irony*. Also see *figures of speech*, above.

Turn (Italian "Volta"): the point in a *sonnet* where the mood or argument changes. The turn may occur between the octave and sestet, i.e., after the eighth line, or in the final couplet, depending on the kind of sonnet.

Vers libre: see *free verse* above.

Verse: a general term for works of poetry, usually referring to poems that incorporate some kind of metric structure. The term may also describe a line of poetry, though more frequently it is applied to a stanza.

Villanelle: a poem usually consisting of 19 lines, with five 3-line stanzas (tercets) rhyming *aba*, and a concluding quatrain rhyming *abaa*. The first and third lines of the first tercet are repeated at fixed intervals throughout the rest of the poem. See, for example, Thomas's "Do Not Go Gentle Into That Good Night."

Zeugma: a *figure of speech* (trope) in which one word links or "yokes" two others in the same sentence, often to comic or ironic effect. For example, a verb may govern two objects, as in Pope's line "Or stain her honour, or her new brocade."

Biographical Notes

ADCOCK, FLEUR (New Zealand, b. 1934) settled in England in 1963, and has published a number of poetry collections since then, including THE INNER HARBOUR (1979), BELOW LOUGHRIGG (1979), and THE INCIDENT BOOK (1986). She has edited an anthology of contemporary New Zealand poetry.

ANGELOU, MAYA (U.S., b. 1928), author of the autobiographical novel I KNOW WHY THE CAGED BIRD SINGS, is a poet, novelist, playwright, and performer. An African-American activist, she was involved with Martin Luther King's civil rights movement in the 1960s.

ARNOLD, MATTHEW (England, 1822-1888), son of Thomas Arnold, founder of Rugby school, also became an educator after graduating from Oxford. He served briefly as a tutor at Oxford, then as Inspector of schools, and for ten years as professor of poetry at Oxford. One of his best-known poems, "Thyrsis" (1867), commemorates his friend Arthur Hugh Clough. For the last thirty years of his life, he published mainly prose, and is known almost as much for his CULTURE AND ANARCHY (1869), and his essays on literary and social criticism, as he is for his poetry.

ATWOOD, MARGARET (Canada, b. 1939), one of Canada's best-known novelists and poets, is a writer of international prominence. Her numerous honors include the Governor-General's Award for THE CIRCLE GAME (1967), and she was a Booker Prize finalist for her novel THE HANDMAID'S TALE. Her collections of poetry include POWER POLITICS (1973), TWO-HEADED POEMS (1978), and INTERLUNAR (1984).

AUDEN, W. H. (U.S., 1907-1973) was born in England, educated at Oxford, and travelled widely in Europe, Iceland, and China before settling in the U.S. in 1939. He taught at colleges and universities throughout the eastern U.S., and was elected Professor of Poetry at Oxford in 1956. He was a playwright and critic, as well as a prolific poet. Among the honors he received for his work were a Guggenheim Fellowship (1942), a Pulitzer Prize (1948), a Bollingen Prize (1954), and a National Book Award (1956).

AVISON, MARGARET (Canada, b. 1918), born in Ontario, graduated from the University of Toronto, and served as Writer in Residence at the University of Western Ontario in 1973. She won the Governor-General's Award in 1960 for her collection WINTER SUN. Much of her poetry, including her collection THE DUMBFOUNDING (1982), explores Biblical and Christian myth.

AWOONOR, KOFI (Ghana, b. 1935), has taught at the State University of New York at Stoneybrook, and served as his country's ambassador to Brazil. His collections of poetry include REDISCOVERY (1964), NIGHT OF MY BLOOD (1971), and UNTIL THE MORNING AFTER: SELECTED POEMS 1963-85 (1987).

BARAKA, IMAMU AMIRI (U.S., b. 1934), born LeRoi Jones, is a poet and playwright. As a political activist, he conveys his messages for Black empowerment through essays, tales, and speeches. He was instrumental in planning several Black Power conferences and arts festivals, and in the 1960s, founded the Black Arts Theatre and Repertory School.

BARBAULD, ANNA LAETITIA (England, 1743-1825) was the daughter of a clergyman and a schoolteacher. Her first collection of poems was published in 1773. Among her many activities, she established a school for young women, engaged in anti-slavery debates, published numerous essays, and edited literary works.

BAXTER, JAMES K. (New Zealand, 1926-1972), educated in New Zealand and England, published his first book of poems, BEYOND THE PALISADE (1944) at age 18, but worked as a laborer, journalist, and teacher before becoming established as a poet of international renown. He wrote over 30 books of verse (some published posthumously), over a dozen plays, and a number of critical works. Among his most acclaimed collections are IN FIRES OF NO RETURN (1958), HOWRAH BRIDGE AND OTHER POEMS (1961), and PIG IS-LAND LETTERS (1966).

BEHN, APHRA (England, 1640-1689), the first professional woman writer, was widely travelled. Among her many adventures, she was involved with a slave uprising in Surinam. After her husband died, she was sent as a spy to Holland, and, back in London, was briefly imprisoned for debt. She began her career as a professional writer in 1670, producing 16 plays and a number of poems up until her death. Her grave is in Westminster Abbey.

BERRYMAN, JOHN (U.S., 1914-1972) grew up on a farm in Oklahoma. He taught English at such universities as Princeton and Harvard. His best-known works include HOMAGE TO MISTRESS BRADSTREET (1956), THE DREAM SONGS (1969), and DELUSIONS, ETC. (1972). His work garnered Pulitzer and Bollingen prizes as well as a National Book Award. However, as his own father had done, Berryman eventually committed suicide.

BETJEMAN, JOHN (Britain, 1906-1984) was born in London. Knighted in 1969 and named Poet Laureate in 1972, he produced numerous collections of poetry, as well as books about landscape and architecture, particularly of churches. His poetic work includes OLD LIGHTS FOR NEW CHANCELS: VERSES TOPOGRAPHICAL AND AMATORY (1940), NEW BATS IN OLD BELFRIES (1945), and SUMMONED BY BELLS (1960), a verse autobiography.

BIRNEY, EARLE (Canada, b. 1904), originally from Calgary, has spent much of his life in Vancouver, British Columbia. A playwright, novelist, and writer of criticism as well as a prolific poet, he has edited CANADIAN POETRY MAGAZINE and PRISM INTERNA-TIONAL, and has taught literature and creative writing at the University of British Columbia. His many honors include Governor-General's awards, fellowships, and the Stephen Leacock Medal (1950). Among his more recent collections of poetry are THE BEAR ON THE DELHI ROAD (1973), NEAR FALSE CREEK MOUTH (1975), and GHOST IN THE WHEELS: SELECTED POEMS 1920-1976 (1978).

BISHOP, ELIZABETH (U.S., 1911-1979) was born in Massachusetts and was a graduate of Vassar College. She won a Pulitzer Prize for her second book of poetry, NORTH AND SOUTH: A COLD SPRING (1956) and a National Book Award for COMPLETE POEMS (1969). After living for many years in Brazil, she served as poet in residence at Harvard from 1969 to 1977.

BLAKE, WILLIAM (England, 1757–1827) received little formal education, apart from an apprenticeship to an engraver and a brief period as a student at the Royal Academy of

Arts in London. As an artist and poet, he designed, illustrated, and published his own work, which ranged from the lyrics of SONGS OF INNOCENCE AND EXPERIENCE to mystical and prophetic works like JERUSALEM: THE EMANATION OF THE GIANT AL-BION. Regarded in his own day as an eccentric, he was not recognized until later as a remarkable artist and important poet. Poor for most of his life, he was buried in an un-marked grave.

BOWERING, GEORGE (Canada, b. 1935), from British Columbia, is a prolific writer of novels and short stories as well as poetry. In 1968 he helped to found the controversial poetry magazine TISH. His first collection of poems was STICKS AND STONES (1963). Two later volumes, ROCKY MOUNTAIN FOOT (1968) and THE GANGS OF KOSMOS (1969) together won a Governor-General's award. His book-length poems include GEORGE VANCOUVER (1970) and KERRISDALE ELEGIES (1984), and among his many works are the novel BURNING WATER (1980) and URBAN SNOW (1992).

BRADSTREET, ANNE (England, c. 1612-1672), considered both an English and American poet, emigrated with her Puritan husband to Massachusetts in 1630. She published THE TENTH MUSE LATELY SPRUNG UP IN AMERICA in 1650. Of her many poems on subjects from family life to Biblical history, she is particularly known for her personal and domestic verse.

BRAND, DIONNE (Canada-Caribbean, b. 1953), born in Trinidad, moved to Toronto in 1970. She has worked within the Black community as an educational advocate, and is also involved with women's issues. Widely published in journals and anthologies across Canada, she has written five books of poetry, as well as fiction and essays.

BRATHWAITE, EDWARD K. (Barbados, b. 1930) was educated at Cambridge University and has taught in Ghana and the West Indies. He writes plays, screenplays, history, and literary criticism as well as poetry. Many of his poems reflect an interest in jazz rhythms and moods. Collections include THE ARRIVANTS: A NEW WORLD TRILOGY (1973), SUN POEM (1982), SELF (1987), and SHAR (1990).

BRONTË, EMILY (England, 1818-1848) grew up with her two sisters, Charlotte and Anne, in Haworth, a town in the Yorkshire moors. She and her sisters wrote prolifically from an early age. Except for occasional travel and teaching abroad, the sisters spent their lives in Haworth. Most of Emily's poems, as well as her novel WUTHERING HEIGHTS (1847), were published under the pseudonym "Ellis Bell." She died of tuberculosis.

BROWNING, ELIZABETH BARRETT (England, 1806-1861) suffered ill health and spent much of her youth in a darkened room. Encouraged by her father to write, by 1844 she had produced two books. POEMS (1844) elicited an admiring letter from the poet Robert Browning. Courting secretly, they eloped and married in 1846, an act for which her father never forgave her. Settled with Robert Browning in Italy, she published CASA GUIDI WIN-DOWS in 1851 and her verse novel, AURORA LEIGH, in 1856.

BROWNING, ROBERT (England, 1812-1889) wrote from an early age, and briefly tried writing drama before turning to the form that secured his fame, the dramatic monologue. When he began to court Elizabeth Barrett in 1845, the two were established poets; they married in secret the next year and lived in Italy with their one child. After Elizabeth's death in 1861, Robert returned to England with his son and continued to produce poetry until his death. Among his best-known books are MEN AND WOMEN (1855), DRAMATIS PERSONAE (1864), and THE RING AND THE BOOK (1868). A popular and respected writer, he received burial in Westminster Abbey.

BUNTING, BASIL (England, 1900-1985), once jailed as a conscientious objector during World War I, was a journalist as well as a poet. Among his best-known works are BRIGGFLATS (1966), WHAT THE CHAIRMAN TOLD TOM (1967), and COLLECTED POEMS (1978). He taught for a time at universities in California and British Columbia.

BURNS, ROBERT (Scotland, 1759-1796) grew up on a family farm. In 1786 he published a collection of poems in Scottish dialect, and was hailed as a rural literary genius. A songwriter as well as poet (best-known for "Auld Lang Syne"), he nonetheless remained a farmer until poverty forced him to sell his property in 1791. Burns is often considered the "Scottish national poet," but his poems have remained popular throughout the English-speaking world.

CAMPION, THOMAS (England, 1567-1620) was trained as a lawyer and became a medical doctor and musician as well as poet; indeed, it is for his music that Campion is best known. In OBSERVATIONS IN THE ART OF ENGLISH POETRY he argued that English poetry should reject rhyme and rhythm based on stressed syllables, and instead follow the classical model of quantitative metres. Many of Campion's finest poems are the lyrics he composed for his songs for the lute.

CARMAN, BLISS (Canada, 1861-1929) was born in New Brunswick, receiving his education in Fredericton, Edinburgh, and Harvard. For a time he studied law, but later served as a literary editor and staff writer for a number of periodicals, including ATLANTIC MONTHLY. Following the publication of LOW TIDE ON GRAND PRÉ (1893), he published great quantities of verse, two plays, and several volumes of essays. Along with Roberts, Lampman, and Scott, Carman is seen as one of the "Confederation" poets, who formed the first distinctly Canadian school of writers.

CARROLL, LEWIS (England, 1832-1898) was the pseudonym of Charles Lutwidge Dodgson, an Oxford mathematics scholar and a deacon in the Anglican Church. Author of numerous mathematical treatises, in 1855 he began contributing stories and poems to THE COMIC TIMES under his pseudonym. He is most famous for his children's books, ALICE'S ADVENTURES IN WONDERLAND (1865) and THROUGH THE LOOKING GLASS (1871), through which are scattered songs, parodies, and nonsense verses.

CAVENDISH, MARGARET, DUCHESS OF NEWCASTLE (England, 1623-1673), was born into aristocracy and, in 1645, married the Marquis (later Duke) of Newcastle, who was also a poet. In 1653 she published POEMS, AND FANCIES and PHILOSOPHICALL FANCIES, and later wrote numerous stories, plays, letters, and philosophical and scientific speculations.

CHAUCER, GEOFFREY (England, c. 1343-1400), raised in London of a wealthy family, as an adult became involved in military campaigns against the French; served at Court and as a royal emissary abroad; and held posts as a senior customs official and Clerk of the King's Works. He began THE CANTERBURY TALES sometime after 1386, and they remained unfinished at his death in 1400. Chaucer's importance as a poet was widely recognized during his lifetime, and he was buried at Westminster Abbey.

CHUDLEIGH, LADY MARY (England, 1656-1710) was married and had three children. Among her many verses celebrating women's friendships and criticizing husbands' conduct, she published THE LADY'S DEFENCE (1699), a satirical response to a sermon about the need for women to obey their husbands.

CLOUGH, ARTHUR HUGH (England, 1819-1861), born in Liverpool and educated at Rugby School and Oxford, was a close friend of the poet Matthew Arnold. Like many intellectuals of his time, he was affected by religious doubt, and became increasingly skeptical about the Church of England.

COHEN, LEONARD (Canada, b. 1934), born in Montréal, is widely known not only for his poetry and fiction, but as a professional singer and composer. His collections of poetry include his first work, LET US COMPARE MYTHOLOGIES (1956); SELECTED POEMS (1968), for which he declined a Governor-General's award; DEATH OF A LADY'S MAN (1978); and most recently, BOOK OF MERCY (1984). He has also published numerous song albums.

COLEMAN, WANDA (U.S., b. 1946) was born in California and struggled with poverty before she became established as a poet with her collection HEAVY DAUGHTER BLUES (1978). A performance poet in the African-American oral tradition, she has also published MAD DOG BLACK LADY (1979) and IMAGOES (1983).

COLERIDGE, SAMUEL TAYLOR (England, 1772-1834), the son of a Devon vicar, abandoned his clerical studies at Cambridge after an ill-considered love affair. In 1798 he received an annuity that allowed him to devote himself to writing. His most famous poems—"The Rime Of The Ancient Mariner," "Kubla Khan," "Christabel"—date from 1797-98, during which time he also collaborated with Wordsworth to produce LYRICAL BALLADS. "Kubla Khan" is the famous fragment written under the influence of opium; Coleridge struggled with his addiction to this drug over the next twenty years.

COUZYN, JENI (Canada, b. 1942) was born in South Africa and now lives in England. Her collections of poetry include LIFE BY DROWNING: SELECTED POEMS (1983, 1985) and SINGING DOWN THE BONES (1989). She has also edited THE BLOODAXE BOOK OF CONTEMPORARY WOMEN POETS (1985).

COWPER, WILLIAM [pronounced "Cooper"] (England, 1731-1800) was trained in the law but declined to practice it; throughout his life he was provided by family and friends with a small income. A victim of depression, he became engaged—though never married—to a widow, Mary Unwin, whose death in 1796 left him in despair. Between bouts of mental illness, Cowper composed the lyric, satirical, and religious poetry for which he is remembered.

CRAWFORD, ISABELLA VALANCY (Canada, 1850-1887) was born in Dublin, and moved with her family to Ontario in 1858. Their lives were beset with difficulties; most of the Crawford children died young, and the father, Dr. S. D. Crawford, was tried and convicted for misappropriation of public funds. He died in 1875. Living in poverty with her mother, Isabella supported herself through her writing. Though she wrote many short stories and poems that were published mainly in American magazines, her work was never collected in her lifetime.

CREELEY, ROBERT (U.S., 1926), born in Massachusetts, is a prolific writer of fiction, plays, screenplays, and literary criticism. He attended Black Mountain College, North Carolina, and became associated with the anti-academic poetry movement at the college. During the 1960s, he travelled throughout the U.S. and Canada, teaching at various universities and writing numerous books of poetry. Among his major collections are SELECTED POEMS (1976) and THE COLLECTED POEMS OF ROBERT CREELEY: 1945-1975 (1982). He has also published selected writings and correspondence of Charles Olson.

CULLEN, COUNTEE (U.S., 1903-1946) was born in New York City, attended Harvard, and taught French at a junior high school until his death. A Guggenheim Fellow, he was a leading figure in the "Harlem Renaissance" of the 1920s. His poetry does subtly incorporate Black oral traditions, but much of his work is in the lyric mode of 19th-century English Romanticism.

CUMMINGS, E. E. (U.S., 1894-1962), born in Massachusetts, attended Harvard and was co-founder of the Harvard Poetry Society. He was a prisoner of war for three months during World War I, an experience which inspired his one work of fiction, THE ENORMOUS ROOM (1922). After the war, Cummings went to Paris to study painting, eventually displaying his art in shows in Paris and New York. As a poet (best known in lower case as e. e. cummings), he was highly experimental and anti-authoritarian; in fact, his work was initially rejected by publishers. His output included over 12 volumes of poetry and four plays, and he was honored for his work with several distinguished poetry awards, a National Book Award, and a Bollingen Prize.

CURNOW, ALLEN (New Zealand, b. 1911), worked as a newspaper reporter in New Zealand and England, then joined the University of Auckland, where he taught until 1976. A central figure in New Zealand poetry, he published his first collection, VALLEY OF DECISION, in 1933. Among his major contributions may be counted A BOOK OF NEW ZEALAND VERSE (1951) and THE PENGUIN BOOK OF NEW ZEALAND VERSE (1960), anthologies that helped to establish a distinct tradition of poetry in New Zealand.

DICKINSON, EMILY (U.S., 1830-1886), born in Massachusetts, was gregarious in her youth, but became a recluse in her later years. Although she travelled a little, she preferred isolation, writing about love, nature, God, and death. Hardly any of her work appeared during her lifetime. Her poems were first gathered posthumously in 1890, and since that time she has won recognition as a major American poet.

H. D. (Hilda Doolittle) U.S., 1886-1961), born in Pennsylvania, was a close friend of the poet Ezra Pound and helped him establish the Imagist movement. She wrote numerous volumes of poetry after World War I; in 1925, her COLLECTED POEMS firmly established her reputation as an Imagist poet. Much of her work uses classical Greek mythology as subject matter.

DONNE, JOHN (England, 1572-1631), born into a prosperous Catholic London family, attended Oxford and, by the 1590s, had established a reputation as both a poet and practitioner of love. Donne held various political posts, including Member of Parliament, but his clandestine marriage at age 29 to Ann More, who was 17, resulted in dismissal, disgrace, and many years of poverty. In mid-life, however, he entered the Anglican church and rose to become Dean of St. Paul's Cathedral.

DRYDEN, JOHN (England, 1631-1700), born in Northamptonshire and educated at Cambridge, was the most influential writer of his time, producing a large body of plays, translations, and criticism, as well as poetry. His best-known work includes the blank-verse tragedy ALL FOR LOVE (1678), the essay OF DRAMATIC POESIE (1668), and the satires ABSALOM AND ACHITOPHEL (1681) and MACFLECKNOE (1682). He was made Poet Laureate in 1668 and Historiographer Royal in 1670, but lost these positions after the Revolution of 1688. He was buried in Westminster Abbey.

EBERHART, RICHARD (U.S., b. 1904), from Minnesota, spent a short time tutoring the son of King Prajadhipok of Siam before serving as a professor of English at several American universities. He has published such collections as A BRAVERY OF EARTH (1930), SONG AND IDEA (1942), THE VASTNESS AND INDIFFERENCE OF THE WORLD (1965), WAYS OF LIGHT (1980), and MAINE POEMS (1989). A recipient of the Bollingen and Pulitzer Prizes for his work, he now lives in New Hampshire and, in 1979, was appointed Poet Laureate for that state.

ELIOT, T. S. (England, 1888-1965), born in the U.S., entered Harvard in 1906. After further education in France and England, he eventually settled in London, working as a clerk in Lloyd's Bank until 1925. He became a British citizen in 1927. He founded and edited the CRITERION (1922-1939), and was a member of the publishing firm Faber and Faber, serving as one of the firm's directors from 1926 until his death. His earlier collections of poetry include PRUFROCK AND OTHER OBSERVATIONS (1917) and THE WASTE LAND (1922). Eliot's poetry after his confirmation into the Anglican Church in 1927—including ASH-WEDNESDAY (1930) and FOUR QUARTETS (1935-1942)—shows an increasingly religious influence. More whimsically, Eliot's OLD POSSUM'S BOOK OF PRACTICAL CATS (1939) provided the lyrics for Andrew Lloyd Webber's musical CATS. He also wrote seven plays and numerous essays and received a quantity of awards and honors, including an Order of Merit from King George VI and a Nobel Prize for Literature, both in 1948.

EMERSON, RALPH WALDO (U.S., 1803-1882), born in Boston and educated at Harvard, worked for a time as a schoolmaster, and served as a pastor before retiring from the ministry. After travelling in Great Britain and Europe—and meeting such writers as Wordsworth, Coleridge, and Carlyle—he established himself as a public lecturer in 1833. Emerson became one of the most renowned proponents of New England Transcendentalism, a mode of Romantic thought that places the supernatural and the natural within one great Unity. He is known as much for his numerous essays and lectures as for his poems.

EZEKIEL, NISSIM (India, b. 1924) writes plays, screenplays, and literary criticism as well as poetry, has taught literature at Bombay University, and has served as writer-in-residence at the National University of Singapore. A TIME TO CHANGE AND OTHER POEMS (1952) was his first collection. More recent work includes HYMNS IN DARKNESS (1976), LATTER-DAY PSALMS (1982), and COLLECTED POEMS, 1952-88 (1989).

FINCH, ANNE, COUNTESS OF WINCHILSEA (England, 1661-1720), of aristocratic family, married a Court officer in 1684. After retiring with her husband to Kent, she published MISCELLANY POEMS ON SEVERAL OCCASIONS, WRITTEN BY A LADY (1713). Her verses center on married life, women's friendship, and nature.

FROST, ROBERT (U.S., 1874-1963), born in San Francisco and educated at Harvard, had little success with his early poems. He turned to mill work, teaching, and farming; then in 1912, he and his wife Elinor moved to England, mingling with other writers and poets. In 1913, A BOY'S WILL was published to critical acclaim in England, and with another volume, NORTH OF BOSTON (1914), Frost's reputation as a poet became established in the United States as well. Frost was a fine teacher and a noted public reader, and his presentations helped to encourage a renewed public interest in poetry. He was the recipient of four Pulitzer Prizes, the Bollingen Prize, and a host of other honors during his lifetime.

GINSBERG, ALAN (U.S., b. 1926), a native of Newark, New Jersey, is best known for his associations with two major sociocultural events: the San Francisco Beat movement in the 1950s, and "flower power" (a phrase he coined) in the 1960s. His publications have reflected and shaped these movements: they include HOWL AND OTHER POEMS (1956), REALITY SANDWICHES (1963), and T.V. BABY POEMS (1967). In 1973, FALL OF AMERICA: POEMS OF THESE STATES won a National Book Award.

GORDON, GEORGE, LORD BYRON (England-Scotland, 1788-1824) grew up with his mother in Scotland in reduced circumstances. He became a baron at the age of 10, when his great-uncle died, and attended Harrow and Cambridge. In the first part of 1812, Byron's long poem CHILDE HAROLD made him a celebrity. He was in the public eye as much for his romantic involvements as for his satirical, dramatic, and lyrical poetry. On the continent, he became an active supporter of revolutionary causes, and died of a fever contracted while helping Greek nationalists plan the overthrow of their Turkish rulers.

GRAVES, ROBERT (England, 1895-1985), from London, was educated at Oxford and served in World War I. His war experiences are graphically recorded in his memoir GOODBYE TO ALL THAT (1929). As a professor of English, he taught in Egypt, then moved to Majorca until the Spanish Civil War, returning to Majorca after World War II. He served as professor of poetry at Oxford in the 1960s. Although Graves wrote great quantities of verse and published numerous collections of his poetry, he was also a prolific novelist, his best known works including I, CLAUDIUS and CLAUDIUS THE GOD (both 1934).

GRAY, THOMAS (England, 1716-1771) attended Cambridge and remained based there, leading a quiet and financially secure life as a poet and scholar. He became Regius Professor of Modern History in 1768. His poetic output was limited, and he is remembered mainly for his ELEGY, which became famous immediately upon its publication in 1751.

HARDY, THOMAS (England, 1840-1928) studied architecture and practiced this profession successfully in London from 1861 until the early 1870s. When he began writing full-time, he produced novels like FAR FROM THE MADDING CROWD (1874), THE MAYOR OF CASTERBRIDGE (1886), and TESS OF THE D'URBERVILLES (1891). However, in 1896, after the publication and hostile reception of JUDE THE OBSCURE, he turned mainly to lyric poetry, publishing WESSEX POEMS AND OTHER VERSES in 1898, then seven other volumes of poetry. He was buried in Westminster Abbey.

HEANEY, SEAMUS (Northern Ireland, b. 1939) established his reputation as one of Ireland's most important poets with his collection DEATH OF A NATURALIST (1966). Some of his other works of poetry include WINTERING OUT (1972), NORTH (1976), BOG POEMS (1975), and THE GOVERNMENT OF THE TONGUE (1988). He has served as Boylston Professor of Rhetoric and Oratory at Harvard University and Professor of Poetry at Oxford.

HERBERT, GEORGE (England, 1593-1633), of a noble family, established himself at Cambridge as an outstanding scholar. He became a deacon in 1624 and a priest in 1630, and acted as rector to a parish near Salisbury before his early death from consumption. His reputation as a poet rests entirely on THE TEMPLE, a collection of about 160 short poems, most of them religious, published shortly after his death.

HERRICK, ROBERT (England, 1591-1674), a graduate of Cambridge, lived first in London, where he joined Ben Jonson's circle. After taking Holy Orders in 1623, he served many years as a cleric in Devonshire.

HINE, DARYL (Canada, b. 1936), born in Vancouver British Columbia and trained as a classical scholar, now lives in the United States. He has written over a dozen books of poetry, including THE CARNAL AND THE CRANE (1957), THE DEVIL'S PICTURE BOOK: POEMS (1960), RESIDENT ALIEN: POEMS (1975), and the critically acclaimed SELECTED POEMS (1981). His most recent collection is POSTSCRIPTS (1990).

HOPE, A.D. (Australia, b. 1907), a literary critic and teacher as well as poet, published his first collection—THE WANDERING ISLANDS (1955)—relatively late in life. His other works include THE DRIFTING CONTINENT (1979), THE TRAGICAL HISTORY OF DR. FAUSTUS (1982), and LADIES FROM THE SEA (1989). He was for many years Professor of English at the Australian National University.

HOPKINS, GERARD MANLEY (England, 1844-1889), born in London and educated at Oxford, converted to Catholicism and was ordained as a Jesuit priest in 1877. After serving in a number of parishes, he was appointed professor of classics in Dublin. He burnt the poems he wrote before his conversion, but later, wrote numerous poems that were both religious and considered highly innovative in their uses of language and rhythm. Mainly out of concern for his religious vocation, he did not publish his poetry; it was not until 1918 that the first edited collection of his poems became available.

HOUSMAN, A. E. (England, 1859-1936), while initially a first-class scholar in classics at Oxford, failed his final examinations. Working as a clerk in the Patent Office in London, he studied on his own and eventually rose to the position of professor of Latin at University

College, London, a post he held until 1911 before moving on to Cambridge, where he stayed until his death. A meticulous textual critic as well as poet, he produced only two volumes of verse during his lifetime, one being A SHROPSHIRE LAD (1896).

HOWARD, HENRY, EARL OF SURREY (England, c. 1517-1547), son of the Duke of Norfolk, was involved for most of his adult life in Court politics. When he fell out of favor with Henry VIII after some ill-considered remarks, Surrey was executed on Tower Hill. As a poet, he developed the sonnet into the form used by Shakespeare. He was also the first English poet to write in blank verse.

HUGHES, LANGSTON (U.S., 1902-1967), from Missouri, was a Black journalist, poet, novelist and dramatist who campaigned against racism in all his writing. He served as visiting professor and poet-in-residence at universities in Georgia and Chicago, and published 17 books of verse, including THE WEARY BLUES (1926), MONTAGE OF A DREAM DEFERRED (1951), and ASK YOUR MAMA: 12 MOODS FOR JAZZ (1961), which are noted for blending poetry with jazz structures.

HUGHES, TED (England, b. 1930) has written extensively in areas of drama, children's fiction, screenwriting, and literary criticism. His first poetry collection was THE HAWK IN THE RAIN (1957); among his numerous others are CROW: FROM THE LIFE AND SONGS OF THE CROW (1971, 1972), PROMETHEUS ON HIS CRAG: 21 POEMS (1973), GAUDETE (1977), ADAM AND THE SACRED NINE (1979), and WOLFWATCHING (1989). At one time married to the poet Sylvia Plath, he has edited and published much of her posthumous work. He has served as Britain's Poet Laureate since 1984.

JARRELL, RANDALL (U.S., 1914-1965) born in Nashville, Tennessee, studied at Vanderbilt, and during World War II served in the Army Air Corps. He taught at universities throughout the U.S., and reviewed for such journals as THE PARTISAN REVIEW and THE YALE REVIEW. Among his best-known works of poetry are BLOOD FOR A STRANGER (1942), LITTLE FRIEND, LITTLE FRIEND (1945), THE WOMAN AT THE WASHINGTON ZOO (1960), and his last, THE LOST WORLD (1965), published after a nervous breakdown. He was killed in a car accident.

JONSON, BEN (England, 1572-1637) had served as a soldier before entering the theatre professionally in the mid 1590s. He is best known as a playwright, producing among other works VOLPONE, THE ALCHEMIST, and BARTHOLOMEW FAIR. Though Jonson made many literary and personal enemies, he was nonetheless first to be appointed Poet Laureate in 1616.

KEATS, JOHN (England, 1795-1821) trained for some years in the medical profession, but by 1817 decided to devote himself to literature. His first volumes of poetry, POEMS (1817) and ENDYMION: A ROMANCE (1818), brought mixed reviews, but established him as a promising member of the London literary community. In 1818-19, despite an unhappy love affair and serious financial problems, he wrote his finest poetry, including the great odes and "Hyperion." His second volume—LAMIA, ISABELLA, THE EVE OF SAINT AGNES, AND OTHER POEMS (1820)—was well received; however, in 1820 he contracted tuberculosis, and within a year he was dead.

KIPLING, RUDYARD (England, 1865-1936), born in India of English parents, was educated in England. After a period as a journalist in India, he lived in London from 1889 on. Although many know him best for his fiction—especially the Mowgli stories—he was also a prolific writer of verse, with over two dozen books of poems published between 1881 (SCHOOLBOY LYRICS) and 1931 (EAST OF SUEZ: BEING A SELECTION OF EASTERN VERSES). Among the many honors he received for his work was the Nobel Prize for Literature in 1907.

KIZER, CAROLYN (U.S., b. 1925), from Washington state, studied in Nationalist China for a year and worked in Pakistan as a specialist in literature for the U.S. State Department. She has served as professor and visiting poet in universities throughout the U.S. Her poetry, which explores feminist themes and relations among women, includes THE UNGRATEFUL GARDEN (1961), KNOCK UPON SILENCE (1965), and MERMAIDS IN THE BASEMENT: POEMS FOR WOMEN (1984).

KLEIN, A. M. (Canada, 1909-1972) was born in the Ukraine, and his family moved to Montréal in 1910. Educated in the traditions of Orthodox Judaism, and later at McGill University, he began publishing poetry in periodicals in 1927. His collections include HATH NOT A JEW. . . (1940), THE ROCKING CHAIR AND OTHER POEMS (1948), which won a Governor-General's award, and THE SECOND SCROLL (1951), written after a fact-finding trip to Israel.

LAMPMAN, ARCHIBALD (Canada, 1861-1899) was educated at the University of Toronto, and worked as a high school teacher and post office clerk. He was the author of four volumes of poetry, though only two were published in his lifetime; many of these poems describe the Canadian landscape and environment. After Lampman's death, the poet Duncan Campbell Scott compiled several collections, including THE POEMS OF ARCHIBALD LAMPMAN (1900).

LANE, PATRICK (Canada, b. 1939) born in Nelson, British Columbia, is a poet and novelist, much of whose early work centers on the West Coast working class. His books of poetry include SEPARATIONS (1969), THE SUN HAS BEGUN TO EAT THE MOUNTAINS (1972), POEMS NEW AND SELECTED (1979), which won a Governor-General's award, and WINTER (1990). He lives in Saskatoon.

LARKIN, PHILIP (England, 1922-1985) blended poetry with a career as a librarian, and also wrote articles about jazz. He was a leading member of the group of anti-romantic English poets known as "The Movement." He published his first collection, THE NORTH SHIP, in 1945, and his second book of poems came out a decade later (THE LESS DECEIVED, 1955). Among his other books of poetry are THE WHITSUN WEDDINGS (1964) and HIGH WINDOWS (1974), and he received much recognition, including several honorary degrees, for his work.

LAWRENCE, D. H. (England, 1885-1930) was born of a working-class family and was educated in Nottingham. He worked for a firm of surgical appliance makers and as a teacher before turning to writing full-time in 1912—also the year he eloped with Frieda Weekley, the German wife of a professor of French at Nottingham University. They married in Germany in 1914. After an unhappy period in England, they travelled to Italy, Australia,

Mexico, and the south of France, where Lawrence finally succumbed to tuberculosis. Generally best known for his novels, including SONS AND LOVERS (1913), WOMEN IN LOVE (1920), and the controversial LADY CHATTERLEY'S LOVER (the first version published in 1928), he also produced volumes of poetry, short stories, and essays.

LAYTON, IRVING (Canada, b. 1912) was born in Romania; the family emigrated to Canada in 1913. A graduate of McGill, he taught at Concordia, Guelph and York universities. His first collection of poetry, HERE AND NOW, appeared in 1945, and was succeeded by a lengthy list of publications that have brought him wide recognition, including a Governor-General's award for A RED CARPET FOR THE SUN (1959).

LEAPOR, MARY (England, 1722-1746) worked as a maid, and kept house for her father until her untimely death from measles. Her writing won the attention of members of the local gentry, who published her work posthumously as POEMS UPON SEVERAL OCCASIONS (1748). The novelist Samuel Richardson organized the publication of a second volume in 1750.

LEE, DENNIS (Canada, b. 1939), born in Toronto, writes children's verse, history, and literary criticism as well as poetry. His first collection, KINGDOM OF ABSENCE (1967), was followed by CIVIL ELEGIES (1968), which in an enlarged edition won a Governor-General's award in 1972. Among his best-known children's verse collections are ALLIGATOR PIE (1974), GARBAGE DELIGHT (1977), and JELLY BELLY (1983).

LePAN, DOUGLAS (Canada, b. 1914), a graduate of the University of Toronto and of Oxford University, served in World War II both in England as a staff advisor and in Italy with the Canadian artillery. He has combined writing with distinguished careers in the diplomatic corps, as an academic, and as a university administrator. LePan has published five books of poetry and a novel; he has won Governor-General's Awards both for fiction and for poetry.

LEVERTOV, DENISE (U.S., b. 1923), born in England, was educated at home, and during World War II served as a nurse. She has been an antiwar activist and has taught at several major American universities. She has written several volumes of literary criticism and over 20 collections of poetry, including RELEARNING THE ALPHABET (1970), FOOTPRINTS (1972), and FREEING OF THE DUST (1975). Her most recent collection is EVENING TRAIN (1992).

LIVESAY, DOROTHY (Canada, b. 1909), from Winnipeg, was educated at the universities of Toronto and British Columbia. In the 1930s and 1940s, she combined political and feminist activism; her poetry from this time includes DAY AND NIGHT (Governor-General's Award, 1944) POEMS FOR PEOPLE (Governor-General's Award, 1947), and CALL MY PEOPLE HOME (1950). Her later poetry, including THE UNQUIET BED (1967) and PLAINSONGS (1969), centered on women's experience.

LONGFELLOW, HENRY WADSWORTH (U.S., 1807-1882), born and educated in Maine, spent time travelling and studying in Europe and Spain before serving as Chair of Modern Languages at Bowdoin College, Maine, and later, as Smith Professor of Modern Languages at Harvard. He produced his first volume of poetry, OUTRE MER, in 1835, and soon established his reputation with POEMS ON SLAVERY (1842), one of his best-known works, THE SONG OF HIAWATHA (1855), and TALES OF A WAYSIDE INN (1863).

LORDE, AUDRE (U.S., 1934-1992), active in the Black Power and feminist movements, used poetry to express activist political and lesbian concerns. Her poetry collections include THE BLACK UNICORN (1978) and OUR DEAD BEHIND US (1986).

LOWELL, ROBERT (U.S., 1917-1977), from Boston, was educated at Kenyon College and taught at universities throughout the eastern U.S. and in England. He published LAND OF UNLIKENESS, his first book of poems, in 1944. The different stages of his life as a poet are represented in such collections as LORD WEARY'S CASTLE (1946), FOR THE UNION DEAD (1964), THE DOLPHIN (1973), and DAY BY DAY (1977). He received the Pulitzer Prize in 1947 and a National Book Award in 1960, among other honors.

MACDIARMID, HUGH (Scotland, 1892-1978) was the pseudonym of Christopher Murray Grieve. He was educated in Edinburgh and edited a number of literary journals there. An ardent Scottish nationalist, he sought to revive interest in the Scots language. Among his best-known works are A DRUNK MAN LOOKS AT THE THISTLE (1926, 1956), and the book-length poem IN MEMORIAM JAMES JOYCE (1955).

MACEWEN, GWENDOLEN (Canada, 1941-1989), was born in Toronto and published her first poem at age 17. Her collection THE SHADOW-MAKER (1969) won a Governer-General's award; other books of poems include THE FIRE EATERS (1976) and THE T.E. LAWRENCE POEMS (1982). She also wrote children's books, short stories, and novels.

MACKENZIE, KENNETH (Australia, 1913-1955) studied arts and law at the University of Western Australia, and wrote fiction and two books of poetry: OUR EARTH (1937) and THE MOONLIT DOORWAY (1944). He is perhaps best known for his novel THE REFUGE: A CONFESSION (1954).

MACLEISH, ARCHIBALD (U.S., 1892-1982), from Illinois, had a varied career as a Librarian of Congress in Washington, D.C., as Assistant Secretary of State, and as Chair of a U.S. delegation to UNESCO in London. Also a noted teacher, he served as Boylston Professor of Rhetoric and Oratory at Harvard until 1962. He produced numerous books of verse, plays, screenplays, and literary and political critique, receiving Pulitzer Prizes for poetry in 1933 and 1953, the Bollingen Prize in 1952, and a National Book Award in 1953.

MACNEICE, LOUIS (England, 1907-1963), born in Belfast and educated at Oxford, served as lecturer and visiting professor in England and the U.S. He also wrote and produced radio plays and documentaries for the BBC, and published 19 books of verse, including BLIND FIREWORKS (1929, his first), AUTUMN JOURNAL: A POEM (1939), TEN BURNT OFFERINGS (1952), and THE BURNING PERCH (1963). After leaving the BBC in 1949, he became director of the British Institute in Athens.

MACPHERSON, JAY (Canada, b. 1931) was born in England; her family moved to Canada when she was nine. A professor of English at the University of Toronto, she established her reputation as a poet with THE BOATMAN (1957), which won a Governor-General's award. Another major collection is POEMS TWICE TOLD (1981).

MARLATT, DAPHNE (Canada, b. 1942) was born in Australia and educated in Canada and the U.S. She now lives on Salt Spring Island, British Columbia. Her poetry includes FRAMES (1968)—which retells Hans Christian Andersen's "The Snow Queen"—,VANCOUVER POEMS (1972), STEVESTON (1974), and TOUCH TO MY TONGUE (1984).

MARLOWE, CHRISTOPHER (England, 1564-1593) is best known as a playwright. His reputation became established with such plays as THE JEW OF MALTA, DOCTOR FAUSTUS, and EDWARD THE SECOND. He also produced narrative poetry, such as HERO AND LEANDER, and lyrical poetry, embodied in THE PASSIONATE SHEPHERD. Marlowe is thought to have been an atheist, and an agent in the secret service of Elizabeth I. He died violently in a tavern, under circumstances that remain mysterious.

MARVELL, ANDREW (England, 1621-1678) attended Cambridge and travelled widely in Europe in his youth. In the 1650s he lived for a time in Yorkshire, where he tutored the daughter of Lord Fairfax and composed much of his best poetry. Holding strong political views, Marvell succeeded Milton as Cromwell's Latin Secretary and was MP for Hull from 1659 to the end of his life.

MELVILLE, HERMAN (U.S., 1819-1891), whose New York family was originally wealthy, grew up in financial straits. He went to sea at age 19, spending several years aboard whalers. These experiences inspired his best-known writing—the novels TYPEE (1846), MOBY-DICK (1851), and BILLY BUDD (published posthumously in 1924). In some of his poetry, notably BATTLE-PIECES AND ASPECTS OF THE WAR (1866), he commented critically on the Civil War. He was buried, almost forgotten, in the Bronx.

MERRILL, JAMES (U.S., b. 1926), from New York City, has written eleven books of poems, as well as several novels and plays. He has received the Pulitzer Prize and two National Book Awards, among other honors. One of his best-known works is a long narrative poem, THE CHANGING LIGHT AT SANDOVER (1982).

MILLAY, EDNA ST. VINCENT (U.S., 1892-1950), born in Maine and educated at Vassar, received recognition at a young age with the publication of her long poem "Renascence" in 1912. During the 1920s, she lived the life of a bohemian writer in Greenwich Village, winning the Pulitzer Prize for her collection THE HARP-WEAVER (1923). Her later poetry, protesting the rise of Fascism in Europe during the 1930s, was not well received, and her popularity eventually declined.

MILTON, JOHN (England, 1608-1674) began to write poetry while at Cambridge. He used his father's moderate wealth to build a life of private study and contemplation", but then began to produce much polemical writing, including a series of tracts in favor of divorce, and AREOPAGITICA, his plea against censorship. For some years he acted as Latin Secretary to Oliver Cromwell's Council of State. PARADISE LOST, a Biblical epic regarded as Milton's greatest poetic work, was published in 1667, by which time the poet had been blind for 16 years.

MONTAGU, LADY MARY WORTLEY (England, 1689-1762) eloped and had two children before she and her husband separated. She was in the center of a glittering court society that included Alexander Pope. After a bout with smallpox that deeply scarred her face, she spent most of the remainder of her life abroad, writing verses and essays.

MOORE, MARIANNE (U.S., 1887-1972), from Missouri, was educated at Bryn Mawr, and began her working life teaching typing and stenography. Her career as a writer dates from 1915, when she published a short satire on war. From 1925-1929 she edited the literary monthly THE DIAL. She won the Bollingen and Pulitzer Prizes for her COLLECTED PO-EMS (1951) and received many honorary degrees.

MUSGRAVE, SUSAN (Canada, b. 1951), originally from California, now lives in British Columbia. Her first poetry collection, SONGS OF THE SEA-WITCH (1970), was published when she was 18. Her works include SKULD (1971), THE IMPSTONE (1976), and TARTS AND MUGGERS (1982).

NORTJE, ARTHUR (South Africa, 1942-1970), born in the Cape Province, was educated in South Africa and at Oxford, then went on to teach English in British Columbia and Toronto. Much of his poetry explores themes of exile from home. Shortly after he returned to Oxford in 1970 to work toward a doctorate, he died of an overdose of drugs.

NOWLAN, ALDEN (Canada, 1933-1983), from Nova Scotia, was first a farmworker, then a news editor. He published his first collection of poetry, THE ROSE AND THE PURITAN, in 1958. He won a Governor-General's award for BREAD, WINE, AND SALT (1967) and was also a Guggenheim Fellowship recipient. His last two collections were SMOKED GLASS (1977) and I MIGHT NOT TELL EVERYBODY THIS (1982).

ONDAATJE, MICHAEL (Canada, b. 1943), born in Ceylon (now Sri Lanka), moved to Canada in 1962. His work includes novels, plays, screenplays, and literary criticism. Among his best-known works of poetry are THE COLLECTED WORKS OF BILLY THE KID (1970), and THERE'S A TRICK WITH A KNIFE I'M LEARNING TO DO (1979). Both of these earned him Governor-General's awards. In 1992, he won the Booker Prize for his novel THE ENGLISH PATIENT.

OWEN, WILFRED (England, 1893-1918), now one of the best-known English war poets, served in two regiments during World War I. He had begun writing poetry at the age of 10, and applied this long training in poetic form to observing experiences in the trenches. While in hospital recovering from shell-shock in 1917, he met Siegfried Sassoon, who encouraged him in his work. Owen was killed in action on November 4, 1918, a week before the Armistice.

PAGE, P.K. (Canada, b. 1916) was born in England; her family settled in Alberta in 1919. AS TEN AS TWENTY (1946) was her first book of poems. For a number of years, she lived abroad, while her husband served as Canadian ambassador to Australia, Brazil, and Mexico. In 1954, her collection THE METAL AND THE FLOWER won a Governor-General's award. More recent poetry includes EVENING DANCE OF THE GREY FLIES (1981). She has also been a National Film Board scriptwriter and has published fiction and essays.

PARKER, DOROTHY (U.S., 1893-1967), from New Jersey, wrote satirical poetry, short stories, and essays. In the 1920s, she was the leader of the notorious "Algonquin Round Table," a group of New York-based writers noted for their acid wit. Her collections of poetry include SUNSET GUN (1928) and NOT SO DEEP AS A WELL (1936). She died in New York.

PHILIPS, KATHERINE (England, 1631-1664), the daughter of a successful London merchant, was brought up as a Puritan but had Royalist sympathies. "The Matchless Orinda," as she was known, was a prolific writer of verse. After her death from smallpox in London, a collection called POEMS, BY THE MOST DESERVEDLY ADMIRED MRS. KATHERINE PHILIPS, THE MATCHLESS ORINDA was published in 1667.

PIERCY, MARGE (U.S., b. 1936), born in Detroit, and a graduate of Michigan and Northwestern, is a feminist writer who produces fiction as well as poetry. She has won two Borestone Mountain poetry awards. Her best-known novel is WOMAN ON THE EDGE OF TIME (1976). Her most recent poetry collections include CIRCLES IN THE WATER (1982), MY MOTHER'S BODY (1985), and AVAILABLE LIGHT (1988).

PLATH, SYLVIA (U.S., 1932-1963), born in Boston, had already published many poems and stories by age 17. She married poet Ted Hughes in 1956. During a career in which she tried to balance teaching, writing, marriage, and motherhood, she published her poetry collection COLOSSUS (1960) and a novel, THE BELL JAR (1963). Eventually she took her own life. Posthumous collections include ARIEL (1965) and CROSSING THE WATER (1971).

POE, EDGAR ALLAN (U.S., 1809-1849) was born in Boston; his mother, an actor, was soon deserted by his father. Poe was educated in London as well as in the United States. Rejecting offers to join his stepfather's family business, he published his first collection, TAMERLANE AND OTHER POEMS, in 1827, and served some time in the U.S. Army under an assumed name. Later, he worked as a journalist and editor, and published three other poetry collections—including THE RAVEN AND OTHER POEMS (1845)—as well as his famous works of horror fiction. He died under mysterious circumstances after being found unconscious on the streets of Baltimore.

POPE, ALEXANDER (England, 1688-1744), the son of a London draper, was one of the first English writers to support himself primarily on the basis of his published writings. He was acclaimed for his translations of Homer's ILIAD and ODYSSEY into heroic couplets, as well as for his versification in ESSAY ON CRITICISM and ESSAY ON MAN. Though prevented by ill health from having a full life, much of his work—such as THE RAPE OF THE LOCK and THE DUNCIAD—is known for its brilliant comedy and ironic wit.

PORTER, PETER (Australia, b. 1929) emigrated to England in 1951, and worked in advertising and journalism before becoming established as a freelance writer and poet. His earliest work, ONCE BITTEN, TWICE SHY (1961) and POEMS ANCIENT AND MODERN (1964), is often highly satirical. Recent collections include COLLECTED POEMS (1983), MARS (1988), and POSSIBLE WORLDS (1989).

POUND, EZRA (U.S., 1885-1972), born in Idaho, was educated at the University of Pennsylvania. In 1908 he began a series of travels throughout Europe, taking up residence in London, Paris, and later, Italy. By 1912 he had attained some prominence as a poet, and helped found the Imagist movement. During World War II, he broadcast his support for Fascism over Italian radio, and was arrested by the U.S. Army in 1945. Declared insane after medical examination, he was found unfit to stand trial for treason and was committed to a hospital in Washington, D.C. until 1958, when the charges were finally dismissed. Pound's contributions to poetry, including the great CANTOS, were recognized with a Bollingen Prize in 1948 and an Academy of American Arts Fellowship in 1963.

PRATT, E. J. (Canada, 1882-1964), born in Newfoundland, attended the University of Toronto and taught English at Victoria College there until 1953. From 1936-1942 he edited the CANADIAN POETRY MAGAZINE. His first collection of poetry, NEWFOUNDLAND VERSE (1923) was followed by a number of others, including THE WITCHES' BREW (1925) and three which won Governor-General's awards: THE FABLE OF THE GOAT AND OTHER POEMS (1932), BRÉBEUF AND HIS BRETHREN (1940), and TOWARDS THE LAST SPIKE (1952).

PURDY, A.W. (Canada, b. 1918), recipient of the Order of Canada in 1982, spent many years as a factory worker in Vancouver and Montréal before publishing his first collection of poems, THE ENCHANTED ECHO, in 1944. He has since produced 24 volumes of poetry and numerous essays, and has also written for radio and television. His collection CARIBOO HORSES (1965) won him a Governor-General's award.

RALEIGH, SIR WALTER (England, c. 1552-1618), as a soldier fought in Ireland and Spain, and as an explorer sailed to Virginia, the West Indies, and South America. Though a frequent favorite of Elizabeth I, several times he fell out of favor at Court and was imprisoned in the Tower. A small number of poems are attributed to him; his writing also includes two books recounting his travels and an unfinished HISTORY OF THE WORLD, much of it written during his longest period of imprisonment (1603-1616). He was executed in 1618.

RANSON, JOHN CROWE (U.S., 1888-1974), born in Tennessee, was a Rhodes Scholar at Oxford. He taught English at several universities in the U.S. and edited the noted literary journal THE KENYON REVIEW. He wrote several books of poetry, his best known including CHILLS AND FEVER (1924) and TWO GENTLEMEN IN BONDS (1927).

REED, HENRY (England, 1914-1986) was a teacher and free-lance journalist, but was best known as a writer for radio. His many radio plays were produced in the U.S. as well as in London. He wrote one book of verse: A MAP OF VERONA (1946, 1947).

RICH, ADRIENNE (U.S., b. 1929), a native of Baltimore, has written extensively on sexual identity, especially the experiences of women and lesbians. Her poetry includes THE DREAM OF A COMMON LANGUAGE (1978), THE FACT OF A DOORFRAME (1984), and AN ATLAS OF THE DIFFICULT WORLD (1991). She has also written several collections of essays, including OF WOMAN BORN (1976) and ON LIES, SECRETS, AND SILENCE (1979).

ROBERTS, CHARLES G. D. (Canada, 1860-1943), born and educated in New Brunswick, taught English in Nova Scotia, and served in the British and Canadian armies during World War I. He wrote much poetry and fiction, including animal stories and historical novels. IN DIVERS TONES (1886) and SONGS OF THE COMMON DAY (1893) are among his best known works of poetry. Considered by many to be the father of Canadian literature, he was knighted in 1935.

RODRIGUEZ, JUDITH (Australia, b. 1936) was born in Perth and now lives in Sydney. She has taught literature at universities in Jamaica and London as well as Australia. An artist who creates linocut prints as well as poetry, she has written two prize-winning collections: WATER LIFE (1976) and MUDCRAB AT GAMBARO'S (1980).

ROETHKE, THEODORE (U.S., 1908-1963), from Michigan, was an English professor who taught for many years at the University of Washington, Seattle. His nine books of verse, and four larger collections of poetry, were honored with a number of grants and fellowships, including a Fulbright, two National Book Awards, and a Bollingen Prize. His poetry collections include THE LOST SON AND OTHER POEMS (1948), PRAISE TO THE END! (1951), and THE WAKING (1953).

ROSSETTI, CHRISTINA (England, 1830-1893), sister of the Pre-Raphaelite poet Dante Gabriel Rossetti, published GOBLIN MARKET in 1862, a work which was highly praised for its originality, and COLLECTED POEMS in 1875. Suffering from thyroidic illness in 1870, she spent her later years in semi-retirement.

ROSSETTI, DANTE GABRIEL (England, 1828-1882), of Italian parentage and also the brother of Christina Rossetti, was born and educated in London. Choosing to study art and painting, in 1848 he co-founded the Pre-Raphaelite Brotherhood group of artists and writers, whose goal was to return English painting to the simplicity and pure colors of pre-Renaissance art. Starting with "The Blessed Damozel," which he wrote when he was 18, many of his poems and paintings explored medieval and Renaissance themes. He suffered from nervous depression in the last years of his life.

SASSOON, SIEGFRIED (England, 1886-1967), educated at Cambridge, served as an Army officer during World War I before becoming literary editor for the London DAILY HERALD in 1919. An autobiographical writer as well as poet, his well-known MEMOIRS OF A FOX-HUNTING MAN (1928) reflects his fondness for the life of an English country gentleman. But he is perhaps best known for his war poetry, exemplified in such works as THE OLD HUNTSMAN AND OTHER POEMS (1917) and COUNTER-ATTACK (1918).

SCOTT, DUNCAN CAMPBELL (Canada, 1862-1947), from Ottawa, held a number of civil service posts with the Canadian government. Since his position as a clerk in Indian Affairs involved travel, much of his poetry details the lives of native peoples in Canada's north. In 1921 he became President of the Royal Society of Canada. He wrote eleven books of poetry in all, including LABOR AND THE ANGEL (1898) and NEW WORLD LYRICS AND BALLADS (1905).

SCOTT, F. R. (Canada, 1899-1985), born in Québec City, was educated at Oxford and at McGill University in Montréal where he taught law from 1928 until his retirement in 1968.

SERVICE, ROBERT (Canada, 1874-1958), born in England, emigrated to Canada in 1896, then moved to France in 1912. He held a variety of jobs, including ambulance driver, intelligence officer in the Canadian Army, banker, and war correspondent. Among his many books of poetry, perhaps his best known are SONGS OF A SOURDOUGH (1907) and RHYMES OF A ROLLING STONE (1912), which include his narrative ballads about the Alaska gold rush.

SEXTON, ANNE (U.S., 1928-1974), born in Massachusetts, studied writing under Robert Lowell. Establishing her reputation as a "confessional" poet, she published books of poetry probing her own mental condition, including TO BEDLAM AND PART WAY BACK (1960), TRANSFORMATIONS (1971), and THE BOOK OF FOLLY (1972). She committed suicide in 1974.

SHAKESPEARE, WILLIAM (England, 1564-1616), raised in Stratford-on-Avon, married Anne Hathaway and fathered three children before moving to London and entering the theatre c. 1590. An actor and playwright as well as writer of poems and sonnets, he wrote plays at a prolific rate of almost two per year from the early 1590s until well into the 17th century. It is believed he retired to Stratford in his last years. His collected plays were first published in 1623, relatively soon after his death; this is an indication that he was recognized in his own age, as he has been in every subsequent age, as a most extraordinary writer.

SHELLEY, PERCY BYSSHE (England, 1792-1822) had a privileged upbringing, but he and a friend were expelled from Oxford in 1811 after publishing a pamphlet on THE NECESSITY OF ATHEISM. After the collapse of his first marriage to Harriet Westbrook, he fell in love with Mary Godwin (who wrote FRANKENSTEIN while with Shelley in Geneva); they were married in 1816 on the Continent. In 1818, the Shelleys moved to Italy, where—despite financial and domestic problems—Shelley produced his greatest work, including "Adonais," "The Triumph of Life," and his famous essay "Defence of Poetry" (1821). He drowned with two others while sailing off the coast of Italy.

SIDNEY, SIR PHILIP (England, 1554—1586), mourned at his funeral as "the worthiest knight that ever lived," was regarded more for his learning and manner than for his importance as a courtier. His writings include the DEFENCE OF POESY—sometimes considered the first work of literary criticism in English—and the prose romance ARCADIA, considered by some as the first English novel. He died at age 32 of a wound received in a military engagement.

SITWELL, EDITH (England, 1887-1964), was born into an eccentric and highly literary family. Her poem-sequence FAÇADE (1922) was set to music by William Walton and read by Sitwell herself, sitting behind a screen. Her most successful poems, in such volumes as STREET SONGS (1942), were inspired by World War II. She "discovered" the young Dylan Thomas and remained his lifelong friend.

SLESSOR, KENNETH (Australia, 1901-1971) served as a news reporter, staff writer, editor, war correspondent, and later, as a literary editor in Sydney. He published seven books of poems, books about Australian life and culture, and literary criticism. His poetry collections include EARTH-VISITORS (1926) and FIVE BELLS: XX POEMS (1939).

SMART, CHRISTOPHER (England, 1722-1771), educated at Cambridge, had established himself as an outstanding classical scholar by age 25. At the same time he was beginning to show signs of psychological illness—a kind of religious mania—that would burden him for the rest of his life. His poetry reflects this mania. Chronically poor, he was imprisoned several times for indebtedness, and died in a debtor's prison.

SMITH, STEVIE (England, 1902-1971) began her professional life as secretary to a magazine-publishing firm and published her own first work, NOVEL ON YELLOW PAPER, in 1936. That novel and her first book of poetry, A GOOD TIME WAS HAD BY ALL (1937), established her reputation as a writer. She went on to produce two further novels and nine volumes of poetry.

SMITH, A. J. M. (Canada, 1902-1980) was born in Montréal and educated at McGill. In 1936, with F.R. Scott, A.M. Klein, E.J. Pratt, and others, (the "Montreal Group"), he published NEW PROVINCES: POEMS OF SEVERAL AUTHORS, a landmark volume in the history of Canadian poetry. He produced NEWS OF THE PHOENIX AND OTHER POEMS in 1943, for which he received a Governor-General's award, and followed this with five other collections through 1978. He also wrote much literary criticism and edited a number of literary anthologies.

SNODGRASS, W.D. (U.S., b. 1926), from Pennsylvania, studied at Iowa under Robert Lowell, and published his first collection of poetry, HEART'S NEEDLE, in 1959. It received a Pulitzer Prize. His other poetic works include REMAINS: POEMS (1970), THE FUHRER BUNKER (1977), SELECTED POEMS (1987), and AUTUMN VARIATIONS (1990).

SOUSTER, RAYMOND (Canada, b. 1921) was born in Toronto and worked as a banker with the Canadian Imperial Bank of Commerce for over four decades. His collections A LOCAL PRIDE (1962), THE COLOUR OF THE TIMES (1964), for which he won a Governor-General's award, and AS IS (1967) established his reputation. More recent work includes IT TAKES ALL KINDS: NEW POEMS (1986) and RUNNING OUT THE CLOCK (1991).

SPENDER, STEPHEN (England, b. 1909), born in London, was educated at Oxford, where he was a close friend of W.H. Auden. For a time he lived in Germany; then during the Spanish Civil War he worked for the Republican side. He coedited the literary journals HORIZON and ENCOUNTER, and became professor of English Literature at the University of London.

SPENSER, EDMUND (England, c. 1552-1599) entered the service of the Earl of Leicester in 1579, after attending Cambridge, and published his first important poem, THE SHEPHEARDES CALENDER, that same year. Spenser lived much of his adult life in Ireland, where he held a number of official posts. The publication of his romantic epic THE FAERIE QUEENE (1590, 1596) cemented his poetic reputation. He was buried at Westminster Abbey.

STAFFORD, WILLIAM (U.S., b. 1914), born in Kansas and living in Oregon, has been an English professor and is a writer of poetry, literary criticism, and history. He has published a number of collections, including DOWN IN MY HEART (1947), TRAVELING THROUGH

THE DARK (1962), A GLASS FACE IN THE RAIN: NEW POEMS (1982), and most recently, AN OREGON MESSAGE (1987).

STEVENS, WALLACE (U.S., 1879-1955), from Pennsylvania, combined two careers: poet and business executive. Educated at Harvard and at the New York University Law School, he was admitted to the bar in 1904 and practiced law for several years. In 1916, he joined the Hartford Accident and Indemnity Company, becoming its Vice-President in 1934. As a poet, he published his first collection, HARMONIUM, in 1923. This was followed by IDEAS OF ORDER (1935) and THE MAN WITH THE BLUE GUITAR AND OTHER POEMS (1937). He received Pulitzer and Bollingen Prizes as well as a National Book Award.

SWIFT, JONATHAN (Ireland, 1667-1745) was born and educated in Ireland, but sought advancement in England. In 1713 he was made Dean of St. Patrick's Cathedral in Dublin. Though he claimed to detest Ireland, he became a great defender of Irish rights. Often accused of misogyny, Swift nonetheless had a life-long friendship with Esther Johnson, the "Stella" of his letters. GULLIVER'S TRAVELS (1726) was his most famous work, and the only one of his many writings to bring him any payment.

TENNYSON, LORD ALFRED (England, 1809-1892), son of a clergyman, began to write poetry while at Cambridge, and published his first volume in 1827. In 1833 he was deeply affected by the death of his close friend Arthur Hallam, and began the poem that was to become IN MEMORIAM (1850). The publication of his 1842 POEMS established Tennyson's reputation, and in 1850 he was appointed Poet Laureate. He continued to produce a substantial quantity of poetry, including the 12-book Arthurian sequence, IDYLLS OF THE KING, completed in 1888. He was buried in Westminster Abbey.

THESEN, SHARON (Canada, b. 1946) lives and teaches in Vancouver, British Columbia. From 1978 to 1989, she served as editor of THE CAPILANO REVIEW. Her poetry collections include ARTEMIS HATES ROMANCE (1980), CONFABULATIONS: POEMS FOR MALCOLM LOWRY (1984), and THE PANGS OF SUNDAY (1990).

THOMAS, DYLAN (Wales, 1914-1953) was born in Swansea, where he worked as a journalist before moving to London. Besides poetry, he wrote plays, such as UNDER MILK WOOD (1953), short stories, and autobiographical pieces. During World War II, he produced film scripts, and began his successful career as a public reader of poetry. He visited North America four times from 1950 to 1953, giving poetry readings, and died suddenly in New York City.

TYNES, MAXINE (Canada, b. 1950), a poet, educator, and free-lance broadcaster, is from Nova Scotia. Recipient of the People's Poet of Canada award in 1988, she has produced three volumes of poetry: BORROWED BEAUTY (1987), WOMAN TALKING WOMAN (1990), and SAVE THE WORLD FOR ME (1991).

WADDINGTON, MIRIAM (Canada, b. 1917), from Winnipeg, was a child caseworker for hospitals and family clinics before becoming a teacher and writer. Her first two books of poetry, GREEN WORLD (1945) and THE SECOND SILENCE (1955), celebrate children's experiences. Later works include THE GLASS TRUMPET (1966), DRIVING HOME: POEMS NEW AND SELECTED (1972), and COLLECTED POEMS (1986).

WALCOTT, DEREK (Caribbean, b. 1930), born on the island of St. Lucia, began publishing poetry at age 14 and put out his first collection, TWENTY-FIVE POEMS (1948), when he was 18. Since then, he has written many volumes of poems, including THE CASTAWAY AND OTHER POEMS (1965), for which he won a Royal Society of Literature award; ANOTHER LIFE (1973); and POEMS OF THE CARIBBEAN (1983). He has also had considerable success as a dramatist. In 1992 he won the Nobel Prize for Literature.

WAYMAN, TOM (Canada, b. 1946) lives in British Columbia. Much of his poetry focuses on working class conditions; his collections include FREE TIME: INDUSTRIAL POEMS (1977), and he has edited GOING FOR COFFEE: POETRY ON THE JOB (1981) and EAST OF MAIN: AN ANTHOLOGY OF POETRY FROM EAST VANCOUVER (1989).

WEBB, PHYLLIS (Canada, b. 1927) was born in Victoria British Columbia, has travelled extensively in Europe and North America, and served for a time as writer-in-residence at the University of Alberta. In the 1960s she was a producer for CBC Radio. Her collections of poems include THE SEA IS ALSO A GARDEN (1962), NAKED POEMS (1965), and THE VISION TREE: SELECTED POEMS (1982), for which she won a Governor-General's award.

WHITMAN, WALT (U.S., 1819-1892), born and educated in New York state, had a varied career as a newspaper reporter, editor, carpenter, Civil War nurse, and civil servant for the Bureau of Indian Affairs and the Attorney-General. While living with his parents in Brooklyn, he wrote and published LEAVES OF GRASS (1855). Between 1865 and 1891, Whitman wrote eight more volumes of poetry, and eventually received critical acclaim in his later years. He suffered a stroke at age 54 that left him paralyzed, though still able to give public readings.

WILBUR, RICHARD (U.S., b. 1921), a professor of English, has published poetry, songs, lyrics, and translations and has served as President of the American Academy of Arts and Letters. His collection POEMS (1957) won a Pulitzer Prize. Among his many other notable works of poetry are THINGS OF THIS WORLD: POEMS (1956), THE POEMS OF RICHARD WILBUR (1963), THE MIND READER (1976), and NEW AND COLLECTED POEMS (1988).

WILKINSON, ANNE (Canada, 1910-1961), was born in Toronto, a member of the well-known Osler family. She established her reputation as a poet with COUNTERPOINT TO SLEEP (1951) and THE HANGMAN TIES THE HOLLY (1955). A founder-editor of TAMARACK REVIEW, she was also an accomplished social historian and writer of children's fiction.

WILLIAMS, WILLIAM CARLOS (U.S., 1883-1963), received a wide-ranging education in the U.S., Switzerland, and Paris before beginning medical training at the University of Pennsylvania. While practicing medicine full-time in his birthplace–Rutherford, New Jersey–from 1910 until the mid-1950s, he produced over 20 volumes of poetry as well as several plays and a quantity of fiction and essays. One of his best-known and most acclaimed poetic works is the five-volume PATERSON, a historical tracing of life along the Passaic River in New Jersey, published between 1946 and 1958. Williams received numerous honors and awards for his poetry, including the Pulitzer and Bollingen Prizes.

WORDSWORTH, WILLIAM (England, 1770-1850) in his youth attended Cambridge and travelled extensively in revolutionary France. After receiving a legacy in 1795, he was able to devote himself to poetry, living with his sister Dorothy—an accomplished writer and diarist—and producing with his friend Coleridge the volume LYRICAL BALLADS (1798). In 1802 he married Mary Hutchinson, and spent the rest of his life in the Lake Country. He was appointed Poet Laureate in 1843.

WRIGHT, JUDITH (Australia, b. 1915) was educated at the University of Sydney and spent a year in Europe before returning to Australia. THE MOVING IMAGE (1946) was her first volume of poems. Other collections include WOMAN TO MAN (1949), THE GATEWAY (1953), FIVE SENSES (1963), THE DOUBLE TREE: SELECTED POEMS 1942-1976 (1978), and most recently, A HUMAN PATTERN (1990). She has also written several works of poetic criticism.

WROTH, LADY MARY (England, 1587-1651) was a noted composer of sonnets and lyric poetry. Married to a jealous husband who, upon his death in 1614, left her in debt, she published the first romance by a woman in 1621. She is best known today for her sonnet sequence, PAMPHILIA TO AMPHILANTHUS, in which she takes a woman's perspective in exploring conflicts between love and selfhood.

WYATT, SIR THOMAS (England, c. 1503-1542) educated at Cambridge, served in various high offices and undertook diplomatic missions under Henry VIII. At one point he was briefly imprisoned in the Tower of London on suspicion of having been one of Anne Boleyn's lovers. Wyatt and the Earl of Surrey were the first poets to incorporate the sonnet form into English, though few of Wyatt's own poems appeared in print during his lifetime.

YEATS, WILLIAM BUTLER (Ireland, 1865-1939) originally intended to be an artist like his father, but left art school to concentrate on literature. Though his earlier poetry was in the Romantic tradition, he was also heavily influenced by the Irish peasant life he saw around him, as well as by Irish nationalism and folklore. A prolific playwright as well as poet, he had a longstanding but unrequited passion for the Irish actress and nationalist Maud Gonne. He also spent a great deal of time with the writer Lady Gregory, with whom he co-founded the Irish Literary Theatre in 1899. Later in life, he gained a deep interest in symbolic systems and spirituality. He was awarded the Nobel Prize for Literature in 1923.

YOUNG, PATRICIA (Canada, b. 1954) has published four volumes of poetry. She won the League of Canadian Poets national poetry competition in 1989 and has received the Pat Lowther Memorial award, among other honors.

Index of Authors & Titles

Index of First Lines

Helen Vendler *The Odes of John Keats*
Cambridge Mass: Harvard UNIV
Press, 1983

PRINTED IN CANADA